CAN ONE LIVE AFTER AUSCHWITZ?

Cultural Memory
in
the
Present

Mieke Bal and Hent de Vries, Editors

CAN ONE LIVE AFTER AUSCHWITZ?

A Philosophical Reader

Theodor W. Adorno

Edited by Rolf Tiedemann
Translated by
Rodney Livingstone and Others

STANFORD UNIVERSITY PRESS

STANFORD, CALIFORNIA

2003

Can One Live after Auschwitz? A Philosophical Reader was originally published in German in 1997 as *"Ob nach Auschwitz noch sich leben lasse": Ein philosophisches Lesebuch,* by Suhrkamp Verlag. © Suhrkamp Verlag Frankfurt am Main 1997

Stanford University Press
Stanford, California

Printed in the United States of America
on acid-free, archival-quality paper.

Library of Congress Cataloging-in-Publication Data

Adorno, Theodor W., 1903–1969.
   [Ob nach Auschwitz noch sich leben lasse. English]
   Can one live after Auschwitz? : a philosophical reader / Theodor W. Adorno ; edited by Rolf Tiedemann ; translated by Rodney Livingstone and others.
       p. cm.—(Cultural memory in the present)
   ISBN 0-8047-3143-8 (cloth : alk. paper)—ISBN 0-8047-3144-6 (pbk : alk. paper)
   1. Philosophy.   2. Holocaust, Jewish (1939–1945)   I. Tiedemann, Rolf.
II. Title.   III. Series
B3199.A330213 2003
193–DC21   2003001161

Original Printing 2003

Last figure below indicates year of this printing:
12   11   10   09   08   07   06   05   04   03

Typeset by TBH Typecast, Inc. in 11/13.5 Adobe Garamond

Contents

handwritten marginalia:

p. 50
65-66 the INDIVIDUAL
68-70 new / now / death
74 capitalism / wealth
83 apo-
85-89 society, death (160)

handwritten marginalia:

Prelloz 467-69
Marx: 114

CAN ONE LIVE AFTER AUSCHWITZ?

Introduction

"NOT THE FIRST PHILOSOPHY, BUT A LAST ONE":
NOTES ON ADORNO'S THOUGHT

Rolf Tiedemann

> The fact that the power of facts has grown so horrifyingly, and that all theory, even true theory, seems like a mockery of this—this has engraved itself on the organ of theory, namely, language, scarring it permanently. Practice, which emasculates theory, reappears at its heart as a destructive force, without even a glance at any possible practice. Actually, it is no longer possible to say anything. Action is the only form left to theory.
> —Bar Harbor, Summer 1939[1]

"Whether one can *live* after Auschwitz"[2] was no mere rhetorical question in Adorno's eyes, but a question of the greatest seriousness. He thought it inconceivable that "life will continue 'normally' or even that culture might be 'rebuilt'" (4: 61–62).[3] Yet that is precisely what has happened. The Holocaust and the Shoah have been converted by the culture industry into aspects of the everyday television experience to which life itself has been reduced. In extreme contrast to the many authors moved to fluent rhetoric about Auschwitz today, Adorno, one of the most eloquent writers of German, seemed to be struck dumb whenever he attempted to describe what had happened. A sense of shame prevented Adorno from "writing elegantly about Auschwitz" (cf. 10.2: 597–98). The same thinker who battled against the protocol statements of the positivists was forced to make use of them himself. The same man whose composer's ear abhorred repetitions found them piling up whenever he faced the task of discussing "the administrative murder of millions of innocent people" (10.2: 557).[4]

Around 1950, Adorno protested that in Germany "reminding people of Auschwitz was held to be the expression of a tedious resentment" (10.1: 53), and toward the end of the 1950s, when he gave his lecture "The Meaning of Working through the Past," he deplored a rejection of the past that would cheat the murder victims even of their right to be remembered. Present-day German society exhibits something like the opposite characteristic. In a ceremonious competition that has spread like a plague, one expert on remembrance seeks to outdo the next with the size of his memorial and the number of dead whose names are inscribed in it. Adorno spoke in his day of "an empty and cold forgetting" (10.2: 566).[5] Today we see a no less empty and cold act of remembrance, a routine of memorialization that has been aptly captured by the malicious New York joke that there's no business like Shoah Business. The philosopher who wrote *Minima Moralia* and *Negative Dialectics* did not exempt himself. Instead he turned the question of "whether there can be life after Auschwitz" on himself by going on to ask "whether in particular a person could go on living who had accidentally escaped and should by rights have been murdered as well. The continued existence of such a person calls for the same coldness, that fundamental principle of bourgeois subjectivity, without which Auschwitz would not have been possible." He called this coldness the "drastic guilt of those who were spared" (6: 355–56). And how should a man come to terms with his guilt if he not only had the good luck to escape scot-free but had never even been in danger? How can he go on living if his name was never even on the lists of those wanted by the police? In Adorno's mind, the impossibility of an authoritative answer was identical to the impossibility of philosophy after Auschwitz. Despite this, Adorno never ceased to philosophize. He insisted on the necessity of philosophy, even though he had no illusions about its irrelevance to the world at large.

In the 1940s, in exile in California, Adorno wrote *Dialectic of Enlightenment* together with his older friend Max Horkheimer. This was the "key work for the understanding of the age."[6] Its authors set themselves the ambitious task of discovering "why humanity, instead of entering a truly human state, is sinking into a new kind of barbarism" (3: 11). This question was one that gave neither Adorno nor Horkheimer any peace for the rest of their lives; it became the focal point of their thought, and in comparison everything else seemed irrelevant. What took place in Auschwitz and the other death camps implied the collapse of the existing civilization that had been built up so laboriously. But it also spelled the revocation of what Adorno ironically termed the "Western legacy of positivity" (6: 372–73), in other words, the innermost substance of traditional philosophy. The "universal cheerfulness" that unwaveringly assigns "meaning," no matter what, to existing reality should by rights have been banished from philosophy once and for all by the sight of the station ramp and the gas chambers. In one of his last texts, an epilogue to *Negative Dialectics*, Adorno referred to a letter in which Marx expressed the fear that civilization might revert to barbarism and commented on what he took to be Marx's view that revolution was the ultima ratio against that regression: "But the fear that must have motivated Marx is out of date. The regression has taken place. To expect it to happen in the future, now that we have witnessed Auschwitz and Hiroshima, is to succumb to the pathetic consolation that things might always get even worse" (10.2: 769).

Philosophy, which, according to Hegel, is "its own time comprehended in thoughts,"[7] has failed abysmally in its efforts to comprehend the rupture that civilization has experienced, let alone to give it any "meaning." For much of the time it has ceased even to try, instead contenting itself either with inconclusive reflections on the existence of existing things or with the analysis of the linguistic premises of thought as such and in general. More recently, philosophers appear to be preoccupied with their own abolition. Adorno refused to play any of these games, and continued in his thinking to reflect upon actual history and the processes eroding it. In *Negative Dialectics* he cites the Lisbon earthquake of 1755 as an instance when philosophy was forced by history to change its axiomatic beliefs: a natural catastrophe "cured" Voltaire of Leibniz's theodicy (see 6: 354). In *Candide* (1759), Voltaire attacked as incompatible with experience the "unscrupulous optimism" that blathers on about the best of all possible worlds. In the meantime, however, philosophical experience has itself been called into question; no philosophy can presume even to approach a social catastrophe like Auschwitz. "It is uncertain . . . whether philosophy, as an activity of the comprehending spirit, has any part to play at the present time. . . . It seems too late for contemplation. What we find before us in all its absurdity resists comprehension" (10.2: 469). Ultimately, however, Adorno seems, at least at times, to have clung to the paradoxical hope that philosophy might not be entirely closed to the idea of practice, of interventions that might bring about change.

At an early stage, Adorno and Horkheimer had seen anti-Semitism as setting the seal on the collapse of civilization. Later, especially after their return to Germany, they did not think it beneath them to translate their theoretical insights into practical applications. They made concrete efforts in both politics and education to combat anti-Semitism and help establish a democratic consciousness. Nonetheless, there was a time when everyone colluded in accusing Adorno, in particular, of an excessive love of theory and a distaste for practice. During the Student Movement, which coincided with the last years of Adorno's life and cast a shadow over them, he was forced to defend himself against many of his own students, who could not rid themselves soon enough of the theoretical stance they had so inadequately learned, and who wished to impose their own pseudo-practice upon their teacher. The fact is that Adorno never rejected practice, even though he perceived only too clearly the link between every action, every form of activism, and oppression, the principle of domination itself. This notwithstanding, Adorno never hesitated to urge, and even to require, respect for a moral law that seemed to have become obsolete since Kant and that took the form of a "new categorical imperative."

Hitler has imposed a new categorical imperative on human beings in their state of unfreedom: to arrange their thoughts and actions in such a way that Auschwitz should never be repeated, that nothing of the sort should ever happen again. This imperative is as resistant to explanation as was the given nature of Kant's imperative in its day. To treat it discursively would be an outrage: it gives us a bodily sensation of an external moral factor. "Bodily," because it represents our active sense of abhorrence in the face of the intolerable physical pain to which individuals are exposed. (6: 358)

The category of the "external factor [*Das Hinzutretende*]"[8] is one that Adorno explicated in his metacritique of Kant's practical philosophy (see 6: 266ff.); it was a pièce de résistance of his materialism. The way to think about it is to bear in mind the element of factual reality without which rational insight and moral action would never meet up in empirical society. It is the factor that alone enables thought, the *res cogitans*, to communicate with the *res extensa* and ultimately go some way to overcoming the causality of nature. This external factor is what raises man above the *lex naturae*; it is the "impulse" behind his activity, the motor force that enables him to go beyond existing reality. "According to the rules of rationality it [the external factor] contains an irrational aspect" (6: 227). It is in this sense that

Adorno's theoretical philosophy, which is concerned above all with the discursive knowledge of reality, requires the imperative that the horror of genocide must not be allowed to recur, an imperative that neither needs nor is capable of further explanation: an external, nondeducible, practical motive without which theory after Auschwitz would have no chance of success.

Auschwitz, the German name for a little provincial Polish town that in Poland goes by the innocuous name of Oświęcim, stands in Adorno's texts merely as a signal that is intended to summon up the things that took place there and in other death camps. Adorno was never able to speak directly about what happened in them, and yet at the same time it was, if not an eloquent theme, at least a "never-ending task" of his thinking. An exemplary instance of the difficulties of speaking theoretically about what the murderers termed the "Final Solution" can be found in the misunderstandings that have accumulated around what is perhaps Adorno's best-known saying: "To write poetry after Auschwitz is barbaric." This statement was misunderstood not just by poets, who were afraid that they were to be deprived en masse of their vocation. It was also misunderstood by Günther Anders, who took it to be a prohibition on the writing of poems, a prohibition that he wished to extend even further.[9]

In truth, Adorno's sentence ended up rebounding on its own author for having criticized culture as a whole on the grounds that it failed to do justice to the suffering of the victims, or was even complicit with it: "Even the most radical reflection of the mind on its own failure is limited by the fact that it remains only reflection, without altering the existence to which its failure bears witness" (10.1: 27–28).[10] "Reflection of the mind on its own failure" is the prime task facing philosophy today. This means, however, that philosophy sees the culture to which it belongs as complicit in the descent of society into a new barbarism. However philosophy reflects on this decline and reacts to it will prove to be false: silence confirms what has happened, while talking is unable to change it:

Even the most extreme consciousness of doom threatens to degenerate into idle chatter. Cultural criticism finds itself faced with the final stage of the dialectic of culture and barbarism. To write poetry after Auschwitz is barbaric. And this corrodes even the knowledge of why it has become impossible to write poetry today. Absolute reification, which presupposed intellectual progress as one of its elements, is now preparing to absorb the mind entirely. Critical intelligence cannot be equal to this challenge as long as it confines itself to self-satisfied contemplation. (10.1: 30)[11]

In Adorno's sentence, "to write poetry" is a synecdoche; it stands for art as such and ultimately for culture as a whole. Adorno wrote in *Negative Dialectics* that Auschwitz "is the irrefutable proof that culture has failed": "The fact that it could happen in the midst of all the traditions of philosophy, art, and the sciences with all their enlightenment, says more than just that these traditions and mind in general were unable to take hold of men and change them. . . . All culture after Auschwitz, together with the urgent critique of culture, is garbage" (6: 359).

Every way out, every Hölderlin-like "saving grace" seems to be barred from a historico-philosophical point of view: "Whoever pleads for the preservation of a radically guilty and shabby culture becomes its accomplice, while anyone who resists culture directly promotes the barbarism which culture revealed itself to be" (6: 360). Adorno did not wish to forbid any poet to write poetry, innocent as such an activity is, particularly when it is compared to the atrocities committed by others; he insisted merely that writing poetry before Auschwitz and writing poetry after were separated by an unbridgeable gulf. His contributions to aesthetic theory are a series of attempts to create a "theodicy" for art in a situation in which art has become objectively questionable, indeed, in which it no longer seems permissible. The authentic poet may well discover an apologia for writing poetry in Adorno's aesthetics:[12] "The concept of a resurrection of culture after Auschwitz is illusory and senseless, and for that reason every work of art that does come into being is forced to pay a bitter price. But because the world has outlived its own demise it needs art as its unconscious chronicle" (10.2: 506).

Partly, no doubt, because there seemed no end to the misunderstandings, when he came to write *Negative Dialectics* and to discuss the pragmatic activity of writing poems, Adorno retracted the sentence he had formulated almost twenty years previously: "A perennial suffering has just as much right to find expression as a victim of torture has to scream. For this reason it may have been wrong to write that after Auschwitz poetry could no longer be written" (6: 355). However, if poems are still possible after Auschwitz, the only ones that are conceivable are those that do not have the suffering in the death camps as their subject, since the opposite would be impossible. The only poems possible are those that are concerned with commemorating that suffering, that have absorbed it and have thereby transcended the aesthetic.

In the two decades after 1949, following his return from California, Adorno's philosophy had an incomparable impact in post-fascist Germany and a decisive influence on cultural life, essentially through its intention, if such it was, to focus on memory. In this respect his philosophy converged with modern works of art, such as Picasso's *Guernica* and Schoenberg's *Survivor of Warsaw*, works brought into existence against a background of their own historico-philosophical impossibility. For the last time, philosophy: this Adorno-like variant on Kafka's dictum[13] might well be inscribed in the history of philosophy itself. But just as the hopes of the 1970s for a changed society were doomed to disappointment and ended up in the following decade in a neoconservative restoration, Adorno's philosophy, too, seems to have succumbed to what Hegel called the "fury of destruction."

After the so-called turning point [i.e., the Fall of the Berlin Wall in 1989], middle-of-the-road German values took over. Today, while the spokesmen of the political class cultivate an official culture of commemoration, the majority can devote themselves all the more single-mindedly to their business affairs—including the building of new poison-gas factories on Israel's doorstep. Adorno's philosophy of remembering recent events has long since been superseded by a revitalized interest in chthonic origins, yet another supposedly "new" mythology deriving from a misunderstanding of Nietzsche conjoined with a renaissance of Heidegger. Such a development had long been inconceivable. Indeed, a moment like this—when the intelligentsia,[14] following in the footsteps of the politicians, has settled down among its exact opposites—may be unfavorable not only to a renewed reading of Adorno's work but to awareness of history in general. Returning to the pre-Socratics means retreating from real history; it filters out memory and screens out experience, thus ratifying trends instinctively followed by society itself. We are witnessing not the end of history, as these neophytes would like us to believe, but the elimination of historical consciousness. This deprives thought not of its best products but of everything.

From Adorno, by contrast, we might learn that without memory, without what Kant termed "reproduction in the imagination," no worthwhile knowledge can be obtained. We might learn that—unlike a theory prevalent ever since Plato and accepted by Kant, too—memory is no timelessly valid thing, no transcendental synthesis, but something that possesses that "temporal core" of which Walter Benjamin was the first to speak. For philosophy in the age following Auschwitz, this temporal core is to be found in the screams of the victims. Since then, "the need to enable suffering to speak . . . [has been] the precondition of all truth" (6: 29). If philosophy is still possible today, it must be a philosophy in which the suffering in the death camps is present in every one of its sentences, a philosophy that recalls not the shadow of the tall plane trees on the banks of the Ilisus but Celan's "shadow / of the scar up in the air."[15]

In summer 1939, even before the outbreak of war, Horkheimer and Adorno drew up plans for an empirical research project on anti-Semitism for the Institute for Social Research, which had left Germany in 1933 and had become domiciled in New York. Their efforts to obtain financial support dragged on and delayed the start of the project for a long time. Early in 1943, the first reports of the German death camps reached the United States, and it is remarkable how accurate the historical facts they contained actually were. The chapter in *Dialectic of Enlightenment* (1947) entitled "Elements of Anti-Semitism"—which, like the rest of the book, Adorno wrote jointly with Horkheimer—was a first attempt to produce a theory that would do justice to the events in Germany. But this ambition ultimately could not be fulfilled because no theory of anti-Semitism can explain what German anti-Semites did in the death camps.

This was doubtless one reason why the two men took up again in 1944 the older project of an empirical study and, together with other members of the Institute for Social Research, brought it to completion in the five volumes of *Studies in Prejudice*. The centerpiece of this work was the socio-psychological study entitled *The Authoritarian Personality*, published in 1950. Adorno subsequently wrote that the theoretical "Elements of Anti-Semitism" had been "decisive" for his contribution to this study (cf. 10.2: 721). Much earlier, in August 1940, Adorno had written in a letter to Horkheimer:

I am gradually coming to realize, partly under the impression of the latest news from Germany, that I simply cannot free myself from the fate of the Jews in Germany. It frequently seems to me that everything we have been wont to see from the standpoint of the proletariat has now been transferred to the Jews in a terrifyingly concentrated form. I wonder whether we should not say . . . the things that we really want to say in connection with the Jews, who represent the opposite extreme to the concentration of power.[16]

These lines provide us with a key to Adorno's thinking from 1940 on, but they also shed light on particular elements of his writings from an earlier period to which their author would have granted "the status of a dreamlike anticipation" (1: 384).[17] "From the standpoint of the proletariat"—that is how the Critical Theory of Horkheimer and his collaborators had viewed history, following Marx: as the history of class struggles. But they had also seen it as a progressive process, in tendency at least, which would be brought sooner or later to a successful conclusion by the proletariat: the proletariat as the class of classes, the ultimate subject-object of history, thanks to whom class struggle would end and the emancipation of humanity would be completed.

This way of seeing could no longer be sustained in the light of the "fate of the Jews in Germany." It was plain that class struggles of the past had been succeeded by something worse, by the "concentration of power," domination as such, a completely rationalized system of manipulation. Human beings, far from organizing themselves as a proletariat into the subject of history, were being definitively degraded in the camps to mere objects of the most brutal oppression, and beyond that, had already entered into what Max Weber had prophetically termed the "house of bondage." The culture industry helped to accelerate the course of events and to predispose individuals to their utter reification. Enlightened thought, Marxism above all, had failed where it was needed most. Reflection and observation, two modes of theoretical behavior that had been revered for two millennia, proved to be impotent. Where had the history of mankind gone wrong? It is this question that *Dialectic of Enlightenment* seeks to answer; in the chapter "Elements of Anti-Semitism" the answer was to be given "in connection with the Jews."

With the "Elements of Anti-Semitism" an idea came into its own that had been haunting Adorno for a long time, one that he had frequently appealed to in the course of his productive misunderstanding of ideas of Benjamin and that also differed from Horkheimer's thinking: the idea of a prehistory of philosophy. For Adorno, Auschwitz was no "marginal situation," as it was for Jaspers (see 11: 129), no accidental and hence reparable catastrophe of history. On the contrary, in *Dialectic of Enlightenment* the authors wished to explain anti-Semitism in terms "of the dominant reason and of the world corresponding to its image" (3: 17). At an earlier stage, Adorno, not without a certain naïveté, had gone in search of the "archaic, historical archetypes" of the phenomena he wished to decode. This procedure now lost the last traces of innocence when he applied it to anti-Semitism. Philosophical theory cannot simply accept that the death camps are prefigured in an existing social structure[18] or are the product of this or that historical cause. Theory finds itself compelled to reinterpret history by going right back to its archaic beginnings.

Auschwitz cannot be brought into analogy with the destruction of the Greek city-states as a mere gradual increase in horror, before which one can preserve tranquillity of mind. Certainly, the unprecedented torture and humiliation of those abducted in cattle trucks does shed a deathly-livid light on the most distant past, in whose mindless, planless violence the scientifically confected was already teleologically latent. (4: 268)[19]

  That is how it is put in one of the reflections of *Minima Moralia*: a compressed model of the philosophical prehistory of anti-Semitism developed simultaneously in *Dialectic of Enlightenment*. If at a later stage Adorno liked to talk about a "modified" conception of philosophy, one that he attempted to fill out in *Negative Dialectics*, it can be said that the first step on this path of modification was taken in "Elements of Anti-Semitism," written over two decades before. Beneath the "deathly-livid light" that was ignited in the middle of the twentieth century, it became absolutely essential to review the "basic concepts" of reason with whose aid Western philosophy has attempted to bring human beings an enlightenment about themselves and their world for two and a half thousand years. "Enlightenment, understood in the widest sense as the advance of thought," as it is formulated in the first sentence of *Dialectic of Enlightenment*, can be said to have utterly failed in its supreme aim of "liberating human beings from fear" (3: 19). If that was the case, then Adorno's philosophy may be said to have reinstated the Kantian "tribunal" of rational critique. In the process the traditional categories we use to explain the world—from the concept of the bourgeois individual to that of the Absolute that confers meaning, from the concept of experience to that of means-ends rationality—are subjected to a scrutiny from which none of these concepts emerges unchanged. Each is stripped of its "affirmative nature," while its negative aspect is retained and extended—extended indeed to the point where "the perfected negativity, once it is faced squarely, comes together in the mirror-writing of its own opposite" (4: 283).

The yellow patch that was imposed on Jews in Germany to make them stand out from other Germans served as well to make them indistinguishable from each other. Qualities specific to an individual were meant to vanish behind the ethnic identity he shared with the many. The individual Jew ceased to be a real, living, suffering human being. As a member of the Jewish people he was reduced to a mere instance, an abstraction, in whom concrete difference merged in indistinguishable sameness. This imposition of exemplary quality by the anti-Semites upon the Jews reminded Adorno of similar methods going back to the prehistory of civilization and constituting essential prerequisites for its history. Ever since socially organized labor emerged, it has followed the same pattern: given nature enters into the labor process, but only to the extent that it is needed for the purpose at hand. Whatever is not needed is left lying by the wayside on the road of progress; as a merely potential human quality, it is treated with disdain. The situation with scientific reason is not much different, so Adorno maintained: as scientific discourse pushes natural qualities ever further into the background, phenomena are encountered only as instances of their own concepts. Wherever there is a discursive surplus, it is neglected, and in the end obliterated, in the interest of fungibility. The identity of the concept negates the nonidentity of the thing.

In this sense the process of selection on the station platform in the extermination camps shed a "deathly-livid light" on the thinking habits of the logicians who in all simplicity declared those habits to be purely mental. "The indifference to the individual expressed in logic" (3: 228)[20] is of the same type that has destroyed people throughout history, treated the individual as a negligible quantity, and locked up deviants and outsiders. Even where—and this was rare enough—people's lives and well-being were not directly threatened, but simply remained in the sphere of the mind, in culture and the sciences, Adorno was convinced that a subterranean process was at work destroying the nonidentical. But as society makes its own tendencies prevail over individuals, and does so indeed by liquidating them, it comes to resemble the camps. And as it does so, we see at the same time an impoverishment of knowledge, knowledge showing itself to be progressively less interested in concrete reality and its divergence from the conceptual. Where knowledge takes cognizance of the world and its inhabitants only in their exemplary functions, where it perceives each thing only as an instance of something else, and nothing as a thing in its own right, there thought has abdicated. Just as "anti-Semitic views always reflected stereotyped thinking," so too the "schema" that has replaced observation of and reflection about things, what Adorno calls "intellectual categories" (see 3: 226–27),[21] manifests a stereotypical mode of perception. Truth in the emphatic sense of the word, that is, a truth that does not just subsume its object under something more abstract but unravels its very core, seems to have become entirely obsolete since Auschwitz. Among the masters at every level of the hierarchy, a concept of truth that attempts to go beyond mere groping for a falsifiable correctness evokes no more than a weary smile.

This is the weariness of a dominance that "is no longer needed for economic reasons" (3: 192);[22] it is the smile of a power that unceasingly contrives to renew the principle of oppression. Domination is the open secret of an enduring prehistory. After Aristotle's *Politics* had recommended a hierarchically organized system of government as a universal principle, valid equally for the home and the polis, St. Paul clothed terrestrial power in the mantle of the divine. According to Critical Theory, "all the oppression that man has ever inflicted on man culminates in the modern age in the cold inhumanity of free wage-labor" (8: 373),[23] and the Enlightenment, which intended something quite different, was based on a rationality that has merged with domination. Instead of replacing the domination of man by man with "the administration of things," as Marxism envisaged, capitalism as it developed established a domination of men by things in which class privilege reproduced itself.

Then, in the twentieth century, exploitation and the domination that had come to prevail unplanned, solely through the mechanisms of the marketplace, was superseded once again by dictatorships and tyrannies with their direct use of terror. Adorno's philosophy undertakes to track down and denounce oppression—that is to say, class relations—even in the most unexpected places, in the small gestures of everyday, those "dregs of the phenomenal world," of which Freud has spoken. "All collaboration, all the human worth of social mixing and participation, merely masks a tacit acceptance of inhumanity," Adorno writes in *Minima Moralia*. "Condescension, and thinking oneself no better, are the same. To adapt to the weakness of the oppressed is to affirm in it the pre-condition of power, and to develop in oneself the coarseness, insensibility, and violence needed to exert domination" (4: 27).[24]

If, originally, the domination of men was modeled on the domination of nature, then the latter always meant the domination of man's own nature in the first instance; the principle of the domination of nature is inseparable from that of self-preservation. In the early 1960s, Adorno read Elias Canetti's *Crowds and Power,* in which power is derived from the principle of survival. Adorno noted, not without satisfaction, the similarity to his and Horkheimer's theory in *Dialectic of Enlightenment*.[25] Self-preservation, Spinoza's *suum esse conservare,* is the essence of more than just a dominating rationality; Spinoza himself grounds virtue in it, and according to Adorno, it even "appears sublimated into the purely logical principle of identity."[26] Self-preservation in a less sublimated and indeed extraordinarily robust form underpins the hardened bourgeois self, its "hidebound particularism," of which Adorno writes in *Dialectic of Enlightenment* that "in the existing order, constitutes precisely the universal." Adorno's critique is aimed at the "cold, stoical character that existing society imposes on human beings" (3: 193).[27]

Coldness as the constituent of bourgeois subjectivity, which was one of the components of Auschwitz, derives from the principle of self-preservation for its own sake, the counterpart to destruction for its own sake, which determined the actions of the caring, music-loving family men who stood revealed as monsters in the camps. Self-examination, which alone might have been able to overcome the narrow-minded instinct for self-preservation, could not do so. The anti-Semitic pogroms and the extermination camps "demonstrate[d] the impotence of what might have restrained them—reflection, meaning, ultimately truth" (3: 195).[28] Reflection, signification, and truth have gradually, laboriously emerged in the course of history from the rationality of self-preservation and opposed themselves to it. Until modern times they embodied the substantial values of philosophy no less than of culture in general: values that perished in Auschwitz alongside the victims.

Nevertheless, Adorno did not subscribe to the social contract that unites the majority of philosophers today, however divided they are in other respects: that is to say, the agreement that speculation is intellectual poetry, metaphysics must be relegated to the history of philosophy, and Hegel's Absolute is a bad joke. They may be all these things, and perhaps even more superfluous than their detractors suspect, but even so, for Adorno that is not the whole story. Adorno would probably have kept Kafka's epithet "the weightless, merry journey" in reserve for the modern project of "post-metaphysical thought"; such thought assuredly does not succeed in "tearing the block out of its base," but it will no doubt manage to "tear the straps to shreds." He knew his own philosophy was chained to concrete existence, and he sought materialistically to keep in the closest possible contact with it. What he wanted was precisely not to "tear out" his "block," that is, to eliminate through thought the element alien to thought, but rather to enter into it and attempt to unlock it from within.[29] The altered conception of philosophy that Adorno subscribed to was concerned with "the transition from philosophy to interpretation; this elevates neither the symbol nor the symbolized to the status of an absolute, but seeks the truth at the point where thought secularizes the irretrievable primal image of sacred texts" (6: 64).

As interpretation, philosophy renounces the claim made by systems to construct the world once again in the shape of ideas by virtue of a sovereign subjectivity; in other words, to conjure up the truth as a whole from one's pocket. However, an interpretative philosophy is not just content with less than is implied by the traditional notion of the system. It aims at more. As fragile as it is radical, it wishes at long last to achieve what had always been denied to systems of every kind, and what they had all "systematically" avoided, namely, to "break open the insoluble" (6: 38). For interpretation, truth is neither the construction of an adequate statement from concepts nor the revelation of a sacred text, nor is it the ἀλήθεια of the ontologies. Rather, it aspires to the utterly secular, which philosophy ever since Plato has turned away from in contempt; it aspires to the transitory and the mortal: "For the concept what is a matter of urgency is what it fails to cover, what its abstracting mechanism eliminates, what is not already the example of a concept" (6: 20).

Society's abstracting mechanism, which is the underlying basis of logic's, has begun by eliminating the individual, the single person, with whom Adorno concerns himself the more urgently the more the individual is neglected by society. In his thought metaphysics has slipped "into the questions of material existence." "The somatic stratum of life, bereft of meaning, is the theater of suffering, which in the camps burned to ashes every soothing element of mind and culture, the mind's objective form, without any consolation" (6: 358). Systematic after its own fashion, Adorno's philosophy binds itself to this stratum and, declaring its solidarity with the injuries of mankind, refuses to squeeze meaning out of suffering. In so doing, it becomes materialist, albeit in the eccentric sense that objective realities owe their existence to subjective experience. "The need to enable suffering to speak is the precondition of all truth. For suffering is objectivity that weighs upon the subject; what the subject experiences as its innermost subjectivity, its expression, is mediated objectively" (6: 29). The expression given to suffering in Adorno's writings has become the last refuge of metaphysics, which can be seen as something that transcends material existence, by however small a margin.

This refuge has its home in language. In the introduction to *Negative Dialectics*, Adorno expounds his concept of philosophical experience. Probably for the first time since Walter Benjamin, he examines the question of philosophical discourse, the indispensable element of expression, its linguistic nature (see 6: 65–66). Once the totality, the "great whole," has been entirely discredited as the primary object of philosophy, and once "as good as nothing remains of its metaphysical truth-content" (6: 399), the experience of small things, of unimportant and unobtrusive things, acquires a completely new dignity. "That which recedes becomes smaller and smaller, more and more insignificant, just as Goethe portrayed it in an extreme form in the parable of the mysterious chest in the *New Melusine*; that is the epistemological as well as the historico-philosophical reason for the fact that metaphysics migrates into the micrological" (6: 399).[30]

The interpretative immersion in the smallest things sets out to understand how these things communicate with one another. The intention is to discover their affinities and thus come closer to the specific nature of objects than one can come through the fetishism of concepts and procedures, the systematic construction of identity. Adorno's talk of "the thing itself [*die Sache selbst*]," generally regarded as a scandal, is concerned with the coherence of the nonidentical, an experience of the object that becomes possible for the subject without violence, by surrendering to it, through the pure act of "looking on" referred to in Hegel's *Phenomenology of Mind*.[31] It is here that Adorno finds "the refuge of the mimetic element of knowledge, that of the elective affinity of the knower and the known" (6: 55).

Adorno was much preoccupied with the doctrine of homology that can be traced back to antiquity, evidently to Parmenides, according to which only something like can recognize a likeness.[32] He defined his own version of this in *Negative Dialectics*: "Only as language can like recognize like" (6: 65). Against all the objections of the professional philosophers, Adorno retained his faith in the possibility of a metaphysical experience that could be salvaged by language. Unlike the narrator of *New Melusine*, such a metaphysics would not be bent on unveiling the secret of small things at any price, but would respect their impenetrability and would assist the individual in asserting his distinctiveness as against other individuals. But the aspect of society that has receded even further into the distance than it had previously, namely, the real reconciliation of difference, is also prohibitively difficult for thought. Adorno believed that he could most easily look to art to provide him with models for his conception of experience. An instance is Valéry's "yearning . . . for a type of thought that would be free from its own coercive character" (11: 201). A great part of Adorno's work on art was concerned to track down this yearning, the deepest layer of meaning of Adorno's "minima metaphysica," and to translate it into philosophy, or at least to make it productive for philosophy. "Even before Auschwitz, it was an affirmative lie to confer any positive meaning on existence in the face of historical experience. . . . Because works of art subject the contexts from which meaning arises to ever sterner tests, they turn against them and against meaning in general" (7: 229). Thus Adorno discovered in art a way of expressing the impossible situation of a philosophy that continues unperturbed to inquire into the meaning of existence.

Adorno's idea of metaphysics as micrological is the counterpart to all first philosophy that, with Aristotle's *Metaphysics*, searches for the πρῶται ἀρχαί and αἰτίαι, the first reasons and causes of existence. *Against Epistemology: A Metacritique*, Adorno's principal philosophical work before *Negative Dialectics*, contains an immanent epistemological critique of the philosophy of origins: a hierarchy based on a first thing on which everything else is built—regardless of how this is defined—and a factual reality derived from this and subordinated to it. Adorno rejected the *pronunciamento* of fundamental ontology against modernity, according to which origins possess a higher solemnity and true value, and must be sought out, like the Mothers in *Faust*. He opposed to this the dialectic, which he viewed as an attempt "to see the newness of the old, instead of just the oldness of the new" (5: 46). Faced with the catastrophe of a modernity that endures, the origins seem to be essentially less idyllic than philosophers imagine in their Black Forest chalets or their professorial chairs. "Luridly the horror of the ending lights up the deception of the origin" (4: 258). In exile and even in innocent works of art a different view could be gleaned; but it is philosophy as a whole after Auschwitz that really brings this insight home: "If the age of the interpretation of the world is past, and the task now is to change it, then philosophy must take its leave. . . . This is not the time for the First Philosophy, but for a Last One" (5: 47). What made Adorno hold onto such a last philosophy was the memory of the victims. Because of them and because of this memory, he insisted, almost with enthusiasm, that "the thought that does not de-capitate itself leads to transcendence and to the idea of a world constitution in which not only is present suffering abolished, but even the suffering that lies in the past and is beyond recall might be revoked" (6: 395).[33] Adorno situated this idea leading to transcendence in a scientific "no-man's-land" from which he liked to send reports. In the gaps he found between the ostensible claims of the different disciplines, which were separated from each other by barbed wire, he looked for "the inextinguishably ontic," the "nonidentical" aspect of things themselves. By that he meant the lack of identity between things and their conceptual copies. "No-man's-land" doubtless means both things: on the one hand, a land without domination, a nature that has hitherto avoided being organized by subjectivity, and, on the other hand, nature deformed, nature at its greatest point of deformation, the "terrain / with the unmistakable track" where Celan wrote his poem "The Straitening [*Engführung*]," the terrain of "the latest rejection."[34] In an account of the games he played in childhood, Adorno once revealed the meaning of "no-man's-land" in his vocabulary: "The land . . . that I occupied when playing on my own was a no-man's-land. Later on, in the war, the word surfaced to describe the devastated space between two fronts. However, it is the faithful translation of the Greek—Aristophanic—word 'utopia,' one that I understood all the better for not knowing anything about it" (10.1: 305). Today, when no one wants to hear of this word any more because no one ever understood it, a last ray of the messianic light may break into the no-man's-land of Adorno's thought, into his fallible and insecurely based "last philosophy." Adorno frequently quoted the last sentence in Benjamin's essay on Goethe's *Elective Affinities*: "Only for the sake of those without hope, has hope been given to us."[35]

Translated by Rodney Livingstone

Note on Sources

For each of the essays in this volume, a parenthetical line at its end gives the date of first publication (and of composition, when the two are not very close), followed, when applicable, by the location of the German text in Theodor W. Adorno, *Gesammelte Schriften*, ed. Rolf Tiedemann in collaboration with Gretel Adorno, Susan Buck-Morss, and Klaus Schultz (Frankfurt am Main: Suhrkamp, 1970–86), abbreviated GS. The exception is Chapter 21, which first appeared in German in Theodor W. Adorno, *Metaphysik: Begriff und Probleme*, ed. Rolf Tiedemann, Nachgelassene Schriften, vol. 14 (Frankfurt am Main: Suhrkamp, 1998), pp. 161–226. Its dates of first delivery are given in the text. Previous English publication for the essays not newly translated for this volume can be found in "Credits," pp. 471–72, below.

PART ONE

TOWARD A NEW CATEGORICAL IMPERATIVE

The Meaning of Working
through the Past

The question "What does working through the past mean?" requires explication.[1] It follows from a formulation, a modish slogan that has become highly suspect during the last years. In this usage "working through the past" does not mean seriously working upon the past, that is, through a lucid consciousness breaking its power to fascinate. On the contrary, its intention is to close the books on the past and, if possible, even remove it from memory. The attitude that everything should be forgotten and forgiven, which would be proper for those who suffered injustice, is practiced by those party supporters who committed the injustice. I wrote once in a scholarly dispute: in the house of the hangman one should not speak of the noose, otherwise one might seem to harbor resentment.[2] However, the tendency toward unconscious and not-so-unconscious defensiveness against guilt is so absurdly associated with the thought of working through the past that there is sufficient reason to reflect upon a domain from which even now there emanates such a horror that one hesitates to call it by name.

One wants to break free of the past: rightly, because nothing at all can live in its shadow, and because there will be no end to the terror as long as guilt and violence are repaid with guilt and violence; wrongly, because the past that one would like to evade is still very much alive. National Socialism lives on, and even today we still do not know whether it is merely the ghost of what was so monstrous that it lingers on after its own death, or whether it has not yet died at all, whether the willingness to commit the unspeakable survives in people as well as in the conditions that enclose them.

I do not wish to go into the question of neo-Nazi organizations.[3] I consider the survival of National Socialism *within* democracy to be potentially more menacing than the survival of fascist tendencies *against* democracy. Infiltration indicates something objective; ambiguous figures make their *comeback* [E] and occupy positions of power for the sole reason that conditions favor them.[4]

Nobody disputes the fact that in Germany it is not merely among the so-called incorrigibles, if that term must be used, that the past has not yet been mastered. Again and again one hears of the so-called guilt complex, often with the association that it was actually first created by the construction of a German collective guilt. Undoubtedly there is much that is neurotic in the relation to the past: defensive postures where one is not attacked, intense affects where they are hardly warranted by the situation, an absence of affect in the face of the gravest matters, not seldom simply a repression of what is known or half-known. Thus we often found in group experiments in the Institute for Social Research that mitigating expressions and euphemistic circumlocutions were chosen in the reminiscences of deportation and mass murder, or that a hollow space formed in the discourse; the universally adopted, almost good-natured expression *Kristallnacht*, designating the pogrom of November 1938, attests to this inclination. A very great number claim not to have known of the events at that time, although Jews disappeared everywhere and although it is hardly believable that those who experienced what happened in the East constantly kept silent about what must have been for them an unbearable burden; surely one may assume that there is a relation between the attitude of "not having known anything about it" and an impassive and apprehensive indifference. In any case the determined enemies of National Socialism knew quite early exactly what was going on.[5]

We[6] all are also familiar with the readiness today to deny or minimize what happened—no matter how difficult it is to comprehend that people feel no shame in arguing that it was at most only five and not six million Jews who were gassed. Furthermore, the quite common move of drawing up a balance sheet of guilt is irrational, as though Dresden compensated for Auschwitz. Drawing up such calculations, the haste to produce counterarguments in order to exempt oneself from self-reflection, already contain something inhuman, and military actions in the war, the examples of which, moreover, are called "Coventry" and "Rotterdam," are scarcely comparable to the administrative murder of millions of innocent people. Even their innocence, which cannot be more simple and plausible, is contested.[7] The enormity of what was perpetrated works to justify this: a lax consciousness consoles itself with the thought that such a thing surely could not have happened unless the victims had in some way or another furnished some kind of instigation, and this "some kind of" may then be multiplied at will.[8] The blindness disregards the flagrant disproportion between an extremely fictitious guilt and an extremely real punishment. At times the victors are made responsible for what the vanquished did when they themselves were still beyond reach, and responsibility for the atrocities of Hitler is shifted onto those who tolerated his seizure of power and not to the ones who cheered him on. The idiocy of all this is truly a sign of something that psychologically has not been mastered, a wound, although the idea of wounds would be rather more appropriate for the victims.

Despite all this, however, talk of a guilt complex has something untruthful to it. Psychiatry, from which the concept is borrowed with all its attendant associations, maintains that the feeling of guilt is pathological, unsuited to reality, psychogenic, as the analysts call it. The word "complex" is used to give the impression that the guilt—which so many ward off, abreact, and distort through the silliest of rationalizations—is actually no guilt at all but rather exists in them, in their psychological disposition: the terribly real past is trivialized into merely a figment of the imagination of those who are affected by it. Or is guilt itself perhaps merely a complex, and bearing the burden of the past pathological, whereas the healthy and realistic person is fully absorbed in the present and its practical goals? Such a view would draw the moral from the saying: "And it's as good as if it never happened," which comes from Goethe but, at a crucial passage in *Faust*, is uttered by the devil in order to reveal his innermost principle, the destruction of memory.[9] The murdered are to be cheated out of the single remaining thing that our powerlessness can offer them: remembrance. The obstinate conviction of those who do not want to hear anything of it does indeed coincide with a powerful historical tendency. Hermann Heimpel on several occasions has spoken of how the consciousness of historical continuity is atrophying in Germany, a symptom of that societal weakening of the ego Horkheimer and I had already attempted to derive in *Dialectic of Enlightenment*.[10] Empirical findings, for example, that the younger generation often does not know who Bismarck and Kaiser Wilhelm I were, have confirmed this suspicion of the loss of history.[11]

Thus the forgetting of National Socialism surely should be understood far more in terms of the general situation of society than in terms of psychopathology. Even the psychological mechanisms used to defend against painful and unpleasant memories serve highly realistic ends. These ends are revealed by the very people maintaining the defense, for instance, when in a practical frame of mind they point out that an all-too-vivid and persistent recollection of what happened can harm the German image abroad. Such zeal does not accord well with the declaration of Richard Wagner, who was nationalistic enough, to the effect that being German means doing something for its own sake—provided that it is not defined a priori as business.[12] The effacement of memory is more the achievement of an all-too-alert consciousness than its weakness when confronted with the superior strength of unconscious processes. In the forgetting of what has scarcely transpired there resonates the fury of one who must first talk himself out of what everyone knows, before he can then talk others out of it as well.

Surely the impulses and modes of behavior involved here are not immediately rational insofar as they distort the facts they refer to. However, they are rational in the sense that they rely on societal tendencies and that anyone who so reacts knows he is in accord with the spirit of the times. Such a reaction immediately fits in well with the desire to get on with things. Whoever doesn't entertain any idle thoughts doesn't throw any wrenches into the machinery. It is advisable to speak along the lines of what Franz Böhm so aptly called "nonpublic opinion."[13] Those who conform to a general mood, which to be sure is kept in check by official taboos but which for that reason possesses all the more virulence, simultaneously qualify both as party to it and as independent agents. The German resistance movement after all remained without a popular base, and it's not as if such a base was magically conjured up out of Germany's defeat just like that. One can surely surmise that democracy is more deeply rooted now than it was after the First World War:[14] in a certain sense National Socialism—antifeudal and thoroughly bourgeois—by politicizing the masses even prepared, against its will, the ground for democratization. The Junker caste as well as the worker's movement have disappeared. For the first time something like a relatively homogeneous bourgeois milieu has developed. But the belated arrival of democracy in Germany, which did not coincide with the peak of economic liberalism and which was introduced by the Allied victors, cannot but have had an effect on the relationship of Germans to democracy. That relationship is only rarely expressed directly, because for the time being things are going so well under democracy and also because it would go against the community of interests institutionalized by political alliances with the West, especially with America.[15] However, the resentment against *re-education* [E] is sufficiently explicit. What can be said is that the system of political democracy certainly is accepted in Germany in the form of what in America is called *a working proposition* [E], something that has functioned well up until now and has permitted and even promoted prosperity. But democracy has not become naturalized to the point where people truly experience it as their own and see themselves as subjects of the political process. Democracy is perceived as one system among others, as though one could choose from a menu between communism, democracy, fascism, and monarchy: but democracy is not identified with the people themselves as the expression of their political maturity. It is appraised according to its success or setbacks, whereby special interests also play a role, rather than as a union of the individual and the collective interests, and the parliamentary representation of the popular will in modern mass democracies already makes that difficult enough. In Germany one often hears Germans among themselves making the peculiar remark that they are not yet mature enough for democracy. They make an ideology out of their own immaturity, not unlike those adolescents who, when caught committing some violent act, talk their way out of it with the excuse that they are just teenagers. The grotesque character of this mode of argumentation reveals a flagrant contradiction within consciousness. The people who play up their own naïveté and political immaturity in such a disingenuous manner, on the one hand, already feel themselves to be political subjects who should set about determining their own destiny and establishing a free society. On the other hand, they come up against the limits strictly imposed upon them by the existing circumstances. Because they are incapable of penetrating these limits with their own thought, they attribute this impossibility, which in truth is inflicted upon them, either to themselves, to the great figures of the world, or to others. It is as though they divide themselves yet once more into subject and object. Moreover, the dominant ideology today dictates that the more individuals are delivered over to objective constellations, over which they have, or believe they have, no power, the more they subjectivize this powerlessness. Starting from the phrase that everything depends on the person, they attribute to people everything that in fact is due to the external conditions, so that in turn the conditions remain undisturbed. Using the language of philosophy, one indeed could say that the people's alienation from democracy reflects the self-alienation of society.

Among these objective constellations, the development of international politics is perhaps the most salient. It appears to justify retrospectively Hitler's attack against the Soviet Union. Since the Western world essentially defines itself as a unity in its defense against the Russian threat, it looks as though the victors in 1945 had foolishly destroyed the tried and tested bulwark against Bolshevism, only to rebuild it a few years later. It is a quick jump from the obvious statement "Hitler always said so" to the extrapolation that he was also right about other things. Only edifying armchair orators could quickly ease themselves over the historical fatality that in a certain sense the same conception that once motivated the Chamberlains and their followers to tolerate Hitler as a watchdog against the East has survived Hitler's downfall. Truly a fatality. For the threat that the East will engulf the foothills of Western Europe is obvious, and whoever fails to resist it is literally guilty of repeating Chamberlain's *appeasement* [E].[16] What is forgotten is merely—merely!—the fact that precisely this threat was first produced by Hitler's campaign, who brought upon Europe exactly what his expansionist war was meant to prevent, or so thought the *appeasers* [E]. Even more than the destiny of single individuals, it is the destiny of political entanglements that constitutes the nexus of guilt. The resistance to the East contains its own dynamic, which reawakens the German past. Not merely in terms of ideology, because the slogans of struggle against Bolshevism have always served to mask those who harbor no better intentions toward freedom than do the Bolsheviks themselves. But also in terms of reality. According to an observation that had already been made during the era of Hitler, the organizational power of totalitarian systems imposes some of its own nature upon its adversaries. As long as the economic disparity persists between East and West, the fascist variety has better chances of success with the masses than the East's propaganda has, whereas admittedly, by contrast, one is not yet pushed to the fascist ultima ratio. However, the same character types are susceptible to both forms of totalitarianism. Authoritarian personalities are altogether misunderstood when they are construed from the vantage point of a particular political-economic ideology; the well-known oscillations of millions of voters before 1933 between the National Socialist and Communist parties is no accident from the social-psychological perspective, either. American studies have

shown that this personality structure does not correlate so easily with political-economic criteria. It must be defined in terms of character traits
such as a thinking oriented along the dimensions of power and powerlessness, a rigidity and an inability to react, conventionality, the lack of self-reflection, and ultimately an overall inability to experience. Authoritarian
personalities identify themselves with real, existing power per se, prior to
any particular contents. Basically, they possess weak egos and therefore require the compensation of identifying themselves with, and finding security in, great collectives. The fact that one meets figures everywhere who resemble those in the film *Wir Wunderkinder* is due neither to the depravity
of the world as such nor to the supposedly peculiar traits of the German
national character.[17] It is due rather to the identity of those conformists—
who before the fact already have a connection to the levers of the whole apparatus of political power—as potential followers of totalitarianism. Furthermore, it is an illusion to believe that the National Socialist regime
meant nothing but fear and suffering, although it certainly was that even
for many of its own supporters. For countless people life was not at all bad
under fascism. Terror's sharp edge was aimed only at a few, relatively well-
defined groups. After the crises of the era preceding Hitler, the predominant feeling was that "everything's being taken care of," and that did not
just mean an ideology of *KdF* trips and flower boxes in the factories.[18]
Compared with the laissez-faire of the past, to a certain degree Hitler's
world actually protected its own people from the natural catastrophes of
society to which they had been abandoned. A barbaric experiment in state
control of industrial society, it violently anticipated the crisis-management
policies of today. The often-cited "integration," the organizational tightening of the weave in the societal net that encompassed everything, also afforded protection from the universal fear of falling through the mesh and
disappearing. For countless people it seemed that the coldness of social
alienation had been done away with thanks to the warmth of togetherness,
no matter how manipulated and contrived; the *völkisch* community of the
unfree and the unequal was a lie and at the same time also the fulfillment
of an old, indeed long-familiar, evil bourgeois dream. The system that offered such gratification certainly concealed within itself the potential for its
own downfall. The economic efflorescence of the Third Reich in large
measure was due to its rearmament for the war that brought about the catastrophe. But the weakened memory I mentioned earlier resists accepting
these arguments. It tenaciously persists in glorifying the National Socialist

era, which fulfilled the collective fantasies of power harbored by those people who, individually, had no power and who, indeed, could feel any self-
worth at all only by virtue of such collective power. No analysis, however
illuminating, can afterward remove the reality of this fulfillment or the instinctual energies invested in it. Even Hitler's *va banque* gamble was not as
irrational as it seemed to average liberal thought at the time or as its failure
seems to historical hindsight today. Hitler's calculation, to exploit the temporary advantage gained over the other nations thanks to a massively accelerated armaments program, was by no means foolish in consideration of
what he wanted to achieve. Whoever delves into the history of the Third
Reich and especially of the war will feel again and again that the particular
moments in which Hitler suffered defeat seem to be accidental and that
only the course of the whole appears necessary, the ultimate victory of the
superior technical-economic potential of the rest of the world that did not
want to be swallowed up: so to speak, a statistical necessity, but by no
means a discernible step-by-step logic. The surviving sympathy for National Socialism has no need for laborious sophistry in order to convince
itself and others that things could just as well have gone differently, that in
fact only some mistakes were made, and that Hitler's downfall was a world-
historical accident the world spirit may perhaps yet rectify.

On the subjective side, in the psyche of people, National Socialism
increased beyond measure the collective narcissism, simply put: national
vanity. The individual's narcissistic instinctual drives, which are promised
less and less satisfaction by a callous world and which nonetheless persist
undiminished as long as civilization denies them so much, find substitute
satisfaction in the identification with the whole.[a] This collective narcissism was severely damaged by the collapse of Hitler's regime, but the damage occurred at the level of mere factuality, without individuals making
themselves conscious of it and thereby coping with it. This is the social-
psychological relevance of talk about an unmastered past. Also absent is
the panic that, according to Freud's theory in *Group Psychology and the*
Analysis of the Ego,[19] sets in whenever collective identifications break apart.
If the lessons of the great psychologist are not to be cast to the wind, then
there remains only one conclusion: that secretly, smoldering uncon-

[a] See Theodor W. Adorno, "Opinion Delusion Society," in *Critical Models:*
Interventions and Catchwords, trans. Henry Pickford (New York: Columbia University Press, 1998), pp. 105–26.

sciously and therefore all the more powerfully, these identifications and the collective narcissism were not destroyed at all, but continue to exist. Inwardly the defeat has been as little ratified as after 1918. Even in the face of the obvious catastrophe the collective Hitler integrated has held together and clung to chimerical hopes like those secret weapons that in truth the other side possessed. Furthermore, social-psychology adds the expectation that the damaged collective narcissism lies in wait of being repaired and seizes upon anything that brings the past into agreement with the narcissistic desires, first in consciousness, but that it also, whenever possible, construes reality itself as though the damage never occurred. To a certain degree this has been achieved by the economic boom, the feeling of "how industrious we are." But I doubt whether the so-called economic miracle—in which, to be sure, everyone participates even while speaking of it with some disdain—social-psychologically really reaches as deeply as one might suppose in times of relative stability. Precisely because famine continues to reign across entire continents when technically it could be eliminated, no one can really be so delighted at his prosperity. Just as individually, for instance, in films, there is resentful laughter when a character sits down to a very good meal and tucks the napkin under his chin, so too humanity begrudges itself the comfort it all too well knows is still paid for by want and hardship; resentment strikes every happiness, even one's own. Satiety has become an insult a priori, whereas the sole point of reproach about it would be that there are people who have nothing to eat; the alleged idealism that especially in today's Germany so pharisaically sinks its teeth into an alleged materialism frequently owes its self-proclaimed profundity merely to repressed instincts.[20] Hatred of comfort engenders in Germany discomfort at prosperity, and it transfigures the past into a tragedy. However, this malaise does not at all issue solely from dark and troubled waters but rather once again from far more rational ones. The prosperity is due to an economic upswing, and no one trusts its unlimited duration. If one seeks consolation in the view that events like the Black Friday of 1929 and the resultant economic crisis could hardly repeat themselves, then this already implicitly contains the reliance on a strong state power that, one then expects, will offer protection if economic and political freedom no longer work. Even in the midst of prosperity, even during the temporary labor shortage, the majority of people probably feel secretly that they are potentially unemployed, recipients of charity, and hence really objects, not subjects, of society: this is the fully legitimate and reasonable cause of their discomfort. It is obvious that at any given moment this discomfort can be dammed up, channeled toward the past, and manipulated in order to provoke a renewal of the disaster.

Today the fascist wish-image unquestionably blends with the nationalism of the so-called underdeveloped countries, which now, however, are instead called "developing countries." Already during the war the *slogans* [E] about Western plutocracies and proletarian nations expressed sympathy with those who felt shortchanged in the imperialist competition and also wanted a place at the table. It is difficult to discern whether and to what extent this tendency has already joined the anticivilization, anti-Western undercurrent of the German tradition and whether in Germany itself there exists a convergence of fascist and communist nationalism. Nationalism today is at once both obsolete and up-to-date. Obsolete, because in the face of the compulsory coalition of nations into great blocs under the supremacy of the most powerful country, which is already dictated by the development in weapons technology alone, the individual sovereign nations, at least in advanced continental Europe, have forfeited their historical substance. The idea of the nation, in which the common economic interests of free and independent citizens once united against the territorial barriers of feudalism, has itself become a barrier to the obvious potential of society as a totality. But nationalism is up-to-date insofar as the traditional and psychologically supremely invested idea of nation, which still expresses the community of interests within the international economy, alone has sufficient force to mobilize hundreds of millions of people for goals they cannot immediately identify as their own. Nationalism does not completely believe in itself anymore, and yet it is a political necessity because it is the most effective means of motivating people to insist on conditions that are, viewed objectively, obsolete. This is why, as something ill at ease with itself, intentionally self-deluded, it has taken on grotesque features nowadays.[21] Admittedly nationalism, the heritage of barbarically primitive tribal attitudes, never lacked such traits altogether, but they were reined in as long as liberalism guaranteed the right of the individual—also concretely as the condition of collective prosperity. Only in an age in which it was already toppling has nationalism become completely sadistic and destructive.[22] The rage of Hitler's world against everything that was different—nationalism as a paranoid delusional system—was already of this caliber. The appeal of precisely these features is hardly any less today. Paranoia, the persecution mania that persecutes those upon whom it projects what it itself desires, is contagious. Collective delusions, like anti-Semitism, confirm the pathology of the individual, who shows that psychologically he is no longer a match for the world and is thrown back upon an illusory inner realm. According to the thesis of the psychoanalyst Ernst Simmel, they may well spare a half-mad person from becoming completely so.[23] To the extent that the delusional mania of nationalism openly manifests itself in the reasonable fear of renewed catastrophes, so, too, does it promote its own diffusion. Delusional mania is the substitute for the dream that humanity would organize the world humanely, a dream the actual world of humanity is resolutely eradicating. Everything that took place between 1933 and 1945 goes together with pathological nationalism.

That fascism lives on, that the oft-invoked working through of the past has to this day been unsuccessful and has degenerated into its own caricature, an empty and cold forgetting, is due to the fact that the objective conditions of society that engendered fascism continue to exist. Fascism essentially cannot be derived from subjective dispositions. The economic order, and to a great extent also the economic organization modeled upon it, now as then renders the majority of people dependent upon conditions beyond their control and thus maintains them in a state of political immaturity. If they want to live, then no other avenue remains but to adapt, submit themselves to the given conditions; they must negate precisely that autonomous subjectivity to which the idea of democracy appeals; they can preserve themselves only if they renounce their self. To see through the nexus of deception, they would need to make precisely that painful intellectual effort that the organization of everyday life, and not least of all a culture industry inflated to the point of totality, prevents. The necessity of such adaptation, of identification with the given, the status quo, with power as such, creates the potential for totalitarianism. This potential is reinforced by the dissatisfaction and the rage that very constraint to adapt produces and reproduces. Because reality does not deliver the autonomy or, ultimately, the potential happiness that the concept of democracy actually promises, people remain indifferent to democracy, if they do not in fact secretly detest it.[24] This form of political organization is experienced as inadequate to the societal and economic reality; just as one must adapt, so would one like the forms of collective life also to adapt, all the more so since one expects from such adaptation the *streamlining* [E] of the state as a gigantic business enterprise within a certainly less than friendly competition of all against all. Those whose real powerlessness shows no sign of ceasing cannot tolerate even the semblance of what would be better; they would prefer to get rid of the obligation of autonomy, which they suspect cannot be a model for their lives, and prefer to throw themselves into the melting pot of the collective ego.[25]

I have exaggerated the somber side, following the maxim that only exaggeration per se today can be the medium of truth.[26] Do not mistake my fragmentary and often rhapsodic remarks for Spenglerism; Spenglerism itself makes common cause with the catastrophe. My intention was to delineate a tendency concealed behind the smooth facade of everyday life before it overflows the institutional dams that, for the time being, are erected against it. The danger is objective, not primarily located in human beings. As I said, there is much that indicates that democracy with all it implies has a more profound hold on people than it did during the Weimar period. By failing to emphasize what is so obvious, I have neglected what circumspect consideration must not ignore: that within the German democracy from 1945 to today the material life of society has reproduced itself more richly than during any other time in living memory, and this is also relevant from a social-psychological perspective. It certainly would not be all too optimistic to affirm that the German democracy is not doing badly these days and that therefore the real reappraisal of the past is also doing fine, provided that it is given enough time and much else besides. Except that the concept of having enough time contains something naive and at the same time contemplative in the bad sense. We are not simply spectators of world history, free to frolic more or less at will within its grand chambers, nor does world history, whose rhythm increasingly approaches that of the catastrophe, appear to allow its subjects the time in which everything would improve on its own.[27] This bears directly on democratic pedagogy. Above all, enlightenment about what has happened must work against a forgetfulness that all too easily turns up together with the justification of what has been forgotten—for instance,[28] parents who must endure embarrassing questions from children about Hitler and, in response, indeed to whitewash their own guilt, speak of the good aspects and say that in fact it was not so awful. In Germany it is fashionable to complain about civic education, and certainly it could be better, but sociology already has data indicating that civic education, when it is practiced earnestly and not as a burdensome duty, does more good than is generally believed. However, if one takes the objective potential for the survival of National Socialism as seriously as I believe it must be taken, then this sets limits even for a pedagogy that promotes enlightenment. Whether it be sociological or psychological, such a pedagogy in practice will probably reach in general only those people who are open to it anyway and who therefore are hardly susceptible to fascism.[29] Yet it is certainly not at all superfluous to fortify this group with enlightened instruction against the nonpublic opinion. On the contrary, one could easily imagine that out of this group something like cadres could develop, whose influence in the most diverse contexts would then finally reach the whole of society, and the chances for this are all the more favorable, the more conscious the cadres become. Obviously, the work of enlightenment will not be limited to these groups. Here I will refrain from a question that is very difficult and laden with the greatest responsibility: namely, how far it is advisable to go into the past when attempting to raise public awareness, and whether precisely the insistence on it does not provoke a defiant resistance and produce the opposite of what it intends. It seems to me, rather, that what is conscious could never prove so fateful as what remains unconscious, half-conscious, or preconscious. Essentially it is a matter of the way in which the past is made present; whether one remains at the level of reproach or whether one withstands the horror by having the strength to comprehend even the incomprehensible. For this, however, it would be necessary to educate the educators themselves. But such education is gravely impaired by the fact that what in America are called the *behavioral sciences* [E] are either not represented at all or woefully underrepresented in Germany at present. It is absolutely imperative that universities strengthen a sociology that would work together with the historical research about our own era. Instead of holding forth with secondhand profundities about the Being of man,[30] pedagogy should set itself the task *re-education* [E] is so vehemently accused of having superficially handled. Criminology in Germany is not yet up to modern standards at all. But, above all, one should think of psychoanalysis, which is still being repressed today as much as ever. Either it is altogether absent, or it is replaced by tendencies that, while boasting of overcoming the much-maligned nineteenth century, in truth fall back behind Freudian theory, even turning it into its very opposite. A precise and undiluted knowledge of Freudian theory is more necessary and relevant today than ever. The hatred of it is directly of a piece with anti-Semitism, by no means simply because Freud was a Jew but rather because psychoanalysis consists precisely in the critical self-reflection that makes anti-Semites livid with rage. Although it is so difficult to carry out something like a mass analysis because of the time factor alone, nonetheless, if rigorous psychoanalysis found its institutional place, its influence upon the intellectual climate in Germany would be a salutary one, even if that meant nothing more than taking it for granted that one should not lash outward but should reflect about oneself and one's relation to whatever obdurate consciousness habitually rages against. In any case, however, attempts to work subjectively against the objective potential for disaster should not content themselves with corrections that would hardly approach the severity of what must be confronted.[31] Likewise, attention to the great achievements of Jews in the past, however true they may be, are hardly of use and smack of propaganda. And propaganda, the rational manipulation of what is irrational, is the prerogative of the totalitarians. Those who resist totalitarians should not imitate them in a way that would only do themselves a disservice. Panegyrics to the Jews that isolate them as a group already give anti-Semitism a running start. Anti-Semitism is so difficult to refute because the psychic economy of innumerable people needed it and, in an attenuated form, presumably still needs it today. Whatever happens by way of propaganda remains ambiguous. I was told the story of a woman who, upset after seeing a dramatization of *The Diary of Anne Frank*, said: "Yes, but *that* girl at least should have been allowed to live." To be sure even that was good as a first step toward understanding. But the individual case, which should stand for, and raise awareness about, the terrifying totality, by its very individuation became an alibi for the totality the woman forgot.[32] The perplexing thing about such observations remains that even on their account one cannot advise against productions of the Anne Frank play and the like, because their effect nonetheless feeds into the potential for improvement, however repugnant they also are and however much they seem to be a profanation of the dignity of the dead. I also do not believe that too much will be accomplished by community meetings, encounters between young Germans and young Israelis, and other organized promotions of friendship. All too often the presupposition is that anti-Semitism in some essential way involves the Jews and could be countered through concrete experiences with Jews, whereas the genuine anti-Semite is defined far more by his incapacity for any experience whatsoever, by his unresponsiveness. If anti-Semitism primarily has its foundation in objective society, and only derivatively in anti-Semites, then—as the National Socialist joke has it—if the Jews had not already existed, the anti-Semites would have had to invent them. As far as wanting to combat anti-Semitism in individual subjects is concerned, one should not expect too much from the recourse to facts, which anti-Semites most often will either not admit or will neutralize by treating them as exceptions. Instead, one should apply the argumentation directly to the subjects whom one is addressing. They should be made aware of the mechanisms that cause racial prejudice within them. A working through of the past understood as enlightenment is essentially such a turn toward the subject, the reinforcement of a person's self-consciousness and hence also of his self. This should be combined with the knowledge of the few durable propaganda tricks that are attuned exactly to those psychological dispositions we must assume are present in human beings. Since these tricks are fixed and limited in number, there is no overwhelming difficulty in isolating them, making them known, and using them as a kind of vaccine. The problem of how to carry out practically such a subjective enlightenment probably could only be resolved by the collective effort of teachers and psychologists, who would not use the pretext of scholarly objectivity to shy away from the most urgent task confronting their disciplines today. Yet in view of the objective power behind the continuing potential of anti-Semitism, subjective enlightenment will not suffice, even if it is undertaken with a radically different energy and in radically deeper psychological dimensions than it has been up to now. If one wishes to oppose the objective danger objectively, then no mere idea will do, not even the idea of freedom and humanitarianism, which indeed—as we have learned in the meantime—in its abstract form does not mean very much to people. If the fascist potential links up with their interests, however limited those interests may be, then the most effective antidote is still a persuasive, because true, demonstration of their own interests and, moreover, their most immediate ones. One would really be guilty of speculative psychologizing in these matters if one disregarded the fact that the war and the suffering it brought upon the German population, although, indeed, being insufficient to remove the fascist potential, nonetheless offers some counterweight against it. If people are reminded of the simplest things—that open or disguised fascist revivals will cause war, suffering, and privation under a coercive system and, in the end, probably the Russian domination of Europe, in short, that they lead to a politics of catastrophe—then this will impress people more deeply than invoking ideals or even the suffering of others, which is always relatively easy to get over, as La Rochefoucauld already knew.[33] Compared with this prospect, the present *malaise* [E] signifies little more than the luxury of a certain mood. Despite all the psychological repression, Stalingrad and the night bombings are not so forgotten that everyone cannot be made to understand the connection between the revival of a politics that led to them and the prospect of a third Punic war. Even if this succeeds, the danger will still exist. The past will have been worked through only when the causes of what happened then have been eliminated. Only because the causes continue to exist does the captivating spell of the past remain to this day unbroken.[34]

(1960; GS 10.2: 555–72)
Translated by Henry W. Pickford

2

Education after Auschwitz

The premier demand upon all education is that Auschwitz not happen again. Its priority before any other requirement is such that I believe I need not and should not justify it. I cannot understand why it has been given so little concern until now. To justify it would be monstrous in the face of the monstrosity that took place. Yet the fact that one is so barely conscious of this demand and the questions it raises shows that the monstrosity has not penetrated people's minds deeply, itself a symptom of the continuing potential for its recurrence as far as people's conscious and unconscious is concerned. Every debate about the ideals of education is trivial and inconsequential compared to this single ideal: never again Auschwitz. It was the barbarism all education strives against. One speaks of the threat of a relapse into barbarism. But it is not a threat—Auschwitz *was* this relapse, and barbarism continues as long as the fundamental conditions that favored that relapse continue largely unchanged. That is the whole horror. The societal pressure still bears down, although the danger remains invisible nowadays. It drives people toward the unspeakable, which culminated on a world-historical scale in Auschwitz. Among the insights of Freud that truly extend even into culture and sociology, one of the most profound seems to me to be that civilization itself produces anticivilization and increasingly reinforces it. His writings *Civilization and Its Discontents* and *Group Psychology and the Analysis of the Ego* deserve the widest possible diffusion, especially in connection with Auschwitz.[1] If barbarism

itself is inscribed within the principle of civilization, then there is something desperate in the attempt to rise up against it.

Any reflection on the means to prevent the recurrence of Auschwitz
is darkened by the thought that this desperation must be made conscious
to people, lest they give way to idealistic platitudes.[2] Nevertheless, the attempt must be made, even in the face of the fact that the fundamental
structure of society, and thereby its members, who have made it so, are the
same today as twenty-five years ago. Millions of innocent people—to quote
or haggle over the numbers is already inhumane—were systematically murdered. That cannot be dismissed by any living person as a superficial phenomenon, as an aberration of the course of history to be disregarded when
compared to the great dynamic of progress, of enlightenment, of the supposed growth of humanitarianism. The fact that it happened is itself the
expression of an extremely powerful societal tendency. Here I would like to
refer to a fact that, very characteristically, seems to be hardly known in Germany, although it furnished the material for a best-seller like *The Forty
Days of Musa Dagh*, by Werfel.[3] Already in the First World War the
Turks—the so-called "Young Turk Movement" under the leadership of En-
ver Pascha and Talaat Pascha—murdered well over a million Armenians.
The highest German military and government authorities apparently were
aware of this but kept it strictly secret. Genocide has its roots in this resurrection of aggressive nationalism that has developed in many countries
since the end of the nineteenth century.

Furthermore, one cannot dismiss the thought that the invention of
the atomic bomb, which can obliterate hundreds of thousands of people literally in one blow, belongs in the same historical context as genocide. The
rapid population growth of today is called a population explosion; it seems
as though historical destiny responded by readying counterexplosions, the
killing of whole populations. This only to intimate how much the forces
against which one must act are those of the course of world history.

Since the possibility of changing the objective—namely, societal and
political—conditions is extremely limited today, attempts to work against
the repetition of Auschwitz are necessarily restricted to the subjective dimension. By this I also mean essentially the psychology of people who do
such things. I do not believe it would help much to appeal to eternal values, at which the very people who are prone to commit such atrocities
would merely shrug their shoulders. I also do not believe that enlighten-

ment about the positive qualities possessed by persecuted minorities would be of much use. The roots must be sought in the persecutors, not in the victims, who are murdered under the paltriest of pretenses. What is necessary is what I once in this respect called the turn to the subject.[4] One must come to know the mechanisms that render people capable of such deeds, must reveal these mechanisms to them, and strive, by awakening a general awareness of those mechanisms, to prevent people from becoming so again. It is not the victims who are guilty, not even in the sophistic and caricatured sense in which still today many like to construe it. Only those who unreflectingly vented their hate and aggression upon them are guilty. One must labor against this lack of reflection, must dissuade people from striking outward without reflecting upon themselves. The only education that has any sense at all is an education toward critical self-reflection. But since according to the findings of depth psychology, all personalities, even those who commit atrocities in later life, are formed in early childhood, education seeking to prevent the repetition must concentrate upon early childhood. I mentioned Freud's thesis on discontent in culture. Yet the phenomenon extends even further than he understood it, above all, because the pressure of civilization he had observed has in the meantime multiplied to an unbearable degree. At the same time the explosive tendencies he first drew attention to have assumed a violence he could hardly have foreseen. The discontent in culture, however, also has its social dimension, which Freud did not overlook though he did not explore it concretely. One can speak of the claustrophobia of humanity in the administered world, of a feeling of being incarcerated in a thoroughly societalized, closely woven, netlike environment. The denser the weave, the more one wants to escape it, whereas it is precisely its close weave that prevents any escape. This intensifies the fury against civilization. The revolt against it is violent and irrational.

A pattern that has been confirmed throughout the entire history of persecutions is that the fury against the weak chooses for its target especially those who are perceived as societally weak and at the same time—either rightly or wrongly—as happy. Sociologically, I would even venture to add that our society, while it integrates itself ever more, at the same time incubates tendencies toward disintegration. Lying just beneath the surface of an ordered, civilized life, these tendencies have progressed to an extreme degree. The pressure exerted by the prevailing universal upon everything particular, upon the individual people and the individual institutions, has a tendency to destroy the particular and the individual together with their power of resistance. With the loss of their identity and power of resistance, people also forfeit those qualities by virtue of which they are able to pit themselves against what at some moment might lure them again to commit atrocity. Perhaps they are hardly able to offer resistance when the established authorities once again give them the order, so long as it is in the name of some ideal in which they half or not at all believe.

When I speak of education after Auschwitz, then, I mean two areas: first, children's education, especially in early childhood; then, general enlightenment, which provides an intellectual, cultural, and social climate in which a recurrence would no longer be possible, a climate, therefore, in which the motives that led to the horror would become relatively conscious. Naturally, I cannot presume to sketch out the plan for such an education even in rough outline. Yet I would like at least to indicate some of its nerve centers. Often, for instance, in America, the characteristic German trust in authority has been made responsible for National Socialism and even for Auschwitz. I consider this explanation too superficial, although here, as in many other European countries, authoritarian behavior and blind authority persist much more tenaciously than one would gladly admit under the conditions of a formal democracy. Rather, one must accept that fascism and the terror it caused are connected with the fact that the old established authorities of the *Kaiserreich* decayed and were toppled, while the people psychologically were not yet ready for self-determination. They proved to be unequal to the freedom that fell into their laps. For this reason the authoritarian structures then adopted that destructive and, if I may put it so, insane dimension they did not have earlier, or at any rate had not revealed. If one considers how visits of potentates who no longer have any real political function induce outbreaks of ecstasy in entire populations, then one has good reason to suspect that the authoritarian potential even now is much stronger than one thinks. I wish, however, to emphasize especially that the recurrence or nonrecurrence of fascism in its decisive aspect is a question not of psychology but of society. I speak so much of the psychological only because the other, more essential aspects lie so far out of reach of the influence of education, if not of the intervention of individuals altogether.

Very often well-meaning people, who don't want it to happen again, invoke the concept of bonds. According to them, the fact that people no longer had any bonds is responsible for what took place. In fact, the loss of authority, one of the conditions of the sadistic-authoritarian horror, is connected with this state of affairs. To normal common sense it is plausible to appeal to bonds that check the sadistic, destructive, and ruinous impulse with an emphatic "You must not." Nevertheless, I consider it an illusion to think that the appeal to bonds—let alone the demand that everyone should again embrace social ties so that things will look up for the world and for people—would help in any serious way. One senses very quickly the untruth of bonds that are required only so that they produce a result— even if it be good—without the bonds' being experienced by people as something substantial in themselves. It is surprising how swiftly even the most foolish and naive people react when it comes to detecting the weaknesses of their betters. The so-called bonds easily either become a ready badge of shared convictions—one enters into them to prove oneself a good citizen—or produce spiteful resentment, psychologically the opposite of the purpose for which they were drummed up.[5] They amount to heteronomy, a dependence on rules, on norms that cannot be justified by the individual's own reason. What psychology calls the superego, the conscience, is replaced in the name of bonds by external, unbinding, and interchangeable authorities, as one could observe quite clearly in Germany after the collapse of the Third Reich. Yet the very willingness to connive with power and to submit outwardly to what is stronger, under the guise of a norm, is the attitude of the tormentors that should not arise again. It is for this reason that the advocacy of bonds is so fatal. People who adopt them more or less voluntarily are placed under a kind of permanent compulsion to obey orders. The single genuine power standing against the principle of Auschwitz is autonomy, if I might use the Kantian expression: the power of reflection, of self-determination, of not cooperating.

I once had a very shocking experience: while on a cruise on Lake Constance I was reading a Baden newspaper, which carried a story about Sartre's play *Morts sans sépulchre*, a play that depicts the most terrifying things.[6] Apparently the play made the critic uneasy. But he did not explain this discontent as being caused by the horror of the subject matter, which is the horror of our world. Instead, he twisted it so that, in comparison with a position like that of Sartre, who engages himself with the horror, we could maintain—almost maintain, I should say—an appreciation of the higher things: so that we could not acknowledge the senselessness of the horror. To the point: by means of noble existential cant the critic wanted to avoid confronting the horror. Herein lies, not least of all, the danger that the horror might recur, that people refuse to let it draw near and indeed even rebuke anyone who merely speaks of it, as though the speaker, if he does not temper things, were the guilty one, and not the perpetrators.

With the problem of authority and barbarism I cannot help thinking of an idea that for the most part is hardly taken into account. It comes up in an observation in the book *The SS State*, by Eugen Kogon, which contains central insights into the whole complex and which hasn't come near to being absorbed by science and educational theory the way it deserves to be.[7] Kogon says that the tormentors of the concentration camp where he spent years were for the most part young sons of farmers. The cultural difference between city and country, which still persists, is one of the conditions of the horror, though certainly neither the sole nor the most important one. Any arrogance toward the rural populace is far from my intentions. I know that one cannot help having grown up in a city or a village. I note only that probably debarbarization has been less successful in the open country than anywhere else.[8] Even television and the other mass media probably have not much changed the state of those who have not completely kept up with the culture. It seems to me more correct to say this and to work against it than to praise sentimentally some special qualities of rural life that are threatening to disappear. I will go so far as to claim that one of the most important goals of education is the debarbarization of the countryside. This presupposes, however, a study of the conscious and unconscious of the population there. Above all, one must also consider the impact of modern mass media on a state of consciousness that has not yet come anywhere close to the state of bourgeois liberal culture of the nineteenth century.

In order to change this state of consciousness, the normal primary school system, which has several problems in the rural environment, cannot suffice. I can envision a series of possibilities. One would be—I am improvising here—that television programs be planned with consideration of the nerve centers of this particular state of consciousness. Then I could imagine that something like mobile educational groups and convoys of volunteers could be formed, who would drive into the countryside and in discussions, courses, and supplementary instruction attempt to fill the most menacing gaps. I am not ignoring the fact that such people would make themselves liked only with great difficulty. But then a small circle of followers would form around them, and from there the educational program could perhaps spread further.

However, there should arise no misunderstanding that the archaic tendency toward violence is also found in urban centers, especially in the larger ones. Regressive tendencies, that is, people with repressed sadistic traits, are produced everywhere today by the global evolution of society. Here I'd like to recall the twisted and pathological relation to the body that Horkheimer and I described in *Dialectic of Enlightenment.*[9] Everywhere where it is mutilated, consciousness is reflected back upon the body and the sphere of the corporeal in an unfree form that tends toward violence. One need only observe how, with a certain type of uneducated person, his language—above all when he feels faulted or reproached—becomes threatening, as if the linguistic gestures bespoke a physical violence barely kept under control. Here one must surely also study the role of sport, which has been insufficiently investigated by a critical social psychology. Sport is ambiguous. On the one hand, it can have an antibarbaric and antisadistic effect by means of *fair play* [E], a spirit of chivalry, and consideration for the weak. On the other hand, in many of its varieties and practices it can promote aggression, brutality, and sadism, above all in people who do not expose themselves to the exertion and discipline required by sports but instead merely watch: that is, those who regularly shout from the sidelines. Such an ambiguity should be analyzed systematically. To the extent that education can exert an influence, the results should be applied to the life of sport.

All this is more or less connected with the old authoritarian structure, with modes of behavior, I could almost say, of the good old authoritarian personality. But what Auschwitz produced, the characteristic personality types of the world of Auschwitz, presumably represents something new. On the one hand, those personality types epitomize the blind identification with the collective. On the other hand, they are fashioned in order to manipulate masses, collectives, as Himmler, Höss, and Eichmann did. I think the most important way to confront the danger of a recurrence is to work against the brute predominance of all collectives, to intensify the resistance to it by concentrating on the problem of collectivization. That is not as abstract as it sounds in view of the passion with which especially young and progressively minded people desire to integrate themselves into something or other. One could start with the suffering the collective first inflicts upon all the individuals it accepts. One has only to think of one's own first experiences in school. One must fight against the type of *folkways*

[E] [*Volkssitten*], initiation rites of all shapes that inflict physical pain—often unbearable pain—upon a person as the price that must be paid in order to consider oneself a member, one of the collective.[10] The evil of customs such as the *Rauhnächte* and the *Haberfeldtreiben* and whatever else such long-rooted practices might be called is a direct anticipation of National Socialist acts of violence.[11] It is no coincidence that the Nazis glorified and cultivated such monstrosities in the name of "customs." Science here has one of its most relevant tasks. It could vigorously redirect the tendencies of folk studies [*Volkskunde*], which were enthusiastically appropriated by the Nazis, in order to prevent the survival, at once brutal and ghostly, of these folk pleasures.

This entire sphere is animated by an alleged ideal that also plays a considerable role in traditional education: the ideal of being hard. This ideal can also, ignominiously enough, invoke a remark of Nietzsche, although he truly meant something else.[12] I remember how the dreadful Boger during the Auschwitz trial had an outburst that culminated in a panegyric to education instilling discipline through hardness. He thought hardness necessary to produce what he considered to be the correct type of person.[13] This educational ideal of hardness, in which many may believe without reflecting about it, is utterly wrong. The idea that virility consists in the maximum degree of endurance long ago became a screen-image for masochism that, as psychology has demonstrated, aligns itself all too easily with sadism. Being hard, the vaunted quality education should inculcate, means absolute indifference toward pain as such. In this the distinction between one's own pain and that of another is not so stringently maintained. Whoever is hard with himself earns the right to be hard with others as well and avenges himself for the pain whose manifestations he was not allowed to show and had to repress. This mechanism must be made conscious, just as an education must be promoted that no longer sets a premium on pain and the ability to endure pain. In other words, education must take seriously an idea in no wise unfamiliar to philosophy: that anxiety must not be repressed. When anxiety is not repressed, when one permits oneself to have, in fact, all the anxiety that this reality warrants, then precisely by doing that, much of the destructive effect of unconscious and displaced anxiety will probably disappear.

People who blindly slot themselves into the collective already make themselves into something like inert material, extinguish themselves as self-determined beings.[14] With this comes the willingness to treat others as an amorphous mass. I called those who behave in this way "the manipulative character" in *Authoritarian Personality*, indeed at a time when the diary of Höss or the recordings of Eichmann were not yet known.[15] My descriptions of the manipulative character date back to the last years of the Second World War. Sometimes social psychology and sociology are able to construct concepts that only later are empirically verified. The manipulative character—as anyone can confirm in the sources available about those Nazi leaders—is distinguished by a rage for organization, by the inability to have any immediate human experiences at all, by a certain lack of emotion, by an overvalued realism. At any cost he wants to conduct supposed, even if delusional, *Realpolitik*. He does not for one second think or wish that the world were any different than it is; he is obsessed by the desire of *doing things* [E] [*Dinge zu tun*], indifferent to the content of such action. He makes a cult of action, activity, of so-called *efficiency* [E] as such, which reappears in the advertising image of the active person. If my observations do not deceive me and if several sociological investigations permit generalization, then this type has become much more prevalent today than one would think. What at that time was exemplified in only a few Nazi monsters could be confirmed today in numerous people, for instance, in juvenile criminals, gang leaders, and the like, about whom one reads in the newspapers every day. If I had to reduce this type of manipulative character to a formula—perhaps one should not do it, but it could also contribute to understanding—then I would call it the type of *reified consciousness*. People of such a nature have, as it were, assimilated themselves to things. And then, when possible, they assimilate others to things. This is conveyed very precisely in the expression "to finish off [*fertigmachen*]," just as popular in the world of juvenile rowdies as in the world of the Nazis. This expression defines people as finished or prepared things in a doubled sense. According to the insight of Max Horkheimer, torture is a manipulated and somewhat accelerated adaptation of people to collectives.[16] There is something of this in the spirit of the age, though it has little to do with spirit. I merely cite the saying of Paul Valéry before the last war, that inhumanity has a great future.[17] It is especially difficult to fight against it because those manipulative people, who actually are incapable of true experience, for that very reason manifest an unresponsiveness that associates them with certain mentally ill or psychotic characters, namely, schizoids.

In the attempt to prevent the repetition of Auschwitz, it seems essential to me first of all to gain some clarity about the conditions under which the manipulative character arises, and then, by altering those conditions, to prevent as far as possible its emergence. I would like to make a concrete proposal: to study the guilty of Auschwitz with all the methods available to science, in particular, with long-term psychoanalysis, in order, if possible, to discover how such a person develops. Those people would be able yet to do some good, in contradiction to their own personality structure, by making a contribution so that such things do not happen again. This could be done only if they would want to collaborate in the investigation of their own genesis. Certainly it will be difficult to induce them to speak; by no means should anything related to their own methods be employed in order to learn how they became what they are. In the meantime, however, in their collective—precisely in the feeling that they are all old Nazis together—they feel so secure that hardly any of them has shown the least sentiment of guilt. Yet presumably there exist even in them, or at least in many, psychologically sensitive points conducive to changing this attitude, for instance, their narcissism: baldly put, their vanity. They might have a sense of importance if they could speak of themselves freely, like Eichmann, who apparently recorded whole libraries of tape. Finally, one can assume that even in these persons, if one digs deep enough, one will find vestiges of the old authority of conscience, which today frequently is in a state of dissolution. Once we learn the external and internal conditions that make them what they are—if I may assume hypothetically that these conditions can in fact be brought forth—then it will be possible to draw practical consequences so that the horror will not happen again. Whether the attempt helps somewhat or not cannot be known before it is undertaken; I don't want to overestimate it. One must remember that individuals cannot be explained automatically by such conditions. Under similar conditions some people develop in one way and other people completely differently. Nevertheless it would be worth the effort. Simply posing such questions already contains a potential for enlightenment. For this disastrous state of conscious and unconscious thought includes the erroneous idea that one's own particular way of being—that one is just so and not otherwise—is nature, an unalterable given, and not a historical evolution. I mentioned the concept of reified consciousness. Above all, this is a consciousness blinded to all historical past, all insight into one's own conditionedness, and posits as absolute what exists contingently. If this coercive mechanism were once ruptured, then, I think, something would indeed be gained.

Furthermore, in connection with reified consciousness one should also observe closely the relationship to technology, and certainly not only within small groups. The relationship here is just as ambiguous as in sports, to which it is related, incidentally. On the one hand, each epoch produces those personalities—types varying according to their distribution of psychic energy—it needs societally. A world where technology occupies such a key position as it does nowadays produces technological people, who are attuned to technology. This has its good reason: in their own narrow field they will be less likely to be fooled, and that can also affect the overall situation. On the other hand, there is something exaggerated, irrational, pathogenic in the present-day relationship to technology. This is connected with the "veil of technology." People are inclined to take technology to be the thing itself, as an end in itself, a force of its own, and they forget that it is an extension of human dexterity. The means—and technology is the epitome of the means of self-preservation of the human species—are fetishized, because the ends—a life of human dignity—are concealed and removed from the consciousness of people.[18] As long as one formulates this as generally as I just did, it should provide insight. But such a hypothesis is still much too abstract. It is by no means clear precisely how the fetishization of technology establishes itself within the individual psychology of particular people, or where the threshold lies between a rational relationship to technology and the overvaluation that finally leads to the point where one who cleverly devises a train system that brings the victims to Auschwitz as quickly and smoothly as possible forgets about what happens to them there. With this type, who tends to fetishize technology, we are concerned—baldly put, with people who cannot love. This is not meant to be sentimental or moralistic but rather describes a deficient libidinal relationship to other persons. Those people are thoroughly cold; deep within themselves they must deny the possibility of love, must withdraw their love from other people initially, before it can even unfold. And whatever of the ability to love somehow survives in them they must expend on devices.[19] Those prejudiced, authoritarian characters whom we examined at Berkeley in *Authoritarian Personality* provided us with much proof of this. A test subject—the expression itself already comes from reified consciousness—said of himself, "*I like nice equipment*" [E] [*Ich habe hübsche Ausstattungen, hübsche Apparaturen gern*],[20] completely indifferent about what equipment it was. His love was absorbed by things, machines as such.

The alarming thing about this—alarming, because combating it can seem so hopeless—is that this trend goes hand in hand with that of the entire civilization. To struggle against it means to stand against the world spirit; but with this I am only repeating what I mentioned at the outset as the darkest aspect of an education opposed to Auschwitz.

As I said, those people are cold in a specific way. Surely a few words about coldness in general are permitted. If coldness were not a fundamental trait of anthropology, that is, the constitution of people as they in fact exist in our society, if people were not profoundly indifferent toward whatever happens to everyone else except for a few to whom they are closely and, possibly, by tangible interests bound, then Auschwitz would not have been possible, people would not have accepted it. Society in its present form—and no doubt as it has been for centuries already—is based not, as has been ideologically assumed since Aristotle, on appeal, on attraction, but rather on the pursuit of one's own interests against the interests of everyone else.[21] This has settled into the character of people to their innermost center. What contradicts my observation, the herd drive of the so-called *lonely crowd* [E] [*die einsame Menge*],[22] is a reaction to this process, a banding together of people completely cold who cannot endure their own coldness and yet cannot change it. Every person today, without exception, feels too little loved, because every person cannot love enough. The inability to identify with others was unquestionably the most important psychological condition for the fact that something like Auschwitz could have occurred in the midst of more or less civilized and innocent people. What is called fellow traveling was primarily business interest: one pursues one's own advantage before all else and, simply not to endanger oneself, does not talk too much. That is a general law of the status quo. The silence under the terror was only its consequence.[23] The coldness of the societal monad, the isolated competitor, was the precondition, as indifference to the fate of others, for the fact that only very few people reacted. The torturers know this, and they put it to the test ever anew.

Understand me correctly. I do not want to preach love. I consider it futile to preach it; no one has the right to preach it since the lack of love, as I have already said, is a lack belonging to *all* people without exception as they exist today. To preach love already presupposes in those to whom one appeals a character structure different from the one that needs to be changed. For the people whom one should love are themselves such that they cannot love, and therefore in turn are not at all that lovable. One of the greatest impulses of Christianity, not immediately identical with its dogma, was to eradicate the coldness that permeates everything. But this attempt failed, surely because it did not reach into the societal order that produces and reproduces that coldness. Probably the warmth among people that everyone longs for has never been present at all except during short periods and in very small groups, perhaps even among peaceful savages. The much maligned utopians saw this. Thus Charles Fourier defined attraction as something that first must be produced through a humane societal order; he also recognized that this condition would be possible only when the drives of people are no longer repressed, but fulfilled and released.[24] If anything can help against coldness as the condition for disaster, then it is the insight into the conditions that determine it and the attempt to combat those conditions, initially in the domain of the individual. One might think that the less is denied to children, the better they are treated, the greater would be the chance of success. But here too illusions threaten. Children who have no idea of the cruelty and hardness of life are then truly exposed to barbarism when they must leave their protected environment. Above all, however, it is impossible to awaken warmth in the parents, who are themselves products of this society and who bear its marks. The exhortation to give more warmth to children amounts to pumping out warmth artificially, thereby negating it. Moreover, love cannot be summoned in professionally mediated relations like that of teacher and student, doctor and patient, lawyer and client. Love is something immediate and in essence contradicts mediated relationships. The exhortation to love—even in its imperative form, that one *should* do it—is itself part of the ideology coldness perpetuates. It bears the compulsive, oppressive quality that counteracts the ability to love. The first thing therefore is to bring coldness to the consciousness of itself, of the reasons why it arose.

In conclusion, permit me to say a few words about some possibilities for making conscious the general subjective mechanisms without which Auschwitz would hardly have been possible. Knowledge of these mechanisms is necessary, as is knowledge of the stereotypical defense mechanisms that block such a consciousness.[25] Whoever still says today that it did not happen or was not all that bad already defends what took place and unquestionably would be prepared to look on or join in if it happens again. Even if rational enlightenment, as psychology well knows, does not straightaway eliminate the unconscious mechanisms, then it reinforces, at least in the preconscious, certain counterimpulses and helps prepare a climate that does not favor the uttermost extreme. If the entire cultural consciousness really became permeated with the idea of the pathogenic character of the tendencies that came into their own at Auschwitz, then perhaps people would better control those tendencies.[26]

Furthermore, one should work to raise awareness about the possible displacement of what broke out in Auschwitz. Tomorrow a group other than the Jews may come along, say, the elderly, who indeed were still spared in the Third Reich, or the intellectuals, or simply deviant groups. As I indicated, the climate that most promotes such a resurrection is the revival of nationalism. It is so evil because, in the age of international communication and supranational blocs, nationalism cannot really believe in itself anymore and must exaggerate itself to the extreme in order to persuade itself and others that it is still substantial.

Concrete possibilities of resistance nonetheless must be shown. For instance, one should investigate the history of euthanasia murders, which in Germany, thanks to the resistance the program met, were not perpetrated to the full extent planned by the National Socialists. The resistance was limited to the group concerned: precisely this is a particularly conspicuous, very common symptom of the universal coldness. The coldness, however, on top of everything else, is narrow-minded in view of the insatiability that lies within the principle of the persecutions. Virtually anyone who does not belong directly to the persecuting group can be overtaken; there is thus a drastic, egoistic interest that can be appealed to. Finally, inquiry must be made into the specific, historically objective conditions of the persecutions. So-called national revival movements in an age in which nationalism is obsolete are obviously especially susceptible to sadistic practices.

All political instruction finally should be centered upon the idea that Auschwitz should never happen again. This would be possible only when it devotes itself openly, without fear of offending any authorities, to this most important of problems. To do this education must transform itself into sociology, that is, it must teach about the societal play of forces that operates beneath the surface of political forms. One must submit to critical treatment—to provide just one model—such a respectable concept as that of "reason of state"; in placing the right of the state over that of its members, the horror is potentially already posited.

Walter Benjamin asked me once in Paris during his emigration, when I was still returning to Germany sporadically, whether there were really enough torturers back there to carry out the orders of the Nazis. There were enough. Nevertheless the question has its profound legitimacy. Benjamin sensed that the people who *do* it, as opposed to the bureaucratic desktop murderers and ideologues, operate contrary to their own immediate interests, are murderers of themselves while they murder others. I fear that the measures of even such an elaborate education will hardly hinder the renewed growth of desktop murderers. But that there are people who do it down below, indeed as servants, through which they perpetuate their own servitude and degrade themselves, that there are more Bogers and Kaduks: against this, however, education and enlightenment can still manage a little something.

(1967; GS 10.2: 674–90)
Translated by Henry W. Pickford

PART TWO

DAMAGED LIFE

3

Selections from *Minima Moralia*

Grassy seat. Our relationship to parents is beginning to undergo a sad, shadowy transformation. Through their economic impotence they have lost their awesomeness. Once we rebelled against their insistence on the reality principle, the sobriety forever prone to become wrath against those less ready to renounce. But today we are faced with a generation purporting to be young, yet in all its reactions insufferably more grown-up than its parents ever were; which, having renounced before any conflict, draws from this its grimly authoritarian, unshakable power. Perhaps people have at all times felt the parental generation to become harmless, powerless, with the waning of its physical strength, while their own generation already seemed threatened by the young: in an antagonistic society the relation between generations, too, is one of competition, behind which stands naked power. But today it is beginning to regress to a state versed, not in the Oedipus complex, but in parricide. One of the Nazis' symbolic outrages is the killing of the very old. Such a climate fosters a late, lucid understanding with our parents, as between the condemned, marred only by the fear that we, powerless ourselves, might now be unable to care for them as well as they cared for us when they possessed something. The violence done to them makes us forget the violence they did. Even their rationalizations, the once-hated lies with which they sought to justify their particular interest as a general one, reveal in them an inkling of the truth, an urge to resolve a conflict whose existence their children, proof against all uncertainty, cheerfully deny. Even the outdated, inconsistent, self-doubting ideas of the older generation are more open to dialogue than the slick stupidity of Junior. Even the neurotic oddities and deformities of our elders stand for character, for something humanly achieved, in comparison to pathic health, infantilism raised to the norm. One realizes with horror that earlier, opposing one's parents because they represented the world, one was often secretly the mouthpiece, against a bad world, of one even worse. Unpolitical attempts to break out of the bourgeois family usually lead only to deeper entanglement in it, and it sometimes seems as if the fatal germ-cell of society, the family, were at the same time the nurturing germ-cell of uncompromising pursuit of another. With the family there passes away, while the system lasts, not only the most effective agency of the bourgeoisie, but also the resistance that, though repressing the individual, also strengthened, perhaps even produced him. The end of the family paralyzes the forces of opposition. The rising collectivist order is a mockery of a classless one: together with the bourgeois it liquidates the Utopia that once drew sustenance from motherly love.

How nice of you, Doctor. There is nothing innocuous left. The little pleasures, expressions of life that seemed exempt from the responsibility of thought, not only have an element of defiant silliness, of callous refusal to see, but directly serve their diametrical opposite. Even the blossoming tree lies the moment its bloom is seen without the shadow of terror; even the innocent "How lovely!" becomes an excuse for an existence outrageously unlovely, and there is no longer beauty or consolation except in the gaze falling on horror, withstanding it, and in unalleviated consciousness of negativity holding fast to the possibility of what is better. Mistrust is called for in the face of all spontaneity, impetuosity, all letting oneself go, for it implies pliancy toward the superior might of the existent. The malignant deeper meaning of ease, once confined to the toasts of conviviality, has long since spread to more appealing impulses. The chance conversation in the train, when, to avoid dispute, one consents to a few statements that one knows ultimately to implicate murder, is already a betrayal; no thought is immune to communication, and to utter it in the wrong place and in wrong agreement is enough to undermine its truth. Every visit to the cinema leaves me, against all my vigilance, stupider and worse. Sociability itself connives at injustice by pretending that in this chill world we can still talk to each other, and the casual, amiable remark contributes to perpetuating silence, in that the concessions made to the interlocutor debase him once more in the person of speaker. The evil principle that was always latent in affability unfurls its full bestiality in the egalitarian spirit. Condescension, and thinking oneself no better, are the same. To adapt to the weakness of the oppressed is to affirm in it the precondition of power, and to develop in oneself the coarseness, insensibility, and violence needed to exert domination. If, in the latest phase, the condescending gesture has been dropped and only the adaptation remains visible, this perfect screening of power only allows the class-relationship it denies to triumph more implacably. For the intellectual, inviolable isolation is now the only way of showing some measure of solidarity. All collaboration, all the human worth of social mixing and participation, merely masks a tacit acceptance of inhumanity. It is the sufferings of men that should be shared: the smallest step toward their pleasures is one toward the hardening of their pains.

Le Bourgeois revenant. Absurdly, the fascist regimes of the first half of the twentieth century have stabilized an obsolete economic form, multiplying the terror needed to maintain it now that its senselessness is blatant. Thereby has private life also been marked. With the strengthening of external authority the stuffy private order, particularism of interests, the long-outdated form of the family, the right of property and its reflection in character, have also reconsolidated themselves. But with a bad conscience, a scarcely concealed awareness of untruth. Whatever was once good and decent in bourgeois values, independence, perseverance, forethought, circumspection has been corrupted utterly. For while bourgeois forms of existence are truculently conserved, their economic precondition has fallen away. Privacy has given way entirely to the privation it always secretly was, and with the stubborn adherence to particular interests is now mingled fury at being no longer able to perceive that things might be different and better. In losing their innocence, the bourgeois have become impenitently malign. The caring hand that even now tends the little garden as if it had not long since become a "lot," but fearfully wards off the unknown intruder, is already that which denies the political refugee asylum. Now objectively threatened, the subjectivity of the rulers and their hangers-on becomes totally inhuman. So the class realizes itself, taking upon itself the destructive will of the course of the world. The bourgeois live on like specters threatening doom.

Proprietary rights. It is the signature of our age that no one, without exception, can now determine his own life within even a moderately comprehensible framework, as was possible earlier in the assessment of market relationships. In principle everyone, however powerful, is an object. Even the profession of general no longer offers adequate protection. No agreements, in the fascist era, are binding enough to secure headquarters against air attacks, and commandants observing traditional caution are hanged by Hitler and beheaded by Chiang Kai-shek. It follows directly from this that anyone who attempts to come out alive—and survival itself has something nonsensical about it, like dreams in which, having experienced the end of the world, one afterwards crawls from a basement—ought also to be prepared at each moment to end his life. This is the mournful truth that has emerged from Zarathustra's exuberant doctrine of freely chosen death. Freedom has contracted to pure negativity, and what in the days of Art Nouveau was known as a beautiful death has shrunk to the wish to curtail the infinite abasement of living and the infinite torment of dying, in a world where there are far worse things to fear than death.—The objective end of humanism is only another expression for the same thing. It signifies that the individual as individual, in representing the species of man, has lost the autonomy through which he might realize the species.

Refuge for the homeless. The predicament of private life today is shown by its arena. Dwelling, in the proper sense, is now impossible. The traditional residences we grew up in have grown intolerable: each trait of comfort in them is paid for with a betrayal of knowledge, each vestige of shelter with the musty pact of family interests. The functional modern habitations designed from a *tabula rasa* are living-cases manufactured by experts for philistines, or factory sites that have strayed into the consumption sphere, devoid of all relation to the occupant: in them even the nostalgia for independent existence, defunct in any case, is sent packing. Modern man wishes to sleep close to the ground like an animal, a German magazine decreed with prophetic masochism before Hitler, abolishing with the bed the threshold between waking and dreaming. The sleepless are on call at any hour, unresistingly ready for anything, alert and unconscious at once. Anyone seeking refuge in a genuine, but purchased, period-style house embalms himself alive. The attempt to evade responsibility for one's residence by moving into a hotel or furnished rooms makes the enforced conditions of emigration a wisely chosen norm. The hardest hit, as everywhere, are those who have no choice. They live, if not in slums, in bungalows that by tomorrow may be leaf-huts, trailers, cars, camps, or the open air. The house is past. The bombings of European cities, as well as the labor and concentration camps, merely proceed as executors, with what the immanent development of technology had long decided was to be the fate of houses. These are now good only to be thrown away like old food cans. The possibility of residence is annihilated by that of socialist society, which, once missed, saps the foundations of bourgeois life. No individual can resist this process. He need only take an interest in furniture design or interior decoration to find himself developing the artsy-craftsy sensibilities of the bibliophile, however firmly he may oppose arts-and-crafts in the narrower sense. From a distance the difference between the Vienna Workshops and the Bauhaus is no longer so considerable. Purely functional curves, having broken free of their purpose, are now becoming just as ornamental as the basic structures of Cubism. The best mode of conduct, in the face of all this, still seems an uncommitted, suspended one: to lead a private life, as far as the social order and one's own needs will tolerate nothing else, but not to attach weight to it as to something still socially substantial and individually appropriate. "It is even part of my good fortune not to be a house-owner," Nietzsche already wrote in *The Gay Science*.[1] Today we should have to add: it is part of morality not to be at home in one's home. This gives some indication of the difficult relationship in which the individual now stands to his property, as long as he still possesses anything at all. The trick is to keep in view, and to express, the fact that private property no longer belongs to one, in the sense that consumer goods have become potentially so abundant that no individual has the right to cling to the principle of their limitation; but that one must nevertheless have possessions, if one is not to sink into that dependence and need that serves the blind perpetuation of property relations. But the thesis of this paradox leads to destruction, a loveless disregard for things that necessarily turns against people, too; and the antithesis, no sooner uttered, is an ideology for those wishing with a bad conscience to keep what they have. Wrong life cannot be lived rightly.

Baby with the bathwater. Among the motifs of cultural criticism, one of the most long-established and central is that of the lie: that culture creates the illusion of a society worthy of man, which does not exist; that it conceals the material conditions upon which all human works rise; and that, comforting and lulling, it serves to keep alive the bad economic determination of existence. This is the notion of culture as ideology, which appears at first sight common both to the bourgeois doctrine of violence and to its adversary, both to Nietzsche and to Marx. But precisely this notion, like all expostulation about lies, has a suspicious tendency to become itself ideology. This can be seen on the private level. Inexorably, the thought of money and all its attendant conflicts extends into the most tender erotic, the most sublime spiritual relationships. With the logic of coherence and the pathos of truth, cultural criticism could therefore demand that relationships be entirely reduced to their material origin, ruthlessly and openly formed according to the interests of the participants. For meaning, as we know, is not independent of genesis, and it is easy to discern, in everything that cloaks or mediates the material, the trace of insincerity, sentimentality, indeed, precisely a concealed and doubly poisonous interest. But to act radically in accordance with this principle would be to extirpate, with the false, all that was true also, all that, however impotently, strives to escape the confines of universal practice, every chimerical anticipation of a nobler condition, and so to bring about directly the barbarism that culture is reproached with furthering indirectly. In the cultural critics after Nietzsche this reversal of position has always been obvious: Spengler endorsed it enthusiastically. But Marxists are not proof against it either. Cured of the Social-Democratic belief in cultural progress and confronted with growing barbarism, they are under constant temptation to advocate the latter in the interests of the "objective tendency," and, in an act of desperation, to await salvation from their mortal enemy, who, as the "antithesis," is supposed in blind and mysterious fashion to help prepare the good end. Apart from this, emphasis on the material element, as against the spirit as a lie, gives rise to a kind of dubious affinity with that political economy that is subjected to an immanent criticism, comparable to the complicity between police and underworld. Since Utopia was set aside and the unity of theory and practice demanded, we have become all too practical. Fear of the impotence of theory supplies a pretext for bowing to the almighty production process, and so fully admitting the impotence of theory. Traits of malice are not alien even to authentic Marxist language, and today there is a growing resemblance between the business mentality and sober critical judgment, between vulgar materialism and the other kind, so that it is at times difficult properly to distinguish subject and object.—To identify culture solely with lies is more fateful than ever, now that the former is really becoming totally absorbed by the latter, and eagerly invites such identification in order to compromise every opposing thought. If material reality is called the world of exchange value, and culture, whatever refuses to accept the domination of that world, then it is true that such refusal is illusory as long as the existent exists. Since, however, free and honest exchange is itself a lie, to deny it is at the same time to speak for truth: in the face of the lie of the commodity world, even the lie that denounces it becomes a corrective. That culture so far has failed is no justification for furthering its failure, by strewing the store of good flour on the spilt beer like the girl in the fairy tale. People who belong together ought neither to keep silent about their material interests, nor to sink to their level, but to assimilate them by reflection into their relationships and so surpass them.

Savages are not more noble. There is to be found in African students of political economy, in Siamese at Oxford, and more generally in diligent art-historians and musicologists of petit-bourgeois origins, a ready inclination to combine with the assimilation of new material an inordinate respect for all that is established, accepted, acknowledged. An uncompromising mind is the very opposite of primitivism, neophytism, or the "noncapitalist world." It presupposes experience, a historical memory, a fastidious intellect, and above all an ample measure of satiety. It has been observed time and again how those recruited young and innocent to radical groups have defected once they felt the force of tradition. One must have tradition in oneself, to hate it properly. That snobs show more aptitude than proletarians for avant-garde movements in art throws light on politics too. Latecomers and newcomers have an alarming affinity for positivism, from Carnap-worshipers in India to the stalwart defenders of the German masters Matthias Grünewald and Heinrich Schütz.[1] It would be poor psychology to assume that exclusion arouses only hate and resentment; it arouses too a possessive, intolerant kind of love, and those whom repressive culture has held at a distance can easily enough become its most diehard defenders. There is even an echo of this in the sentential language of the worker who wants, as a Socialist, to "learn something," to partake of the so-called heritage, and the philistinism of the Bebels[2] lies less in

their incomprehension of culture than in the alacrity with which they accept it at face value, identify with it, and in so doing, of course, reverse its
meaning. Socialism is in general no more secure against this transformation than against lapsing theoretically into positivism. It can happen easily
enough that in the Far East Marx is put in the place vacated by Driesch
and Rickert.[3] There is some reason to fear that the involvement of non-
Western peoples in the conflicts of industrial society, long overdue in itself,
will be less to the benefit of the liberated peoples than to that of rationally
improved production and communications, and a modestly raised standard of living. Instead of expecting miracles of the precapitalist peoples,
older nations should be on their guard against their unimaginative, indo-
lent taste for everything proven, and for the successes of the West.

Out of the firing line. Reports of air attacks are seldom without the
names of the firms that produced the planes: Focke-Wulff, Heinkel, Lan-
caster feature where once the talk was of cuirassiers, lancers, and hussars.
The mechanism for reproducing life, for dominating, and for destroying it
is exactly the same, and accordingly industry, state, and advertising are
amalgamated. The old exaggeration of skeptical liberals, that war was a
business, has come true: state power has shed even the appearance of independence from particular interests in profit; always in their service really, it
now also places itself there ideologically. Every laudatory mention of the
chief contractor in the destruction of cities helps to earn it the good name
that will secure it the best commissions in their rebuilding.

Like the Thirty Years' War, this too—a war whose beginning no one
will remember when it comes to an end—falls into discontinuous cam-
paigns separated by empty pauses: the Polish campaign, the Norwegian,
the Russian, the Tunisian, the Invasion. Its rhythm, the alternation of jerky
action and total standstill for lack of geographically attainable enemies, has
the same mechanical quality that characterizes individual military instruments and that too is doubtless what has resurrected the pre-liberal form
of the campaign. But this mechanical rhythm completely determines the
human relation to the war, not only in the disproportion between individual bodily strength and the energy of machines, but in the most hidden
cells of experience. Even in the previous conflict the body's incongruity
with mechanical warfare made real experience impossible. No one could
have recounted it as even the Artillery-General Napoleon's battles could be

recalled. The long interval between the war memoirs and the conclusion of peace is not fortuitous: it testifies to the painful reconstruction of memory, which in all the books conveys a sense of impotence and even falseness, no matter what terrors the writers have passed through. But the Second War is as totally divorced from experience as is the functioning of a machine from the movements of the body, which only begins to resemble it in pathological states. Just as the war lacks continuity, history, an "epic" element, but seems rather to start anew from the beginning in each phase, so it will leave behind no permanent, unconsciously preserved image in the memory. Everywhere, with each explosion, it has breached the barrier against stimuli beneath which experience, the lag between healing oblivion and healing recollection, forms. Life has changed into a timeless succession of shocks, interspaced with empty, paralyzed intervals. But nothing, perhaps, is more ominous for the future than the fact that, quite literally, these things will soon be past thinking on, for each trauma of the returning combatants, each shock not inwardly absorbed, is a ferment of future destruction. Karl Kraus was right to call his play *The Last Days of Mankind*. What is being enacted now ought to bear the title: "After Doomsday."

The total obliteration of the war by information, propaganda, commentaries, with cameramen in the first tanks and war reporters dying heroic deaths, the mishmash of enlightened manipulation of public opinion and oblivious activity: all this is another expression for the withering of experience, the vacuum between men and their fate, in which their real fate lies. It is as if the reified, hardened plaster-cast of events takes the place of events themselves. Men are reduced to walk-on parts in a monster documentary film that has no spectators, since the least of them has his bit to do on the screen. It is just this aspect that underlies the much-maligned designation "phony war." Certainly, the term has its origin in the fascist inclination to dismiss the reality of horror as "mere propaganda" in order to perpetrate it unopposed. But like all fascist tendencies, this too has its source in elements of reality, which assert themselves only by virtue of the fascist attitude malignantly insinuating them. The war is really phony, but with a phoniness more horrifying than all the horrors, and those who mock at it are principal contributors to disaster.

Had Hegel's philosophy of history embraced this age, Hitler's robot bombs would have found their place beside the early death of Alexander and similar images, as one of the selected empirical facts by which the state of the world spirit manifests itself directly in symbols. Like fascism itself, the robots career without a subject. Like it, they combine utmost technical perfection with total blindness. And like it they arouse mortal terror and are wholly futile. "I have seen the world spirit," not on horseback, but on wings and without a head, and that refutes, at the same stroke, Hegel's philosophy of history.

The idea that after this war life will continue "normally" or even that culture might be "rebuilt"—as if the rebuilding of culture were not already its negation—is idiotic. Millions of Jews have been murdered, and this is to be seen as an interlude and not the catastrophe itself. What more is this culture waiting for? And even if countless people still have time to wait, is it conceivable that what happened in Europe will have no consequences, that the quantity of victims will not be transformed into a new quality of society at large, barbarism? As long as blow is followed by counterblow, catastrophe is perpetuated. One need only think of revenge for the murdered. If as many of the others are killed, horror will be institutionalized, and the precapitalist pattern of vendettas, confined from time immemorial to remote mountainous regions, will be reintroduced in extended form, with whole nations as the subjectless subjects. If, however, the dead are not avenged and mercy is exercised, fascism will, despite everything, get away with its victory scot-free, and, having once been shown so easy, will be continued elsewhere. The logic of history is as destructive as the people that it brings to prominence: wherever its momentum carries it, it reproduces equivalents of past calamity. Normality is death.

To the question what is to be done with defeated Germany, I could say only two things in reply. Firstly: at no price, on no conditions, would I wish to be an executioner or to supply legitimations for executioners. Secondly: I should not wish, least of all with legal machinery, to stay the hand of anyone who was avenging past misdeeds. This is a thoroughly unsatisfactory, contradictory answer, one that makes a mockery of both principle and practice. But perhaps the fault lies in the question and not only in me.

Cinema newsreel: the invasion of the Marianas, including Guam. The impression is not of battles, but of civil engineering and blasting operations undertaken with immeasurably intensified vehemence, also of "fumigation," insect extermination on a terrestrial scale. Works are put in hand, until no grass grows. The enemy acts as patient and corpse. Like the Jews under fascism, he features now as merely the object of technical and administrative measures, and should he defend himself, his own action immediately takes on the same character. Satanically, indeed, more initiative is in a sense demanded here than in old-style war: it seems to cost the subject his whole energy to achieve subjectlessness. Consummate inhumanity is the realization of Edward Grey's humane dream, war without hatred.

Autumn 1944

Johnny-Head-in-Air. The relation of knowledge to power is one not only of servility but of truth. Much knowledge, if out of proportion to the disposition of forces, is invalid, however formally correct it may be. If an émigré doctor says, "For me, Adolf Hitler is a pathological case," his pronouncement may ultimately be confirmed by clinical findings, but its incongruity with the objective calamity visited on the world in the name of that paranoiac renders the diagnosis ridiculous, mere professional preening. Perhaps Hitler is "in-himself" a pathological case, but certainly not "for-him." The vanity and poverty of many of the declarations against fascism by émigrés is connected with this. People thinking in the forms of free, detached, disinterested appraisal were unable to accommodate within those forms the experience of violence that in reality annuls such thinking. The almost insoluble task is to let neither the power of others nor our own powerlessness stupefy us.

Back to culture. The claim that Hitler has destroyed German culture is no more than an advertising stunt of those who want to rebuild it from their telephone desks. Such art and thought as were exterminated by Hitler had long been leading a severed and apocryphal existence, whose last hideouts fascism swept out. Anyone who did not play the game was forced into inner emigration years before the Third Reich broke out: at the latest with the stabilization of the German currency, coinciding with the end of expressionism, German culture stabilized itself in the spirit of the Berlin illustrated magazines, which yielded little to that of the Nazis' "Strength through Joy," Reich autobahns, and jaunty exhibition-hall classicism. The whole span of German culture was languishing, precisely where it was most liberal, for its Hitler, and it is an injustice to the editors of Mosse and Ullstein[1] or to the reorganizers of the *Frankfurter Zeitung* to reproach them with time-serving under Nazism. They were always like that, and their line of least resistance to the intellectual wares they produced was continued undeflected in the line of least resistance to a political regime among whose ideological methods, as the führer himself declared, comprehensibility to the most stupid ranked highest. This has led to fatal confusion. Hitler eradicated culture, Hitler drove Mr. X into exile, therefore Mr. X is culture. He is indeed. A glance at the literary output of those émigrés who, by discipline and a sharp separation of spheres of influence, performed the feat of representing the German mind shows what is to be expected of a happy reconstruction: the introduction of Broadway methods on the Kurfürstendamm, which differed from the former in the Twenties only through its lesser means, not its better intentions. Those who oppose cultural fascism should start with Weimar, the "Bombs on Monte Carlo," and the Press Ball, if they do not wish to finish by discovering that equivocal figures like Fallada[2] spoke more truth under Hitler than the unambiguous celebrities who successfully transplanted their prestige.

Invitation to the dance. Psychoanalysis prides itself on restoring the capacity for pleasure, which is impaired by neurotic illness. As if the mere concept of a capacity for pleasure did not suffice gravely to devalue such a thing, if it exists. As if a happiness gained through speculation on happiness were not the opposite, a further encroachment of institutionally planned behavior-patterns on the ever-diminishing sphere of experience. What a state the dominant consciousness must have reached when the resolute proclamation of compulsive extravagance and champagne jollity, formerly reserved to attachés in Hungarian operettas, is elevated in deadly earnest to a maxim of right living. Prescribed happiness looks exactly what it is; to have a part in it, the neurotic thus made happy must forfeit the last vestige of reason left to him by repression and regression, and to oblige the analyst, display indiscriminate enthusiasm for the trashy film, the expensive but bad meal in the French restaurant, the serious drink, and the lovemaking taken like medicine as "sex." Schiller's dictum that "Life's good, in spite of all," *papier-mâché* from the start, has become idiocy now that it is blown into the same trumpet as omnipresent advertising, with psychoanalysis, despite its better possibilities, adding its fuel to the flames. As people have altogether too few inhibitions and not too many, without being a whit the healthier for it, a cathartic method with a standard other than successful adaptation and economic success would have to aim at bringing people to a consciousness of unhappiness both general and—inseparable from it—personal, and at depriving them of the illusory gratifications by which the abominable order keeps a second hold on life inside them, as if it did not already have them firmly enough in its power from outside. Only when sated with false pleasure, disgusted with the goods offered, dimly aware of the inadequacy of happiness even when it is that—to say nothing of cases where it is bought by abandoning allegedly morbid resistance to its positive surrogate—can men gain an idea of what experience might be. The admonitions to be happy, voiced in concert by the scientifically epicurean sanatorium-director and the highly strung propaganda chiefs of the entertainment industry, have about them the fury of the father berating his children for not rushing joyously downstairs when he comes home irritable from his office. It is part of the mechanism of domination to forbid recognition of the suffering it produces, and there is a straight line of development between the gospel of happiness and the construction of camps of extermination so far off in Poland that each of our own countrymen can convince himself that he cannot hear the screams of pain. That is the model of an unhampered capacity for happiness. He who calls it by its name will be told gloatingly by psychoanalysis that it is just his Oedipus complex.

On the morality of thinking. Naïveté and sophistication are concepts so endlessly intertwined that no good can come of playing one off against the other. The defense of the ingenuous, as practiced by irrationalists and intellectual-baiters of all kinds, is ignoble. Reflection that takes sides with naïveté condemns itself: cunning and obscurantism remain what they always were. Mediately to affirm immediacy, instead of comprehending it as mediated within itself, is to pervert thought into an apologia of its antithesis, into the immediate lie. This perversion serves all bad purposes, from the private pigheadedness of "life's-like-that" to the justification of social injustice as a law of nature. However, to wish on these grounds to erect the opposite as a principle, and to call philosophy—as I once did myself— the binding obligation to be sophisticated, is hardly better. It is not only that sophistication, in the sense of worldly-wise, hard-boiled shrewdness, is a dubious medium of knowledge, forever liable, through its affinity to the practical orders of life and its general mental distrust of theory, itself to revert to a naïveté engrossed with utilitarian goals. Even when sophistication is understood in the theoretically acceptable sense of that which widens horizons, passes beyond the isolated phenomenon, considers the whole, there is still a cloud in the sky. It is just this passing-on and being unable to linger, this tacit assent to the primacy of the general over the particular, which constitutes not only the deception of idealism in hypostatizing concepts but also its inhumanity, which has no sooner grasped the particular than it reduces it to a through-station, and finally comes all too quickly to terms with suffering and death for the sake of a reconciliation occurring merely in reflection—in the last analysis, the bourgeois coldness that is only too willing to underwrite the inevitable. Knowledge can widen horizons only by abiding so insistently with the particular that its isolation is dispelled. This admittedly presupposes a relation to the general, though not one of subsumption, but rather almost the reverse. Dialectical mediation is not a recourse to the more abstract, but a process of resolution of the concrete in itself. Nietzsche, who too often thought in over-wide horizons himself, was nevertheless aware of this: "He who seeks to mediate between two bold thinkers," he writes in *The Gay Science*, "stamps himself as mediocre: he has not the eyes to see uniqueness: to perceive resemblances everywhere, making everything alike, is a sign of weak eyesight."[1] The morality of thought lies in a procedure that is neither entrenched nor detached, neither blind nor empty, neither atomistic nor consequential. The double-edged method that has earned Hegel's *Phenomenology* the reputation among reasonable people of unfathomable difficulty, that is, its simultaneous demands that phenomena be allowed to speak as such—in a "pure looking-on"—and yet that their relation to consciousness as the subject, reflection, be at every moment maintained, expresses this morality most directly and in all its depth of contradiction. But how much more difficult has it become to conform to such morality now that it is no longer possible to convince oneself of the identity of subject and object, the ultimate assumption of which still enabled Hegel to conceal the antagonistic demands of observation and interpretation. Nothing less is asked of the thinker today than that he should be at every moment both within things and outside them—Münchhausen pulling himself out of the bog by his pigtail becomes the pattern of knowledge that wishes to be more than either verification or speculation. And then the salaried philosophers come along and reproach us with having no definite point of view.

Morality and temporal sequence. While literature has treated all the psychological species of erotic conflict, the simplest external source of conflict has remained unnoticed because of its obviousness. It is the phenomenon of prior engagement: a loved person refuses herself to us not through inner antagonisms and inhibitions, too much coldness or repressed warmth, but because a relationship already exists that excludes another. Abstract temporal sequence plays in reality the part one would like to ascribe to the hierarchy of feelings. In being previously engaged there is, apart from the freedom of choice and decision, also an accidental element that seems in flat contradiction to the claims of freedom. Even, and precisely, in a society cured of the anarchy of commodity production, there could scarcely be rules governing the order in which one met people. Such an arrangement would amount to the most intolerable interference with freedom. Thus the priority of the fortuitous has powerful arguments on its side: someone ousted by a newcomer is always misused, a shared past life annulled, experience itself deleted. The irreversibility of time constitutes an objective moral criterion. But it is one intimately related to myth, like abstract time itself. The exclusiveness implicit in time gives rise, by its inherent law, to the exclusive domination of hermetically sealed groups, finally to that of big business. Nothing is more touching than a loving woman's anxiety lest love and tenderness, her best possession just because they cannot be possessed, be stolen away by a newcomer, simply because of her newness, itself conferred by the prerogative of the older. But from this touching feeling, without which all warmth and protection would pass away, an irresistible path leads, by way of the little boy's aversion for his younger brother and the fraternity student's contempt for his "fag," to the immigration laws that exclude all non-Caucasians from Social-Democratic Australia, and right up to the fascist eradication of the racial minority, in which, indeed, all warmth and shelter explode into nothingness. Not only were all good things, as Nietzsche knew, once bad things: the gentlest, left to follow their own momentum, have a tendency to culminate in unimaginable brutality.

It would serve no purpose to try to point to a way out of this entanglement. Yet it is undoubtedly possible to name the fatal moment that brings the whole dialectic into play. It lies in the exclusive character of what comes first. The original relationship, in its mere immediacy, already presupposes abstract temporal sequence. Historically, the notion of time is itself formed on the basis of the order of ownership. But the desire to possess reflects time as a fear of losing, of the irrecoverable. Whatever is, is experienced in relation to its possible nonbeing. This alone makes it fully a possession and, thus petrified, something functional that can be exchanged for other, equivalent possessions. Once wholly a possession, the loved person is no longer really looked at. Abstraction in love is the complement of exclusiveness, which manifests itself deceptively as the opposite of abstract, a clinging to this one unique being. But such possessiveness loses its hold on its object precisely through turning it into an object, and forfeits the person whom it debases to "mine." If people were no longer possessions, they could no longer be exchanged. True affection would be one that speaks specifically to the other, and becomes attached to beloved features and not to the idol of personality, the reflected image of possession. The specific is not exclusive: it lacks the aspiration to totality. But in another sense it is exclusive, nevertheless: the experience indissolubly bound up with it does not, indeed, forbid replacement, but by its very essence precludes it. The protection of anything quite definite is that it cannot be repeated, which is just why it tolerates what is different. Underlying the property relation to human beings, the exclusive right of priority, is the following piece of wisdom: after all, they are all only people; which one it is does not really matter. Affection that knows nothing of such wisdom need not fear infidelity, since it is proof against faithlessness.

Folly of the wise. Schiller's verbal demeanor calls to mind the young man of low origins who, embarrassed in good society, starts shouting to make himself heard: power and insolence mixed. German tirading and sententiousness are modeled on the French, but rehearsed in the beer hall. In his limitless and implacable demands, the petit bourgeois sticks his chest out, identifying himself with a power that he does not have, outdoing it in his arrogance to the point of absolute spirit and absolute horror. Between the grandiose sublimity embracing the whole of humanity that all idealists have in common—a sublimity ever ready to trample inhumanly on anything small as mere existence—and the coarse ostentation of bourgeois men of violence, there is an intimate collusion. The dignity of spiritual giants is prone to hollow booming laughter, exploding, smashing. When they say Creation, they mean the compulsive will-power with which they puff themselves up and intimidate all questions: from the primacy of practical reason it was always only a step to hatred of theory. Such a dynamic inheres in all idealistic movement of thought: even Hegel's immeasurable effort to remedy the dynamic with itself fell victim to it. The attempt to deduce the world in words from a principle is the behavior of someone who would like to usurp power instead of resisting it. Schiller, accordingly, was primarily concerned with usurpers. In the classical apotheosis of the sovereignty over nature, the vulgar and inferior mirrors itself by assiduous negation. Close behind the ideal stands life. The rose scents of Elysium, much too voluble to be credited with the experience of a single rose, smell of the tobacco smoke in a magistrate's office, and the soulful moon on the backdrop was fashioned after the miserable oil-lamp by whose meager light the student sweats for his exam. Weakness posing as strength betrayed the thought of the allegedly rising bourgeoisie to ideology, even when the class was thundering against tyranny. In the innermost recesses of humanism, as its very soul, there rages a frantic prisoner who, as a fascist, turns the world into a prison.

A word for morality. Amoralism, with which Nietzsche chastised the old untruth, is itself now subject to the verdict of history. With the decay of religion and its palpable philosophical secularizations, restrictive prohibitions lost their inherent authority, their substantiality. At first, however, material production was still so undeveloped that it could be proclaimed with some reason that there was not enough to go round. Anyone who did not criticize political economy as such had to cling to the limiting principle that was then articulated as unrationalized appropriation at the expense of the weak. The objective preconditions of this have changed. It is not only the social nonconformist or even the narrow-minded bourgeois who must see restriction as superfluous in the face of the immediate possibility of superfluity. The implied meaning of the master-morality, that he who wants to live must fend for himself, has in the meantime become a still more miserable lie than it was when a nineteenth-century piece of pulpit-wisdom. If in Germany the common citizen has proved himself a blond beast, this has to do not with national peculiarities but with the fact that blond bestiality itself, social rapine, has become in the face of manifest abundance the attitude of the backwoodsman, the deluded philistine, that same "hard-done-by" mentality that the master-morality was invented to combat. If Cesare Borgia were resurrected today, he would look like David Friedrich Strauss,[1] and his name would be Adolf Hitler. The cause of amorality has been espoused by the same Darwinists whom Nietzsche despised, and who proclaim as their maxim the barbaric struggle for existence with such vehemence, just because it is no longer needed. True distinction has long ceased to consist in taking the best for oneself, and has become instead a satiety with taking that practices in reality the virtue of giving, which in Nietzsche occurs only in the mind. Ascetic ideals constitute today a more solid bulwark against the madness of the profit-economy than did the hedonistic life sixty years ago against liberal repression. The amoralist may now at last permit himself to be as kind, gentle, unegoistic, and openhearted as Nietzsche already was then. As a guarantee of his undiminished resistance, he is still as alone in this as in the days when he turned the mask of evil upon the normal world, to teach the norm to fear its own perversity.

Mélange. The familiar argument of tolerance, that all people and all races are equal, is a boomerang. It lays itself open to the simple refutation of the senses, and the most compelling anthropological proofs that the Jews are not a race will, in the event of a pogrom, scarcely alter the fact that the totalitarians know full well whom they do and whom they do not intend to murder. If the equality of all who have human shape were demanded as an ideal instead of being assumed as a fact, it would not greatly help. Abstract utopia is all too compatible with the most insidious tendencies of society. That all men are alike is exactly what society would like to hear. It considers actual or imagined differences as stigmas indicating that not enough has yet been done, that something has still been left outside its machinery, not quite determined by its totality. The technique of the concentration camp is to make the prisoners like their guards, the murdered, murderers. The racial difference is raised to an absolute so that it can be abolished absolutely, if only in the sense that nothing that is different survives. An emancipated society, on the other hand, would not be a unitary state, but the realization of universality in the reconciliation of differences. Politics that are still seriously concerned with such a society ought not, therefore, propound the abstract equality of men even as an idea. Instead, they should point to the bad equality today, the identity of those with interests in films and in weapons, and conceive the better state as one in which people could be different without fear. To assure the black that he is exactly like the white man, while he obviously is not, is secretly to wrong him still further. He is benevolently humiliated by the application of a standard by which, under the pressure of the system, he must necessarily be found wanting, and to satisfy which would in any case be a doubtful achievement. The spokesmen of unitary tolerance are, accordingly, always ready to turn intolerantly on any group that remains refractory: intransigent enthusiasm for blacks does not exclude outrage at Jewish uncouthness. The melting pot was introduced by unbridled industrial capitalism. The thought of being cast into it conjures up martyrdom, not democracy.

Unmeasure for unmeasure. What the Germans have done passes understanding, particularly by psychology, just as, indeed, their horrors seem to have been committed rather as measures of blind planning and alienated terrorization than for spontaneous gratification. According to eyewitness reports, the torturing and murdering was done without pleasure, and perhaps for that reason so utterly without measure. Nevertheless, a consciousness that wishes to withstand the unspeakable finds itself again and again thrown back on the attempt to understand, if it is not to succumb subjectively to the madness that prevails objectively. The thought obtrudes that the German horror is a kind of anticipated revenge. The credit system, in which everything, even world conquest, can be advanced, also determines the actions that will put an end to it and the whole market economy, including the suicide of dictatorship. In the concentration camps and the gas chambers the ruin of Germany is being, as it were, discounted. No one who observed the first months of National Socialism in Berlin in 1933 could fail to perceive the moment of mortal sadness, of half-knowing self-surrender to perdition, that accompanied the manipulated intoxication, the torchlight processions, and the drumbeating. How disconsolate sounded the favorite German song of those months, "Nation to Arms," along the Unter den Linden. The saving of the Fatherland, fixed from one day to the next, bore from the first moment the expression of catastrophe that was rehearsed in the concentration camps, while the triumph in the streets drowned all forebodings. This premonition of catastrophe need not be explained by the collective unconscious, though this may clearly have had a voice in the matter. Germany's position in the competition between imperialist powers was, in terms of the available raw materials and of her industrial potential, hopeless in peace and war. Everybody, and nobody, was stupid enough to overlook this. To commit Germany to the final struggle in this competition was to leap into the abyss, so the others were pushed into it first, in the belief that Germany might thereby be spared. The chances of the National Socialist enterprise compensating, by record-breaking terror and temporal priority, for its disadvantage in total volume of production, were minute. It was the others who had believed in such a possibility, rather than the Germans, whom even the conquest of Paris brought no joy. While they were winning everything, they were already frenzied like those with nothing to lose. At the beginning of German imperialism stands Wagner's *Twilight of the Gods*, that inflamed prophecy of the nation's own doom, the composition of which was undertaken at the same time as the victorious campaign of 1870. In the same spirit, two years before the Second World War, the German people were shown on film the crash of their Zeppelin at Lakehurst. Calmly, unerringly, the ship went on its way, then suddenly dropped like a stone. When no way out is left, the destructive drive becomes entirely indifferent to the question it never posed quite clearly: whether it is directed against others or against its own subject.

People are looking at you. Indignation over cruelty diminishes in proportion as the victims are less like normal readers, the more they are swarthy, "dirty," dago-like. This throws as much light on the crimes as on the spectators. Perhaps the social schematization of perception in anti-Semites is such that they do not see Jews as human beings at all. The constantly encountered assertion that savages, blacks, Japanese are like animals, monkeys, for example, is the key to the pogrom. The possibility of pogroms is decided in the moment when the gaze of a fatally wounded animal falls on a human being. The defiance with which he repels this gaze—"after all, it's only an animal"—reappears irresistibly in cruelties done to human beings, the perpetrators having again and again to reassure themselves that it is "only an animal," because they could never fully believe this even of animals. In repressive society the concept of man is itself a parody of divine likeness. The mechanism of "pathic projection" determines that those in power perceive as human only their own reflected image, instead of reflecting back the human as precisely what is different. Murder is thus the repeated attempt, by yet greater madness, to distort the madness of such false perception into reason: what was not seen as human and yet is human is made a thing, so that its stirrings can no longer refute the manic gaze.

Little folk. Those who deny objective historic forces find a ready-made argument in the outcome of the war. The Germans should really have won: that they did not was due to the stupidity of their leaders. Now Hitler's decisive moments of "stupidity," his refusal, in the thick of war, to make war on England, his attacks on Russia and America, have a precise social meaning, which developed according to its own dialectic ineluctably from one reasonable step to the next and to catastrophe. But even if it had been stupidity, it would have been historically comprehensible; stupidity is not a natural quality, but one socially produced and reinforced. The German ruling clique drove toward war because they were excluded from a position of imperial power. But in their exclusion lay the reason for the blind and clumsy provincialism that made Hitler's and Ribbentropp's policies uncompetitive and their war a gamble. That they were as badly informed about the Tory balance between general class interests and British special interests, and about the strength of the Red Army, as were their own masses behind the cordon of the Third Reich is inseparable from the historical causes of National Socialism and almost from its strength. The sole chance of success for their reckless adventure lay in their knowing no better, and this was also the reason for its failure. Germany's industrial backwardness forced its politicians—anxious to regain lost ground and, as have-nots, specially qualified for the role—to fall back on their immediate, narrow experience, that of the political facade. They saw nothing before them except cheering assemblies and frightened negotiators: this blocked their view of the objective power of a greater mass of capital. It was immanent revenge on Hitler that he, the executioner of liberal society, was yet in his own state of consciousness too "liberal" to perceive how industrial potential outside Germany was establishing, under the veil of liberalism, its irresistible domination. He, who recognized the untruth in liberalism as did no other bourgeois, could yet not recognize the power behind him, the social tendency for which Hitler was really no more than drummer. His consciousness regressed to the standpoint of his weaker, short-sighted opponents, which he had first adopted in order to make shorter work of them. Germany's hour necessarily accorded with such stupidity. For only leaders who resembled the people of the country in their ignorance of the world and global economics could harness them to war and their pigheadedness to an enterprise wholly unhampered by reflection. Hitler's stupidity was a ruse of reason.

Uninformed opinion. The Third Reich failed to produce a single work of art, a single mental structure capable of satisfying even the meager liberalistic requirement of "quality." The demolition of humanity, and the conservation of works of the mind, were as incompatible as air-raid shelter and stork's nest, and the regenerated, martial culture looked, on its first day, like the cities on their last, a heap of rubble. To this culture, at least, the population practiced passive resistance. But the cultural energies allegedly released by National Socialism were in no way absorbed by the technical, political, or military spheres. The whole thing is truly barbarism, and triumphs as such even over its own barbaric spirit. This can be seen in the sphere of strategy. The fascist era has not brought about a flowering of strategy, but abolished it. The great military conceptions were inseparable from cunning, imagination: almost from private astuteness and initiative. They were part of a discipline relatively independent of the production process. The object was to derive decisive advantages from specialized innovations, such as diagonal battle lines or the accuracy of artillery. There was something of the bourgeois virtue of self-reliant enterprise in all this. Hannibal was a scion of merchants, not of heroes, and Napoleon of a democratic revolution. The element of bourgeois competition in the conduct of war has blown up in the face of fascism. The fascists raised to an absolute the basic idea of strategy: to exploit the temporary discrepancy between one nation with a leadership organized for murder, and the total potential of the rest. Yet by taking this idea to its logical conclusion in inventing total war, and by erasing the distinction between army and industry, they themselves liquidated strategy. Today it is as antiquated as the sound of military bands and paintings of battleships. Hitler sought world dominion through concentrated terror. The means he used, however, were unstrategic—the accumulation of overwhelming forces at particular points, the crude frontal breakthrough, the mechanical encirclement of the enemy stranded by armored spearheads. This principle, wholly quantitative, positivistic, without surprises, thus everywhere "public" and merging with publicity, no longer sufficed. The Allies, infinitely wealthier in economic resources, needed only to outdo the Germans in their own tactics to crush Hitler. The torpor and apathy of the war, the general defeatism that helped to protract its catastrophes, were conditioned by the decay of strategy. When all actions are mathematically calculated, they also take on a stupid quality. As if in mockery of the idea that anybody ought to be able to run the state, this war is conducted, despite the radar and the artificial harbors, as if by a schoolboy sticking flags into a chart. Spengler saw in the downfall of the West the promise of a golden age of engineers. The prospect coming into view, however, is the downfall of technology itself.

Pseudomenos. The magnetic power exerted by patently threadbare ideologies is to be explained, beyond psychology, by the objectively determined decay of logical evidence as such. Things have come to a pass where lying sounds like truth, truth like lying. Each statement, each piece of news, each thought has been preformed by the centers of the culture industry. Whatever lacks the familiar trace of such preformation lacks credibility, the more so because the institutions of public opinion accompany what they send forth with a thousand factual proofs and all the plausibility that total power can lay hands on. Truth that opposes these pressures not only appears improbable but is, in addition, too feeble to make any headway in competition with their highly concentrated machinery of dissemination. The extreme case of Germany is instructive of the general mechanism. When the National Socialists began to torture, they not only terrorized the peoples inside and outside Germany but were the more secure from exposure the more wildly the horror increased. The implausibility of their actions made it easy to disbelieve what nobody, for the sake of precious peace, wanted to believe, while at the same time capitulating to it. Trembling voices persuade themselves that, after all, there is much exaggeration: even after the outbreak of the war, details about the concentration camps were unwanted in the English press. Every horror necessarily becomes, in the enlightened world, a horrific fairy tale. For the untruth of truth has a core that finds an avid response in the unconscious. It is not only that the unconscious wishes horrors to come about; fascism is itself less "ideological," insofar as it openly proclaims the principle of domination that is elsewhere concealed. Whatever humane values the democracies can oppose it with, it can effortlessly refute by pointing out that they represent not the whole of humanity but a mere illusory image that fascism has had the courage to discard. So desperate have people become in civilization, however, that they are forever ready to abandon their frail better qualities as soon as the world does their worse ones the obligation of confessing how evil it is. The political forces of opposition, however, are compelled to make constant use of lies if they are not themselves to be completely wiped out as destructive. The deeper the divergence of an opposition from the established order, which at least affords it refuge from a blacker future, the more easily fascists can pin it down to untruths. Only the absolute lie now has any freedom to speak the truth. The confounding of truth and lies, making it almost impossible to maintain a distinction, and a labor of Sisyphus to hold onto the simplest piece of knowledge, marks the victory in the field of logical organization of the principle that lies crushed on that of battle. Lies have long legs: they are ahead of their time. The conversion of all questions of truth into questions of power, a process that truth itself cannot escape if it is not to be annihilated by power, not only suppresses truth, as in earlier despotic orders, but has attacked the very heart of the distinction between true and false, which the hirelings of logic were in any case diligently working to abolish. So Hitler, of whom no one can say whether he died or escaped, survives.

The paragraph. What the Nazis did to the Jews was unspeakable. Languages had no word for it, for even mass murder, when confronted with the planned, systematic, and total nature of the killing, would have sounded like something from the good old days of the head teacher from Degerloch.[1] Despite everything, an expression had to be found if the victims, who were anyway too numerous for them all to be remembered by name, were to be spared the obloquy of being consigned to oblivion. For this reason the term *genocide* [E] was introduced in English. But the act of codification that is enshrined in the International Declaration of Human Rights has ensured that the unspeakable has been cut down to size at the very moment that it is protested against. Elevating it into a concept simultaneously acknowledges its possibility. It becomes an institution to be prohibited, rejected, and debated. The day will come when discussions will take place about whether some new monstrous act falls within the definition of genocide; whether the nations have the right to intervene, a right of which they have no real wish to avail themselves; and whether, given the unforeseen difficulties in applying the term in practice, the whole concept of "genocide" should not be deleted from the statutes. Shortly thereafter, medium-sized headlines will appear in the papers: "Genocidal Measures in East Turkistan Almost Complete."

Deviation. The decay of the workers' movement is corroborated by the official optimism of its adherents. This seems to grow with the immovable consolidation of the capitalist world. The founders of the movement never regarded success as guaranteed, and therefore throughout their lives said dire things to the workers' organizations. Today, when the enemy's power and control over the consciousness of the masses has been immeasurably strengthened, the attempt radically to alter this consciousness by withholding assent to it is considered reactionary. Suspicion falls on anyone who combines criticism of capitalism with that of the proletariat, which is more and more becoming a mere reflection of the tendencies of capitalist development. Once it crosses class boundaries, the negative element of thought is frowned upon. Kaiser Wilhelm's words of wisdom, "I tolerate no Jeremiahs," have penetrated the ranks of those he wanted to crush. Anyone who pointed, for example, to the lack of any spontaneous resistance by the German workers was told in reply that things were so much in a state of flux that such judgments were impossible; anyone who was not on the spot, right among the poor German victims of aerial warfare—victims, however, who had few objections to air raids as long as they were directed at the other side—had no right to open his mouth, and in any case agrarian reforms were imminent in Rumania and Yugoslavia. Yet the further the rational expectation diminishes that society's doom can really be averted, the more reverently they repeat the old prayers: masses, solidarity, Party, class struggle. While not a single idea in the critique of political economy is firmly believed any longer by the adherents of the left-wing platform, while their newspapers daily and witlessly trumpet forth theses that outdo all revisionism yet signify nothing and can be replaced at will tomorrow by the opposite, the ears of the faithful partyliners show a musician's sensitivity to the faintest disrespect for the slogans that have jettisoned theory. Hurrah-optimism has a fitting counterpart in international patriotism. The staunch supporter must swear allegiance to a people, no matter which. In the dogmatic concept of the people, however, the acceptance of an alleged common destiny among men as the authority for action, the idea of a society liberated from the compulsion of nature, is implicitly denied.

Even this frantic optimism is the perversion of a motif that has seen better days: the refusal to wait. Confidence in the state of technology made people see change as imminent, a palpable possibility. Conceptions entailing long intervals of time, precautions, elaborate measures for public enlightenment were suspected of abandoning the goal they claimed to pursue. At that time optimism, amounting to a disregard for death, expressed an autonomous will. All that is left is its shell, belief in the power and greatness of the organization as such, devoid of any willingness for individual action, indeed, imbued with the destructive conviction that while spontaneity is no longer possible, the Red Army will win in the end. The constantly enforced insistence that everybody should admit that everything will turn out well places those who do not under suspicion of being defeatists and deserters. In the fairy tale, the toads who came from the depths were messengers of great joy. Today, when the abandonment of utopia looks as much like its realization as the Antichrist resembles the Paraclete, "toad" has become a term of abuse among those who are themselves in the depths. The optimism of the left repeats the insidious bourgeois superstition that one should not talk of the devil but look on the bright side. "The gentleman does not find the world to his liking? Then let him go and look for a better one"—such is the popular parlance of socialist realism.

Passing muster. For the so-called man of affairs with interests to pursue, plans to realize, the people he comes into contact with are metamorphosed automatically into friends or enemies. In looking at them with a view to deciding how well they fit in with his intentions, he reduces them from the outset to objects: some are usable, others an obstacle. Every differing opinion appears on the system of coordinates provided by the predecided purposes without which the practical man is lost, as tiresome resistance, sabotage, intrigue; all agreement, though it may stem from the basest interests, becomes support, something of use, a testimony of alliance. Thus impoverishment of the relation to others sets in: the capacity for seeing them as such and not as functions of one's own will withers, as does that, above all, of fruitful contrast, the possibility of going beyond oneself by assimilating the contradictory. These are replaced by an appraising knowledge of people for which the best are in the end the lesser evil, and the worst not the greatest. This way of reacting, however, the pattern of all administration and "personnel policy," tends of its own accord, and in advance of any education of the political will or commitment to exclusive programs, toward fascism. Anyone who has once made it his concern to judge people's suitability sees those judged, by a kind of technological necessity, as insiders or outsiders, as belonging or alien to the race, as accomplices or victims. The fixed, inspecting, hypnotic, and hypnotized stare that is common to all the leaders of horror has its model in the appraising look of the manager asking an interview candidate to sit down, and illuminating his face in such a way as to divide it pitilessly into bright, utilizable parts, and dark, disreputable areas of incompetence. The last stage is the medical examination to decide between capacity for work and liquidation. The New Testament words "He who is not for me is against me" lay bare the heart of anti-Semitism down the centuries. It is a basic feature of domination that everyone who does not identify with it is consigned for

Anti-Semitism

mere difference to the enemy camp: it is no accident that "catholicism" is the Greek word for the Latin "totality," which the National Socialists have realized. It means the equation of the dissimilar, whether it be the "deviationist" or the members of a different race, with the opponent. In this respect National Socialism has attained to historical consciousness of itself: Carl Schmitt defined the very essence of politics by the categories of friend and enemy.[1] Progress to such consciousness makes its own regression to the behavior patterns of the child, which either likes things or fears them. The a priori reduction to the friend-enemy relationship is one of the primal phenomena of the new anthropology. Freedom would be not to choose between black and white but to abjure such prescribed choices.

Picture-book without pictures. The objective tendency of the Enlightenment, to wipe out the power of images over man, is not matched by any subjective progress on the part of enlightened thinking toward freedom from images. While the assault on images irresistibly demolishes, after metaphysical Ideas, those concepts once understood as rational and genuinely attained by thought, the thinking unleashed by the Enlightenment and immunized against thinking is now becoming a second figurativeness, though without images or spontaneity. Amid the network of now wholly abstract relations of people to each other and to things, the power of abstraction is vanishing. The estrangement of schemata and classifications from the data subsumed beneath them, indeed, the sheer quantity of the material processed, which has become quite incommensurable with the horizons of individual experience, ceaselessly enforces an archaic retranslation into sensuous signs. The little silhouettes of men or houses that pervade statistics like hieroglyphics may appear in each particular case accidental, mere auxiliary means. But it is not by chance that they have such a resemblance to countless advertisements, newspaper stereotypes, toys. In them representation triumphs over what is represented. Their outsize, simplistic, and therefore false comprehensibility corroborates the incomprehensibility of the intellectual processes themselves, from which their falseness—their blind, unthinking subsumption—is inseparable. The omnipresent images are none, because they present the wholly general, the average, the standard model, as something unique or special, and so deride it. The abolition of the particular is turned insidiously into something particular. The desire for particularity has silted up while still at the stage of a need, and is reproduced on all sides by mass culture, on the pattern of the comic strip. What was once called intellect is superseded by illustrations. It is not only that people are no longer able to imagine what is not shown and drilled into them in abbreviated form. Even the joke, in which once the freedom of the mind collided with the facts and exploded them, has gone over to illustration. The pictorial jokes filling magazines are for the most part pointless, devoid of meaning. They consist of nothing beyond a challenge to the eye to compete with the situation. One is supposed, schooled by countless precedents, to see what is "going on" more quickly than the moments of significance in the situation can unfold. What is acted out by such pictures and then reenacted by the well-versed onlooker, in the instantaneous sizing-up of the situation, the unresisting submission to the empty predominance of things, is the jettisoning of all meaning like ballast. The joke of our time is the suicide of intention. He who "cracks" it is rewarded by admission to the collective of laughers, who have cruel things on their side. If one strove to understand such jokes by thinking, one would fall helplessly behind the runaway tempo of things, which tear along even in the simplest caricature as in the mad race at the end of a film cartoon. Cleverness turns straight into stupidity in the face of regressive progress. The only comprehension left to thought is horror at the incomprehensible. Just as the reflective onlooker, meeting the laughing placard of a toothpaste beauty, discerns in her flashlight grin the grimace of torture, so from every joke, even from every pictorial representation, he is assailed by the death sentence on the subject, which is implicit in the universal triumph of subjective reason.

Monad. The individual owes his crystallization to the forms of political economy, particularly to those of the urban market. Even as the opponent of the pressure of socialization he remains the latter's most particular product and its likeness. What enables him to resist, that streak of independence in him, springs from monadological individual interest and its precipitate, character. The individual mirrors in his individuation the preordained social laws of exploitation, however mediated. This means too, however, that his decay in the present phase must itself be deduced not individualistically but from the social tendency that asserts itself by means of individuation and not merely as its enemy. On this point reactionary cultural criticism diverges from the other kind. Reactionary criticism often enough attains insight into the decay of individuality and the crisis of society, but places the ontological responsibility for this on the individual as such, as something discrete and internal: for this reason the accusation of shallowness, lack of faith and substance, is the last word it has to say, and return to the past its solace. Individualists like Huxley and Jaspers damn the individual for his mechanical emptiness and neurotic weakness, but the trend of their condemnation is rather to sacrifice the individual himself than to criticize the social *principium individuationis*. As half-truths their polemics are already the whole untruth. Society is seen by them as an unmediated community of men, from whose attitudes the whole follows, instead of as a system not only encompassing and deforming them, but even reaching down into that humanity which once conditioned them as individuals. By this exclusively human interpretation of the situation as it is, the crude material reality that binds human beings to inhumanity is accepted even while being accused. In its better days, when it reflected historically, the bourgeoisie was well aware of such interconnections, and it is only since its doctrine has degenerated to obtuse apologetics against socialism that it has forgotten them. It is not the least merit of Jakob Burckhardt's history of Greek civilization to have connected the drying-up of Hellenistic individuality not only with the objective decline of the *polis* but precisely with the cult of the individual: "But following the deaths of Demosthenes and Phocion, the city is surprisingly depleted of political personalities, and not only of them: Epicurus, born as early as 342 of an Attic cleruch family on Samos, is the last Athenian of any kind to have world-historical importance." The situation in which the individual was vanishing was at the same time one of unbridled individualism, where "all was possible": "Above all, individuals are now worshiped instead of gods."[1] That the setting-free of the individual by the undermining of the *polis* did not strengthen his resistance but eliminated him and individuality itself, in the consummation of dictatorial states, provides a model of one of the central contradictions that drove society from the nineteenth century to fascism. Beethoven's music, which works within the forms transmitted by society and is ascetic toward the expression of private feelings, resounds with the guided echo of social conflict, drawing precisely from this asceticism the whole fullness and power of individuality. That of Richard Strauss, wholly at the service of individual claims and dedicated to the glorification of the self-sufficient individual, thereby reduces the latter to a mere receptive organ of the market, an imitator of arbitrarily chosen ideas and styles.

Within repressive society the individual's emancipation not only benefits but damages him. Freedom from society robs him of the strength for freedom. For however real he may be in his relations to others, he is, considered absolutely, a mere abstraction. He has no content that is not socially constituted, no impulse transcending society that is not directed at assisting the social situation to transcend itself. Even the Christian doctrine of death and immortality, in which the notion of absolute individuality is rooted, would be wholly void if it did not embrace humanity. The single man who hoped for immortality absolutely and for himself alone would in such limitation only inflate to preposterous dimensions the principle of self-preservation that the injunction "He that loses his life, shall save it" holds in check. Socially, the absolute status granted to the individual marks the transition from the universal mediation of social relation—a mediation that, as exchange, always also requires curtailment of the particular interests realized through it—to direct domination, where power is seized by the strongest. Through this dissolution of all the mediating elements within the individual himself, by virtue of which he was, in spite of everything, also a part of a social subject, he regresses, impoverished and coarsened, to the state of a mere social object. As something abstractly realized, in Hegel's sense, the individual cancels himself out: the countless people who know nothing but their naked, prowling interest are those who capitulate the moment organization and terror overtake them. If today the trace of humanity seems to persist only in the individual in his decline, it admonishes us to make an end of the fatality that individualizes men, only to break them completely in their isolation. The saving principle is now preserved in its antithesis alone.

Bequest. Dialectical thought is an attempt to break through the coercion of logic by its own means. But since it must use these means, it is at every moment in danger of itself acquiring a coercive character: the ruse of reason would like to hold sway over the dialectic too. The existing cannot be overstepped except by means of a universal derived from the existing order itself. The universal triumphs over the existing through the latter's own concept and therefore, in its triumph, the power of mere existence constantly threatens to reassert itself by the same violence that broke it. Through the absolute rule of negation, the movement of thought as of history becomes, in accordance with the pattern of immanent antithesis, unambiguously, exclusively, implacably positive. Everything is subsumed under the principal economic phases and their development, which each in turn historically shape the whole of society; thought in its entirety has something of what Parisian artists call *le genre chef d'oeuvre*. That calamity is brought about precisely by the stringency of such development; that this stringency is itself linked to domination is, at the least, not made explicit in critical theory, which, like traditional theory, awaits salvation from stage-by-stage progression. Stringency and totality, the bourgeois intellectual ideals of necessity and generality, do indeed circumscribe the formula of history, but for just this reason the constitution of society finds its precipitate in those great, immovable, lordly concepts against which dialectical criticism and practice are directed. If Benjamin said that history had hitherto been written from the standpoint of the victor, and needed to be written from that of the vanquished,[1] we might add that knowledge must indeed present the fatally rectilinear succession of victory and defeat, but should also address itself to those things that were not embraced by this dynamic, which fell by the wayside—what might be called the waste product and blind spot that have escaped the dialectic. It is in the nature of the defeated to appear, in their impotence, irrelevant, eccentric, derisory. What transcends the ruling society is not only the potentiality it develops but also all that which did not fit properly into the laws of historical movement. Theory must needs deal with cross-grained, opaque, unassimilated material, which as such admittedly has from the start an anachronistic quality, but is not wholly obsolete since it has outwitted the historical dynamic. This can most readily be seen in art. Children's books like *Alice in Wonderland* or *Struwwelpeter*, of which it would be absurd to ask whether they are progressive or reactionary, contain incomparably more eloquent ciphers even of history than the high drama of Hebbel, concerned though it is with the official themes of tragic guilt, turning points of history, the course of the world and the individual, and in Satie's pert and puerile piano pieces there are flashes of experience undreamed of by the school of Schoenberg, with all its rigor and all the pathos of musical development behind it. The very grandeur of logical deductions may inadvertently take on a provincial quality. Benjamin's writings are an attempt in ever new ways to make philosophically fruitful what has not yet been foreclosed by great intentions. The task he bequeathed was not to abandon such an attempt to the estranging enigmas of thought alone, but to bring the intentionless within the realm of concepts: the obligation to think at the same time dialectically and undialectically.

Late extra. In central passages of Poe and Baudelaire the concept of newness emerges. In the former, in the description of the maelstrom and the shudder it inspires—equated with "the novel"—of which none of the traditional reports is said to give an adequate idea; in the latter, in the last line of the cycle *La Mort*, which chooses the plunge into the abyss, no matter whether hell or heaven, "*au fond de l'inconnu pour trouver du nouveau* [in the depths of the unknown to find the new]." In both cases it is an unknown threat that the subject embraces and that, in a dizzy reversal, promises joy. The new, a blank place in consciousness, awaited as if with shut eyes, seems the formula by means of which a stimulus is extracted from dread and despair. It makes evil flower. But its bare contour is a cryptogram for the most unequivocal reaction. It circumscribes the precise reply given by the subject to a world that has turned abstract, the industrial age. The cult of the new, and thus the idea of modernity, is a rebellion against the fact that there is no longer anything new. The never-changing quality of machine-produced goods, the lattice of socialization that enmeshes and assimilates equally objects and the view of them, converts everything encountered into what always was, a fortuitous specimen of a species, the doppelgänger of a model. The layer of unpremeditatedness, freedom from intentions, on which alone intentions flourish, seems consumed. Of it the idea of newness dreams. Itself unattainable, newness installs itself in the place of overthrown divinity amidst the first consciousness of the decay of experience. But its concept remains chained to that sickness, as its abstraction attests, impotently reaching for a receding concreteness. For a "prehistory of modernity"[1] it would be instructive to analyze the change in the meaning of the word "sensation," the exoteric synonym for the Baudelairian *nouveau*. The word became familiar to the educated European through epistemology. In Locke it means simple, direct perception, the opposite of reflection. It then became the great Unknown, and finally the arouser of masses, the destructive intoxicant, shock as a consumer commodity. To be still able to perceive anything at all, regardless of its quality, replaces happiness, since omnipotent quantification has taken away the possibility of perception itself. In place of the fulfilled relation of experience to its subject matter, we find something merely subjective, physically isolated, feeling that is exhausted in the reading on the pressure gauge. Thus the historical emancipation from being-in-itself is converted into the form of perception, a process that nineteenth-century sense-psychology accommodated by reducing the underlying level of experience to a mere "basic stimulus," of whose particular constitution the specific sense-energies were independent. Baudelaire's poetry, however, is full of those lightning flashes seen by a closed eye that has received a blow. As phantasmagoric as these lights is the idea of newness itself. What flashes thus, while serene contemplation now attains merely the socially preformed plaster casts of things, is itself repetition. The new, sought for its own sake, a kind of laboratory product, petrified into a conceptual scheme, becomes in its sudden apparition a compulsive return of the old, not unlike that in traumatic neuroses. To the dazzled vision the veil of temporal succession is rent to reveal the archetypes of perpetual sameness: this is why the discovery of the new is satanic, an eternal recurrence of damnation. Poe's allegory of the "novel" is that of the breathlessly spinning yet in a sense stationary movement of the helpless boat in the eye of the maelstrom. The sensations in which the masochist abandons himself to the new are as many regressions. So much is true in psychoanalysis that the ontology of Baudelairian modernity, like all those that followed it, answers the description of infantile partial-instincts. Its pluralism is the many-colored fata morgana in which the monism of bourgeois reason sees its self-destruction glitter deceptively as hope. This false promise makes up the idea of modernity, and everything modern, because of its never-changing core, has scarcely aged before it takes on a look of the archaic. The *Tristan* that rises in the middle of the nineteenth century as an obelisk of modernity is at the same time a soaring monument to the compulsion to repeat. The new is ambivalent in its enthronement. While it embraces everything that strives beyond the oneness of an ever more rigid established order, it is at the same time absorption by newness which, under the weight of that oneness, decisively furthers the decomposition of the subject into convulsive moments of illusory living, and so also furthers total society, which modishly ousts the new. Baudelaire's poem about the martyr of sex, the murder victim, allegorically celebrates the sanctity of pleasure in the fearsomely liberating still-life of crime, but his intoxication before the naked headless body already resembles that which drove the prospective victims of Hitler's regime to buy, in paralyzed greed, the newspapers in which stood the measures announcing their own doom. Fascism was the absolute sensation: in a statement at the time of the first pogroms, Goebbels boasted that at least the National Socialists were not boring. In the Third

Reich the abstract horror of news and rumor was enjoyed as the only stimulus sufficient to incite a momentary glow in the weakened sensorium of
the masses. Without the almost irresistible force of the craving for headlines, in which the strangled heart convulsively sought a primeval world,
the unspeakable could not have been endured by the spectators or even by
the perpetrators. In the course of the war, even news of calamity was finally
given full publicity in Germany, and the slow military collapse was not
hushed up. Concepts like sadism and masochism no longer suffice. In the
mass society of technical dissemination they are mediated by sensational-
ism, by cometlike, remote, ultimate newness. It overwhelms a public
writhing under shock and oblivious of who has suffered the outrage, itself
or others. Compared to its stimulus value, the content of the shock becomes really irrelevant, as it was ideally in its invocation by poets; it is even
possible that the horror savored by Poe and Baudelaire, when realized by
dictators, loses its quality as sensation, burns out. The violent rescuing of
all qualities in the new was devoid of quality. Everything can, as the new,
divested of itself, become pleasure, just as desensitized morphine addicts
finally grab indiscriminately at any drug, including atropine. Sensation has
submerged, together with differentiation between qualities, all judgment:
it is really this that makes it an agent of catastrophic degeneration. In the
terror of regressive dictatorship, modernity, the dialectical image of
progress, has culminated in explosion. Newness in collective form, of
which there was already a hint in Baudelaire's journalistic streak, as in Wagner's drumbeating, is in fact a stimulating and paralyzing narcotic extract
boiled out of external life: not for nothing were Poe, Baudelaire, Wagner
addictive types. Newness only becomes mere evil in its totalitarian format,
where all the tension between individual and society, which once gave rise
to the category of the new, is dissipated. Today the appeal to newness, of no
matter what kind, provided only that it is archaic enough, has become universal, the omnipresent medium of false mimesis. The decomposition of
the subject is consummated in his self-abandonment to an ever-changing
sameness. This drains all firmness from characters. What Baudelaire com-
manded through the power of images, comes unbid to will-less fascination.
Faithlessness and lack of identity, pathic subservience to situations, are induced by the stimulus of newness, which, as a mere stimulus, no longer
stimulates. Perhaps in this lassitude mankind's renunciation of the wish for
children is declared, because it is open to everyone to prophesy the worst:

the new is the secret figure of all those unborn. Malthus is one of the fore-fathers of the nineteenth century, and Baudelaire had reason to extol infertile beauty. Mankind, despairing of its reproduction, unconsciously projects its wish for survival into the chimera of the thing never known, but this resembles death. Such a chimera points to the downfall of an all-embracing constitution that virtually no longer needs its members.

Boy from the heath. Things one fears for no real reason, apparently obsessed by an *idée fixe*, have an impertinent tendency to come about. The question one most shuns is raised with perfidiously amiable interest by a subordinate; the person one wishes most anxiously to keep away from one's beloved will unfailingly invite her, be it from a distance of three thousand miles, thanks to well-meaning introductions, and bring about ominous acquaintances. It is debatable how far one promotes these terrors oneself: whether one's over-anxious silence puts the question into the insidious listener's mouth; whether one provokes the fatal contact by asking the mediator, in foolishly destructive confidence, not to mediate. Psychology knows that he who imagines disasters in some way desires them. But why do they come so eagerly to meet him? Something in reality strikes a chord in paranoid fantasy and is warped by it. The sadism latent in everyone unerringly divines the weakness latent in everyone. And the fantasy of persecution is contagious: wherever it occurs spectators are driven irresistibly to imitate it. This succeeds most easily when one gives the fantasy a helping hand by doing what the other fears. "One fool makes many"—the bottomless solitude of the deluded has a tendency to collectivization and so quotes the delusion into existence. This pathic mechanism harmonizes with the social one prevalent today, whereby those socialized into desperate isolation hunger for community and flock together in cold mobs. So folly becomes an epidemic: insane sects grow with the same rhythm as big organizations. It is the rhythm of total destruction. The fulfillment of persecution fantasies springs from their affinity to bloody realities. Violence, on which civilization is based, means the persecution of all by all, and the persecution maniac puts himself at a disadvantage only by blaming on his neighbor what is perpetrated by the whole, in a helpless attempt to make the incommensurable commensurable. He is burnt because he seeks to grasp directly, as with his bare hands, the objective delusion that he resembles, whereas the absurd order consists precisely in its perfected indirectness. He is sacrificed to safeguard the tissue of beguilement. Even the worst, most senseless representations of events, the wildest projections, contain the unconscious effort of consciousness to recognize the fatal law by which society perpetuates its existence. Aberration is really only short-circuited adaptation: the patent imbecility of one calls the imbecility of the whole by its right name mistakenly in another, and the paranoiac is a caricature of the right life, in that he chooses on his own initiative to emulate the wrong one. But just as in a short-circuit sparks are scattered, in reality one delusion communicates like lightning with another. The points of communication are the overwhelming confirmations of persecution fantasies, which, mocking the invalid with being right, only plunge him deeper into them. The surface of life then at once closes together again, proving to him that things are not so bad and he is insane. He subjectively anticipates the state where objective madness and individual helplessness merge directly, as when fascism, a dictatorship by persecution maniacs, realizes all the persecution fears of its victims. Whether exaggerated suspicions are paranoiac or true to reality, a faint private echo of the turmoil of history, can therefore be decided only retrospectively. Horror is beyond the reach of psychology.

Il servo padrone. The mindless tasks imposed by authoritarian culture on the subject classes can be performed only at the cost of permanent regression. Their formlessness is, precisely, the product of social form. The barbarians engendered by culture have, however, always been used by it to keep alive its own barbaric nature. Domination delegates the physical violence on which it rests to the dominated. In being allowed the satisfaction of exercising their distorted instincts in collectively approved and proper ways, they learn to do those things that the noble need for the continued indulgence of their nobility. The self-education of the ruling clique, with all its concomitant discipline, stifling of spontaneous impulses, cynical skepticism, and blind lust to command, would not be possible if the oppressors did not themselves submit, through hirelings among the oppressed, to a part of the oppression they inflict on others. This is doubtless why the psychological differences between the classes are so much less than the objective economic gap. The harmony of the irreconcilable helps to perpetuate the bad totality. The baseness of the superior puts him on a level with his upstart subordinate. From the domestic servants and governesses tormenting upper-class children to show them what life is like, by way of the teachers from Westerwald extirpating in them, along with the use of foreign words, all joy in language, and then the officials and employees leaving them to stand in queues, the noncommissioned officers treading on them, there is a straight line to Gestapo torturers and the bureaucrats of the gas chambers. The delegation of power to the lower orders finds a prompt and sympathetic response in the upper orders themselves. Someone appalled by the good breeding of his parents will seek refuge in the kitchen, basking in the cook's vitality, which secretly reflects the principle of the parental good breeding. The refined are drawn to the unrefined, whose coarseness deceptively promises what their own culture denies. They do not know that the indelicacy that appears to them as anarchic nature is nothing but a reflex action produced by the compulsion they struggle to resist. Mediating between the class solidarity of the higher orders and their blandishments to delegates of the lower classes is a justified feeling of guilt toward the poor. But the rebel who has been put in his place, who has been made to feel to the core of his being "how things are done here," has ended up one of them himself. Bettelheim's observation on the identification of the victims of the Nazi camps with their executioners implies a verdict on the higher nurseries of social horticulture, the English public school, the German military academy. Topsy-turviness perpetuates itself: domination is propagated by the dominated.

Model of virtue. Everyone has heard of the connection between repression and morality as instinctual renunciation. But moral ideas not only suppress the rest, they are directly derived from the existence of the suppressors. Since Homer, Greek linguistic usage has intertwined the concepts of goodness and wealth. *Kalokagathia*, held up by the humanists to modern society as a model of aesthetico-moral harmony, always laid heavy stress on possessions, and Aristotle's *Politics* openly admits the fusion of inner worth with status in its definition of nobility as "inherited wealth, combined with excellence." The conception of the *polis* in the classical age, embracing both inward and outward existence, the individual's position in the city-state and his self as a unity, made it possible to attribute moral rank to riches without arousing the crude suspicions even at that time befitting the doctrine. If visible influence in the existing state is the measure of a man, then it is only consistent to accredit the material wealth that tangibly underwrites his influence to his character, since moral substance itself

is seen, no differently from in Hegel's philosophy of later years, as constituted by his participation in objective social reality. It was the advent of
Christianity that first negated this identification, with its proposition that
a camel could pass more easily through a needle's eye than a rich man enter heaven. But the special theological premium on poverty indicates how
deeply the general consciousness was stamped by the morality of possessions. Fixed property was a means of differentiation from nomadic disorder, against which all norms were directed; to be good and to have goods
coincided from the beginning. The good man is he who rules himself as he
does his own property: his autonomous being is modeled on material
power. The rich should therefore not be accused of immorality—the reproach has ever been part of the armature of political repression—but
rather made aware that, to the others, they represent morality. In it, goods
are reflected. Wealth as goodness is an element in the world's mortar: the
tenacious illusion of their identity prevents the confrontation of moral
ideas with the order in which the rich are right, while at the same time it
has been impossible to conceive concrete definitions of morality other than
those derived from wealth. The further the individual and society diverge
in later periods through the competition of interests, and the more the individual is thrown back on himself, the more doggedly he clings to the notion of the moral nature of wealth. Wealth shall vouch for the possibility
of reuniting what is sundered, the inward and the outward. Such is the secret of intramundane asceticism, the businessman's boundless exertion—
falsely hypostatized by Max Weber—*ad maiorem dei gloriam.* Material success joins individual and society not merely in the comfortable and by now
questionable sense that the rich man can escape solitude, but far more radically: if blind, isolated self-interest is pursued far enough, it turns, as economic power, into social predominance and manifests itself as an incarnation of the all-uniting principle. He who is rich or attains riches feels that
he has accomplished "on his own initiative," as a self, what the objective
spirit, the truly irrational predestination of a society held together by brutal economic inequality, intends. So the rich man can claim as goodness
what really only betokens its absence. He himself and others perceive him
as the realization of the general principle. Because this is one of injustice,
the unjust man regularly becomes just, and not merely in illusion, but supported by the supreme might of the law by which society reproduces itself.
The wealth of individuals is inseparable from the progress of society in
"prehistory." The rich control the means of production. Technical advances

in which society as a whole participates are therefore put down primarily to "their"—today industry's—progress, and the Fords necessarily seem benefactors to the extent that they actually are so within the framework of the existing relations of production. Their preestablished privilege makes it appear as if they are relinquishing something belonging to them—that is, the increase of use-values—while they are really, in the blessings they administer, only letting a part of the profit flow back where it came from. Hence the delusive character of the moral hierarchy. Certainly, poverty has always been glorified as asceticism, the social condition for gaining the very riches in which morality becomes manifest; nevertheless, as is known, "what a man is worth" means his bank balance, and in German commercial jargon to say "the man is good" means that he can pay. However, what the reason of state of an omnipotent economy confesses so cynically, extends unavowed to the behavior of individuals. The private generosity that the rich can supposedly afford, the aura of happiness surrounding them, some of which is reflected on those they allow to approach them, all this helps to veil them. They remain the nice, the right people, the better sort, the good. Wealth insulates from overt injustice. While the policeman beats up strikers with a rubber truncheon, the factory owner's son can drink an occasional whiskey with a progressive writer. By all the desiderata of private morality, even the most advanced, the rich man could—if only he could— indeed be better than the poor. This possibility, admittedly neglected in reality, plays a part in the ideology of those without it: even the confidence-trickster, who may in any case be preferable to the legitimate corporation bosses, enjoys the fame, after his arrest, of having had such a lovely house, and the highly paid executive acquires human warmth by serving opulent dinners. The barbaric success-religion of today is consequently not simply contrary to morality: it is the homecoming of the West to the venerable morals of our ancestors. Even the norms that condemn the present world are themselves the fruits of its iniquities. All morality has been modeled on immorality and to this day has reinstated it at every level. The slave morality is indeed bad: it is still the master morality.

Rosenkavalier. The elegant attract by the expectation that they will be free in private from greed for advantages already theirs, and from the blinkered myopia that results from constricting circumstances. One imagines them capable of adventurous thinking, serene indifference to their own interests, sophisticated reactions, and believes that their sensitivity must recoil, at least in thought, from the brutality on which their privilege depends, whereas the victims have scarcely even the possibility of perceiving what makes them such. If, however, the severance of production from the private sphere turns out to be itself a piece of necessary social illusion, this expectation of spiritual unrestraint must be disappointed. Not even the subtlest snobbism has *dégoût* for its objective precondition, but rather insulates the snob from its realization. It is an open question how far the eighteenth-century French aristocracy did indeed have the playfully suicidal share in the Enlightenment and the preparation for the Revolution that revulsion from the terrorists of virtue is so fond of imagining. The bourgeoisie, at any rate, has remained pure even in its late phase from any such penchants. None but the *déclassés* dance out of line on the volcano. Subjectively, too, society life is so thoroughly stamped by the economic principle, whose kind of rationality spreads to the whole, that emancipation from egoistic interests, even merely as an intellectual luxury, is denied to it. Just as they are incapable of themselves enjoying their immeasurably increased wealth, they are unable to think against themselves. To no avail the quest for frivolity. The perpetuation of the real difference between upper and lower strata is assisted by the progressive disappearance of differences in the mode of consciousness between the two. The poor are prevented from thinking by the discipline of others, the rich by their own. The rulers' consciousness is inflicting on all intellect what earlier was done to religion. Culture is being turned by the *haute bourgeoisie* into an element of ostentation. A person's intelligence or education is ranked among the qualities that make him suitable for inviting or marrying, like good horsemanship, love of nature, charm, or a faultlessly fitting dinner jacket. About knowledge they are incurious. Usually these blithe spirits are as totally absorbed by everyday practicalities as the petite bourgeoisie. They furnish houses, prepare parties, show virtuosity in booking hotel and airline reservations. For the rest, they sustain themselves on the offal of European irrationalism. They bluntly justify their own hostility to mind, sensing subversion—not even wrongly—in thought itself, in its independence of anything given, existent. Just as in Nietzsche's day educated philistines believed in progress, the unfaltering elevation of the masses, and the greatest possible happiness for the greatest possible number, so today they believe, without quite knowing it themselves, in the opposite, the revocation of 1789, the incorrigibility of human nature, the anthropological impossibility of happiness—in other words, that the workers are too well-off. The profound insights of the day before yesterday have been reduced to the ultimate in banality. Of Nietzsche and Bergson, the last socially accepted philosophies, nothing is left but the murkiest anti-intellectualism in the name of the nature its apologists despoil. "What most vexes me about the Third Reich," a general director's Jewish wife, later murdered in Poland, said in 1933, "is that we can no longer use the word 'earthy,' because it has been commandeered by the Nazis," and even after the defeat of the fascists, a fine-featured Austrian lady of the manor, meeting at a cocktail party a workers' leader mistakenly thought radical, could do nothing in her enthusiasm for his personality but repeat bestially: "and moreover he's so utterly unintellectual, so utterly unintellectual." I remember my fright when an aristocratic girl of vague origins, scarcely able to speak German without an affectedly foreign accent, confessed to me her sympathy for Hitler, with whose image hers seemed incompatible. At the time I thought a winsome feeble-mindedness must be concealing from her who she was. But she was shrewder than I, for what she represented no longer existed, and her class consciousness, in deleting her individual destiny, helped her being-in-itself, her social character, to emerge. People at the top are closing ranks so tightly that all possibility of subjective deviation has gone, and difference can be sought only in the more distinguished cut of an evening dress.

The bad comrade. In a real sense, I ought to be able to deduce fascism from the memories of my childhood. As a conqueror dispatches envoys to the remotest provinces, fascism had sent its advance guard there long before it marched in: my schoolfellows. If the bourgeois class has from time immemorial nurtured the dream of a brutal national community, of oppression of all by all, children already equipped with Christian names like Horst and Jürgen and surnames like Bergenroth, Bojunga, and Eckhardt enacted the dream before the adults were historically ripe for its realization. I felt with such excessive clarity the force of the horror toward which they were straining, that all subsequent happiness seemed revocable, borrowed. The outbreak of the Third Reich did, it is true, surprise my political judgment, but not my unconscious fear. So closely had all the motifs of permanent catastrophe brushed me, so deeply were the warning signs of the German awakening burned into me, that I recognized them all in the features of Hitler's dictatorship: and it often seemed to my foolish terror as if the total State had been invented expressly against me, to inflict on me after all those things from which, in my childhood, its primeval form, I had been temporarily dispensed. The five patriots who set upon a single schoolfellow, thrashed him, and, when he complained to the teacher, defamed him a traitor to the class—are they not the same as those who tortured prisoners to refute claims by foreigners that prisoners were tortured? They whose hallooing knew no end when the top boy blundered—did they not stand grinning and sheepish round the Jewish detainee, poking fun at his maladroit attempt to hang himself? They who could not put together a correct sentence but found all of mine too long—did they not abolish German literature and replace it with their "writ [*Schrifttum*]"? Some covered their chests with mysterious insignia and wanted, far from the sea, to become naval officers when the navy had long ceased to exist: they proclaimed themselves detachment and unit leaders, legitimists of the illegitimate. The crabbed intelligent ones, who had as little success in class as the gifted amateur constructor without connections had under liberalism, who therefore, to please their parents, busied themselves with fretsaw work or even, for their own pleasure, spun out intricate designs in colored inks at their drawing boards on long afternoons, helped the Third Reich to its cruel efficiency, and are being cheated once again. Those, however, who were always truculently at loggerheads with the teachers, interrupting the lessons, nevertheless sat down, from the day, indeed the very hour of their matriculation, with the same teachers, at the same table and the same beer, in male confederacy, vassals by vocation, rebels who, crashing their fists on the table, already signaled their worship for their masters. They needed only to miss promotion to the next class to overtake those who had left their class, and take revenge on them. Now that they, officials and recruits, have stepped visibly out of my dream and dispossessed me of my past life and my language, I no longer need to dream of them. In fascism the nightmare of childhood has come true.

1935

Expensive reproduction. Society is integral even before it undergoes totalitarian rule. Its organization also embraces those at war with it by coordinating their consciousness to its own. Even those intellectuals who have all the political arguments against bourgeois ideology at their fingertips undergo a process of standardization that—despite crassly contrasting content, through readiness on their part to accommodate themselves—approximates them to the prevalent mentality to the extent that the substance of their viewpoint becomes increasingly incidental, dependent merely on their preferences or the assessment of their own chances. What they subjectively fancy radical belongs objectively so entirely to the compartment in the pattern reserved for their like that radicalism is debased to abstract prestige, legitimation for those who know what an intellectual nowadays has to be for and what against. The good things they opt for have long since been just as accepted, in numbers just as restricted, in their hierarchy of values just as fixed, as those of student fraternities. While they inveigh against official kitsch, their views, like dutiful children, are allowed to partake only of preselected nutrition, clichés against clichés. The habitations of such young bohemians resemble their intellectual household. On the walls the deceptively faithful color reproductions of famous Van Goghs like *Sunflowers* or *Café at Arles*, on the bookshelf boiled-down socialism and psychoanalysis and a little sexology for libertines with inhibitions. Added to this the Random House edition of Proust—Scott Moncrieff's translation deserved a better fate, cut-price exclusivity even in its appearance, the compactly economical "omnibus" shape, a mockery of the author whose every sentence put out of action some received opinion, while now as a prize-winning homosexual he fills a similar need for youth as do the books about forest animals and the North Pole expedition in the German home. Also the gramophone with the *Lincoln*-cantata of some stalwart spirit deeply concerned with railway stations, together with the duly marveled-at Oklahoma folklore and a few noisy jazz records that make you feel at once collective, audacious, and comfortable. Every opinion earns the approbation of friends; every argument is known by them beforehand. That all cultural products, even nonconformist ones, have been incorporated into the distribution mechanisms of large-scale capital, that in the most developed country a product that does not bear the imprimatur of mass production can scarcely reach a reader, viewer, listener at all denies deviationary longings their subject matter in advance. Even Kafka is becoming a fixture in the sublet studio. The intellectuals themselves are already so heavily committed to what is endorsed in their isolated sphere that they no longer desire anything that does not carry the highbrow tag. Ambition aims solely at expertise in the accepted stock-in-trade, hitting on the correct slogan. The outsiderishness of the initiates is an illusion; they are merely biding their time. To see them as renegades is to assess them too high; they mask mediocre faces with horn-rimmed spectacles betokening "brilliance," though with plain-glass lenses, solely in order to better themselves in their own eyes and in the general rat race. They are already just like the rest. The subjective precondition of opposition, uncoordinated judgment, is dying out, while its gesticulations continue to be performed as a group ritual. Stalin only needs to clear his throat and they throw Kafka and Van Gogh on the rubbish heap.

Juvenal's error. Difficult to write satire. Not only because our situation, which needs it more than any ever did, makes a mockery of mockery. The medium of irony has itself come into contradiction with truth. Irony convicts its object by presenting it as what it purports to be, and without passing judgment, as if leaving a blank for the observing subject, measures it against its being-in-itself. It shows up the negative by confronting the positive with its own claim to positivity. It cancels itself out the moment it adds a word of interpretation. In this it presupposes the idea of the self-evident, originally of social resonance. Only when a compelling consensus of subjects is assumed, is subjective reflection, the performance of the conceptual act, superfluous. He who has laughter on his side has no need of proof. Historically, therefore, satire has for thousands of years, up to Voltaire's age, preferred to side with the stronger party, which could be relied on, with authority. Usually it acted on behalf of older strata threatened by more recent stages of enlightenment, which sought to support their traditionalism with enlightened means: its inexhaustible theme was the decay of morals. For this reason what was once a deft rapier appears to later generations as a decidedly cumbersome cudgel. This double-tongued spiritualization of appearances is always intended to show the satirist as amusing, on the crest of progress; the yardstick applied, however, is that of whatever is endangered by progress, while the latter is nevertheless so far presupposed as the prevalent ideology that the phenomenon pronounced degenerate is condemned without being done the justice of rational debate. Aristophanean comedy, in which obscenity is supposed to expose loose living, counted, as a modernistic *laudatio temporis acti*, on the mob it slandered. With the triumph of the bourgeois class in the Christian era the function of irony then slackened. It early defected to the oppressed, especially those who in reality were no longer so. Certainly, as prisoner of its own form, it never entirely divested itself of its authoritarian inheritance, its unrebellious malice. Only with the bourgeois decline was it sublimated into an appeal to ideas of humanity that no longer tolerated any reconciliation with the established order and its consciousness. But even these ideas included their own self-evidence: no doubt concerning objective, immediate obviousness was entertained; no witticism of Karl Kraus wavers over the decision who is decent and who a scoundrel, what is intelligence and what stupidity, what is language and what journalism. To this presence of mind his formulations owe their force. Just as, in their instantaneous grasp of the matter in hand, no question holds them up, so they admit no question. The more emphatically, however, Kraus's prose posits its humanity as invariant, the more backward-looking it becomes. It condemns corruption and decadence, the literati and the futurists, without having any other advantage over the zealots of an intellectual state of nature than a perception of its worthlessness. That in the end his intransigence toward Hitler showed itself pliable toward Schuschnigg attests not to want of courage but to the antinomy of satire. It needs something to hold onto, and the self-styled malcontent had to bow to its positivity. Even the denunciation of the hack journalist contains, besides its truth, its critical element, something of the common sense that cannot bear the inflated windbag. The hatred for those who would seem more than they are nailed them down to their real nature as an undisputed fact. The infallible eye for anything trumped-up, for unsubstantiated but commercially angled intellectual pretensions, unmasks those who failed to measure up to their own higher standard. This higher standard is power and success and manifests itself, in their bungled attempt to reach it, as itself a lie. But equally these impostors have always incarnated utopia: even false jewelry gleams with a helpless childhood dream, and this too is damned, called before the forum of success, because it failed. All satire is blind to the forces liberated by decay. Which is why total decay has absorbed the forces of satire. The scorn of the leaders of the Third Reich for emigrants and liberal statesmen, a scorn whose power was now no more than that of mere biceps, was the last. The impossibility of satire today should not be blamed, as sentimentality is apt to do, on the relativism of values, the absence of binding norms. Rather, agreement itself, the formal a priori of irony, has given way to universal agreement of content. As such it presents the only fitting target for irony and at the same time pulls the ground from under its feet. Irony's medium, the difference between ideology and reality, has disappeared. The former resigns itself to confirmation of reality by its mere duplication. Irony used to say: such it claims to be, but such it is; today, however, the world, even in its most radical lie, falls back on the argument that things are like this, a simple finding that coincides, for it, with the good. There is not a crevice in the cliff of the established order into which the ironist might hook a fingernail. Crashing down, he is pursued by the mocking laughter of the insidious object that disempowered him. The gesture of the unthinking That's-how-it-is is the exact means by which the world dispatches each of its victims, and the transcendental agreement inherent in irony becomes ridiculous in the face of the real unanimity of those it ought to attack. Pitted against the deadly seriousness of total society, which has absorbed the opposing voice, the impotent objection earlier quashed by irony, there is now only the deadly seriousness of comprehended truth.

Consecutio temporum. When my first composition teacher, trying to knock the atonal nonsense out of me, found his tales of erotic scandals about the new composers proving ineffective, he switched his attack to what he suspected as my weak spot, by showing himself up-to-date. The ultramodern, his argument ran, was no longer modern; the stimulations I sought were already numb; the expressive figures that excited me belonged to an outdated sentimentality; and the new youth had, as he liked to put it, more red blood corpuscles. His own pieces, in which oriental themes were regularly extended by the chromatic scale, betrayed the same ultra-subtle deliberations as the maneuvers of a conservatory director with a bad conscience. But I was soon to discover that the fashion he opposed to my modernity did actually resemble, in the primeval habitat of the great salons, what he had hatched up in the provinces. Neoclassicism, that form of reaction that not only fails to acknowledge itself as such but even passes off its reactionary moment as ahead of its time, was the advance-guard of a massive tendency that under fascism and mass culture quickly learned to be rid of tender concern for the endlessly tiresome sensibilities of artists, and to combine the spirit of Courths-Mahler[1] with that of technical progress. The modern has really become unmodern. Modernity is a qualitative, not a chronological, category. Just as it cannot be reduced to abstract form, with equal necessity it must turn its back on conventional surface coherence, the appearance of harmony, the order corroborated merely by replication. The stalwarts of the fascist fighting leagues, thundering fulsomely against futurism, saw more clearly in their rage than did the Moscow censors who placed cubism on the Index because, in its private impropriety, it failed to measure up to the spirit of the collective age, or the brazen theater critics who find a play by Strindberg or Wedekind passé but a piece of underground reportage up-to-date. All the same, their blasé philistinism utters an appalling truth: that the procession of total society, which would like to force its organization on all expression, is in fact leaving behind the power that opposes what Lindbergh's wife called the wave of the future, that is, the critical construction of being. This is not merely outlawed by a corrupt public opinion, but the prevailing absurdity affects its very substance. The might of what is, constraining the mind to follow its example, is so overwhelming that even the unassimilated expression of protest assumes in the face of it a homespun, aimless, inexperienced quality reminiscent of the provincialism that once so prophetically suspected modernity of backwardness. Matching the psychological regression of individuals who exist without a self is a regression of the objective spirit, in which obtuseness, primitivism, and the bargain-sale set up what historically has long since decayed as the newest historical power, and consign to the day before yesterday everything that does not zealously join the march of regression. This quid pro quo of progress and reaction makes orientation in contemporary art almost as difficult as in politics, and furthermore paralyzes production itself, where anyone who clings to extreme intentions is made to feel like a backwoodsman, while the conformist no longer lingers bashfully in arbors, literary or horticultural,[2] but hurtles forward, rocket-powered, into the pluperfect.

Toy shop. Hebbel, in a surprising entry in his diary, asks what takes away "life's magic in later years." "It is because in all the brightly-colored contorted marionettes, we see the revolving cylinder that sets them in motion, and because for this very reason the captivating variety of life is reduced to wooden monotony. A child seeing the tightrope-walkers singing, the pipers playing, the girls fetching water, the coachmen driving, thinks all this is happening for the joy of doing so; he can't imagine that these people also have to eat and drink, go to bed, and get up again. We, however, know what is at stake." Namely, earning a living, which commandeers all those activities as mere means, reduces them to interchangeable, abstract labor-time. The quality of things ceases to be their essence and becomes the accidental appearance of their value. The "equivalent form"[1] mars all perceptions: what is no longer irradiated by the light of its own self-determination as "joy in doing," pales to the eye. Our organs grasp nothing sensuous in isolation, but notice whether a color, a sound, a movement is there for its own sake or for something else; wearied by a false variety, they steep all in gray, disappointed by the deceptive claim of qualities still to be there at all, while they conform to the purposes of appropriation, indeed largely owe their existence to it alone. Disenchantment with the contemplated world is the sensorium's reaction to its objective role as a "commodity world." Only when purified of appropriation would things be colorful and useful at once: under universal compulsion the two cannot be reconciled. Children, however, are not so much, as Hebbel thought, subject to illusions of "captivating variety," as still aware, in their spontaneous perception, of the contradiction between phenomenon and fungibility that the resigned adult no longer sees, and they shun it. Play is their defense. The unerring child is struck by the "peculiarity of the equivalent form": "use-value becomes the form of manifestation, the phenomenal form of its opposite, value."[2]

In his purposeless activity the child, by a subterfuge, sides with use-value against exchange value. Just because he deprives the things with which he plays of their mediated usefulness, he seeks to rescue in them what is benign toward men and not what subserves the exchange relation that equally deforms men and things. The little trucks travel nowhere, and the tiny barrels on them are empty; yet they remain true to their destiny by not performing, not participating in the process of abstraction that levels down that destiny, but instead abide as allegories of what they are specifically for. Scattered, it is true, but not ensnared, they wait to see whether society will finally remove the social stigma on them, whether the vital process between men and things, praxis, will cease to be practical. The unreality of games gives notice that reality is not yet real. Unconsciously they rehearse the right life. The relation of children to animals depends entirely on the fact that Utopia goes disguised in the creatures whom Marx even begrudged the surplus value they contribute as workers. In existing without any purpose recognizable to men, animals hold out, as if for expression, their own names, utterly impossible to exchange. This makes them so beloved of children, their contemplation so blissful. I am a rhinoceros, signifies the shape of the rhinoceros. Fairy tales and operettas know such images, and the ridiculous question of the woman: how do we know that Orion is really called Orion, rises to the stars.

Novissimum organum. It has long been demonstrated that wage labor formed the masses of the modern epoch, indeed, created the worker himself. As a general principle the individual is not merely the biological basis, but the reflection of the social process; his consciousness of himself as something in-itself is the illusion needed to raise his level of performance, whereas in fact the individuated function in the modern economy as mere agents of the law of value. The inner constitution of the individual, not merely his social role, could be deduced from this. Decisive here, in the present phase, is the category of the organic composition of capital. By this the theory of accumulation meant the "growth in the mass of the means of production, as compared with the mass of the labor-power that vivifies them."[1] If the integration of society, particularly in totalitarian states, designates subjects more and more exclusively as partial moments in the network of material production, then the "alteration of the technical composition of capital" is prolonged within those encompassed, and indeed constituted, by the technological demands of the production process. The organic composition of man is growing. That which determines subjects as means of production and not as living purposes increases with the proportion of machines to variable capital. The pat phrase about the "mechanization" of man is deceptive because it thinks of him as something static that, through an "influence" from outside, an adaptation to conditions of production external to him, suffers certain deformations. But there is no substratum beneath such "deformations," no ontic interior on which social mechanisms merely act externally: the deformation is a sickness not in men but in the society that begets its children with the "hereditary taint" that biologism projects onto nature. Only when the process that begins with the metamorphosis of labor power into a commodity has permeated men through and through and objectified each of their impulses as formally commensurable variations of the exchange relationship is it possible for life to reproduce itself under the prevailing relations of production. Its consummate organization demands the coordination of people that are dead. The will to live finds itself dependent on the denial of the will to live: self-preservation annuls all life in subjectivity. Compared to this, all the achievements of adaptation, all the acts of conformity described by social psychology and cultural anthropology, are mere epiphenomena. The organic composition of man refers by no means only to his specialized technical faculties, but—and this the usual cultural criticism will not at any price admit—equally to their opposite, the moments of naturalness that once themselves sprung from the social dialectic and are now succumbing to it. Even what differs from technology in man is now being incorporated into it as a kind of lubrication. Psychological differentiation, originally the outcome both of freedom and of the division of labor that dissects man according to sectors of the production process, is finally itself entering the service of production. "The specialized 'virtuoso,'" one dialectician wrote thirty years ago, "the vendor of his objectified and reified faculties . . . lapses into a contemplative attitude towards the workings of his own objectified and reified faculties. This phenomenon can be seen at its most grotesque in journalism. Here it is subjectivity itself, knowledge, temperament and powers of expression that are reduced to an abstract mechanism, functioning autonomously and divorced both from the personality of their 'owner' and from the material and concrete nature of the subject-matter in hand. The journalist's 'lack of convictions,' the prostitution of his experiences and beliefs is comprehensible only as the apogee of capitalist reification."[2] What was here noted among the "degenerate manifestations" of the bourgeoisie, which it still itself denounced, has since emerged as the social norm, as the character of irreproachable existence under late industrialism. It has long ceased to be a matter of the mere sale of the living. Under a priori salability the living has made itself, as something living, a thing, equipment. The ego consciously takes the whole man into its service as a piece of apparatus. In this reorganization the ego as business manager delegates so much of itself to the ego as business mechanism that it becomes quite abstract, a mere reference point: self-preservation forfeits its self. Character traits, from genuine kindness to the hysterical fit of rage, become capable of manipulation, until they coincide exactly with the demands of a given situation. With their mobilization they change. All that is left are the light, rigid, empty husks of emotions, matter transportable at will, devoid of anything personal. They are no longer the subject; rather, the subject responds to them as to his internal object. In their unbounded docility toward the ego, they are at the same time estranged from it: being wholly passive they nourish it no longer. This is the social pathogenesis of schizophrenia. The severance of character traits both from their instinctual basis and from the self, which commands them where it formerly merely held them together, causes man to pay for his increasing inner organization with increasing disintegration. The consummation of the division of labor within the individual, his radical objectification, leads to his morbid scission. Hence the "psychotic character," the anthropological precondition of all totalitarian mass movements. Precisely this transition from firm characteristics to push-button behavior patterns—though apparently enlivening—is an expression of the rising organic composition of man. Quick reactions, unballasted by a mediating constitution, do not restore spontaneity but establish the person as a measuring instrument deployed and calibrated by a central authority. The more immediate its response, the more deeply in reality mediation has advance: in the prompt, unresistant reflexes the subject is entirely extinguished. So too, biological reflexes, the models of the present social ones, are—when measured against subjectivity—objectified, alien: not without reason are they often called "mechanical." The closer organisms are to death, the more they regress to such twitching. Accordingly the destructive tendencies of the masses that explode in both varieties of totalitarian state are not so much death wishes as manifestations of what they have already become. They murder so that whatever to them seems living shall resemble themselves.

Knackery. Metaphysical categories are not merely an ideology concealing the social system; at the same time they express its nature, the truth about it, and in their changes are precipitated those in its most central experiences. Thus death comes within the scope of history, and the latter in turn can be understood only through it. Its dignity used to resemble that of the individual. His autonomy, economic in origin, culminated in the conception of his absoluteness once the theological hope of immortality, which had empirically relativized it, began to pale. To this corresponded the emphatic image of death in which the individual, the basis of all bourgeois behavior and thinking, was entirely wiped out. Death was the absolute price of absolute value. Now it shares the ruin of the socially defunct individual. Where it is draped in the old dignity, it exudes the lie that was always latent in it: that of naming the impenetrable, predicating the subjectless, incorporating the unassimilable. In contemporary consciousness, however, the truth and untruth of its dignity are done with, not because of otherworldly hopes, but in the face of the hopeless debility of the here and now. "The modern world," the radical Catholic Charles Péguy noted as early as 1907, "has succeeded in debasing what is perhaps the most difficult thing in the world to debase, because this thing has in it, as if in its very texture, a particular kind of dignity, a singular incapacity to be debased: it debases death."[1] If the individual whom death annihilates is himself nothing, bereft of self-command and of his own being, then the annihilating power becomes also nothing, as if in a facetious application of Heidegger's formula of the nothing that anihilates. The radical replaceability of the individual makes his death practically—and in utter contempt—revocable, as it was once conceived to be with paradoxical pathos by Christianity. But as a "negligible quantity" death is entirely assimilated. For every person, with all his functions, society has a stand-in ready, to whom the former is in any case no more than an intrusive occupier of his workplace, a candidate for death. So the experience of death is turned into that of the exchange of functionaries, and anything in the natural relationship to death that is not wholly absorbed into the social one is turned over to hygiene. In being seen as no more than the exit of a living creature from the social combine, death has been finally domesticated: dying merely confirms the absolute irrelevance of the natural organism in the face of the social absolute. If the culture industry anywhere bears witness to the changes in the organic composition of society, it is in the scarcely veiled admission of this state of affairs. Under its lens death begins to be comic. Certainly, the laughter that greets it in a certain genre of production is ambiguous. It still announces fear of the amorphous thing under the net that society has woven over the whole of nature. But the webbing is so thick and dense that remembrance of nature's uncovered state seems childish, sentimental. After the breakdown of the detective story in the books of Edgar Wallace, which seemed by their less rational construction, their unsolved riddles, and their crude exaggeration to ridicule their readers, and yet in so doing magnificently anticipated the collective imago of total terror, the type of the murder comedy has come into being. While continuing to claim to make fun of a bogus awe, it demolishes the images of death. It presents the corpse as what it has become, a stage prop. It still looks human and is yet a thing, as in the film *A Slight Case of Murder*, where corpses are continuously transported to and fro, allegories of what they already are. Comedy savors to the full the false abolition of death that Kafka had long before described in panic in the story of Gracchus the hunter: for the same reason, no doubt, music too is starting to become comic. What the National Socialists perpetrated against millions of people—the parading and patterning of the living like dead matter, then the mass production and cost-cutting of death—threw its prefiguring shadow on those who felt moved to chortle over corpses. What is decisive is the absorption of biological destruction by conscious social will. Only a humanity to whom death has become as indifferent as its members, that has itself died, can inflict it administratively on innumerable people. Rilke's prayer for "one's own death" is a piteous attempt to conceal the fact that nowadays people merely snuff out.

Don't exaggerate. Criticism of tendencies in modern society is automatically countered, before it is fully uttered, by the argument that things have always been like this. Excitement—so promptly resisted—merely shows want of insight into the invariability of history, an unreasonableness proudly diagnosed by all as hysteria. The accuser is further informed that the motive of his attack is self-aggrandizement, a desire for special privileges, whereas the grounds for his indignation are common knowledge, trivial, so that no one can be expected to waste his interest on them. The obviousness of disaster becomes an asset to its apologists—what everyone knows no one need say—and under cover of silence is allowed to proceed unopposed. Assent is given to what has been drummed into people's heads by philosophy of every hue: that whatever has the persistent momentum of existence on its side is thereby proved right. One need only be discontented to be at once suspect as a world reformer. Connivance makes use of the trick of attributing to its opponent a reactionary and untenable theory of decline—for is not horror indeed perennial?—in order by the alleged error in his thinking to discredit his concrete insight into the negative, and to blacken him who remonstrates against darkness as an obfuscator. But even if things have always been so, although neither Timur nor Genghis Khan nor the English colonial administration in India systematically burst the lungs of millions of people with gas, the eternity of horror nevertheless manifests itself in the fact that each of its new forms outdoes the old. What is constant is not an invariable quantity of suffering, but its progress toward hell: that is the meaning of the thesis of the intensification of antagonisms. Any other would be innocuous and would give way to conciliatory phrases, abandoning the qualitative leap. He who registers the death camps as a technical mishap in civilization's triumphal procession, the martyrdom of the Jews as world-historically irrelevant not only falls short of the dialectical vision but reverses the meaning of his own politics: to hold ultimate calamity in check. Not only in the development of forces of production but also in the increasing pressure of domination does quantity change into quality. If the Jews as a group are eradicated while society continues to reproduce the life of the workers, then the argument that the former were bourgeois and their fate unimportant for the great dynamic of history becomes economic sophistry, even insofar as mass murder is indeed explicable by the falling rate of profit. Horror consists in its always remaining the same—the persistence of "prehistory"—but is realized as constantly different, unforeseen, exceeding all expectation, the faithful shadow of developing productive forces. The same duality defines violence, as Marx demonstrated, in material production: "There are characteristics which all stages of production have in common, and which are established as general ones by the mind; but the so-called *general pre-conditions* of all production are nothing more than . . . abstract moments with which no real historical stage of production can be grasped."[1] In other words, to abstract out historically unchanged elements is not to observe neutral scientific objectivity but to spread, even when correct, a smoke screen behind which whatever is tangible and therefore assailable is lost to sight. Precisely this the apologists will not admit. On one hand they rave about the *dernière nouveauté* and on the other they deny the infernal machine that is history. Auschwitz cannot be brought into analogy with the destruction of the Greek city-states as a mere gradual increase in horror, before which one can preserve tranquillity of mind. Certainly, the unprecedented torture and humiliation of those abducted in cattle trucks does shed a deathly-livid light on the most distant past, in whose mindless, planless violence the scientifically confected was already teleologically latent. The identity lies in the nonidentity, in what, not having yet come to pass, denounces what has. The statement that things are always the same is false in its immediateness, and true only when introduced into the dynamics of totality. He who relinquishes awareness of the growth of horror not merely succumbs to cold-hearted contemplation but fails to perceive, together with the specific difference between the newest and that preceding it, the true identity of the whole, of terror without end.

(1951; from GS 4)
Translated by Edmund Jephcott

PART THREE

ADMINISTERED WORLD, REIFIED THOUGHT

4

Reflections on Class Theory

I

According to theory,[1] history is the history of class struggles. But the concept of class is bound up with the emergence of the proletariat. Even when it was still revolutionary, the bourgeoisie called itself the third estate. By extending the concept of class to prehistory, theory denounces not just the bourgeois, whose freedom, together with their possessions and education, perpetuates the tradition of the old injustice. It also turns against prehistory itself. It destroys the illusion of a good-natured patriarchy that had been assumed by prehistory following the victory of inexorable capitalist calculation. The venerable unity of a traditional structure, the natural right of hierarchy in a society that was presented as having grown organically, turned out to be a unity of interested parties. That hierarchy had always been a coercive organization designed for the appropriation of the labor of others. Natural law is historical injustice that has become obsolete; the articulated organism is a system of divisiveness; the picture of the estates is the ideology that—with its themes of honest merit, loyal work, and, lastly, the exchange of equivalents—was ideally suited to the newly installed bourgeoisie.

By exposing the historical necessity that had brought capitalism into being, political economy became the critique of history as a whole, whose immutable nature was the source of the privileged status of capitalism as well as its forbears. To recognize the catastrophic violence in the latest form of injustice, that is to say, the latent injustice contained in fair exchange, means simply to identify it with the prehistory that it destroyed. If all the oppression that man has ever inflicted on man culminates in the modern age in the cold inhumanity of free wage labor, then the past is revealed in conditions and things—the romantic contrast to industrial reason—as the trace of former suffering. The archaic silence of pyramids and ruins becomes conscious of itself in materialist thought: it is the echo of factory noise in the landscape of the immutable. Jacob Burckhardt hazards the suggestion that the parable of the cave in Plato's *Republic*, with its sublime symbolism of the doctrine of eternal ideas, derived from the horrendous image of the Athenian silver mines.[a] This implies that the philosophical idea of eternal truth had sprung from the contemplation of present torment. All history is the history of class struggles because it was always the same thing, namely, prehistory.

II

This gives us a pointer as to how we can recognize what history is. From the most recent form of injustice, a steady light reflects back on history as a whole. Only in this way can theory enable us to use the full weight of history to gain an insight into the present without succumbing in resignation to the burden of the past. Members of the bourgeoisie and their supporters have been loud in their praise of Marxism on account of its dynamism, in which they detect the same industrious mimicry of history that characterizes their own efforts. According to the appreciative comments of Ernst Troeltsch in his book on historicism, Marxist dialectic has "preserved its constructive power and its ability to adapt to the fundamental mobility of the real."[b] This praise of the constructive ability to adapt arouses our distrust of that fundamental mobility. Dynamism is merely one side of dialectic: it is the side preferred by the belief in practicality, masterful action, the indefatigable "can-do" attitude, because constant change is the best way to conceal the old untruth.

[a] See Jakob Burckhardt, *Griechische Kulturgeschichte*, vol. 1, 4th ed. (Stuttgart: Kröner, 1908), p. 164 n. 5.

[b] Ernst Troeltsch, *Der Historismus und seine Probleme* (Tübingen: J. C. B. Mohr, 1922), p. 315.

The other, less popular aspect of dialectic is its static side. The self-movement of the concept, the conception of history as a syllogism, as it is to be found in Hegel's philosophy, is no developmental doctrine. It was only turned into one by the collusive misunderstanding of the humanities. The law that, according to the Hegelian dialectic, governs the restlessly destructive unfolding of the ever-new consists in the fact that at every moment the ever-new is also the old lying close at hand. The new does not add itself to the old but remains the old in distress, in its hour of need, as it becomes topical as an immanent contradiction through its act of reflection, its indispensable confrontation with the universal in the old. Thus throughout all its antithetical mediations, history remains one vast analytic proposition. That is the historical essence of the metaphysical doctrine of the identity of subject and object in the Absolute. The system of history, the elevation of the temporal to the totality of meaning, abolishes time and reduces it to an abstract negation.

As a philosophy, Marxism remained true to this. It confirms Hegelian idealism as prehistory's knowledge of its own identity. But it puts it back on its feet by unmasking that identity as prehistorical. For Marxism, the identical truly becomes a state of need, the need of the human beings who are merely articulated by the concept. The irreconcilable power of the negative that sets history in motion is the power of what exploiters do to the victims. As a shackle binding one generation to the next, it functions as an obstacle to both freedom and history. The systematic unity of history, which is supposed to give meaning to individual suffering or else demote it from on high to the level of something fortuitous, is the philosophical appropriation of the labyrinth in which men have toiled to this day, the epitome of suffering.

Within the sphere of influence of the system, the new—progress—is, like the old, a constant source of new disaster. Knowing the new does not mean adapting oneself to it and to the movement of history; it means resisting its inflexibility and conceiving of the onward march of the battalions of world history as marking time. Theory knows of no "constructive force" but only of one that lights up the contours of a burned-out prehistory with the glow of the latest disaster in order to perceive the parallel that exists between them. The latest thing is always the old terror, the myth, which consists in that blind continuum of time that continually retracts itself, with patient, stupidly omniscient malice, just like Oknos's ass, which eats the rope as fast as he twines it. Only he who recognizes that the new is the same old thing will be of service to whatever is different.

III

The latest phase of class society is dominated by monopolies; it tends toward fascism, the form of political organization worthy of it. While it vindicates the doctrine of class struggle with its concentration and centralization, extreme power and extreme impotence directly confronting one another in total contradiction, it makes people forget the actual existence of hostile classes. The monopolies are assisted much more by such forgetfulness than by the ideologies that have meanwhile become so attenuated that they declare themselves to be lies in order to show those who believe in them how impotent they really are. The total organization of society by big business and its ubiquitous technology has taken such utter possession of the world and the imagination that even to conceive of the idea that things might be otherwise calls for an almost hopeless effort. The diabolical image of harmony, the invisibility of the classes caused by the petrified mold in which they are held fast, can only gain such power over people's minds because the idea that the oppressed, the workers of the world, might unite as a class and put an end to the horror seems doomed in the light of the present distribution of power and impotence.

The leveling of mass society that is so bitterly lamented by cultural conservatives and their sociological henchmen is in truth nothing but the desperate elimination of difference from the identity of the masses. They, the prisoners of the system, strive to bring about this leveling by imitating their stunted rulers in the hope of receiving a pittance in their old age, if only they can prove themselves worthy. The belief that they might be able to form an organized class and conduct a class war crumbles in the minds of the dispossessed along with liberal illusions. This is not very different from the way in which, once upon a time, the desire of the bourgeoisie to dress itself up as an estate could be undermined by the mockery of revolutionary workers' associations. Class struggle is dismissed and sent to join the ranks of ideals, where it has to make do with slogans about tolerance and humanity in the speeches of trade-union leaders. The age when people could build barricades now lies almost as firmly in the past as the time when a craftsman's trade was a solid foundation for life.

The omnipotence of repression and its invisibility are the same thing. The classless society of car drivers, cinema goers, and comrades makes a mockery not only of those who do not belong but even of those who do, the objects of domination who dare not admit as much to others or even to themselves because simply knowing one is such an object is punished by gnawing fear for one's job and one's life. So great has the tension become between the poles that never meet that it has ceased to exist. The immeasurable pressure of domination has so fragmented the masses that it has even dissipated the negative unity of being oppressed that forged them into a class in the nineteenth century. In exchange, they find they have been directly absorbed into the unity of the system that is oppressing them. Class rule is set to survive the anonymous, objective form of the class.

IV

This makes it essential to scrutinize the concept of class closely enough for us to take hold of it and simultaneously change it. Take hold of it, because its basis, the division of society into exploiters and exploited, not only continues unabated but is increasing in coercion and solidity. Change it, because the oppressed who today, as predicted by the theory, constitute the overwhelming majority of mankind are unable to experience themselves as a class. Those among them who claim the name mean by it for the most part their own particular interest in the existing state of affairs, much as the leaders of industry make use of the word "production."

The distinction between exploiters and exploited is not so visible as to make it obvious to the exploited that solidarity should be their ultima ratio; conformity appears more rational to them. Membership in the same class by no means translates into equality of interests and action. The contradictory nature of the concept of class that is wreaking such havoc today is to be sought less among the labor aristocracy than in the egalitarian character of the bourgeoisie. If the critique of political economy means the critique of capitalism, then the concept of class, its center, is modeled on the bourgeoisie itself. As the anonymous unity of the owners of the means of production and their various appendages, the bourgeoisie is the class par excellence. But the egalitarian character that makes it so is dissolved by the critique of political economy, not just in comparison with the proletariat but also as a defining factor of the bourgeoisie itself. Free competition among capitalists entails the same injustice as they, when taken collectively, commit against wage laborers.

For exploitation does not occur just in the process of exchange but is rather produced through the system as such. Equal rights and equal opportunities among the competing parties are largely a fiction. Their success depends on the power of their capital outside the competitive process, a power they already possess on entering the marketplace. It depends further on the political and social power they represent, on old and new conquistador spoils, on their affiliation with feudal property that a competitive economy has never entirely liquidated, and on their relations with the direct governing apparatus of the military. The equality of interests reduces itself to sharing in the booty of the large owners, something that is granted when all owners concede to the large ones the principle of sovereign ownership that guarantees them their power and the scope for expanded production: the class as a whole must be prepared for utter surrender to the principle of property ownership, by which is meant the property of the large owners in the first instance.

Bourgeois class consciousness aspires to protection from above, the concession that the truly dominant owners make to those who sell themselves to them body and soul. Bourgeois tolerance wants to be tolerated. It does not mean justice for those at the bottom of the pile, not even for those members of its own class who find themselves condemned by those above them "in the spirit of objectivity." The law of the exchange of equivalents and its reflexes in the political and the legal systems is the compact that regulates the relations between the core of the class and its majority, the bourgeois vassals, and it regulates them tacitly in the interests of existing power relations. In other words, real though the class is, it is also ideology in equal measure. If theory shows that there is something questionable about the idea of fair exchange, bourgeois freedom, and humanity, this sheds light on the dual nature of the class. This duality consists in the fact that its formal equality has the function both of oppressing the class with which it is contrasted and of using the strongest to control members of its own.

Theory denounces the bourgeois class as a unity, a class against the proletariat, in order to expose the fact that the universal interest it claims to represent possesses a particularist dimension. But this particularist unity is necessarily a non-unity in itself. The egalitarian form of the class serves as an instrument to protect the privilege of the dominant segment over its supporters while concealing it. The critique of liberal society cannot stop short at the concept of class, which is both as true and as false as the liberal system itself. Its truth is its critical aspect: it designates the unity in which particular bourgeois interests are made real. Its untruth lies in the non-unity of the class. Its immanent determination by the state of power relations is the tribute it is forced to pay to its own particularity, which its unity benefits. Its real non-unity is veiled by its no less real unity.

V

In the market economy the untrue aspect of the concept of class was latent; in monopoly capitalism it has become as visible as its truth—the survival of classes—has become invisible. Competition and its struggles have led to the disappearance of much of the unity of the class, which previously held the competitors together in the form of the rules of the game and of common interests. It is so easy for the bourgeoisie to deny its own class character to the proletariat because in fact its organization has cast off the consensual form of like interests that had constituted it as a class in the eighteenth and nineteenth centuries. It has replaced this with the direct economic and political command of the large capitalists that used the same threat of the police against both their own supporters and the workers. This imposes on both sections of the population the same function and the same need, and it is this that makes it almost impossible for the workers to see that class relations are at work.

Theory's prognosis of a few owners and an overwhelming mass of the expropriated has come true, but instead of becoming glaringly obvious, this has been conjured out of existence by the mass society in which class society has culminated. The ruling class disappears behind the concentration of capital. This latter has reached a magnitude and acquired a weight of its own that enables capital to present itself as an institution, as the expression of society as a whole. By virtue of its omnipotence, the particular is able to usurp the totality: this overall social aspect of capital is the endpoint of the old fetish character of the commodity according to which relations between men are reflected back to them as relations between things.

Today, the entire order of existence has turned into such things. In this social order, the proletariat discovers that with the free market, which for the workers had always been a lie, the path to the formation of a class is now objectively blocked. And now it is even closed off by the conscious will and practical measures of the rulers in the name of the great totality, in other words, them. However, if the workers wish to live, they must fall into line. Everywhere, self-preservation pushes them via the collective in the direction of conspiratorial cliques. The division between leader and led to be found in the ruling class reproduces itself compulsively further down the ladder. The trade unions become monopolies, and their officials become bandits who call for blind obedience from those permitted to become members. They terrorize outsiders but are loyally prepared to share the spoils with other monopolists, if these have not already taken over the entire organization in the form of open fascism.

This development has put an end to the episode of liberalism; the dynamics of yesterday are unmasked as the ossified prehistory of today, namely, the anonymous class as the dictatorship of the self-appointed elite. Even political economy, the conception of which theory grimly gave to liberalism, is proving to be ephemeral. Economics is a special case of economizing, lack prepared for domination. The laws of exchange have not led to a form of rule that can be regarded as historically adequate for the reproduction of society as a whole at its present stage. Instead, it was the old form of rule that had joined the economic apparatus so that, once in possession, it might smash it and thus make its own life easier. By abolishing the classes in this way, class rule comes into its own. In the image of the latest economic phase, history is the history of monopolies. In the image of the manifest act of usurpation that is practiced nowadays by the leaders of capital and labor acting in consort, it is the history of gang wars and rackets.

VI

Marx died before he could develop the theory of class, and the working class let the matter rest there. Even in its rudimentary form, the theory was not merely the most effective tool of agitation but an active instrument of conflict in the age of bourgeois democracy, the proletarian mass party, and strikes, before the open victory of monopoly and the growth of unemployment had become second nature. Only the revisionists entered into a discussion of the class question, and they did so in order to cloak the initial stages of their betrayal with the denial of class war, their statistical appreciation of the middle strata, and their praise of a generalized progress.

The hypocritical denial of the existence of classes moved the responsible exponents of theory to guard the concept of class as a pedagogic tactic, without attempting to take it any further. This was a source of weakness, and it means that the theory must take some of the blame for the degeneration of practice. Bourgeois sociology of all nations exploited this weakness to the full. Bourgeois sociology may have been deflected from its own course by Marx, as if by a magnet, and become the more strident in its own defense, the more it insisted on value-free neutrality. Nevertheless, its positivist ideology, its close adherence to the facts, was able to score points wherever the facts put a stunted theory in the wrong.

For the theory had declined to the point where even in its own eyes statements of fact had become an article of faith. The nominalism characteristic of its method of research reduced the essential fact, namely, class, to an ideal type and banished it to the realm of methodology, while abandoning reality to a cult of unique events that the theory merely garnished. This pattern went hand in hand with studies that found the concept of class—for instance, in its specific political equivalent of the Party—guilty of possessing those oligarchic features that the theory had neglected or treated reluctantly in an appendix entitled "Monopoly Capitalism." The more thoroughly the facts were cleansed of the concrete concept—namely, the concept of their relation to the present state of exploitation, which is contained in all factual material and determines it—the more easily they fitted into the abstract concept that applies to all times and places and over which that general framework has no influence precisely because it is an abstraction.

Oligarchy, integration, and division of labor cease to be aspects of the history of domination, a dark forest you can no longer see because it is obscured by the green trees of people's own lives. Instead, they become general categories of the socialization of mankind. The skepticism toward the so-called metaphysics of class becomes the norm in the realm of formal sociology: classes are said not to exist because of the unshakable facts. The facts are unshakable because they are made to take the place of class, and wherever the sociological gaze seeks the stones of class, it discovers only the bread of the elites, and learns daily that you simply cannot dispense with ideology. And since sociology always acts in this way, the cleverest thing it can do is to leave the forms of socialization unscathed and, perhaps with bleeding heart, adopt the cause of the unavoidable elite as one's own ideology.

It would be a sign of pure impotence to try to ward off this deeply rooted delusion by appealing to counterexamples—by denying the oligarchic nature of the mass party, or by refusing to acknowledge that the theory really had become ideology in the mouths of its officials. To argue in that way would mean importing the spirit of apologia into the theory against which the apologists of the bourgeoisie have already spun their web.

Nothing helps but to turn the truth of the sociological concepts against the untruth that produced them. What sociology can advance against the reality of classes is nothing but the principle of class society: the universality of socialization is the form in which domination has historically been able to prevail. This abstract unity has been assembled from blind facts, and from these sociology imagines it has been able to perfect its mirage of a classless society. But in reality this unity means the demotion of human beings to objects, a demotion brought about by the system of domination and adopted by the classes themselves today. The sociologists' neutrality reiterates that social act of violence, and the blind facts that conceal this are the ruins to which the world has been reduced by an ordered system with which the sociologists get on famously.

The general laws are no argument against the lawless future because their universality is the logical form of the repression that must be abolished if mankind is not to relapse into the state of barbarism from which it has never emerged. That democracy is oligarchy is the fault not of human beings who, according to the opinion and the interest of their mature leaders, are not mature enough for democracy, but of the inhumanity that inscribes privilege in the objective necessities of history. The fact that the dialectic of class ends in a naked clique system spells the end of sociology, which always intended that very thing. Its formal invariant factors turn out to be predictions of the latest material trends. The theory that learns how to identify the different gangs within the classes today is a parody of the formal sociology that denies the existence of class in order to make those gangs permanent.

VII

The aspect of the Marxist theory of class that is most susceptible to an apologist critique seems to be the theory of pauperization. Shared poverty turns proletarians into a class. Their poverty follows from their place in the

production process of the capitalist economy and develops with that
process to the point where the poverty becomes unbearable. In this way
poverty becomes a force in the revolution that aims to stamp out poverty.
The proletariat has nothing to lose but its chains and has everything to
gain: the choice will not be difficult, and bourgeois democracy is progressive enough to give scope for the formation of class organizations that will
bring about the revolution by weight of numbers.

Against this argument all the statistics can be marshalled. The proletariat does have more to lose than its chains. Measured against conditions
in England a century ago as they were evident to the authors of the *Communist Manifesto*, their standard of living has not deteriorated but improved. Shorter working hours; better food, housing, and clothing; protection for family members and for the worker in his old age; an average
increase in life expectancy—all these things have come to the workers with
the development of the technical forces of production. There can be no
question of their being driven by hunger to join forces and make a revolution. This puts the possibility of organization and mass revolution in
doubt. The individual thrives better in an organization of special interests
than in one opposed to them; the concentration of technical and military
resources on the side of the employers is so formidable as to consign old-
style uprisings to the tolerated realm of heroic memory. Moreover, it is
quite improbable that bourgeois democracy, where its facade still exists,
would permit the emergence of a mass party that really contemplates the
revolution it talks about. Thus the traditional argument about pauperization collapses. To try and shore it up with a makeshift concept of "relative
pauperization," as was attempted at the time of the revisionist debate, could
occur only to social-democratic counterapologists whose ears have been so
deafened by their own shouts that they could not even hear the ridicule
that the term "relative pauperization" would bring down on their heads.

What is essential here is the concept of pauperization itself, not its
sophisticated modification. However, it is a strict concept from economics,
defined by the absolute law of accumulation. The industrial reserve army,
overpopulation, and pauperism grow in proportion to "functioning capital,"[c] and at the same time they depress wages. Pauperization is the flip side

---

[c] Karl Marx, *Capital*, ed. Friedrich Engels, vol. 1 (London: Lawrence &
Wishart, 1967), p. 644.

of the free play of economic forces in the liberal system, whose theory is reduced ad absurdum by the Marxist analysis: with the growth in social wealth there is also, under capitalist relations of production with their immanent systemic compulsions, a corresponding growth in social poverty. Presupposed here is the undisturbed, autonomous running of the mechanisms of the economy postulated by liberal theory, in other words, the coherence of the *tableau économique* to be analyzed in each case. All other modifying factors are consigned to the various "circumstances" "the analysis of which does not concern us here."[d] However, this shows that the pauperization thesis is itself dependent upon the dual nature of class, the distinction between direct and indirect repression that its concept contains. Pauperization does exist to the degree that the bourgeois class really is an anonymous and unconscious class, and that both it and the proletariat are dominated by the system.

As a purely economic necessity, the process of pauperization is absolute: if liberalism were the liberalism for which Marx takes it, there would be the same pauperism even in times of peace that is to be found today in the countries defeated in war. But the ruling class is not just governed by the system; it rules through the system and ultimately dominates it. The further modifying factors lie outside the system of political economy but are central to the history of domination. In the process of liquidating the economy, they are not modifying factors but the essence. To this extent they affect pauperization: pauperization must not become visible lest it blow the system apart. In its blindness the system is dynamic, and it accumulates poverty, but the self-preservation it brings about through its dynamism also peters out vis-à-vis poverty in a static condition that has always been the pedal point of the prehistorical dynamism. The less the acquisition of alien labor under monopoly conditions is carried out through the laws of the marketplace, the feebler, too, the reproduction of society as a whole. The pauperization theory implies the direct application of market categories in the shape of competition among the workers, leading to a fall in the price of the commodity of labor power, whereas in reality this competition with all it entails has become as questionable as competition between capitalists.

The dynamics of poverty are brought to a halt by the process of accumulation. The improvement or stabilization of the economic situation

[d] Ibid.

of the lower classes is extraeconomic: the higher standard of living is paid for out of income or monopoly profits, not out of variable capital. It is unemployment benefit, even if it is called by some other name, or indeed even if the semblance of work and wages is maintained: in the minds of the rulers, it is a gift, a handout. Goodwill and psychology have nothing to do with it. The rationale of such progress is the system's consciousness of the conditions that enable it to be perpetuated, not the unconscious mathematics of the processes concerned. Thus Marx's prognosis finds itself verified in an unsuspected way: the ruling class is so well fed by alien labor that it resolutely adopts as its own cause the idea that its fate is to feed the workers and to "secure for the slaves their existence within slavery" in order to consolidate its own. At the start, the pressure of the masses, the potential revolution, could bring about a change of course. Later, with the strengthening of the monopolistic centers, the position of the working classes was improved further by the prospect of benefits beyond their own firmly defined economic systems—rather than directly through colonial profits. The final consolidation of power is included in all elements of the calculation. The theater of a cryptogenic—as it were, censored—poverty, however, is that of political and social impotence. It turns all men into mere administrative objects of the monopolies and their states, on a par with those paupers of the liberal era who have been allowed to die out in our own age of high civilization. This impotence permits wars to be waged in all nations. Just as war confirms the *faux frais* [incidental expenses] of the power apparatus as profitable investments once the war is over, it also cashes in the credit of poverty that the dominant cliques cleverly managed to defer, although that same cleverness finds itself confronting an immovable barrier when it comes to poverty itself. Poverty can be eliminated only by the overthrow of the dominant cliques, and not by a process of manipulation, however disguised.

VIII

"If something falls, give it an extra push." Nietzsche's dictum expresses in the form of a maxim a principle that defines the actual practice of class society. It becomes a maxim only against the ideology of love in a world full of hate. Nietzsche belongs to the tradition of bourgeois thinkers since the Renaissance whose indignation with the untruth of society drives them cynically to play off its truth as an ideal against the ideal. Through this critical force of confrontation, they come to the aid of that other truth that they fiercely deride as the untruth into which it has been transformed by the magic of prehistory. However, the maxim says more than the thesis of *bellum omnium contra omnes* [the war of all against all], which stands at the gateway to the age of competition. The alliance of pushing and falling is a symbol of the ancient double character of class that is only becoming visible today. The objective tendency of the system is always duplicated, stamped, and legitimated by the conscious will of those who control it. For the blind system is the domination itself; this is why it always benefits the rulers, even when it seems to threaten them. The midwife services of the ruling classes testify to their knowledge of this and restore the meaning of the system whenever it is concealed by the objective character of the historical process, its alienated shape. There is a tradition of free bourgeois actions, from the Gunpowder Plot—and perhaps even the mutilation of the statues of Hermes in Athens [in BC 415]—down to the Reichstag fire, and of intrigues such as the bribing of the Hindenburgs and the meeting with Schroeder, the banker,[2] upon which the connoisseur of the objective tendency looks down with disdain. He evidently regards such episodes as mere coincidences that the world antispirit seizes upon in order to bring about its own triumph. However, such actions are perhaps not as coincidental as all that; they are acts of freedom testifying that the objective historical trend is a delusion unless it harmonizes with the subjective interests of those who use history to order history about.

Reason is a good deal more cunning even than Hegel believed. Its secret is less that of the passions than of freedom itself. In prehistory freedom is the power of the cliques over the anonymous catastrophes that go by the name of fate. The cliques are overwhelmed by the illusion of essence that they have themselves brought into play, and for that reason they only appear to be overwhelmed. History is progress in the consciousness of their own freedom passing right through historical objectivity, and this freedom is nothing but the flip side of the unfreedom of others. That is the true interaction between history and the gangs, the "inner identity . . . in which . . . necessity is raised to freedom."[e]

[e] G. W. F. Hegel, *The Science of Logic*, trans. A. V. Miller (London: Allen & Unwin, 1969), p. 570.

Idealism, which is rightly accused of transfiguring reality, is at the same time the most terrible truth about the world: even in its moments of positive assertion, its doctrine of freedom, it transparently contains the covering image of its opposite, and where it claims men have escaped, that is precisely the point in prehistory where they have succumbed to their fate. Not, indeed, in the Prussian state but in Hitler's charisma freedom comes into its own as the repetition of necessity. If the masses are reluctant to listen to any more talk of freedom, this is not simply their fault, nor a reflection of the way the word has been abused. They suspect that the world of coercion was in fact always the world of freedom, command, assertion, and that the free man is the man who is in a position to take liberties. Anything truly different has no name, and what stands in for it at present—solidarity, tenderness, consideration, reflection—has precious little to do with the freedom of the men who are free today.

IX

The social impotence of the proletariat is the product of conflicting tendencies. On the one hand, there is economic pauperization, on the other, the extraeconomic improvement of the standard of living. This impotence was not foreseen by the theory. The predominating insight into the first tendency goes hand in hand with the expectation that the pressure of poverty would lead directly to the power to resist the oppressor. However, the idea of impotence is not alien to the theory. It appears under the name of dehumanization. Just as industry calls for victims of physical mutilation, sickness, and deformation, it also threatens to deform consciousness. The theory explicitly mentions the brutalization of the workers who compulsively do to those who are dependent upon them what has been done to them, as well as their growing alienation from the mechanized labor process that they can no longer comprehend.

But the theory does not inquire how people so affected could become capable of action that calls not just for cleverness, an overview, and presence of mind, but also for extreme self-sacrifice. The danger of psychologism was averted at the outset—it is no coincidence that the author of *Psychology of Socialism* finally became a fascist, just like the sociologist of political parties[3]—long before bourgeois philosophy doggedly set out to defend its objective nature. Marx refused to be drawn into the psychology of the working class. Such a psychology presupposes individuality and a kind of autarchic view of motivation in the individual. Such individuality is itself a socially constructed concept, which comes under the rubric of political economy. Even among the competing members of the bourgeoisie, the individual is in great measure ideology, and those at the bottom of the heap are denied individuality by the property system. This can only be called dehumanization.

The dichotomy between bourgeoisie and proletariat negates the bourgeois conception of man as well as the concepts of the bourgeois economy. That conception is retained only so that its contradictory nature can be exposed; it is not there to be confirmed by a Marxist "anthropology." The disappearance of the autonomy of the market economy and the bourgeois individuality formed by it also spells the disappearance of its opposite, the blood-stained dehumanization of those rejected by society. The figure of the worker who comes home drunk at night and beats his wife and children is pushed right into the background: his wife has more to fear from the social worker who counsels her than from him.

Nor are we confronted by the stultification of the worker allegedly unable to comprehend the work process in which he is involved. The great intensification of the division of labor does indeed distance the worker further and further from the end product with which the craftsman was thoroughly conversant. But at the same time, the individual work processes are increasingly undifferentiated, so that the man who can perform one can perform virtually all and can understand the whole operation. The man on the production line at Ford who always has to perform the same action knows very well how the finished car works, since it contains no secrets that cannot be imagined on the model of that action. Even the distinction between the worker and the engineer, whose work is itself increasingly mechanized, is gradually turning into a question of privilege. The demand for technical specialists during the war showed how flexible the different technicians were and how the distinctions between specializations have been eroded.

However, none of this does any more to mitigate the impotence of the workers, initially at least, than, previously, stark poverty had turned into revolution. It is no easier for the alert mechanics of today to become individuals than it was for the dulled inmates of the workhouse a century ago, and of course it is unlikely that their individuality will accelerate the revolution. In the meantime, the work process that they understand shapes them even more thoroughly than the process they did not understand shaped them in times past; it becomes a "technological veil." The workers have their share of the dual character of class. The system may have called a halt to the process of dehumanization that jeopardizes the ruling classes until the latter take it over in the service of their own inhumanity. But in return, Marx's insight that the system produces the proletariat has been fulfilled on a scale that was absolutely unforeseeable.

By virtue of their needs and the omnipresent requirements of the system, men have truly become its products: under the monopoly system the process of dehumanization is perfected on the backs of the civilized as an all-encompassing reification, not as naked coercion; indeed, this dehumanization is what that civilization is. The totalizing character of society proves itself in the fact that it does not just take utter possession of its members but creates them in its own image. This is ultimately the point of that polarization into power and impotence. The monopolistic power confers the rewards on which the stability of the system depends today only upon those people who resemble it. This process of leveling, civilizing, and slotting-in consumes all the energy that might be used to do things differently, to the point where a conditioned universal humanity gives birth to the barbarism that in fact it is.

By reproducing the life of society in a planned way, the ruling classes reproduce the impotence of those that are planned. Thus domination becomes an integral part of human beings. They do not need to be "influenced," as liberals with their ideas of the market are wont to imagine. Mass culture simply makes them yet again what they already are thanks to the coercion of the system. It keeps a watchful eye on the anomalies, introduces the official complement of practice in the shape of "public morality," and provides people with models for imitation. The task of influencing people who beg to differ cannot be entrusted to films that stretch the credulity even of the like-minded: the vestiges of the ideologies that mediated between autonomy and domination disappear along with the vestiges of autonomy. Dehumanization is no external power, no propaganda, however conceived, no exclusion from culture. It is precisely the intrinsic reality of the oppressed in the system, who used formerly to stand out because of their wretchedness, whereas today their wretchedness lies in the fact that they can never escape, that they suspect that the truth is propaganda, while swallowing the propaganda culture that is fetishized and distorted into the madness of an unending reflection of themselves.

—This means, however, that the dehumanization is also its opposite. In reified human beings reification finds its outer limits. They catch up with the technical forces of production in which the relations of production lie hidden: in this way these relations lose the shock of their alien nature because the alienation is so complete. But they may soon also lose their power. Only when the victims completely assume the features of the ruling civilization will they be capable of wresting them from the dominant power. The only remaining differentiating factor is reduced to naked usurpation. Only in its blind anonymity could the economy appear as fate: its spell is broken by the horror of the seeing dictatorship. The mimicking of the classless society by class society has been so successful that, while the oppressed have all been co-opted, the futility of all oppression becomes manifest. The ancient myth proves to be quite feeble in its new omnipotence. Even if the dynamic at work was always the same, its end today is not the end.

(written 1942; first published 1972; GS 8: 373–91)
Translated by Rodney Livingstone

5

Late Capitalism or Industrial Society?

THE FUNDAMENTAL QUESTION
OF THE PRESENT STRUCTURE OF SOCIETY

I would like to say something about the alternatives: late capitalism or industrial society. Anyone unfamiliar with the present state of the controversy within the social sciences could be forgiven for suspecting that this was a dispute about nomenclature. Experts might be thought to be tormented by the vain anxiety that the present phase was one thing or the other and hence deserved to be called by one name rather than the other. In reality, however, there is a crucial matter of substance at issue. What is at stake is whether the capitalist system still predominates according to its model, however modified, or whether the development of industry has rendered the concept of capitalism obsolete, together with the distinction between capitalist and noncapitalist states and even the critique of capitalism.

In other words, the question is whether it is true that Marx is out of date. According to this claim, widespread among sociologists today, the world is so completely determined by the unprecedented growth in technology that the social relations that once characterized capitalism—namely, the transformation of living labor into a commodity, with the consequent conflict between classes—have now lost their relevance or can even be consigned to the realm of superstition. At the same time, we can note the unmistakable signs of convergence between the technically most advanced nations, the United States and the Soviet Union. In terms of living standards and consciousness, particularly in the most important Western nations, class differences are far less in evidence now than in the decades

during and following the Industrial Revolution. The predictions of class
theory, such as pauperization and the collapse of capitalism, have been insufficiently realized for their meaning not to be distorted beyond recognition. To speak of "relative pauperization" is ludicrous. Even if Marx's by no
means unambiguous law of the falling rate of profit had turned out to be
true, we would have to concede that capitalism has discovered resources
within itself that have postponed its collapse until the Greek Calends.
These resources include, at the top of the list, the immense growth in technical potential and with it the vast increase in consumer goods available to
all the members of the advanced industrialized nations. At the same time,
faced with this technical development, the relations of production have
proved to be more flexible than Marx had expected.

The criteria of class relations that empirical sociologists like to call
criteria of social stratification, that is to say, distinctions of income, living
standards, and education, are generalizations of findings about single individuals. In this sense we may call them subjective. In contrast, the old definition of class was meant to be objective, independent of indices derived
directly from the lives of their subjects, however much such indices may
express objective social realities. Marxist theory was based on the position
of employers and workers in the process of production, and ultimately referred to the ownership of the means of production. In the dominant
schools of sociology today, this premise is rejected as dogmatic. The dispute needs to be resolved theoretically, not simply through the presentation of facts, which may well contribute to the critique but may also, according to Critical Theory, obscure social structures. Even the opponents
of dialectics are no longer willing to postpone indefinitely the development
of a theory that takes account of the proper interests of sociology. The controversy is essentially one of *interpretation*—unless we are to banish the desire for a solution to the limbo of the nonscientific.

A dialectical theory of society is concerned with structural laws that
govern the facts, manifest themselves in them, and are modified by them.
By structural laws, it understands tendencies that follow, more or less
strictly, from the historical constituents of the overall system. The Marxist
models for this were the law of value, the law of accumulation, and the law
of the collapse [of capitalism]. By structure, dialectical theory does not
mean patterns in which, as far as possible, sociological findings can be entered completely, continuously, and free from contradiction. Thus it means
not systematic knowledge but rather the system of society that exists prior

to the procedures and data of scientific knowledge. Such a theory is the last to resist the facts and may certainly not twist them in order to satisfy some preconceived thesis. For in that case it would undoubtedly lapse into dogmatism and would repeat in the mind what the powers-that-be in Eastern Europe enacted in reality through the instrument of dialectical materialism. That is to say, it would immobilize things that according to their own logic can only be conceived to be in motion. Thus a fetishism of objective laws is created corresponding to the fetishism of facts. A dialectical theory overborne by the painful dominance of these laws does not glorify them but criticizes them, just as it criticizes the illusion that individual and concrete facts determine the course of the world. Under its spell the individual and concrete probably do not yet exist. The word "pluralism" lends support to the utopian belief that utopia already exists; it serves to mollify us. This explains why a dialectical theory that reflects on itself critically may not make itself at home in the medium of the universal. To break out of that medium is indeed its intention.

Nor is it immune to the false distinction between explicit theorizing and empirical research. Recently, a Russian intellectual with considerable influence explained to me that sociology was a new science in the Soviet Union. What he meant was empirical sociology. The idea that this could have anything to do with the theory of society that possesses the status of state religion in his country was as little apparent to him as the fact that Marx conducted empirical research. Reified consciousness does not end where the concept of reification has been given a place of honor. Bluster about concepts such as "imperialism" or "monopoly," regardless of their scope and of the realities corresponding to these words, is false and irrational. It is on a par with the attitude that takes seriously its own blindly nominalist idea of "the facts" and so rejects the notion that such concepts as "exchange society" have an objective reality and a universal coercive force that goes beyond the facts and that cannot always be translated into operationally defined realities. Both tendencies must be resisted. In this sense our subject, late capitalism or industrial society, testifies to our intention to practice self-criticism in the spirit of freedom.

A simple answer to the question raised by our subject can be neither expected nor sought. Alternatives that force us to decide for one or the other, even if only at the level of theory, are themselves predicaments modeled on dilemmas taken from an unfree society and transferred to minds whose task is to break the yoke of unfreedom by obstinately insisting on reflection. The dialectician, above all, should not let himself be forced into a clear-cut distinction between late capitalism and industrial society, any more than he should let himself be satisfied by a facile "on the one hand and on the other." *Pace* Brecht's advice, he must avoid simplification because the routine habit of thought will suggest to him a routine answer, just as it will suggest to his opponents the opposite answer. Anyone who does not blind himself to the priority that structure has over facts will not, unlike most of his opponents, be tempted to dismiss contradictions as errors in logic and attempt to eliminate them by ensuring the coherence of the scientific framework. Instead, he will pursue them back into the social structure, which has been antagonistic ever since society began, as has been all too crassly demonstrated by foreign-policy conflicts, the permanent threat of war, and, most recently, the Russian invasion of Czechoslovakia. This consciousness of the contradictions inherent in the structure of society is ignored by the opposite mode of thinking, which constantly projects the logical idea of contradiction-free statements onto whatever intellectual problems present themselves. The task is not to choose between these two approaches, either for scientific reasons or on grounds of taste. Instead, the task is to realize that the relation between these approaches expresses the contradiction that characterizes the present situation. To articulate this at the level of theory is the task of sociology.

Many of the prognoses of dialectical theory contradict one another. Some simply fail to come true. Certain analytical categories lead to impasses that can be eliminated only by highly artificial arguments. Other predictions, originally closely intertwined with them, have been spectacularly vindicated. Given the claims made by dialectics, even people who do not believe that prognoses are the point of theory will not be satisfied with the assertion that prognoses are partly true and partly false. These divergences call in turn for theoretical explanation. The fact that we cannot speak of a proletarian class consciousness in the most influential capitalist countries does not of itself refute the claim that classes exist, even though this claim runs counter to the prevailing wisdom. Class was defined by the relation of its members to the means of production, not by their consciousness.

Plausible explanations for the absence of class consciousness are scarcely lacking. We have, for example, the fact that the workers were not becoming pauperized but were increasingly being integrated into bourgeois society and its views, a development that was not to be foreseen during and immediately after the Industrial Revolution, when the industrial proletariat was recruited from the ranks of the paupers and still found themselves halfway outside society. It is not the case that social existence directly creates class consciousness. Because of their integration into society, the masses have no more control of their social destiny today than they possessed 120 years ago. In consequence, they not only have lost any sense of class solidarity but also fail to grasp fully that they are the objects and not the subjects of the social process that as subjects they nevertheless sustain. Class consciousness, on which, according to Marxian theory, the qualitative leap was supposed to depend, was also in its view an epiphenomenon. However, in the countries that are prototypical for class relations, such as North America, class consciousness did not exist for long periods of time, if indeed it ever existed at all. But if that is the case, and if the question of the proletariat just becomes a puzzle, then quantity changes into quality, and the suspicion that conceptual myths are being created can be suppressed only by decree; it cannot remain hidden from thought.

History finds it hard to part company with the centerpiece of Marxian theory, the doctrine of surplus value. This was supposed to provide an objective economic explanation of class relations and the growth of class antagonism. But if, thanks to technological progress and industrialization, the share of living labor from which alone surplus value is supposed to arise shrinks and even becomes marginal, at least in tendency, this cannot but affect that core doctrine, the theory of surplus value. The current absence of an objective theory of value is determined, not just by the school of economic thinking that almost alone enjoys academic respectability today, but also by the prohibitive difficulties in explaining the formation of classes objectively in the absence of a theory of surplus value.

Non-economists have observed that even so-called neo-Marxists use elements of subjective economics to plug the gaps in their treatment of the crucial problems. It is not just the weakening of the theoretical impulse that we have to blame for this. It is conceivable that contemporary society is evading the difficulties of formulating a coherent theory. Marx had it easier in this respect, since the developed system of liberal economics was available to him. He needed only to inquire whether capitalism fit into this system in order to produce a quasi-systematic theory of his own, in determinate negation of the system he found before him.

In the meantime, the market economy has become so full of holes as to rule out any such confrontation. The irrational nature of contemporary society inhibits a rational account of it in the realm of theory. The possibility that the steering of economic processes might be transferred to the political powers does indeed follow from the dynamics of the deductive system, but also tends toward an objective irrationality. It is this, and not the sterile dogmatism of its supporters, that can help explain why we have had no convincing objective theory of society for so long. On this interpretation, this failure is the expression, not of the critical progress of the scientific spirit, but of an enforced resignation. The failure to produce a theory of society runs parallel to the regression of society itself.

Such a theory would find many weighty facts in its path. *Without* making use of capitalism as a key concept, they could only be interpreted at the cost of violent and arbitrary distortions. Human beings continue to be subject to domination by the economic process. Its objects have long since ceased to be just the masses; they now include those in charge and their agents. The latter, in accordance with the older theory, have largely been reduced to functions of their own apparatus of production. The much-discussed question of the managerial revolution, following the alleged transfer of power from the legal owners to a managerial bureaucracy, is of secondary importance. The former process continues to produce and reproduce itself as it always did. Even if the classes no longer resemble those depicted in Zola's *Germinal*, a structure is created that the anti-socialist Nietzsche anticipated with the formula "a flock, but no shepherd." However, the formula conceals something he did not want to see, namely, the ancient social oppression. Only now that oppression has become anonymous. If the old pauperization theory has turned out not to be literally true, it has done so in the no less alarming sense that unfreedom, dependency upon an apparatus that has escaped the control of those who use it, has spread out universally over mankind.

The widely lamented immaturity of the masses simply reflects the fact that they are now no more the autonomous masters of their lives than they ever were. As in myth, their lives befall them, like fate. Empirical studies indicate, moreover, that even subjectively, in terms of their consciousness of reality, class distinctions have by no means been abolished to the degree that has sometimes been supposed. Even the theories of imperialism have not been rendered obsolete by the great powers' withdrawal from their colonies. The process they described survives today in the con-

flicts between the two monstrous power blocs. The allegedly obsolete doctrine of social antagonisms that were supposed to lead to ultimate collapse
has been superseded by manifest political conflicts in our own day.
Whether and to what extent class relations were displaced onto the relations between the leading industrial states, on the one hand, and the vigorously courted underdeveloped nations, on the other, is not a question I
can go into here.

In terms of critical, dialectical theory, I would like to propose as an
initial, necessarily abstract answer that contemporary society undoubtedly
is an industrial society according to the state of its *forces* of production. Industrial labor has everywhere become the model of society as such, regardless of the frontiers separating differing political systems. It has developed
into a totality because methods modeled on those of industry are necessarily extended by the laws of economics to other realms of material production, administration, the sphere of distribution, and those that call themselves culture. In contrast, however, society is capitalist in its *relations* of
production. People are still what they were in Marx's analysis in the middle of the nineteenth century: appendages of the machine, not just literally
workers who have to adapt themselves to the nature of the machines they
use, but far beyond that, figuratively, workers who are compelled right
down to their most intimate impulses to subordinate themselves to the
mechanisms of society and to adopt specific social roles without reservation. Production takes place today, as then, for the sake of profit. And far
exceeding what was foreseeable in Marx's day, human needs that were potentially functions of the production apparatus have now become such
functions in fact, rather than the production apparatus becoming a function of human needs. People are now totally controlled. Admittedly, even
though they are fixed and adapted to the interests of the apparatus, human
needs are still present, dragged along, as it were, and the apparatus can,
therefore, make an effective appeal to them. But the use-value side of
commodities has now lost all its remaining spontaneous "naturalness." Not
only are needs satisfied indirectly, via their exchange value, but in the economically relevant sectors they are generated by the profit motive, even at
the expense of the objective needs of consumers, such as adequate homes,
to say nothing of education and information about the most important
matters affecting their lives. In the realm of goods that go beyond the bare
necessities of life, the tendency is for exchange values to become detached,
consumed—a phenomenon that appears in empirical sociology couched in

such terms as "prestige" and "status symbols," although these do not capture their objective essence.

In the advanced industrial societies, as long as no natural economic catastrophes occur in defiance of Keynes, people have learned to prevent an all-too-visible poverty, if not to the degree imagined in the thesis of the affluent society. However, the spell cast over mankind by the system has been strengthened by the process of integration, insofar as such comparisons have meaning. It is undeniable that with the increasing satisfaction of material needs, despite their deformation by the apparatus, a life without deprivation has become incomparably more attainable. Even in the poorest countries no one need go hungry any longer. At the same time, the fact that the veil concealing the consciousness of what is possible has become more transparent is demonstrated by the panic created everywhere by forms of social enlightenment that are not catered to in official systems of communication. What Marx and Engels, who desired a human organization of society, denounced as utopia, claiming that it merely sabotaged such an organization, became a tangible possibility. Today, criticism of utopias has degenerated into the stock inventory of ideology, while the triumph of technical productivity deludes us into believing that utopia, which is irreconcilable with the relations of production, has nevertheless been made real. But the contradictions in their new, international form—I am thinking of the arms race in East and West—make the possible impossible.

To see through all this requires, of course, that even though criticism always invites us to do so, we should not blame technology, that is to say, the forces of production, or succumb to a kind of theoretical Luddism on an expanded scale. It is not technology that is the catastrophe but its imbrication with the social relations that embrace it. We should merely remind ourselves that it is the concern for profit and domination that has canalized technological development: on occasion it coincides in a disastrous way with the need to exercise control. Not for nothing has the invention of weapons of destruction become the new prototype of technology. And, by contrast, those technologies that turn their backs on domination, centralism, and violence against nature, and that would doubtless help to heal much of what is damaged literally and figuratively by the technology we have, are allowed to wither away.

For all its protestations to the contrary, for all its dynamism and its growth in production, contemporary society displays certain static tendencies. These belong to the relations of production. Those have ceased to be just property relations; they now also include relations ranging from those of the administration on up to those of the state, which functions now as an all-inclusive capitalist organization. In that their rationalization resembles technical rationality, the rationality of the forces of production, they have undoubtedly become more flexible. This creates the impression that the universal interest is to preserve the status quo and that the only ideal is full employment, not liberation from heteronomous labor. But this situation, which in foreign-policy terms is in any case highly unstable, is only temporarily in equilibrium, the product of forces whose tension threatens to tear it apart. Within the dominant relations of production, mankind is virtually its own reserve army and is supported as such. Marx's expectation that historically the primacy of the forces of production was assured, and that this would necessarily burst asunder the relations of production, proved all too optimistic. In this respect Marx, the sworn enemy of German idealism, remained true to its affirmative view of history. Trust in the world spirit helped to buttress later versions of the world order that was supposed to be overthrown, according to the Eleventh Thesis on Feuerbach.[1] The sheer instinct for survival enabled the relations of production to remain in control of the liberated forces of production through a series of ad hoc devices and stratagems. The signature of the age is the predominance of the relations of production over the forces of production, even though in the eyes of the latter the relations of production were no more than a laughingstock. The fact that the extended arm of mankind can reach distant, empty planets but is incapable of establishing a permanent peace on earth makes visible the absurd goal toward which the social dialectic is moving.

This persistent predominance of the relations of production was not what Marx had hoped for. It was caused not least by the fact that society was able to absorb into itself what Veblen termed the "underlying population." Only a man who puts the happiness of the whole abstractly before that of living individuals might regret such absorption. For its part, this development depended on that of the forces of production. It was not identical, however, with their priority over the relations of production. The absorption of the underlying population should never be thought of in mechanistic terms. To achieve the predominance of the forces of production would have called for the spontaneous action of those people who were interested in changing social relations, and by now their numbers have surpassed many times those of the industrial proletariat. However, objective interest and subjective spontaneity go in completely different directions. Spontaneity dried up under the disproportionate weight of the given. Marx's dictum that theory becomes a real force when it grips the masses was flagrantly overturned by the course of events. If the organization of society, whether by accident or design, uses the culture industry, the consciousness industry, and the monopolistic control of opinion to bar the way to the most basic knowledge and experience of the most dangerous processes and the most essential critical ideas, and if, going far beyond that, society paralyzes people's ability to imagine the world in concrete terms as being anything other than it appears to be, then the fixed and manipulated state of mind becomes a real force, too. But it becomes the force of repression, which is just as potent in its own way as had been, once upon a time, its opposite, namely, free spirit, which wished to do away with repression once and for all.

Conversely, in a certain sense the term "industrial society" seems to suggest that the technocratic element in Marx, whom some people would like to argue out of existence, had an immediate validity, as if the nature of society followed directly from the state of the forces of production, independently of the social conditions governing them. It is astonishing how little is said about these conditions in established sociological circles, and how little they are analyzed. The best aspect of this argument—which by no means needs be the best—is simply forgotten. This is the emphasis on totality, to use Hegel's term, the ether that permeates the whole of society. However, this ether is anything but ethereal; it is, rather, the *ens realissimum*. If it seems abstract, that is the fault not of fantastic, willful thinking, hostile to the facts, but of the exchange relation, the objective abstraction to which the social process of life is subject. The power of this abstraction over human beings is more palpable than the power of any other single institution that has been tacitly constructed on the basis of this principle, which is thus drummed into people. The impotence of the individual in the face of the totality is the drastic expression of the power of the exchange relation. In sociology, of course, with its traditional tendency to classify phenomena, the sustaining social relations, the social conditions of production, appear far less powerful than that concrete universal. They are neutralized into concepts like power or social control. The use of such categories helps to conceal the sting and with it, one would like to say, what is truly social about society, namely, its structure.

However, simply to regard the forces of production and the relations of production as polar opposites would be unworthy of a dialectical theory. They are interlocking phenomena: the one contains the other within it. It is this that seduces us into focusing simply on the forces of production, even though it is the relations of production that have the upper hand. The forces of production are mediated more than ever by the relations of production, so completely, perhaps, that the latter appear to be the essence; they have become second nature. They are responsible for the fact that, in crazy contradiction to what is possible, human beings in large parts of the planet live in penury. Even where goods abound, they seem to be under a curse. Needs, which tend to have the quality of illusion about them, infect goods with this illusion. It would be possible to distinguish real needs and false ones, without conceding the right of some bureaucracy somewhere in the world to regulate them. For good or ill, the whole of society is to be found in these needs; they may well be the first port of call for market surveys, but they are not the top priority in the administered world. What would be required to distinguish between true needs and false ones is an insight into the structure of society as a whole, together with all its mediations. The fictitious element that deforms the gratification of all needs today is perceived unconsciously, but not questioned; it doubtless contributes to the present discontents of culture.

Even more important, however, than the almost impenetrable process of exchange between needs, gratification, and the interest in profit or power is the constant threat to the single need upon which all others depend, namely, sheer survival. Enclosed within a horizon in which a bomb can fall at any moment, even the most sumptuous provision of consumer goods seems like a mockery. But the international conflicts that are being intensified to the point of a truly total war have a clear connection with the relations of production in the most literal sense. The threat of one catastrophe is deferred by that of others. The relations of production would find it hard to maintain their position so persistently without the apocalyptic cataclysms of renewed economic crises. For in this way a disproportionate amount of the social product, which otherwise would be unable to find a market, is diverted for the production of weapons of destruction. The same process can be seen in the Soviet Union, notwithstanding the elimination of the market economy. The economic reasons for this are clear: the desire for rapid growth in production in a backward economy produced a rigid dictatorial administration. The unleashing of the forces of production led to a renewal of restrictive relations of production: production for its own sake became the goal and prevented the attainment of the true goal of an unconfined freedom. Under both systems there is a truly diabolical parody of the bourgeois concept of socially useful labor, which proved itself in the marketplace by its ability to produce a profit, never by its transparent usefulness for human beings or for their happiness. However, for the relations of production to dominate mankind in this way assumes that the forces of production have achieved a certain level.

While the two things need to be distinguished, anyone who wishes to comprehend the jinxed nature of the situation must always understand the one in order to grasp the other. Overproduction, which ensnares and replaces seemingly subjective needs, gushes from a technical apparatus that has made itself so autonomous that below a certain level of production, it becomes irrational, in other words, unprofitable. Overproduction is, therefore, necessarily precipitated by relations of production. In only one respect have the relations of production failed to shackle the forces of production: that of total annihilation. But the dirigiste methods for controlling the masses presuppose a concentration and centralization that have a technological dimension as well as an economic one, something that would have to be shown from a study of the mass media. For this would demonstrate how, from a few points, the consciousness of countless people can be brought into line simply by the selection and presentation of news and commentary.

The relations of production have not been revolutionized, and their power is greater than ever. However, at the same time, since they are objectively anachronistic, they are debilitated, damaged, and undermined. They no longer function autonomously. Economic intervention is not, as the older liberal school believed, an alien element grafted on from outside, but an intrinsic part of the system, the epitome of self-defense. Nothing could provide a more telling illustration of the concept of dialectic. One finds an analogy here with Hegel's *Philosophy of Right*, in which bourgeois ideology and the dialectic of bourgeois society are so deeply intertwined. Hegel summoned the state to assist the intrinsic dialectic of society, which he believed would otherwise collapse. He issued this summons even though the state was supposed to stand outside the conflicts of society and mitigate these social antagonisms with the aid of the police. Invasion by forces extrinsic to the system is likewise an instance of immanent dialectics for Hegel. Similarly, at the opposite pole, Marx conceived of the overthrow of the relations of production both as imposed by the course of history and at the same time as caused only by an action qualitatively different from the coherent system of society.

But if it is argued that late capitalism has been rescued from the anarchy of commodity production by intervention and, beyond that, by large-scale planning, and has therefore ceased to be true capitalism, we may reply that the social fate that befalls the individual is as arbitrary as it ever was. The fact is that the model according to which capitalism operated was never as pure as liberal apologias supposed. As early as Marx, the model took the form of ideological critique; that is to say, it was supposed to show how little the conception that bourgeois society had of itself corresponded to the reality. Ironically, this critical dimension—the fact that even in its heyday liberalism was no such thing—can today be translated into the assertion that capitalism is no such thing any more. This, too, points to a transformation. Those aspects of bourgeois society that had always been irrational, that is, unfree and unfair—by contrast to the rationality of free and fair exchange—have now been intensified to the point where the entire system is breaking down. But this very fact is now viewed as positive from the standpoint of a system whose integrated nature is really a cover for inner disintegration. What is alien to the system stands revealed as one of its constituents and is to be found at the very heart of its politics. With the trend toward intervention, the system's resilience has been confirmed, but so, indirectly, has the theory of its collapse. The transition to a form of domination independent of the mechanisms of the market is the system's goal. The slogan "unified [*formiert*] society" incautiously blurted this out.[2] Such a regression on the part of liberal capitalism had its correlative in the regression of consciousness, of human beings, to a more backward form of society than is on offer today. People lose the qualities that they can no longer use and that only hamper them; the core of their individuality has begun to decay.

Only in more recent times have traces of a countervailing trend become visible among various sections of the younger generation: resistance to blind conformism, the freedom to choose rational goals, revulsion from the world's deceptions and illusions, the recollection of the possibility of change. Whether, by contrast, the socially increasing impulse to destroy will triumph after all remains to be seen. Subjective regression favors the regression of the system. Because it has become dysfunctional (to apply a concept that Merton used rather differently), the consciousness of the masses has become identical with the system as it has grown increasingly alienated from the rationality of the fixed, identical self, which had still been implicit in the concept of the functional society.

The idea that the forces and relations of production are one and the same today, and that the notion of society can be easily constructed solely by reference to the forces of production, is the current shape of socially necessary illusion. It is socially necessary because elements of the social process that were formerly separate—and this includes living human be-ings—have been brought down to a kind of common denominator. Material production, distribution, and consumption are administered jointly. Their boundaries flow into one another, even though earlier within the overall social process they were at once different from one another and re-lated, and for that reason they respected what was qualitatively different. Everything is now one. The totality of the processes of mediation, which amounts in reality to the principle of exchange, has produced a second, deceptive immediacy. This enables people to ignore the evidence of their own eyes and forget difference and conflict or repress it from consciousness. But this consciousness of society is illusion, because while it does justice to the process of technological and organizational standardization, it overlooks the fact that this standardization is not fully rational but remains subject to blind, irrational laws. No overall social subject exists. We could formulate this illusion by saying that all social phenomena today are so completely mediated that even the element of mediation is distorted by its totalizing nature. It is no longer possible to adopt a vantage point outside the hurly-burly that would enable us to give the horror a name; we are forced to adopt its inconsistencies as our starting point.

This is what Horkheimer and I meant when we spoke, some decades ago, of the technological veil. The false identity between the organization of the world and its inhabitants, an identity created by the expansion of technology, amounts to the affirmation of the relations of production, for whose beneficiaries we seek today almost as vainly as for the proletarians, who have become all but invisible. The system has become independent, even of those who are in control, but this process has now reached its limits. It has now become fate and finds its expression in what Freud called ubiquitous, free-flowing anxiety; free-flowing because it is no longer able to attach itself to living beings, whether to individuals or classes. But ultimately, what has been liberated are the relations between human beings that had been buried beneath the relations of production. Hence the overpowering order of things remains its own ideology and is thus virtually impotent. Impenetrable though its spell is, it is only a spell. If sociology is going to do anything more than provide agents and interests with the information they want, if it is going to achieve anything of what was envisaged at its birth, it must face up to the task of employing methods that have not succumbed to universal fetishism, and thus make its contribution, however modest, to breaking this spell.

hope

(1969; GS 8: 354–70)
Translated by Rodney Livingstone

6

Progress

FOR JOSEF KÖNIG

For a theoretical account of the category of progress, it is necessary to scrutinize the category so closely that it loses its semblance of obviousness, in both its positive and its negative usages. And yet such proximity also makes the account more difficult. Even more than other concepts, the concept of progress dissolves upon attempts to specify its exact meaning, for instance, what progresses and what does not. Whoever wants to define the concept precisely easily destroys what he is aiming at. The subaltern prudence that refuses to speak of progress before it can distinguish progress in what, of what, and in relation to what displaces the unity of the moments, which within the concept reciprocally elaborate each other, into a mere juxtaposition. By insisting on exactitude where the impossibility of the unambiguous appertains to the subject matter itself, dogmatic epistemology misses its object, sabotages insight, and helps to perpetuate the bad by zealously forbidding reflection upon what, in the age of both utopian and absolutely destructive possibilities, the consciousness of those entangled would like to discover: whether there is progress. Like every philosophical term, "progress" has its equivocations; and as in any such term, these equivocations also register a commonality. What at this time should be understood by the term "progress" one knows vaguely, but precisely: for just this reason one cannot employ the concept roughly enough. To use the term pedantically merely cheats it out of what it promises: an answer to the doubt and the hope that things will finally get better, that people will at last be able to breathe a sigh of relief. For this reason alone one cannot say precisely what progress should mean to people, because the crisis of the situation is precisely that while everyone feels the crisis, the words bringing resolution are missing. Only those reflections about progress have truth that immerse themselves in progress and yet maintain distance, withdrawing from paralyzing facts and specialized meanings. Today reflections of this kind come to a point in the contemplation of whether humanity[1] is capable of preventing catastrophe. The forms of humanity's own global societal constitution threaten its life, if a self-conscious global subject does not develop and intervene. The possibility of progress, of averting the most extreme, total disaster, has migrated to this global subject alone. Everything else involving progress must crystallize around it. Material needs, which long seemed to mock progress, have been potentially eliminated; thanks to the present state of the technical forces of production no one on the planet need suffer deprivation anymore. Whether there will be further want and oppression—which are the same thing—will be decided solely by the avoidance of catastrophe through the rational establishment of the whole society as humanity. Kant's sketch of a doctrine of progress, indeed, was anchored to the "idea of the human being":[a] "The highest purpose of nature—i.e. the development of all natural capacities—can be fulfilled for mankind only in society, and nature intends that man should accomplish this, and indeed all his appointed ends, by his own efforts. This purpose can be fulfilled only in a society which has not only the greatest freedom, and therefore a continual antagonism among its members, but also the most precise specification and preservation of the limits of this freedom in order that it can co-exist with the freedom of others. The highest task which nature has set for mankind must therefore be that of establishing a society in which *freedom under external laws* would be combined to the greatest possible extent with irresistible force, in other words of establishing a perfectly *just civil constitution*. For only through the solution and fulfillment of this task can nature accomplish its other intentions with our species."[b] The concept of history, in which progress would have its place,

---

[a] Immanuel Kant, "Idea for a Universal History with a Cosmopolitan Purpose," trans. H. B. Nisbet, in *Political Writings*, ed. Hans Reiss, 2d ed. (Cambridge: Cambridge University Press, 1991), p. 43, "Second Proposition" (translated as "an idea in [man's] mind").

is emphatic, the Kantian universal or cosmopolitan concept, not one of any particular sphere of life. But the dependence of progress on the totality comes back to bite progress. An awareness of this problem animates Benjamin's polemic against the coupling of progress and humanity in "Theses on the Concept of History," perhaps the most weighty critique of the idea of progress held by those who are reckoned in a crudely political fashion as progressives: "Progress as pictured in the minds of Social Democrats was, first of all, the progress of humanity itself (and not just advances in people's skills and knowledge)."[c] As little as humanity *tel quel* progresses by the advertising slogan of the ever new and improved, so little can there be an idea of progress without the idea of humanity; the sense of the Benjamin passage should then also be more a reproach that the Social Democrats confused progress of skills and knowledge with that of humanity, rather than that he wanted to eradicate progress from philosophical reflection. In Benjamin progress obtains legitimation in the doctrine that the idea of the happiness of unborn generations—without which one cannot speak of progress—inalienably includes the idea of redemption.[d] This confirms the concentration of progress on the survival of the species: no progress is to be assumed that would imply that humanity in general already existed and therefore could progress. Rather, progress would be the very establishment of humanity in the first place, whose prospect opens up in the face of its extinction. This entails, as Benjamin further teaches, that the concept of universal history cannot be saved; it is plausible only as long as one can believe in the illusion of an already existing humanity, coherent in itself and moving upward as a unity. If humanity remains entrapped by the totality it itself fashions, then, as Kafka said, no progress has taken place at all,[2] while mere totality nevertheless allows progress to be entertained in thought. This can be elucidated most simply by the definition of humanity as that which excludes absolutely nothing. If humanity were a totality that no longer held within it any limiting principle, then it would also be free of the coercion that subjects all its members to such a principle and thereby would no longer be a totality: no forced unity. The passage

[b] Ibid., pp. 45–46.

[c] Walter Benjamin, "Theses on the Philosophy of History," in *Illuminations: Essays and Reflections*, ed. Hannah Arendt, trans. Harry Zohn (New York: Schocken, 1968), p. 260, thesis 13; trans. modified.

[d] See ibid., pp. 253–54, thesis 2.

from Schiller's "Ode to Joy," "And who never could, let him steal away / weeping from this league,"[3] which in the name of all-encompassing love banishes whoever has not been granted it, unintentionally admits the truth about the bourgeois, at once totalitarian and particular, concept of humanity. In the verse, what the one who is unloved or incapable of love undergoes in the name of the idea of humanity unmasks this idea, no differently from the affirmative violence with which Beethoven's music hammers it home; it is hardly a coincidence that the poem with the word "steal" in the humiliation of the one who is joyless, and to whom therefore joy is once again denied, evokes associations from the spheres of property and criminology. Perpetual antagonism is integral to the concept of totality, as in the politically totalitarian systems; thus the evil mythical festivals in fairy tales are defined by those who are not invited. Only with the decomposition of the principle of totality that establishes limits, even if that principle were merely the commandment to resemble totality, would there be humanity and not its deceptive image.

Historically the conception of humanity was already implicit in the middle Stoa's theorem of the universal state, which objectively at least amounted to progress, no matter how strange its idea otherwise might have been to pre-Christian antiquity. The fact that this Stoic theorem immediately reconciled itself with the founding of Rome's imperial claims betrays something of what the concept of progress underwent through its identification with increasing "skills and knowledge." Existing humanity is substituted for the unborn generations, and history immediately becomes salvation history. That was the prototype for the idea of progress until Hegel and Marx. In the Augustinian *civitas dei* this idea is connected to redemption by Christ, as historically successful redemption; only an already redeemed humanity can be seen as though, after it had been chosen and by dint of the grace it had been vouchsafed, it were moving in the continuum of time toward the heavenly kingdom. Perhaps it was the unfortunate fate of later thinking about progress that it inherited from Augustine the immanent teleology and the conception of humanity as the subject of all progress, while Christian soteriology faded into speculations about the philosophy of history. In this way the idea of progress was taken up into the *civitas terrena*, its Augustinian counterpart. Even in the dualistic Kant, the *civitas terrena* should progress according to its own principle, its "nature." Within such enlightenment, however, which first of all puts progress toward humanity in people's own hands and thereby concretizes the idea of progress as one to be realized, lurks the conformist confirmation of what merely exists. It receives the aura of redemption after redemption has failed to appear and evil has persisted undiminished. This incalculably far-ranging modification of the concept of progress could not have been avoided. Just as the emphatic claim of successful redemption became a protest in th face of post-Christian history, so, inversely, in the Augustinian theologoumenon of an immanent movement of the species toward the blessed state there already lay the motive of irresistible secularization. The temporality of progress itself, its simple concept, links it to the empirical world; yet without such a temporality the heinous aspects of the way of the world would first truly be immortalized in thought, the Creation itself would become the work of a Gnostic demon. In Augustine one can recognize the inner constellation of the ideas of progress, redemption, and the immanent course of history, which should not dissolve into one another, lest they reciprocally destroy each other. If progress is equated with redemption as transcendental intervention per se, then it forfeits, along with the temporal dimension, its intelligible meaning and evaporates into a historical theology. But if progress is mediatized into history, then the idolization of history threatens and with it, in the reflection of the concept as in the reality, the absurdity that it is progress itself that inhibits progress. Expedient expositions of an immanent-transcendent concept of progress pass sentence on themselves by their very nomenclature.

The greatness of the Augustinian doctrine was its for-the-first-time. It contains all the abysses of the idea of progress and strives to master them theoretically. The structure of his doctrine unabatedly expresses the antinomian character of progress. Already in Augustine, as then again at the height of secular philosophy of history since Kant, there is an antagonism at the center of this historical movement that would be progress since it is directed toward the kingdom of heaven; the movement is the struggle between the earthly and the heavenly. All thought about progress since then has received its draft from the weight of the historically mounting disaster. While redemption in Augustine forms the *telos* of history, the history neither leads directly to redemption, nor is redemption completely unmediated by history. Redemption is embedded in history by the divine world plan but is opposed to it after the Fall. Augustine realized that redemption and history can exist neither without each other nor within each other but only in tension, the accumulated energy of which finally desires nothing less than the sublation of the historical world itself. For the sake of nothing less than this, however, can the idea of progress still be thought in the age of catastrophe. Progress should be no more ontologized, unreflectedly ascribed to Being, than should decline, though indeed the latter seems to be the preference of recent philosophy. Too little of what is good has power in the world for progress to be expressed in a predicative judgment about the world, but there can be no good, not a trace of it, without progress. If, according to a mystical doctrine, all innerworldly events down to the most insignificant happenstance are of momentous consequence for the life of the absolute itself, then certainly something similar is true for progress. Every individual trait in the nexus of deception is nonetheless relevant to its possible end. Good is what wrenches itself free, finds a language, opens its eyes. In its condition of wresting free, it is interwoven in history that, without being organized unequivocally toward reconciliation, in the course of its movement allows the possibility of redemption to flash up.

According to conventional thought, the moments in which the concept of progress has its life are partly philosophical and partly societal. Without society the notion of progress would be completely empty; all its elements are abstracted from society. If society had not passed from a hunting and gathering horde to agriculture, from slavery to the formal freedom of subjects, from the fear of demons to reason, from deprivation to provisions against epidemics and famine and to the overall improvement of living conditions, if one thus sought *more philosophico* to keep the idea of progress pure, say, to spin it out of the essence of time, then it would not have any content at all. But once the meaning of a concept necessitates moving to facticity, this movement cannot be stopped arbitrarily. The idea of reconciliation itself—the transcendent *telos* of all progress, measured by finite criteria—cannot be broken loose from the immanent process of enlightenment that removes fear and, by erecting the human being as an answer to human beings' questions, wins the concept of humanitarianism that alone rises above the immanence of the world. Nonetheless, progress is not tantamount to society, is not identical with it; indeed, like society, progress is at times its own opposite. Philosophy in general, as long as it was at all useful, was also a doctrine of society, except that ever since it consigned itself without demur to societal power, philosophy has professedly had to isolate itself from society; the purity into which philosophy regressed is the bad conscience of its impurity, its complicity with the world. The concept of progress is philosophical in that it articulates the movement of society while[3] contradicting it. Having arisen societally, the concept of progress requires critical confrontation with real society. The aspect of redemption, no matter how secularized, cannot be removed from the concept of progress. The fact that it can be reduced neither to facticity nor to the idea indicates its own contradiction. For the element of enlightenment within it, which terminates in the reconciliation with nature by soothing nature's terror, is kindred to the aspect of the domination of nature.[4] The model of progress, even if displaced onto the godhead, is the control of external and internal, or human, nature. The oppression exercised by such control, which has its highest form of intellectual reflection in the identity principle of reason, reproduces this antagonism. The more identity is posited by imperious spirit, the more injustice is done to the nonidentical. The injustice is passed on through the resistance of the nonidentical. The resistance in turn reinforces the oppressing principle, while what is oppressed, poisoned, limps along further. Everything within the whole progresses: only the whole itself to this day does not progress. Goethe's "And all pressing, all struggling / Is eternal calm in God the Master"[5] codifies this experience, and the Hegelian doctrine of the process of world spirit, the absolute dynamic, as a returning into itself or even its game with itself comes very close to the Goethean aphorism. Only one nota bene could be added to the sum of its intuition: that this whole stands still in its movement, that it knows nothing beyond itself, for it is not the divine absolute, but rather its opposite rendered unfamiliar by thought. Kant neither bowed to this deception nor absolutized the rupture. When, in the most sublime passage of his philosophy of history, he teaches that the antagonism, the entanglement of progress in myth, in nature's hold upon the domination of nature, in short, in the realm of unfreedom, tends by means of its own law toward the realm of freedom—Hegel's "cunning of reason" later came out of this[6]—then this says nothing less than that the conditions for the possibility of reconciliation are its contradiction and that the conditions for the possibility of freedom are unfreedom.[7] Kant's doctrine stands at a watershed. It conceptualizes the idea of this reconciliation as immanent in the antagonistic "development" by deriving it from a design nature harbors for human beings. By contrast, the dogmatic-rationalistic rigidity with which such a design is presumed in nature—as though nature itself were not included in the development and its own concept thereby altered—is the impress of the violence the identity-positing spirit inflicts upon nature. The static quality of the concept of nature is a function of the dynamic concept of reason; the more this concept usurps from the realm of the nonidentical, the more nature becomes a residual *caput mortuum*, and precisely this makes it easier to equip nature with the qualities of eternity that sanctify its ends. The idea of "design" cannot be conceived at all except with the provision that reason is attributed to nature itself. Still, following metaphysical custom, which Kant in this passage uses when speaking of the concept of nature, bringing it close to the transcendent thing-in-itself, nature remains as much a product of spirit as it is in the *Critique of Pure Reason*. If spirit conquered nature, by making itself at every stage equal to nature according to Bacon's program, then at the Kantian stage spirit has projected itself back onto nature, insofar as nature is absolute and not merely constituted, for the sake of a possibility of reconciliation in which, however, the primacy of the subject is not in the least diminished. In the passage where Kant comes closest to the concept of reconciliation, in the thought that the antagonism terminates in its abolition, appears the catchword of a society in which freedom is "bound up with irresistible power."[8] Yet even the talk of power recalls the dialectic of progress itself. While the perpetual oppression that unleashed progress at the same time always arrested it, this oppression—as the emancipation of consciousness—first made the antagonism and the whole extent of the deception recognizable at all, the prerequisite for settling the antagonism. The progress that the eternal invariant brought forth is that finally progress can begin, at any moment. Should the image of progressing humanity remind one of a giant who, after sleeping from time immemorial, slowly stirs himself awake and then storms forth and tramples everything that gets in his way, nonetheless, his unwieldy awakening is the sole potential for attaining political maturity—that nature's tenacity, into which even progress integrates itself, will not have the final word. For aeons the question of progress made no sense. The question arose only after the dynamic became free, from which the idea of freedom could then be extrapolated. If progress—since Augustine the translation of the natural course of life between birth and death of the individual onto the species as a whole—may be as mythical as the notion of the course the command of fate prescribes to the constellations, then the idea of progress is just as much inherently antimythological, exploding the circulation to which it belongs. Progress means: to step out of the magic spell, even out of the spell of progress, which is itself nature, in that humanity becomes aware of its own inbred nature and brings to a halt the domination it exacts upon nature and through which domination by nature continues. In this way it could be said that progress occurs where it ends.

This imago of progress is encoded in a concept that all camps today unanimously defame, that of decadence. The artists of *Jugendstil* declared their adherence to it. Certainly the reason for this is not only that they wished to express their own historical situation, which in many ways seemed to them biological morbidity. Their urgency to immortalize their condition in an image was animated by the impulse—and in this they agreed profoundly with the *Lebensphilosophen*—that truth was preserved only in that part of them that appeared to prophesy their own and the world's downfall. Hardly anyone could have expressed this more concisely than Peter Altenberg: "Mistreatment of horses. It will stop only when passersby become so irritable and decadent that they, no longer in control of themselves, mad and desperate in such cases, commit crimes and shoot down the cringing and cowardly coachman. . . . Inability to tolerate the mistreatment of horses is the deed of the decadent neurasthenic man of the future! Until now people have had only enough wretched strength not to have to bother with *other peoples'* affairs of this sort."[c] Thus Nietzsche, who condemned pity, collapsed in Turin when he saw a coachman beating his horse. Decadence was the fata morgana of this progress that has not yet begun. The ideal, even if it be narrow-minded and willfully obstinate, of a complete, life-renouncing distance from any type of purpose was the reverse image of the false purposefulness of industry, in which everything exists for something else. The irrationalism of *décadence* denounced the unreason of the dominant reason. A separated, arbitrary, privileged happiness is sacred to irrationalism because it alone vouches for what has escaped, while that immediate notion of happiness of the whole—according to the current liberalist formula, the greatest possible happiness for the greatest possible number of people—barters happiness away to the apparatus, the sworn enemy of happiness, whose only goal is self-preservation, even where happiness is proclaimed to be the goal. In just such a spirit the sen-

[c] Peter Altenberg, *Auswahl aus seinen Büchern*, ed. Karl Kraus (Vienna: Anton Scholl, 1932), pp. 122ff.

timent dawns on Altenberg that extreme individuation is the placeholder for humanity: "For insofar as an individuality tending in some direction or other has a justification . . . , it should be nothing other than a first, a forerunner in some organic development of the human in general that yet *lies in the natural course of possible development for all human beings*! It is worthless to be '*the only one*,' a miserable trifling of fate with the individual. To be '*the first*' is everything! . . . He knows that the whole of mankind comes behind him! He is merely sent in advance by God! . . . *All* people will one day be wholly fine, wholly delicate, wholly loving. . . . *True* individuality means being alone and *in advance* that which later *everyone, everyone* must become!"[f] Humanity can be thought only through this extreme form of differentiation, individuation, not as a comprehensive generic concept.

The prohibition against any brushed-in portrait of utopia that the dialectical theories of both Hegel and Marx issued keenly sniffs out any betrayal of utopia. Decadence is the nerve center where the dialectic of progress becomes, as it were, bodily appropriated by consciousness. Whoever rails and rages against decadence inevitably takes up the standpoint of sexual taboo, the violation of which constitutes the antinomian ritual of decadence. In the insistence upon this taboo, for the sake of the unity of nature-dominating ego, there rumbles the voice of deceived, unreflective progress. Yet for that reason progress can be convicted of its own irrationality because it always bewitches the means it uses into the ends it truncates. Of course, the opposing position of decadence remains abstract, and not least of all because of this it incurred the curse of being ridiculous. Decadence mistakes the particularity of happiness, which it must insist upon, for immediate utopia, for realized humanity, whereas decadence itself is disfigured by unfreedom, privilege, and class domination; it indeed owns up to all of these, but also glorifies them. Its wish-image, unfettered erotic availability, would also be perpetual slavery, as in Wilde's *Salomé*.

The explosive tendency of progress is not merely the Other to the movement of a progressing domination of nature, not just its abstract negation; rather, it requires the unfolding of reason through the very domination of nature. Only reason, the principle of societal domination inverted into the subject, would be capable of abolishing this domination. The possibility of wresting free is effectuated by the pressure of negativity. Yet reason, which wants to escape nature, first of all shapes nature into

[f] Ibid., pp. 135ff.

what it must fear. The concept of progress is dialectical in a strictly un-metaphorical sense, in that its organon, reason, is one; a nature-dominating level and a reconciling level do not exist separate and disjunct within reason, rather, both share all its determinations. The one moment inverts into its other only in that it literally reflects itself, in that reason applies reason to it-self and in its self-restriction emancipates itself from the demon of identity. Kant's incomparable greatness proved itself not least in that he incorrupt-ibly maintained the unity of reason even in its contradictory uses—the nature-dominating, what he called theoretical, causal-mechanical, and the power of judgment snuggling up to nature in reconciliation—and displaced reason's difference strictly onto the self-limitation of nature-dominating reason. A metaphysical interpretation of Kant should not impute a latent ontology to him[9] but instead read the structure of his entire thought as a di-alectic of enlightenment, which the dialectician par excellence, Hegel, does not notice, because in the consciousness of Unitary Reason he erases its lim-its and thereby falls into the mythical totality he considers to be "recon-ciled" in the absolute idea. Progress comprehends not merely, as in the Hegelian philosophy of history, the compass of what belongs to dialectic; rather, it is dialectical in its own concept, like the categories of the *Science of Logic*. Absolute domination of nature is absolute submission to nature and yet arches beyond this in self-reflection, myth that demythologizes myth. But the claim of the subject would then no longer be theoretical and also not contemplative. The notion of the domination of pure reason as a being-in-itself, separated from praxis, subjugates even the subject, deforms it into an instrument to be used toward an end. The beneficial self-reflection of reason, however, would be its transition to praxis: reason would see through itself as a moment of praxis and would recognize, instead of mistaking itself for the absolute, that it is a mode of behavior. The antimythological ele-ment in progress cannot be conceived without the practical act that reins in the delusion of spirit's autarky. Hence progress can hardly be ascertained by disinterested contemplation.

Those who from time immemorial and with perpetually new phrases want the same thing—that there be no progress—have the most perni-cious pretense of all. It is sustained by the false inference that because there has been no progress up until now, there never will be any. It presents the inconsolable return of the same as the message of Being, which must be hearkened to and respected, although Being itself, which has had this message put into its mouth, is a cryptogram of myth, the liberation from which would be a moment of freedom. In the translation of historical desperation into a norm that must be adhered to, there echoes that abominable construal of the theological doctrine of original sin, the idea that the corruption of human nature legitimates domination, that radical evil legitimates evil. This conviction wields a catch phrase with which it obscurantistically condemns progress in modern times: the belief in progress. The attitude of those who defame the concept of progress as insipid and positivistic is usually positivistic itself. They explain the way of the world, which repeatedly thwarted progress and which also always was progress, as evidence that the world plan does not tolerate progress and that whoever does not renounce it commits sacrilege. In self-righteous profundity one takes the side of the terrible, slandering the idea of progress according to the schema that whatever human beings fail at is ontologically refused them, and that in the name of their finitude and mortality they have the duty to wholeheartedly appropriate both of these qualities. A sober response to this false reverence would be that while indeed progress from the slingshot to the megaton bomb may well amount to satanic laughter, in the age of the bomb a condition can be envisaged for the first time in which violence might vanish altogether. Nonetheless, a theory of progress must absorb whatever is cogent in the invectives against belief in progress as an antidote to the mythology from which such a theory suffers. Least of all would it befit a doctrine of progress that has been brought to self-consciousness to deny that a shallow doctrine exists simply because derision of the latter belongs to the treasure chamber of ideology. Despite Condorcet, the much-maligned idea of progress of the eighteenth century is less shallow than that of the nineteenth: in Rousseau the doctrine of radical perfectibility is combined with that of the radical corruptness of human nature. As long as the bourgeois class was oppressed, at least in terms of political forms, it took "progress" as its slogan to oppose the prevailing stationary condition: the slogan's pathos was the echo of this situation. Not until the bourgeois class had occupied the decisive positions of power did the concept of progress degenerate into the ideology that ideological profundity then accused the eighteenth century of harboring. The nineteenth century came up against the limit of bourgeois society, which could not fulfill its own reason, its own ideals of freedom, justice, and humane immediacy, without running the risk of its order being abolished. This made it necessary for society to credit itself, untruthfully, with having achieved what it had failed. This falsity, with which the educated citizens then reproached the belief in progress held by the uneducated or reformist labor leaders, was an expression of bourgeois apologetics. Of course, when the shadows of imperialism descended, the bourgeoisie quickly abandoned that ideology and resorted to the desperate one of counterfeiting the negativity that the belief in progress had disputed away into a metaphysical substance.

Whoever rubs his hands with humility and satisfaction while remembering the sinking of the Titanic, because the iceberg supposedly dealt the first blow to the idea of progress, forgets or suppresses the fact that this accident, which, incidentally, was by no means fateful, occasioned measures that in the following half century protected sea voyages from unplanned natural catastrophes. Part of the dialectic of progress is that historical setbacks, which themselves are instigated by the principle of progress—what could be more progressive than the race for the blue ribbon?—also provide the condition needed for humanity to find the means to avert them in the future. The nexus of deception surrounding progress reaches beyond itself. It is mediated to that order in which the category of progress would first gain its justification, in that the devastation wrought by progress can be made good again, if at all, only by its own forces, never by the restoration of the preceding conditions that were its victim. The progress of the domination of nature, which, in Benjamin's simile, proceeds in the reverse direction of that true progress that would have its *telos* in redemption, nevertheless is not entirely without hope.[10] Both concepts of progress communicate with each other, not only in averting the ultimate disaster, but rather in every actual form of easing the persistent suffering.

The belief in interiority is felt to be a corrective to the belief in progress. But not this interiority, not the ability of human beings to improve, guarantees progress. Already in Augustine the notion of progress—he could not yet use the word—is as ambivalent as the dogma of a successful redemption in the face of an unredeemed world demands it to be. On the one hand, progress is historical according to the six epochs of the world that correspond to the periodization of human life; on the other hand, progress is not of this world but internal, in Augustine's language, mystical. *Civitas terrena* and *civitas dei* are held to be invisible realms, and no one can say who among the living belongs to the one or the other; that decision is made by the secret election to grace, the same divine will that moves history in accordance with its plan. Yet already in Augustine, according to the insight of Karl Heinz Haag, the interiorization of progress allows the world to be assigned to the powers that be, and therefore, as with Luther later, Christianity is to be commended because it preserves the political state.[11] Platonic transcendence, which in Augustine is fused with the Christian idea of salvation history, makes it possible to cede the this-worldly to the principle against which progress is conceived and to allow, only on the Day of Judgment and in spite of all philosophy of history, the abrupt restoration of undisturbed creation. This ideological mark has remained to this day engraved on the interiorization of progress. As opposed to this mark, interiority itself, as a historical product, is a function of progress or of its contrary. The constitutive qualities of human beings make up merely one aspect in innerworldly progress and nowadays certainly not the primary one. The argument claiming that there is no progress because none occurs within interiority is false, because it feigns an immediately humane society, in its historical process, whose law is based on what human beings themselves are. But it is the essence of historical objectivity that whatever is made by human beings, their institutions in the broadest sense, evolves independently of its creators and becomes second nature. That false conclusion then permits the thesis of the constancy of human nature, whether it be extolled or deplored. Innerworldly progress has its mythical aspect, as Hegel and Marx recognized, in that it occurs above the heads of subjects and forms them in its own image; it is foolish to deny progress just because it cannot completely manage its objects, the subjects. In order to halt what Schopenhauer called the wheel that unrolls itself, surely that human potential is needed that is not entirely absorbed by the necessity of historical movement.[12] The idea that progress offers a way out is blocked today because the subjective aspects of spontaneity are beginning to atrophy in the historical process. To desperately posit an isolated, allegedly ontological concept of the subjectively spontaneous against societal omnipotence, as the French existentialists do, is too optimistic, even as an expression of despair; one cannot conceive of a versatile spontaneity outside of its entwinement with society. It would be illusory and idealistic to hope that spontaneity would be enough here and now. One cherishes such hope solely in a historical hour in which no support for hope is in sight. Existentialist decisionism is merely the reflex reaction to the seamless totality of the world spirit. Nevertheless, this totality itself is also semblance. The rigidified institutions, the relations of production, are not Being as such, but even in their omnipotence they are man-made and revocable. In their relationship to the subjects from which they originate and which they enclose, they remain thoroughly antagonistic. Not only does the whole demand its own modification in order not to perish, but by virtue of its antagonistic essence it is also impossible for it to extort that complete identity with human beings that is relished in negative utopias. For this reason innerworldly progress, adversary of the other progress, at the same time remains open to the possibility of this other, no matter how little it is able to incorporate this possibility within its own law.

Yet it can be plausibly asserted that things do not proceed with as much vim and vigor in the intellectual spheres—art, especially law, politics, anthropology—as in the material forces of production. Hegel himself, and Jochmann more extremely, expressed this about art; the idea of non-synchrony in the movement of superstructure and substructure was then formulated as a principle by Marx in the proposition that the superstructure revolutionizes itself more slowly than the substructure.[13] Apparently no one was astonished that spirit, fleeting and mobile, should be thought stationary in contrast to the *rudis indigestaque moles* of what, even in the context of society, is not named "material" for nothing. Analogously, psychoanalysis teaches that the unconscious, from which even consciousness and the objective forms of spirit are fed, supposedly is ahistorical. Certainly that which itself is subsumed in a brutal classification under the concept of culture and which contains within itself even subjective consciousness raises a perennial objection to the ever-sameness of what merely exists. But it perennially finds its objection futile. The ever-sameness of the whole, human beings' dependence upon vital necessities, the material conditions of their self-preservation, hides, as it were, behind its own dynamic, the growing increase of alleged societal wealth, and ideology benefits from this. However, it can easily be proved to spirit, which would like to transcend this situation and which is the actual dynamic principle, that it has failed, and this pleases ideology no less. Reality produces the semblance of developing upward and remains *au fond* what it was. Spirit, which, to the extent that it is not a part of the apparatus, seeks innovation, in its hopelessly repeated attempts only knocks its head in, as when an insect flying toward the light collides with a windowpane. Spirit is not what it enthrones itself as, the Other, the transcendent in its purity, but rather is also a piece of natural history. Because natural history has appeared in society as a dynamic since the time of the Eleatics and Plato, spirit imagines that it has the Other, that which is removed from the *civitas terrena* in the immutable self-same, and its forms—logic, above all, which is latently inherent in all that is spiritual—are tailored accordingly. In these forms spirit is seized by something stationary, against which spirit struggles while remaining a part of it. Reality's spell over spirit prevents spirit from doing what its own concept wants to do when faced with the merely existent: to fly. Because more tender and fleeting, spirit is all the more susceptible to oppression and mutilation. As the placeholder of what progress could be, above and beyond all progress, spirit stands askew to the progress that takes place, and this in turn bestows honor upon the placeholder. Through less than complete complicity with progress, spirit reveals what progress is really up to. However, wherever it can be judged with reason that spirit as being-for-itself progresses, there spirit itself participates in the domination of nature simply because it is not, as it fancies itself to be, χωρίς, but rather is entwined with that life process from which it separated itself in conformity with the law of this process. All progress in the cultural spheres is that of the domination of material, of technique. The truth content of spirit, on the contrary, is not indifferent to this. A quartet by Mozart is not simply better made than a symphony of the Mannheim school, but by being better constructed and more consistent it also ranks higher in an emphatic sense. By contrast, it is problematic to determine whether, thanks to the development of perspectival technique, the painting of the high Renaissance truly surpassed so-called primitive painting, whether the best of artworks occur in the incomplete mastery of the material, as a for-the-first-time, something emerging abruptly that vanishes as soon as it becomes a readily available technique. Progress in the mastery of material in art is in no way immediately identical with the progress of art itself. If the gold background had been defended against the use of perspective in the early Renaissance, that would have been not only reactionary but also objectively untrue because contrary to what its own logic demanded; even the complexity of progress unfolds itself only in the course of history. *À la longue* what should persevere and prevail in the afterlife of spiritual creations beyond their momentary progressiveness is their quality, ultimately their truth content, but this only by virtue of a process of progressing consciousness. The notion of the canonical essence of Greek antiquity, which still survived in the dialecticians Hegel and Marx, is not simply an undissolved rudiment of the cultural tradition but in all its dubiousness also the precipitate of a dialectical insight. In order to express its contents, art, and in the spiritual sphere not only art, must inevitably absorb the increasing domination of nature. However, it thereby also works surreptitiously against what it wants to say and distances itself from what it nonverbally, nonconceptually opposes to the increasing domination of nature. This might help explain why the apparent continuity of so-called intellectual developments often breaks off, indeed often with an appeal—no matter how motivated by misunderstanding—for a return to nature. The blame for this lies with—among other, especially social, aspects—the fact that spirit is terrified by the contradiction in its own development and that it tries—vainly, of course—to rectify this contradiction through recourse to what it has estranged itself from and what it therefore mistakenly believes to be invariant.

The paradox that there is some progress and yet there is none is perhaps nowhere so graphic as in philosophy, where the very idea of progress has its home. No matter how compelling might be the transitions, mediated by critique, from one authentic philosophy to another, nonetheless the assertion that there was progress between them—Plato and Aristotle, Kant and Hegel, or even in a philosophical universal history as a whole—remains dubious. But the cause for this is not the invariance of the alleged philosophical object, that of true Being, whose concept has dissolved irrevocably in the history of philosophy; nor would a merely aesthetic view of philosophy be defensible that places an imposing architecture of thought or even the ominous great thinkers higher than the truth, which in no way coincides with the immanent closure and rigor of these philosophies. It is a completely pharisaical and false verdict to conclude that progress in philosophy leads it away from what the jargon of bad philosophy baptizes as its concern: in this way, need would become the guarantor of truth content. On the contrary, the unavoidable and dubious progress of that which receives its limit from its theme—the limit—is posited by the principle of reason, without which philosophy cannot be thought, because without this principle there can be no thought. One concept after another plunges into the Orcus of the mythical.[14] Philosophy lives in symbiosis with science and cannot break from it without turning into dogmatism and ultimately relapsing into mythology. Yet the content of philosophy should be to express what is neglected or excised by science, by the division of labor, by the forms of reflection entailed by the bustle of self-preservation. For this reason philosophy's progress simultaneously recedes from the necessary goal of its progress; the force of experience that philosophy registers is weakened the more it is honed down by the scientistic apparatus. The movement philosophy as a whole performs is the pure self-sameness of its principle. Every time it pays the price of what it would need to conceptually grasp and can grasp only by virtue of self-reflection, through which it relinquishes the standpoint of stubborn immediacy or, in Hegelian terminology, the philosophy of reflection. Philosophical progress is deceitful because the tighter it connects arguments, the more airtight and unassailable its propositions become, the more it becomes identity-thinking. Philosophical progress weaves a net over its objects that, by plugging up the holes of what it is not, impudently thrusts itself in place of its object of inquiry. Indeed, finally it seems, in harmony with the actual retrogressive tendencies of society, that vengeance is exacted on the progress of philosophy for having hardly been progress at all. To assume that there has been progress from Hegel to the logical positivists, who dismiss him as obscure or meaningless, is nothing but funny. Even philosophy is not immune to falling prey to that kind of regression, whether into narrow-minded scientification or into the denial of reason, which certainly is no better than the maliciously derided belief in progress.

In bourgeois society, which created the concept of total progress, the convergence of this concept with the negation of progress originates in this society's principle: exchange. Exchange is the rational form of mythical ever-sameness. In the like-for-like of every act of exchange, the one act revokes the other; the balance of accounts is null. If the exchange was just, then nothing should really have happened, and everything stays the same. At the same time the assertion of progress, which conflicts with this principle, is true to the extent that the doctrine of like-for-like is a lie. From time immemorial, not just since the capitalist appropriation of surplus value in the commodity exchange of labor power for the cost of its reproduction, the societally more powerful contracting party receives more than the other. By means of this injustice, something new occurs in the exchange: the process, which proclaims its own stasis, becomes dynamic. The truth of the expansion feeds on the lie of the equality. Societal acts are supposed to reciprocally sublate themselves in the overall system and yet do not. Wherever bourgeois society satisfies the concept it cherishes as its own, it knows no progress; wherever it knows progress, it violates its own law, in which this offense already lies, and by means of the inequality immortalizes the injustice progress is supposed to transcend. But this injustice is at once also the condition for possible justice. The fulfillment of the repeatedly broken exchange contract would converge with its abolition; exchange would disappear if truly equal things were exchanged; true progress would not be merely an Other in relation to exchange, but rather exchange that has been brought to itself. Thus thought both Marx and Nietzsche, antipodes of each other; Zarathustra postulates that man will be redeemed from revenge.[15] For revenge is the mythical prototype of exchange; as long as domination persists through exchange, myth will dominate as well. The interlocking of the ever-same and the new in the exchange relation manifests itself in the imagoes of progress under bourgeois industrialism. What seems paradoxical about these imagoes is that something different ever appears at all, that the imagoes grow old, since the ever-sameness of the exchange principle intensifies by virtue of technology into domination by repetition within the sphere of production. The life process itself ossifies in the expression of the ever-same: hence the shock of photographs from the nineteenth century and even the early twentieth century. The absurdity explodes: that something happens where the phenomenon says that nothing more could happen; its attitude becomes terrifying.[16] In this experience of terror, the terror of the system forcibly coalesces into appearance; the more the system expands, the more it hardens into what it has always been. What Benjamin called "dialectics at a standstill" is surely less a Platonizing residue than the attempt to raise such paradoxes to philosophical consciousness. Dialectical images: these are the historically objective archetypes of that antagonistic unity of standstill and movement that defines the most universal bourgeois concept of progress.[17]

Hegel as well as Marx bore witness to the fact that even the dialectical view of progress needs correction. The dynamic they taught is conceived, not as a simple dynamic per se, but on the contrary as one unified with its opposite, with something steadfast, in which alone a dynamic first becomes legible at all. Marx, who criticized all notions of the natural growth of society as fetishistic, likewise rejected, against Lassalle's Gotha Program, the absolutization of the dynamic in the doctrine of labor as the single source of societal wealth, and he conceded the possibility of a relapse into barbarism.[18] It may be more than mere coincidence that Hegel, despite his famous definition of history, has no detailed theory of progress and that Marx himself seems to have avoided the word, even in the constantly cited programmatic passage from the preface to *Critique of Political Economy*. The dialectical taboo on concept fetishes, the legacy of the old, antimythological Enlightenment in its self-reflective phase, extends even to the category that used to soften up reification: progress, which deceives as soon as it—as a single aspect—usurps the whole. The fetishization of progress reinforces its particularity, its restrictedness to techniques.[19] If progress were truly master of the whole, the concept of which bears the marks of its violence, then progress would no longer be totalitarian. Progress is not a conclusive category. It wants to cut short the triumph of radical evil, not to triumph as such itself. A situation is conceivable in which the category would lose its meaning, and yet which is not the situation of universal regression that allies itself with progress today. In this case, progress would transform itself into the resistance to the perpetual danger of relapse. Progress is this resistance at all stages, not the surrender to their steady ascent.

(1964; GS 10.2: 617–38)
Translated by Henry W. Pickford

7

Cultural Criticism and Society

To anyone in the habit of thinking with his ears, the words "cultural criticism" [*Kulturkritik*] must have an offensive ring, not merely because, like "automobile," they are pieced together from Latin and Greek. The words recall a flagrant contradiction. The cultural critic is not happy with civilization, to which alone he owes his discontent. He speaks as if he represented either unadulterated nature or a higher historical stage. Yet he is necessarily of the same essence as that to which he fancies himself superior. The insufficiency of the subject—criticized by Hegel in his apology for the status quo—which in its contingency and narrowness passes judgment on the might of the existent, becomes intolerable when the subject itself is mediated down to its innermost makeup by the notion to which it opposes itself as independent and sovereign. But what makes the content of cultural criticism inappropriate is not so much lack of respect for that which is criticized as the dazzled and arrogant recognition that criticism surreptitiously confers on culture. The cultural critic can hardly avoid the imputation that he has the culture that culture lacks. His vanity aids that of culture: even in the accusing gesture, the critic clings to the notion of culture, isolated, unquestioned, dogmatic. He shifts the attack. Where there is despair and measureless misery, he sees only spiritual phenomena, the state of man's consciousness, the decline of norms. By insisting on this, criticism is tempted to forget the unutterable, instead of striving, however impotently, so that man may be spared.

The position of the cultural critic, by virtue of its difference from the prevailing disorder, enables him to go beyond it theoretically, although often enough he merely falls behind. But he incorporates this difference into the very culture industry that he seeks to leave behind and that itself needs the difference in order to fancy itself culture. Characteristic of culture's pretension to distinction, through which it exempts itself from evaluation against the material conditions of life, is that it is insatiable. The exaggerated claims of culture, which in turn inhere in the movement of the mind, remove it ever further from those conditions, as the worth of sublimation becomes increasingly suspect when confronted both by a material fulfillment near enough to touch and by the threatening annihilation of uncounted human beings. The cultural critic makes such distinction his privilege and forfeits his legitimation by collaborating with culture as its salaried and honored nuisance. This, however, affects the substance of criticism. Even the implacable rigor with which criticism speaks the truth of an untrue consciousness remains imprisoned within the orbit of that against which it struggles, fixated on its surface manifestations. To flaunt one's superiority is, at the same time, to feel in on the job. Were one to study the profession of critic in bourgeois society as it progressed toward the rank of cultural critic, one would doubtless stumble on an element of usurpation in its origins, an element of which a writer like Balzac was still aware. Professional critics were first of all "reporters": they oriented people in the market of intellectual products. In so doing, they occasionally gained insights into the matter at hand, yet remained continually traffic agents, in agreement with the sphere as such if not with its individual products. Of this they bear the mark even after they have discarded the role of agent. That they should have been entrusted with the roles of expert and then of judge was economically inevitable although accidental with respect to their objective qualifications. Their agility, which gained them privileged positions in the general competition—privileged, since the fate of those judged depends largely on their vote—invests their judgments with the semblance of competence. While they adroitly slipped into gaps and won influence with the expansion of the press, they attained that very authority their profession already presupposed. Their arrogance derives from the fact that, in the forms of competitive society in which all being is there merely *for* something else, the critic himself is also measured only in terms of his marketable success—that is, in terms of his *being for* something else. Knowledge and understanding were not primary, but at most by-products, and the more they are lacking, the more they are replaced by one-upmanship and conformity. When the critics in their playground—art—no longer understand what they judge and enthusiastically permit themselves to be degraded to propagandists or censors, it is the old dishonesty of trade fulfilling itself in their fate. The prerogatives of information and position permit them to express their opinion as if it were objectivity. But it is solely the objectivity of the ruling mind. They help to weave the veil.

The notion of the free expression of opinion, indeed, that of intellectual freedom itself in bourgeois society, upon which cultural criticism is founded, has its own dialectic. While the mind has extricated itself from a theological-feudal tutelage, it has fallen increasingly under the anonymous sway of the status quo. This regimentation, the result of the progressive societalization of all human relations, did not simply confront the mind from without; it immigrated into its immanent consistency. It imposes itself as relentlessly on the autonomous mind as heteronomous orders were formerly imposed on the mind that was bound. Not only does the mind mold itself for the sake of its marketability, and thus reproduce the socially prevalent categories. Rather, it grows to resemble ever more closely the status quo, even where it subjectively refrains from making a commodity of itself. The network of the whole is drawn ever tighter, modeled after the act of exchange. It leaves the individual consciousness less and less room for evasion, preforms it more and more thoroughly, cuts it off a priori, as it were, from the possibility of differencing itself, as all difference degenerates to a nuance in the monotony of supply. At the same time, the semblance of freedom makes reflection upon one's own unfreedom incomparably more difficult than formerly, when such reflection stood in contradiction to manifest unfreedom, thus strengthening dependence. Such moments, in conjunction with the social selection of the "spiritual and intellectual leaders," result in the regression of spirit and intellect. In accordance with the predominant social tendency, the integrity of the mind becomes a fiction. Of its freedom it develops only the negative moment, the heritage of the planless-monadological condition, irresponsibility. Otherwise, however, it clings ever more closely as a mere ornament to the material base that it claims to transcend. The strictures of Karl Kraus against freedom of the press are certainly not to be taken literally. To invoke seriously the censors against hack writers would be to drive out the devil with Beelzebub. Nev-

ertheless, the brutalization and deceit that flourish under the aegis of freedom of the press are not accidental to the historical march of the mind.
Rather, they represent the stigma of that slavery within which the liberation of the mind—a false emancipation—has taken place. This is nowhere
more striking than where the mind tears at its bonds: in criticism. When
the German fascists defamed the word and replaced it with the inane notion of "art appreciation," they were led to do so only by the rugged interests of the authoritarian state, which still feared the passion of a Marquis
Posa in the impertinence of the journalist. But the self-satisfied cultural
barbarism that clamored for the abolition of criticism, the incursion of the
wild horde into the preserve of the mind, unawares repaid kind in kind.
The bestial fury of the Brownshirt against "carping critics" arises not
merely from his envy of a culture that excludes him and against which he
blindly rebels, nor is it merely his resentment of the person who can speak
out the negative moment that he himself must repress. Decisive is that the
critic's sovereign gesture suggests to his readers an autonomy he does not
have, and arrogates for itself a position of leadership that is incompatible
with his own principle of intellectual freedom. This is innervated by his
enemies. Their sadism was idiosyncratically attracted by the weakness,
cleverly disguised as strength, of those who, in their dictatorial bearing,
would have willingly excelled the less clever tyrants who were to succeed
them. Except that the fascists succumbed to the same naïveté as the critics,
the faith in culture as such, which reduced it to pomp and approved spiritual giants. They regarded themselves as physicians of culture and removed
the thorn of criticism from it. They thus not only degraded culture to the
Official but in addition failed to recognize the extent to which culture and
criticism, for better or for worse, are intertwined. Culture is true only
when implicitly critical, and the mind that forgets this revenges itself in the
critics it breeds. Criticism is an indispensable element of culture that is itself contradictory: in all its untruth still as true as culture is untrue. Criticism is unjust not when it dissects—this can be its greatest virtue—but
rather when it parries by not parrying.

The complicity of cultural criticism with culture lies not in the mere
mentality of the critic. Far more, it is dictated by his relation to that with
which he deals. By making culture his object, he objectifies it once more.
Its very meaning, however, is the suspension of objectification. Once culture itself has been debased to "cultural goods," with its hideous philosophical rationalization, "cultural values," it has already defamed its *raison*

d'être. The distillation of such "values"—the echo of commercial language is by no means accidental—places culture at the will of the market. Even the enthusiasm for foreign cultures includes the excitement over the rarity in which money may be invested. If cultural criticism, even at its best with Valéry, sides with conservatism, it is because of its unconscious adherence to a notion of culture that, during the era of late capitalism, aims at a form of property that is stable and independent of stock-market fluctuations. This idea of culture asserts its distance from the system in order, as it were, to offer universal security in the middle of a universal dynamic. The model of the cultural critic is no less the appraising collector than the art critic. In general, cultural criticism recalls the gesture of bargaining, of the expert questioning the authenticity of a painting or classifying it among the Master's lesser works. One devaluates in order to get more. The cultural critic evaluates and hence is inevitably involved in a sphere stained with "cultural values," even when he rants against the mortgaging of culture. His contemplative stance toward culture necessarily entails scrutinizing, surveying, balancing, selecting: this piece suits him, that he rejects. Yet his very sovereignty, the claim to a more profound knowledge of the object, the separation of the idea from its object through the independence of critical judgment, threatens to succumb to the thinglike form of the object when cultural criticism appeals to a collection of ideas on display, as it were, and fetishizes isolated categories such as mind, life, and the individual.

But the greatest fetish of cultural criticism is the notion of culture as such. For no authentic work of art and no true philosophy, according to their very meaning, has ever exhausted itself in itself alone, in its being-in-itself. They have always stood in relation to the actual life-process of society from which they distinguished themselves. Their very rejection of the guilt of a life that blindly and callously reproduces itself, their insistence on independence and autonomy, on separation from the prevailing realm of purposes, implies, at least as an unconscious element, the promise of a condition in which freedom is realized. This remains an equivocal promise of culture as long as its existence depends on a bewitched reality and, ultimately, on control over the work of others. That European culture in all its breadth—that which reached the consumer and which today is prescribed for whole populations by managers and psychotechnicians—degenerated to mere ideology resulted from a change in its function with regard to material *praxis*: its renunciation of interference. Far from being culture's "sin," the change was forced upon culture by history. For it is only in the process of withdrawing into itself—only indirectly, that is—that bourgeois culture conceives of a purity from the corrupting traces of a totalitarian disorder that embraces all areas of existence. Only insofar as it withdraws from a *praxis* that has degenerated into its opposite, from the ever-changing production of what is always the same, from the service of the customer who himself serves the manipulator—only insofar as it withdraws from Man, can culture be faithful to man. But such concentration on substance that is absolutely one's own, the greatest example of which is to be found in the poetry and theoretical writings of Paul Valéry, contributes at the same time to the impoverishment of that substance. Once the mind is no longer directed at reality, its meaning is changed despite the strictest preservation of meaning. Through its resignation before the facts of life and, even more, through its isolation as one "field" among others, the mind aids the existing order and takes its place within it. The emasculation of culture has angered philosophers from the time of Rousseau and the "ink-splattering age" of Schiller's *Robbers*, to Nietzsche, and, finally, to the preachers of commitment for its own sake. This is the result of culture's becoming self-consciously cultural, which in turn places culture in vigorous and consistent opposition to the growing barbarism of economic hegemony. What appears to be the decline of culture is its coming to pure self-consciousness. Only when neutralized and reified does Culture allow itself to be idolized. Fetishism gravitates toward mythology. In general, cultural critics become intoxicated with idols drawn from antiquity to the dubious, long-evaporated warmth of the liberalist era, which recalled the origins of culture in its decline. Cultural criticism rejects the progressive integration of all aspects of consciousness within the apparatus of material production. But because it fails to see through the apparatus, it turns toward the past, lured by the promise of immediacy. This is necessitated by its own momentum and not merely by the influence of an order that sees itself obliged to drown out its progress in dehumanization with cries against dehumanization and progress. The isolation of the mind from material production heightens its esteem but also makes it a scapegoat in the general consciousness for that which is perpetrated in practice. Enlightenment as such—not as an instrument of actual domination—is held responsible. Hence, the irrationalism of cultural criticism. Once it has wrenched the mind out of its dialectic with the material conditions of life, it seizes it unequivocally and straightforwardly as the principle of fatality, thus undercutting the mind's own resistance. The cultural critic is

barred from the insight that the reification of life results not from too much enlightenment but from too little, and that the mutilation of man that is the result of the present[particularistic rationality]is the stigma of total irrationality. The abolition of this irrationality, which would coincide with the abolition of the divorce between mental and physical work, appears as chaos to the blindness of cultural criticism: whoever glorifies order and form as such must see in the petrified divorce an archetype of the Eternal. That the fatal fragmentation of society might some day end is, for the cultural critic, a fatal destiny. He would rather that everything end than that mankind put an end to reification. This fear harmonizes with the interests of those interested in the perpetuation of material denial. Whenever cultural criticism complains of "materialism," it furthers the belief that the sin lies in man's desire for consumer goods, and not in the organization of the whole that withholds these goods from man: for the cultural critic, the sin is satiety, not hunger. Were mankind to possess the wealth of goods, it would shake off the chains of that civilized barbarism that cultural critics ascribe to the advanced state of the human spirit rather than to the retarded state of society. The "eternal values" of which cultural criticism is so fond reflect the perennial catastrophe. The cultural critic thrives on the mythical obduracy of culture.

Because the existence of cultural criticism, no matter what its content, depends on the economic system, it is involved in the fate of the system. The more completely the life process, including leisure, is dominated by modern social orders—those in the East, above all—the more all spiritual phenomena bear the mark of the order. On the one hand, they may contribute directly to the perpetuation of the system as entertainment or edification, and are enjoyed as exponents of the system precisely because of their socially preformed character. Familiar, stamped and Approved by Good Housekeeping, as it were, they insinuate themselves into a regressive consciousness, present themselves as "natural," and permit identification with powers whose preponderance leaves no alternative but that of false love. Or, on the other hand, by being different they become rarities and once again marketable. Throughout the liberalist era, culture fell within the sphere of circulation. Hence, the gradual withering away of this sphere strikes culture to the quick. With the elimination of trade and its irrational loopholes by the calculated distributive apparatus of industry, the commercialization of culture culminates in absurdity. Completely subdued, administered, thoroughly "cultivated," in a sense, it dies out. Spengler's denunciation: that mind and money go together, proves correct. But because of his sympathy with direct rule, he advocated a structure of existence divested of all economic as well as spiritual mediations. He maliciously threw the mind together with an economic type that was in fact obsolete. What Spengler failed to understand was that no matter to what extent the mind is a product of that type, it implies at the same time the objective possibility of overcoming it. Just as culture sprang up in the marketplace, in the traffic of trade, in communication and negotiation as something distinct from the immediate struggle for individual self-preservation, just as it was loosely tied to trade in the era of mature capitalism, just as its representatives were counted among the class of "third persons" who supported themselves in life as middlemen, so culture, considered "socially necessary" according to classical rules, in the sense of reproducing itself economically, is in the end reduced to that as which it began, to mere communication. Its alienation from human affairs terminates in its absolute docility before a humanity that has been enchanted and transformed into clientele by the suppliers. In the name of the consumer, the manipulators suppress everything in culture that enables it to go beyond the total immanence in the existing society and allow only that to remain which serves society's unequivocal purpose. Hence, "consumer culture" can boast of being not a luxury but rather the simple extension of production. Political slogans, designed for mass manipulation, unanimously stigmatize, as "luxury," "snobbism," and "highbrow," everything cultural that displeases the commissars. Only when the established order has become the measure of all things does its mere reproduction in the realm of consciousness become truth. Cultural criticism points to this and rails against "superficiality" and "loss of substance." But by limiting its attention to the entanglement of culture in commerce, such criticism itself becomes superficial. It follows the pattern of reactionary social critics who pit "productive" against "predatory" capital. In fact, all culture shares the guilt of society. It ekes out its existence only by virtue of injustice already perpetrated in the sphere of production, much as does commerce (cf. *Dialectic of Enlightenment*). Consequently, cultural criticism shifts the guilt: such criticism is ideology as long as it remains mere criticism of ideology. Totalitarian regimes of both kinds, seeking to protect the status quo from even the last traces of insubordination, which they ascribe to culture even at its most servile, can conclusively convict culture and its introspection of servility. They suppress the mind, in itself already grown intolerable, and so feel themselves to be purifiers and revolutionaries. The ideological function of cultural criticism bridles its very truth, which lies in its opposition to ideology. The struggle against deceit works to the advantage of naked terror. "When I hear the word 'culture,' I reach for my gun," said the spokesman of Hitler's Imperial Chamber of Culture.

Cultural criticism is, however, able to reproach culture so penetratingly for prostituting itself, for violating in its decline the pure autonomy of the mind, only because culture originates in the radical separation of mental and physical work. It is from this separation, the original sin, as it were, that culture draws its strength. When culture simply denies the separation and feigns harmonious union, it falls back behind its own notion. Only the mind that, in the delusion of being absolute, removes itself entirely from the merely existent truly defines the existent in its negativity. As long as even the least part of the mind remains engaged in the reproduction of life, it is its sworn bondsman. The antiphilistinism of Athens was both the most arrogant contempt of the man who need not soil his hands for the man from whose work he lives, and the preservation of an image of existence beyond the constraint that underlies all work. In projecting its own uneasy conscience onto its victims as their "baseness," such an attitude also accuses that which they endure: the subjugation of men to the prevailing form in which their lives are reproduced. All "pure culture" has always been a source of discomfort to the spokesmen of power. Plato and Aristotle knew why they would not permit the notion to arise. Instead, in questions concerning the evaluation of art, they advocated a pragmatism that contrasts curiously with the *pathos* of the two great metaphysicians. Modern bourgeois cultural criticism has, of course, been too prudent to follow them openly in this respect. But such criticism secretly finds a source of comfort in the divorce between "high" and "popular" culture, art and entertainment, knowledge and noncommittal *Weltanschauung*. Its antiphilistinism exceeds that of the Athenian upper class to the extent that the proletariat is more dangerous than the slaves. The modern notion of a pure, autonomous culture indicates that the antagonism has become irreconcilable. This is the result both of an uncompromising opposition to being-for-something-else, and of an ideology that in its hubris enthrones itself as being-in-itself.

Cultural criticism shares the blindness of its object. It is incapable of allowing the recognition of its frailty to arise, a frailty set in the division of mental and physical work. No society that contradicts its very notion—

that of mankind—can have full consciousness of itself. A display of subjective ideology is not required to obstruct this consciousness, although in times of historical upheaval it tends to contribute to the objective blindness. Rather, the fact that every form of repression, depending on the level of technology, has been necessary for the survival of society, and that society as it is, despite all absurdity, does indeed reproduce its life under the existing conditions, objectively produces the semblance of society's legitimation. As the epitome of the self-consciousness of an antagonistic society, culture can no more divest itself of this semblance than can cultural criticism, which measures culture against culture's own ideal. The semblance has become total in a phase in which irrationality and objective falsity hide behind rationality and objective necessity. Nevertheless, by virtue of their real force, the antagonisms reassert themselves in the realm of consciousness. Just because culture affirms the validity of the principle of harmony within an antagonistic society, albeit in order to glorify that society, it cannot avoid confronting society with its own notion of harmony and thereby stumbling on discord. The ideology that affirms life is forced into opposition to life by the immanent drive of the ideal. The mind that sees that reality does not resemble it in every respect but is instead subject to an unconscious and fatal dynamic, is impelled even against its will beyond apologetics. The fact that theory becomes real force when it moves men is founded in the objectivity of the mind itself, which, through the fulfillment of its ideological function, must lose faith in ideology. Prompted by the incompatibility of ideology and existence, the mind, in displaying its blindness, also displays its effort to free itself of ideology. Disenchanted, the mind perceives naked existence in its nakedness and delivers it up to criticism. The mind either damns the material base, in accordance with the ever-questionable criterion of its "pure principle," or becomes aware of its own questionable position, by virtue of its incompatibility with the base. As a result of the social dynamic, culture becomes cultural criticism, which preserves the notion of culture while demolishing its present manifestations as mere commodities and means of brutalization. Such critical consciousness remains subservient to culture insofar as its concern with culture distracts from the true horrors. From this arises the ambivalent attitude of social theory toward cultural criticism. The procedure of cultural criticism is itself the object of permanent criticism, both in its general presuppositions—its immanence in the existing society—and in its concrete judgments. For the subservience of cultural criticism is revealed in its specific content, and only in this may it be grasped conclusively. At the same time, a dialectical theory that does not wish to succumb to "Economism," the sentiment which holds that the transformation of the world is exhausted in the increase of production, must absorb cultural criticism, the truth of which consists in bringing untruth to consciousness of itself. A dialectical theory that is uninterested in culture as a mere epiphenomenon helps pseudo-culture to run rampant and collaborates in the reproduction of the evil. Cultural traditionalism and the terror of the new Russian despots are in basic agreement. Both affirm culture as a whole, sight unseen, while proscribing all forms of consciousness that are not made-to-order. They are thus no less ideological than is criticism when it calls a disembodied culture before its tribunal, or holds the alleged negativity of culture responsible for real catastrophes. To accept culture as a whole is to deprive it of the ferment that is its very truth—negation. The joyous appropriation of culture harmonizes with a climate of military music and paintings of battle scenes. What distinguishes dialectical from cultural criticism is that it heightens cultural criticism until the notion of culture is itself negated, fulfilled and surmounted in one.

Immanent criticism of culture, it may be argued, overlooks what is decisive: the role of ideology in social conflicts. To suppose, if only methodologically, anything like an independent logic of culture is to collaborate in the hypostasis of culture, the ideological *proton pseudos*. The substance of culture, according to this argument, resides not in culture alone but in its relation to something external, to the material life-process. Culture, as Marx observed of juridical and political systems, cannot be fully "understood either in terms of itself . . . or in terms of the so-called universal development of the mind." To ignore this, the argument concludes, is to make ideology the basic matter and thus to establish it firmly. And in fact, having taken a dialectical turn, cultural criticism must not hypostatize the criteria of culture. Criticism retains its mobility in regard to culture by recognizing the latter's position within the whole. Without such freedom, without consciousness transcending the immanence of culture, immanent criticism itself would be inconceivable: the spontaneous movement of the object can be followed only by someone who is not entirely engulfed by it. But the traditional demand of ideology critique is itself subject to a historical dynamic. The critique was conceived against idealism, the philosophical form that reflects the fetishization of culture. Today, however, the definition of consciousness in terms of being has become a means of dispensing with all consciousness that does not conform to existence. The objectivity of truth, without which the dialectic is inconceivable, is tacitly replaced by vulgar positivism and pragmatism—ultimately, that is, by bourgeois subjectivism. During the bourgeois era, the prevailing theory was the ideology and the opposing *praxis* was in direct contradiction. Today, theory hardly exists any longer, and the ideology drones, as it were, from the gears of an irresistible *praxis*. No notion dares to be conceived anymore that does not cheerfully include, in all camps, explicit instructions as to who its beneficiaries are—exactly what the polemics once sought to expose. But the unideological thought is that which does not permit itself to be reduced to "operational terms" and instead strives solely to help things themselves to that articulation from which they are otherwise cut off by the prevailing language. Since the moment arrived when every advanced economic and political council agreed that what was important was to change the world and that to interpret it was *allotria*, it has become difficult simply to invoke the "Theses" against Feuerbach. Dialectics also includes the relation between action and contemplation. In an epoch in which bourgeois social science has, in Scheler's words, "plundered" the Marxian notion of ideology and diluted it to universal relativism, the danger involved in overlooking the function of ideologies has become less than that of judging intellectual phenomena in a subsumptive, uninformed, and administrative manner and assimilating them into the prevailing constellations of power, which the intellect ought to expose. As with many other elements of dialectical materialism, the notion of ideology has changed from an instrument of knowledge into its straitjacket. In the name of the dependence of superstructure on base, all use of ideology is controlled instead of criticized. No one is concerned with the objective substance of an ideology as long as it is expedient.

Yet the very function of ideologies becomes increasingly abstract. The suspicion held by earlier cultural critics is confirmed: in a world that denies the mass of human beings the authentic experience of intellectual phenomena by making genuine education a privilege and by shackling consciousness, the specific ideological content of these phenomena is less important than the fact that there should be anything at all to fill the vacuum of the expropriated consciousness and to distract from the open secret. Within the context of its social effect, the particular ideological doctrine that a film imparts to its audience is presumably far less important than the interest of the homeward bound moviegoer in the names and marital affairs of the stars. Vulgar notions such as "amusement" and "diversion" are more appropriate than pretentious explanations that designate one writer as a representative of the lower middle class, another of the upper middle. Culture has become ideological not only as the quintessence of subjectively devised manifestations of the objective mind, but even more as the sphere of private life. The illusory importance and autonomy of private life conceals the fact that private life drags on only as an appendage of the social process. Life transforms itself into the ideology of reification—a death mask. Hence, the task of criticism must be not so much to search for the particular interest groups to which cultural phenomena are to be assigned, as to decipher the general social tendencies that are expressed in these phenomena and through which the most powerful interests realize themselves. Cultural criticism must become social physiognomy. The more the whole divests itself of all spontaneous elements, is socially mediated and filtered, is "consciousness," the more it becomes "culture." In addition to being the means of subsistence, the material process of production finally unveils itself as that which it always was, from its origins in the exchange relationship as the false consciousness that the two contracting parties have of each other: ideology. Inversely, however, consciousness becomes at the same time increasingly a mere transitional moment in the functioning of the whole. Today, ideology means society as appearance. Although mediated by the totality behind which stands the rule of partiality, ideology is not simply reducible to a partial interest. It is, as it were, equally near the center in all its pieces.

The alternatives—either calling culture as a whole into question from outside under the general notion of ideology, or confronting it with the norms it itself has crystallized—cannot be accepted by Critical Theory. To insist on the choice between immanence and transcendence is to revert to the traditional logic criticized in Hegel's polemic against Kant. As Hegel argued, every method that sets limits and restricts itself to the limits of its object thereby goes beyond them. The position transcending culture is in a certain sense presupposed by dialectics as the consciousness that succumbs in advance to the fetishization of the intellectual sphere. Dialectics means intransigence toward all reification. The transcendent method, which aims at totality, seems more radical than the immanent method, which presupposes the questionable whole. The transcendent critic assumes an as it were Archimedean position above culture and the blindness of society, from which consciousness can bring the totality, no matter how massive, into flux. The attack on the whole draws strength from the fact that the semblance of unity and wholeness in the world grows with the advance of reification; that is, with division. But the summary dismissal of ideology that in the Soviet sphere has already become a pretext for cynical terror, taking the form of a ban on "objectivism," pays that wholeness too high an honor. Such an attitude buys up culture *en bloc* from society, regardless of the use to which it is put. If ideology is defined as socially necessary appearance, then the ideology today is society itself insofar as its integral power and inevitability, its overwhelming existence-in-itself, surrogates the meaning that that existence has exterminated. The choice of a standpoint outside the sway of existing society is as fictitious as only the construction of abstract utopias can be. Hence, the transcendent criticism of culture, much like bourgeois cultural criticism, sees itself obliged to fall back upon the idea of "naturalness,"which itself forms a central element of bourgeois ideology. The transcendent attack on culture regularly speaks the language of false escape, that of the "nature boy." It despises the mind and its works, contending that they are, after all, only man-made and serve only to cover up "natural" life. Because of this alleged worthlessness, the phenomena allow themselves to be manipulated and degraded for purposes of domination. This explains the inadequacy of most socialist contributions to cultural criticism: they lack the experience of that with which they deal. In wishing to wipe away the whole as if with a sponge, they develop an affinity for barbarism. Their sympathies are inevitably with the more primitive, more undifferentiated, no matter how much it may contradict the level of intellectual productive forces. The blanket rejection of culture becomes a pretext for promoting what is crudest, "healthiest," even repressive; above all, the perennial conflict between individual and society, both drawn in like manner, which is obstinately resolved in favor of society according to the criteria of the administrators who have appropriated it. From there it is only a step to the official reinstatement of culture. Against this struggles the immanent procedure as the more essentially dialectical. It takes seriously the principle that it is not ideology in itself that is untrue but rather its pretension to correspond to reality. Immanent criticism of intellectual and artistic phenomena seeks to grasp, through the analysis of their form and meaning, the contradiction between their objective idea and that pretension. It names what the consistency or inconsistency of the work itself expresses of the structure of the existent. Such criticism does not stop at a general recognition of the servitude of the objective mind, but seeks rather to transform this knowledge into a heightened perception of the thing itself. Insight into the negativity of culture is binding only when it reveals the truth or untruth of a perception, the consequence or lameness of a thought, the coherence or incoherence of a structure, the substantiality or emptiness of a figure of speech. Where it finds inadequacies it does not ascribe them hastily to the individual and his psychology, which are merely the facade of the failure, but instead seeks to derive them from the irreconcilability of the object's moments. It pursues the logic of its aporias, the insolubility of the task itself. In such antinomies criticism perceives those of society. A successful work, according to immanent criticism, is not one that resolves objective contradictions in a spurious harmony but one that expresses the idea of harmony negatively by embodying the contradictions, pure and uncompromised, in its innermost structure. Confronted with this kind of work, the verdict "mere ideology" loses its meaning. At the same time, however, immanent criticism holds in evidence the fact that the mind has always been under a spell. On its own it is unable to resolve the contradictions under which it labors. Even the most radical reflection of the mind on its own failure is limited by the fact that it remains only reflection, without altering the existence to which its failure bears witness. Hence immanent criticism cannot take comfort in its own idea. It can be neither vain enough to believe that it can liberate the mind directly by immersing itself in it, nor naive enough to believe that unflinching immersion in the object will inevitably lead to truth by virtue of the logic of things if only subjective knowledge of the false whole is kept from intruding from the outside, as it were, in the determination of the object. The less the dialectical method can today presuppose the Hegelian identity of subject and object, the more it is obliged to be mindful of the duality of moments. It must relate the knowledge of society as a totality and of the mind's involvement in it to the claim inherent in the specific content of the object that it be apprehended as such. Dialectics cannot, therefore, permit any insistence on logical neatness to encroach on its right to go from one genus to another, to shed light on an object in itself hermetic by casting a glance at society, to present society with the bill that the object does not redeem. Finally, the very opposition between knowledge which penetrates from without and that which bores from within becomes suspect to the dialectical method, which sees in it a symptom of precisely that reification that the dialectic is obliged to accuse. The abstract categorizing and, as it were, administrative thinking of the former corresponds in the latter to the

fetishism of an object blind to its genesis, which has become the prerogative of the expert. But if stubbornly immanent contemplation threatens to
revert to idealism, to the illusion of the self-sufficient mind in command of
both itself and reality, transcendent contemplation threatens to forget the
effort of conceptualization required and content itself instead with the prescribed label, the petrified invective, most often "petit bourgeois," the
ukase dispatched from above. Topological thinking, which knows the place
of every phenomenon and the essence of none, is secretly related to the
paranoic system of delusions, which is cut off from experience of the object. With the aid of mechanically functioning categories, the world is divided into black and white and thus made ready for the very domination
against which concepts were once conceived. No theory, not even that
which is true, is safe from perversion into delusion once it has renounced
a spontaneous relation to the object. Dialectics must guard against this no
less than against enthrallment to the cultural object. It can subscribe neither to the cult of the mind nor to hatred of it. The dialectical critic of culture must both participate in culture and not participate. Only then does
he do justice to his object and to himself.

The traditional transcendent critique of ideology is obsolete. In principle, the method succumbs to the very reification that is its critical theme.
By transferring the notion of causality directly from the realm of physical
nature to society, it falls back behind its own object. Nevertheless, the transcendent method can still appeal to the fact that it employs reified notions
only insofar as society itself is reified. Through the crudity and severity of
the notion of causality, it claims to hold up a mirror to society's own crudity and severity, to its debasement of the mind. But the sinister, integrated
society of today no longer tolerates even those relatively independent, distinct moments to which the theory of the causal dependence of superstructure on base once referred. In the open-air prison that the world is becoming, it is no longer so important to know what depends on what; such
is the extent to which everything is one. All phenomena rigidify, become
insignias of the absolute rule of that which is. There are no more ideologies
in the authentic sense of false consciousness, only advertisements for the
world through its duplication and the provocative lie that does not seek belief but commands silence. Hence, the question of the causal dependence
of culture, a question that seems to embody the voice of that on which culture is thought only to depend, takes on a backwoods ring. Of course, even
the immanent method is eventually overtaken by this. It is dragged into

the abyss by its object. The materialistic transparency of culture has not made it more honest, only more vulgar. By relinquishing its own particularity, culture has also relinquished the salt of truth, which once consisted in its opposition to other particularities. To call it to account before a responsibility it denies is only to confirm cultural pomposity. Neutralized and ready-made, traditional culture has become worthless today. Through an irrevocable process its heritage, hypocritically reclaimed by the Russians, has become expendable to the highest degree, superfluous, trash. And the hucksters of mass culture can point to it with a grin, for they treat it as such. The more total society becomes, the greater the reification of the mind and the more paradoxical its effort to escape reification on its own. Even the most extreme consciousness of doom threatens to degenerate into idle chatter. Cultural criticism finds itself faced with the final stage of the dialectic of culture and barbarism. To write poetry after Auschwitz is barbaric. And this corrodes even the knowledge of why it has become impossible to write poetry today. Absolute reification, which presupposed intellectual progress as one of its elements, is now preparing to absorb the mind entirely. Critical intelligence cannot be equal to this challenge as long as it confines itself to self-satisfied contemplation.

(written in 1949; first published in 1951; GS 10.1: 11–30)
Translated by Samuel Weber and Shierry Weber Nicholsen

8

The Jargon of Authenticity

In the early 1920s, a number of people interested in philosophy, sociology, and theology planned a meeting. The majority of them had changed from one faith to another. What they had in common was an emphasis on their recent acquisition of their religion, not the religion itself. They were all dissatisfied with the idealism that held sway in universities at the time. Philosophy led them, from motives of freedom and autonomy, to choose what Kierkegaard had called positive theology. Consciously or not, they were less concerned about specific dogmas, the truth content of revelation, than about a wholesome effect, the appeasement of spiritual and very real anguish that they hoped would result from their resolve.

A friend who was attracted by this group at the time was slightly offended that he had not been invited. He was, they hinted to him, not authentic enough for the task. True enough, impressed by Kierkegaard's *Concluding Unscientific Postscript*, he was working on an existentialist philosophy with a theological flavor, but he remained mindful of the boundary between philosophy and religion. He hesitated to make the leap, suspecting that a religion conjured up out of autonomous thinking would thereby subordinate itself to such thinking, and would thus nullify itself as the absolute that it aspired to be. He described his attitude as that of a person in a state of waiting. In the circle of which I have been speaking, that was enough to disqualify him. A further factor was their aversion to critical thinking and to an element of nonconformity, of a failure to fit promptly into a social role.

The mood of the gathering was presumably festive. In this respect, modern celebrations resemble archaic ones in the sense that they are only really enjoyable for the participants if someone has been excluded, a wicked fairy or a black man. The assembled company consisted of anti-intellectual intellectuals. They confirmed their higher mutual understanding by excluding as a negative influence someone who had not made the same positive commitments as they professed to one another. What they defended intellectually, they chalked up to their own ethos, just as if the Gospels contained nothing about the Pharisees.

Even forty years later, a retired bishop could walk out of the conference of a Protestant academy because an invited speaker questioned the possibility of sacred music today. He, too, felt he had been given a dispensation about, or had been warned against, dealing with people who do not toe the line, as if such independent thought were a subjective fault, not something with an objective explanation. People of this type combine the tendency to put themselves in the right, as Rudolf Borchardt put it, with the fear of exposing their ideas to criticism, as if they were not entirely convinced by them themselves. Now as then, they sense the danger that what they call the concrete might easily be swallowed up by the abstraction they find so suspect and that cannot be eradicated from the medium of thought, of concept. They imagine that concreteness is vouchsafed by sacrifice, starting with that of their own intellect. Heretics dubbed them the Authentics.

This was long before the appearance of *Being and Time*. Heidegger introduced "authenticity" *tout court* into philosophy as a term in the context of an existential ontology. In the same way, he energetically poured ideas into philosophy that the Authentics had agitated for less theoretically, and so won over people whose aspirations were rather vaguer. Thanks to him, it became possible to dispense with the demands of religion. Heidegger's book acquired its aura because it presented the goals toward which the German intelligentsia was obscurely striving before 1933 in terms that were phenomenologically illuminating and solidly authoritative. Despite this, his writing and that of all those who followed him still contains a faint theological echo to this day. For the theological velleities of those years trickled into his language and spread far beyond the circle of literati who postured as an elite at the time.

Gradually, of course, the consecrated feel of the language of authenticity came to apply to the cult of authenticity rather than to Christianity, even where it resembled Christianity, owing to the temporary lack of another available authority. Disregarding its specific contents, this language shaped its ideas to fit an authoritarian potential even where it imagined itself to be resisting authoritarianism. Fascism was not simply the conspiracy that it was; it was also the manifestation of a powerful social trend. Language gave it asylum; in language the simmering catastrophe found expression as if it were salvation.

In Germany the jargon of authenticity is a spoken and, even more, a written language. It is the trademark of a socialized exclusiveness, at once aristocratic and homely. It extends from philosophy and theology via educational theory, adult education, and youth organizations down to the elevated diction of senior figures in commerce and the civil service. While the jargon overflows with its pretensions to profound human experience, it has become as standardized as the world it officially negates. This is partly because of its mass reception and partly because it asserts its message automatically by virtue of its pure nature, and this cuts it off from the experience that ought to animate it. The jargon comprises a modest vocabulary and an equally modest set of guiding signals. Authenticity itself is not foremost among them; it serves rather to illuminate the ether in which the jargon thrives, as well as the conviction that feeds it. As examples we might start by mentioning "existential," "at the point of decision," "task," "appeal," "encounter," "genuine dialogue," "concern," and "commitment."

A number of nonjargon terms with a similar tone could be added to the list. Some, like "concern" [*Anliegen*], can be found in the Grimms' *German Dictionary* and could still be used innocently even by Walter Benjamin. It acquired its present connotations only after coming within this field of tension—"field of tension," too, is part of the relevant language. Our purpose here is not to set up an *Index verborum prohibitorum* of fashionable noble nouns but to examine their function in the jargon. Independently of their context and their content, they sound as if they expressed something more exalted than their meaning. It is hardly a coincidence that Walter Benjamin should have introduced the term "aura" at the very moment when, according to his own theory, what he meant by it was in the process of dissolving.[a] Sacred, but without religious content,

---

[a] See Walter Benjamin, "The Work of Art in the Age of Mechanical Repro-

the keywords of the jargon of authenticity are the products of the disintegration of aura.

This goes hand in hand with a vagueness that puts them at the disposal of any number of meanings in the disenchanted world. The jargon's constant invective against reification is itself reified. It fits Richard Wagner's definition of bad art as effects without cause. Where the Holy Spirit runs out, people speak with mechanical tongues. The hinted-at but absent secret is public. Whoever does not possess it has only to speak as if he does and everyone else doesn't. The expressionist slogan "Every human being is one of the Chosen," which occurs in a play by Paul Kornfeld, a dramatist who was murdered by the Nazis, can be used, once the fake Dostoyevsky has been subtracted, to inflate the ideological self-esteem of a petite bourgeoisie that is threatened and humiliated by social changes. It deduces its own superiority from its failure to keep pace with developments, both actual and intellectual. It is a crying shame that Nietzsche did not live long enough to feel revulsion at the jargon of authenticity. For in the twentieth century he is the outstanding example of the phenomenon of German rancor.

Expressions and situations from an everyday world that has largely become obsolete constantly swell up as if they were empowered and guaranteed by an Absolute about which our sense of reverence prevents us from speaking. The concept of "task" [*Auftrag*] is prototypical. When people waffle on about the educational tasks of the German nation, this creates confusion between the legislative organs of the democratic state, whose institutions are supposed to instruct the people, and the remembered idea of a prophet who listens for the voice of God. While shrewder minds are chary of appealing to divine revelation, the speakers of the jargon in their search for power arrange for the ascension of the Word over the realm of the factual, the conditional, and questionable, by uttering it, even in print, as if it contained a direct blessing from on high. Ambiguity is the signature of a language whose favorite philosophy has listed ambiguity in its catalogue of vices.[b] General philosophical concepts and ideas, such as those of Being, are so forcefully irradiated by the jargon that their conceptual nature, their mediation by the thinking subject, dissolves beneath the glare:

---

duction," in his *Illuminations*, ed. Hannah Arendt, trans. Harry Zohn (London: Jonathan Cape, 1970), pp. 222ff.

   [b] See Martin Heidegger, *Being and Time*, trans. John Macquarrie and Edward Robinson (Oxford: Blackwell, 1985), pp. 217–19.

they then entice us as if they were concrete beings. Transcendence and concreteness become shimmering realities; away with a thinker who wished to make distinctions.

But the untruth can be recognized by its bloated nature. One man wrote after a long absence that he was now existentially secure; it required some reflection to realize that this meant he had no real financial worries. A center planned for international discussions—whatever they may turn out to be good for—was given the name of House of Encounters. The visible house, solidly built on firm foundations, becomes a holy place by virtue of the encounters, which are supposed to be superior to discussions because they take place between existing, living human beings who, after all, could just as well have discussions. Such oscillations produce a permanent tremolo. The jargon is the Wurlitzer organ of the spirit. It must have been used to write that sermon from Huxley's *Brave New World* that was recorded on tape and whose prefabricated emotion will bring the rebellious masses to heel, if indeed they can ever again manage to band together. By inserting it mechanically into the mechanically produced sound, the Wurlitzer organ humanizes the vibrato, which was once the medium of subjective expression, for advertising purposes.

In the same way, the jargon provides people with patterns for a humanity that unfree labor has driven out of them, if indeed traces of free labor have ever existed. Heidegger has established the principle of authenticity against the "they" [*man*] and "idle talk" [*Gerede*], without blinding himself (as we can see from a number of turns of phrase) to the fact that there is no complete gulf between what he treats as two existential types, indeed that their own dynamic leads them to merge. But he did not foresee that what he called authenticity, once it had become a term, would gradually acquire the same anonymity of the exchange society against which *Being and Time* had protested in its unsociological way. For allowing itself to be used in this way, the jargon is rewarded by a nudging and winking smile of complicity that might well figure in Heidegger's own phenomenology of idle talk. The jargon confirms the adepts in their belief that they possess an exalted, nontrivial sensibility while pacifying the constantly festering suspicion of rootlessness.

In professional groups engaged in what is called intellectual work, but whose members are also employed, dependent, and economically weak, the jargon is endemic, a survival of the age of handicraft. Such groups possess a specific function in addition to the general social one. In many respects their education and their consciousness lag behind the spirit with which they are actively occupied in accordance with the social division of labor. They would like to use the jargon in order to bridge the gap; their members would like to present themselves both as the possessors of a really classy culture—even the shabby old jargon sounds modern to them—and also as unique individuals: the more innocent ones among them are probably not ashamed to call it the personal touch. The stereotypes of the jargon are also fantasies of subjective activity. They appear to guarantee that you are not doing what in fact you are doing when you use the jargon, namely, bleating along with the crowd. After all, this is supposed to be something you have achieved on your own, as a distinctive, free person.

The formal affectation of autonomy replaces its content. Pompously labeled "commitment," such content is borrowed from elsewhere. What pseudo-individuality provides in the culture industry, the jargon provides for those who despise the culture industry. The jargon is the German symptom of progressive semiliteracy; it is attractive to people who feel doomed by history, or at least on the way down, but who wish to present themselves to their equals and themselves as an inner elite: a language of those at the bottom as a language of those on top. Implicitly, a guarantee of reliability is being issued on behalf of the universal through a particularity stamped by the universal; the regulation fastidious tone seems to be the voice of the universal itself. The most important benefit is that of a character reference. Regardless of what it says, the voice that resonates in this way signs onto a social contract; reverence for a status quo that seems a priori to be more than it is puts an end to all insubordination. The pure tone drips with positive affirmation, without ever condescending to put in a plea for the existing order of things. It even escapes the suspicion of ideology, which has long since been socialized. What is successfully rescued is the dichotomy between the subversive and the constructive that fascism used to stifle critical ideas. Simply being there is enough to guarantee the merit of a thing; it is protected by the double sense of "positive," meaning on the one hand given, existing, and on the other hand worthy of approval. Positive and negative are objectified prior to all living experience, as if they were qualities in themselves, not determined as positive or negative by thought, and as if the path to such a definition were not itself that of permanent negation.

Meanwhile, in the higher echelons of the hierarchy of authenticity, negativities are freely distributed. Heidegger monopolizes the taboo concept of destruction and the black concepts of anxiety, care, and death, while, for his part, Jaspers occasionally annexes the opposite of security: "Today, philosophy is the only possibility for the consciously insecure."[c] But in the end, it is the positive that leaps out at us. The entire panoply of horror—endangerment, risk, putting oneself on the line—does not amount to very much. Even one of the original Authentic women once spoke about how the light of redemption shone at the heart of the Dostoyevskian hell, only to receive the reply that, if that were so, hell was like a short railway tunnel. With even more important Authentics, praise is even scarcer than it is with the parson. They would prefer to reap the harvest from a scorched earth. They faithfully exploit a phenomenon observed by social psychologists, but with the opposite intention. This is the discovery that negative judgments, regardless of their content, have a greater chance of acceptance than positive ones.[d] Brow-furrowing thought descends to farce, to an egregious begging the question; this is why the cleverest among them defend the vicious circle. Questions, a key prop of the jargon, must needs constantly emphasize their radicality because they are adapted to answers that block the possibility of anything too radical. Here is a paradigmatic example from Jaspers:

Existential philosophy would be lost were it to claim once again that it knows what man is. It would again give us blueprints with which to study the varieties of human and animal life; it would again become anthropology, psychology, and sociology. Its meaning is possible only if it remains groundless in its concreteness. This philosophy awakens what it does not know; it enlightens and moves, but it does not pin down. For the man who is under way it is the expression that enables him to steer his course, the means by which he preserves his highest moments so that he can make them reality through his life. . . . Because it remains without an object, insight into existence leads to no conclusion.[e]

[c] Karl Jaspers, *Die geistige Situation der Zeit* (1931), 5th ed. (Berlin: W. de Gruyter, 1947), p. 128.

[d] See *Gruppenexperiment: Ein Studienbericht*, revised by Friedrich Pollock, vol. 2 of *Frankfurter Beiträge zur Soziologie*, commissioned by the Institute for Social Research [Institut für Sozialforschung], ed. Theodor W. Adorno and Walter Dirks (Frankfurt am Main: Europäische Verlagsanstalt, 1955), pp. 482ff.

[e] Jaspers, *Die geistige Situation der Zeit*, pp. 146–47.

The grandiose question "All or nothing?," which could reject any answer as reification, is vacuous. It is suited at best to a witch-hunt for the inauthentic; apart from that, it is good only for enabling us to avoid making a firm statement of any kind out of sheer seriousness and to hold ourselves cautiously at the ready. The old Protestant motif of an absurd faith had been tied to the decision of the individual subject and handed down from Lessing to Kierkegaard in the shape of the pathos of existence, in opposition to any fixed conclusions alien to the subject. Here, it allies itself strategically with a critique of the positive sciences, sciences from which, as Kierkegaard had asserted, the subject has been excluded. The radical question is given substance at the expense of any answer and is thus protected against any unpleasantness. In the jargon there is only a difference of expertise, not an essential distinction between being secure and being insecure: even the insecure are safe, as long as they have joined the chorus. This makes possible such pieces of writing as this one from Hans Schwitzke's "Three Fundamental Theses on Television":

The situation with sermons is quite different. Here a pastor confessed his faith in an existential manner for over ten minutes in a single, unchanging close-up. And because of the high degree of human conviction that he radiated, his testimony, backed up as it was by his image on the screen, not only was completely credible, but made the observer forget utterly the mediating apparatus. In front of the television screen, as if in a church, a kind of congregation came into being among the chance viewers who directly faced the speaker and felt that he had established a connection between them and the object of his sermon, the word of God. There can be no explanation for this surprising process, other than that everything depends upon the man who speaks, the man who has courage and significance enough to throw himself into the breach with his entire substance and existence in the exclusive service of the cause to which he bears witness and the viewers with whom he feels a bond.[f]

This is a media commercial for authenticity. The preacher's "word"—as if his words and God's were one and the same—is by no means "backed up by his image on the screen." At best, depending on the credibility of his speech, we may wish to credit him with being trustworthy. If his presence on the screen makes us forget the mediating apparatus,

[f] Heinz Schwitzke, "Drei Grundthesen zum Fernsehen," *Rundfunk und Fernsehen*, 1953, no. 2, pp. 11–12.

the jargon of authenticity, which rejoices at this, commits itself to a philosophy of "as if": by a process of staging, the here and now of a cult ritual is simulated, a ritual that is annulled by its universal presence on television. However, nothing can be imagined of the existential mode in which the preacher makes his confession of faith "in a single, unchanging close-up," except for the obvious fact that the preacher has no choice but to be projected onto the screen as an empirical person and may perhaps seem likeable to some of his viewers, although the claim that he has formed a congregation cannot be demonstrated. From the sphere of "risk" he has imported the turn of phrase "he has thrown himself into the breach with his entire substance and existence." But the preacher who explains on television why the church has become too narrow for him does so without the slightest risk to himself, whether of contradiction by others or of inner struggle. If he were forced to experience moments of temptation while trapped between floodlights and microphone, the jargon would have been ready and waiting with additional praise for his existentiality.

The benefit of the negative is transferred to the positive, in parodic reversal of the Hegelian dialectic; positive negativity is made to warm the heart. In accordance with the code of the jargon, the negative words confess their secret positive nature. The metaphysical need that is supposed to inspire the terrifying words, particularly about the "nothing," creates what it desires by virtue of its own emphatic utterance. The ominous words are numinous, as are the whitewashed words of the man who feels secure on Sundays; they lie as close to the positive as the menacing Last Trump has always been. The jargon exploits the ambiguity of the term "metaphysics" as it wishes, switching at will between Being and Nothing. It may mean the preoccupation with metaphysical themes, even when the metaphysical substance is disputed. Or it may mean the affirmative doctrine of the transcendent world on the Platonic model.

In such a practice, metaphysical need, the state of mind that appeared early on in Novalis's essay *Christendom or Europe* and that the young Lukács called transcendental homelessness, has been flattened out into a standard item of general culture. Ever since Kierkegaard, the theological emancipation of the numinous from a sclerotic dogma has formed part of an worldly secularization. The insatiable demythologization of the divine whose echo we constantly hear in the tremulous tones of deeply troubled questioning chains the divine in mystical heresy to anyone who relates to it. Substance is supposed to exist only in the relationship whose opposite pole is "the absolutely different" and that therefore eludes all definition, which it stigmatizes as reification. Because of this, an inflated transcendence is humanized still further. A complete demythologization reduces transcendence to an abstraction, a concept, and subjectivizes it without restraint. Enlightenment triumphs within obscurantism, against its will and notwithstanding its attacks. Nevertheless, unbeknownst to itself, the sovereign power of the subject once again conjures up myth in all dialectical theology: its highest achievement is blind. In such contradictions the Authentics sheepishly celebrate commitments, instead of plunging into speculation, which alone might justify commitments in the eyes of radical doubters. Their relation to speculation is ambivalent; they would like best of all to reserve it for gurus. Yet others preach the absence of a reliable ground for philosophy in order to provide a better contrast to the possibilities of rescue that are supposed to emerge in extreme, albeit imaginary, dangers. They come up against ungrounded thought as soon as that thinking refuses, through its attitude, to sanction a priori commitments that are as unavoidable as the happy end in a film. If the happy end fails to appear, then even the existentialists will give existentialism a hard time:

Only against this background can we begin to perceive the whole greatness of existential ethics. It once again establishes a resolute ethical position on the foundations of modern historical relativism. But this opens the door to the risk inherent in an existential adventurism. Completely unconstrained by any particular commitment and without the constancy that derives from loyalty to a cause, the adventurer can enjoy the daring of his engagement as a last, sublime pleasure. The existentialist is especially exposed to the temptation of inconstancy and disloyalty because of the unconditional nature of any given momentary engagement.[g]

The metaphysical need that the jargon pushes to the fore has a worldly aspect. But the jargon promptly denies it by spiritualizing it. The more assiduously it celebrates its everyday experience, in implicit mockery of Kierkegaard's wish to unify the sublime and the mundane, the more it muddies the categories and the more the everyday becomes the groundless guarantee of one's own transcendence, while transcendence becomes the deceptive closeness of the here and now:

[g] Otto Friedrich Bollnow, *Die Neue Geborgenheit* (Stuttgart: W. Kohlhammer, 1956), pp. 37–38.

Heidegger's concluding remarks, in which he comments on the "housing shortage" as one of the great problems of our time, point to the fundamental importance of a dwelling for the whole of human existence: "The real problem of dwelling," he says here, "lies not simply in the shortage of dwellings, although this problem really is not one to be lightly dismissed"; but behind this problem, there is another, deeper problem: this is that man has lost his essence and hence cannot find peace. "The real problem of dwelling lies in the fact that mortal men . . . still have to learn what dwelling is." But to learn what dwelling is means to understand the necessity of getting a place of shelter in the face of danger, and of settling down in it with peace of mind. But the converse is also true: the possibility of settling down is connected in a menacing way with the availability of a dwelling.[h]

The safe space of shelter is simply inferred from the necessity that man should "get" a dwelling for himself. The linguistic lapse, arising from the unresisted babble of the jargon, swiftly eradicates everything for which the jargon was first devised. It shudders complacently at the prospect of homelessness. But the game with the housing shortage is more serious than the pose of existential seriousness: it is the lurking fear of unemployment, even in periods of glorious full employment, which is endemic in all members of the advanced capitalist nations. This fear is resisted by administrative means and is therefore projected onto the Platonic starry firmament. Everyone knows in his heart of hearts that, given the present stage of technological development, the work he does is expendable, so that he feels that his wages are a form of unemployment benefit in disguise, something arbitrarily diverted from the gross domestic product in order to maintain existing relations of production, and capable of being revoked at any time. Whoever is not provided with ration cards can in principle be deported tomorrow; the dictatorships have already set the migration of nations in motion once, right up to Auschwitz. This can be continued. There is no need to affix an existential label to the anxiety that the jargon distinguishes so punctiliously from worldly, empirical fear. Its primary meaning is that everyone who is caught up in the socialized but antagonistic society constantly feels threatened by it, even though it sustains him, without being able to specify in concrete instances the source of this global threat.

In the new security, however, the declassed individual who knows how far he can go can cheekily cock a snook at society. On the one hand, he has nothing to lose; on the other, the administered world still preserves

[h] Ibid., p. 170.

the compromises of bourgeois society in the sense that, in its own interest, it shrinks from extreme measures, from the liquidation of its own members, and for the time being it still has palliatives at its disposal in the grand plan of the economy. We may suspect that if we look at the social basis of the jargon's reinterpretation of complete negativity into the positive, what we shall find is the blackmailing self-confidence of the fear-driven consciousness. Even the cheap, automated suffering produced by the loss of meaning is not simply the suffering caused by the vacuum that allegedly arose from the general movement of the Enlightenment, although precisely that was the diagnosis of the more ambitious obscurantists. After all, *taedium vitae* has been reported from periods when the state religion was quite unquestioned. It was as familiar to the Church Fathers as to those moderns who parrot Nietzsche's judgment on modern nihilism while deluding themselves that this enables them to leave both Nietzsche and nihilism behind them, a Nietzschean nihilism that they have turned on its head.

In social terms, the feeling of meaninglessness is a reaction to the far-reaching dispensation from work within the framework of an enduring absence of social freedom. The free time of individuals denies them the freedom they had secretly hoped for, and chains them to eternal sameness, to the machinery of production—even where it releases them. It is with this eternal sameness that they must compare the apparent possibility of freedom, and they become the more confused, the less the closed facade of consciousness that is based on that of society allows the conception of freedom to peek through. The anthropological condition of so-called human emptiness, which the Authentics claim is unalterable, could be changed, the desire for fulfilment could be granted, as soon as it was no longer denied. Not, of course, just by the injection of a spiritual meaning or a mere verbal substitute. The constitution of society trains people essentially to reproduce themselves, and the implicit compulsion to do so is extended into their souls as soon as it loses its external power. By virtue of a self-preservation that has been inflated into a totality, what you already are becomes the goal for which you strive. If the grip of a tautological life were to be loosened, then the zealously proclaimed nullity of the subject might dissolve, too, that shadow of a condition in which everyone is literally his own best friend.

In the assertion of meaning at any price, an assertion that pays no heed to Hegel's insight into the impossibility of restoring meaning to anything consumed by the reflective consciousness, the old antisophistical bias becomes pervasive in so-called mass society. In the jargon, it hastens to use thought to denounce thought, the accusation Nietzsche leveled at Kant, who had spoken of "quibbling" [*Vernünfteln*] with the same overtone of authoritarian contempt as Hegel used in speaking of "reasoning." The form assumed for well over a generation now by this emotion is the accusation of the lack of a firm foundation. Its demagoguery profits from the venerable ambiguity of hostility to sophistry. Consciousness is false if it thinks itself superior to a thing and judges it externally, without, as Hegel said, being a part of it. And shameful as it is for such consciousness to ridicule the idea of truth it insists on, it is no less shameful for it to descend into ideology the moment it puffs itself up and proclaims that thought must have a firm foundation.

The Hegelian dialectic had refuted every philosophy based on an oracular first pronouncement, but as an absolute idealism it was unable to shake off the terrorism of a philosophy of origins: the dogma that an idea can be legitimated only if it is based on an absolute first thing, a premise beyond all doubt. The jargon of authenticity becomes all the more terroristic the less it says about its own first principle on the understanding that it is self-evident. The regression of a resurrected metaphysics to a predialectical stage is transfigured by the jargon into the road back to the primal truth. The hostility to sophistry in the final stage of a reconstructed mythology is an ossified philosophy of origins. The Authentics denounce sophistry instead of showing that they are equal to its challenge, but their own projects perpetuate its arbitrary nature. They communicate with sophistry by proclaiming their favorite thesis that everything depends on man, the unctuously revived assertion that man is the measure of all things, an assertion they have adapted for their own purposes.

The social model of its chosen bogeyman is comparable to the freedom of domicile in an earlier age, which once helped thought achieve its emancipation. Only now, in a bourgeois society permeated by reason, the mobility of people and ideas represents less of a threat to settled groups of people, who are in any case scarcely to be found anymore in the advanced industrial societies. Instead, such mobility challenges the continuing irrationality of the total system. For this reason the jargon is compelled to assume the existence of transitory social forms, and must defend as substantial forms that no longer exist. If it wished to mount the barricades for the existing social order, a society based on exchange, it would have to come out in support not just of an obvious evil but also of its underlying principle, which could revoke it, namely, the rationality that it both promises and disappoints. Rationality in its bourgeois form has always called for an element of the irrational in order to maintain itself as what it is: an enduring injustice through justice. Such irrationality in the midst of the rational is the working climate of authenticity.

This can mean that, in the present unjust system, a literal and metaphorical mobility always turns into an injustice for those who cannot quite keep up with developments. They experience social progress as an act of violence; their suffering at its hands is the breeding ground of both authenticity and its jargon. The latter deflects suffering from its object, the specific constitution of society. For the designated victims of this rhetoric of antisophistry are themselves condemned, and have been ever since the sphere of circulation was integrated into the sphere of production. It is only because of this that the jargon has such success with its efforts to convert the native's fear of the migrant, the mute person's fear of the man who can speak out, into something like a metaphysical or moral judgment: because it has already been uttered in real terms, because the gesture of the genuinely rooted coincides with that of the historical victors. This is the substance of authenticity, the sacred source of its strength. Taciturnity and silence are such an effective counterpoint to existential and existentialist claptrap because order itself resorts to speechlessness of both sign and command. The jargon fills the vacuum created by the socially necessary disintegration of language. In the face of a dawning social entropy, a reflection of the human falls on the officiously persuasive rhetoric of the recent past. If philosophy were to recuperate the genuine experiences that have assumed such distorted shape in the jargon and return them from the distilled essences and possibilities of Being to the society from which they had originated (supposing that the word "origin" means anything at all), then philosophy would be able to overcome the duality of mobility and rootedness, of ungrounded reason and authenticity. It would recognize that both are but aspects of the same guilt-laden totality, in which businessmen and heroes are complementary halves. Liberalism gave birth to the culture industry, whose forms are such a source of indignation to the jargon of authenticity, even though it is one of them. That same liberalism was a forerunner of fascism, which then destroyed it and its clientele. Of course, the bloodguilt that can be heard to echo in the jargon is incomparably greater than the stratagems of liberal mobility, whose principle is incompatible with that of direct violence.

The allegedly unspoiled world is posited as the antithesis to the damaged world with its socialized consciousness, the "malaise" on which the jargon feeds. Through its linguistic form, remote from all social considerations, the unspoiled world is equated with agrarian conditions or at least a simple barter economy, the phantasm of an undivided community, closed and protective, a world that moves in a steady rhythm and unbroken continuity. This conception is the residue of romanticism, but is transferred without ado into the modern conditions that it contradicts. Hence the categories of the jargon are mobilized as though they had not sprung from historical and ephemeral social conditions but belonged directly to human beings as their inalienable possibility.

"Man" is the ideology of dehumanization. Conclusions are drawn from categories that remind us of more or less organic social conditions in which the institutions of exchange do not yet have complete power over relations between human beings. For these categories, it is inferred that their underlying essence, man, is himself nature and can be immediately made real in contemporary human beings. Past forms of socialization, from before the division of labor, are surreptitiously elided into the eternal forms of eternal human beings. Their reflection falls upon conditions that have already fallen victim to a progressive rationalization and that, when compared to those rationalized conditions, appear more human.

What lesser Authentics are pleased to call the image of man they situate in a zone in which it is no longer permissible to inquire how those conditions came into being; what sufferings were inflicted on the subjugated with the shift to permanent settlement; and whether the undivided state, unenlightened and coercive at the same time, had prepared and deserved its own demise.

The talk of man was popular not just in an old-fashioned way, in the spirit of half-timbered houses and gabled roofs, but also in the more fashionable manner of a radicalism that strips away superfluous epiphenomena and concerns itself with the underlying naked creature concealed beneath all cultural disguises. But because it is concerned with man and not the conditions that man has created and that have hardened in opposition to them, we are released from criticizing them, as if criticism were altogether too shallow.

The theme of Kant's *Ideas on a Universal History from a Cosmopolitan Point of View* was that a condition worthy of human beings could be created not from a pure idea but only through antagonism, from its own force. This idea is now completely suppressed. Even the meaning of the word "man" has undergone significant historical changes. In the expressionist literature of the time of the First World War, it could still be defined by the protest against the flagrant inhumanity that invented the notion of human material together with the battle of matériel.

The ancient reification of bourgeois society, which comes into its own at great moments of history when it becomes human mobilization, becomes palpable at such times and, polemically, even turns into its own counterconcept. The sentence "Man is good" was false, but at least needed no metaphysical or anthropological sauce. After all, even the expressionist "O Man," which had been a manifesto against everything merely made by man and was usurped, tended to ignore human violence, and with that it risked becoming tainted by what it opposed. This could be shown in the writings of Franz Werfel. The image of man implied in the jargon, however, is the sellout of that "O Man" and the negative truth about it.

To convey an idea of the change in the function of the word "man," it is sufficient to consider two similar titles. Around the time of the German November revolution in 1918, a book appeared by the pacifist Ludwig Rubiner, with the title *Man in the Middle*; in the 1950s a book was published with the title *Man in the Middle of Business Operations*. Thanks to its abstract nature, the concept of man can be squirted like lubricating oil into the very machinery that it once denounced, and its passion, which has long since dissipated, becomes part of the ideology that insists that the business operation is there for the sake of the human beings who are in reality its appendages. What is meant is that the organization of labor has to look after the workers so that its productivity will increase.

However, like Elsie, the contented cow in the American advertisement, the cliché about man that we are encouraged to cultivate would hardly be so seductive unless it were based on a valid perception: namely, the realization that in the final analysis the overpowering conditions of society really have been created by men and can therefore be abolished by them. This overpowering strength, like that of myth, has something fetishistic and illusory about it. But even though there is something illusory about the appearance of institutions—they reflect the ossified relations between men—this appearance has real power over men, and that explains why the appeal to inalienable and in fact long since alienated human essences is a downright lie. It is not "man" who created the institutions but particular men in particular configurations with nature and with one another. This imposed institutions upon men just as men erected institutions, namely, without consciousness. All of this was incisively formulated in the run-up to the revolutions of 1848, particularly in Marx's critique of Feuerbach's anthropology and the Young Hegelians. In the realm of the jargon this has been studiously forgotten, possibly because the Authentics are proud of their ignorance of historical continuity, as if such ignorance were itself proof of human immediacy.

The *vox angelica* with which the jargon of authenticity intones the word "man" has its origin in the unnamed theological doctrine that man was made in the image of God. Hence the emotive force of the jargon-word "man." But it is also secular. Its specific cachet points back to a linguistic feature of *Jugendstil*[1] that the jargon was responsible for preparing for the mass market. The historical link connecting *Jugendstil* and the jargon was doubtless the Youth Movement. Prototypical was the title of a play by Gerhart Hauptmann: *Lonely People*. In one of her novels, Franziska von Reventlow satirized a professor from the bohemian circles in the Schwabing district of Munich around 1910, who described everyone whom he thought fit to join the fancy-dress festivities as "a miraculous person." A related phenomenon was the mannerism of actors during the early Reinhardt era, who were given to placing one hand on their heart and opening their eyes wide.

Once the original religious image has been shattered, the transcendence that in the great religions had been separated from the likeness by powerful taboos—"thou shalt not make unto thee a graven image"—is transferred to the likeness as a hidden quality. It is said to be miraculous because there are no more miracles. That is the mystery of every attempt to make authenticity concrete: the existing thing is erected as its own imago. There no longer is anything to which the miraculous human being, who is miraculous just because he is only a human being, must bow down. Even so, the jargon treats him with the reverence that man used to show to God.

The goal is an unquestioned humility without reference to an object. This is said to be human virtue as such. It always went well with the hubris of the sovereign subject. The fact that the object of humility was hidden encouraged the adherents of the jargon to hypostatize and reify it. That had always been implicit in the concept of reverence, even in Goethe. Jaspers celebrates it explicitly, independently of its object, and condemns its absence. He finds it easy to make the transition to hero worship:

Gazing at the historical examples of human greatness, the power of reverence holds fast to the measure of what man is and of what he is capable. Reverence does not allow the destruction of what it has seen. It remains true to whatever tradition was effective in its process of development; it grasps the origin of its substance in particular human beings in whose shadow reverence has become conscious; it preserves the past in the shape of a piety that never yields. Through memory, what has ceased to have reality in the world remains present, as an absolute claim.[i]

However, despite the cult of historical figures and of greatness as such, the word "man" no longer puts its trust in human dignity, as idealism did. As the relevant philosophers argue, the substance of man lies in his impotence and nullity, a condition to which in modern society he actually can be said to be coming closer and closer. Such a historical situation is projected onto the nature of man as such, and is thereby transfigured and immortalized simultaneously. Conversely, since man is sublime by virtue of his nothingness, the jargon robs him of all the features derived from the Enlightenment and also from German idealism that contained a criticism of the conditions in which his soul was denied its divine right. The jargon goes hand in hand with a conception of man from which every memory of natural rights has been expunged, even though man himself is elevated into something like a category of nature. Theology held out the hope of eternal life to a mankind caught up in the intolerable transience of a false and unfulfilled life. This vanishes in the celebration of transience as an absolute.

The gestural language of the jargon lays down that suffering, evil, and death are to be accepted, not changed. The public is to be trained in a difficult balancing act: they must understand their nothingness as a form of Being; avoidable or at least corrigible need must be revered as the essence of humanity; and because of man's innate fallibility, he must learn to respect authority as such. Although authority no longer ventures to claim that it has been sent by God, it retains all the insignia it once bor-

---

[i] Jaspers, *Die geistige Situation der Zeit*, p. 170.

rowed from God the father. But because it no longer has any legitimation beyond its mere existence, blind and opaque, it becomes radically evil.

This is what constitutes the affinity between the all-inclusive rhetoric of man and the totalitarian state. What the former shares with the latter is its way of leveling human subjects in the face of absolute force. Hjalmar Schacht once claimed that the Third Reich was the true democracy because it could produce such comfortable majorities that there was scarcely any need to falsify the voting figures. In this respect it is in tune with the worldview of the jargon, although for the time being, at least, the latter can boast a greater innocence.

By virtue of their share in the image of man, all men are equal in their impotence. To be human becomes the most general and empty form of privilege: it is strictly appropriate to a consciousness that no longer tolerates privilege yet remains completely under its spell. But such a universal humanity is itself ideology—the shameful caricature of the equality that is supposed to exist among everyone with a human face. It is ideology because it conceals the unmitigated differences of social power, the distinctions of hunger and abundance, of intellect and pliable idiocy. You hear people making an appeal with chaste emotion to the humanity in human beings, at no cost to the speakers. Whoever resists that appeal finds himself condemned as a monster by the guardians of the jargon, and can be thrown to its victims as a sop. He, and not those in power, is made out to be the arrogant enemy of the people who drags their human dignity in the mud.

(essay version, 1963; not in GS)
Translated by Rodney Livingstone

9

Crowds and Power

CONVERSATION WITH ELIAS CANETTI

ADORNO. I know that your views differ greatly from Freud's in many respects and that you are very critical of him. But on one point of method you undoubtedly do agree with him. This is on a matter that he often emphasized, particularly at a time when psychoanalysis was still in its formative stages and had not yet hardened. He claimed that his intention was not to repudiate or dispute the findings of other established sciences but merely to add something they had neglected. Admittedly, the reasons for the neglect of this additional element were, he believed, of great importance, and indeed they even held the key to human society, something that you also believe. You could best explain this, if you wished, by pointing to the crucial role played by death in your work, as indeed in many of what we might broadly call the anthropological works of our day. That is to say, you could use the complex of death—if I can use such a pompous expression to describe something so fundamental— to give our listeners an idea, a model, of what this neglected dimension actually is. You could explain to them what aspects of the experience of death you find so important, and so show them the usefulness of the method. This would enable your listeners to see not just that it becomes possible to discuss things that are otherwise ignored, but that there is something dangerous in regarding such matters as self-evident and that you would like to mitigate this danger by elevating it into consciousness in the spirit of Enlightenment.

CANETTI. I believe you are right to say that reflections on death play a great role in my study. To give an example of what you are saying, I could point to the question of survival, a question about which I do not think enough has been said. The moment in which one person survives another is very *concrete*, and I believe that the experience has very important consequences. I believe that this experience is obscured by convention, by the things we are *supposed* to feel when we witness the death of another human being. Hidden beneath these conventions there are certain feelings of satisfaction that can even extend to feelings of triumph—in battle, for example—and if such feelings occur frequently and accumulate, this can give rise to something quite dangerous. And this dangerous accumulation of experiences of other people's deaths is, I believe, one of the essential seeds of power. I give this example bluntly and without discussing it in further detail. You were really speaking about Freud, and I would be the first to admit that Freud's new way of tackling things and his refusal to allow himself to be deflected or deterred made a deep impression on me in my formative period. It is certainly true that I am no longer so persuaded of his conclusions today and that I disagree with a number of his special theories. But I still have nothing but the deepest respect for his way of tackling problems.

ADORNO. I set some store by the fact that the very place you have put your finger on is one where there is a powerful affinity between us. In *Dialectic of Enlightenment*, Horkheimer and I analyzed the problem of self-preservation, of a self-sustaining rationality, and in the process we made a similar discovery about the principle of self-preservation in its first, classical formulation in Spinoza's philosophy, a principle that you in your terminology call the motif of survival, the experience of surviving. We discovered that when self-preservation grows "wild," that is to say, when it loses its relationships with those around it, it turns into a destructive force and also always into a self-destructive force. You did not know what we had written, and we were ignorant of your writing on this topic. I believe that our agreement on this point is not a coincidence, but that it points to an objective reality that has sprung from the crisis of the contemporary situation, which turns out to be a crisis of this self-preservation, of an instinct for survival, gone wild. And this crisis has an immediate relevance today.

CANETTI. I am delighted to learn that your own thinking has led you in the same direction, and I believe that the argument is strengthened by the fact that we have reached the same conclusions independently.

ADORNO. I agree. Yet there is a problem of methodology that cannot really be ignored, particularly in this context, that is to say, our attempt to situate your thinking. What strikes the thinking reader of your book, and may even scandalize him, regardless of whether he calls himself a philosopher or a sociologist, is what I might call the subjectivity of your approach. By subjectivity, I do not mean the subjectivity of the ideas, of the author. On the contrary, the freedom of subjective thinking, that is to say, the idea that thinking should not be bound by the prevailing rules of a scientific discipline or respect the boundaries of the division of labor—that is something that I find very appealing. What I mean by subjectivity here is the idea of using as your starting point the subjects you propose to observe; in other words, your starting point is the different points of view. I am very conscious that the basic terms you use (and in this you are not so very far from Freud)—"crowds" and "power"—are terms that you ultimately derive from real conditions, that is, from real crowds and real power, in short, from the experience of real things. And in the last analysis, I would do much the same myself. Nevertheless, the reader of your book cannot quite rid himself of the feeling that as your book develops the imagined nature of these concepts or facts—the two seem to merge with each other—is more important than the concepts or facts themselves. An example is the concept of the invisible crowds, which plays a great part in your thinking. So I should like to put to you a really quite simple question, which will give our listeners a clearer impression of what is at stake. The question is: How do you assess the real significance of crowds and power, or the representatives of power, in relation to the pictures or, as the psychoanalysts would say, the imagoes of crowds and power with which you have been concerned?

CANETTI. I would like to step back a little in order to answer this question. (*Adorno.* I think that would be very helpful.) You mention my concept of the invisible crowds. Well, I should like to point out that the invisible crowds appear only in the short fourteenth chapter of the book, and are preceded by thirteen other chapters in which I discuss real crowds in great detail. My approach to the subject is, I believe, as real as real can be. I start with what I call the fear of being touched. I believe that individuals feel threatened by other people, and because of that they try to protect themselves from contact with the unfamiliar by creating a space around themselves and by striving to keep other people at a safe distance. Everyone knows that we all try to avoid jostling other people and do not like to be jostled. Despite all our precautionary measures people never entirely lose this fear of being touched. And now, it is a truly remarkable fact that human beings are able to lose themselves completely in a crowd. This is a really important paradox. A person loses his fear of being touched only when he finds himself packed in a crowd, when he is surrounded by other people so tightly that he doesn't know who is pushing him. At such a moment, he loses his fear of physical contact with other people. The fear of being touched turns into its opposite; and I believe that one of the reasons why people like to become part of a crowd, to join a crowd, is the relief they feel at this process of reversal. I think that this is a very real approach to the problem. It starts off from a concrete experience that everyone who has been in a crowd is familiar with. In the later chapters, I explore other aspects of real crowds. I talk about open and closed crowds. I emphasize that crowds always want to get bigger, and that this compulsion to grow is of crucial importance for it. I talk about the feeling of equality in the crowd and many other matters that I cannot go into here. Then, in chapter 14, I come to the concept of the invisible crowd, and perhaps I can say something briefly about that. It is very striking for anyone who has studied religions, especially primitive religions, how these religions are full of crowds that people cannot actually see. We need only think of the spirits that are so important in primitive religions. There are countless instances that show that people genuinely believe that the air is full of these spirits, that these spirits manifest themselves in massive quantities—and that this even enters our universal religion. We know the role played in Christianity by the idea of the devil, the idea of angels. In the Middle Ages there was much evidence to prove this. Sightings of devils were reported on a massive scale. Richalm, a medieval Cistercian abbot, said that when he closed his eyes, he felt devils surrounding him like a coat of dust. Now, these invisible crowds play a major role in the different religions and in the minds of believers. Nevertheless, I would not call them unreal, since people believe in these spirits and so for them they are real. And in order to understand that, we need only remind ourselves that such invisible crowds also exist in our own day. We no longer call them devils, but they are perhaps just as dangerous, just as aggressive, and we fear them just as much. We all believe in bacteria. Very few people have actually peered into a microscope and seen them, but all of us believe we are at risk from millions of bacteria that are always present, that can turn up anywhere, and this idea is very prevalent.

So much for the invisible crowds that in a sense I would describe as real, and I believe, Mr. Adorno, that in this instance we can speak of the invisible crowds having a kind of reality.

ADORNO. Yes, and if I might reply to that right away, I would ask you to forgive my epistemologist's pedantry. In the first place, there is a difference between the primitive mind, which does not make such a sharp distinction between imagination and reality, and the developed Western mind, which is actually based on that distinction. Merely because archaic thought, primitive thought, does not distinguish between the imagining of genies or whatever spirits are involved, and their actual existence, this does not mean that they have objectively become more real. We cannot escape our own nature, and this tells us that the world is not populated with spirits. In this sense, what you have just said confirms me in my view that in your thinking there is a certain predominance of the imagination, of whatever has been transposed into the world of ideas, over the drastically immediate reality. For I do not believe—and it is perhaps not unimportant for you to clarify your intentions in this regard—that you would defend the kind of view to be found, on the one hand, in Ludwig Klages and, at the opposite end of the spectrum, in Oskar Goldberg, that these pictures, these imagoes, are collective beings with the kind of immediate reality comparable to the reality of the masses in modern mass society.

CANETTI. No, I would certainly not claim that. Nevertheless, this led me to posit a concept that appears to me to be important: this is the concept of crowd symbols. And I would like to say something about them. By crowd symbols I understand collective entities that do not consist of human beings but are nevertheless felt to be crowdlike. Among these entities I would include ideas such as fire, the sea, the forest, grain, treasure, and heaps of different sorts: heaps of harvested crops, for example. Now these entities undoubtedly exist, but they function as mass symbols in the minds of individuals. It would be necessary to look at these symbols individually to explain why they have this function and what their meanings are. To give a practical example, perhaps I should say that these mass symbols were of decisive importance for the formation of national consciousness. (*Adorno.* Absolutely.) When people think of themselves as belonging to a nation at moments of national crisis, let us say at moments of national turmoil such as the outbreak of war, when they think of themselves as Englishmen or Frenchmen or Germans, what they have in mind is a crowd or a crowd symbol, something that they can relate to themselves. This something exercises an extraordinary power in their minds and has important implications for their actions. I think you would agree with me that the power of such mass symbols on the individual mind is indisputable.

ADORNO. I would agree absolutely. I believe, for example, that you really hit upon something very important with your idea of the forest as an imago, as a crowd symbol. I think these things are highly productive. I think that these categories really advance our ideas considerably, particularly when they are compared with the rather sketchy, archaic symbols that we encounter in Freud, or Jung's somewhat arbitrary archetypes. However, I may say that it is not for nothing that you have assigned a central role to the concept of the symbol and that even after this explanation your interest is still focused essentially on categories that are already internalized and directed toward the imagination. Now, the question I should like to ask you is something quite simple and straightforward. It is the kind of question that suggests itself in the context of a psychoanalytically oriented social theory, too. The question is whether you believe that these symbols really are the key to the problems of contemporary society that are of primary importance to you as well as to me, or whether or not the actual, real masses, that is to say, the enormous pressure exerted on the political decision-making process by the sheer number of human beings has an even greater importance for modern society than these factors of the imagination, these sociopsychological issues to which you have drawn attention. And this remains true even though we must bear in mind that the organization of society potentially makes it both harder and easier to sustain their lives. I may perhaps simply point out in this connection that it has been shown that even movements like fascism and National Socialism, movements that seemed to be nothing more than extreme dictatorships, from which every democratic attention to the will of the people had been ruthlessly eliminated, still possessed, latently at least, what the sociologist Arkadi Gurland called an element of compromise. By that I mean that even in these forms of domination, which so tyrannized the masses, a certain concern for the real interests of the masses, for their real interests and existence, kept breaking through, however subterranean this aspect of the process may have been. And what I am concerned with here—and this is something that you could perhaps talk about—is this question. In your conception of society and the masses, what importance do you attach to this pressure, this living weight of the masses, in contrast to the entire realm of the symbolical?

CANETTI. Well, there of course I would say that the value, the importance of the real masses is incomparably greater. I would not hesitate for a moment; I would even go so far as to say that the dictatorships we have seen consist entirely of masses, and that without the growth of the masses—and this is especially important—without the conscious and artificial stimulation of larger and larger masses, the power of the dictatorships would be quite inconceivable. That is a fact that actually formed my starting point in this entire study. Any human being, any contemporary of the events of the last fifty years, ever since the outbreak of the First World War, that is to say, anyone who has witnessed wars, revolutions, the inflation, and then the fascist dictatorship, will surely feel the need under the impact of these things to come to grips with the question of the masses. I would really be very upset if anyone were misled into thinking that the reality of the masses is not the crucial thing for me, merely because I have also investigated other aspects of the subject in the course of a study lasting many years.

ADORNO. This seems to me to be of fundamental importance for the proper understanding of your intentions. If I can throw in another theoretical comment, it would be a kind of mediation—though not in the sense of a compromise, but rather in the sense in which the concept of mediation occurs in Hegel—if we were to assume that, as you have rightly seen, the categories of crowds and power are deeply intertwined and that the real pressure of actual crowds and power has grown to the point where it becomes infinitely difficult for the individual to resist or to assert himself as individual. And this mediating process has also increased the symbolic significance of these categories. To put it another way, in their inwardness, in their emotional life, people seem to revert to an archaic stage in which these internalized categories have acquired such a corporeal significance that they become fully identified with them. The only way for them to be able to acquiesce in their own disempowerment through these mutually complementary categories is for them to reinterpret them so as to make them seem meaningful, numinous, and perhaps even irrational and, for that reason, sacred. This, it seems to me, is the link between the growing symbolic significance of these things and their reality. There is just one qualification that I think it important to make. This is that the irrational symbolism that then recurs is not precisely what it was previously, thanks to this pressure, but has now become a sort of product of the actual situation in which human beings find themselves, and of the world of images to which they have recourse, or to which they regress. And it is my idea that the ominous and even catastrophic connotations that so easily attach themselves nowadays to such concepts as "leader" or "masses," particularly when they are associated with each other in a kind of short-circuiting process—that these connotations are present because we are not really dealing with the archaic societies in which they had some validity, but instead these archaic societies are somehow conjured up. And anything that is conjured up from the past, but has no contemporary truth, is transformed by its own untruth in the present into a kind of poisonous substance.

CANETTI. I think that this raises a number of points that I could respond to. I might even like to correct what you have said a little, if you have no objection. By and large I accept what you say. But perhaps I ought also to say that one of the essential points that keep cropping up when we think about the masses today is the fact of these archaic elements that are to be found in them. I do not know if you would agree with me that these elements are particularly important and that they merit special attention. It is not possible just to study the masses as they exist at present, even though there are a lot of them and they take many forms. I think it is important to trace them back to something that has existed for a long time, has appeared very often, and has assumed a variety of shapes.

ADORNO. I agree with you completely. It is precisely these archaic features that appear in mass formations that modern social psychology has repeatedly drawn attention to. The first to do so was Gustave Le Bon in his *The Crowd: A Study of the Popular Mind*[1] What Le Bon did was to give a purely descriptive account of the different aspects of these archaic, irrational modes of behavior of the masses. He then reduced them to the rather vague and problematic notion of suggestion. This was then followed by Freud in what, in my view at least, was a very important little essay, "Group Psychology and the Analysis of the Ego."[2] Freud attempted to underpin Le Bon's account of the masses—which he acknowledged—with a psychogenetic foundation. Since you have entered a debate with a very substantial tradition of social thought, I think it would be very helpful if you could explain to us the specific differences between your theories and those of Le Bon and Freud, and we might also mention the American sociologist William McDougall.

CANETTI.   To do that I would have to take a few steps back first and look at the question of what form the masses took in primitive societies, for it is quite obvious that since primitive societies contain only small numbers of people, they cannot lead to the mass formations that we know today.

ADORNO.   That is the very question that has been on my lips the entire time. Can we talk about masses in primitive societies where there are so terribly few people? It is very good that you have raised this question.

CANETTI.   In that case I think that I shall have to introduce a further concept. I have talked about the *pack*, and by "pack" I understand a small group of people in a particular state of excitement that is very similar to the state of excitement of our modern masses. The difference is that it is limited in size, whereas our masses can grow without limit. Packs appear in societies consisting of small groups—sometimes as few as ten, twenty, or thirty people who wander around, looking for food. The famous models for such small groups in the ethnographic literature are the hordes of the Australian aborigines. Now, it is very striking that in certain conditions such hordes, as they are called by the anthropologists, form small excited groups that have a definite goal and that pursue it with great energy and in a high state of excitement.

One type of horde, for example, is the hunting pack. Its target is a very large animal that cannot be killed by single individuals; several people have to come together to hunt such an animal. Or else a large number of animals have appeared. People want to hunt as many of them as possible at one time; they do not want them to escape; they might disappear again, or else a drought might occur, and there would be a shortage of animals. So people band together, and they hunt down this animal or these animals. The concept of the hunting pack is so self-evident that little needs be said about it.

The second kind of pack—and this is also obvious—is when one pack opposes another, and that brings us to the war pack. If two packs threaten each other, then you have something that, once it has expanded on a huge scale, is very familiar to us from the war. But this situation already exists in early societies when one pack fights another.

The third form, one that may be less obvious, is one that I have perhaps been the first to identify as the "lamenting pack." When a group consisting of a few people loses one of their number, the group tends to draw together in order to mark this death in one way or another. They will start by attempting to hold the dying man back, to keep him in the group. When he has died, they will turn to some rite or other that will detach him from the group, reconcile him to his fate, and prevent him from becoming a dangerous enemy to the group. There is a whole host of very important ceremonies, and there is scarcely a single nation on earth that does not possess one of them. All the phenomena that belong in this context are what I call lamenting packs.

We now come to the fourth kind of pack, and this may be the most interesting kind for us. The people who existed only in very small numbers wanted to grow more and more numerous. If there were more of them, they could hunt more. If there were more of them, they could survive better in a war against other groups of people who were attacking them. There is a whole host of rites and ceremonies concerned with population increase. By increase I mean increasing the number not just of people but also of the animals and the plants they live on. And everything connected with this I call the increase pack.

These four kinds of pack seem to me to be firmly established. I believe that there is much evidence of their existence, and it appears to me also that they continue to have an influence down to our own day, although it should be said that the first three forms are a kind of archaic survival. In our modern world the hunting pack has become a hysterical mob. We know of cases of lynchings when people suddenly attack someone . . . (*Adorno*. As in a pogrom!) That can be traced back to this early example of the hunting pack. We know about war; that is all too familiar to us. We also know about lamenting, and perhaps we know more than just the attenuated form of lamenting in which we find it today, namely, in the religions. Lamenting plays an enormous part in Christianity and in other religions. However, the increase pack has changed. Of course, it was entirely dependent upon the changes in the relations of production, and when we speak of the importance of the relations of production, we are thinking, or so I believe, primarily of things pertaining to the increase pack. So it is not simply an archaic form; it is something that has undergone qualitative changes. These changes are so extensive that in our society, where it manifests itself as production, it has changed beyond all recognition. I think it is important—and I do not know how far you would agree with me about this—to make a sharp distinction between the forms that are essentially archaic and those that have entered into our modern existence in such a way as to become a truly contemporary part of our lives.

ADORNO.   Perhaps I can start by attempting to cream off the essence of what you have been saying. It contains a very important truth. According to you, the concept of the masses is not, as is often thought nowadays, purely quantitative. By relating the concept of the masses to that of the pack, you define it in terms of a number of qualitative distinctions of the kind you have mentioned: hunting, war—which then appears as a more rational, more intensified, and more highly developed form of the hunt—lamenting, and what you call increase. I believe that these distinctions are important because they enable us to see how superficial the phrases are that we hear so much of today about the age of the masses. For people really behave as if this was purely a question of numbers, in the sense in which a poem by Stefan George contained the line "Your very number is a crime," whereas the crime is a matter not of numbers but of these qualitative factors that you have referred to. Now, of these categories of the pack the first three speak for themselves, although, as I am sure you would agree, they cannot be distinguished from each other in any simple way, but are mutually interdependent. The hunting pack and the war pack doubtless merge, although the war pack may be thought of as organized in contrast to what we might call the spontaneous hunting pack, and it thus represents the negation of the latter's immediacy.

CANETTI.   If I can just intervene briefly, I would say that I am even convinced that the war pack originally emerged from the hunting pack (*Adorno. . . . emerged from. Precisely!*) The crucial factor was the need to take revenge on someone who had probably committed murder, and so people banded together to avenge this murder. If the group to which the murderer belonged defended itself, you had a second pack, and this provides us with the model of the war pack.

ADORNO.   Quite so! I think that is also the generally accepted view of the ethnologists on this point nowadays. (*Canetti.* Indeed.) To be frank, I have a certain difficulty with the concept of the increase pack, for this business with the desire to grow seems a little problematic. This desire is ambivalent at the very least. We must recollect that the imperative to grow that is characteristic of the great religions, above all Judaism and Catholicism, is to be found among the very religions that distinguish themselves from the mythical or magic natural religions. We must presume that at more primitive stages—I have in mind the notion of a hetaeristic phase of human development—this particular question of human growth was not an issue of the deepest concern, and that in fact people did not value it at all. I would instead be inclined to think that this commandment to grow is a product of history and that it is linked to the notion of property, of fixed, inheritable property. Only when there is such a thing as property that has to be maintained, that is, fetishized, made independent, and passed down—only at that point does it become imperative to produce heirs who can take the property over. This means that the impulse to grow and increase is a secondary, not a primary, factor.

It might be interesting if you could say something about this. And I would like then to add a few words myself about what seems to me to be a very productive aspect of this concept of the increase pack.

CANETTI. I have collected a large number of examples and perhaps should mention two. In the *Shih Ching*, the classic *Book of Songs* of the Chinese, there is a poem about locusts that equates the number of locusts with the number of descendants, and it sees this as something desirable. The poem is short, and I should like to read it to you: "The locusts' wings say: hurry, hurry. Oh, may your sons and grandsons be an army beyond number. The locusts' wings say: bind up, bind up. Oh, may your sons and grandsons continue in an endless line. The locusts' wings say: unite, unite. Oh, may your sons and grandsons be forever at one."

So what we have here are large numbers, unbroken succession, and unity—three wishes for one's offspring. The fact that the swarms of locusts are used as the symbol for offspring is especially striking because locusts were of course an object of fear. (*Adorno.* They were normally negatively cathected.) Nevertheless, their monstrous numbers were exactly what people wanted for their descendants.

ADORNO. But doesn't this come from a very late stage of a society that is already organized and institutionalized, that has a state and an organized religion—in contrast to natural conditions?

CANETTI. That could perhaps be argued. The *Shih Ching* is very ancient, but . . . (*Adorno.* But it still presupposes a highly developed and even a hierarchical society.) That may well be true. That is why I should like to give you another example. This one is particularly interesting since it involves totemic myths that were published only about fifteen years ago. They were recorded by the younger Strehlow among the Aranda tribe. I should like to tell you about them. It is about the origin of the totem of the opossums, which are also called bandicoots in Australia, and in this context the following story is told. The ancestor of the bandicoot totem, old Karora, is said to lie in everlasting sleep at the bottom of a pond; he has been asleep from time immemorial. One day a host of bandicoots emerge from his navel and his armpits, and he is completely surrounded by them. But he is still asleep. The sun rises. He stretches himself, stands up and feels hungry. He then notices that he is surrounded by a vast throng of bandicoots. He tries to grab them and does manage to catch one of these bandicoots. He cooks it in the boiling sun and eats it—in other words, he eats one of these creatures that has come from himself. He goes back to sleep, and during the same night, a bull-roarer falls out of his armpit; it takes on another shape and becomes a human being. This is his first son, who grows larger, and the next day he recognizes him as his son. The following night more such sons arrive, and they always come from his armpits. This process is repeated night after night. He ends up with as many as fifty sons coming out of his armpits at one time, and he sends his sons out in search of bandicoots, which they then catch and cook and on which they live.

We have here a kind of double process of growth. On the one hand, he is the ancestor of the bandicoots that have suddenly come into being in such huge quantities; then, after that, a large number of sons come from him, the father. We should perhaps call him a mass mother, since he really is a composite being, consisting either of bandicoots or of sons. And what is very interesting is the relationship between the bandicoots and the sons. The one group feeds on the other. So he has produced the food and also his own sons. He is the ancestor of the totem that passes for the bandicoot totem, and this totem means simply that bandicoots and human beings that belong to this totem are closely related. The human beings, his human sons, are the younger brothers of these bandicoots. There are many other similar traditional stories that we could set beside this myth. I believe that we can really speak of a powerful impulse to increase here.

ADORNO. I would say that this would take us too far afield. I do not think we can fully discuss the matter here since we are dealing with an ambivalent phenomenon. There is undoubtedly an archaic element that gives rise to diversity, to the amorphousness and the multiplicity of forms. But there is also the opposite element, and it is probably no longer possible, or so it seems to me, to distinguish clearly between what is primary and what is secondary, as indeed it is in general difficult to separate them so that such discussions tend not to lead very far.

Today, however, it looks as if the idea of growth is simultaneously desired and feared—and there are well-known economic and social reasons for this. And these ambivalent attitudes can be seen both in individuals and families and also in nations and mankind as a whole. For mankind can sense in its quantitative growth the danger threatening its survival within its existing forms of organization, and beyond that it is tormented by what are surely imaginary doubts, in part, at least, about whether this old planet earth will be able to go on feeding a human race that has expanded so uncontrollably.

CANETTI. I should like to interject here that this idea that the earth is overpopulated is also an ancient and mythical anxiety. (*Adorno.* Very old!) It can be found among the ancient Persians and already existed among nations that tended strongly toward growth and increasingly emphasized the desire to grow.

ADORNO. This ambivalence undoubtedly contains the very profound consciousness that, on the one hand, all possible forms of life, everything that can at all exist, actually has the right to exist, but that, on the other hand, because of the forms, the institutions, in which people have always lived and still live to this day, every human being who arrives represents something of a threat, however remote, to the continued existence of all other human beings. I would add that this ambivalence has real causes, however remote, and not just psychological ones.

But perhaps I may come to a small point that—whatever the outcome of our disagreement here—seems to be a very productive aspect of your theory of growth. In one passage in your book you argue that productivity, the growth in the quantity of goods, has become a kind of self-justifying activity or, as I would put it, has been fetishized. Now, from the standpoint of an economic theory of society it is easy to give rational, or pseudo-rational, reasons to explain how this could have happened. In other words, under existing conditions the apparatus of production, and with it the relations of production as a whole, can be kept going only by constantly creating new lots of buyers for their products, thus creating that curious reversal of primary and secondary in which human beings, for whom allegedly everything exists, are in fact just dragged along by the machine that has been made from them.

I believe that at this point your theory fulfills a very useful function. It would be very hard to understand why this cult of production for the sake of production should thrive everywhere on earth, without any distinction between political systems, unless there were something in human subjectivity, in people's subconscious, in their entire archaic inheritance to which it made a powerful appeal.

For otherwise there would be the obvious objection: why should we continue to produce more and more goods if what has been produced has long since proved to be sufficient to satisfy our needs? The fact that no one actually puts this question seems to me to be proof that this apparatus of production is able to mobilize huge sources of libido in the masses to which its own constant and ultimately problematic expansion can relate. This is why I think that your approach is extremely productive, even if one were inclined, as I am, not to place this desire or drive to grow at the very start, as you do.

Perhaps I may return once more to the question I asked you earlier, namely, about the difference between your theories about the masses and those of Le Bon and Freud, which of course are very well known. For the fact is that the productivity of a theory often lies in minute divergences from related theories.

CANETTI. Perhaps you would allow me to stress the differences between my theory and Freud's, since I find . . .

ADORNO. Le Bon's is not really a theory; it is more a description of a relatively narrow phenomenon. I mean, the masses he describes really are just the masses that only appear in quite specific situations, such as great fires, theaters burning down, and the like, and they are of course not at all prototypical for the concept of the masses in general. I think it far better for you to talk about Freud than Le Bon.

CANETTI. As far as Freud is concerned, there are a number of things to be said. Freud speaks of two concrete crowds that he gives as examples. One is the church; the other, the army. The fact that he fixes upon what we might call two hierarchically articulated groups in order to explain his theory of the crowd appears to me to be very revealing about him. For me the army is not a crowd at all. The army is a collection of people that is held together by a specific chain of command in such a way that it does *not* become a crowd. In an army it is extremely important that an order can split off two people or five; three hundred can be split off and sent somewhere or other as a single unit. An army is divisible at any time. At given moments, moments of flight or unusually fierce attack, an army can become a crowd, but in principle it is not a crowd at all in my sense of the term. So for me it is significant that Freud should use the army to explain his theory. Another important point of disagreement is that Freud really speaks only of crowds that have a leader. He always sees an individual at the head of a crowd.

ADORNO. Of course, that is connected with his theory of the primal father, the father of the horde.

CANETTI. However and I imagine that you will agree with me here there are also crowds of quite a different kind. a fleeing crowd, for example. People in one place who suddenly find themselves threatened . . .

ADORNO. He thinks of them as the decomposition of the crowd; this is quite consistent with his point of view.

CANETTI. No, I think it is important to distinguish between a fleeing crowd and a crowd in a panic. (*Adorno.* That's right, a crowd in a panic.) A fleeing crowd is still a crowd, just like a herd that all run at the same time. A panic is (*Adorno.* A disintegration . . .) . . . a fragmentation of the crowd, when everyone just wants to save his own skin. A fleeing crowd that has not yet panicked and that is still a unified mass has no leader. It has a direction. The direction is: away from danger! Despite this, it displays quite explicit features of crowd behavior that can be explained and that are very significant. I believe also that a lynch mob does not always have a leader, either. You will rightly object that lynch mobs are very often incited by demagogues of one sort or another . . .

ADORNO. Historically, above all, it has always been the case that lynch mobs are never spontaneous, but the objects of manipulation. That was true as early as the pogroms during the Crusades.

CANETTI. That is certainly correct. Nevertheless, I believe that there is such a thing as a lynch mob before and beyond this directed crowd that looks to a leader. Then there are other cases as well. You will recollect that I also describe a feast crowd. (*Adorno.* Yes.) That is doubtless an example that has absolutely nothing to do with a leader. What we have there is a gathering of people and a great quantity of produce that they wish to enjoy together in a state of pleasure and excitement. Everything is in motion;

you cannot even identify a particular direction, and there can be no question of a leader. I believe that the Freudian concept of the crowd is too dependent on Le Bon's.

ADORNO. He bases himself on Le Bon. What he has produced is actually a commentary or interpretation, a genetic interpretation of Le Bon's phenomenology of the crowd.

CANETTI. And I have a further point to make. Even if we stick to this limited definition of the crowd as Freud attempts to explain it, basing himself on Le Bon's account, there are other objections to be raised. What concerns me the most is his concept of identification. I believe that this concept has not been fully thought through; it is insufficiently precise and lacks real clarity. Freud says in many passages of his writings when he speaks of identification that he is talking about a model. For example, a child identifies himself with his father and actually wants to become like his father. His father is his model. Now this is true enough. But what is really involved in this relation to the model has never really been spelled out in detail. You will certainly have noticed with astonishment that so much of my book has been devoted to the problems of transformation. The second volume is due to say a lot more about transformation. I have really made it my task to make a fresh study of transformation in all its aspects, and in such a way as to enable me to say what a model really is, what really takes place between a model and the person who models himself on him. Only then will we perhaps have a clearer idea of identification. Until that has been accomplished, I would be inclined to avoid the entire concept of identification. Nor will you find the concept in my portrayal of the crowd. I attempt there to dispense with identification altogether. I have mentioned a number of points here, but there are others.

ADORNO. This critique seems to me to be highly productive and accurate in many respects. This is because of Freud's basic tendency to replace a theory of society with an individual psychology that is expanded to include the social collectivity. The effect of this is always to bring him hard up against the invariable, immutable, basic facts of the unconscious at the expense of essential historical qualifications. This has the consequence that his social theory always remains a little abstract. So I would completely agree that such entities as the army and the church cannot simply be subsumed under the concept of the crowd but are instead reactions to it. They do indeed contain this archaic element of the crowd that Freud had in mind, but it is negated and held in check by the hierarchical factors and a particular mode of rationality. And if we take this further, we shall see that the so-called mass phenomena that we are concerned with today cannot simply be considered to be primary manifestations of the archaic concept of the crowd, as Freud undoubtedly considered them during the First World War. Instead, they must be regarded as reaction-formations, namely regressions to social stages that are no longer reconcilable with present realities.

As far as festivals are concerned, it is undoubtedly true that we cannot really talk of leaders on such occasions. Perhaps I can refer here to a very important study of festivals that appeared many years ago. It is by Roger Caillois, the French cultural anthropologist. He regards the festival as a reaction-formation, as a reversal of the strict hierarchical rites in very rigid, barbaric societies, which in a sense are able to maintain their own institutional survival only by overturning their own rules and by permitting, and even making obligatory in certain exceptional circumstances, things that are normally forbidden. In this sense what you would call a feast crowd could also be seen as a dynamic historical phenomenon, not a primary one.

If I may make one further point, what impressed me most about your book was something that does not so much form part of the theory of the crowd as belong to the theory of power, which is admittedly an inseparable corollary to it. I am thinking here of your theory of the command. This seems to me to have an essential, enlightening function because you say something there—and I may perhaps refer once more to our *Dialectic of Enlightenment*—that normally tends to disappear behind the facade of society. This is that behind every social, socially approved, socially required mode of behavior there is, however distantly, something like direct physical force, in other words, the threat of annihilation. And I believe that only if we are clear in our minds that society, and with it the survival of mankind, has the threat of death as its foundation will we become properly aware of the terrible interlocking nature of survival, as you call it, and death, in the way that you have formulated it.

For this reason I think it would be very welcome if you could, by way of conclusion, say a few words, Mr. Canetti, about your theory of the command.

CANETTI. Gladly, although it cannot really be summed up in a few words. I derive the notion of command—biologically—from the order to flee. I believe that the threat of an animal that feeds on other animals leads to their taking flight. A lion on the prowl that reveals its presence to other animals by its roar has the effect of making them flee. And this seems to me to be the germ of the command as it subsequently developed and became an important institution in human society. It is in origin the command to flee. It drives a threatened animal from the source of danger. That is a very important fact, for in our society this has had the force of a model; it is indeed built into our society. Orders are handed out without people realizing or suspecting that they are simultaneously receiving a death threat. But however commands are issued, this death threat lies behind them. And by carrying out death sentences, as is customary in most societies, the terrible threat underlying the command is reinforced. You are warned that if you do not do what is asked of you, then what you see happening in this execution will be done to you. (*Adorno.* Every execution addresses the others, those who are not executed.)

And one more point, very briefly. My study of the command has led me to the conclusion that a command can be broken down into its impulse, the motor energy that leads to its being carried out, and another part that I call the sting. This sting has the same form as the command, and the same content, but it remains stuck in the person who has carried out the order. The position is that a man who has obeyed a command feels no joy at having done so. He may not know it; he probably does not give it a thought. But the sting from this command remains stuck in him, and this sting is completely unalterable. That is particularly important. In this way people can store up the stings from commands within themselves, and these stings may have been inflicted twenty or thirty years previously. It is all still in them, and through a kind of reversal, it all wants to come to the surface again. People want to free themselves from these stings; they feel oppressed by them; and they often seek out situations that are the exact reverse of the original situation in which they received commands, in order to get rid of the stings. The consequence of this is obvious. It is simply a fact that everyone who lives in a society is simply full of such stings resulting from commands he has had to obey. They can be so numerous that he is driven to commit quite monstrous acts because he is suffocating from these stings.

ADORNO. I think this is very suggestive, above all, because it tells us in a very original and unconventional way that the threat of direct force survives in all mediations, and that every attempt to escape from this impasse remains under the spell of this mythical circular process, namely, to do to others what has been done to oneself. Nietzsche's great statement that our task is to redeem mankind from revenge refers to precisely the situation that you have described. And by describing it, by describing this magic spell in your book, you aim, if I have understood you correctly, to utter the magic words that have bewitched mankind, and by uttering them, to help us finally to escape from the spell.

(1972; not in GS)
Translated by Rodney Livingstone

PART FOUR

ART, MEMORY OF SUFFERING

10

Heine the Wound

Anyone who wants to make a serious contribution to remembering Heine on the centennial of his death and not merely deliver a formal speech will have to speak about a wound, about what in Heine and his relationship to the German tradition causes us pain and what has been repressed, especially in Germany since the Second World War. Heine's name is an irritant, and only someone who addresses that without whitewashing it can hope to be of aid.

The National Socialists were not the first to defame Heine. In fact, they almost honored him when they put the now famous words "Author Unknown" under his poem "The Lorelei," thus unexpectedly sanctioning as a folksong the secretly scintillating verses that remind one of Parisian Rhine nymphs from a long-lost Offenbach opera. Heine's *Book of Songs* had a stupendous influence, extending far beyond literary circles. In its train, lyric poetry was ultimately drawn down into the language of commerce and the press. This is why Heine came to have such a bad name among those responsible for culture around 1900. The George Circle's verdict may be ascribed to nationalism, but that of Karl Kraus cannot be erased. Since that time Heine's aura has been painful and guilt-laden, as though it were bleeding. His own guilt became an alibi for those of his enemies whose hatred for the Jewish middleman ultimately paved the way for the unspeakable horror.

One who confines himself to Heine as a prose writer avoids the annoyance; Heine's stature as a prose writer in the utterly dismal level of the era between Goethe and Nietzsche is immediately evident. This prose is not limited to Heine's capacity for conscious pointed linguistic formulation, a polemical power extremely rare in Germany and in no way inhibited by servility. August von Platen had the opportunity to experience it when he made an anti-Semitic attack on Heine and was disposed of in a way that would probably be called existential nowadays—if the concept of the existential were not so carefully preserved from contamination by the real existence of human beings. But in its substance Heine's prose goes far beyond such bravura pieces. After Leibniz gave Spinoza the cold shoulder, the whole German Enlightenment failed, at least in that it lost its social sting and confined itself to subservient affirmation; of all the famous names in German literature, Heine alone, for all his affinities with romanticism, retains an undiluted concept of enlightenment. The discomfort he arouses despite his conciliatory stance comes from that harsh climate. With polite irony he refuses to smuggle right back in through the back door—or the basement door to the depths—what he has just demolished. It is questionable whether he had such a strong influence on the young Marx as many young sociologists would like to think. Politically, Heine was not a traveling companion one could count on: even of socialism. But in contrast to socialism, he held fast to the idea of uncurtailed happiness in the image of a just society, an idea quickly enough disposed of in favor of slogans like "Anyone who doesn't work won't eat." His aversion to revolutionary purity and stringency is indicative of Heine's distrust of mustiness and asceticism, elements whose traces are already evident in many early socialist documents and which, much later, worked in favor of disastrous developmetal tendencies. Heine the individualist—and he was so much an individualist that even in Hegel he heard only individualism—did not bow to the individualistic concept of inwardness. His idea of sensuous fulfillment encompasses fulfillment in external things, a society without coercion and deprivation.

The wound, however, is Heine's lyric poetry. At one time its immediacy was enchanting. It interpreted Goethe's dictum on the occasional poem to mean that every occasion found its poem and everyone considered the opportunity to write to be something favorable. But at the same time, this immediacy was thoroughly mediated. Heine's poems were ready mediators between art and an everyday life bereft of meaning. For them as for the feuilletonist, the experiences they processed secretly became raw materials that one could write about. The nuances and tonal values that they discovered, they made interchangeable, delivered them into the power of a prepared, ready-made language. For them the life to which they matter-of-factly bore witness was venal; their spontaneity was one with reification. In Heine commodity and exchange seized control of sound and tone, whose very nature had previously consisted in the negation of the hustle and bustle of daily life. So great had the power of a mature capitalist society become at that time that lyric poetry could no longer ignore it without descending into provincial folksiness. In this respect, Heine, like Baudelaire, looms large in the modernism of the nineteenth century. But Baudelaire, the younger of the two, heroically wrests dream and image from modernity itself, from the experience of implacable destruction and dissolution, which by then was further advanced; indeed he transfigures the loss of all images, transforming that loss itself into an image. The forces of this kind of resistance increased along with those of capitalism. In Heine, whose poems were still set to music by Schubert, they had not reached such a high level of intensity. He surrendered more willingly to the flow of things; he took a poetic technique of reproduction, as it were, that corresponded to the industrial age and applied it to the conventional romantic archetypes, but he did not find archetypes of modernity.

It is just this that later generations find embarrassing. For since the existence of a bourgeois art in which artists have to earn their livelihoods without patrons, they have secretly acknowledged the law of the marketplace alongside the autonomy of their laws of form, and have produced for consumers. It was only that this dependency was not visible behind the anonymity of the marketplace. It allowed the artist to appear pure and autonomous in the eyes of himself and others, and this illusion itself was accepted at face value. Heine the advocate of enlightenment unmasked Heine the romantic, who had been living off the good fortune of autonomy, and brought the commodity character of his art, previously latent, to the fore. He has not been forgiven for that. The ingratiating quality of his poems, which is overacted and hence becomes self-critical, makes it plain that the emancipation of the spirit was not the emancipation of human beings and hence was also not that of the spirit.

But the rage of the person who sees the secret of his own degradation in the confessed degradation of someone else is directed with sadistic assurance to Heine's weakest point, the failure of Jewish emancipation. For

Heine's fluency and self-evidence, which is derived from the language of communications, is the opposite of a native sense of being at home in language. Only someone who is not actually inside language can manipulate it like an instrument. If the language were really his own, he would allow the dialectic between his own words and words that are pregiven to take place, and the smooth linguistic structure would disintegrate. But for the person who uses language like a book that is out of print, language itself is alien. Heine's mother, whom he loved, did not have full command of German. His lack of resistance to words that are in fashion is the excessive mimetic zeal of the person who is excluded. Assimilatory language is the language of unsuccessful identification. There is a well-known anecdote according to which the youthful Heine, when asked by the elderly Goethe what he was working on, replied "a Faust" and was thereupon ungraciously dismissed. Heine explained this incident in terms of his shyness. His impertinence sprang from the impulse of the person who wants for the life of him to be accepted and is thereby doubly irritating to those who are already established, who drown out their own guilt at excluding him by holding the vulnerability of his adaptation up to him. This continues to be the trauma of Heine's name today, and it can be healed only if it is recognized rather than left to go on leading an obscure, preconscious existence.

The possibility of that, however, is contained, as a potential for rescue, within Heine's poetry itself. For the power of the one who mocks impotently exceeds his impotence. If all expression is the trace left by suffering, then Heine was able to recast his own inadequacy, the muteness of his language, as an expression of rupture. So great was the virtuosity of this man, who imitated language as if he were playing it on a keyboard, that he raised even the inadequacy of his language to the medium of one to whom it was granted to say what he suffered. Failure, reversing itself, is transformed into success. Heine's essence is fully revealed, not in the music composed to his poems, but only in the songs of Gustav Mahler, written forty years after his death, songs in which the brittleness of the banal and the derivative is used to express what is most real, in the form of a wild, unleashed lament. It was not until Mahler's songs about the soldiers who flew the flag out of homesickness, not until the outbursts of the funeral march in his Fifth Symphony, until the folksongs with their harsh alternation of major and minor, until the convulsive gestures of the Mahlerian orchestra, that the music in Heine's verses was released. In the mouth of a stranger, what is old and familiar takes on an extravagant and exaggerated quality, and precisely that is the truth. The figures of this truth are the aesthetic breaks; it forgoes the immediacy of rounded, fulfilled language.

The following stanzas appear in the cycle of poems that Heine, the emigrant, called *Der Heimkehr* [*The Return Home*]:

> Mein Herz mein Herz ist traurig,
> Doch lustig leuchtet der Mai;
> Ich stehe, gelehnt an der Linde,
> Hoch auf der alten Bastei.
>
> Da drunten fließt der blaue
> Stadtgraben in stiller Ruh;
> Ein Knabe fährt im Kahne,
> Und angelt und pfeift dazu.
>
> Jenseits erheben sich freundlich,
> In winziger, bunter Gestalt,
> Lusthäuser und Gärten und Menschen,
> und Ochsen und Wiesen und Wald.
>
> Die Mägde bleichen Wäsche,
> Und springen im Gras herum:
> das Mühlrad staubt Diamanten,
> Ich höre sein fernes Gesumm.
>
> Am alten grauen Turme
> Ein Schilderhäuschen steht;
> Ein rotgeröckter Bursche
> Dort auf und nieder geht.
>
> Er spielt mit seiner Flinte,
> Die funkelt im Sonnenrot,
> Er präsentiert und schultert—
> Icht wollt, er schösse mich tot.

> My heart, my heart is heavy,
> Though joyously shines the May,
> As I stand 'neath the lime-tree leaning
> High on the ramparts gray.
>
> The moat winds far beneath me;
> On its waters calm and blue
> A boy in his boat is drifting,

Fishing and whistling too.

Beyond, like a smiling picture,
Little and bright, lie strewed
Villas and gardens and people
Cattle and meadows and wood.

The maidens are bleaching linen—
They skip on the grass and play;
The mill-wheel scatters diamonds,
Its drone sounds, far away.

A sentry-box is standing
The old gray keep below,
And a lad in a coat of scarlet
Paces there to and fro.

He handles and plays with his musket—
It gleams in the sunset red,
He shoulders and presents it—
I would that he shot me dead![1]

It has taken a hundred years for this intentionally false folksong to become a great poem, a vision of sacrifice. Heine's stereotypical theme, unrequited love, is an image for homelessness, and the poetry devoted to it is an attempt to draw estrangement itself into the sphere of intimate experience. Now that the destiny that Heine sensed has been fulfilled literally, however, the homelessness has also become everyone's homelessness; all human beings have been as badly injured in their beings and their language as Heine the outcast was. His words stand in for their words: there is no longer any homeland other than a world in which no one would be cast out any more, the world of a genuinely emancipated humanity. The wound that is Heine will heal only in a society that has achieved reconciliation.

(1956; GS II:95–100)
Translated by Shierry Weber Nicholsen

11

Notes on Kafka

FOR GRETEL

> Si Dieu le Père a créé les choses en les nommant, c'est en leur ôtant leur nom, ou
> en leur donnant un autre que l'artiste les recréé. [If God the Father created all
> things by naming them, the artist, by unnaming or renaming them, recreates
> things.]
> —Marcel Proust

I

Kafka's popularity, that comfort in the uncomfortable that has made of him an information bureau of the human condition, be it eternal or modern, and that knowingly dispenses with the very scandal on which his work is built, leaves one reluctant to join the fray, even if it is to add a dissenting opinion. Yet it is just this false renown, fatal variant of the oblivion Kafka so bitterly desired for himself, that compels one to dwell on the enigma. Of that which has been written on him, little counts; most is existentialism. He is assimilated into an established trend of thought while little attention is paid to those aspects of his work that resist such assimilation and that, precisely for this reason, require interpretation. As though Kafka's Sisyphean labors would have been necessary, as though the maelstrom force of his work could be explained, if all he had to say was that man had lost the possibility of salvation or that the way to the absolute is barred, that man's life is dark, confused, or, in currently fashionable terminology, "suspended in nothingness," and that the only alternative left is for him to do his duty, humbly and without great aspirations, and to integrate himself into a collective that expects just this and that Kafka would not have

had to affront had he been of one mind with it. To qualify such an interpretation by arguing that Kafka of course did not say this in so many words
but rather worked as an artist with realistic symbolism is to admit a dissatisfaction with formulas but not much more. For an artistic representation
is either realistic or symbolic; no matter how densely organized the symbols may be, their own degree of reality cannot detract from the symbolic
character. Goethe's play *Pandora* is no less rich in sensuous depiction than
a novel by Kafka, and yet there can be no doubt concerning the symbolism
of Goethe's fragment, even though the power of the symbols—as with El-
pore, who embodies hope—may exceed what was originally intended. If
the notion of the symbol has any meaning whatsoever in aesthetics—and
this is far from certain—then it can only be that the individual moments
of the work of art point beyond themselves by virtue of their interrelations,
that their totality coalesces into meaning. Nothing could be less true of
Kafka. Even in a work such as Goethe's, which plays so profoundly with allegorical moments, these still relinquish their significance, by virtue of their
context, to the thrust of the whole. In Kafka, however, everything is as
hard, defined, and distinct as possible; in this his works resemble the novel
of adventure, as described by James Fenimore Cooper in his preface to *The
Red Rover*: "The true Augustan age of literature can never exist until works
shall be as accurate in their typography as a 'log-book,' and as sententious
in their matter as a 'watch-bill.'" Nowhere in Kafka does there glimmer the
aura of the infinite idea; nowhere does the horizon open. Each sentence is
literal, and each signifies. The two moments are not merged, as the symbol
would have it, but yawn apart, and out of the abyss between them blinds
the glaring ray of fascination. Here too, in its striving not for symbol but
for allegory, Kafka's prose sides with the outcasts, the protest of his friend
notwithstanding. Walter Benjamin rightly defined it as parable. It expresses
itself not through expression but by its repudiation, by breaking off. It is a
parabolic system the key to which has been stolen; yet any effort to make
this fact itself the key is bound to go astray by confounding the abstract
thesis of Kafka's work, the obscurity of the existent, with its substance.
Each sentence says "interpret me," and none will permit it. Each compels
the reaction "That's the way it is," and with it the question "Where have I
seen that before?"; the *déjà vu* is declared permanent. Through the power
with which Kafka commands interpretation, he collapses aesthetic distance. He demands a desperate effort of the allegedly "disinterested" ob-

server of an earlier time, overwhelms him, suggesting that far more than his intellectual equilibrium depends on whether he truly understands; life and death are at stake. Among Kafka's presuppositions, not the least is that the contemplative relation between text and reader is shaken to its very roots. His texts are designed not to sustain a constant distance between themselves and their victim but rather to agitate his feelings to a point where he fears that the narrative will shoot toward him like a locomotive in a three-dimensional film. Such aggressive physical proximity undermines the reader's habit of identifying himself with the figures in the novel. It is by reason of this principle that surrealism can rightfully claim him. He is Turandot set down in writing. Anyone who sees this and does not choose to run away must stick out his head or, rather, try to batter down the wall with it at the risk of faring no better than his predecessors. As in fairy tales, their fate serves not to deter but to entice. As long as the word has not been found, the reader must be held accountable.

II

Far more than for most other writers, it may be said of Kafka that not *verum* but *falsum* is *index sui*. He himself, however, contributed to the spread of the untruth. His two great novels, *The Castle* and *The Trial,* seem to bear the mark of philosophical theorems, if not in their details then in their general outlines, which, despite all intellectual profundity, in no way belie the title given to a collection of Kafka's theoretical writings, *Reflections on Sin, Pain, Hope and the True Way.* Still, the content of the title is not canonic for the literary work. The artist is not obliged to understand his own art, and there is particular reason to doubt whether Kafka was capable of such understanding. In any case, the aphorisms are hardly equal to his most enigmatic stories and episodes, such as "Care of a Family Man" or "The Bucket Rider." Kafka's works protected themselves against the deadly aesthetic error of equating the philosophy that an author pumps into a work with its metaphysical substance. Were this so, the work of art would be stillborn; it would exhaust itself in what it says and would not unfold itself in time. To guard against this short circuit, which jumps directly to the significance intended by the work, the first rule is: take everything literally; cover up nothing with concepts invoked from above. Kafka's authority is textual. Only fidelity to the letter, not oriented understanding, can be of help. In an art that is constantly obscuring and revoking itself, every determinate statement counterbalances the general proviso of indeterminateness. Kafka sought to sabotage this rule when he let it be announced at one point that messages from the castle must not be taken "literally." All the same, if one is not to lose all ground on which to stand, one must cling to the fact that at the beginning of *The Trial*, it is said that someone must have been spreading rumors about Josef K., "for without having done anything wrong, he was arrested one fine morning." Nor can one throw to the winds the fact that at the beginning of *The Castle*, K. asks "What village is this that I have wandered into? Is there a castle here?" and hence cannot possibly have been summoned there. He also knows nothing of Count Westwest, whose name is mentioned only once and who is thought of less and less until he is entirely forgotten, like the Prometheus of one of Kafka's fables, who merges with the rock to which he is chained and is then forgotten. Nevertheless, the principle of literalness, probably a reminiscence of the Torah exegesis of Jewish tradition, finds support in many of Kafka's texts. At times, words, metaphors in particular, detach themselves and achieve a certain autonomy. Josef K. dies "like a dog," and Kafka reports the "Investigations of a Dog." Upon occasion the literalness is driven to the point of a pun. Thus, in the story of Barnabas's family in *The Castle*, the official, Sortini, is described as having remained "at the nozzle" during the Fire Department party. The colloquial German expression for devotion to duty is taken seriously, the respectable person stays at the nozzle of the fire hose, and simultaneously an allusion is made, as in parapraxes, to the crude desire that drives the functionary to write the fateful letter to Amalia— Kafka, disparager of psychology, is abundantly rich in psychological insights, such as that into the relation between instinctual and obsessive personality. Without the principle of literalness as criterion, the ambiguities of Kafka would dissolve into indifferent equivalence. This principle, however, invalidates the most commonly held conception of the author, one that seeks to unite in him the claim to profundity with equivocation. Cocteau rightly pointed out that the introduction of anything startling in the form of a dream invariably removes its sting. It was to prevent such misuse that Kafka himself interrupted *The Trial* at a decisive point with a dream—he published the truly horrifying piece in *A Country Doctor*—and by contrast confirmed the reality of everything else, even if it should be that dream-reality suggested periodically in *The Castle* and *America* by passages so agonizingly drawn out that they leave the reader gasping for air. Among the moments of shock, not the least results from the fact that Kafka takes dreams *à la lettre*. Because everything that does not resemble the dream and its prelogical logic is excluded, the dream itself is excluded. It is not the horrible that shocks, but its self-evidence. No sooner has the surveyor driven the bothersome assistants from his room in the inn than they climb back through the window without the novel's stopping for one word more than required to communicate the event; the hero is too tired to drive them away again. The attitude that Kafka assumes toward dreams should be the reader's toward Kafka. He should dwell on the incommensurable, opaque details, the blind spots. The fact that Leni's fingers are connected by a web, or that the executioners resemble tenors, is more important than the Excursus on the law. It is true both of the mode of representation and of the language. Gestures often serve as counterpoints to words: the prelinguistic that eludes all intention upsets the ambiguity, which, like a disease, has eaten into all signification in Kafka. "'The letter,' began K., 'I have read it. Do you know the contents?' 'No,' said Barnabas, whose look seemed to imply more than his words. Perhaps K. was as mistaken in Barnabas's goodness as in the malice of the peasants, but his presence remained a comfort." Or: "'Well,' she said extenuatingly, 'there was a reason for laughing. You asked if I knew Klamm, and you see I'—here she involuntarily straightened up a little, and her triumphant glance, which had no connection whatever with what she was saying, swept over K.—'I am his mistress.'" Or, in the scene of Frieda's parting from the surveyor: "Frieda had let her head fall on K.'s shoulder; their arms round each other, they walked silently up and down. 'If we had only,' said Frieda after a while, slowly, quietly, almost serenely, as if she knew that only a very short respite of peace on K.'s shoulder was reserved for her and she wanted to enjoy it to the utmost, 'If we had only gone away somewhere at once that night, we might be in peace now, always together, your hand always near enough for mine to grasp; oh, how much I need your companionship, how lost I have felt without it ever since I've known you! To have your company, believe me, is the only dream I've had, that and nothing else.'" Such gestures are the traces of experiences covered over by signification. The most recent state of a language that wells up in the mouths of those who speak it, the second Babylonian confusion, which Kafka's sober diction tirelessly opposes, compels him to invert the historical relation of concept and gesture. The gesture is the "that's the way it is"; language, the configuration of which should be truth, is, as a broken one, untruth. "'Also you should be far more reticent, nearly everything you have just said could have been implied in your behavior with the help of a word here and there, and in any case does not redound particularly to your credit.'" The experiences sedimented in the gestures will eventually have to be followed by interpretation, one that recognizes in their mimesis a universal that has been repressed by sound common sense. In the scene of Josef K.'s arrest at the beginning of *The Trial*, there is the following passage: "Through the open window, he had another glimpse of the old woman who with genuine senile inquisitiveness had moved along to the window exactly opposite, in order to see all that could be seen." Is there anyone who has lived in boarding houses and has not felt himself observed by the neighbors in precisely the same manner; together with the repulsive, the familiar, the unintelligible, and the inevitable, such a person has seen the image of fate suddenly light up. The reader who succeeds in solving such rebuses will understand more of Kafka than all those who find in him ontology illustrated.

III

Here one may object that an interpretation can no more rely on this than on anything else in Kafka's deranged cosmos, that such experiences are nothing but contingent and private psychological projections. Anyone who believes that the neighbors are watching him from their windows or that the telephone speaks to him with its own singing voice—and Kafka's writing teems with such statements—is suffering from delusions of persecution and of relation, and anyone who seeks to make a kind of system out of such things has been infected by the paranoia; for such a person Kafka's works serve solely to rationalize his own psychological injuries. This objection can be answered only through reflection on the relation of Kafka's work itself to the zone of psychology. His words "for the last time, psychology," are well known, as is his remark that everything of his could be interpreted psychoanalytically except that this interpretation would in turn require further interpretation *ad indefinitum*; yet neither such verdicts, nor the venerable haughtiness that is the most recent ideological defense of materialism, should tempt one to accept the thesis that Kafka has nothing to do with Freud. It would be a bad sign for his much-praised profundity if one refused to acknowledge what exists in those depths. In their conception of hierarchy, Kafka and Freud are hardly to be distinguished. In *Totem and Taboo*, Freud writes: "A king's taboo is too strong for his subject because the social difference between them is too great. But a minister may serve as a harmless intermediary between them. Transposed from the language of taboo into that of normal psychology this means the following: the subject, who fears the great temptation involved in contact with the king, can still tolerate dealings with an official whom he does not need to envy so much and whose position may even appear within his grasp. The minister, however, can temper his envy of the king by considering the power which he has been allotted. Thus smaller differences in the magical power leading to temptation are less to be feared than particularly great ones." In *The Trial*, a high official says, "Not even I can bear the sight of even the third door-keeper," and there are analogous moments in *The Castle*. This also sheds light on a decisive complex in Proust, snobbism as the will to soothe the dread of the taboo by winning acceptance among the initiates: "For it was not just Klamm's proximity as such that was worth striving for but rather the fact that it was he, K., only he, no one else with his wish or with any other, who approached Klamm, not in order to rest with him but rather to pass beyond him, farther, into the castle." The expression *délire de toucher*, which Freud cites and which is equally germane to the sphere of the taboo, exactly describes the sexual magic that drives people together in Kafka, especially those of lower social station with those of a higher class. Even the "temptation" suspected by Freud—that of murdering the father figure—is alluded to in Kafka. At the conclusion of the chapter in *The Castle* in which the landlady explains to the surveyor that it is utterly impossible for him to speak with Herr Klamm in person, he has the last word: "'Well, what are you afraid of? You're surely not afraid for Klamm, are you?' The landlady gazed silently after him as he ran down the stairs with the assistants following." To come closest to understanding the relation between the explorer of the unconscious and the parabolist of impenetrability, one must remember that Freud conceived of an archetypal scene such as the murder of the primal father, a prehistorical narrative such as that of Moses, or the young child's observation of its parents having sexual relations, not as products of the imagination but in large measure as real events. In such eccentricities Kafka follows Freud with the devotion of a Till Eulenspiegel to the limits of absurdity. He snatches psychoanalysis from the grasp of psychology. Psychoanalysis itself is already in a certain sense opposed to the specifically psychological inasmuch as it derives the individual from amorphous and diffuse drives, the Ego from the Id. Personality is transformed from something substantial into a mere organizational principle of somatic impulses. In Freud as in Kafka the validity of the soul is excluded; Kafka, indeed, took virtually no notice of it from the very beginning. He distinguishes himself from the far older, scientifically inclined Freud, not through a more delicate spirituality, but rather through a skepticism toward the Ego that, if anything, exceeds that of Freud. This is the function of Kafka's literalness. As though conducting an experiment, he studies what would happen if the results of psychoanalysis were to prove true not merely metaphorically but in the flesh. He accepts psychoanalysis insofar as it convicts civilization and bourgeois individuation of their illusoriness; he explodes it by taking it more exactly at its word than it does itself. According to Freud, psychoanalysis devotes its attention to the "dregs of the world of appearances." He is thinking of psychic phenomena, parapraxes, dreams, and neurotic symptoms. Kafka sins against an ancient rule of the game by constructing art out of nothing but the refuse of reality. He does not directly outline the image of the society to come—for in his as in all great art, asceticism toward the future prevails—but rather depicts it as a montage composed of waste products, which the new order, in the process of forming itself, extracts from the perishing present. Instead of curing neurosis, he seeks in it itself the healing force, that of knowledge: the wounds with which society brands the individual are seen by the latter as ciphers of the social untruth, as the negative of truth. His power is one of demolition. He tears down the soothing facade to which a repressive reason increasingly conforms. In the process of demolition—never was the word more popular than in the year of Kafka's death—he does not stop at the subject, as does psychology, but drives through to the bare material existence that emerges in the subjective sphere through the total collapse of a submissive consciousness, divested of all self-assertion. The flight through man and beyond into the nonhuman—that is Kafka's epic course. The decline of genius, the spasmodic lack of resistance that so completely converges with Kafka's morality, is paradoxically rewarded by the compelling authority of its expression. Such a posture, relaxed virtually to the breaking point, is heir to what was formerly metaphor, significance, mind, and it inherits it as though it were a physical reality of its own, as "spiritual body." It is as though the philosophical doctrine of the "categorical intuition," which was becoming well known at the time that Kafka wrote, were to be honored in hell. The windowless monad preserves itself as the magic lantern, mother of all images, as in Proust and Joyce. That above which individuation lifts itself, what it conceals and what it drove from itself, is common to all but can be grasped only in solitude and undistracted concentration. To fully participate in the process that produces the abnormal experiences that in Kafka define the norm, one must have experienced an accident in a large city; uncounted witnesses come forward, proclaiming themselves acquaintances, as though the entire community had gathered to observe the moment when the powerful bus smashed into the flimsy taxicab. The permanent *déjà vu* is the *déjà vu* of all. This is the source of Kafka's success, which becomes betrayal only when the universal is distilled from his writings and the labors of deadly allusion are avoided. Perhaps the hidden aim of his art as a whole is the manageability, technification, collectivization of the *déjà vu*. The best, which is forgotten, is remembered and imprisoned in a bottle like the Cumaean sibyl. Except that in the process it changes into the worst: "I want to die," and that is denied it. Made eternal, the transient is overtaken by a curse.

IV

Eternalized gestures in Kafka are the momentary brought to a standstill. The shock is like a surrealistic arrangement of that which old photographs convey to the viewer. Such a snapshot, unclear, almost entirely faded, plays its role in *The Castle*. The landlady shows K. a photograph she has kept as a relic of her contact with Klamm and through him with the hierarchy. Only with difficulty can K. recognize anything in it. Yesterday's gaudy tableaux, drawn from the sphere of the circus—for which Kafka, with the avant-garde of his generation, felt an affinity—are frequently introduced into his work; perhaps everything was originally supposed to become a tableau and only an excess of intention prevented this, through long dialogues. Anything that balances on the pinnacle of the moment like a horse on its hind legs is snapped, as though the pose ought to be preserved forever. The most gruesome example of this is probably to be found in *The Trial*: Josef K. opens the lumber room, in which his warders had been beaten a day earlier, to find the scene faithfully repeated, including the appeal to himself. "At once K. slammed the door shut and then beat on it with his fists, as if that would shut it still more securely." This is the gesture of Kafka's own work, which—as Poe had already begun to do—turns away from the most extreme scenes as though no eye could survive the sight. In it what is perpetually the same and what is ephemeral merge. Over and over again, Titorelli paints that monotonous genre picture, the heath. The sameness or intriguing similarity of a variety of objects is one of Kafka's most persistent motifs; all possible demi-creatures step forward in pairs, often marked by the childish and the silly, oscillating between affability and cruelty like savages in children's books. Individuation has become such a burden for men and has remained so precarious that they are mortally frightened whenever its veil is raised a little. Proust was familiar with the shiver of discomfort that comes over someone who has been made aware of his resemblance to an unknown relative. In Kafka, this becomes panic. The realm of the *déjà vu* is populated by doubles, *revenants*, buffoons, Hasidic dancers, boys who ape their teachers and then suddenly appear ancient, archaic; at one point, the surveyor wonders whether his assistants are fully alive. Yet there are also images of what is coming, men manufactured on the assembly line, mechanically reproduced copies, Huxleyian Epsilons. The social origin of the individual ultimately reveals itself as the power to annihilate him. Kafka's work is an attempt to absorb this. There is nothing mad in his prose, unlike that of the writer from whom he learned decisively, Robert Walser; every sentence has been shaped by a mind in full control of itself; yet, at the same time, every sentence has been snatched from the zone of insanity into which all knowledge must venture if it is to become such in an age when sound common sense only reinforces universal blindness. The hermetic principle has, among others, the function of a protective measure: it keeps out the onrushing delusion, which would mean, however, its own collectivization. The work that shatters individuation will at no price want to be imitated; for this reason, surely, Kafka gave orders for it to be destroyed. No tourist trade was to blossom where it had gone, yet anyone who imitated its gestures without having been there would be guilty of pure effrontery in attempting to pocket the excitement and power of alienation without the risk. The result would be impotent affectation. Karl Kraus, and to a certain extent Schoenberg, reacted much like Kafka in this respect. Yet such inimitability also affects the situation of the critic. Confronted by Kafka, he occupies a position no more enviable than that of the disciple; it is, in advance, an apology for the world. Not that there is nothing to criticize in Kafka's work. Among the defects, which become obvious in the great novels, monotony is the most striking. The presentation of the ambiguous, uncertain, inaccessible, is repeated endlessly, often at the expense of the vividness that is always sought. The bad infinity of the matter represented spreads to the work of art. This fault may well reflect one in the content, a preponderance of the abstract idea, itself the myth that Kafka attacks. The portrayal seeks to make the uncertain still more uncertain but provokes the question Why the effort? If everything is questionable to begin with, then why not restrict oneself to the given minimum? Kafka would have replied that it was just this hopeless effort that he demanded, much as Kierkegaard sought to irritate the reader through his diffuseness and thus startle him out of aesthetic contemplation. Discussions concerning the virtues and deficiencies of such literary tactics are so fruitless because criticism can address itself only to that in a work wherein it seeks to be exemplary, where it says, "as I am, so shall it be." But precisely this claim is rejected by Kafka's disconsolate "that's the way it is." Nevertheless, at times the power of the images he conjures up cracks through their protective covering. Several subject the reader's self-awareness, to say nothing of the author, to a severe test: "The Penal Colony" and "The Metamorphosis," reports that had to await those of Bettelheim, Kogon, and Rousset for their equals, much as the bird's-eye photos of bombed-out cities redeemed, as it were, Cubism, by realizing that through which the latter broke with reality. If there is hope in Kafka's work, it is in those extremes rather than in the milder phases: in the capacity to stand up to the worst by making it into language. Are these, then, the works that offer the key to an interpretation? There are grounds to think so. In "The Metamorphosis," the path of the experience can be reconstructed from the literalness as an extension of the lines. "These traveling salesmen are like bugs," is the German expression that Kafka must have picked up, speared up like an insect. Bugs—not *like* bugs. What becomes of a man who is a bug as big as a man? As big as adults must appear to the child, and as distorted, with gigantic, trampling legs and far-off, tiny heads, were one to catch and isolate the child's terrified vision; it could be photographed with an oblique camera. In Kafka, an entire lifetime is not enough to reach the next town, and the stoker's ship, the surveyor's inn, are of dimensions so enormous that one would have to return to a long-forgotten past to find a time when man saw his own products similarly. Anyone who desires such vision must transform himself into a child and forget many things. He recognizes his father as the ogre he has always feared in infinitesimal omens; his revulsion against cheese rinds reveals itself as the ignominious, prehuman craving for them. The "boarders" are visibly shrouded in the horror—their emanation—that hitherto clung almost imperceptibly to the word. Kafka's literary technique fastens onto words as Proust's involuntary recollection does to sensuous objects, only with the opposite result: instead of reflection on the human, the trial run of a model of dehumanization. Its pressure forces the subject into a regression that is, so to speak, biological and that prepares the ground for Kafka's animal parables. The crucial moment, however, toward which everything in Kafka is directed is that in which men become aware that they are not themselves—that they themselves are things. The long and fatiguing imageless sections, beginning with the conversation with the father in "The Judgment," serve the purpose of demonstrating to men what no image could, their unidentity, the complement of their copylike similarity. The lesser motives, conclusively demonstrated to the surveyor by the landlady and then also by Frieda, are alien to him—Kafka brilliantly anticipated the concept of the Ego-alien later developed by psychoanalysis. But the surveyor admits these motives. His individual and his social character are split as widely as in Chaplin's *Monsieur Verdoux*; Kafka's hermetic memoranda contain the social genesis of schizophrenia.

V

Kafka's world of images is sad and dilapidated, even where it sets its sights high, as in "The Natural Theater of Oklahoma"—as though he had foreseen the migration of workers from this state—or in the "Care of a Family Man": the fund of flash photographs is as chalky and mongoloid as a petit-bourgeois wedding by Henri Rousseau; the odor is that of unaired beds; the color, the red of mattresses whose sheets have been lost; the dread Kafka evokes, that of vomiting. And yet most of his work is a reaction to unlimited power. To this power, that of the raging patriarch, Benjamin gave the name "parasitic": it lives off the life it oppresses. But characteristically, the parasitic moment is displaced. Gregor Samsa, not his father, becomes the bug. It is not the powerful but the impotent who appear superfluous; none of them performs socially useful work. Even the fact that the accused bank clerk, Josef K., being preoccupied with his trial, cannot do his job properly, is recorded. They creep around among properties that have long since been amortized and that grant them their existence only as charity, since they have outlived themselves. The displacement is modeled on the ideological habit of glorifying the reproduction of life as an act of grace on behalf of those who have at their disposal the means of production, those who "provide" work. It describes a social whole in which those whom society holds in its grip and through whom it maintains itself become superfluous. But the shabbiness in Kafka goes further. It is the cryptogram of capitalism's highly polished, glittering late phase, which he excludes in order to define it all the more precisely in its negative. Kafka scrutinizes the smudges left behind in the deluxe edition of the book of life by the fingers of power. No world could be more homogeneous than the stifling one that he compresses to a totality by means of petit-bourgeois dread; it is logically airtight and empty of meaning, like every system. Everything that he narrates belongs to the same order of reality. All of his stories take place in the same spaceless space, and all holes are so tightly plugged that one shudders whenever anything is mentioned that does not fit in, such as Spain and southern France at one point in *The Castle*; all of America, however, is incorporated into that space in the image of steerage. Mythologies are interconnected like Kafka's labyrinthine descriptions. The inferior, abstruse, deformed, however, is as essential to their continuum as are corruption and criminal asociality to totalitarian domination, and the love of excrement to the cult of hygiene. Intellectual and political systems desire nothing that does not resemble them. The more powerful they become, the more they seek to bring existing reality under a single heading, the more they oppress it, and the farther they remove themselves from it. Precisely for this reason, the slightest "deviation" becomes a threat to their basic principle, as intolerable as are the strangers and solitaries to the powers-that-be in Kafka. Integration is disintegration, and in it the mythic spell converges with the rationality of domination. The so-called problem of contingency, which has been the cause of so much agony to philosophical systems, is their own creation. It is only because of their pure inexorability that whatever slips through their net becomes a mortal enemy, just as the mythical queen cannot rest while there is still someone, far beyond the mountains, the child of the fairy tale, who is more beautiful than she. There is no system without its residue. From this Kafka prophesies. If it is true that everything that happens in his compulsive world combines the expression of utter necessity with that of the utter contingency peculiar to shabbiness, then it is no less true that he deciphers the notorious law in his mirror-writing. Consummate untruth is the contradiction of itself; it need not, therefore, be explicitly contradicted. Kafka unmasks monopolism by focusing on the waste products of the liberal era that it liquidates. This historical moment, not anything allegedly metatemporal illuminating history from above, is the crystallization of his metaphysics; there is no eternity for him other than that of the endlessly repeated sacrifice, which culminates in the image of the last one. "Only our notion of time permits us to speak of the Last Judgment; actually, it is a summary court in perpetual session." The last sacrifice is always yesterday's. Precisely for this reason virtually every overt reference to anything historical—"The Bucket Rider," drawn from the coal shortage, is a rare exception—is avoided in Kafka. His work assumes a hermetic stance toward history as well: a taboo hangs over this concept. To the eternity of the historical moment there corresponds an attitude that sees the way of the world as naturally fallen and invariant; the moment, the absolutely transient, is the likeness of the eternity of passing away, of damnation. The name of history may not be spoken since what would truly be history, the Other, has not yet begun. "To believe in progress is to believe that there has not yet been any." In the midst of apparently static living conditions, those of peasants and artisans in a simple commodity economy, Kafka depicts everything historical as condemned, just as those conditions themselves are condemned. His scenery is always obsolete; the "long, low building" that functions as a school is said to combine "remarkably a look of great age with a provisional appearance." Human beings are not very different. The obsolete is the stigma of the present; Kafka has taken an inventory of such marks. Yet for children, who have to do with the disintegration of the historical world, the obsolete is also the image of that in which history as such first appears; it is the "child's image of modernity," the hope bequeathed them that history might yet come to be. "The feeling of one who is in need and help comes, one who is happy not because he is saved—he is not saved—but rather because new, young people come, confident, ready to take up the struggle, ignorant, of course, of what stands before them, yet in an ignorance which does not cause the observer to lose hope but rather fills him with awe, with joy, with tears. Hatred of him against whom the struggle is waged is also present." For this struggle there is a call to arms: "In our house, this enormous suburban house, a rented barracks overgrown with indestructible medieval ruins,

there was proclaimed today, on a misty, icy winter morning, the following
call to arms: 'Fellow Tenants, I possess five toy guns. They are hanging in
my closet, one on each hook. The first is mine, the rest are for anyone who
wants them. Should there be more than four, the others will have to bring
their own weapons and deposit them in my closet. For there will have to be
unity; without unity we will not move forward. Incidentally, I only have
guns which are entirely useless for any other purpose, the mechanism is ru-
ined, the wads are torn off, only the hammers still snap. Therefore, it will
not be very difficult to procure more such weapons should they be needed.
But fundamentally, I will be just as happy, in the beginning, with people
who have no guns. Those of us who do, will, at the crucial moment, take
the unarmed into our midst. This is a strategy which proved itself with the
first American farmers against the Indians; why shouldn't it prove itself here
as well, since the conditions are, after all, similar? We can even forget about
guns, then, for the duration, and even the five guns are not absolutely necessary, and they will be used simply because they are already here. If the
other four do not want to carry them, then they can forget about them. I
alone will carry one, as the leader. But we shouldn't have a leader, and so I,
too, will destroy my gun or lay it aside.' That was the first call to arms. In
our house no one has the time or desire to read such calls, much less consider them. Soon the little papers were swimming along in the stream of
dirt which originates in the attic, is nourished by all the corridors, and
spills down the stairs to struggle there with the opposing stream that swells
upwards from below. But a week later came a second call: 'Fellow Tenants!
So far no one has reported to me. I was, insofar as the necessity of earning
my living allowed, constantly at home, and during the time of my absence,
when the door to my room was always left open, a sheet of paper lay on my
table on which anyone who so desired could enroll. No one has done so.'"
This is the figure of the revolution in Kafka's narratives.

VI

Klaus Mann insisted that there was a similarity between Kafka's world and
that of the Third Reich. And while it is true that any direct political allusion would have violated the spirit of a work whose "hatred of him against
whom the struggle is waged" was far too implacable to have sanctioned any
kind of aesthetic realism, any acceptance of the facade of reality at face

value—nevertheless, it is National Socialism far more than the hidden dominion of God that his work cites. Dialectical theology fails in its attempt
to appropriate him, not merely because of the mythical character of the
powers at work, an aspect that Benjamin rightly emphasized, but also because in Kafka, unlike *Fear and Trembling*, ambiguity and obscurity are attributed not exclusively to the Other as such but to human beings and to
the conditions in which they live. Precisely that "infinite qualitative distinction" taught by Kierkegaard and Barth is leveled off; there is no real
distinction, Kafka writes, between town and castle. Kafka's method was
verified when the obsolete liberal traits that he surveyed, stemming from
the anarchy of commodity production, changed into the forms of fascist
organization. And it was not only Kafka's prophecy of terror and torture
that was fulfilled. "State and Party"—they meet in attics, live in taverns,
like Hitler and Goebbels in the *Kaiserhof,* a band of conspirators installed
as the police. Their usurpation reveals that inherent in the myth of power.
In *The Castle* the officials wear a special uniform, as the SS did—one that
any pariah can make himself, if need be. In fascism, too, the elites are self-
appointed. Arrest is assault, judgment violence. The Party always allowed
its potential victims a dubious, corrupt chance to bargain and negotiate, as
do Kafka's inaccessible functionaries; he could have invented the expression "protective custody" had it not already become current during the
First World War. Gisa, the blonde schoolmistress, cruel and fond of animals—probably the only pretty girl depicted by Kafka who is free from
mutilation, as though her hardness scorned the Kafkaesque maelstrom—
stems from the pre-Adamic race of Hitler *Jungfrauen,* who hated the Jews
long before there were any. Acts of unbridled violence are performed by
figures in subordinate positions, types such as noncommissioned officers,
prisoners of war, and concierges. They are all *déclassés,* caught up in the collapse of the organized collective and permitted to survive, like Gregor
Samsa's father. As in the era of defective capitalism, the burden of guilt is
shifted from the sphere of production to the agents of circulation or to
those who provide services: traveling salesmen, bank employees, waiters.
The unemployed (in *The Castle*) and emigrants (in *America*) are dressed
and preserved like fossils of the process of *déclassement.* The economic tendencies whose relics they represent almost before those tendencies had pre-
vailed, were by no means as foreign to Kafka as his hermetic procedure
might suggest. A glimpse of this is to be found in a remarkable empirical
passage from *America,* the first of his novels: "It was some kind of whole-

sale ordering and transporting business, which, to the best of Karl's memory, was unlike anything in Europe. The business consisted in serving as a middleman; not, however, between producers and consumers, or perhaps the sellers, but rather in distributing all goods and basic products among the large factory cartels." It was this very monopolistic apparatus of distribution, "of gigantic dimensions," that destroyed trade and traffic, the Hippocratic face of which Kafka immortalized. The historical verdict is the product of disguised domination, and thus becomes integrated into the myth, that of blind force endlessly reproducing itself. In the latest phase of this force, that of bureaucratic control, he recognizes the earliest stage; its waste products become prehistorical. The rents and deformations of the modern age are in his eyes traces of the Stone Age; the chalk figures on yesterday's school blackboard, left unerased, become the true cave drawings. The daring foreshortening in which such regressions appear, however, also reveals the trend of society. With his transposition into archetypes, the bourgeois comes to an end. The loss of his individual features, the disclosure of the horror teeming under the stone of culture, marks the disintegration of individuality itself. The horror, however, consists in the fact that the bourgeois was unable to find a successor; "no one has done so." Perhaps this is what is meant by the tale of Gracchus, the once wild hunter, a man of force who was unable to die. Just as the bourgeoisie failed to die. History becomes hell in Kafka because the chance that might have saved was missed. This hell was inaugurated by the late bourgeoisie itself. In the concentration camps, the boundary between life and death was eradicated. A middle ground was created, inhabited by living skeletons and putrefying bodies, victims unable to take their own lives, Satan's laughter at the hope of abolishing death. As in Kafka's twisted epics, what perished there was that which had provided the criterion of experience—life lived out to its end. Gracchus is the consummate refutation of the possibility banished from the world: to die after a long and full life.

VII

The hermetic character of Kafka's writings offers the temptation not merely to set the idea of his work in abstract opposition to history—as he himself frequently does—but in addition to refine the work itself out of history with ready profundity. Yet it is precisely this hermetic quality that links it to the literary movement of the decade surrounding the First World War; one of the focal points of this movement was Prague, and its milieu was Kafka's. One must have read Kurt Wolff's black, soft-bound editions of "The Last Judgment," "The Judgment," "Metamorphosis," and the "Stoker" chapter to have experienced Kafka in his authentic horizon, that of expressionism. His epic temperament sought to avoid its characteristic linguistic gesture, although lines like "Pepi, proud, head tossed back, smile never changing, irrefutably aware of her dignity, twirling her braid at every turn, hurried back and forth" or "K. stepped out onto the stoop in the wildly swirling wind and peered into the darkness" display his consummate mastery of the style. Proper names, especially in the shorter prose pieces, stripped of first names, like Wese and Schmar, recall the list of characters in expressionist plays. It is no rarity for Kafka's language to disavow its content as audaciously as in that ecstatic description of the little barmaid—its verve sweeps the narrative up out of the desolate stagnancy of the story. In his liquidation of the dream through its ubiquity, Kafka, the epic writer, follows the expressionist impulse farther than any but the most radical of the poets. His work has the tone of the ultraleft; to level it down to the "universally human" is to falsify it conformistically. Debatable formulations such as the "trilogy of solitude" retain their value because they emphasize a precondition inherent in every line of Kafka. The hermetic principle is that of completely estranged subjectivity. It is no accident that Kafka resisted all social involvement in the controversies on which Brod reports; only for the sake of such resistance did this involvement become thematic in *The Castle*. He is Kierkegaard's pupil solely with regard to "objectless inwardness." This inwardness explains extreme traits. What is enclosed in Kafka's glass ball is even more monotonous, more coherent, and hence more horrible than the system outside, because in absolute subjective space and in absolute subjective time there is no room for anything that might disturb their intrinsic principle, that of inexorable estrangement. Again and again, the space-time continuum of "empirical realism" is exploded through small acts of sabotage, like perspective in contemporary painting; as, for instance, when the land surveyor, wandering about, is surprised by nightfall, which comes much too soon. The undifferentiated character of autarchic subjectivity strengthens the feeling of uncertainty and the monotony of compulsive repetition. Inwardness, revolving in itself and devoid of all resistance, is denied all those things that might put a stop to its interminable movement and that thus take on an aura of mystery. A spell hangs over Kafka's space; imprisoned in itself, the subject holds its breath, as though it were not permitted to touch anything unlike itself. Under this spell pure subjectivity turns into mythology, and spiritualism, carried to its logical extreme, turns into the cult of nature. Kafka's eccentric interest in nudism and nature-cures, his tolerance, however qualified, of Rudolf Steiner's wild superstitions, are not rudiments of intellectual insecurity but rather conform to a principle, which, in implacably denying itself all basis of differentiation, itself loses the power to differentiate and threatens to succumb to the very regression that Kafka uses with such mastery as a literary technique—to the equivocal, amorphous, nameless. "The mind sets itself in opposition to nature as a free and autonomous entity because it sees nature as demonic, both in external reality and in itself. In that the autonomous mind appears as something physical; however, nature takes possession of it at the point when it emerges in its most historical form—the objectless interior. . . . The natural element of the mere, inherently 'historical' mind may be called mythical." Absolute subjectivity is also subjectless. The self lives solely through transformation into otherness; as the secure residue of the subject that cuts itself off from everything alien, it becomes the blind residue of the world. The more the I of expressionism is thrown back upon itself, the more like the excluded world of things it becomes. By virtue of this similarity Kafka forces expressionism—the chimerical aspect of which he, more than any of his friends, must have sensed, and to which he nevertheless remained faithful—into the form of a torturous epic; pure subjectivity, being of necessity estranged from itself as well and having become a thing, assumes the dimensions of objectivity, which expresses itself through its own estrangement. The boundary between what is human and the world of things becomes blurred. This forms the basis of the frequently noted affinity with Klee. Kafka called his writing "scribbling." The thinglike becomes a graphic sign; his spellbound figures do not determine their actions but rather behave as if each had fallen into a magnetic field.[a] It is precisely this as it were external determination of persons existing inwardly that gives Kafka's prose the inscrutable semblance of sober objectivity. The zone in

[a] This dooms all dramatizations. Drama is possible only insofar as freedom—even in its painful birth pangs—is visible; all other action is futile. Kafka's figures are struck by a flyswatter even before they can make a move; to drag them onto the tragic stage as heroes is to make a mockery of them. André Gide would

which it is impossible to die is also the no-man's-land between man and thing: within it meet Odradek, which Benjamin viewed as an angel in Klee's style, and Gracchus, the humble descendant of Nimrod. The understanding of these most advanced, incommensurable productions, and of several others that similarly evade current conceptions of Kafka, may one day provide the key to the whole. His entire work, however, is permeated by the theme of depersonalization in sex. Just as, according to the rite of the Third Reich, girls were not permitted to refuse medal-of-honor winners, Kafka's spell, the great taboo, extinguishes all the lesser taboos that pertain to the sphere of the individual. The textbook example of this is the punishing of Amalia and her family—by tribal rite—because she refuses to submit to Sortini. In the ruling powers, the family triumphs as an archaic collective over its later, individualized form. Helpless, driven together like animals, men and women are coupled. Kafka fashioned his own neurotic guilt feelings, his infantile sexuality as well as his obsession with "purity," into an instrument with which to etch away the approved notions of eroticism. The absence of choice and of memory that characterizes the life of white-collar workers in the huge cities of the twentieth century becomes, as later in Eliot's *The Waste Land*, the image of an archaic past. It is anything but hetaeric. In the suspension of its rules, patriarchal society reveals its true secret, that of direct, barbaric oppression. Women are reified as mere means to an end: as sexual objects and as connections. But in the gloom Kafka gropes for an image of happiness. It emerges out of the hermetically secluded subject's incredulity at the paradox that it can be loved all the same. As incomprehensible as the inclination displayed by all women for the prisoner in *The Trial* is all hope; Kafka's disenchanted eros is also ecstatic masculine gratitude. When poor Frieda calls herself Klamm's beloved, the word's aura is brighter than at the most sublime moments in Balzac or Baudelaire; when, while denying the presence of the surveyor hidden under the table to the searching innkeeper, "she places her little foot on his chest," and then bends down and "quickly kisses" him, she finds the gesture for which one can wait an

---

have remained the author of "Paludes" had he not made the mistake of attempting to do *The Trial*; amid the rising tide of illiteracy, he, at least, ought not to have forgotten that for works of art that deserve the name, the medium is not a matter of indifference. Adaptations should be reserved for the culture industry.

entire lifetime in vain; and the hours that the two spend lying together "in little puddles of beer and other garbage which covered the floor" are those of fulfillment in a world so foreign that "even the air did not have a particle of the air at home." This dimension was made accessible to lyric poetry by Brecht. In both writers, however, the language of ecstasy is far removed from that of expressionism. Confronted by the task of squaring the circle, of finding words for the space of objectless inwardness, in spite of the fact that the scope of every word transcends the absolute immediacy of that which it is supposed to evoke—the contradiction on which all expressionist literature founders—Kafka mastered it ingeniously through the visual element. As the medium of gestures, it asserts its priority. Only the visible can be narrated, yet in the process it becomes completely alien, a picture. In the most literal sense, Kafka saves the idea of expressionism not by listening in vain for "primal sounds" but by transferring the practices of expressionist painting to literature. His attitude toward expressionist painting is similar to that of Utrillo to the picture postcards that are supposed to have served as the models for his frosty streets. In the eyes of the panic-stricken person who has withdrawn all affective cathexis from objects, they petrify into a third thing, neither dream, which can only be falsified, nor the aping of reality, but rather its enigmatic image composed of its scattered fragments. Many decisive parts in Kafka read as though they had been written in imitation of expressionist paintings that should have been painted but never were. At the end of *The Trial*, Josef K.'s eye falls "on the top story of the house bordering on the quarry. As a light sprung on, the shutters flew open, a man, weak and thin in the distance and height, leaned suddenly far out and stretched his arms out even farther. Who was it? A friend? a good man?" This kind of transfer is at the heart of Kafka's picture-world. This world is built on the strict exclusion of everything musical, in the sense of being like music, on the refusal to reject myth through antithesis; according to Brod, Kafka was unmusical, judged by usual criteria. His mute battle-cry against myth is: not to resist. And this asceticism endows him with the most profound relation to music in passages such as the song of the telephone in *The Castle*, the musicology in the "Investigations of a Dog," and in one of the last completed stories, "Josephine." By avoiding all musical effects, his brittle prose functions like music. It breaks off its meaning like broken pillars of life in nineteenth-century cemeteries, and the lines that describe the break are its hieroglyphics.

VIII

An expressionist epic is a paradox. It tells of something about which nothing can be told, of the totally self-contained subject, which is unfree and which, in fact, can hardly be said to exist. Dissociated into the compulsive moments of its own restrictive and confined existence, stripped of identity with itself, its life has no continuity; objectless inwardness is space in the precise sense that everything it produces obeys the law of timeless repetition. This law is not unrelated to the ahistorical aspect of Kafka's work. Form that is constituted through time as the unity of inner meaning is not possible for him; the verdict condemning the large epic that he carries out was observed by Lukács in authors as early as Flaubert and Jacobsen. The fragmentary quality of the three large novels, works that, moreover, are hardly covered any more by the concept of the novel, is determined by their inner form. They do not permit themselves to be brought to an end as the totality of a rounded temporal experience. The dialectic of expressionism in Kafka forces the novel form ever closer to the serialized adventure story. Kafka loved such novels. By adopting their technique he at the same time dissociated himself from the established literary mores. To the list of his known literary models should be added, in addition to Walser, surely the beginning of Poe's "Arthur Gordon Pym" and several chapters of Kürnberger's *Amerikamüde*, such as the description of a New York apartment. Above all, however, Kafka allied himself with apocryphal literary genres. Universal suspicion, a trait etched deeply into the physiognomy of the present age, he learned from the detective novel. In detective novels, the world of things has gained mastery over the abstract subject, and Kafka uses this aspect to refashion things into ever-present emblems. The large works are rather like detective novels in which the criminal fails to be exposed. Even more instructive is his relationship to Sade, regardless of whether or not Kafka knew him. Like the innocents in Sade—not to mention those in American grotesque films and the "funnies"—Kafka's subject, especially the emigrant Karl Rossmann, passes from one desperate and hopeless situation to the next; the stations of the epic adventure become those of a modern passion. The closed complex of immanence becomes concrete in the form of a flight from prisons. In the absence of contrast, the monstrous becomes the entire world, as in Sade, the norm, whereas the unreflective adventure novel, by concentrating on extraordinary events, thus confirms the rule of the ordinary. In Sade and Kafka, however, reason is at work; by making madness the stylistic principle, the objective insanity is allowed to emerge. Both authors are in the tradition of enlightenment, although they represent different stages. In Kafka its disenchanting touch is his "that's the way it is." He reports what actually happens, though without any illusion concerning the subject, which, possessing the greatest degree of self-awareness—of its nullity—throws itself on the junk pile, no different from what the death machine does to its victims. He wrote the consummate Robinson Crusoe story, that of the phase in which each man has become his own Robinson, adrift with his accumulated things on a rudderless raft. The connection between the Robinson Crusoe legend and allegory, originating in Defoe himself, is not alien to the great tradition of the enlightenment. It is part of the early-bourgeois struggle against religious authority. In the Eighth Part of the *Axiomata*, directed against the orthodox chief pastor Goeze, by an author Kafka esteemed highly, Lessing, there is the story of a "discharged Lutheran preacher from the Pfalz" and his family, "which consisted of foundlings of both sexes." Their ship is wrecked, and the family saves itself and a catechism on a small, uninhabited group of islands in the Bermudas. Generations later a Hessian minister finds their descendants on the island. They speak a German "in which he thought he hear nothing but phrases and expressions from Luther's catechism." They are orthodox, "with the exception of a few trivia. The catechism had naturally been used up during the 150 years and they had nothing remaining except the boards of the cover. This cover, they said, contains everything we know. 'It used to contain it, my dear friends,' said the chaplain. 'It still does, it still contains it!' they said. 'We ourselves cannot read, of course, and we hardly even know what reading is. But our fathers heard their fathers read from it. And our forefathers knew the man who engraved the cover. The man's name was Luther, and he lived soon after Christ.'" Perhaps even closer to Kafka's style is Lessing's "Parable," which shares with the later writer a moment, unintentional certainly, of obscurity. The man to whom it was addressed, Goeze, misunderstood it completely. The parable form as such, however, is hardly to be separated from a rationalistic intention. By embedding human meaning and theories in natural materials—is not Aesop's ass a descendant of Ocnos's?—the mind recognizes itself in them. It thus breaks the spell of myth by staring it in the eye without giving ground. Several passages from Lessing's parable, which he intended to reissue under the title "The Palace on Fire," exemplify this all the more for the fact that they are far removed from that awareness of being caught in myth which dawns in analogous passages in Kafka. "A wise, resourceful king of a great, great realm had in his capital city a palace of immeasurable size and extraordinary architecture. The size was immeasurable because he had gathered within it all the people whom he needed as assistants or agents for his government. The architecture was extraordinary because it violated all the accepted rules. . . . After many, many years, the entire palace was still as pure and as perfect as when it had left the hands of its builders—from the outside somewhat puzzling, from within light and harmony everywhere. Anyone who claimed to know something about architecture was particularly offended by the exterior, which was broken up by a few scattered windows, large and small, round and rectangular, but which therefore had all the more doors and gates of different shapes and sizes. . . . It was difficult to understand why so many varied entrances were necessary, since one large portal on each side would have been more decorous and no less efficient. For few people were willing to concede that for each person who was summoned to the palace, the shortest and easiest way to where he was needed was through one of the many small entrances. And thus all kinds of disputes arose among the supposed experts, of whom the most contentious were generally those who had had the least opportunity to see the interior of the palace. Moreover, there was something that one would have thought would simplify and end the dispute but which instead complicated it still more and provided the richest fuel for its stubborn survival. Namely, there were certain old plans that were believed to stem from the original architects of the palace, and these plans were marked up with words and signs, for which the language and character were as good as lost. . . . Once, when the dispute over the plans was not so much settled as dormant—once at midnight the watchman's voice suddenly rang out: 'Fire! fire in the palace!' . . . Everyone leaped from his bed and, acting as though the fire were not in the palace but in his own house, ran for what he considered his most precious possession—his plan. If we can only save that, everyone thought. Even if the palace burns down there, its authenticity is safe here! . . . With all this zealous quibbling the palace might indeed have burned to the ground, if it had burned. But the startled watchman had mistaken the northern lights for a conflagration." It would require only the slightest shift in accent for this story, a link connecting Pascal and Kierkegaard's *Diapsalms to Myself*, to become one by Kafka. Had Lessing merely placed stronger emphasis on the bizarre and monstrous lines of the edifice at the expense of its utility, had he only used the statement that even if the palace burns down there, its authenticity is preserved in the plans, as a favorite answer of all those ministries whose sole legal principle is "quod non est in actis non est in mundo," and the apology for religion against its pedantic exegesis would have become the denunciation of the noumenal power itself through the medium of its own exegesis. The increased obscurity and ambiguity of the parabolic intention are consequences of the enlightenment. The more its rationalism reduces objective matters to human dimensions, the more barren and unintelligible become the outlines of the merely existing world that man can never entirely dissolve into subjectivity and from which he has already drained everything familiar. Kafka reacts in the spirit of the enlightenment to its reversion to mythology. He has often been compared to the cabala. Whether justifiably or not can be decided only by those who know that text. If, however, it is true that, in its late phase, Jewish mysticism vanishes and becomes rational, then this fact affords insight into the affinity of Kafka, a product of the late enlightenment, to antinomian mysticism.

IX

Kafka's theology, if one can speak of such at all, is antinomian with respect to the very God that Lessing defended against orthodoxy, the God of the enlightenment. This God, however, is a *deus absconditus*. Kafka thus becomes, not a proponent of dialectical theology, as is often asserted, but its accuser. Its "absolute difference" converges with the mythic powers. Totally abstract and indeterminate, purged of all anthropomorphic and mythological qualities, God becomes an ominously ambiguous and threatening deity, who evokes nothing but dread and terror. His "purity"—patterned after the mind—which expressionist inwardness sets up as absolute, recreates the archaic terror of nature-bound man in the horror of that which is radically unknown. Kafka's work preserves the moment in which the purified faith was revealed to be impure, in which demythologizing appeared as demonology. He remains a rationalist, however, in his attempt to rectify the myth that thus emerges, to reopen the trial against it, as though before an appellate court. The variations of myths that were found in his unpublished writings bear witness to his efforts in search of such a corrective. The

Trial novel is itself the trial of the trial. Kafka used motifs from Kierkegaard's *Fear and Trembling* not as heir but as critic. In Kafka's statement to whomever it may concern, he describes the court that sits in judgment over men in order to convict law itself. Concerning the latter's mythic character he left no doubt. At one point in *The Trial*, the goddesses of justice, war, and the hunt are treated as one. Kierkegaard's theory of objective despair affects absolute inwardness itself. Absolute estrangement, abandoned to the existence from which it has withdrawn, is examined and revealed as the hell that it inherently was already in Kierkegaard, although unconsciously. As hell seen from the perspective of salvation. Kafka's artistic alienation, the means by which objective estrangement is made visible, receives its legitimation from the work's inner substance. His writing feigns a standpoint from which the creation appears as lacerated and mutilated as it itself conceives hell to be. In the Middle Ages, Jews were tortured and executed "perversely"—i.e. inversely; as early as Tacitus, their religion was branded as perverse in a famous passage. Offenders were hung head down. Kafka, the land surveyor, photographs the earth's surface just as it must have appeared to these victims during the endless hours of their dying. It is for nothing less than such unmitigated torture that the perspective of redemption presents itself to him. To include him among the pessimists, the existentialists of despair, is as misguided as to make him a prophet of salvation. He honored Nietzsche's verdict on the words "optimism" and "pessimism." The light source that shows the world's crevices to be infernal is the optimal one. But what for dialectical theology is light and shadow is reversed. The absolute does not turn its absurd side to the finite creature—a doctrine that already in Kierkegaard leads to things much more vexing than mere paradox and that in Kafka would have amounted to the enthroning of madness. Rather, the world is revealed to be as absurd as it would be for the *intellectus archetypus*. The middle realm of the finite and the contingent becomes infernal to the eye of the artificial angel.

This is the point to which Kafka stretches expressionism. The subject objectifies itself in renouncing the last vestiges of complicity. Of course, this is apparently contradicted by the theory that can be read out of Kafka, as well as by the stories of the Byzantine respect that he, not without scurrility, personally paid to strange powers. But the often-noted irony of these traits is itself part of the didactic content. It was not humility that Kafka preached but rather the most tried and tested mode of behavior against myth—cunning. The only chance, in Kafka's eyes, however feeble and minute, of preventing the world from being all-triumphant was to concede it the victory from the beginning. Like the youngest boy in the fairy tale, one must make oneself completely unobtrusive, small, a defenseless victim, instead of insisting on one's rights according to the mores of the world, that of exchange, which unremittingly reproduce injustice. Kafka's humor hopes to reconcile myth through a kind of mimicry. In this as well he follows that tradition of enlightenment that reaches from the Homeric myth to Hegel and Marx, in whom the spontaneous deed, the act of freedom, coincides with the culmination of the objective trend. Since then, however, the crushing burden of human existence has exceeded all bounds in relation to the subject, and with this development the untruth of the abstract utopia has also increased. As was done thousands of years ago, Kafka seeks salvation in the incorporation of the powers of the adversary. The subject seeks to break the spell of reification by reifying itself. It prepares to complete the fate that befell it. "For the last time, psychology"—Kafka's figures are instructed to leave their psyches at the door, at a moment of the social struggle in which the sole chance for the bourgeois individual lies in the negation of his own composition, as well as of the class situation that has condemned him to be what he is. Like his countryman Gustav Mahler, Kafka sides with the deserters. Instead of human dignity, the supreme bourgeois concept, there emerges in him the salutary recollection of the similarity between man and animal, an idea upon which a whole group of his narratives thrives. Immersion in the inner space of individuation, which culminates in such self-contemplation, stumbles upon the principle of individuation, the postulation of the self by the self, officially sanctioned by philosophy, the mythic defiance. The subject seeks to make amends by abandoning this defiance. Kafka does not glorify the world through subordination; he resists it through nonviolence. Faced by the latter, power must acknowledge itself as that which it is, and it is on this fact alone that he counts. Myth is to succumb to its own reflected image. The heroes of *The Trial* and *The Castle* become guilty not through their guilt—they have none—but because they try to get justice on their side. "The original sin, the ancient injustice committed by man, consists in his protest—one which he never ceases to make—that he has suffered injustice, that the original sin was done against him." It is for this reason that their clever speeches, especially those of the land surveyor, have something of the

inane, doltish, naive about them—their sound reasoning strengthens the
delusion against which it protests. Through reification of the subject, demanded by the world in any event, Kafka seeks to beat the world at its own
game—the moribund become harbinger of Sabbath rest. This is the other
side of Kafka's theory of the unsuccessful death—the fact that the mutilated creation cannot die any more is the sole promise of immortality that
the rationalist Kafka permits to survive the ban on images. It is tied to the
salvation of things, of those that are no longer enmeshed in the network of
guilt, those that are nonexchangeable, useless. This is what is meant in his
work by the phenomenon of obsolescence, in its innermost layer of meaning. His world of ideas—as in the "Natural Theater of Oklahoma"—resembles a world of shopkeepers; no theologoumenon could describe it
more accurately than the title of an America film comedy, *Shopworn Angel.*
Whereas the interiors, where men live, are the homes of the catastrophe,
the hideouts of childhood, forsaken spots like the bottom of the stairs, are
the places of hope. The resurrection of the dead would have to take place
in the auto graveyards. The innocence of what is useless provides the counterpoint to the parasitical: "Idleness is the beginning of all vice, the crown
of all virtue." According to the testimony brought by Kafka's work, in a
world caught in its own toils, everything positive, every contribution, even
the very work that reproduces life, helps increase that entanglement. "Our
task is to do the negative—the positive has already been given us." The
only cure for the half-uselessness of a life that does not live would be its entire inutility. Kafka thus allies himself with death. The creation gains priority over the living. The self, innermost fortress of myth, is smashed, repudiated as the illusion of mere nature. "The artist waited until K. had
calmed himself, and then, finding no other way out, decided to continue
writing. The first small stroke that he made was a deliverance for K., although the artist appeared to accomplish it only in overcoming the greatest resistance; the writing, moreover, was no longer as beautiful, above all
there seemed to be lack of gold; pale and uncertain the line progressed, the
letter grew very large. It was a J and was almost finished when the artist
stamped furiously with his foot into the mound on the grave, causing the
earth to fly up into the air. At last K. understood him; there was no longer
any time left to plead with him. With all his fingers he clawed at the dirt,
which offered scarcely any resistance. Everything seemed prepared. A thin
surface crust seemed to have been put here only for the sake of appearance;

directly beneath it yawned a large hole with steep walls, into which K., turned over on his back by a soft breeze, sank. While below, his head still straining upwards, he was already being absorbed into the impenetrable depths, above his name, lavishly embellished, flashed across the stone. Enchanted by this sight he awoke." The name alone, revealed through a natural death, not the living soul, vouches for that in man which is immortal.

(written 1942–53; first published 1953; GS 10.1: 254–87)
Translated by Samuel Weber and Shierry Weber Nicholsen

12

Commitment

Since Sartre's essay *What Is Literature?* there has been less theoretical debate about committed and autonomous literature. But the controversy remains as urgent as only something that concerns spirit and not the immediate survival of human beings can be today. Sartre was moved to write his manifesto because he—and he was certainly not the first to do so—saw works of art lying in state next to one another in a pantheon of elective culture, decaying into cultural commodities. Works of art violate one another through their coexistence. Each one, without the author necessarily having willed it, strives for the utmost, and none really tolerates its neighbor next to it. This kind of salutary intolerance characterizes not only individual works but also types of art, like the different approaches the half-forgotten controversy about committed and autonomous art was concerned with. These are two "attitudes to objectivity," and they are at war with one another even when intellectual life exhibits them in a false peace. The committed work of art debunks the work that wants nothing but to exist; it considers it a fetish, the idle pastime of those who would be happy to sleep through the deluge that threatens us—an apolitical stance that is in fact highly political. In this view, such a work distracts from the clash of real interests. The conflict between the two great power blocs no longer spares anyone. The possibility of spirit itself is so dependent on that conflict that only blindness would insist on rights that can be smashed to bits tomorrow. For autonomous works of art, however, such considerations, and the

conception of art that underlines them, are themselves already the catastrophe of which committed works warn spirit. If spirit renounces the freedom and the duty to objectify itself in pure form, it has abdicated. Any
works that are still created are busy conforming to the naked existence they
are opposed to, as ephemeral as committed works consider autonomous
works, which from the day they are created belong in the academic seminar where they will inevitably end. The sharp point of this antithesis is a
reminder of just how problematic matters are with art today. Each of the
two alternatives negates itself along with the other: committed art, which
as art is necessarily detached from reality, because it negates its difference
from reality; *l'art pour l'art* because through its absolutization it denies
even the indissoluble connection to reality that is contained in art's autonomy as its polemical a priori. The tension in which art has had its life up
to the most recent period vanishes between these two poles. In the meantime, contemporary literature itself raises doubts about the omnipotence
of these alternatives. Contemporary literature is not so completely subjugated to the way of the world that it is suited to the formation of political
fronts. The Sartrean goats and the Valéryan sheep cannot be separated.
Commitment as such, even if politically intended, remains politically ambiguous as long as it does not reduce itself to propaganda, the obliging
shape of which mocks any commitment on the part of the subject. The opposite, however, what the Soviet catalogue of sins calls formalism, is opposed not only by the officials over there and not only by libertarian existentialism: the so-called abstract texts are easily reproached with a lack of
scandalousness, a lack of societal aggressiveness, even by avant-gardists. On
the other hand, Sartre has the highest praise for Picasso's *Guernica*; he
could easily be accused of formalist sympathies in music and painting. He
reserves his concept of commitment for literature on account of its conceptual nature: "The writer deals with meanings."[1] Certainly, but not only
with meanings. Although no word that enters into a work of literature divests itself fully of the meanings it possesses in communicative speech, still,
in no work, not even the traditional novel, does this meaning remain un-
transformed; it is not the same meaning the word had outside the work.
Even the simple "was" in an account of something that did not exist acquires a new, formal quality by virtue of the fact that it "was" not. This
continues in the higher levels of meaning in a literary work, up to what
was once thought of as its Idea. The special status Sartre accords literature

must also be questioned by anyone who does not immediately subsume the genres of art under the general, overarching concept of art. The residues in literary works of meanings from outside those works are the indispensable nonartistic element in art. The work's formal law can be inferred not from those meanings but only from the dialectic of the two moments. That law governs what the meanings are transformed into. The distinction between writers and literati is a shallow one, but the subject matter of a philosophy of art, such as even Sartre intends, is not its journalistic aspect. Still less is it that for which German offers the term *Aussage* [message]. That term vibrates intolerably between what an artist wants from his product and the demand for a metaphysical meaning that expresses itself objectively. Here in Germany that is generally an uncommonly serviceable Being. The social function of talk about committed art has become somewhat confused. The person who demands, in a spirit of cultural conservatism, that the work of art say something allies himself with the political counterposition in opposing the afunctional hermetic work of art. Those who sing the praises of binding ties will be more likely to find Sartre's *No Exit* profound than to listen patiently to a text in which language rattles the cage of meaning and through its distance from meaning rebels from the outset against a positive assumption of meaning. For Sartre, the atheist, by contrast, the conceptual meaning of the literary work remains the precondition for commitment. Works that the bailiff takes action against in the East may be denounced demagogically by guardians of the genuine message because they allegedly say something they do not say at all. Hatred of what the National Socialists were already calling cultural bolshevism during the Weimar Republic has outlived the age of Hitler, when it was institutionalized. Today it flares up about works of the same kind as forty years ago, including some whose origins go back a long way and whose link with tradition is unmistakable. In the newspapers and periodicals of the radical right there is, as always, a contrived outrage about what is said to be unnatural, overly intellectual, unhealthy, and decadent; they know whom they are writing for. This is in accord with the insights of social psychology into the authoritarian character. Among the existentialia of that character are conventionalism, respect for the rigid facade of opinion and society, defense against impulses that cause confusion about that facade or strike something personal in the unconscious, something that cannot be admitted at any cost. Literary realism of any provenance whatsoever, even if it calls itself critical or socialist, is more compatible with this antagonistic attitude toward everything strange or upsetting than are works that through their very approach, without swearing by political slogans, put the rigid coordinate system of the authoritarian character out of action, a coordinate system that such people then hold to all the more stubbornly the less they are capable of spontaneously experiencing something not already officially approved. The desire to take Brecht out of the repertory [in West Germany] should be attributed to a relatively superficial layer of political consciousness; and it was probably not very strong, or it would have taken a much crasser form after August 13 [i.e., when the Berlin Wall was put up]. When, by contrast, the social contract with reality is canceled, in that literary works no longer speak as though they were talking about something real, one's hair stands on end. Not the least of the weaknesses in the debate about committed art is that the debate did not reflect on the effect exerted by works whose formal law disregards matters of effect. As long as what is communicated in the shock of the unintelligible is not understood, the whole debate resembles shadowboxing. Confusions in evaluating an issue do not, of course, change anything in the issue itself, but they do necessitate a rethinking of the alternatives.

In terms of theory, commitment should be distinguished from tendentiousness, or advocacy of a particular partisan position. Committed art in the strict sense is not intended to lead to specific measures, legislative acts, or institutional arrangements, as in older ideological pieces directed against syphilis, the duel, the abortion laws, or the reform schools. Instead, it works toward an attitude: Sartre, for instance, aims at choice as the possibility of existence, as opposed to a spectatorlike neutrality. The very thing that gives committed art an artistic advantage over the tendentious piece, however, makes the content to which the author is committed ambiguous. In Sartre the category of decision, originally Kierkegaardian, takes on the legacy of the Christian "He who is not for me is against me," but without the concrete theological content. All that is left of that is the abstract authority of the choice enjoined, without regard for the fact that the very possibility of choice is dependent on what is to be chosen. The prescribed form of the alternatives through which Sartre wants to prove that freedom can be lost negates freedom. Within a situation predetermined in reality, it fails and becomes empty assertion. Herbert Marcuse provided the correct label for the philosophical idea that one can accept or reject torture inwardly: nonsense. It is precisely this, however, that is supposed to leap out at us from Sartre's dramatic situations. The reason they are so ill suited to serve as models for Sartre's own existentialism is that—and here we must credit Sartre's truthfulness—they contain within themselves the whole administered world that existentialism ignores; it is unfreedom that can be learned from them. Sartre's theater of ideas sabotages the very thing for which he thought up the categories. But this is not an individual failing on the part of his plays. Art is a matter not of pointing up alternatives but rather of resisting, solely through artistic form, the course of the world, which continues to hold a pistol to the heads of human beings. When, however, committed works of art present decisions to be made and make those decisions their criteria, the choices become interchangeable. As a consequence of that ambiguity, Sartre has stated very openly that he does not expect any real change in the world to be accomplished through literature; his skepticism bears witness to historical changes both in society and in the practical function of literature since Voltaire. The locus of commitment shifts to the writer's views, in accordance with the extreme subjectivism of Sartre's philosophy, which for all its materialist undertones resounds with German speculative philosophy. For Sartre the work of art becomes an appeal to the subject because the work is nothing but the subject's decision or nondecision. He will not grant that even in its initial steps every work of art confronts the writer, however free he may be, with objective requirements regarding its construction. Confronted with these demands, the writer's intention becomes only a moment in the process. Sartre's question "Why write?" and his derivation of writing from a "deeper choice" are unconvincing because the author's motivations are irrelevant to the written work, the literary product. Sartre comes close to acknowledging this when he remarks that, as Hegel was well aware, works increase in stature the less they remain bound up with the empirical person who produces them. When, using Durkheimian terminology, Sartre calls the work a *fait social*, a social fact, he is involuntarily citing the idea of a deeply collective objectivity that cannot be penetrated by the mere subjective intentions of the author. This is why he wants to link commitment not to the writer's intention but to the fact that the writer is a human being.[2] But this definition is so general that any distinction between commitment and human works or behavior of any kind is lost. It is a question of the writer's engaging himself in the present, *dans le présent*; but since the writer cannot escape the present in any case, no program can be inferred from this. The obligation the writer takes on is far more precise: it is not one of choice but one of substance. When Sartre talks about dialectics, his subjectivism pays so little heed to the particular Other that the subject becomes in divesting itself of itself and through which it becomes subject in the first place that for him any and all literary objectification becomes suspect as rigidity. But because the pure immediacy and spontaneity that he hopes to salvage are not defined by anything they confront, they degenerate to a second-order reification. To move the drama and the novel beyond mere expression—for Sartre the prototype would be the cry of the person being tortured—he has to have recourse to a flat objectivity, removed from the dialectic of work and expression: the communication of his own philosophy. That philosophy appoints itself the substance of literature as only in Schiller. But by the criterion of the literary work, what is communicated, however sublime it might be, is hardly more than material. Sartre's plays are vehicles for what the author wants to say; they have failed to keep pace with the evolution of aesthetic forms. They operate with traditional plots and exalt them with an unshaken faith in meanings that are to be transferred from art to reality. The theses illustrated, or sometimes expressly stated, however, misuse the impulses whose expression is the motivation for Sartre's dramaturgy by providing examples, and in doing so they disavow themselves. The sentence "Hell is other people," which concludes one of Sartre's most famous plays,[3] sounds like a quotation from *Being and Nothingness*; moreover, it could just as well read, "Hell is we ourselves." The conjunction of readily graspable plots and equally graspable and distillable ideas has brought Sartre great success and made him, certainly against his own intentions, acceptable to the culture industry. The high level of abstraction of his *pièces à thèse* misled him into setting some of his best works, the filmscript *The Die Is Cast* and the drama *Dirty Hands*, among the political leaders and not in obscurity among the victims. Similarly, the current ideology that Sartre hates confuses the deeds and the sufferings of paper-doll leaders with the objective course of history. Sartre participates in weaving the veil of personalization, the idea that those who are in charge, and not an anonymous machinery, make the decisions, and that there is still life on the heights of the social command posts; Beckett's characters, who are in the process of kicking the bucket, know the score on that one. Sartre's approach prevents him from recognizing the hell he is rebelling against. Many of his phrases could be echoed by his mortal enemies. The idea that it is a matter of choice in and of itself would even coincide with the Nazi slogan "Only sacrifice makes us free"; in Fascist Italy, absolute dynamism made similar philosophical pronouncements. The weakness in Sartre's conception of commitment strikes at the cause to which Sartre is committed.

Brecht too, who glorifies the Party directly in many of his plays, like the dramatization of Gorki's *The Mother* or *The Measures Taken*, occasionally wanted, at least according to his theoretical writings, primarily to educate spectators to a detached, thoughtful, experimental attitude, the opposite of the illusionary stance of empathy and identification. Since *St. Joan*, his dramaturgy has surpassed Sartre's considerably in its tendency to abstractness. Except that Brecht, more consistent than Sartre and the greater artist, has raised abstraction itself to a formal principle, that of a didactic *poésie* that excludes the traditional concept of the dramatic character. Brecht understood that the surface of social life, the sphere of consumption, of which the psychologically motivated actions of individuals are also to be considered a part, conceals the essence of society. As the law of exchange, that essence is itself abstract. Brecht distrusts aesthetic individuation as an ideology. This is why he wants to turn the gruesomeness of society into a theatrical phenomenon by dragging it out into the open. The people on his stage visibly shrivel up into the agents of social processes and functions that they are, indirectly and without realizing it, in empirical reality. Unlike Sartre, Brecht no longer postulates an identity between living individuals and the social essence, nor the absolute sovereignty of the subject. But the process of aesthetic reduction he undertakes for the sake of political truth works against political truth. That truth requires countless mediations, which Brecht disdains. What has artistic legitimacy as an alienating infantilism—Brecht's first plays kept company with Dada—becomes infantility when it claims theoretical and social validity. Brecht wanted to capture the inherent nature of capitalism in an image; to this extent his intention was in fact what he disguised it from the Stalinist terror as being—realistic. He would have refused to cite that essence, imageless and blind, as it were, through its manifestations in the damaged life, removed from meaning. But this burdened him with an obligation to theoretical accuracy in what he unequivocally intended. His art disdains the quid pro quo in which what presents itself as doctrine is simultaneously exempted, by virtue of its aesthetic form, from the requirement that what it teaches be cogent. Critique of Brecht cannot gloss over the fact that—for objective reasons that go beyond the adequacy of his work—he did not satisfy the norm that he established for himself as though it were a means of salvation. *St. Joan* was the central work of his dialectical theater; even *Good Woman of Szechuan* varied it through reversal: just as Joan aids the bad through spontaneous goodness, so the person who wills the good must make herself bad. *St. Joan* is set in a Chicago that is a middle ground between economic data and a Wild West fairy tale of capitalism from *Mahagonny*. The more intimately Brecht involves himself with the former and the less he aims at imagery, the more he misses the essence of capitalism the parable is about. Events in the sphere of circulation, where competitors are cutting one another's throats, take the place of appropriation of surplus value in the sphere of production, but in comparison with the latter, the cattle dealers' brawls over loot are epiphenomena that could not possibly bring about the great crisis on their own; and the economic events that appear as the machinations of the rapacious dealers are not only childish, as Brecht no doubt wanted them to be, but also unintelligible by any economic logic, no matter how primitive. The reverse side of this is a political naïveté that could only bring a grin to the faces of Brecht's opponents, a grin that says they have nothing to fear from such silly enemies; they can be as satisfied with Brecht as they are with the dying Joan in the very impressive final scene of his drama. The idea that the leadership of a strike backed by the party would entrust a crucial task to someone who did not belong to the organization is, with the most generous allowance for poetic credibility, just as unthinkable as the idea that the failure of that one individual could cause the strike to fall through.

Brecht's comedy about the resistible rise of the great dictator Arturo Ui throws a harsh and accurate light on what is subjectively empty and illusory in the fascistic leader. The dismantling of leaders, however, like that of the individual generally in Brecht, is extended into the construction of the social and economic contexts in which the dictator acts. In place of a conspiracy of the highly placed and powerful, we have a silly gangster organization, the cauliflower trust. The true horror of fascism is conjured away; fascism is no longer the product of the concentration of social power but rather an accident, like misfortunes and crimes. The goals of political agitation decree this; the opponent must be scaled down, and that promotes false politics, in literature as in the political praxis of the period before 1933. Contrary to all dialectics, the ridiculousness to which Ui is consigned takes the teeth out of fascism, a fascism Jack London had accurately prophesied decades earlier. The anti-ideological writer paves the way for the degradation of his own doctrine to ideology. The tacitly accepted affirmation that one part of the world is no longer antagonistic is complemented by jokes about everything that belies the theodicy of the current situation. Not that respect for world-historical greatness would prohibit laughter about housepainters, although the use of the word "housepainter" against Hitler speculates awkwardly on bourgeois class consciousness. And the group that staged the seizure of power was most certainly a gang. This kind of elective affinity, however, is not extraterritorial but rooted in society itself. This is why the comic quality in fascism, which Chaplin's film [*The Great Dictator*] also captured, is also its most extreme horror. If that is suppressed, if paltry exploiters of greengrocers are made fun of when it is really a question of key economic positions, then the attack fails. *The Great Dictator* also loses its satirical force and becomes offensive in the scene in which a Jewish girl hits one storm trooper after another on the head with a pan without being torn to pieces. Political reality is sold short for the sake of political commitment; that decreases the political impact as well. Sartre's candid doubt about whether *Guernica* had "won a single person to the Spanish cause" certainly holds true for Brecht's didactic drama as well. Hardly anyone needs to be taught the *fabula docet* that can be derived from it: that the world does not operate justly. The dialectical theory to which Brecht summarily declared allegiance has left few traces there. The demeanor of the didactic drama recalls the American expression "preaching to the saved." In actuality the primacy of doctrine over pure form that Brecht intended becomes a moment of form itself. When suspended, form turns against its own illusory character. Its self-criticism is akin to functionalism in the sphere of the applied visual arts. The heteronomously determined correction of form, the eradication of the ornamental for the sake of function, increases the autonomy of form. That is the substance of Brecht's literary work: the didactic drama as an artistic principle. Brecht's medium, the alienation of immediately occurring events, is more a medium of the constitution of form than a contribution to the work's practical efficacy. To be sure, Brecht did not talk as skeptically about effect as Sartre did, but the shrewd and sophisticated Brecht was hardly fully convinced about it; he once wrote sovereignly that if he were fully honest with himself, the theater was ultimately more important to him than the alteration of the world it was supposed to serve. Not only does the artistic principle of simplification purify the real political dynamics of the illusory differentiations they take on in the subjective reflection of social objectivity, but at the same time, the very objectivity whose distillation the didactic play strives for is falsified. If one takes Brecht at his word and makes politics the criterion of his committed theater, then his theater proves false by that criterion. Hegel's *Logic* taught that essence must appear. But in that case a representation of essence that fails to take into account its relationship to appearance is inherently as false as the substitution of the lumpen proletariat for those behind fascism. Brecht's technique of reduction would be legitimate only in the domain of *l'art pour l'art*, which his version of commitment condemns as he condemns Lucullus.

Contemporary literary Germany likes to distinguish between Brecht the writer and Brecht the politician. People want to rescue this important figure for the West and if possible set him on a pedestal as a pan-German writer and thereby neutralize him, put him *au dessus de la mêlée*. It is certainly true that Brecht's literary power, like his cunning and indomitable intelligence, shot out beyond the official credo and the prescribed aesthetics of the People's Democracies. For all that, Brecht should be defended against this kind of defense. His work, with its obvious weaknesses, would not have such power if it were not thoroughly permeated with politics; even in its most questionable products, like *The Measures Taken*, this produces an awareness that something extremely serious is at stake. To this extent Brecht has fulfilled his claim to provoke thought through the theater. It is useless to distinguish the existing or fictitious beauties of his works from their political intention. Immanent criticism, which is the only dialectical criticism, should, however, synthesize the question of the validity of his work with that of his politics. In Sartre's chapter "Why Write?" he says, quite correctly, "Nobody can suppose for a moment that it is possible to write a good novel in praise of anti-Semitism."[4] Nor in praise of the Moscow Trials, even if the praise was bestowed before Stalin had Zinoviev and Bukharin murdered. The political untruth defiles the aesthetic form. Where the social problematic is artificially straightened out for the sake of the *thema probandum* that Brecht discusses in the epic theater, the drama crumbles within its own framework. *Mother Courage* is an illustrated primer that tries to reduce to absurdity Montecuccoli's dictum that war feeds war. The camp follower who uses war to pull her children through is supposed to become responsible for their downfall by doing so. But in the play this guilt does not follow logically either from the war or from the behavior of the little canteen operator. If she had not been absent at precisely the critical moment, the disaster would not have occurred, and the fact that she has to be absent to earn something has no specific relationship to what happens. The pictorial technique that Brecht has to use to make his thesis graphic interferes with its proof. A political-social analysis such as Marx and Engels outlined for Lassalle's drama about Franz von Sickingen would show that the simplistic equation of the Thirty Years War with a modern war omits precisely what decides Mother Courage's actions and fate in the Grimmelshausen prototype. Because the society of the Thirty Years' War is not the functional society of modern war, no closed functional totality in which the life and death of a private individual could be directly linked with economic laws can be stipulated, even poetically, for the former. Brecht needed those wild, old-fashioned times nonetheless, as an image of the present day, for he himself well knew that the society of his own time could no longer be grasped directly in terms of human beings and things. Thus the construction of society leads him astray, first to a false construction of society and then to events that are not dramatically motivated. Political flaws become artistic flaws, and vice versa. But the less works have to proclaim something they cannot fully believe themselves, the more internally consistent they become, and the less they need a surplus of what they say over what they are. Furthermore, the truly interested parties in all camps still no doubt survive war quite well, even today.

Such aporias are reproduced even in the literary fiber, the Brechtian tone. However little doubt there is about the tone and its unmistakable quality—things on which the mature Brecht may have placed little value—the tone is poisoned by the falseness of its politics. Because the cause he championed is not, as he long believed, merely an imperfect socialism but a tyranny in which the blind irrationality of social forces returns, with Brecht's assistance as a eulogist of complicity, his lyrical voice has to make itself gravelly to do the job better, and it grates. The rough-and-tumble adolescent masculinity of the young Brecht already betrays the false courage of the intellectual who, out of despair about violence, shortsightedly goes over to a violent praxis of which he has every reason to be afraid. The wild roaring of *The Measures Taken* out-shouts the disaster that occurred, a disaster it feverishly tries to depict as salvation. Even the best part of Brecht is infected by the deceptive aspect of his commitment. The language bears witness to the extent of the divergence between the poetic subject and what it proclaims. In order to bridge the gap, Brecht's language affects the speech of the oppressed. But the doctrine it champions requires the language of the intellectual. Its unpretentiousness and simplicity are a fiction. The fiction is revealed as much by the marks of exaggeration as by the stylized recourse to outmoded or provincial forms of expression. Not infrequently it is overly familiar; ears that have preserved their sensitivity cannot help hearing that someone is trying to talk them into something. It is arrogant and almost contemptuous toward the victims to talk like them, as though one were one of them. One may play at anything, but not at being a member of the proletariat. What weighs heaviest against commitment in art is that even good intentions sound a false note when they are noticeable; they do so all the more when they disguise themselves because of that. There is some of this even in the later Brecht, in the linguistic gesture of wisdom, the fiction of the old peasant saturated with epic experience as the poetic subject. No one in any country of the world has this kind of down-to-earth, south German "muzhik" experience any more. The ponderous tone becomes a propaganda technique that is designed to make it seem that life is lived properly once the Red Army takes over. Because there is truly nothing in which that humanity, which is palmed off as having already been realized, can be demonstrated, Brecht's tone makes itself an echo of archaic social relationships that are irrevocably in the past. The late Brecht was not all so far from the officially approved version of humanness. A Western journalist might well praise *Caucasian Chalk Circle* as a Song of Songs about motherliness, and who is not moved when the splendid young woman is held up as an example to the lady who is plagued by migraines. Baudelaire, who dedicated his work to the person who formulated the phrase *l'art pour l'art*, was less suited for such a catharsis. Even ambitious and virtuoso poems like "The Legend of the Origin of the Book Tao Te Ching" are marred by the theatrics of utter simplicity. Those whom Brecht considers classics denounced the idiocy of rural life, the stunted consciousness of those who are oppressed and in poverty. For him, as for the existential ontologist, this idiocy becomes ancient truth. His whole oeuvre is a Sisyphean endeavor to somehow reconcile his highly cultivated and differentiated taste with the boorish, heteronomous demands he took on in desperation.

I do not want to soften my statement that it is barbaric to continue to write poetry after Auschwitz; it expresses, negatively, the impulse that animates committed literature. The question one of the characters in Sartre's *The Dead without Tombs* asks, "Does living have any meaning when men exist who beat you until your bones break?" is also the question whether art as such should still exist at all; whether spiritual regression in the concept of committed literature is not enjoined by the regression of society itself. But Hans Magnus Enzensberger's rejoinder also remains true, namely, that literature must resist precisely this verdict, that is, be such that it does not surrender to cynicism merely by existing after Auschwitz. It is the situation of literature itself and not simply one's relation to it that is paradoxical. The abundance of real suffering permits no forgetting; Pascal's theological "On ne doit plus dormir" ["Sleeping is no longer permitted"] should be secularized. But that suffering—what Hegel called the awareness of affliction—also demands the continued existence of the very art it forbids; hardly anywhere else does suffering still find its own voice, a consolation that does not immediately betray it. The most significant artists of the period have followed this course. The uncompromising radicalism of their works, the very moments denounced as formalist, endows them with a frightening power that impotent poems about the victims lack. But even Schoenberg's *Survivors of Warsaw* remains caught in the aporia in which it has involved itself as an autonomous artistic construction of heteronomy intensified to the point where it becomes hell. There is something awkward and embarrassing in Schoenberg's composition—and it is not the aspect that irritates people in Germany because it does not allow them to repress what they want at all costs to repress. When it is turned into an image, however, for all its harshness and discordance it is as though the embarrassment one feels before the victims were being violated. The victims are turned into works of art, tossed out to be gobbled up by the world that did them in. The so-called artistic rendering of the naked physical pain of those who were beaten down with rifle butts contains, however distantly, the possibility that pleasure can be squeezed from it. The morality that forbids art to forget this for a second slides off into the abyss of its opposite. The aesthetic stylistic principle, and even the chorus's solemn prayer, make the unthinkable appear to have had some meaning; it becomes transfigured, something of its horror removed. By this alone an injustice is done the victims, yet no art that avoided the victims could stand up to the demands of justice. Even the sound of desperation pays tribute to a heinous affirmation. Then works of lesser stature than the highest are also readily accepted, part of the process of "working through the past." When even genocide becomes cultural property in committed literature, it becomes easier to continue complying with the culture that gave rise to the murder. One characteristic of such literature is virtually ever-present: it shows us humanity blossoming in so-called extreme situations, and in fact precisely there, and at times this becomes a dreary metaphysics that affirms the horror, which has been justified as a "boundary situation," by virtue of the notion that the authenticity of the human being is manifested there. In this cozy existential atmosphere the distinction between victim and executioner becomes blurred, since, after all, both are equally vulnerable to the possibility of nothingness, something generally, of course, more bearable for the executioners.

The adherents of that metaphysics, which has in the meantime degenerated to an idle sport of opinions, inveigh as they did before 1933 against the brutalization, distortion, and artistic perversion of life, as though the authors were responsible for what they protest against because what they write reflects the horror. A story about Picasso provides a good illustration of this mode of thinking, which continues to flourish beneath the silent surface of Germany. When an occupying German officer visited him in his studio and asked, standing before the *Guernica*, "Did you make that?," Picasso is said to have responded, "No, you did." Even autonomous works of art like *Guernica* are determinate negations of empirical reality; they destroy what destroys, what merely exists and as mere existence recapitulates the guilt endlessly. It was none other than Sartre who recognized the connection between the autonomy of the work and a will that is not inserted into the work but rather is the work's own gesture toward reality: "The work of art," he wrote, "does not *have an end*; there we agree with Kant. But the reason is that it *is* an end. The Kantian formula does not account for the appeal which issues from every painting, every statue, every book."[5] It need only be added that this appeal does not stand in any direct relationship to the thematic commitment of the literary work. The unqualified autonomy of works that refrain from adaptation to the market involuntarily becomes an attack. That attack, however, is not an abstract one, not an invariant stance taken by all works of art toward a world that does not forgive them for not completely fitting in. Rather, the work of art's detachment from empirical reality is at the same time mediated by that reality. The artist's imagination is not a *creatio ex nihilo*; only dilettantes and sensitive types conceive it as such. By opposing empirical reality, works of art obey its forces, which repulse the spiritual construction, as it were, throwing it back upon itself. There is no content, no formal category of the literary work that does not, however unrecognizably transformed and unawarely, derive from the empirical reality from which it has escaped. It is through this relationship, and through the process of regrouping its moments in terms of its formal law, that literature relates to reality. Even the avant-garde abstractness to which the philistine objects and which has nothing to do with the abstractness of concepts and ideas is a reflection of the abstractness of the objective law governing society. One can see this in the works of Beckett. They enjoy the only fame now worthy of the name: everyone shrinks from them in horror, and yet none can deny that these eccentric novels and plays are about things everyone knows and no one wants to talk about. Philosophical apologists may find it convenient to view Beckett's oeuvre as an anthropological sketch, but in fact it deals with an extremely concrete historical state of affairs: the dismantling of the subject. Beckett's *ecce homo* is what has become of human beings. They look mutely out from his sentences as though with eyes whose tears have dried up. The spell they cast and under which they stand is broken by being reflected in them. The minimal promise of happiness that they contain, which refuses to be traded for any consolation, was to be had only at the price of a thoroughgoing articulation, to the point of worldlessness. All commitment to the world has to be canceled if the idea of the committed work of art is to be fulfilled, the polemical alienation that Brecht the theoretician had in mind, and that he practiced less and less the more he devoted himself sociably to the human. This paradox, which may sound too clever, does not require much support from philosophy. It is based on an extremely simple experience: Kafka's prose and Beckett's plays and his genuinely colossal novel *The Unnamable* have an effect in comparison to which official works of committed art look like children's games—they arouse the anxiety that existentialism only talks about. In dismantling illusion they explode art from the inside, whereas proclaimed commitment only subjugates art from the outside, hence only illusorily. Their implacability compels the change in attitude that committed works only demand. Anyone over whom Kafka's wheels have passed has lost both his sense of being at peace with the world and the possibility of being satisfied with the judgment that the course of the world is bad: the moment of confirmation inherent in a resigned acknowledgment of the superior power of evil has been eaten away. The more ambitious the work, of course, the greater its chance of foundering and failure. The loss of tension that can be observed in works of painting and music that move away from representation and intelligible meaning has in many respects infected the literature referred to, in an abominable expression, as texts. Such works approach irrelevance and inconspicuously degenerate into handicrafts—into the kind of repetitive formulaic play that has been debunked in other species of art, decorative patterns. This often gives legitimacy to the crude demand for commitment. Works that challenge a mendacious positivity of meaning easily verge on meaninglessness of a different kind, positivist formal arrangements, idle play with elements. In doing so they succumb to the sphere they began by differentiating themselves from; an extreme case is a literature that undialectically confuses itself with science and vainly equates itself with cybernetics. The extremes meet: what cuts off the last act of communication becomes the prey of communication theory. There is no firm criterion for distinguishing between the determinate negation of meaning and the mere positivity of a meaninglessness that diligently grinds along of its own accord. Least of all can an appeal to humanity and a cursing of mechanization serve to draw such a line. Those works that through their very existence become the advocates of the victims of a nature-dominating rationality are in their protest by their very nature also always interwoven with the process of rationalization. To deny that process would be to be disempowered, both aesthetically and socially: a higher-order native soil. The organizing principle in every work of art, the principle that creates its unity, is derived from the same rationality that its claim to totality would like to put a stop to.

Historically, the question of commitment has taken different forms in French and German consciousness. Aesthetically, the principle of *l'art pour l'art* has been dominant in France, overtly or covertly, and has been allied with academic and reactionary tendencies. This explains the rebellion against it.[6] In France there is a touch of the pleasant and the decorative even in works of the extreme avant-garde. This is why the appeal to existence and commitment sounded revolutionary there. The reverse is true in Germany. For a tradition extending deep into German idealism—its first famous document, canonized in the intellectual history of the schoolmasters, was Schiller's treatise on the theater as a moral institution—art's freedom from purposefulness, which was, however, first elevated theoretically to a pure and incorruptible moment of the judgment of taste by a

German, Kant, was suspect. Not so much, however, on account of the absolutization of spirit coupled with it; that is precisely what had its fling in
German philosophy—to the point of hubris. Rather, on account of the
face the purposeless work of art turns toward society. It calls to mind the
sensuous pleasure in which even the most extreme dissonance, and precisely that dissonance, participates, in sublimated form and through negation. German speculative philosophy saw the moment of transcendence
contained within the work of art itself—that its own inherent essence is always more than its existence—and inferred from it evidence of its morality. In terms of this latent tradition, the work of art is to be nothing for itself, because otherwise—and Plato's design for state socialism already
stigmatized it in this way—it inspires effeminacy and discourages action
for the sake of action, the German version of original sin. Antagonism to
happiness, asceticism, the sort of ethos that always invokes names like
Luther and Bismarck, have no use for aesthetic autonomy; and there is certainly an undercurrent of servile heteronomy beneath the pathos of the
categorical imperative, which, on the one hand, is supposed to be reason
itself but, on the other hand, is merely something given, something to be
blindly obeyed. Fifty years ago there was the same kind of opposition to
Stefan George and his school as to French aestheticism. Today that stink,
which the bombs did not get rid of, is in league with the outrage over the
alleged unintelligibility of contemporary art. A petit-bourgeois hatred of
sex is at work there; Western ethical philosophers and the ideologues of socialist realism are in agreement on that. No moral terrorism can control the
fact that the face the work of art turns toward the viewer gives him pleasure, even if it is only the formal fact of temporary liberation from the compulsion of practical ends. Thomas Mann expressed that in his phrase about
art as "higher-order farce," something intolerable to those with good
morals. Even Brecht, who was not free of ascetic traits—they return, transformed, in the resistance of great autonomous art to consumption—while
rightly denouncing the culinary work of art, was much too shrewd not to
realize that the pleasurable aspect of the work's effect cannot be completely
disregarded no matter how implacable the work is. But consumption, and
with it complicity in the bad sense, are not smuggled in on the side
through the primacy of the aesthetic object as an object of pure construction. For while the moment of pleasure always recurs in the work's effect
even if it has been extirpated from it, the principle that governs au-

tonomous works of art is not effect but their inherent structure. They are knowledge in the form of a nonconceptual object. In this lies their dignity. They do not need to persuade human beings of it because it has been given to them. This is why it is now timely to speak in favor of autonomous rather than committed works in Germany. The latter can all too readily claim all the noble values for themselves and do with them as they please. There was no foul deed committed even under fascism that did not clothe itself in a moral justification. Those who are bragging about their ethics and their humanity today are only waiting to persecute those they condemn by their criteria and to carry out in practice the same inhumanity of which they accuse contemporary art in theory. In Germany commitment in art amounts primarily to parroting what everybody is saying, or at least what everybody would like to hear. Hidden in the notion of a "message," of art's manifesto, even if it is politically radical, is a moment of accommodation to the world; the gesture of addressing the listener contains a secret complicity with those being addressed, who can, however, be released from their illusions only if that complicity is rescinded.

Literature that exists for the human being, like committed literature, but also like the kind of literature the moral philistine wants, betrays the human being by betraying what could help him only if it did not act as though it were doing so. But anything that made itself absolute in response, existing only for its own sake, would degenerate into ideology. Art cannot jump over the shadow of irrationality: the fact that art, which is a moment in society even in opposing it, must close its eyes and ears to society. But when art itself appeals to this and arbitrarily restricts thought in accordance with art's contingent nature, making this its *raison d'être*, it fraudulently turns the curse it labors under into its theodicy. An "it shall be different" is hidden in even the most sublimated work of art. If art is merely identical with itself, a purely scientized construction, it has already gone bad and is literally pre-artistic. The moment of intention is mediated solely through the form of the work, which crystallizes into a likeness of an Other that ought to exist. As pure artifacts, products, works of art, even literary ones, are instructions for the praxis they refrain from: the production of life lived as it ought to be. Such mediation is not something in between commitment and autonomy, not some mixture of advanced formal elements and a spiritual content that aims at a real or ostensible progressive politics. The substance of works is not the spirit that was pumped into them; if anything, it is the opposite. The emphasis on the autonomous work, however, is itself sociopolitical in nature. The current deformation of politics, the rigidification of circumstances that are not starting to thaw anywhere, forces spirit to move to places where it does not need to become part of the rabble. At present everything cultural, even autonomous works, is in danger of suffocating in cultural twaddle; at the same time, the work of art is charged with wordlessly maintaining what politics has no access to. Sartre himself expressed that in a passage that does credit to his honesty.[7] This is not the time for political works of art; rather, politics has migrated into the autonomous work of art, and it has penetrated most deeply into works that present themselves as politically dead, as in Kafka's parable about the children's guns, where the idea of nonviolence is fused with the dawning awareness of an emerging political paralysis. Paul Klee too should figure in the discussion about committed and autonomous art, because his work, *écriture* par excellence, had literary roots and would not exist if it had not devoured them. During the First World War or shortly thereafter, Klee drew caricatures showing Kaiser Wilhelm as an inhuman iron-eater. Out of these came, in 1920—one could no doubt trace the development in detail—*Angelus novus*; the machine angel, which no longer bears any overt marks of caricature or commitment but far surpasses both. With enigmatic eyes, the machine angel forces the viewer to ask whether it proclaims complete disaster or the rescue hidden within it. It is, however, to use the words of Walter Benjamin, who owned the picture, an angel that does not give but takes instead.

(1962; GS 11:409–30)
Translated by Shierry Weber Nicholsen

13

Trying to Understand *Endgame*

TO S.B., IN MEMORY OF PARIS, FALL 1958

Beckett's oeuvre has many things in common with Parisian existentialism. It is shot through with reminiscences of the categories of absurdity,
situation, and decision or the failure to decide, the way medieval ruins permeate Kafka's monstrous house in the suburbs. Now and then the windows
fly open and one sees the black, starless sky of something like philosophical anthropology. But whereas in Sartre the form—that of the *pièce à
thèse*—is somewhat traditional, by no means daring, and aimed at effect, in
Beckett the form overtakes what is expressed and changes it. The impulses
are raised to the level of the most advanced artistic techniques, those of
Joyce and Kafka. For Beckett absurdity is no longer an "existential situation" diluted to an idea and then illustrated. In him literary method sur-
renders to absurdity without preconceived intentions. Absurdity is relieved
of the doctrinal universality that in existentialism, the creed of the irre-
ducibility of individual existence, linked it to the Western pathos of the
universal and lasting. Beckett thereby dismisses existentialist conformity,
the notion that one ought to be what one is, and with it easy comprehensibility of presentation. What philosophy Beckett provides, he himself reduces to cultural trash, like the innumerable allusions and cultural tidbits
he employs, following the tradition of the Anglo-Saxon avant-garde and especially of Joyce and Eliot. For Beckett, culture swarms and crawls, the way
the intestinal convolutions of *Jugendstil* ornamentation swarmed and
crawled for the avant-garde before him: modernism as what is obsolete in

modernity. Language, regressing, demolishes that obsolete material. In Beckett, this kind of objectivity annihilates the meaning that culture once was, along with its rudiments. And so culture begins to fluoresce. In this Beckett is carrying to its conclusion a tendency present in the modern novel. Reflection, which the cultural criterion of aesthetic immanence proscribed as abstract, is juxtaposed with pure presentation; the Flaubertian principle of a completely self-contained subject matter is undermined. The less events can be presumed to be inherently meaningful, the more the idea of aesthetic substance as the unity of what appears and what was intended becomes an illusion. Beckett rids himself of this illusion by coupling the two moments in their disparity. Thought becomes both a means to produce meaning in the work, a meaning that cannot be rendered directly in tangible form, and a means to express the absence of meaning. Applied to drama, the word "meaning" is ambiguous. It covers the metaphysical content that is represented objectively in the complexion of the artifact; the intention of the whole as a complex of meaning that is the inherent meaning of the drama; and finally the meaning of the words and sentences spoken by the characters and their meaning in sequence, the dialogic meaning. But these equivocations point to something shared. In Beckett's *Endgame* that common ground becomes a continuum. Historically, this continuum is supported by a change in the a priori of drama: the fact that there is no longer any substantive, affirmative metaphysical meaning that could provide dramatic form with its law and its epiphany. That, however, disrupts the dramatic form down to its linguistic infrastructure. Drama cannot simply take negative meaning, or the absence of meaning, as its content without everything peculiar to it being affected to the point of turning into its opposite. The essence of drama was constituted by that meaning. Were drama to try to survive meaning aesthetically, it would become inadequate to its substance and be degraded to a clattering machinery for the demonstration of worldviews, as is often the case with existentialist plays. The explosion of the metaphysical meaning, which was the only thing guaranteeing the unity of the aesthetic structure, causes the latter to crumble with a necessity and stringency in no way unequal to that of the traditional canon of dramatic form. Unequivocal aesthetic meaning and its subjectivization in concrete, tangible intention was a surrogate for the transcendent meaningfulness whose very denial constitutes aesthetic content. Through its own organized meaninglessness, dramatic action must model itself on what has transpired with the truth content of drama in general. Nor does this kind of construction of the meaningless stop at the linguistic molecules; if they, and the connections between them, were rationally meaningful, they would necessarily be synthesized into the overall coherence of meaning that the drama as a whole negates. Hence interpretation of *Endgame* cannot pursue the chimerical aim of expressing the play's meaning in a form mediated by philosophy. Understanding it can mean only understanding its unintelligibility, concretely reconstructing the meaning of the fact that it has no meaning. Split off, thought no longer presumes, as the Idea once did, to be the meaning of the work, a transcendence produced and vouched for by the work's immanence. Instead, thought transforms itself into a kind of second-order material, the way the philosophical ideas expounded in Thomas Mann's *Magic Mountain* and *Doctor Faustus* have their fate as material does, a fate that takes the place of the sensuous immediacy that dwindles in the self-reflective work of art. Until now this transformation of thought into material has been largely involuntary, the plight of works that compulsively mistook themselves for the Idea they could not attain; Beckett accepts the challenge and uses thoughts *sans phrase* as clichés, fragmentary materials in the *monologue intérieur* that spirit has become, the reified residues of culture. Pre-Beckettian existentialism exploited philosophy as a literary subject as though it were Schiller in the flesh. Now Beckett, more cultured than any of them, hands it the bill: philosophy, spirit itself, declares itself to be dead inventory, the dreamlike leavings of the world of experience, and the poetic process declares itself to be a process of wastage. *Dégoût,* a productive artistic force since Baudelaire, becomes insatiable in Beckett's historically mediated impulses. Anything that no longer works becomes canonical, thus rescuing from the shadowlands of methodology a motif from the prehistory of existentialism, Husserl's universal world-annihilation. Adherents of totalitarianism like Lukács, who wax indignant about the decadence of this truly *terrible simplificateur*, are not ill-advised by the interest of their bosses. What they hate in Beckett is what they betrayed. Only the nausea of satiety, the *taedium* of the spirit, wants something completely different; ordained health has to be satisfied with the nourishment offered, homely fare. Beckett's *dégoût* refuses to be coerced. Exhorted to play along, he responds with parody, parody both of philosophy, which spits out his dialogues, and of forms. Existentialism itself is parodied; nothing remains of its invariant categories but bare existence. The play's opposition to ontology, which outlines something somehow First and Eternal, is unmistakable in the following piece of dialogue, which involuntarily caricatures Goethe's dictum about *das alte Wahre*, what is old and true, a notion that deteriorates to bourgeois sentiment:

> HAMM. Do you remember your father.
>
> CLOV (wearily). Same answer. (Pause.) You've asked me these questions millions of times.
>
> HAMM. I love the old questions. (With fervor.) Ah, the old questions, the old answers, there's nothing like them![a]

Thoughts are dragged along and distorted, like the residues of waking life in dreams, *homo homini sapienti sat*. This is why interpreting Beckett, something he declines to concern himself with, is so awkward. Beckett shrugs his shoulders at the possibility of philosophy today, at the very possibility of theory. The irrationality of bourgeois society in its late phase rebels at letting itself be understood; those were the good old days, when a critique of the political economy of this society could be written that judged it in terms of its own *ratio*. For since then the society has thrown its *ratio* on the scrap heap and replaced it with virtually unmediated control. Hence interpretation inevitably lags behind Beckett. His dramatic work, precisely by virtue of its restriction to an exploded facticity, surges out beyond facticity and in its enigmatic character calls for interpretation. One could almost say that the criterion of a philosophy whose hour has struck is that it prove equal to this challenge.

French existentialism had tackled the problem of history. In Beckett, history swallows up existentialism. In *Endgame*, a historical moment unfolds, namely, the experience captured in the title of one of the culture industry's cheap novels, *Kaputt*. After the Second World War, everything, including a resurrected culture, has been destroyed without realizing it; humankind continues to vegetate, creeping along after events that even the survivors cannot really survive, on a rubbish heap that has made even reflection on one's own damaged state useless. The word *kaputt*, the pragmatic presupposition of the play, is snatched back from the marketplace:

> CLOV. (He gets up on ladder, turns the telescope on the without.) Let's see. (He looks, moving the telescope.) Zero . . . (he looks) . . . zero . . . (he looks) . . . and zero.
>
> HAMM. Nothing stirs. All is—

[a] Samuel Beckett, *Endgame* (New York: Grove, 1958), p. 38. Page numbers in parentheses hereafter refer to this edition.

CLOV. Zer—

HAMM. (violently) Wait till you're spoken to. (Normal voice.) All is . . . all is . . . all is what? (Violently.) All is what?

CLOV. What all is? In a word. Is that what you want to know? Just a moment. (He turns the telescope on the without, looks, lowers the telescope, turns toward Hamm.) Corpsed. [In the German translation quoted by Adorno, "Kaputt!"] (29–30)

The fact that all human beings are dead is smuggled in on the sly. An earlier passage gives the reason why the catastrophe may not be mentioned. Hamm himself is vaguely responsible for it:

HAMM. That old doctor, he's dead naturally?

CLOV. He wasn't old.

HAMM. But he's dead?

CLOV. Naturally. (Pause.) *You* ask *me* that? (24–25)

The situation in the play, however, is none other than that in which "there's no more nature" (11). The phase of complete reification of the world, where there is nothing left that has not been made by human beings, is indistinguishable from an additional catastrophic event caused by human beings, in which nature has been wiped out and after which nothing grows any more:

HAMM. Did your seeds come up?

CLOV. No.

HAMM. Did you scratch round them to see if they had sprouted?

CLOV. They haven't sprouted.

HAMM. Perhaps it's still too early.

CLOV. If they were going to sprout they would have sprouted. (Violently.) They'll never sprout! (13)

The dramatis personae resemble those who dream their own death, in a "shelter" in which "it's time it ended" (3). The end of the world is discounted, as though it could be taken for granted. Any alleged drama of the atomic age would be a mockery of itself, solely because its plot would comfortingly falsify the historical horror of anonymity by displacing it onto human characters and actions and by gaping at the "important people" who are in charge of whether or not the button gets pushed. The violence of the unspeakable is mirrored in the fear of mentioning it. Beckett keeps it nebulous. About what is incommensurable with experience as such one can speak only in euphemisms, the way one speaks in Germany of the murder of the Jews. It has become a total a priori, so that bombed-out consciousness no longer has a place from which to reflect on it. With gruesome irony, the desperate state of things provides a stylistic technique that protects that pragmatic presupposition from contamination by childish science fiction. If Clov had really exaggerated, as his companion, nagging him with common sense, accuses him of doing, that would not change much. The partial end of the world that the catastrophe would then amount to would be a bad joke. Nature, from which the prisoners are cut off, would be as good as no longer there at all; what is left of it would merely prolong the agony.

But at the same time, this historical nota bene, a parody of Kierkegaard's point of contact between time and eternity, places a taboo on history. What existentialist jargon considers the *condition humaine* is the image of the last human being, which devours that of the earlier ones, humanity. Existentialist ontology asserts that there is something universally valid in this process of abstraction that is not aware of itself. It follows the old phenomenological thesis of the *Wesensschau*, eidetic intuition, and acts as though it were aware of its compelling specifications in the particular— and as though it thereby combined apriority and concreteness in a single, magical stroke. But it distills out the element it considers supratemporal by negating precisely the particularity, individuation in time and space, that makes existence existence and not the mere concept of existence. It courts those who are sick of philosophical formalism and yet cling to something accessible only in formal terms. To this kind of unacknowledged process of abstraction, Beckett poses the decisive antithesis: an avowed process of subtraction. Instead of omitting what is temporal in existence—which can be existence only in time—he subtracts from existence what time, the historical tendency, is in reality preparing to get rid of. He extends the line taken by the liquidation of the subject to the point where it contracts into a "here and now," a "whatchamacallit," whose abstractness, the loss of all qualities, literally reduces ontological abstractness *ad absurdum*, the absurdity into which mere existence is transformed when it is absorbed into naked self-identity. Childish silliness emerges as the content of philosophy, which degenerates into tautology, into conceptual duplication of the existence it had set out to comprehend. Modern ontology lives off the unfulfilled promise of the concreteness of its abstractions, whereas in Beckett the concreteness of an existence that is shut up in itself like a mollusk, no longer capable of universality, an existence that exhausts itself in pure self-positing, is revealed to be identical to the abstractness that is no longer capable of experience. Ontology comes into its own as the pathogenesis of the false life. It is presented as a state of negative eternity. Dostoyevsky's messianic Prince Mishkin once forgot his watch because no earthly time was valid for him; for Beckett's characters, Mishkin's antitheses, time can be lost because time would contain hope. Bored, the characters affirm with yawns that the weather is "as usual" (27); this affirmation opens the jaws of hell:

> HAMM. But that's always the way at the end of the day, isn't it, Clov?
>
> CLOV. Always.
>
> HAMM. It's the end of the day like any other day, isn't it, Clov?
>
> CLOV. Looks like it. (13)

Like time, the temporal has been incapacitated; even to say that it didn't exist any more would be too comforting. It is and it isn't, the way the world is for the solipsist, who doubts the world's existence but has to concede it with every sentence. A passage of dialogue equivocates in this way:

> HAMM. And the horizon? Nothing on the horizon?
>
> CLOV (lowering the telescope, turning towards Hamm, exasperated). What in God's name would there be on the horizon? (Pause.)
>
> HAMM. The waves, how are the waves?
>
> CLOV. The waves? (He turns the telescope on the waves.) Lead.
>
> HAMM. And the sun?
>
> CLOV (looking). Zero.
>
> HAMM. But it should be sinking. Look again.
>
> CLOV (looking). Damn the sun.
>
> HAMM. Is it night already then?
>
> CLOV (looking). No.
>
> HAMM. Then what is it?
>
> CLOV (looking). Gray. (Lowering the telescope, turning towards Hamm, louder.) Gray! (Pause. Still louder.) GRRAY! (31)

History is kept outside because it has dried up consciousness's power to conceive it, the power to remember. Drama becomes mute gesture, freezes in the middle of dialogue. The only part of history that is still apparent is its outcome—decline. What in the existentialists was inflated into the be-all and end-all of existence here contracts to the tip of the historical and breaks off. True to official optimism, Lukács complains that in Beckett human beings are reduced to their animal qualities.[b] His complaint tries to ignore the fact that the philosophies of the remainder, that is, those that subtract the temporal and contingent element of life in order to retain only what is true and eternal, have turned into the remains of life, the sum total of the damages. Just as it is ridiculous to impute an abstract subjectivist ontology to Beckett and then put that ontology on some index of degenerate art, as Lukács does, on the basis of its worldlessness and infantilism, so it would be ridiculous to put Beckett on the stand as a star political witness. A work that sees the potential for nuclear catastrophe even in the oldest struggle of all will scarcely arouse us to do battle against nuclear catastrophe. Unlike Brecht, this simplifier of horror resists simplification. Beckett, however, is not so dissimilar to Brecht. His differentiatedness becomes an allergy to subjective differences that have degenerated into the conspicuous consumption of those who can afford individuation. There is a social truth in that. Differentiatedness cannot absolutely and without reflection be entered on the positive side of the ledger. The simplification of the social process that is under way relegates it to the *faux frais*, the "extras," in much the same way that the social formalities by means of which the capacity for differentiation was developed are disappearing. Differentiatedness, once the precondition of humanness [*Humanität*], is gradually becoming ideology. But an unsentimental awareness of this is not regressive. In the act of omission, what is left out survives as something that is avoided, the way consonance survives in atonal harmony. An unprotesting depiction of ubiquitous regression is a protest against a state of the world that so accommodates the law of regression that it no longer has anything to hold up against it. There is a constant monitoring to see that things are one way and not another; an alarm system with a sensitive bell indicates what fits in with the play's topography and what does not. Out of delicacy, Beckett keeps quiet about the delicate things as well as the brutal. The vanity of the individual who accuses society while his "rights" add to the accumulation of injustices is manifested in embarrassing declamations like Karl Wolfskehl's *Deutschlandsgedicht* [*Poem on Germany*]. There is nothing

[b] See Theodor W. Adorno, "Extorted Reconciliation," in *Notes to Literature*, ed. Rolf Tiedemann, trans. Shierry Weber Nicholsen (New York: Columbia University Press, 1991), 1: 226–27; and Georg Lukács, *Realism in Our Time* (New York: Harper & Row, 1964).

like that in Beckett. Even the notion that he depicts the negativity of the age in negative form would fit in with the idea that people in the Eastern satellite states, where the revolution was carried out in the form of an administrative act, must now devote themselves cheerfully to reflecting a cheerful era. Playing with elements of reality without any mirroring, taking no stand and finding pleasure in this freedom from prescribed activity, exposes more than would taking a stand with the intent to expose. The name of the catastrophe is to be spoken only in silence. The catastrophe that has befallen the whole is illuminated in the horrors of the last catastrophe; but only in those horrors, not when one looks at its origins. For Beckett, the human being—the name of the species would not fit well in Beckett's linguistic landscape—is only what he has become. As in utopia, it is its last day that decides on the species. But mourning over this must reflect—in the spirit—the fact that mourning itself is no longer possible. No weeping melts the armor; the only face left is the one whose tears have dried up. This lies at the basis of an artistic method that is denounced as inhuman by those whose humanness has already become an advertisement for the inhuman, even if they are not aware of it. Of the motives for Beckett's reductions of his characters to bestialized human beings, that is probably the most essential. Part of what is absurd in his writing is that it hides its face.

The catastrophes that inspire *Endgame* have shattered the individual, whose substantiality and absoluteness was the common thread in Kierkegaard, Jaspers, and Sartre's version of existentialism. Sartre even affirmed the freedom of victims of the concentration camps to inwardly accept or reject the tortures inflicted upon them. *Endgame* destroys such illusions. The individual himself is revealed to be a historical category, both the outcome of the capitalist process of alienation and a defiant protest against it, something transient himself. The individualistic position constitutes the opposite pole to the ontological approach of every kind of existentialism, including that of *Being and Time*, and as such belongs with it. Beckett's drama abandons that position like an outmoded bunker. If individual experience in its narrowness and contingency has interpreted itself as a figure of Being, it has received the authority to do so only by asserting itself to be the fundamental characteristic of Being. But that is precisely what is false. The immediacy of individuation was deceptive; the carrier of individual experience is mediated, conditioned. *Endgame* assumes that the individual's claim to autonomy and being has lost its credibility. But although the prison of individuation is seen to be both prison and illusion—the stage set is the imago of this kind of insight—art cannot break the spell of a detached subjectivity; it can only give concrete form to solipsism. Here Beckett runs up against the antinomy of contemporary art. Once the position of the absolute subject has been exposed as the manifestation of an overarching whole that produces it, it cannot hold up; expressionism becomes obsolete. Art is denied the transition to a binding universality of material reality that would call a halt to the illusion of individuation. For unlike discursive knowledge of reality, something from which art is not distinguished by degrees but categorically distinct, in art only what has been rendered subjective, what is commensurable with subjectivity, is valid. Art can conceive reconciliation, which is its idea, only as the reconciliation of what has been estranged. Were it to simulate the state of reconciliation by joining the world of mere objects, it would negate itself. What is presented as socialist realism is not, as is claimed, something beyond subjectivism, but rather something that lags behind it and is, at the same time, the pre-artistic complement of subjectivism. The expressionist invocation "O Mensch" ["Oh Man"] is the perfect complement to a social reportage seasoned with ideology. An unreconciled reality tolerates no reconciliation with the object in art. Realism, which does not grasp subjective experience, to say nothing of going beyond it, only mimics reconciliation. Today the dignity of art is measured, not according to whether or not it evades this antinomy through luck or skill, but in terms of how it bears it. In this, *Endgame* is exemplary. It yields both to the impossibility of continuing to represent things in works of art, continuing to work with materials in the manner of the nineteenth century, and to the insight that the subjective modes of response that have replaced representation as mediators of form are not original and absolute but rather a resultant, something objective. The whole content of subjectivity, which is inevitably self-hypostatizing, is a trace and a shadow of the world from which subjectivity withdraws in order to avoid serving the illusion and adaptation the world demands. Beckett responds to this not with a stock of eternal truths but with what the antagonistic tendencies will still—precariously, and subject to revocation—permit. His drama is "fun" the way it might have been fun to hang around the border markers between Baden and Bavaria in old Germany, as though they encompassed the realm of freedom. *Endgame* takes place in a neutral zone between the inner and the outer, between the materials without which no subjectivity could express itself or even exist and an animation that causes the materials to dissolve and blend as though it had breathed on the mirror in which they are seen. So paltry are the materials that aesthetic formalism is, ironically, rescued from its opponents on either side: the materials vendors of Diamat, dialectical materialism, on the one hand, and the cultural spokespersons of authentic expression on the other. The concretism of lemures, who have lost their horizon in more than one sense, passes directly into the most extreme abstraction. The material stratum itself gives rise to a procedure through which the materials, touched tangentially in passing, come to approximate geometric forms; what is most limited becomes most general. The localization of *Endgame* in that zone mocks the spectator with the suggestion of something symbolic, something that, like Kafka, it then withholds. Because no subject matter is simply what it is, all subject matter appears to be the sign of an inner sphere. But the inner sphere of which it would be a sign no longer exists, and the signs do not point to anything else. The strict ration of reality and characters that the drama is allotted and with which it makes do is identical to what remains of subject, spirit, and soul in view of the permanent catastrophe. What is left of spirit, which originated in mimesis, is pitiful imitation; what is left of the soul, which dramatizes itself, is an inhumane sentimentality; and what is left of the subject is its most abstract characteristic: merely existing, and thereby already committing an outrage. Beckett's characters behave in precisely the primitive, behavioristic manner appropriate to the state of affairs after the catastrophe, after it has mutilated them so that they cannot react any differently; flies twitching after the fly swatter has half-squashed them. The aesthetic *principium stilisationis* turns human beings into the same thing. Subjects thrown completely back upon their own resources, worldlessness become flesh, they consist of nothing but the wretched realities of their world, which has shriveled to bare necessity. They are empty personae, truly mere masks through whom sound merely passes. Their phoniness is the result of the disenchantment of spirit as mythology. In order to underbid history and thereby perhaps survive it, *Endgame* takes up a position at the nadir of what the construction of the subject-object laid claim to at the zenith of philosophy: pure identity becomes the identity of what has been annihilated, the identity of subject and object in a state of complete alienation. In Kafka, meanings were decapitated or disheveled; Beckett simply puts a stop to the infinity, in the bad sense, of intentions: their meaning, according to him, is meaninglessness. This is his objective and nonpolemical judgment on existential philosophy, which by means of the equivocations in the concept of meaning transfigures meaninglessness itself into meaning under the name of "thrownness," *Geworfenheit*, and, later, absurdity. Beckett does not oppose this with a *Weltanschauung*; instead, he takes it literally. What becomes of the absurd once the characteristics of the meaning of existence have been demolished is not something universal—if it were, the absurd would turn back into an idea. Instead, the absurd turns into forlorn particulars, which mock the conceptual, a layer composed of minimal utensils, refrigerators, lameness, blindness, and the distasteful bodily functions. Everything waits to be carted off to the dump. This stratum is not a symbolic one but rather the stratum characteristic of a post-psychological condition such as one finds in old people and in those who have been tortured.

Dragged out of the sphere of inwardness, Heidegger's *Befindlichkeiten* [states-of-being] and Jaspers's situations become materialist. The hypostasis of the individual and that of the situation were in harmony in them. "Situation" was temporal existence as such and the totality of the living individual as the primary certainty. It presupposed the identity of the person. Beckett proves himself to be Proust's student and Joyce's friend by returning to the concept of situation its actual content, what the philosophy that exploits it avoids—the dissociation of the unity of consciousness into disparate elements, into nonidentity. But once the subject is no longer unquestionably identical with itself, no longer a self-contained complex of meaning, its boundary with what is outside it becomes blurred, and the situations of inwardness become those of *phusis*, of physical reality. The verdict on individuality, which existentialism retained as an idealist core, condemns idealism. Nonidentity is both the historical disintegration of the unity of the subject and the emergence of something that is not itself subject. That changes what the term "situation" can be used to mean. Jaspers defines it as "a reality for an existing subject who has a stake in it."[c] He subordinates the concept of situation to the subject, which is conceived as stable and identical, just as he assumes that the situation acquires meaning through its relationship to this subject. Immediately afterwards he also calls it "not just a reality governed by natural laws. It is a sense-related reality," which, moreover, remarkably, is for him already conceived as "neither psy-

[c] Karl Jaspers, *Philosophy*, trans. E. G. Ashton (Chicago: University of Chicago Press, 1970), 2: 177.

chological nor physical, but both in one."[d] But when, in Beckett's view, the situation actually becomes both, it loses its existential-ontological constituents: personal identity and meaning. This becomes striking in the concept of the "boundary situation" [*Grenzsituation*]. That concept, too, originates with Jaspers:

Situations like the following: that I am always in situations; that I cannot live without struggling and suffering; that I cannot avoid guilt; that I must die—these are what I call boundary situations. They never change, except in appearance; [with regard to our existence, they are final].[e]

The construction of *Endgame* takes that up with a sardonic "I beg your pardon?" Platitudes like "I cannot live without struggling and suffering; . . . I cannot avoid guilt; . . . I must die" lose their blandness when they are retrieved from the a priori and returned to the sphere of phenomena. The qualities of nobility and affirmation disintegrate; these are the qualities with which philosophy—by subsuming the aconceptual under a concept that causes what ontology pompously calls "difference" to magically disappear—adorns an existence Hegel already called "foul." Beckett picks up existential philosophy, which has been standing on its head, and puts it back on its feet. His play responds to the comedy and ideological distortion in sentences like "Courage in the boundary situation is an attitude that lets me view death as an indefinite opportunity to be myself,"[f] whether Beckett is familiar with them or not. The poverty of the participants in *Endgame* is the poverty of philosophy.

The Beckettian situations of which his drama is composed are the photographic negative of a reality referred to meaning. They have as their model the situations of empirical existence, situations that, once isolated and deprived of their instrumental and psychological context through the loss of personal unity, spontaneously assume a specific and compelling expression—that of horror. Such situations were already to be found in the praxis of expressionism. The horror aroused by Leonhard Frank's schoolteacher Mager, a horror that occasions his murder, is evident in the description of the elaborate manner in which Herr Mager peels an apple in front of his class. His deliberateness, which looks so innocent, is a figure of

[d] Ibid.

[e] Ibid., p. 178; bracketed material omitted in the English translation.

[f] Ibid., p. 197.

sadism: the image of the person who takes his time is like the person who keeps people waiting for a grisly punishment. But Beckett's treatment of these situations, the frightening and artificial derivatives of the perennial simpleminded situation comedy, helps to articulate something that was already evident in Proust. In a posthumous work, *Immediacy and the Interpretation of Meaning*, Heinrich Rickert speculates on the possibility of an objective physiognomy of the spirit, a "soul" in a landscape or a work of art that would not be a mere projection.[g] Rickert cites a passage from Ernst Robert Curtius, who considers it "only partially correct . . . to see in Proust merely or primarily a great psychologist. A Stendhal is accurately characterized by this term. It . . . places him in the Cartesian tradition of the French spirit. But Proust does not acknowledge the distinction between thinking substance and extended substance. He does not divide the world into the psychic and the physical. To view his work from the perspective of the 'psychological novel' is to misunderstand its meaning. In Proust's books the world of sense objects occupies the same space as that of the psychic." Or: "If Proust is a psychologist, then he is one in a completely new sense of the word: he is a psychologist in that he immerses everything real, including sense perception, in a psychic fluid." To show that "the customary notion of the psychic does not fit here," Rickert cites Curtius again: "But the concept of the psychological has thereby lost its opposite—and because of this it can no longer be used for characterization."[h] The physiognomy of objective expression retains its enigmatic character, nonetheless. The situations say something—but what? In this regard art itself, the quintessence of situations, converges with that physiognomy. It combines the most extreme specificity with its radical opposite. In Beckett this contradiction is turned inside out. What normally hides behind a communicative facade is sentenced to appear. Working within a subterranean mystical tradition, Proust continues to cling affirmatively to that physiognomy, as though involuntary memory revealed the secret language of things. In Beckett that becomes the physiognomy of what is no longer human. His situations are the counterimages of the inextinguishable substance con-

[g] See Heinrich Rickert, *Unmittelbarkeit und Sinndeutung* (Tübingen: J. C. B. Mohr, 1939), pp. 133–34.

[h] Ernst Robert Curtius, *Französischer Geist im neuen Europa* (1925), reprinted in his *Französischer Geist im zwanzigsten Jahrhundert* (Bern: Francke, 1952), pp. 312–13; quoted in Rickert, *Unmittelbarkeit und Sinndeutung*, pp. 133–34.

jured up in Proust's, wrested from the tide of schizophrenia, which a terrified healthiness defends itself against by crying bloody murder. In the
realm of schizophrenia, Beckett's drama retains its self-control. It subjects
even schizophrenia to reflection:

> HAMM. I once knew a madman who thought the end of the world had
> come. He was a painter—and engraver. I had a great fondness for him. I
> used to go and see him, in the asylum. I'd take him by the hand and drag
> him to the window. Look! There! All that rising corn! And there! Look!
> The sails of the herring fleet! All that loveliness! (Pause.) He'd snatch away
> his hand and go back into his corner. Appalled. All he had seen was ashes.
> (Pause.) He alone had been spared. (Pause.) Forgotten. (Pause.) It appears
> the case is . . . was not so . . . so unusual. (44)

The madman's perception coincides with that of Clov, who peers out the
window on command. *Endgame* moves away from the nadir only by calling its own name, as one does with a sleepwalker: the negation of negativity. Sticking in Beckett's memory is something like an apoplectic middle-
aged man taking his midday nap with a cloth over his eyes to protect them
from light or flies. The cloth makes him unrecognizable. This run-of-the-
mill image, hardly unfamiliar even optically, becomes a sign only for the
gaze that is aware of the face's loss of identity, of the possibility that its
shrouded state is that of a dead man, of how repulsive the physical suffering is that already places the living man among the corpses by reducing
him to his body.[i] Beckett stares at such things until the everyday family life
from which they are drawn pales into irrelevance: at the beginning is the
tableau of Hamm covered with an old sheet; at the end he brings the hand-
kerchief, his last possession, up to his face:

> HAMM. Old Stancher! (Pause.) You . . . remain. (84)

Such situations, emancipated from their context and from the character's
personality, are structured into a second, autonomous context, the way
music assembles the intentions and expressive features that become submerged in it until their sequence forms a structure in its own right. A key
passage in the play,

[i] Max Horkheimer and Theodor W. Adorno, *Dialectic of Enlightenment*, ed.
Gunzelin Schmid Noerr, trans. Edmund Jephcott (Stanford: Stanford University
Press, 2002), pp. 194–95.

If I can hold my peace, and sit quiet, it will be all over with sound, and motion, all over and done with—(69)

reveals the principle, perhaps in a reminiscence of the way Shakespeare handled his in the players' scene in *Hamlet.*

> HAMM. Then babble, babble, words, like the solitary child who turns himself into children, two, three, so as to be together, and whisper together, in the dark. (Pause.) Moment upon moment, pattering down, like the millet grains of . . . (he hesitates) that old Greek, and all life long you wait for that to mount up to a life. (70)

In the horror of not being in a hurry, such situations allude to the irrelevance and superfluousness of anything the subject is still able to do. Hamm considers riveting down the covers of the garbage cans in which his parents live, but he revokes that decision in the same words he uses to change his mind about urinating, which requires the torment of the catheter:

> HAMM. Time enough. (24)

A slight aversion to medicine bottles, dating back to the moment when one became aware that one's parents were physically weak, mortal, falling apart, is reflected in the question:

> HAMM. Is it not time for my pain-killer? (7)

Speaking to one another has been consistently transformed into Strindbergian nagging:

> HAMM. You feel normal?
> CLOV (irritably). I tell you I don't complain. (4)

and at another point:

> HAMM. I feel a little too far to the left. (Clov moves chair slightly.) Now I feel a little too far to the right. (Clov moves chair slightly.) Now I feel a little too far forward. (Clov moves chair slightly.) Now I feel a little too far back. (Clov moves chair slightly.) Don't stay there [i.e. behind the chair], you give me the shivers. (Clov returns to his place beside the chair.)
> CLOV. If I could kill him I'd die happy. (27)

But the waning of a marriage is the situation in which one scratches oneself:

> NELL. I am going to leave you.

NAGG. Could you give me a scratch before you go?

NELL. No. (Pause.) Where?

NAGG. In the back.

NELL. No. (Pause.) Rub yourself against the rim.

NAGG. It's lower down. In the hollow.

NELL. What hollow?

NAGG. The hollow! (Pause.) Could you not? (Pause.) Yesterday you scratched me there.

NELL (elegiac). Ah yesterday!

NAGG. Could you not? (Pause.) Would you like me to scratch you? (Pause.) Are you crying again?

NELL. I was trying. (19–20)

After the former father and preceptor of his parents has told the allegedly metaphysical Jewish joke about the trousers and the world, he himself bursts out laughing over it. The embarrassment that comes over us when someone laughs about his own words becomes existential; life is still a quintessence only as the quintessence of everything one has to be ashamed of. Subjectivity dismays us as domination in a situation where one person whistles and the other comes running.[j] But what shame protests against has its social value: in the moments when the bourgeois act like true bourgeois, they sully the notion of humanity that is the basis for their own pretensions. Beckett's prototypes are also historical in that they hold up as typical of human beings only the deformations inflicted upon them by the form of their society. There is no room left for others. The bad habits and ticks of the normal personality, which *Endgame* intensifies unimaginably, are the universal form—which has long since put its stamp on all classes and individuals—of a totality that reproduces itself only in and through particularity in the bad sense, the antagonistic interests of individuals. But because there has been no life other than the false life, the catalog of its defects becomes the counterpart of ontology.

In a play that does not forgo the traditional cast of characters, however, this fragmentation into disconnected and nonidentical elements is nevertheless tied up with identity. It is only in opposition to identity, and

[j] Cf. Beckett, *Endgame*, p. 45.

thus falling within its concept, that dissociation as such is possible; otherwise it would be pure, unpolemical, innocent multiplicity. For now, the historical crisis of the individual finds its limit in the individual biological entity that is its arena. Thus the sequence of situations in Beckett, which flows on without opposition from the individuals, ends in the stubborn bodies to which they regress. Judged in terms of this unity, the schizoid situations are comical, like hallucinations. Hence the clowning that one sees immediately in the behavior and the constellations of Beckett's figures.[k] Psychoanalysis explains the clown's humor as a regression to an extremely early ontogenetic stage, and Beckett's drama of regression descends to that level. But the laughter it arouses ought to suffocate the ones who laugh. This is what has become of humor now that it has become obsolete as an aesthetic medium and repulsive, without a canon for what should be laughed about, without a place of reconciliation from which one could laugh, and without anything harmless on the face of the earth that would allow itself to be laughed at. An intentionally idiotic double entendre about the weather reads:

> CLOV. Things are livening up. (He gets up on ladder, raises the telescope, lets it fall.) It did it on purpose. (He gets down, picks up the telescope, turns it on auditorium.) I see . . . a multitude . . . in transports . . . of joy. (Pause.) That's what I call a magnifier. (He lowers the telescope, turns toward Hamm.) Well? Don't we laugh? (29)

Humor itself has become silly, ridiculous—who could still laugh at basic comic texts like *Don Quixote* or *Gargantua*?—and Beckett carries out the sentence on it. Even the jokes of those who have been damaged are damaged. They no longer reach anyone; the pun, of whose degenerate form there is a bit in every joke, covers them like a rash. When Clov, the one who looks through the telescope, is asked about the color and frightens Hamm with the word "gray," he corrects himself with the formulation "light black." That botches a line from Molière's *Miser*, which describes the allegedly stolen cashbox as "grayish red." Jokes, like colors, have had the marrow sucked out of them. At one point the two non-heroes, one blind and one crippled, the stronger already both and the weaker in the process of becoming both, plot a "trick," an escape, "some kind of plan" à la *The*

---

[k] Cf. Günther Anders, *Die Antiquiertheit des Menschen* (Munich: Beck, 1956), p. 217.

Threepenny Opera, not knowing whether it will only prolong life and agony or put an end to both of them in absolute annihilation:

> CLOV. Ah good. (He starts pacing to and fro, his eyes fixed on the ground, his hands behind his back. He halts.) The pains in my legs! It's unbelievable! Soon I won't be able to think any more.
>
> HAMM. You won't be able to leave me. (Clov resumes his pacing.) What are you doing?
>
> CLOV. Having an idea. (He paces.) Ah. (He halts.)
>
> HAMM. What a brain! (Pause.) Well?
>
> CLOV. Wait! (He meditates. Not very convinced.) Yes . . . (Pause. More convinced.) Yes! (He raises his head.) I have it! I set the alarm! (46–47)

This is probably associated with the (perhaps also originally Jewish) joke about the Busch Circus in which stupid August, who catches his wife with his friend on the sofa, cannot decide whether to throw out his wife or his friend, because he cares too much about both of them, and hits on the solution of selling the sofa. But even the last trace of silly sophistic rationality is erased. The only thing that is still funny is the fact that humor itself evaporates along with the meaning of the punch line. This is the way someone starts when, having climbed to the top step of a flight of stairs, he keeps going and steps off into empty space. Extreme crudeness carries out the sentence on laughter, which has long been its accomplice. Hamm lets the torsos of his parents, who have turned into babies in the garbage cans, starve to death, the triumph of the son as father. Chatter accompanies this:

> NAGG. Me pap!
>
> HAMM. Accursed progenitor!
>
> NAGG. Me pap!
>
> HAMM. The old folks at home! No decency left! Guzzle, guzzle, that's all they think of. (He whistles. Enter Clov. He halts beside the chair.) Well! I thought you were leaving me.
>
> CLOV. Oh not just yet, not just yet.
>
> NAGG. Me pap!
>
> HAMM. Give him his pap.
>
> CLOV. There's no more pap.
>
> HAMM (to Nagg). Do you hear that? There's no more pap. You'll never get any more pap. (9)

To the irreparable harm the non-hero adds insult, his indignation at the old people who no longer have any decency, the way old people usually wax indignant about immoral youth. In this ambience, what remains of humanity—the fact that the two old people share their last zwieback with one another—becomes repulsive through the contrast with transcendental bestiality, and what remains of love becomes lip-smacking intimacy. To the extent to which they are still human beings, human things still go on:

NELL. What is it, my pet? (Pause.) Time for love?

NAGG. Were you asleep?

NELL. Oh no!

NAGG. Kiss me.

NELL. We can't.

NAGG. Try. (Their heads strain towards each other, fail to meet, fall apart again.) (14)

Like humor, dramatic categories as a whole are shifted around. All are parodied. But not derided. In its emphatic sense, parody means the use of forms in the era of their impossibility. It demonstrates this impossibility and by doing so alters the forms. The three Aristotelian unities are preserved, but drama itself has to fight for its life. *Endgame* is the epilogue to subjectivity, and the play loses the hero along with subjectivity. The only aspect of freedom still known to it is the powerless and pitiful reflex action of trivial decisions.[1] In this, too, Beckett's play is heir to Kafka's novels. His relationship to Kafka is analogous to that of the serial composers to Schoenberg: he provides Kafka with a further self-reflection and turns him upside down by totalizing his principle. Beckett's critique of the older writer, which points irrefutably to the divergence between what is happening and an objectively pure epic language, contains the same difficulty as the relationship between contemporary integral composition and the inherently antagonistic music of Schoenberg: what is the *raison d'être* of forms when the tension between them and something that is not homogeneous with them has been abolished, without that slowing down progress in the artistic mastery of materials? *Endgame* handles the matter by adopting that question as its own, by making it thematic. The same thing that

[1] See Theodor W. Adorno, "Notes on Kafka," Chap. 11 in the present volume, pp. 229–30 footnote a.

militates against the dramatization of Kafka's novels becomes Beckett's subject matter. The dramatic constituents put in a posthumous appearance. Exposition, complication, plot, peripeteia, and catastrophe return in decomposed form as participants in an examination of the dramaturgical corpse. Representing the catastrophe, for instance, is the announcement that there are no more painkillers (14). Those constituents have collapsed, along with meaning, to which drama once served as an invitation. *Endgame* performs a test-tube study of the drama of the age, a drama that no longer tolerates any of its constituents. For example: at the climax of the plot, tragedy had at its disposal, as the quintessence of antithesis, the technique of stichomythia, an extreme tightening of the dramatic fabric— a dialogue in which a trimeter of one character is followed by a trimeter of another. Dramatic form had relinquished this technique as being too remote from secular society in its stylization and its unconcealed pretentiousness. Beckett makes use of it, as though the detonation had provided access to things that were buried under drama. *Endgame* contains rapid-fire monosyllabic dialogues like the play of question and answer that once took place between the deluded king and the messenger of fate. But whereas in *Oedipus* that served as a medium for a rising curve of tension, here it is a medium in which the interlocutors slacken. Short of breath to the point of being mute, they can no longer manage to synthesize linguistic periods, and they stammer in protocol sentences—whether of the positivist or the expressionist variety one does not know. The asymptote toward which Beckett's drama tends is silence, which was already defined as a rest in the Shakespearean origins of modern tragedy. The fact that *Endgame* is followed by an *acte sans paroles* [act without words], as a kind of epilogue, is *Endgame*'s own *terminus ad quem*. The words in *Endgame* sound like stopgap measures because that state of muteness has not yet been satisfactorily achieved; they are like an accompaniment to the silence they disturb.

What has become of form in *Endgame* can almost be traced in literary history. In Ibsen's *Wild Duck*, Hjalmar Ekdal, a photographer who has gone to seed and is already a potential non-hero, forgets to bring the adolescent Hedwig the promised menu from a sumptuous dinner at old Werle's house, to which, wisely, he has been invited without his family. Psychologically, this is motivated in terms of his careless, egotistical character, but it is also symbolic of Hjalmar, of the course of the action, and of the meaning of the whole: the fruitless sacrifice of the young woman. This anticipates the later Freudian theory of parapraxis, which interprets the "slip" in terms of its relationship both to the person's past experiences and to his wishes, hence to the unity of the person. Freud's hypothesis that all our experiences "have a sense"[m] translates the traditional dramatic idea into a psychological realism in which Ibsen's tragicomedy about the wild duck rekindles the spark of form. When symbolism is emancipated from its psychological determinants it becomes reified and turns into something that exists in itself; the symbol becomes symbolist, as in Ibsen's late work— when, for example, the bookkeeper Foldal in *John Gabriel Borkmann* is run down by "Youth." The contradiction between this kind of consistent symbolism and a conservative realism is responsible for the inadequacy of Ibsen's last plays. But by the same token it becomes a leavening agent for the expressionist Strindberg. His symbols tear themselves free of empirical human beings and are woven into a tapestry in which everything and nothing is symbolic because everything can mean everything. Drama has only to recognize the inevitable ridiculousness of this kind of pan-symbolism, which abolishes itself, and make use of it, and Beckettian absurdity has been reached through the immanent dialectic of form. Meaning nothing becomes the only meaning. The deadliest fear of the characters in the drama, if not of the parodied drama itself, is the fear, disguised as humor, that they might mean something.

> HAMM. We're not beginning to . . . to . . . mean something?
> CLOV. Mean something! You and I, mean something! (Brief laugh.) Ah that's a good one! (32–33)

With the disappearance of this possibility, which has long since been suppressed by the superior power of an apparatus in which individuals are interchangeable or superfluous, the meaning of language disappears as well. Irritated by the degenerate clumsiness of the impulse of life in his parents' trashcan conversation and nervous because "it doesn't end," Hamm asks, "What do they have to talk about? What does anyone still have to talk about?" (23). The play lives up to that question. It is built on the foundation of a prohibition of language, and it expresses that taboo in its own structure. But it does not escape the aporia of expressionist drama:

---

[m] Sigmund Freud, *Introductory Lectures on Psychoanalysis*, trans. James Strachey (New York: Norton, 1966), p. 40.

that even where language tends to reduce itself to pure sound, it cannot divest itself of its semantic element, cannot become purely mimetic[n] or gestural, just as forms of painting that are emancipated from objective representation cannot completely free themselves from resemblance to material objects. Once definitively separated from the values of signification, mimetic values become arbitrary and accidental, and ultimately turn into a second-order convention. The way *Endgame* deals with this distinguishes it from *Finnegans Wake*. Instead of trying to liquidate the discursive element in language through pure sound, Beckett transforms it into an instrument of its own absurdity, following the ritual of the clown, whose babbling becomes nonsense by being presented as sense. The objective decay of language, that bilge of self-alienation, at once stereotyped and defective, which human beings' words and sentences have swollen up into within their own mouths, penetrates the aesthetic arcanum. The second language of those who have fallen silent, an agglomeration of insolent phrases, pseudo-logical connections, and words galvanized into trademarks, the desolate echo of the world of the advertisement, is revamped to become the language of a literary work that negates language.[o] Here Beckett's work converges with the drama of Eugène Ionesco. If one of Beckett's later plays revolves around the imago of the tape recorder, the language of *Endgame* is reminiscent of the abominable party game in which the nonsense talked at a party is secretly taped and then played back to the guests to humiliate them. The shock, which people scurry away from in embarrassed giggles, is developed in full in Beckett's work. Just as, after an intensive reading of Kafka, alert experience thinks it sees situations from his novels everywhere, so Beckett's language effects a healing disease in the sick person: the person who listens to himself talk starts to worry that he sounds the same way. For a long time now, people leaving the movie theater seem to see the film's planned contingency continuing in chance events on the street. Gaps open up between the mechanically assembled phrases of everyday speech. When one of Beckett's two characters asks,

[n] Theodor W. Adorno, "Presuppositions," in *Notes to Literature,* ed. Rolf Tiedemann, trans. Shierry Weber Nicholsen (New York: Columbia University Press, 1992), 2: 95–108; and Horkheimer and Adorno, *Dialectic of Enlightenment,* pp. 18–19.

[o] See Theodor W. Adorno, *Dissonanzen,* 2d ed. (Göttingen: Vandenhoeck & Ruprecht, 1958), pp. 34 and 44, reprinted in GS 14: 39–40, 49–50.

with the routine gesture of someone jaded by the inviolable boredom of existence, "What in God's name could there be on the horizon?" (31), this linguistic shrugging of the shoulders becomes apocalyptic precisely by virtue of its utter familiarity. The slick and aggressive impulse of healthy common sense, "What in God's name could there be?," is blackmailed into confessing its own nihilism. Somewhat later, Hamm, the master, orders Clov, the *soi-disant* servant, to fetch the "gaff" for a circus trick, the vain attempt to push the chair back and forth. A short dialogue follows:

> CLOV. Do this, do that, and I do it. I never refuse. Why?
>
> HAMM. You're not able to.
>
> CLOV. Soon I won't do it any more.
>
> HAMM. You won't be able to any more. (Exit Clov.) Ah the creatures, the creatures, everything has to be explained to them. (43)

Every day millions of bosses beat the fact that "everything has to be explained to them" into their subordinates. Through the nonsense it is supposed to justify in that passage, however—Hamm's explanation negates his own command—the line not only casts a harsh light on the craziness of the cliché, which habit obscures, but also expresses what is deceptive about dialogue: the fact that those who are hopelessly estranged from one another can no more reach one another by conversing than the two old cripples in the trashcans. Communication, the universal law of the cliché, proclaims that there is no communication any more. The absurdity of talk does not unfold in opposition to realism but rather develops out of it. For by its very syntactic form—its logicity, its deductive relationships, its fixed concepts—communicative language postulates the law of sufficient cause. But this requirement is scarcely ever satisfied any more: when human beings converse with one another, in part they are motivated by their psychology, the prelogical unconscious, and in part they pursue ends that, as ends of mere self-preservation, deviate from the objectivity whose illusory image is reflected in logical form. Nowadays, certainly, one can prove this to them with their tape recorders. As both Freud and Pareto understood it, the *ratio* of verbal communication is always rationalization as well. But *ratio* itself sprang from the interest of self-preservation, and hence its compulsive rationalizations demonstrate its own irrationality. The contradiction between rational facade and unalterable irrationality is itself already the absurd. Beckett has only to mark it as such to use it as a principle of selection, and realism, divested of the semblance of rational stringency, comes to its senses.

Even the syntactic form of question and answer is undermined. It presupposes an openness about what is to be said that, as Huxley had already recognized, no longer exists. The predesignated answer can be heard in the question, and this turns the play of question and answer into empty delusion, a futile effort to conceal the unfreedom of informative language under the linguistic gestures of freedom. Beckett strips away this veil, and the philosophical veil as well. The philosophy that calls everything radically into question by confronting it with the void stops itself from the outset—by means of a pathos derived from theology—from reaching the frightening conclusion whose possibility it suggests. Through the form of the question it infiltrates the answer with precisely the same meaning the question calls into doubt; it is no accident that in fascism and pre-fascism these *destructeurs* were able to condemn the destructive intellect so heartily. Beckett, however, spells out the lie implicit in the question mark: the question has become a rhetorical one. If the hell of existentialist philosophy is like a tunnel midway through which one can already see the light from the other end shining, Beckett's dialogue rips up the tracks of conversation; the train no longer reaches the point where it starts to get light. Wedekind's old technique of misunderstanding becomes total. The course of the dialogue itself approaches the aleatory principle of the literary production process. The dialogue sounds as though the law of its progression were not the rationality of statement and rejoinder, nor even their psychological interconnection, but rather a process of hearing something out, akin to the process of listening to music that is emancipated from preexisting forms. The drama listens in order to hear what kind of statement will follow the one before. It is only in relation to the initial spontaneity of these questions that the absurdity of the content becomes clear. This too has its infantile prototype in visitors to the zoo who wait to see what the hippopotamus or the chimpanzee will do next.

In its disintegration, language becomes polarized. On the one hand, it becomes the Basic English, or French, or German of individual words, commands sputtered out archaically in the jargon of a universal disrespect, the familiarity of irreconcilable antagonists; on the other, it becomes the ensemble of its empty forms, a grammar that has abandoned all relationship to its content and with it its synthetic function. The interjections are accompanied by practice sentences, God knows what for. This, too, Beckett broadcasts: one of the rules of *Endgame* is that the asocial partners, and the spectators along with them, are always peeking at one another's cards. Hamm considers himself an artist. He has chosen Nero's *qualis artifex pereo* as the motto for his life. But the stories he projects run aground on syntax:

> HAMM. Where was I? (Pause. Gloomily.) It's finished, we're finished. (Pause.) Nearly finished. (50)

Logic staggers around among the paradigms. Hamm and Clov are talking in their authoritarian, cutting manner:

> HAMM. Open the window.
> CLOV. What for?
> HAMM. I want to hear the sea.
> CLOV. You wouldn't hear it.
> HAMM. Even if you opened the window?
> CLOV. No.
> HAMM. Then it's not worthwhile opening it?
> CLOV. No.
> HAMM (violently). Then open it! (Clove gets up on the ladder, opens the window. Pause.) Have you opened it?
> CLOV. Yes. (64–65)

One is almost tempted to see in Hamm's last "then" the key to the play. Because it is not worthwhile to open the window, because Hamm cannot hear the sea—perhaps it has dried up, perhaps it is no longer moving—he insists that Clov open it: the senselessness of an action becomes the reason for doing it, a belated legitimation of Fichte's free activity for its own sake. This is how contemporary actions seem, and they arouse the suspicion that it was never much different. The logical figure of the absurd, which presents as stringent the contradictory opposite of stringency, negates all the meaningfulness logic seems to provide in order to convict logic of its own absurdity: to convict it of using subject, predicate, and copula to lay out the nonidentical as though it were identical, as though it could be accommodated with forms. It is not as a *Weltanschauung* that the absurd replaces the worldview of rationality; rather, in the absurd that worldview comes into its own.

The preestablished harmony of despair governs the relationship between the forms and the residual content of the play. The ensemble, melted down, consists of only four characters. Two of them are excessively red, as though their vitality were a skin disease; the old people, by contrast, are excessively white, like potatoes sprouting in the cellar. None of them have properly functioning bodies any more. The old people consist only of torsos—they lost their legs, incidentally, not in the catastrophe but apparently in a private accident with the tandem in the Ardennes, "on the road to Sedan" (16), where one army regularly destroys another; one should not imagine that all that much has changed. But even the memory of their particular misfortune becomes enviable in view of the vagueness of the general disaster, and they laugh as they remember it. By contrast to the expressionists' Fathers and Sons, they all have proper names, but all four are one-syllable names, "four letter words" like obscenities. The practical and intimate short forms popular in Anglo-Saxon countries are exposed as mere stumps of names. Only the name of the old mother, Nell, is somewhat familiar, if obsolete; Dickens uses it for the touching figure of the child in *The Old Curiosity Shop*. The three others are invented, as though for billboards. The old man is called Nagg, by association with nagging, and perhaps also through a German association: the married couple is a couple by virtue of its *Nagen*, gnawing. They discuss whether the sawdust in their trashcans has been changed, but it is now sand instead of sawdust. Nagg confirms that it was once sawdust, and Nell responds wearily, "Once!" (17), the way a wife scornfully exposes the expressions her husband frozenly repeats. However petty the debate about sawdust or sand may be, the difference between them is crucial for what is left of the plot, the transition from the minimum to nothing at all. Beckett, too, could claim what Benjamin praised in Baudelaire, the ability to say the most extreme things with the utmost discretion;[P] the consoling platitude that things could always be worse becomes a condemnation. In the realm between life and death, where it is no longer possible even to suffer, everything rides on the distinction between sawdust and sand; sawdust, wretched by-product of the object-world, becomes a scarce commodity, and being deprived of it means an intensification of one's life-long death penalty. The two make their home in trashcans (an analogous motif appears, incidentally, in Tennessee Williams's *Camino Real*, although surely neither of the plays drew on the

---

[P] Walter Benjamin, "On Some Motifs in Baudelaire," in *Illuminations: Essays and Reflections*, ed. Hannah Arendt, trans. Harry Zohn (New York: Schocken, 1968), pp. 183–84.

other): as in Kafka, the colloquial phrase is taken literally. "Today the old people are thrown on the garbage heap," and it happens. *Endgame* is true gerontology. By the criterion of socially useful labor, which they are no longer capable of, the old people are superfluous and should be tossed aside; this notion is distilled from the scientific fussing of a welfare system that underlines the very thing it denies. *Endgame* prepares us for a state of affairs in which everyone who lifts the lid of the nearest trashcan can expect to find his own parents in it. The natural connection between the living has now become organic garbage. The Nazis have irrevocably overthrown the taboo on old age. Beckett's trashcans are emblems of the culture rebuilt after Auschwitz. This subplot, however, goes farther than too far; it extends all the way to the demise of the two old people. They are refused their baby food, their pap, which is replaced by a biscuit that the toothless old people can no longer chew, and they choke to death because the last human being is too squeamish to spare the lives of the next to last. This is linked to the main plot in that the deaths of the two old people move it forward to that exit from life whose possibility constitutes the dramatic tension. This is a variation on *Hamlet*: to croak or to croak, that is the question.

Grimly, the name of Beckett's hero abbreviates Shakespeare's; the name of the now-liquidated dramatic subject, that of the first dramatic subject. There is also an association with one of Noah's sons and hence with the Flood: the father of the black race, who, in a Freudian negation, stands for the white master-race. Finally, in English, "ham actor" means a hack comedian. Beckett's Hamm, keeper of the keys and impotent at the same time, plays what he no longer is, as though he had read the recent sociological literature that defines the *zōon politikon* as a role. Being a "personality" would mean putting on airs as expertly as the impotent Hamm does. Personality may even have been a role from the start, nature behaving like something more than nature. Changing situations in the play provide the occasion for one of Hamm's roles. From time to time a stage direction makes the drastic recommendation that he speak with the "voice of a rational being" (33). In his long-winded tale he affects the "narrative tone" (50). The remembrance of something that cannot be brought back becomes a fraud. The disintegration retrospectively condemns as fictitious the continuity of life, which makes life what it is. The difference in tone between people who are telling stories and people who are speaking directly passes judgment on the identity principle. The two tones alternate in Hamm's long speech, which is a sort of interpolated aria without music. He stops at the breaks, with the artificial pauses of a leading man past his prime. *Endgame* presents the antithesis to existential philosophy's norm that human beings should be what they are because there is nothing else they can be—the idea that this very self is not the self but a slavish imitation of something that does not exist. Hamm's duplicity points up the lie involved in saying "I" and thereby ascribing to oneself the substantiality whose opposite is the contents that the ego synthesizes. The enduring, as the quintessence of the ephemeral, is its ideology. But of thought, which used to be the truth content of the subject, only the gestural shell is retained. The two figures act as though they were thinking something over, without in fact thinking anything over:

> HAMM. The whole thing is comical, I grant you that. What about having a good guffaw the two of us together?
> CLOV (after reflection). I couldn't guffaw again today.
> HAMM (after reflection). Nor I. (60)

Hamm's foil is what he is even in his name: a twice-mutilated clown the last letter of whose name has been amputated. His name sounds the same as an obsolete expression for the devil's "cloven" hoof and is like the current word "glove." He is his master's devil, who threatens him with the worst possible thing—leaving him—and also his master's glove, which Hamm uses to makes contact with the world of objects to which he no longer has direct access. Not only the figure of Clov but also Clov's relationship to Hamm is constructed from such associations. On the old piano edition of Stravinsky's *Ragtime for Eleven Instruments*, one of the most important pieces in his surrealist phase, was a drawing by Picasso, probably inspired by the "Rag" in the title, which shows two seedy figures, precursors of Vladimir and Estragon, the vagabonds who are waiting for Godot. This virtuoso piece of graphic art consists of a single tortuous line. *Endgame*'s double sketch is in the same spirit, as are the battered repetitions that Beckett's whole oeuvre irresistibly drags in. In those repetitions history is annulled. The repetition compulsion is learned by watching the regressive behavior of the prisoner, who tries again and again. Not the least of the ways in which Beckett converges with the most contemporary trends in music is that he, a Western man, amalgamates features of Stravinsky's radical past, the oppressive stasis of a continuity that has disintegrated, with advanced expressive and constructive techniques from the Schoenberg school. The outlines of Hamm and Clov are also drawn with a single line; the process of individuation into properly autonomous monads is denied them. They cannot live without one another. Hamm's power over Clov seems to rest on the fact that he is the only one who knows how to open the larder, much as only the head of the firm knows the combination of the safe. He would be prepared to tell him the secret if Clov would promise to "finish" him—or "us." In a phrase thoroughly characteristic of the texture of the play, Clov responds, "I couldn't finish you," and as though the play were making fun of anyone who assumes rationality, Hamm says, "Then you won't finish me" (36). He is dependent on Clov because only Clov can still do the things necessary to keep them both alive. That, however, is of questionable value, because, like the captain of the ghost ship, both must fear that they will not be able to die. The little thing on which everything hangs is the possibility that something might change. This movement, or its absence, constitutes the plot. To be sure, it is never made more explicit than the reiterated leitmotiv "Something is taking its course" (13; cf. 32), as abstract as the pure form of time. The Hegelian dialectic of master and servant, which Günther Anders discussed in relation to *Godot*, is not "given form" in accordance with the tenets of traditional aesthetics so much as ridiculed. The servant is no longer capable of taking charge and doing away with domination. The mutilated Clov would scarcely be capable of it, and in any case, according to the historico-philosophical sundial of the play, it is too late for spontaneous action. There is nothing left for Clov to do but wander off into a world that does not exist for these recluses and take the chance that he will die in the process. For he cannot even rely on his freedom to die. He does manage to decide to leave and comes in as though to say good-bye: "Panama hat, tweed coat, raincoat over his arm, umbrella, bag" (82), with the emphatic effect of a musical finale. But we do not see his exit; he "halts by the door and stands there, impassive and motionless, his eyes fixed on Hamm, till the end" (82). This is an allegory whose intention has fizzled out. Aside from differences that may be decisive but may also be completely irrelevant, it is identical with the beginning. No spectator, and no philosopher, would be capable of saying for sure whether or not the play is starting all over again. The pendulum of the dialectic has come to a standstill.

The action of the play as a whole is composed on two themes, in musical fashion, as double fugues used to be. The first theme is that things should come to an end, a homely version of Schopenhauer's negation of the will to life. Hamm sets the tone: the characters, who are no longer characters, become the instruments of their situation, as though they had to play chamber music. "Of all Beckett's bizarre instruments, Hamm, in *Endgame*, who sits in his wheelchair, blind and immobile, is the one with the most tones, the most surprising sound."q Hamm's nonidentity with himself motivates the course of the action. While he desires the end, as the end of the agony of an existence that is unending in the bad sense, he is as concerned about his life as a man in the fateful "best years of his life." The minor paraphernalia of health are of excessive importance to him. But he fears not death but rather that death could miscarry—an echo of Kafka's motif in "The Hunter Gracchus."r Just as important to him as his own bodily necessities is the fact that Clov, appointed lookout, sees no sail and no column of smoke, that there is no rat or insect stirring from which the disaster could begin all over again, not even the child who may have survived, who would represent hope, and for whom he lies in wait like Herod the butcher stalking the *agnus dei*. Insecticide, which pointed toward the death camps from the very beginning, becomes the end-product of the domination of nature, which now abolishes itself. Life's sole remaining content is that there shall be nothing living. Everything that exists is to be made identical to a life that is itself death, abstract domination. The second theme is assigned to Clov, the servant. According to an admittedly very obscure story, he came to Hamm looking for a refuge, but he also has much of the son of the enraged, impotent patriarch in him. To put an end to one's obedience to the powerless is the most difficult thing there is; everything insignificant and outmoded is irresistibly opposed to its own abolition. The counterpoint between the two plots is provided by the fact that Hamm's will to death is the same as his life principle, whereas Clov's will to life could well bring about the death of them both; Clov [in the English version, Hamm] says, "Outside of here, it's death" (9). Nor is the antithesis formed by the two heroes a fixed one. Their impulses intermingle; it is Clov who first speaks of the end. The schema the course of the action

---

q Marie Luise Kaschnitz, *Zwischen Immer und Nie: Gestalten und Themen der Dichtung* (Frankfurt am Main: Insel, 1971), p. 207.

r See Adorno, "Notes on Kafka," Chap. 11 in this volume, p. 227.

follows is that of the endgame in chess, a typical and to some extent norm-governed situation separated by a caesura from the midgame with its com-binations. The latter are absent in the play as well. Intrigue and plot are tacitly suspended. Only technical errors or accidents, such as the existence of a living thing somewhere, could give rise to something unforeseen, not the spirit of invention. The field is almost empty, and what happened be-fore can be inferred only with great difficulty from the positions of the few characters. Hamm is the king around whom everything revolves and who can do nothing himself. On the stage, the disproportion between chess as a pastime and the inordinate effort it involves takes the form of the dis-proportion between the athletic actions of the actors and the insignificance of their actions. Whether the game ends in a stalemate or in an eternal check, or whether Clov wins, is not made clear, as though too much cer-tainty about this would provide too much meaning. And in any case it is probably not so important: everything comes to a standstill in a draw just as it does in a mate. The only other thing that stands out is the fleeting im-age of the child (78), a very weak reminiscence of Fortinbras or the Child King. It might even be Clov's own abandoned child. But the oblique light that falls from it into the room is as weak as the impotent helping arms that reach out the window at the end of Kafka's *Trial*.

The final history of the subject is made the theme of an inter-mezzo that can allow itself its symbolism because it reveals its own inade-quacy and thereby the inadequacy of its meaning. The hubris of idealism, the enthronement of human meaning as the creator at the center of his creation, has entrenched itself in that "bare interior" like a tyrant in his last days. There, with an imagination reduced to the smallest proportions, Hamm recapitulates what men once wanted to be, a vision of which they were deprived as much by the course of society as by the new cosmology, and which they nevertheless cannot let go of. Clov is his male nurse. Hamm has him push him in his wheelchair to the middle of the room, the room that the world has become and that is at the same time the interior of his own subjectivity:

> HAMM. Take me for a little turn. (Clov goes behind the chair and pushes it forward.) Not too fast! (Clov pushes chair.) Right round the world! (Clov pushes chair.) Hug the walls, then back to the center again. (Clov pushes chair.) I was right in the center, wasn't I? (25)

The loss of a center which that parodies, because that center was already a lie, becomes the pitiful object of a nagging and impotent pedantry:

> CLOV. We haven't done the round.
>
> HAMM. Back to my place. (Clov pushes chair back to center.) Is that my place?
>
> CLOV. I'll measure it.
>
> HAMM. More or less! More or less!
>
> CLOV (moving chair slightly). There!
>
> HAMM. I'm more or less in the center?
>
> CLOV. I'd say so.
>
> HAMM. You'd say so! Put me right in the center!
>
> CLOV. I'll go and get the tape.
>
> HAMM. Roughly! Roughly! (Clov moves chair slightly.) Bang in the center! (26–27)

But what is being requited in this stupid ritual is not something the subject has done. Subjectivity itself is at fault; the fact that one exists at all. Heretically, original sin is fused with creation. Being, which existential philosophy trumpets as the meaning of being, becomes its antithesis. Panic fear of the reflex movements of the living not only serves as an incitement to indefatigable domination of nature; it is directed to life itself, as the cause of the catastrophe life has become.

> HAMM. All those I might have helped. (Pause.) Helped! (Pause.) Saved. (Pause.) Saved! (Pause.) The place was crawling with them! (Pause. Violently.) Use your head, can't you, use your head, you're on earth, there's no cure for that! (68)

From which he draws the conclusion: "The end is in the beginning and yet you go on" (69). The autonomous moral law reverses itself antinomically; pure domination of nature becomes the duty to exterminate, which was always lurking behind it.

> HAMM. More complications! (Clov gets down.) Not an underplot, I trust. (Clov moves ladder nearer window, gets up on it, turns telescope on the without.)

[In the German edition to which Adorno refers, the dialogue continues as follows:

> CLOV. Oi, oi, oi, oi!
>
> HAMM. A leaf? A flower? A toma . . . (he yawns) . . . to?
>
> CLOV (looking). You'll get your tomatoes right away! Someone! There's someone there!
>
> HAMM (stops yawning). Well, go wipe him out. (Clov gets down from the ladder. Softly.) Someone! (with trembling voice.) Do your duty! (78)]

A question addressed by Clov, the frustrated rebel, to his frustrated master passes judgment on the idealism from which this totalitarian concept of duty is derived:

> CLOV. Any particular sector you fancy? Or merely the whole thing? (73)

That sounds like a test of Benjamin's idea that a single cell of reality, truly contemplated, counterbalances the whole rest of the world. The totality, a pure positing by the subject, is the void. No statement sounds more absurd than this most rational of statements, which reduces "everything" to an "only," the mirage of a world that can be dominated anthropocentrically. As rational as this utmost *Absurdum* may be, however, it is not possible to argue away the absurd aspect of Beckett's play solely because hasty apologetics and a desire for labels have appropriated it. *Ratio*, which has become completely instrumental, devoid of self-reflection and reflection on what it has disqualified, must inquire after the meaning that it itself has expunged. But in the state that makes this question necessary, there is no answer left but the void that the question, as pure form, already is. The historical inevitability of this absurdity makes it seem ontological: that is, the delusoriness of history itself. Beckett's drama demolishes it. The immanent contradiction of the absurd, the nonsense in which reason terminates, opens up the emphatic possibility of something true that cannot even be conceived of anymore. It undermines the absolute claim of the status quo, that which simply is the way it is. Negative ontology is the negation of ontology: it was history alone that produced what the mythical power of the timeless and eternal has appropriated. The historical fiber of situation and language in Beckett does not concretize, *more philosophico*, something ahistorical—precisely this practice on the part of existentialist dramatists is as alien to art as it is philosophically backward. Rather, what is eternal and enduring for Beckett is the infinite catastrophe; it is only the fact that "the

earth is extinguished, though I never saw it lit" (81) that justifies Clov's answer to Hamm's question, "Do you not think this has gone on long
enough?": "I've always thought so" (45). Prehistory lives on; the phantasm
of eternity is only its curse. After Clov has told Hamm, who is completely
paralyzed, what he has seen of the earth, which the latter ordered him to
look at (72), Hamm confides to him, as though confiding his secret:

> CLOV (absorbed). Mmm.
>
> HAMM. Do you know what it is?
>
> CLOV (as before). Mmm.
>
> HAMM. I was never there. (74)

No one has ever set foot on the earth; the subject is not yet a subject. Determinate negation takes dramatic form through its consistent inversion.
The two partners qualify their understanding that there is no nature anymore with the bourgeois phrase "you exaggerate" (11). Presence of mind is
the proven means of sabotaging reflection. It occasions the melancholy
reflection:

> CLOV (sadly). No one that ever lived ever thought so crooked as we. (11)

Where they come closest to the truth, they sense, with double comedy,
that their consciousness is false; this is how a situation that can no longer
be reached by reflection is reflected. But the whole play is constructed by
means of this technique of reversal. It transfigures the empirical world into
what it had already been called in the late Strindberg and expressionism.
"The whole house stinks of corpses. . . . The whole universe" (46). Hamm,
who responds, "To hell with the universe," is just as much a descendant of
Fichte, who despises the world because it is nothing but raw materials and
products, as he is the one who has no hope but the cosmic night, which he
supplicates with poetic quotations. Absolute, the world becomes hell:
nothing exists but it. Beckett uses typography to emphasize Hamm's statement: "Beyond is the . . . [OTHER] hell" (26; capitals omitted in the English version). He lets a twisted secular metaphysics shine through, with a
Brechtian commentary:

> CLOV. Do you believe in the life to come?
>
> HAMM. Mine was always that. (Exit Clov.) Got him that time! (49)

In this conception Benjamin's notion of dialectics at a standstill comes into
its own:

HAMM. It will be the end and there I'll be, wondering what can have brought it on and wondering what can have . . . (he hesitates) . . . why it was so long coming. (Pause.) There I'll be, in the old refuge, alone against the silence and . . . (he hesitates) . . . the stillness. If I can hold my peace, and sit quiet, it will be all over, with sound, and motion, all over and done with. (69)

That stillness is the order that Clov allegedly loves and that he defines as the goal of his activities:

CLOV. A world where all would be silent and still and each thing in its last place, under the last dust. (57)

The Old Testament "dust thou shalt become" is translated into: filth. Excretions become the substance of a life that is death. But the imageless image of death is an image of indifference, that is, a state prior to differentiation. In that image the distinction between absolute domination—the hell in which time is completely confined within space, in which absolutely nothing changes any more—and the messianic state in which everything would be in its right place, disappears. The last absurdity is that the peacefulness of the void and the peacefulness of reconciliation cannot be distinguished from one another. Hope skulks out of the world, which cannot conserve it any more than it can pap and bonbons, and back to where it came from, death. From it the play draws its only consolation, a stoic one:

CLOV. There are so many terrible things now.

HAMM. No, no, there are not so many now. (44)

Consciousness gets ready to look its own end in the eye, as though it wanted to survive it the way these two have survived the destruction of their world. Proust, about whom Beckett wrote an essay in his youth, is said to have tried to record his own death throes; the notes were to be inserted into the description of Bergotte's death. *Endgame* carries out this intention as though it were a mandate bequeathed it in a will.

(1961; GS 11: 281–321)
Translated by Shierry Weber Nicholsen

14

Beethoven's Late Style

The maturity of the late works of major artists does not resemble the ripeness of fruit. They are commonly not round but furrowed or even torn. They often lack sweetness, and their bristly, austere husk resists straightforward tasting. They do not possess the harmony that a neoclassical aesthetics is wont to demand from art. They exhibit more of history than of growth. The routine view tends to explain this by declaring them to be the products of a subjectivity, or rather a "personality," ruthlessly expressing itself. This subjectivity is said to break through the smooth surface of form in order to express itself; it turns harmony into the dissonant outpouring of suffering and scorns sensuous charm in favor of the autocratic gestures of the liberated spirit. This account forces late works to the margins of art and to its interface with personal document. And in fact discussions of Beethoven's last works seldom lack pointers to his life and fate. It is as if art theory were willing to forgo its rights in the face of the dignity due to human mortality and to abdicate in the presence of reality.

This is the only possible explanation for the fact that hardly anyone has raised serious objections to the defects of this approach. These defects become evident as soon as you look at the works themselves, instead of their psychological origins. For the task is to identify their formal laws without crossing the frontier separating art from document. Once that line is crossed, every notebook of Beethoven's conversations has greater significance than the C-sharp minor quartet. However, the formal laws governing the late works are not of the kind that can be subsumed under the

concept of expression. From the late Beethoven we possess highly distanced, "nonexpressive" works. This makes it just as plausible to see them
as modern, polyphonic, and objective as to think of them as products of
that ruthless self-expression. Their discordant nature is not always that of
resoluteness in the face of death or of demonic humor. Frequently it is simply enigmatic, yet it is discernible in passages that are cheerful and even
idyllic in tone. The nonsensuous spirit does not avoid expression marks
like "Cantabile e compiacevole" or "Andante amabile." It is not possible to
reduce his stance to the cliché of "subjectivism." After all, subjectivity in
Beethoven's music as a whole, entirely in keeping with the spirit of Kant's
concept, does not just disrupt artistic form, it creates it. The *Appassionata*
is exemplary in this respect. It is undoubtedly more condensed, more coherent, and "more harmonious" than the last quartets, but it is also more
subjective, autonomous, and spontaneous. Nevertheless, these late works
have the advantage of their mysterious nature. What does it consist in?

Only a technical analysis of the works in question can help us to revise this view of the late works. This would have to begin with one particular feature that is sedulously overlooked by the traditional approach: the
role of conventions. This is well known in the case of Goethe's late works,
or Stifter's. But it can be just as much in evidence in Beethoven, the ostensible representative of a radically personal stance. This fact intensifies the
question. For the first principle of every "subjectivist" approach is to eliminate all conventions or to recast them in tune with the requirements of ex-
pressivity. This is why the middle Beethoven himself drew the traditional
accompaniment figures into his dynamic subjectivism by developing latent
middle voices and through rhythm, tension, and other elements. In this
way he transformed them according to his intentions, wherever he did
not—as in the first movement of the Fifth Symphony—simply generate
them from their thematic core, so that their uniqueness removed them
from the realm of convention once and for all. Contrast the compositions
of the late Beethoven. There—even where their syntax, like that of the last
five piano sonatas, is unique—formulae and phrases drawn from convention are scattered throughout. They are full of ornamental chains of trills,
cadences, and fioriture. Frequently, the conventions become visible in a
quite open, undisguised, and unmodified way: the first theme of the piano
sonata op. 110 contains an unashamedly primitive sixteenth-note accompaniment that would not have been countenanced in his middle style; the
last of the Bagatelles has introductory and concluding measures like the

distraught prelude to an operatic aria—all of this in the midst of the most unyielding rock strata of the multivoiced landscape, in the most restrained impulses of a secluded lyricism. No interpretation of Beethoven or probably of any late style will suffice that explains the fragmentary ruins of the conventions in psychological terms, while remaining indifferent to their structural function. After all, it is only in these structural terms that art discovers its substantive meaning. The relation of the conventions to subjectivity must be understood as the formal law from which the substance of the late works arises, if they are to be anything more than touching relics.

This formal law becomes evident in the thought of death. If the rights of art pale when faced with the reality of death, then the latter can certainly not enter directly into art as its "subject." It is the destiny of living creatures, not of anything they construct, and this explains why it has always appeared in art only indirectly: as allegory. Psychological interpretation fails to take cognizance of this. By declaring mortal subjectivity to be the substance of late works, it hopes to be able to become fully aware of death in the work of art; that remains the illusory pinnacle of its metaphysics. This mode of interpretation does indeed perceive the explosive power of subjectivity in the late work of art. But it seeks that power in the opposite direction from where it is to be found, namely, in the expression of subjectivity. Subjectivity, however, vanishes from the work of art as something mortal and in the name of death. The power of subjectivity in late works of art is the sudden flaring up with which it abandons the work of art. It bursts them asunder, not in order to express itself but so as to cast off the appearance of art. What is left of the works is ruins, and subjectivity communicates itself, as if by means of ciphers, only through the hollowed-out forms from which it escapes. Touched by death, the hand of the master liberates the mass of material that it previously shaped; the cracks and crannies it contains are testimony to the ultimate impotence of the self in the face of existence; they are the master's last achievement. Hence the superabundance of subject-matter in *Faust*, part 2, and in *Wilhelm Meisters Wanderjahre*. Hence, too, the conventions that are no longer permeated and overwhelmed by subjectivity but simply allowed to stand. With the outburst of subjectivity, they splinter into pieces. As splinters, fragmented and abandoned, they end up transforming themselves into expression—expression no longer of the isolated self but of the mythical nature of the living creature and of its demise—while the stages in this process of decline are marked symbolically by the late works of art in momentary pauses.

Thus in Beethoven's last works the conventions become expression in the naked representation of themselves. This is furthered by the often-noted foreshortening of his style: this style aims not so much to purify his musical idiom of clichés as to purify the clichés of the illusion of control by subjective spirit: the liberated cliché, released from its own dynamic, speaks for itself. But only for a moment, since subjectivity, escaping, passes through it, and its intentionality suddenly illuminates it; hence the crescendos and diminuendos that, seemingly independently of the musical structure, subject it to a series of shocks in the late Beethoven.

Beethoven no longer gathers up the landscape, assembling it, as it stands there abandoned and alienated, into a picture. He irradiates it with the fire that subjectivity ignites by bursting out and colliding with the walls of the work, faithful to the idea of its dynamic nature. Even his last works remain processlike. Not as a development but as a spark between poles that no longer tolerate a secure middle path and spontaneous harmony. Between opposite poles in a precise technical sense: on the one side, the harmony, unison, of the significant cliché; on the other side, the polyphony that raises itself above it. It is subjectivity that welds these opposite poles together in a single moment, charging the concentrated polyphony with its tensions, fragmenting their unison, and then escaping, leaving behind the denuded tone; it is subjectivity that introduces the cliché as a memorial to the past into which subjectivity itself enters in fossilized form. But the caesuras, the abrupt breaks that characterize the late Beethoven more than anything else are those moments of eruption; the work falls silent when it is abandoned and turns its hollow interior to the outside world. Only then is it followed by the next fragment, transfixed to its spot by the command of an erupting subjectivity and welded to the previous fragment for good or ill; for the mystery lies between the two, and it can be conjured up only in the particular configuration that they form. This explains the apparent paradox that the late Beethoven is said to be both subjective and objective. What is objective is the crumbling landscape; the subjective side is the light that alone illuminates it. He does not synthesize the two harmoniously. Through the power of dissociation he tears them asunder in time, perhaps to preserve them like that for all eternity. In the history of art, late works are the catastrophes.

(written 1934; first published 1937; GS 17: 13–17)
Translated by Rodney Livingstone

15

Schubert

The entire, useless body was invaded by transparency. Little by little the body became luminous. The blood radiated out. The limbs froze in an incomprehensible gesture. And man ceased to be more than a sign among the constellations.

—Louis Aragon

Crossing the threshold between the deaths of Beethoven and Schubert, you feel a shudder like that experienced by someone who emerges from a rumbling, piled-up, cooling crater into the painfully fine, white light, who becomes aware of dark, gossamer-trailing plants against the background of the lava shapes on the bare, defenseless heights and perceives at last, close to the mountain and yet far above his head, the eternal clouds in their path. Leaving the abyss behind him, he enters the landscape that surrounds it and renders its bottomless depths visible by defining its contours with the mighty stillness of its outline and receiving in readiness the light that the glowing mass had just blindly reached out to. Even if Schubert's music does not contain the power of the active will that arises out of the center of gravity of Beethoven's nature, the chasms and shafts that furrow it lead into the same chthonic depths in which that will had its origins and reveal the demonic image that the act of practical reason was always able to master. But the stars that visibly shine for it are the same as those to which the eager hand reached out in the attempt to grasp that unattainable light. This is how we must think of Schubert's landscape in the strict sense. Unlike Beethoven, he cannot be understood in terms of the spontaneous unity of his personality, and so nothing could falsify the substance of his music more than the attempt to think of him as a personality whose ruling idea was a virtual focal point from which to organize its disparate elements.

Instead, the further the components of Schubert's music diverge from such an internal human reference point, the more they prove themselves to be the signs of an intention that alone prevails over the fragments of the deceptive totality of man's desire to exist as a self-determining spirit. Released from every idealist synopsis and from the premature phenomenological study of "sensuous unity," neither a coherent system nor a purposively growing flower, Schubert's music provides the setting for the meeting of truths that it does not produce but receives, and that can be expressed only by human beings who have received them. Of course, this should not be taken as a denial of the share of personal composition in Schubert's music, and however misguided the common view may be that Schubert, as the lyricist of his own self, simply expressed what he happened to be feeling, it would be no less misguided to eliminate Schubert as human being from his music and instead follow the pattern established in discourse about Bruckner. Such discourse would make Schubert the vessel of divine inspiration or even revelation.

In the same way, talk about artistic intuition always blocks any insight into art, what with its obscure amalgam of a crude psychology of the creative process and an indiscriminate metaphysics of the finished work of art. The two ideas are actually identical although superficially very different, and if one falls by the wayside, the other disappears, too. Both are rooted in a false conception of the lyrical, believed to possess a reality of its own by people with a mistaken sense of loyalty to the sacrilegious overidealization of art in the nineteenth century. They think of the lyrical as part of the real human being or as a fragment of a transcendent reality, whereas art, even lyrical art, remains no more than an image of the real, distinguished from other images only in the sense that its manifestation is connected with the entry of the real as a possibility. With this insight we have a new definition of the proportions of objective and subjective in Schubert's lyrical landscape. The lyric contents are not generated; they are the smallest units of an existing objectivity, as whose images they survive, once the large objective forms have fallen into disuse, their authoritarian legitimation long since faded. However, these images do not simply fall into the souls of people open to poetry like the sun's rays into a plant: in no sense are works of art creatures. They are, rather, things that have been struck, like targets: if you hit the right number, they go into reverse and allow the real to shine through. The force that strikes them is human, not artistic: it is human feeling that moves them. This is how we should understand the identity of subjective and objective in the lyric.

The lyrical artist does not directly reproduce his feeling in the work, but his feeling is the means by which truth can be imported into the work in its incomparably small, crystallized form. Truth does not form part of the work but is represented in it, and the revelation of its image remains the work of man. The artist reveals the image. However, the image of truth is always part of history. The history of the image is that of its disintegration—the disintegration of the appearance of the truth of all the matters of substance it means to convey, and the discovery of its transparent passage to the truth contents that are intended along with it and that emerge fully only with its disintegration. The disintegration of the lyrical image is, in particular, the disintegration of its subjective contents. The subjective contents of the lyrical work of art are simply its subject matter. The truth contents are conveyed together with this, but unity between these contents belongs to the historical moment and is dissolved.

Thus, what has permanence in lyrical works is not, as those who believe in a static nature would have it, constant, fundamental human feelings but the objective characteristics that meet up in the origin of works of art with feelings that are transitory. For their part, the subjectively intended and reproduced contents have the same fate as the great forms, which are determined by their material and which are undermined by the passage of time. The dialectical clash between the two forces—the forms with their deceptive immortality, which can be discerned in the stars, and the contents derived directly from consciousness, which assert themselves as absolute givens—this clash destroys both, and with them the provisional unity of the work. It opens up the work as the scene of its transitory nature and at long last liberates whatever images of truth have been able to elevate themselves to the fragile surface of art.

Only now has the landscape of Schubert's music become visible, just as it has taken until now for us to be able to plumb the Luciferian depths of Beethoven's dynamics. The actual contents of Schubert's music were dialectically liberated after romanticism, to which he can hardly ever be assigned in any simple way. Romanticism read his work as a sign language embodying his subjective intentions and buried the problem of its form in a pedestrian school of criticism. The psychological information that it extracted from him was then inflated and exhausted as speedily as only a bad infinity can be exhausted. However, romanticism left behind the best part of his work, and the cavities of subjectivity it contained, the cracks in the poetic surface, are visibly filled with the precious metal that had previously been concealed beneath handy statements about his psyche.

As evidence of the demise of subjectivity as the driving force in the truth character of the work, we may mention the transformation of Schubert as a human being into the figure of Schwammerl, that loathsome icon of petit-bourgeois sentimentality created by Rudolf Hans Bartsch in his novel of that name.[1] This figure secretly continues to dominate the Austrian literature about Schubert down to the present day, and as the cornerstone of all romantic imaginings about Schubert, it presides over their annihilation in *Das Dreimäderlhaus*.[2] For that is how small a man has to become in order to cease blocking the view he has opened up and from which he cannot be expelled entirely, but which he must animate from the sidelines as a minimal accessory. And it is true that a discordant Schubert who is a figure of fun for shop girls and who resembles them in his erotic gaucheness is actually a better match for the genuine image of his music than the prerevolutionary dreamer who is always sitting on the banks of a stream, listening to the rushing water. And there is a genuine logic in the fact that *Das Dreimäderlhaus* should be linked to Schubert, rather than to Mozart or Beethoven; and the socially determined affinity of Biedermeier with genre postcards, which generates the impulse to associate Schubert with kitsch, turns out in the works themselves to be the continuity of the isolated individual that inhabits the Schubertian landscape.

Even if there are limits to Schubertian form, while that of Beethoven and Mozart endures unimpaired—a question, admittedly, that cannot be settled before it has been explored in all seriousness—the confused, banal, eccentric world of the potpourri, wholly inadequate socially to the existing order, guarantees his themes a second life. In the potpourri, the features of his work that have been fragmented with the demise of subjective unity in him are forged into a new unity, which is not, indeed, capable of being legitimated as such, but which uniquely demonstrates the incomparable nature of those features by confronting them directly. The survival of the theme as theme is guaranteed by the potpourri, for it joins one theme to the next without feeling compelled to draw out the consequences of change from any of them. No theme that has passed away could endure the proximity of another; a terrible rigor mortis weighs upon the opera potpourris of the nineteenth century. In Schubert, by contrast, themes succeed one another pell-mell without ever congealing into a Medusa-like mask. Nevertheless, it is only the blind collection of themes that clears the path to their origins and at the same time opens up access to Schubertian form. For like a kind of musical jigsaw, potpourris aspire to rediscover at random the lost unity of works of art. They will have a chance of achieving this only if that unity is not the product of subjective will, for that would never manage to generate a unity from a game of chance. It would succeed only if unity were to arise spontaneously from the configuration of images.

Of course, this seems to fall into the opposite trap of endorsing a traditional view of Schubert that is based on a false idea of the lyrical. This view regards Schubert's music as a plantlike creation that unfolds organically without reference to any preconceived form (and perhaps without any form), and bursts into bloom. However, the idea of the potpourri in fact negates that organic theory. Any such organic unity would necessarily be teleological: every cell it contained would be the necessary step to the next one, and their interconnections would be the driving motivation of their subjective intention, which has faded away and whose restitution is far from being the point of the potpourri. Wagner's music, established on the model of the organism, does not for the most part allow the potpourri to emerge. But this cannot be said of Weber and Bizet, whose music has affinities with Schubert's. The cells assembled in the potpourri are interrelated in accordance with a different law from one that obtains in the unity of a living being.

Admittedly, by comparison, Schubert's music always appears to have grown rather than to have been made; nevertheless, always fragmentary and never self-sufficient, its growth is crystalline rather than vegetative. Because the transition to the potpourri confirms the original isolation of the elements of his music and thus their basically fragmentary nature, it completely clarifies the nature of the Schubertian landscape. We must not judge it a matter of chance that during the nineteenth century the potpourri emerged as a surrogate for musical form at the same time that the miniature landscape made its appearance as an object of bourgeois use of every kind, down to the picture postcard. All such landscapes converge with the intention of leaping suddenly from history only to cut history off as with a pair of scissors. They continue to have their destiny in history, but only as its scenario: history is never their object. In them the idea of a mythical reality assumes monstrous and depraved forms. Potpourris, too, are timeless in themselves. The total interchangeability of all individual themes in the potpourri points to the simultaneous nature of all events that are aligned without history.

From this simultaneity we can read off the contours of the Schubertian landscape that are reflected as if in an underworld. Every truly legitimate distortion of aesthetic contents is inaugurated by works of art in which the unveiling of the image succeeds to the point where the translucent power of truth goes beyond the image and penetrates the realm of reality. This transparency, for which the work of art has to pay with its life, is an integral part of the crystalline character of the Schubertian landscape. There, fate and reconciliation lie side by side, undifferentiated; their ambiguous eternity is destroyed by the potpourri so that they may be recognized for what they are. It is the landscape prior to death. Life is no more the intended object of Schubert's music than history can preside over the space between the entry of one Schubertian theme and the next.

The hermeneutic problem that Schubert undeniably presents us with has been explored hitherto only in the polemic against romantic psychologism, and even there it was not pursued with the requisite incisiveness. The critique of all musical hermeneutics rightly destroys the idea that music is the poetic reproduction of psychological meanings. But this does not imply that criticism can dispense with the relation to objective truth and that it can replace the bad subjective interpretation of art with a belief in the blind immanence of art. No art has art itself as its object; my point is merely that art's symbolic meaning does not manifest itself in abstract isolation from its concrete materiality. In its origin the meaning is inseparable from that materiality, cutting itself off from it only in the course of history. In history, changing meanings arise from the work, and only the silenced work exists for itself. If Schubert's work, which even in its distortions is more eloquent than any other of his age, was not turned to stone, this was precisely because it does not owe its vitality to an ephemeral subjective dynamic through a conformist process of imitation.

In its origins it is already the inorganic, disjointed, fragmented life of stones, and death is too deeply implanted in it for it to have to fear death.

We have no need here to turn our thoughts to Schubert's psychological reflections, his experiences of death; and the countless anecdotes about Schubert's own premonitions of death have the force only of weak signs. Of
greater significance is his choice of texts, whose energy brings movement
into the Schubertian landscape, even though that landscape is buried soon
enough beneath their mass. In particular, we should remind ourselves that
the two great song-cycles are based on poems in which man is confronted
with images of death, such that as he wanders among them, he seems to be
as tiny as the Schubert to be found in *Das Dreimäderlhaus.* The stream, the
mill, and the black winter wasteland, stretching out timelessly in the twilight of mock suns, as in a dream—these are the insignia of the Schubertian landscape, dried flowers their sorrowful ornament. They release their
objective symbols of death, and their feeling returns to their objective symbols of death.

This is the Schubertian dialectic: it attaches itself to the fading images of existing objectivity with the power of subjective interiority so as to
rediscover them in the minutest cells of concrete musical detail. The allegorical image of death and the maiden perishes in it; not so as to dissolve
into individual feeling, but so that, after the demise of that feeling, the image emerges from the musical figure of sadness and is saved. Admittedly, it
is then qualitatively changed. But such changes succeed only on a small
scale; on a large scale, death prevails. The very cyclical nature of the two
song-cycles can demonstrate this, for their circuitous course is the timeless
one between birth and death, as nature blindly ordains. The figure who
traverses this space is the wanderer. This figure has never been discussed in
terms of its defining significance for the structure of Schubert's works. And
this despite the fact that it gives us a deep insight into the mythical substance of Schubert's art, in contrast to the overt symbolism of Wagner,
from which the wanderer keeps his distance. The difference is that in
Schubert it points to a truth, while in Wagner it is merely a quotation
without substance. In psychoanalysis journeys and travels have been taken
over as an archaic residue objectively symbolizing death, and so we are entitled to look for both in the landscape of death. The eccentric structure of
that landscape, in which every point is equidistant from the center, dis-
closes itself to the wanderer, who traverses it without progressing: all development is the landscape's complete antithesis; the first step is as close to
death as the last; and, moving in a circle, the dissociated points of the landscape are visited without its terrain ever being abandoned.

For Schubert's themes wander like the miller or the man whose lover left him in winter. They have no knowledge of history but only a journey with changing points of view; the only change is a changing light. This explains Schubert's tendency to make use of the same theme two or three times in different works, and to use it in different ways; most memorably, perhaps, in the repetition of that immortal melody that appears as a theme in piano variations, as a variation in the A minor quartet [D. 804],[3] and in the music to *Rosamunde*. It would be foolish to explain this recurrence with reference to the composer's insatiability, given that he might have chosen a hundred other themes, thanks to the melodic inventiveness we have heard more than enough about. The wanderer, however, encounters the same passages, unchanged, but in a different light, passages that are timeless and that occur in isolation. This pattern does not just include the repeated use of the same theme in different works but defines the nature of Schubertian forms as such.

His themes remain without dialectical history. And if Schubert's variations, unlike Beethoven's, never attack the structure of the theme but instead swirl around it, what we have is the circular wandering that characterizes Schubert's form. This does not revolve around an obviously accessible center. On the contrary. Its center proclaims itself solely in its ability to direct everything that manifests itself toward itself. This holds good for the impromptus, the *Moments Musicaux* [D. 780], and, above all, the works in sonata form. What distinguishes them from Beethoven is not just the fundamental negation of all thematic and dialectical progression but also the repetition of unchanging characters. For example, in the first A minor sonata [D. 537], the first movement begins with two ideas that are not contrasted as first and second subjects, but are each contained in both the first and the second thematic group. This cannot be ascribed to any motivic economy that husbands its material for the sake of unity; it can be regarded only as the repetition of the same thing within a profusion spread out before us.

We can see here the origin of that notion of mood and atmosphere that was characteristic of the art of the nineteenth century and especially its landscape painting. Mood is what changes in something that remains timelessly the same without change having any power over it. Once difference starts to creep in, mood is transformed into appearance. This explains why the genuineness of Schubert's changing moods is inseparable from the genuineness of the identical meanings that they revolve around, and if they escape the decline of "mood" art, they owe this to those defined characters. What is repeatable is the actually existing fact, not what has been subjectively created, for that necessarily dissipates itself in time. What jeopardizes the forms of Schumann and Wagner is not the use of repetition as such but merely the repetition of the unrepeatable, which alone has the right to exist at that particular point in the musical form where it arises from the subjective, inner temporal dynamic. The situation is different in Schubert. His themes are manifestations of truth characters, and the talent of the artist is confined to encapsulating their image with feeling and, once their image has appeared, to citing it again and again. However, no citation occurs at the same time as another, and this is why the mood changes.

Schubert's forms are forms that conjure up something that has once appeared, not forms that transform something invented. This foundational a priori has wholly permeated the sonata. Instead of developing mediations, harmonic shifts appear, lighting up different aspects in turn, and leading us into a new landscape that is as bereft of any progression as what went before it. There we find elaborations that abandon any attempt to dissect the themes into motives in order to strike the dynamic spark from their smallest parts. Instead, the unchanging themes are progressively revealed; retrospectively, themes are taken up again that have been traversed but not left behind. And over everything, like a thin, rustling veil, lies the sonata, which overlies the growing crystals only to shatter into fragments. A true analysis of form in Schubert, of the kind that has never yet been attempted, but whose nature is completely clear, would above all have to explore the dialectical relationship between the prescribed sonata pattern and Schubert's second, crystalline form. This results in the creation of Schubertian form in which the creative idea has to assert itself and to triumph over the deceptive dynamics of the sonata. Nothing could strengthen his themes more than the immanent compulsion to dominate a form that spontaneously rejects them as themes.

The founding distinction between creative idea [*Einfall*] and invention, one that is not identical with the dividing line between grace and will but cuts through both, is fixed in Schubert in exemplary fashion. Both treat the objectivities of form dialectically. Invention penetrates them with its constructive power emanating from the subject, and dissolves them in its assertion of the personal identity that freely creates form once again from within itself. The creative idea disperses them through a process of dissociation by preserving their constitutive dignity at the level of detail, where it communicates with subjective intention, once that dignity has evaporated at the macrolevel. Invention creates constructs within the dimensions of an infinite task, and strives to create a totality; the creative idea draws the figures of truth and is rewarded by its ultimate success at the microlevel. This is what is made clear by talk of hitting upon the right image. It is hit both as a target is struck by the marksman and as the reality is captured by a copy. In a photograph a person's features are "well-caught," a "good likeness," if the image resembles the person. Likewise, Schubert's creative ideas capture their undying model, of whose immortality they often enough preserve the traces, just as if those ideas had always been there and were merely being revealed to us. At the same time, however, in these ideas man has discovered the entrance to the realm of truth as surely as an eagle-eyed marksman finds his target. Both the photographer and the marksman hit the mark in a moment, in a flash, rather than in extended time. Schubert's creative ideas resemble them in that respect. The smallest fraction of these ideas stands as a signal of both their preservation and their annihilation. The evidence that Schubert's themes have hit their mark is their appearances as holes in the foreground of form at which he had aimed, and at the same time as gaps enabling us to glimpse an unattainable true form. His themes are asymmetrical, in early mockery of the architecture of tonality.

In its irregularity the autonomy of the captured image prevails over the abstract will to create a pure immanence of form. But it rightly inserts breaks in the structure of subjective intentions and the historical styles that are their corollaries: hence the work must remain fragmentary. The fragmentary nature of Schubert's music material can be seen in his finales. The cyclical nature of the song collections conceals what must become obvious in every temporal sequence of timeless cells as soon as such cells become long enough for a sonata to develop. The unwritability of the finale of the B minor symphony ["The Unfinished," D. 759] should be associated in our minds with the inadequacy of the finale of the "Wanderer" Fantasy [D. 760]. We have here not the failure of a dilettante with an overflowing heart to master the technical construction of the conclusion, but a confrontation with the Tartarean question "whether perfection has not yet been achieved," which dominates the entire realm of Schubert's work.

Confronted with that question, music falls silent. This is why the successful finales from among his works are perhaps the most potent signs of hope that his oeuvre contains.

Admittedly, there is as yet no such sign in the "Wanderer" Fantasy. In the quoting adagio, the bright forest greenery is even retracted into a gloomy, Acherontic ravine. The hermeneutics of death that pervades so many images of Schubert's music, altering their objective character, does not exhaust it. The emotion of death—for the emotion of death is reproduced in the Schubertian landscape, that is to say, sorrow about mankind, not the pain that mankind feels—is alone the gateway to the underworld down to which Schubert conducts us. Faced with this underworld, hermeneutic speech, which was just able to follow the transition to death, falls silent. No metaphor can clear a path through the frost-covered forests, the crystal patterns that spring up only to crash down again like dying dragons. The bright world above, from which again and again the path into this realm sets forth, is little more than a perspective, an intimation of a third dimension. This world above is like a sparse, vegetable covering, like the organic dialectical sonata that overlies Schubert's second form. In his choice of texts, his blind tendency always to follow mythological poems, without making much distinction between Goethe and Mayrhofer, graphically illustrates the failure of all words in that deep abyss, in which the word only produces materials and never has the power to illuminate them truly. The wanderer, striding forth into the depths, follows the words as they fall, never their illumined intentions, and even his human passion becomes the instrument of his gaze as he descends, not into the depths of his soul, but into the vault of his destiny. "I wish to kiss the ground / and pierce ice and snow / with my scalding tears / until I see the earth below."[4] It is right down to these depths that we are led by the harmonies, the apposite principle of natural musical depth: but here we find, not nature as the sensible object of inner human feelings about nature, but rather images of nature that are symbols of chthonic profundity itself, and that as such are as inadequate as ever the poetic word was.

Schubert's moods do not just circle but plunge down, and it is not for nothing that they are linked to harmonic shifts, the penetrating gaze of modulation, which sheds light on sameness from changing depths. Like blinds, those sudden, undeveloping, never-mediating modulations block out the light from above. The introduction of the second group of themes in the first movement of the great B major sonata [D. 960]; the violent chromatic progression, for example, in the first movement of the trio in E-flat major [D. 929]; and, finally, the beginning of the second subject of the C major symphony [D. 944]—they have all transformed the change in key of the sonata into a perspectival incursion into harmonic depths. And the fact that in those three pieces in a major key the second subjects appear to be in the minor signifies a perceptible step into the dark, according to the gender symbolism of the keys, to which Schubert still adhered.

The demonic function of depth is achieved by Schubert's altered chords. In the landscape divided between major and minor they stand ambivalently like mythical nature itself, pointing up and down simultaneously. Their luster is wan, and the expression with which his use of modulation endows them is that of fear: fear of the lethal knowledge of the earth and of the annihilating knowledge of the bare, human self. In this way, the mirror image of the doppelgänger becomes a court suspended above man on the basis of his sorrow. Only the fact that modulation and alteration are scattered through the idiom of tonality gives these chords such power at that precise historical moment. As the adversary of the natural world above, they undermine tonality; following its collapse, modulation and alteration, too, are drawn into that undifferentiated flow of subjective dynamics, and not until Schoenberg, with his emphatic definition of the bass parts, was the strength of Schubertian harmonics again recaptured, only to be eliminated for good. Schubert's treatment of harmony, which is followed into the depths by counterpoint, as the vivid shadow of melody, reaches its nadir in the pure minor key of sorrow. If the emotion of death was the gateway to that descent, the earth itself, the terra firma that has finally been reached, is the physical manifestation of death, and faced with it, the dejected soul recognizes itself to be a woman, ineluctably trapped within nature.

In the last great allegorical poem of the German language, Matthias Claudius's image of Death and the Maiden, the wanderer reaches the heart of his landscape. There, the essence of the minor key is revealed. But just as punishment follows swiftly for a child caught in the act, and just as in the common proverb necessity is the mother of invention, so here consolation follows in the footsteps of sorrow. Rescue is achieved in the smallest steps, the transformation from a minor into a major third. The two come so close together that after the major third has appeared, the minor stands revealed as its shadow. So it comes as no surprise if the qualitative distinction between sorrow and consolation, whose concrete figuration contains Schubert's true response, is overlaid with mediating procedures, nor need we feel astonished that the nineteenth century believed that it could sum up Schubert's basic stance in the concept of "resignation." But the illusion of reconciliation that emanates from "resignation" has nothing in common with the consolation offered by Schubert. In that consolation, hope suggests that the coercion represented by entrapment in the toils of nature does ultimately have limits. However heavily Schubert's sorrow bears down to the depths, and even though the wanderer himself might long to perish without hope in the waters of birth, consolation stands immutably over the dead and guarantees that hope persists; its place is not fixed for all eternity in the depraved magic circle of nature. It is at this point that time catches fire in Schubert's music, and the successful finale comes from a different realm from that of death. Of course, its source is also different from the Beethovian "must." For in contrast with Beethoven's joy—which is more menacingly demanded, more oppressed, more graspable conceptually, but more elusive materially—Schubert's joy is more like hearing an echo that is confused at first, but then becomes self-confident and immediately present. Only once does it unleash a great dynamic: in the climax of the finale of the C major symphony [D. 944], where the melody in the wind section bursts in upon the music like actual voices, severing it from its true foundation as scarcely any music has ever done before.

Aside from this one instance, joy in Schubert tends to take different and curiously bewildering paths. In the great four-handed rondo in A major [D. 951], the expansive sense of well-being sings with such sustained and physical presence as to seem corporeal in perpetuity. It is as different from Beethoven as good food differs from the immortality postulated by practical reason. That joy often includes the lengthening of Schubert's movements, and the saying about "heavenly length" continues to attract as much support as ever. If, in the landscape of death, Schubert's themes stand timelessly side by side, music consolingly fills a rediscovered time far from the finality of death with the anticipated permanence of the Eternal. The repeatability of individual Schubertian motives arises from his timelessness but is transformed into time for time's material fulfillment. That fulfillment, however, has no need of long movements or even the pathos of a large-scale form. It would much rather dwell in a region far beneath the established conventions of an accepted bourgeois musical practice.

For the Schubertian world of authentic joy, of dances and military marches, of the skimpy four-handed piano, of hovering banality and slight drunkenness, is as inappropriate socially to bourgeois and even petit-bourgeois music-making as it ever was to attempts to provide a naive validation of reality. Whoever persists in classifying Schubert as a mere music-maker should reflect that the man in question was socially disadvantaged, and closer in spirit to itinerant folk, to traveling conjurors and magicians, than to the alleged simplicity of the artisan. Thus the joy of Schubert's marches is disrespectful, and the time they register is the time not of psychological development but of the movement of human crowds. Schubert's joy, directly proclaimed, no longer knows anything of form; ready for use, it comes close to the lower reaches of empirical reality, and having broken free of the realm of art.

The man who composed the music expressing such an anarchic joy must have been a dilettante; and when did a revolution appear to the statesman as anything other than dilettantish? But this dilettantism is the dilettantism of a fresh start, and its seal is the autonomous organization that emerges from that new beginning. In Schubert the organization remains a matter of compositional technique, but the image is blurred. Nowhere does it come nearer the truth than in Schubert's use of folklore, but in a completely different sense from that attempted by anyone after him. Schubert did not undertake to compensate for lost proximity with unattainable distance. He was able to achieve transcendent distance in his own immediate vicinity. That distance lies at his doorstep, like Hungary, and is as remote as an incomprehensible language. This is the source of that mystery that pervades the entire Schubertian oeuvre—not just the Hungarian divertissement [D. 818], the F minor fantasy [D.940], and the secondary themes of the rondo in A major [D. 951], but also the oeuvre's subtler ramifications, becoming in turn tangible and phantomlike in the C-flat minor theme from the finale of the A minor quartet [D. 804].

The language of this Schubert is dialect: but a dialect not rooted in a specific locality. It possesses the concreteness of a homeland; but here there is no homeland, only a remembered one. Nowhere is Schubert further removed from the earth than where he evokes it. It reveals itself in the images of death: but when seen in close up, nature cancels itself out. Thus no path leads from Schubert to genre music and an ideology of the soil; the paths lead, on the one hand, merely to the deepest depravity, and, on the other, to the scarcely addressed reality of a liberated music of a transformed humanity. In irregular features, Schubert's music, like a seismograph, has registered the message of the qualitative transformation of mankind. In response we weep indiscriminately, moved equally by the most appalling sentimentality of *Das Dreimäderlhaus* and by the body convulsed. Confronted with Schubert's music, the tears flow from our eyes without consulting our soul: that is the measure of its literal, actual impact upon us. We weep without knowing why, because we have not yet become what that music promises, and because we feel indescribable happiness that the music needs only to be what it is in order to assure us that we will one day become like that. We cannot read them, but the music holds out to our fading eyes, brimful of tears, the ciphers of ultimate reconciliation.

(1928; GS 17: 18–33)
Translated by Rodney Livingstone

16

Wagner's Relevance Today

From the countless points of interest that Wagner's work presents us with I should like arbitrarily to single out one, as is inevitable in a single lecture. It is the question of his relevance, of the attitude to his work today, if indeed we can speak of a general attitude here. What is meant is an advanced consciousness, one that is equal to the challenge of his work and, conversely, one that is advanced in its own right. Almost thirty years ago I wrote a book on Wagner. Four chapters appeared in the *Zeitschrift für Sozialforschung* in 1939; the whole book not until much later, in 1952, shortly after my return to Germany from emigration. Today I would take a different view of much of what the book, *In Search of Wagner*, contains. The central problem, that of the mediation between social, internal-compositional, and aesthetic aspects, is one that should be examined in greater depth today than it was then. But I do not distance myself from the book, or disown the conception underlying it. Our perception of Wagner has now changed fundamentally. This is why I wish to deviate from the older text, not so as to revise what I said then but to take into account what we can now see in Wagner for the first time.

We have now gained a certain distance that we did not have thirty years ago. Wagner no longer represents, as he did in my youth, the world of the parental generation, but that of our grandparents. By way of evidence, just one small symptom. I can remember how my mother complained about the decline of Italian singing, which she attributed to the

Wagnerian style of singing. Today, that Wagnerian singing style is itself on the point of extinction. It is extremely difficult to find singers who are equal to the demands it makes. The well-known, philistine guest system, in which the few famous Wagnerian singers are passed around on loan from one production to the next, is no mere passing excess. Opera is beginning to regress to the stage that Wagner's arrival had shown to be obsolete. Wagner no longer possesses the unlimited authority he had. But what rebelled against that authority was not so much a critical mind at odds with the victor, as a spirit of reaction: the ambivalence toward a former love now about to grow old. Nevertheless, attitudes toward Wagner have now become much freer: the emotional tie to him has now been broken.

If, thanks to this freedom, I can start by saying something about this changed attitude toward Wagner's art, I cannot avoid saying something about politics. There has been too much harm to the living for us to let ourselves be dazzled by what is alleged to be a purely aesthetic discussion. Nevertheless, there can still be changes even in our attitude toward the political implications of Wagner. The spirit of nationalism he embodied, particularly in his works, which was transmitted to National Socialism via Houston Stewart Chamberlain and Alfred Rosenberg, who were able to appeal to him explicitly, has now exploded, or, with the integration of the nations into power blocs, it has at least become less threatening. This means that it has also begun to recede in the works. Of course, this change should not be overestimated. The National Socialist potential continues to smoulder dangerously in Germany, and so it is still present in Wagner, too. That gives us an idea of the most serious difficulty in appreciating his function for the contemporary consciousness. The thunderous applause that can still be met with after a performance of the *Meistersinger,* the feeling of confirmation that the audience can glean from listening to him, still has something of the old virulence. The question of whether to perform Wagner, and how, can be separated only with difficulty from the awareness of such demagogy.

When I wrote the book I attempted to situate it in the pure aesthetics of the music. Perhaps my criticism has earned me the right, if I may strike a personal note, to emphasize what survives of that critique. My own experience of Wagner goes beyond that political element, however little that can be salvaged, and it often seems to me that, having once brought it to the surface, I had cleared away an underlying layer of meaning, which then revealed another, deeper one that I had indeed no need to discover anew for myself. At any rate, the currently fashionable private objections to Wagner's personality and conduct have something unspeakably contemptible about them; whoever drags them to the light of day dirties his hands. If formerly I, too, drew his personality into the discussion, what I had in mind was his social character, those elements of his private personality that were both the stage and the exhibit of social trends. I was not concerned to sit in judgment upon the psychological foibles of Wagner the individual, which some people make so much fuss about. Whatever objections are raised against him, unless the attempt is made to mediate between the artistic productivity concentrated in him and society, it remains no more than pure philistinism, not far removed from the contemptible genre of the biographical novel. Instead, we should remind ourselves of Ernest Newman's great biography, which is anything but an official biography and which stands at the opposite end of the spectrum. Newman had rightly emphasized how hypocritical it was to become indignant about, say, Wagner's extravagance, in light of the fact that in all the years he was in emigration, the theater derived huge profits from his work, while he lived in penury. I mention Newman deliberately; the relevance of Wagner calls for the translation of his truly authentic work, the outstanding achievement of the entire panoply of Wagner biographies.

The hostility to Wagner in purely aesthetic terms was led by the so-called neoclassical movement, itself by no means progressive, which was linked primarily to the name of Igor Stravinsky. It now lies behind us, and not just chronologically; it ran out of steam. The visible sign of its capitulation lies in the fact that in his last years Stravinsky had recourse to the technique that his movement had originally attacked: that of the Schoenberg school. That is to be laid not simply at the door of the zeitgeist but in a failing of neoclassicism; its historical impossibility became a compositional defect. The present trend, which runs in the opposite direction and makes neoclassicism look feeble and ornamental, reveals things that have more to do with Wagner than with those composers who had been pleased to present themselves as his opponents during the last thirty or forty years. The Second Viennese School, namely, Arnold Schoenberg's, which decisively influenced the most recent developments in music, followed directly in Wagner's footsteps. That had been the reproach leveled at Schoenberg's earliest pieces in order to discredit the mature composer.

However, what has changed in Wagner is not just his impact but the work itself. That is the foundation of his relevance today and not any posthumous, second triumph, or the deserved defeat of the neobaroque. Works of art as spiritual creations are not fixed totalities. They constitute a field of tension of every possible intention and force, of internal tendencies and countertendencies, of success and necessary failure. Objectively, new levels of significance keep separating themselves out and emerging; others become a matter of indifference and wither and die. The true relationship with a work of art is not just that we fit it into a changed situation, as we say, but that we decipher something in the work that provokes a different reaction from us historically. The attitude toward Wagner that I think of as my own whenever I encounter it, and that is actually not just mine, can be called ambivalent, to a greater degree even than the old one. It is a pendulum swinging between attraction and repulsion.

This points, however, to the Janus-faced nature of the work itself. Undoubtedly, every significant work exhibits something of the sort. Wagner's more than most. Progressive and reactionary elements are intertwined in his work, just as they are in the reactions he provokes. That people react critically to him at the level of politics goes without saying after all that has happened. But it was also the case beforehand and remained so in view of the possibility that there might be a resurgence of those forces that ought rather to remain dormant, like Erda, their patron goddess. In this respect reality takes precedence over art. It remains an open question how the requisite resistance to Wagner is to be combined with the possibility of new performances. We must not imagine—and here I touch on an issue of central importance—that it is a simple matter to strip out the ideology and find ourselves holding the pure art in our hands as a clean residue. For the gestures of demagogy, persuasion, and collective narcissism enter deeply into the internal complexion of his music. What is suspect about them is amalgamated with its opposite.

By contrast—and that, too, is part of the ambivalent reaction he provokes—Wagner is resisted by all those people who, even today, could not keep pace with the music. This even includes his greatest critic, Nietzsche. The anti-Wagner movement was the first major wave of resentment against modern art in Germany. This led to a disastrous alliance between the anti-Wagner complex and so-called folk music and youth music, the recorder revivalists and the like. They liked to play off newly excavated composers like Heinrich Schütz against Wagner and mobilized forces against him that aspired to simplicity in the face of his subtle and complex art. There is something like a right-wing hostility to Wagner, a petit-bourgeois hatred. No doubt, there is also a good bourgeois element that recoils from him, the insistence on the responsibility and autonomy of the individual. But there is also a bad side, a stuffiness and narrow-mindedness that remains implacably opposed to him. Few composers who have been received into the German pantheon are as liberated erotically as he. Here, too, from very early on the orthodox view with its self-righteous purity sinned against this aspect of Wagner.

Ambivalence is a relationship to something you cannot come to terms with; when you cannot cope with a thing, you remain ambivalent toward it. Faced with this, it is high time we simply exposed ourselves fully to Wagner's work, something that has not been done to this day, for all his outward successes. *Tristan, Parsifal,* the most important parts of the *Ring*— these are all praised rather than truly appreciated. It is grotesque that in the *Ring* the *Valkyrie* still functions as a drawing card because of such passages as Siegmund's "Wintry storms have vanished before Maytime," Wotan's farewell, or the Fire Music, that is to say, the plums, or what the Viennese call *Stückerln* [the best pieces]. As such, they are a blow in the face of the Wagnerian idea. The incomparably grander architecture of *Siegfried* has never truly found its way into public consciousness. At best, the opera-going public lets it wash over it as a jewel of high culture. The unappreciated works are actually the most modern ones, those whose technique is the boldest and the most advanced, and hence furthest away from existing convention. Their modernity should not be thought of superficially, as a matter of technique, simply because they contain more dissonances, enharmonic modulations, and chromaticism than other music. In terms of quality, too, Wagner's modernity towers above the music it has left behind.

Wagner is the first instance of a consistent musical nominalism, if I may be permitted to use this philosophical term. I mean by this that his work is the first in which the primacy of the individual work, and within the individual work, that of the concrete, formed shape, is made to prevail against every convention of whatever kind, against every externally prescribed pattern. He was the first composer to draw the logical conclusion from the contradiction between forms that had been handed down, indeed, the traditional formal language of music as such, and the artistic

tasks that he concretely faced. This contradiction had first announced itself as a low rumble in Beethoven and bore fruit in his late style. Wagner
then accepted without reservation that the authority, the truly universal
nature of musical works of art could be sought only in their concrete particularity and not through their dependence on any universal types.

That is why, in contrast to the views expressed in a book that has received mass distribution, that of Hans Gàl, Wagner's critique of opera deserves to be taken with absolute seriousness both theoretically and artisti-
cally. It must not be trivialized through the simple-minded assertion that
he was an opera composer like other opera composers and that his ideas
were simply makeshifts designed to generate publicity for his own works.
His verdict that the opera was childish, his demand that music should finally grow up, cannot be reversed. As a form, the opera has grown historically and will pass away. Simply to include Wagner in the ranks of opera
composers is to suppress the dynamism that characterizes the history of the
form. It is not for nothing that the number opera is only possible as a stylized act, a ruptured totality, as in Stravinsky's *Rake*. Even anti-Wagnerians
who wish to revive the number opera register or perceive in the irony with
which they deploy numbers or self-contained individual bits that the verdict that Wagner pronounced on such notions as a theoretician and artist
still retains its validity. He looked the antagonism of the universal and particular squarely in the face. Previously it had simply crystallized unconsciously in musical form, and his genius resolved unwaveringly that there
could be no universal except as an extreme of particularity.

This has implications for the content of his music, as well as the
form. In Wagner the artistic consciousness of an antagonistic, self-contra-
dictory world has been radicalized. The traditional forms no longer har-
monize with artistic consciousness, any more than ossified conditions har-
monize with critical knowledge. In this sense Wagner acted productively.
Even more. In the introduction to Hegel's *Philosophy of History*, which has
become popular under the title "The Rational View of World History," I
came across the sentence "Mere desire, the wildness and savagery of the
will, falls outside the theater and the sphere of world history." This sentence from Hegel, who was a classicist both philosophically and aesthetically, was one Wagner failed to heed. In his youth, as is well known, Wagner had been decisively influenced by Feuerbach, before he was converted
to Schopenhauer, and in this sense he was undoubtedly a revolutionary

Young Hegelian. His music quivers with the violence that persists undiminished in the world to this day.

We can raise all sorts of objections to Wagner's mythology; we can unmask it as a sham and accuse it of fostering a romanticism of false beards and stained glass. At the same time, in contrast to all middle-of-the-road, serenely realistic and neoclassical art, it retains, above all in the *Ring*, its decisive truth in that mythical dimension. This truth is that violence breaks through in myth with the same force that it possessed in the primeval world. The *Ring* is modern through and through, but in it the prehistorical world is modernity itself. This fractures the superficial bourgeois facade, and through the cracks you can glimpse enough of the qualities that have only now blossomed and become identifiable, a feature that itself provides proof of Wagner's contemporary relevance. It is undoubtedly true that his preference, the cause for which his music pleads—and Wagner's music, not just his texts, contains a constant plea—is mythology. We may say that he becomes the advocate of violence, just as his principal work glorifies Siegfried, the man of violence. But because violence is openly expressed in his work, and because the work makes no attempt to conceal the terrible pitfalls it ensnares people in, it willy-nilly becomes an attack on myth, despite its mythologizing tendency. Proof of this can be found in the indescribable émigré music of Siegmund's at the beginning of act 2 of the *Valkyrie*. We owe to Richard Strauss the inspired utterance that Wagner used the leitmotiv to redeem us from myth. We may take this to mean that the quasi-rational leitmotiv, with its ability to create identity and unity, is an effective counter to the diffuse and lethal ambiguity of myth that is evoked by the surging waves of Wagnerian music. Self-awareness transforms myth into something of a different order; the reflection of disaster in the memory marks its limits.

The fact that Wagner puts in a plea for myth, but indicts it through the process in which music is given shape, may well provide the key with which to decode his dual nature. His immediate relevance today is not a case of the ordinary artistic revivals. Like much in the nineteenth century, Ibsen, above all, it is fed by unfinished business. This would have to be shown in a series of musical moments. I shall mention a few. Wagner's use of harmony, for a start. In his book, Gàl denies the link between Wagner's use of harmony and modern harmony, atonality. This stands in glaring contradiction to the fact that modern harmony grew out of Wagner's practice at the hands of Schoenberg, from *Verklärten Nacht* on. Needless to say, there is no atonality in Wagner, and it has never occurred to me to claim that there was. All his sonorities and interconnections are explicable in terms of the traditional theory of harmony, for all Wagner's bold innovations, particularly in *Tristan* and *Parsifal.* But we are talking here about a tendency, a potential, not about the literal meaning of the notes. We are talking about the direction of the music, and that does indeed point decisively to atonality. The predominance of harmonic progressions specific to particular contexts over what we might call the tokens of harmony, such as triads and sevenths, points forward to what we find in consistently atonal music, which has done away with musical tokens altogether. In Wagner, we find a predominance of dissonance, not quantitatively but qualitatively. It has more strength, more substantial weight than consonance, and this, too, points convincingly to the new music.

In his books Heinrich Schenker criticized Wagner, whom he could hardly have liked, for having destroyed the *Urlinie,* despite his correct use of harmony. What he meant, in his peculiar terminology, was simply that what was missing in Wagner was the use of the regular harmonic progression of the figured bass and the associated melody to provide the music with a backbone. This is an accurate observation, but Schenker's emphasis is perverse. As the retrospective advocate of the predominance of backbones, of abstract generalities in music, he failed to recognize that the alleged destruction of music, its emancipation from its merely skeletal, abstract organization in favor of a more specific process of shaping, contained what was irresistibly new in music, the presupposition of everything that was to come. The feeling of abandoning terra firma, of drifting into the unknown, is what is exciting and also compelling about Wagner's music. Its innermost structure, the quality that by analogy with the language of painting we might call its *peinture,* can be appreciated only by an ear that is willing to venture out into the unknown. So we may start by saying that what is relevant today is what has not yet been properly recognized and hence appreciated.

I should like to explain this principle further with reference to a specific technical detail. It is not possible to talk about works of art, as distinct from idly chattering about them, without speaking, however briefly, about their concrete technical complexion. It is customary when talking about Wagner's mature works to emphasize the principle of the sequence. I, too, have done this in the past. By sequence we understand the repetition of brief motives in a more developed form—in Wagner these are the leitmotivs—for the most part with a dynamic, intensifying effect. The progress of the music, the actual fiber, the texture, works, then, more or less with the repetition of given material, in contrast to the technique of Viennese classicism, which can be described in Arnold Schoenberg's phrase as the technique of developing variation. However many sequences are to be found in Wagner, it would be wrong to say that they are the sole principle at work, and, above all, they are often varied with immense subtlety. A textbook example is the famous beginning of *Tristan*, with its two sequences on one pattern. It becomes evident as early as the third phrase of the sequence, which varies minimally but decisively from its first state; this leads back to the *forte* entry on the dominant of the paraphrased home key of A minor.

In general, the sequence principle in Wagner is no crutch. It follows naturally from the chromaticism, the prevalence of the minor seconds that crisscross the entire musical material, at any rate in works of the kind I am speaking of. On the one hand, the sequence is meant to establish the context that disappeared with chromaticism, that is to say, with the abolition of any articulation of harmonic progressions of differing weight. On the other hand, however, Wagner is able to snuggle up so closely and in such a modern way to his own material that the chromaticism itself acquires something of the sequential principle: in the sequence, the succession of the various individual musical events corresponds to the repetition of the smallest intervals assigned to them. The identity of the sequential phrases that succeed each other is closely related to the identity of the chromatic steps. Thus even the sequential principle is not a mechanical device, as we musicians find it all too easy to believe; it is connected with the problems and challenges of the internal organization of Wagner's music at a much deeper level than I was able to appreciate thirty years ago.

Admittedly, the position is different in others of Wagner's works. There the sequence plays no very central role at all. These are the less chromatic works. A timely and relevant appreciation of Wagner would have to explore their structure. In *Die Meistersinger* the greatest musical differentiation is combined by and large with an absence of chromaticism, and also the sequences often give way to the colorful succession of individual shapes. Unity is established over great expanses by loosely describing a dramatic curve that advances from one moment to the next. Wagner's sustained use of the diatonic scale enables him to dispense with any sort of surface glue. This gives the music a concrete irregularity inconceivable in traditional music. It remains the prototype for Schoenberg, Berg, and the most recent developments: namely, the trend toward free but condensed structures. The idea of a unity consisting of constantly changing situations, which in Wagner would take their lead from the twists and turns of the action, is one that has not been fully achieved to this day. It would be the model for genuinely informal composing that would be built up out of contrasting but mutually necessary characters. Needless to say, nothing of the kind is either intended or fully elaborated in Wagner. The unfolding of the drama was more important to him than organizing a structure, but, nevertheless, the objective trend in this direction is unmistakable.

By touching upon such difficult structural elements I have reached the problem of so-called form in Wagner. We should begin by establishing a certain order in our terminology, though I would not wish to insist too pedantically on this. Many definitions of music, of rhythm, to say nothing of form, have become so ambiguous and have been so flattened out by overuse that they have come to mean everything and nothing. Wagner may have done away with existing forms and established features of the opera, such as the aria, the recitative, and ensemble. But it would be a mistake to conclude that his own music lacked form; that, as the nineteenth-century critics fumed, it was formless. Such objections are petty and reactionary, even though they have Nietzsche's authority to back them up. The element of truth they contain lies in that peculiar floating feeling, as if the music had no firm ground beneath its feet. In Wagner, the form sends roots into the air. He recoils allergically from that aspect of form that the conservative language of the twentieth century would come to call "ontological." However, music that seems to float in the air as if held by the hand of a secret puppeteer has something static about it, just as Wagner's ostensibly dynamic sequential principle ends up in the feeling of permanent sameness. Similarly, the latest music tends to come closer to painting and drawing, and we find there, too, that the static tendency has grown, thus fulfilling something Wagner had aspired to.

The accusation of formlessness misses its mark, since it confuses the abandonment of traditional forms with the complete absence of organization. The fact is that, even though it possesses no abstract scheme, Wagner's music is highly organized, articulated, and structured. It remains the great achievement of the now unjustly forgotten Alfred Lorenz that he was the first to perceive this. To deny that there is a problem of form in Wagner, as Gàl does, is to dismiss it, or to solve it by ignoring it. The moment traditional formal norms were abandoned, the task of organizing music cogently from within itself became inescapable. Admittedly, the forms proposed by Lorenz, the *Bogen* and the *Bar*, which he overemphasized[1] but which are by no means unimportant for an understanding of Wagner, are themselves far too abstract. They are like mathematical graphs, which are unable to grasp the Wagnerian principle of development and hence, too, to provide a material theory of musical form.

In particular, diagrams fail to do justice to the art of transition, which Wagner placed on the same plane as the art of composition. The task facing Wagner scholarship is to show in detail how his forms are produced and become effective without borrowing from conventions alien to him. This succeeds best, perhaps, in *Siegfried*, which consists magnificently of a single ascending curve constructed in such a way that each of the three acts is based on a similarly rising curve; the steepest ascent comes in act 3, which is probably the climax of Wagner's entire oeuvre. I would like to make the heretical proposal that there ought one day to be a production of the third act of *Siegfried* on its own so that we can focus on it with our entire powers of concentration. Only then will we be able to appreciate its riches fully.

In connection with form I would like to say something about color and orchestration. Wagner's mastery of orchestration is undisputed even by his enemies. The idea of "integrated orchestration" has long since been recognized in his work: the art of translating even the smallest arteries of a composition into a corresponding palette of orchestral color and thus of clarifying them. The orchestration, the timbre, becomes the method with which to render the course of the music visible down to its subtlest detail. In this sense it creates form; but we need to go further. Wagner's art of orchestration not only encompasses the minutest detail but also provides the solution to the question of large-scale form that I have described. We may perhaps say that the general conventions that Wagner did away with were replaced by the entirely novel, highly individual dimension of orchestration. Timbre itself becomes structural. Here, too, *Siegfried* would be the best illustration. Simply to mention the pitch, the highs and the lows are articulated in such a way that both within the acts and in the work as a whole the upsurge of the form corresponds to an upsurge in pitch from the depths to the heights. What Wagner achieves by differentiating the color by dissolving it into its minutest components, he complements by combining the minutest values so that something like an integrated timbre comes into being.

He tends to take a sonority that is subdivided into minimal units, and these he converts into large sound surfaces, like uninterrupted fields of sound. The splinters into which the sword is shattered, as Siegfried says in the cryptic sword songs, are forged together again into great homogeneous units. Only what is infinitesimally small can be welded together in such seamless totalities. Anyone familiar with painting will be able to see at once the elective affinity between impressionism and this double process of differentiation and reintegration. The coherence of the sound pattern arising from this process of fragmentation is one of the most important features of Wagner's method; he creates a totality by reducing it to the minutest models of particularity, which then continually merge into each other, thus producing great, dense textures of sound. This is what brings into being the rounded, encompassing feel of the Wagnerian sound, the feature that I have referred to by using the philosophical term "totality" but that, musically, we would do better to call the "sound surface." No composer can sustain this more consistently or can handle it more subtly than Wagner. Not until our own time has the integrated sound surface, the merging of different sonorities into fields, wholly come into its own In the idea of the incorporation of sound into the total construction.

It is above all in the orchestration that we can see how many of the criticisms of Wagner either were invalid or have been overtaken by subsequent developments. Our parents criticized his music for being noisy. Curiously, this complaint has continued to accompany the history of the new music. In the meantime, people have gradually become aware that the Bayreuth ideal of the concealed orchestra was itself opposed to noise. But here, too, it would be better to consider the purpose of the noise itself and to emphasize the genius of the Wagnerian sound where it opposes the standard of a moderate pleasure in pleasant levels of sound and where it absolutely refuses to allow itself to be enjoyed in a culinary fashion. On occasion, Wagner mobilizes quite extraordinary volumes. But not often. Anyone who is familiar with the scores knows that he makes very sparing use of *fortissimo*. But once he does use *fortissimo*, it becomes a kind of protest against the middle-of-the-road cultural consensus that he denounced in the knights in *Tannhäuser* and derided in the guilds in *Die Meistersinger*. It is a mistake to equate barbarism and loudness in his work, just as it is a mistake to interpret the representation of myth as a direct manifestation of the barbaric. The barbaric ceases to be barbaric once it is reflected in great art; it becomes distanced and is even made the object of criticism. When Wagner goes to extremes, this has a precise function: namely, to objectify the chaotic, the undomesticated, to which his works expose themselves without reservation. The violence of the Wagnerian sound, where it is to be found, is the violence of the thing itself.

Wagner's peculiar transcendence of culture—he is always both above it and beneath it at the same time—is what makes him so very German. Whatever has its aesthetic function in itself, like his sonorities, is self-justifying; it is beautiful in itself. I recently made a very curious observation during a Karajan performance of *Twilight of the Gods* in Vienna: its pleasing sonorities were particularly compelling in the pleasing nature of its sound. In the final episode of the *Ring* the only parts that seem noisy are those that have not been properly resolved musically, those in which the volume is not fully justified by the musical events. An instance is the overextended and uneventful climax of Siegfried's Funeral Music; it seems to be problematic in general, and it is not for nothing that it reminds us of Liszt. The conquest of extremes both of expression and of musical construction since Wagner has provided a retrospective vindication of any thunderous booming in his work. It is no accident that works on the threshold of the new music sympathize with Wagner in their tendency to make use of a threefold *fortissimo*. I have in mind such works as Schoenberg's *Gurrelieder* or Strauss's *Elektra*. At the same time, Wagner never lays it on too thick in his orchestration. His method of composition is always transparent, everything is clear, by contrast to many works of the middle Strauss. If it is true that in Wagner the orchestration and the *Klangfarbenmelodie* [melody of tone colors] always serve to create the fiber and sinews of the composition, this implies that they are aiming not at obfuscation or bombast but at the elucidation of the musical events. These events stand in need of further clarification because they do not appear in a pattern whose meaning is self-evident. You will hear Wagner properly only if you bear this in mind when listening to him. He is already guided by the orchestral ideal of clarity that was to lead to the new music via Mahler and Schoenberg. It follows from the principle of fulfilling the potential of the structure in terms of its sonorities. The Siegfried Idyll, which presents the themes of act 3 of *Siegfried* with the solo forces of a chamber ensemble, is the test case that points to the nature of his oeuvre as a whole.

We can even shed light on what we regard today as the offensive eccentricities of his music. The overlong narratives are one example, the tendency toward musical verbosity. Given the difficulties that abound in converting the wealth of incidents in the *Edda* version of the Siegfried story into subject matter suitable for the stage, it seems superfluous at first to have to endure the repetitions of earlier events and of what we already know in such recitals as Wotan's great narrative in act 2 of the *Valkyrie*, or the repetition of familiar material in the riddle scene between Wotan and Mime in act 1 of *Siegfried*. Nor should we overlook the disturbing and embarrassing nature of many long speeches, even where they are essential to the action, as is Gurnemanz's account of the story of Amfortas and Klingsor. We should not prejudge the question of whether modern interpretations of Wagner should brave the howls of rage of the united guardians of the Grail and cut such passages as long as doing so does not damage the general harmonic structure. But if in the process we were to lose such extraordinary passages as the long story that Wotan tells Brünnhilde, that would only confirm the difficulty that Wagner creates for the modern consciousness. The problem is that it is not possible to separate the dubious from the magnificent, and that the truth of his work and what is questionable about it determine each other. Self-confident practitioners nevertheless feel uncertainty in dealing with him, ultimately because this amalgam of truth and untruth cannot be evaded. Whatever the situation, it is Wagner's profound sense of form that has led him to include these narratives.

The fundamental conception of the *Ring* is one of escorting and narrating; like its source it was not really dramatic at all. If we wished to express it as a paradox, we might say that the *Ring* and other works by the mature Wagner are examples of epic theater, although Brecht, who was a rabid anti-Wagnerian, would hardly have assented to this and would more likely have tried to throttle me for saying so. Wagner was instinctively very well aware that epics do not really permit dramatization if they are enacted in a world that does not contain subjectivity as a given trait of the free individual, but in which subjectivity emerges only in conflict with fate. In this respect Wagner was more perceptive than the better-educated Friedrich Hebbel, who thought himself much cleverer.

However, the epic tendency is not just a question of subject matter. One could rightly object that Greek tragedy also made use of epic materials and that it nevertheless managed to make them dramatic. As a totality, the *Ring*—which, after all, was conceived as a masterpiece, and which we must take to be such in the first instance at least—has the quality of something predetermined, preprogrammed, thanks to that Schopenhauerian influence that colors its innermost musical fiber. From one step to the next you find the fulfilment of events that you had expected and that cannot turn out otherwise. Whereas for Hegel history was progress in the consciousness of freedom, for Wagner, who identified with Hegel's antipode, Schopenhauer, the *Ring* was a "phenomenology of spirit as fate."

It follows that the element of freedom, of open possibility, which is essential to drama, does not exist. From Senta's ballad to Gurnemanz's great narrative, ballads and reports punctuate the entire oeuvre, sometimes in the same way that you find in the great art of the *Lied* in the early nineteenth century. I note in passing that the highly promising question of a comparison of Wagner and certain songs of Schubert's has to my knowledge never been investigated. The use of narrative means that what happens is reported: it all lies in the past as something essentially resolved. This points yet again to the realization that, unlike traditional music—which works with firmly fixed, existing, as it were, forms—Wagner's music works with forms that are supposed to be dynamic, always becoming. The paradox is that his music turns into something static. Ultimately, this is because its absolute dynamic lacks its opposite pole, the other, which would enable it to generate a genuine dynamism. In fact it would be hard to discover contrasting themes in Wagner of the kind you find in Beethoven. Related to this is the way his music is organized in fields. We know from logic that without fixed elements there can be no dynamic ones, that where everything flows, nothing happens. The remarkable coincidence here between the philosophy of Heraclitus and his antipodes, the Eleatics, speaks in favor of this paradox.

In Wagner, incessant change—at once a merit and a defect—terminates in sameness. This is already implicit in his most striking material. For chromaticism, the principle of dynamism, of never-ending transition, of continuation par excellence—which Wagner defined as his method—is in itself lacking in qualities and undifferentiated. One chromatic step resembles another. In this sense chromatic music always sympathizes with identity. If you will permit such reflections on the philosophy of history—and I would be the last to suppress them—we might speculate that Wagner's approach to composition anticipated the dawning horror of the transition from a thoroughly dynamic society to a newly rigid, entirely reified one, one that we might call, using Veblen's term, a new feudalism.

In this connection, too, I should like to dwell on another questionable aspect of Wagner, one that shows how his great achievements and his failings are intertwined. I return here once again to *Twilight of the Gods*. The feebleness of the last act can scarcely be denied and fails to do justice to its subject. Wagner does not live up to his promise to provide music appropriate to the end of the world. The music fades away and fails to satisfy our expectations of the ultimate catastrophe, despite the shudder provoked by passages like Gutrune's scene before Siegfried's body is brought home. For example, Brünnhilde's last aria is incomparably weaker and less coherent than Isolde's, to which it may be compared in certain respects.

I used to explain this striking feebleness with reference to the leitmotiv machine, to Wagner's need to confine himself to the preexisting collection of motives, some of it decades old, even though his fully developed late style had long since left it behind. But such an explanation is too superficial. Thanks to the cyclical element of the tetralogy—with its built-in impossibility of escape, as is already implicit in the title of the *Ring*—everything qualitatively different or novel is blocked from the outset, even though it is called for aesthetically at the critical juncture. There had been a similar quandary earlier on, in the quintet in *Die Meistersinger*, where Wagner's sense of form told him to step outside the magic circle. He responded to this with an inspired melody that did not flow inevitably from the machinery. But he does not pursue this new idea logically, does not allow it to follow its own impulse, but simply economizes, making use of the rather worn stock of themes from the song-contest complex.

However, the ideas I have sketched in connection with act 3 of *Twilight of the Gods* are literally valid in philosophy, in particular in Hegel's *Phenomenology of Spirit*, which I have already referred to. The last chapter of that book bears the title "Absolute Knowledge." The unsuspecting reader who has devoured his way through the *Phenomenology* hopes that absolute knowledge will finally stand revealed with the identity of subject and object and that he will at long last have it in his grasp. But if you read the chapter you will be sorely disappointed, and can even picture Hegel mocking the reader for cherishing such outlandish expectations, even those that have been encouraged by his philosophy. Absolute knowledge turns out to be little other than a kind of recapitulation of what has gone before; the epitome of that movement of the spirit in which it is said to have come home to itself, without the absolute's being expressed in so many words, and which indeed, according to Hegel, could not be expressed as a portable conclusion. In musical terms, in short, it is a reprise, with the element of disappointment characteristic of all reprises. It is likewise in *Twilight of the Gods*. The absolute, the redemption from myth, even if only a catastrophic redemption, is possible only as a reprise. Myth is catastrophe in perpetuity. Whatever abolishes it revitalizes it, and death, the end of the bad infinity, is also absolute regression.

I hope I have succeeded in giving you at least an idea of how Wagner's aesthetic weakness is inseparable from the kernel of his musical conception, that is to say, from the cyclical progression, the doom-laden totality, which prohibits the redemption of what it simultaneously promises. If I have, then you will be able to understand why Wagner's so-called aesthetic faults are not simply to be corrected at will. No individual failing on Wagner's part can be blamed for them. They can be criticized only if we go beyond the purely aesthetic realm. This talk of faults may sound pedantic, but as soon as we talk of the truth in works of art of the highest rank, we must also speak of their defects. To do otherwise is to fail to take them seriously. Wagner's aesthetic weaknesses arise in the metaphysics of repetition, that gesture of "That's how it is; may it always be so. You cannot get away from it; there is no escape." This leads to the question of productions of Wagner today, and I should like to say a few words about that.

The problem is antinomic. As with the narratives and act 3 of *Twilight of the Gods*, so it is with everything in Wagner that is hard to take. It is inseparable from the heart of the matter. If you eliminate the offensive aspects, you are in danger of damaging the core. You are forced to go further than you would like, and this leads to inconsistencies, conflicts, and irritation. If you fail to eliminate them, you do not just lapse into the antiquarian but are compelled to display all sorts of things that are no longer viable today—and this includes not just lilac bushes but musical elements such as sequences and entire formal dimensions. Attempts to evade such antinomies by seeking refuge in so-called timeless verities are completely futile, even though the idea of timelessness is very close to Wagner's own mythology. In Wagner everything has its historical kernel. Like a spider, his spirit dwells at the heart of the huge web of exchange relations that criss-cross the nineteenth century. Even the cozy, Spitzweg[2] mood of act 2 of *Die Meistersinger* is functional since it belongs to the almost irresistible but poisoned attempt to re-create a recent mythical national past with which the modern German nation can become intoxicated.

For this reason it may be the surrealist attempts at production that will turn out to be adequate, even though the surrealism of the 1920s and 1930s is long since obsolete. Such attempts aspire, not to mythologize Wagner by making him timeless, but to open up his historical core by display-ing its debt to history, or by "distanciating" it, as people are all too quick to say nowadays. Max Ernst's idea of showing King Ludwig II disporting himself in the Venusberg is delightful. The latest parodic and aggressive view of act 2 of *Die Meistersinger* in Bayreuth—I have not seen the pro-duction myself—is presumably in the same vein. If it is true that however you approach Wagner you are bound to get it wrong, then the best solu-tion is to highlight the false, incoherent, and antinomic aspects, instead of smoothing them out and creating a kind of harmony that conflicts with what is most profound in Wagner. For this reason, only experimental solu-tions will do nowadays; the only true productions are those that offend against Wagnerian orthodoxy. The guardians of the Grail should not be so touchy. We possess Wagner's precise instructions, and they will continue to be handed down by the historians. But the fury unleashed by modern in-terventions is proof that they hit a raw nerve, the very spot at which we must attempt to resolve the question of Wagner's relevance today. By the same token, it is right to intervene in such explicitly nationalistic passages as Hans Sachs's final speech. Similarly, the music dramas should be freed from the stigma of the shameful anti-Jewish caricatures of Mime and Beckmesser. The director can achieve this by changes of emphasis. If Wag-ner's works are truly full of ambivalences and inconsistencies, the only way to do them justice is through productions that take account of this to bring out the difficulties instead of disguising them with cosmetic effects.

It remains to inquire whether the relevance of Wagner, on which I have tried to shed light from a variety of points of view that are distant from each other, is not merely an artistic relevance, merely a matter of technique. The implied concept of a technique that can be separated from truth content is shallow. But I would like to comment directly on the question of truth content. If we are to seek a formula for that truth, it would have to be a statement about a kind of music that for all its colorful nature is dark and forbidding and that points to the downfall of the world by depicting it. Even the barbaric aspects of Wagner's oeuvre express the fact that the culture that is being destroyed as the anvil in Mime's smithy is destroyed by Siegfried, is no culture at all. The spirit of the world has truly behaved like the Wagnerian unfolding of total negativity. Today, nothing could be graver; this is why the gravity of his work persists. This is confirmed, perhaps for the last time, by the profound affinity between the poetic drafts, whether successful or not, and the nature of the composition. Such an affinity has never again been achieved by art on a grand scale.

Music has become specialized, and its historical curse is that the process of specialization cannot be reversed at will, even though it damages the relevance and authenticity of the work of art. The fault lines in Wagner's works spring from the works' claims to a totality that refuses to declare itself satisfied with the specialized work of art, even though Wagner himself was involved in the process of specialization through technology. His artistry, his professionalism, those features that delighted Nietzsche, implied a rejection of dull craftsmanship; from them everything was to be learned. In Wagner, they serve the concept of a totality that criticized the old fourfold division of opera as well as the division of labor in the guilds and hierarchies down to the present day. Since in Wagner the whole of history appears circular, appears as something in which history has not yet begun, his music issues a wordless protest against that very fact. This was the message gleaned by his friend Bakunin when he heard *The Flying Dutchman* and said that this was just water, but what would this music be like once it became fire. The fact that Wagner was less successful in his representation of fire is itself a piece of metaphysics: beneath the coercion of its own metaphysics, his music retreated into itself. But because it ultimately fails to fulfill what it had promised, it has been passed on to us in its faulty, unfinished form, as something that is incomplete in itself and that still has to be taken further. It is waiting for the thing that will drive it on further until it reaches its goal in itself. That, no doubt, is its true relevance today.

(lecture, 1963; first published 1964; GS 16 543–64)
Translated by Rodney Livingstone

17

Mahler

CENTENARY ADDRESS, VIENNA, 1960

No one who comes to Vienna from Germany to speak on the occasion of Mahler's centenary can escape the feeling that he is bringing coals to Newcastle. Mahler's innovations—and these were his essential contribution—are not comprehensible without reference to the norm from which he deviated, the norm that is itself a deviation. I am speaking of his Austrian idiom, which is also the determining musical tradition of Europe.[1] He gave ten years of his life to the Vienna Opera, years that have gone down in history as the Age of Mahler and that have made a lasting contribution both to music and to the history of interpretation. The standards they set for the entire world of music have continued to this day to exert a pervasive influence on composition. Aware from early on that the so-called tradition was losing its hold, he insisted on clarity and accountability down to the very last note, and combined this with a generous and enthusiastic vision of a composition as a whole.

From the Austrian tradition he inherited that instinct for dwelling on what is musically meaningful, as opposed to any purely mechanical sequence of events. But at the same time he was acutely conscious of the threat to musical form posed by any easygoing, conciliatory attitude of laissez-faire. He resisted this much as his contemporary Karl Kraus assailed the corruption of language in the culture section of the papers. Hence even as an interpreter Mahler has an important place in that intellectual movement of the age that served notice on the dominant conformism. This has the paradoxical effect that the impermanent performances that he rehearsed and conducted have become immortal, even to those who were not present. A person who has lost a loved one often looks for traces of his way of speaking, moving, and gesturing in the people who knew him or at least belonged to the same circle, so that what seems to be the nuance of an intonation may provide the consolation that the dead man is not wholly dead. In the same way, one would like to reconstruct what it was like to have been directed by him from the accounts of those who knew him. I sometimes play with the idea that the features of his face, suffering and tender, powerful and earnest, were shared out among the conductors and composers who succeeded him.

To hear Mahler properly it is essential to be attuned to the consensus that prevails wherever music speaks Austrian. In this respect the extremes meet, since Bruckner was on friendly terms with Mahler, while Webern was probably his most authentic interpreter. The Austrian spoken by his mother is inscribed in passages in early works like the trio of the First Symphony, which is sweet without being sugary, thanks to the richly differentiated levels of harmony. Austrian too is the long *Ländler* melody in the andante of the Second Symphony, which was probably the first piece to attract Mahler lovers to his music. It is enough on its own to refute the accusations of a poverty of melodic inventiveness, if anyone were still brave enough to level that charge. He was capable of such extended melodic passages whenever he required them, even in his maturest phase—in the first trio of the first "Night" music of the Seventh Symphony and in the incomparable F-sharp major theme of the adagio sketch for the Tenth. That he was sparing in his use of melody is due not to his lack of inventiveness but to a symphonic conception in which the whole surpasses even the most beautiful parts. Austrian, lastly, is his counterpoint, the imaginative creation of melodies to be added to those already set, a process of condensation arrived at not by compression but by allowing free rein to the profusion of his ideas. Even in the muted works of his last phase we find a recurrence of the Austrian tone. In the "Dance of Death" in the Ninth, a tune reminiscent of a *Ländler* is played on the fiddle.

There is little point in defending him against the flood of long-since-standardized objections, by presuming to assign him to his appropriate niche in history. What needs to be explained is why the living experience of works that have been collectively repressed is now overdue. The justification lies in the repressed music itself; it lies in what is true in Mahler and will outlive the scandal.

The aim cannot be simply to transform him into a great composer, to salvage his reputation merely by asserting that the great achievements that were unquestionably his were really wonderful. For this would be to acquiesce in the norms of the *juste milieu* and would cheat Mahler of his best claim to fame. What is inauthentic about him is not just the allusions to the popular musical idiom of Austria and Bohemia, which have been criticized for their *déraciné* irony or their mawkish sentimentality. His own musical language is consistently fractured. It challenges the conventional musical belief that music is a pure, unmediated art, a belief that people cling to despite the fact that relations between people have undeniably become more complex and that the world they inhabit is increasingly bureaucratized. When Schoenberg remarked in his important study of Mahler that in the Ninth Symphony the composer's voice could not be heard directly, he put his finger on something that applies more or less to all his works and goes a long way toward explaining the unease and the sense of ambivalence he arouses.

Scarcely a theme, let alone a whole movement, can be taken at face value. A masterpiece like the Fourth Symphony has a hypothetical air about it from the first note to the last. Although the composer claims to love nature, he puts musical immediacy and naturalness in doubt, and this doubt goes to the very core of his musical ideas. Unmistakable and individual though his manner is, he has absolutely nothing in common with the idea of originality as this has been formulated ever since the early romantics, if not earlier.

His themes, which are always conceived as something other and more than what they directly are, are frequently borrowed or else open to the accusation of banality. Indifference to the norms of a fastidious musical culture or, rather, rebellion against them, dominates both the form of the individual detail and the strategy of the entire work. Whereas the traditional formulae remain more or less in force, apart from the very last works, they are disavowed by the concrete shape they are given. It is not merely that the proportions of the parts within the movements are incompatible with the traditional meaning of the overall scheme. The very fiber of the music contradicts the meaning of the formal categories. This applies particularly to the sonata, even though Mahler never completely abandons it before the late period. This means that the listener who is accustomed to listening for the prescribed formal patterns sometimes receives an impression of chaos. The established concept of musical culture is thus faced with a mortal threat. At the climax of the first movement of the First Symphony there is a fanfare that seems to shatter the walls of the securely constructed form. Against all art, its aim is to transform art into an arena for the invasion of an absolute. Mahler's music shakes the foundations of a self-assured aesthetic order in which an infinity is enclosed within a finite totality. It knows moments of breakthrough, of collapse, of episodes that make themselves autonomous, and, finally, of disintegration into centrifugal complexes. In its attitude to form it is recklessly advanced, despite a harmonic, melodic, and coloristic stock-in-trade that seems downright conservative when set beside Strauss or Reger. As the representative of the existing cultural establishment, Debussy had walked out in protest from the Paris premiere of the Second Symphony. He was appalled by what seemed to him a monstrosity of inflated dimensions when measured by the criteria of clarity and distinctness. Later on people became deaf to Mahler's rebellion against the constraints placed on music by private bourgeois conventionality. He was labeled an exponent of the monumentality of the Wilhelminian age and the *Ringstrasse*.[2] This represented a *streamlined* [E] version of the old, spiteful cliché that Mahler's intentions were not matched by his achievements. The Beckmesser-like ridicule of the man who doesn't follow the rules, but learns his tunes from the finches and the tits, was now dressed up as the defense of a newly espoused modernity.

But what the apostles of authenticity really hold against Mahler, namely, his thoroughgoing discontinuity, the musical nonidentity with whatever stands behind it, emerges now as a necessary development. *Weltschmerz*, the disharmony between the aesthetic subject and reality, had been the posture of the musical spirit ever since Schubert. But this had not led composers to modify the formal language of music. That was Mahler's achievement. The soul thrown back on itself no longer feels at home in its traditional idiom. It feels distraught; its language is no longer able to accommodate the direct violence of its suffering. In this respect, although Mahler came from the margins of society and never disowned the experience derived from his background, he is not far removed from Hofmannsthal's high-born Lord Chandos, who finds the words crumbling in his mouth because they no longer say what they ought. But unlike Chandos, Mahler did not conclude that the only solution was to fall silent.

Instead, by attributing to the traditional words and syntax of music intentions that they no longer possessed, he signaled his recognition of the rupture. The inauthenticity of the language of music becomes the expression of its substance. Mahler's tonal chords, plain and unadorned, are the explosive expressions of the pain felt by the individual subject imprisoned in an alienated society. They are the cryptograms of modernism, guardians of the absolute dissonance that after him became the very language of music. Unstylized outbreaks of horror, such as the one in the first trio of the Funeral March in the Fifth Symphony, in which the inhuman voice of command seems to cut across the screams of the victims, were no longer really compatible with the language of tonality, least of all within the compass of the march. The scandal is that he achieved it nevertheless and succeeded in expressing the truly unprecedented with a traditional vocabulary.

Today, when music has discovered a language appropriate to such experiences, we are tempted to wonder whether that very appropriateness does not weaken and make harmonious the unspeakable experiences that flash through Mahler's music and only become reality at a later stage. But it is his banalities, the true fossils of tradition, that really establish its incompatibility with the individual subject. They are indispensable to a consciousness that abandons itself unreservedly to the historical negativity that is approaching. They are also allegories of the "Lower Depths"[3] of the insulted and the socially injured. With supreme genius Mahler, the passionate reader of Dostoyevsky, incorporates them into the language of art. The commonplaces he evokes never remain commonplace. They become eloquent and hence integral parts of the composition. In this way Mahler strives to compensate to some degree for the ancient wrong necessarily committed by the artistic language of music when, in order to realize itself, it excluded everything that did not fit in with its social preconditions, those of educated privilege.

Following the Eighth Symphony, the experience of metaphysical negativity entered Mahler's consciousness. This meant the impossibility of using music to confirm the meaningfulness of the ways of the world, something that had previously been the hallowed custom that allowed for no exception, not even the tragic metaphysics of Richard Wagner. The now famous letter to Bruno Walter makes this plain. It is an early testimony to the fact that the foundations of all music had been severely shaken. This is the source of everything that sounds chaotic to the ear that loves order. Because his music can no longer profess any guaranteed meaning and because, unlike Beethoven's, it must dispense with the hope that meaning will be vouchsafed by the overriding logic of a dynamic structure, he is forced to surrender himself nakedly to individual impulse. Anyone who has allowed the lower depths to enter into composition composes from the bottom up. The only totality known to this symphonic art is one that arises from the temporal stratification of its individual segments.

In Viennese classicism the concept of totality was the undisputed master. Its musical ideal could therefore be called dramatic. If that is so, then Mahler's may be described as epic; it is a cousin to the large-scale novel. Reminiscent of the novel are the rise and fall of passion; the unexpected, seemingly coincidental, but in reality necessary events; the detours, which are actually the main road. From beneath the trembling veil of the old, conciliatory symmetries, we witness the emergence of that musical prose that then became the language of music as such. To understand Mahler means to cast off, as far as is possible, the listening crutches afforded by the traditional patterns. Given the fact that, not infrequently, the movements are very long, this is no petty requirement. Since the music has been composed from the bottom up, it must be heard from the bottom up. The listener must abandon himself to the flow of the work, from one chapter to the next, as with a story when you do not know how it is going to end. You then become aware of a second and superior logic. It follows from the definition of the individual figures, rather than an abstract, preordained design. As Mahler developed, this logic became increasingly marked. The ability to organize a totality became fused with the ability to shape this totality out of the goals of the individual components. Starting from the chance nature of existence, he transformed it into a coherent whole, without having to borrow from sources no longer authenticated. This is what defines Mahler as a great composer. None of the more recent composers has equaled him in his ability to make objective an untrammeled subjectivity. But the forces that led him to such adventurous composing were themselves anything but private and voluntary. He had no illusions about the inexorable decline of forms that behave as if their mere existence could establish a meaning that is no longer present in society. He perceived the direction this decline was taking and complied with it. Hence his power.

Mahler's music is critical of aesthetic illusion and of the culture in which it thrives and from whose superannuated elements it is composed. Wherever he falls below the level of culture, by the same token he stands above it. Having salvaged an amalgam of happiness and misery from his childhood, he refused to subscribe to any adult resignation or self-abnegation, the official social contract of music. By nature he was a *fauviste*, a savage, but not one who is intent on the resurrection of barbarism because he is oppressed by civilization. Instead, his music envisages a human race that rises above the preordained order and its own failures, which works of art normally replicate simply by virtue of their existence. The works of art that he created dream of the abolition of art by that achieved fulfillment which his symphonies conjure up so indefatigably and in so many variations. Hence the contradictory nature of his work. The elements defined by the cliché of the gulf between intention and achievement point not to an aesthetic inadequacy but to the inadequacy of the aesthetic itself. I do not deny that you cannot have the one without the other. Works of art that are superior to the current culture are not able to satisfy its requirements entirely. But the most ambitious works succeed by transforming their weaknesses into strengths. After the last of the *Lieder eines fahrenden Gesellen*, Mahler was able to convert his neurosis, or, rather, the genuine fears of the downtrodden Jew, into a vigor of expression whose seriousness surpassed all aesthetic mimesis and all the fictions of the *stile rappresentativo*.

In the same way, his lack of immediacy and virtuosity as a composer all became part of the creative ferment of his art. The austere, unpolished beginnings developed into the clarity, the unadorned terseness that a generation ago Erwin Stein rightly termed Mahler's matter-of-factness [*Sachlichkeit*]. In the words of the Chorus Mysticus [from the end of Goethe's *Faust*, Part II], which he was not too overawed to set, it really is the case that in his music, "All that is enacted / Here is perfected." Even his monumentality, which offers such an easy target for the ridicule of those who have the advantage of having been born fifty years after him, expresses his refusal to accept an intimacy that had degenerated into a mere ornament and that had become the particular refuge of the most sophisticated composers, like Brahms and Debussy. This monumentality may be problematic in a society built on individualism, and Mahler has to pay the price for that.

But he was sometimes able to achieve one of the ambitions of all modern music since Bach, one that was especially central to the Austrian symphonic tradition. This was the desire to fill the empty flows of time with meaning, to transform it into a permanence full of joy. That fulfillment—which was present in those passages of Schubert that have been described, not without irony, as his "heavenly lengths," or that could be glimpsed in Bruckner, where it was frustrated by his failure to close the gap between the epic design and the traditional formulae of music—has found its true home in Mahler's unaccommodated and fractured symphonies. If all important conceptions of art are built on an inherent paradox, then the paradox of Mahler's music is that he succeeded on the terrain of the large-scale symphony at a time when such works had already become impossible.

In the early works—that is, the first four, closely related symphonies, which are generally known as the "Wunderhorn" symphonies—the basic elements are already to be found. These include his sense of the "way of the world"[4] and the breakthrough to something better, the closeness to dialect, and the discontinuities full of inner torment. But at this stage they are just crudely juxtaposed to each other. They overassert themselves to the point, on occasion, of an intentional musical program. This is the source of their freshness, the inextinguishable aroma of their individual characteristics. Never again would Mahler venture as far as in the first movement of the Third Symphony, which is doubtless the cause of its neglect today. With the trombones savagely erupting from the defined tonal space in the slow passages; the sequence of marches, which are heard not from a fixed reference point but from a series of shifting vantage points and which sweep the ear along in the Dionysian revelry; and, in the closing section of the development, a sound that was already as completely undomesticated as anything in the orchestration of the new music—in all this we perceive Mahler's *Urphänomen*, the fountainhead of his music. Mahler renounces the traditional idea of the symphonic goal and waits, without intervening, for the din to exhaust itself. Only the drum rhythm links it with the recapitulation of the introductory section; the barren passage of time shows through, much like the canvas in early modern paintings.

The fear of his own audacity, which must have overtaken him thereafter, had become productive. In the Fourth Symphony, the epilogue to the Third, all the different strands are brought under control. But the norm against which they are measured, a perspective reduced to that of childhood, remains dislocated. The consequence is not just a work that satisfies traditional standards better than any others and that tempts the obtuse to compare it with Mozart; it is also as puzzling as the damaged paradise of Kafka's Nature Theater of Oklahoma.[5] None of Mahler's symphonies is more deeply impregnated with sorrow than this seraphic work, and it is this that makes it an act of homage to Mozart. Mahler was a late developer who was by no means utterly at home in the details of his craft. It was only with this symphony that he acquired full control of the compositional means available to him. The three great instrumental symphonies that followed are reflections on the image world of those that went before. Of course, with the new professionalism, the world of the latter is now distanced and preserved in a fully organized musical context; recapitulation in the dialectical meaning of the word. It may well be that the much-vaunted tragic character of the Sixth Symphony is itself the expression of that immanent coherence to which Mahler's work increasingly tended. This coherence allows for no escape, so that the life that pulsates in the great finale of the Sixth is destined, not for destruction by the hammer blows of fate, but for an internal collapse: the *élan vital* stands revealed as the sickness unto death. The movement combines the powerful dimensions of an expansive epic ideal of music, the generous elevations of the large-scale novel, with the compelling density of thematic work: the symphonic idea is simultaneously realized and suspended.

Of equal stature to the Sixth is the first movement of the Seventh. Here Mahler's vocabulary is enlarged and sheds that hint of anachronism that hitherto had been inseparable from his boldness. The timbral range of the orchestra embraces everything from the most luminous super major to the darkest shadows. No less rich is his harmony. His use of fourths may have inspired the Chamber Symphony that Schoenberg completed a year later. Even more astonishing are the chordal contrasts of the second theme, which give the music an almost three-dimensional shape. Then, in the Eighth Symphony, the hand of the master attempts retrospectively to complete what had been anticipated as early as the Second. In the hymn "Veni Creator Spiritus" there are passages where the impossibility of making a start turns into violence, as if willfully asserting that the start had been a success.

But there is no stronger argument in Mahler's favor than his impatience with the affirmative nature of the masterpiece. And it was the very idea of affirmation that he found suspect. The idea of a breakthrough, which never left him, became sublimated into the memory of a past life as of a utopia that had never existed. It was in *Das Lied von der Erde* that the desire for subjective expression first broke through the impulse for symphonic objectification. It provided the keyword of "universal loneliness" and thereby became Mahler's most popular work. To this day it has remained the ultimate composition to conquer all hearts, despite its autonomous nature, despite its total organization. What is puzzling, though, is a quality that goes beyond even mastery itself and that is almost impossible to account for in technical terms. The simplest turns of phrase, formulae, are sometimes so saturated with content in *Das Lied von der Erde* that they put one in mind of the everyday speech of an older man whose words go beyond their overt meaning and contain the experience of a lifetime. Written by a man not yet fifty, this work, despite its fragmented form, is one of the greatest achievements of a late musical style since the last Quartets. It is surpassed, if at all, only by the first movement of the Ninth Symphony. It lingers in the same Chinese Dolomite landscape of streams and pines, but frames the compressed fullness of the vocal part within a wide-ranging symphonic objectivity that represents a final leave-taking from the sonata form. Two themes, major and minor, alternate in dialogue. They tell a story that stretches far into the past. Their voices intertwine and drown each other out, mingling with each other until, driven by a third motive, the work becomes ensnared in a passionate present, only to collapse at a sudden blow, of which the listener had had a presentiment from the rhythm of the very first bar. Only shards remain, and the sweetness of a captivating but futile solace. The last work that Mahler completed, whose third movement contains polyphonic passages that strain to escape from the thorough-bass scheme, is the first work of the new music.

Mahler drew the consequences from a development whose implications have only now become fully apparent. It is the perception that the Western idea of unified, internally coherent, as it were systematic music, whose unity is meant to be identical with its meaning, is no longer viable. It has become incompatible with a situation in which people are no longer in command of any authentic experience of such a meaning in their lives. It is incompatible with a world that has ceased to provide them with the categories of unity in happiness, leaving them only with those of standardized compulsion. Mahler is matter-of-fact even in the supreme metaphysical sense, in that he jettisoned the aesthetic illusion of a meaningful totality, which no longer existed, if indeed it ever did. Mahler, whose uncompromising spirituality separated him from the hedonism of his age, from Debussy and Strauss, and whose mind selflessly strove to conceive of something that goes beyond mere existence—Mahler discovered the impossibility of such a task simply by refusing to be deflected from his path. A metaphysician like no other composer since Beethoven, he made the impossibility of metaphysics his central belief, even while battering his head against the brick wall this represented. His world, like that of his compatriot Franz Kafka, is a world infinitely full of hope, although not for us. He passionately wagers everything on the absurd possibility that it will one day be fulfilled. This conviction does not hover over his music abstractly, but permeates its texture right down to the last technical refinements. Technique in Mahler is concretely determined by and directed toward this idea. Mahler's technique centers on the principle of composing logically, in a manner free of caprice and indifferent to effects,[6] and at the same time of transcending logicality. What he longs for is the epiphany of construction and freedom. This would be a lost cause if it were not corroborated by the construction itself. Conversely, the construction would be no more than an arbitrary exercise of power by the would-be sovereign self, if it were not filled with substance that is reconciled with it, rather than subject to it. Of course, in this account of the goal of which Mahler was unconscious, but which is implicit in his music, we may recognize the spiritual return of the quintessential Austrian, purified of all its stifling coziness—that is to say, something passive and yielding, which trusts itself to the surge of inspiration without attempting to tamper with it.

The history of music since Mahler, even in its most recent phase, has maintained this trend toward integration and even taken it to extremes. The principle of motivic elaboration, which goes back to Bach, Beethoven, and Brahms, has been extended to the point where every element of the music is determined by a latent element common to them all. Hence it has virtually excluded the idea of a variety that is to be synthesized. An individual musical fact is viewed from the outset as a functional part of a totality, and hence sheds its own substantiality. Unity, however, is undermined as soon as it ceases to unify a plurality. Without a dialectical counterpart it threatens to degenerate into an empty tautology. The recent tendency to incorporate aleatoric elements into the overall construction implies a critical reflection on this situation.

Mahler would be the staunchest pillar of this criticism. He has elicited from the process of composition a dimension that had been repressed, as he had been, and that has now been revealed as the precondition for all music. It is the dimension of functional characterization, where distinctions tend to be obliterated in the undifferentiated unity of the integral language of the present. In Mahler's music all the individual domains are formulated as definitely and unambiguously as possible. They proclaim: I am a continuation, something that comes after, a coda. Thanks to the clarity of this characterization, which makes everything what it is by virtue of its function, its formal meaning within the totality, the individual domain genuinely becomes something more than itself. It opens itself up to a totality that crystallizes out in consequence, without being brought to bear on the functional elements from outside. This is why these elements never remain constant, but are caught up in a continuous process of change, even though they are all unmistakably themselves.

It has rightly been observed that the first thing that impresses the listener to Mahler's music is that it always develops in an unexpected way. But by the same token, his novelistic, unschematic approach is far removed from the merely episodic or arbitrary. The method he uses is the variation technique. When compared to the total work, the functional elements are too independent, too evidently living beings in process, to be split up in accordance with the rules governing traditional motivic work or to sink their identity in a seamless web. In variation technique each functional element is fixed in a recognizable shape; the structure of themes and shapes is preserved.

However, particular features are modified; classical music comes to incorporate the principle derived from the oral tradition and the folk song, according to which subterfuges, minute variations, are introduced into the repetition of the original melody that transforms the identical into the nonidentical. Mahler is the composer of deviation, right down to the technicalities. Variation, however, the unexpected, is the opposite of the kind of effect used by the school of Berlioz, Liszt, and Strauss to achieve the *imprévu*. Nowhere do Mahler's variations introduce difference for its own sake. For all their irregularity, their sequence in time is subject to a certain organic teleology that can be studied down to the very last interval. Where there is change, there has to be change because tensions and potentials that proclaimed themselves at the figure's appearance are worked through. Why a thing starts off one way and then becomes something else is always precisely motivated. In the first movement of the Fourth Symphony, for ex-

ample, it can be observed how from the outset a theme waits from its beginning to enlarge one of its component intervals, but that this interval is
introduced only after lengthy preparation. It is in the tensions between the
variations that the breathing rate of Mahler's symphonies is established and
the transition from the particular to the totality is achieved.

But it is in the functional figures, as they emerge, persist, and disappear, that the substance of Mahler's music is contained. They are quite simply expression, which becomes both the function and the constituent of
the form. If Mahler's art begins with the idea of breakthrough, this is objectified and fulfilled in these figures. Frequently failure itself, the celebration of the compulsion they are subject to, becomes a substitute for what
has been promised. But in Mahler it is achieved; that is what is so fasci-
nating. And if, on the other hand, Mahler's experience in a society whose
spell cannot be broken means that the image of breakthrough and fulfillment is itself distorted, he nevertheless succeeds in discovering the figure
appropriate to such experience—namely, that of a fully composed-out disintegration and collapse. It is already to be found in outline in parts of the
first movement of the Second Symphony, then in the first two movements
of the Fifth, and finally and utterly in those passages of the andante in the
Ninth that follow the catastrophe.

In the final phase it may be that the idea of a music that evokes transcendental meaning is reduced to a truly Proustian search for things past,
for the pavilion of friends and the blossoming beauty of slender young
girls. But if so, the composition adapts itself to this with figures of disintegration and by renouncing the ambition of integration. It finds its true solace in the strength to look absolute desolation in the face and to love the
world even though there is no hope. Such figures are to be discovered in
the leave-taking movements of *Das Lied von der Erde* and the Ninth Symphony, which dissolve into particles that make no pretense of unity.

Mahler's nonviolent violence, which is formulated in such figures, is
the power of a true humanity. Greatness in composition does not consist
for him, as it did for Luther, in commanding the notes to go where they
belonged. Instead, he follows them where they lead, from a sense of identification with those who are cruelly knocked about and forced into line by
aesthetic norms and indeed by civilization itself. In short, he identifies with
the victims. Ultimately it is because of this self-denying identification with
the Other that Mahler has attracted criticism for his subjectivism. The expression of suffering, both his own and that of those who have to bear the

burdens, no longer knuckles under at the behest of the sovereign subject, which insists that things must be so and not otherwise. This is the source of the offense he gives. In his youth he composed a setting to the poem "Zu Straßburg auf der Schanz."[7] Throughout his life his music sided with those who fall out of the community and are destroyed—with the poor drummer boy, the doomed outpost, the soldier who has to keep beating the drum even after his death. Death itself was for him simply the continuation of the blind earthly disasters in which he was enmeshed.

But the great symphonies, the marches that reverberate through his entire oeuvre, set limits to the sovereign individual, who owes his life and glory to those who dwell in the shadows. In Mahler's music the individual becomes conscious of his own incipient impotence. Aware of the imbalance between himself and the superior might of society, he awakens to a sense of his own utter unimportance. Mahler responds to this by abandoning the sovereign power to posit form, but without writing a single bar that the subject, who is thrown back on himself, would have been unable to fill or to answer for. He does not adjust to the incipient external domination of the age, nor does he deny its power. Instead, his ego is strong enough to help the weak and the speechless to express themselves and to salvage their image in art. The objectivity of his songs and symphonies distinguishes him sharply from all art that makes a pleasant and comfortable home for itself in the private individual. As a metaphor of the unattainability of a harmonious, reconciled totality, this objectivity is essentially negative.[8] His symphonies and marches do not express a discipline that triumphantly subdues all particulars and individuals; instead, they assemble them in a procession of the liberated, which in the midst of unfreedom necessarily sounds like a procession of ghosts. To use the term for an awakening, which occurs in one of his songs, all his music is a reveille.

(1960)

Afterthoughts

The Centenary Exhibition in Vienna provokes the criticism that with their program "Mahler and His Age" the organizers formulated their aims too broadly and that Mahler's specific qualities have been dissipated in the generalities of the age, if indeed it is possible to grasp anything of them at all through the display of visual exhibits. But the very irrelevance of the exhibition to the man it is celebrating enhances our knowledge of him considerably. The period of his maturity coincides more or less exactly with that of Art Nouveau. Names like Roller and, above all, Moll, his wife's stepfather, are both associated with this sphere.[9] But what distances Mahler from his age, and that includes its leading literary figures, is the almost complete absence of the elements of Art Nouveau in his work. Such elements predominate in Richard Strauss; they are present in the young Schoenberg and can even be found in Reger. But of Mahler the most that could be said is that the exotic aspect of his last works reveals an affinity with Art Nouveau. But that aside, he must have sounded retrograde when compared to the standards of what was then thought modern. Neither the slogans nor the formal idiom of Art Nouveau made any impact on his oeuvre. The images that inspire it are late romantic rather than neoromantic; they belong to those that people were in rebellion against. But his anachronistic element, this sense of not having quite kept up with developments, became in him a source of strength that went beyond the capacities of the age. It provided him with a sort of resistance to the process of subjectivization, which enabled him to retain a quite spontaneous hold on the model of the great objective symphonic work. Even though this had now become an impossible project, it nonetheless managed to infiltrate his works and imbue them with something of that past collective authority, as soon as his works were technically in command of themselves. On occasion the most progressive kind of art seeks refuge in the residues of what has been left unfinished or unworked out. This bypasses the sphere of what is regarded as *up to date* [E] by taking up and rethinking what has been left to one side. That lack of concern with himself, with the composing subject, which is evident in his music and which must have struck his contemporaries as a lack of discrimination, was potentially the saving grace of self-obliviousness. It legitimated his symphonies as the language of the age after the style of the isolated human being, which he never achieved, had become obsolete and a matter of indifference.

"Die Lichter, die aus deinen Wunden strahlen" ["The lights that radiate from your wounds"]: this line by Stefan George reads like a motto to Mahler, his older contemporary. But the fact that in his case the scars of failure are transformed into the bearers of expression and therewith to the fermentation of a second success, is no merely private peculiarity. His music inquires how the sonata form can be reconstituted from the inside so that it is no longer violently imposed on the living specificities within it, but is at one with them. This is the squaring of the circle, comparable to that Sisyphean philosophical labor of reconciling rationalism and empiricism. All supreme art has some paradox of this sort. It is not inadequate talent but the insolubility of an objectively posed problem that jeopardizes a work. And the threat is all the greater the more profoundly the work is conceived and the more boldly it exposes itself to its own impossibility. Or, rather, in authentic artists a subjective flaw becomes the site of an objective historical failure. Not the worst criterion of art is to ask whether its failure is adventitious or whether its chance nature gives expression to a necessity. In Mahler's case this becomes the signature of his work.

The peculiar preponderance of march music in Mahler calls for a better explanation than the notion that he was fixated on childhood impressions. The behavioral patterns objectified in the march stand in intimate relationship to the novelistic structure of the Mahlerian symphony. The march is a collective form of walking. It assembles the unconnected occurrences of daily experience in a single figure. At the same time it suggests a unidirectional, irreversible movement toward a specific goal. To retract, turn about, or repeat are alien to it, even though such elements constantly enter the march from the dance. The time consciousness of the march seems to be the musical equivalent of narrative time. "*Time marches on*" [E]. This is just as much a metaphor of an unconcentrated, linear, but menacing concept of time as it is of the impulsive movement that corresponds to such a concept, if, indeed, it does not originate in it in the first place. Mahler's marches intend all this. His ingenuity led him to excavate them from his childhood as the fundamental models of an experience of time, which in a lively consciousness stripped of its illusions is all the more potent, the less it obtrudes in the workings of the work of art.

The criticism that could be made of the principal theme of the Sixth Symphony is that it smacks of the official. It sounds a little like the epithet "tragic," which even at that time had degenerated into a cultural reminiscence, and not only in music. But emphatic though the theme is, and even though a genuinely symphonic gesture has assumed theatrical overtones, it is more than mere trappings. Because the theme appears forced on its entry at the very beginning, it is compelled to justify itself by universal mediation—that is, by elaboration. The Sixth is so completely integrated that nothing is allowed to remain an isolated detail, but everything becomes what it is by virtue of its place in the totality. In order to understand such works the listener should not cling to themes but instead should propose them to himself, and await events. As soon as it starts to develop, the movement casts off its "official" tone. At the point where the accompanying march rhythm is dropped, the full, rounded orchestral sound of the opening is split open as if it were going to bleed. The principal motive leaps from the violins to the immoderate trombones; the violins play a counterpoint against it, and the entire high-pitched woodwind section plays a semiquaver, without a bass to carry the harmony. Only after this disruptive interlude does the march return with the crotchets of the opening, followed by a shrill oboe melody. After only a few bars of motivic intervention every hint of the conventional gives way to Mahler's heartrending tone.

There is something sinister about the scherzo of the Sixth, not least because, thanks to the put-on crescendi and the chromatic *fauxbourdon* passages in the middle voices, the orchestra seems to swell like a body threatening to burst and cause untold damage. The three-dimensionality of the orchestra, its spatial volume, as it were, becomes the vehicle of expression. It perhaps assumes this function because Mahler's laborious development of a full, corporeal orchestral sound established itself only in the instrumental works of his middle period, whereas the first three symphonies at least sound curiously two-dimensional, as if lacking in spatial depth, simply because of his efforts to achieve maximum clarity in his orchestration. This spatial depth appeared for the first time in Mahler's polyphonic orchestral thinking, where it at once became an element of the musical meaning, the expression.

The trio in the same movement operates, as is well known, with the frequent alternation of 3/8 and 4/8 time. But since it too is polyphonic in structure, the irregularity of the meter leads to such overlapping of the entries of the different parts that what has a strong beat in one voice has a weaker beat in another. This results in a highly idiosyncratic process of rhythmic interference, an unstable sense of the main emphases when it is heard as a whole. The metric irregularity is not confined to externals, the succession of beats, but extends into the core, into the simultaneous composition of the music. Under the impact of what Bartok and Stravinsky have accustomed us to think of as rhythmic, these rhythmic innovations of Mahler's have been forgotten and have been largely neglected by later composers. Down to the present there is no aspect of music in which less has changed than in rhythm—the dimension that has been the most talked about of all. Of this too Mahler is a reminder.

From the andante moderato of the Sixth we can hear how Mahler's sense of form has sapped the vigor of the traditional patterns, without ever breaking with them openly. It begins as if it were one of the *Kindertoten-lieder*, with a cantabile melody in the upper part, which is followed by an alternative theme. Initially the two complexes alternate regularly. But the sense of elevation to which the development or, if you wish, the final section of the movement leads endows this passage with such verve that it seems to burst its confines and then gradually ebb away. For this its intensity requires a lengthier period in order that it should not seem out of proportion and so that the development should not break off suddenly.

But after the broad, flowing movement, no space would be left for a recapitulation of the chief thematic complex. It would make an academic, tacked-on impression, like a mere formal doubling of that descending movement that covers the resolution span of the elaborated section. For this reason it is diverted at the end so that it unobtrusively and without interruption takes over the function of the coda of the entire movement. For the sake of balance Mahler omits the recapitulation that would normally reinstate the balance.

This exemplifies the subtlety and delicacy with which Mahler's sense of the irreversibility of time announces itself in his mature symphonic work. His principle of the variation technique, the deviation, is applied to subverting the large-scale forms. In consequence the entire movement ends up in a different place from the one intended by the composer or, rather, by the overall structural design. According to a theory in contemporary painting, this is, in general, the kernel of truth contained in the most hackneyed concept of originality. Originality is a historical concept, not a fixed one. As long ago as the eighteenth century, Goethe had praised the painter Hackert in his autobiography, observing that "he had gradually risen to the production of some originals." However, the idea that the path of music is one of diversion is so much more compelling than the logic of its own forms because diversion provides an aesthetic formulation of the actual experience that every life runs at cross-purposes to its own premises. It is diversion itself that is the inescapable reality.

Mahler's music can be said to be "concretely determined toward its idea." Lest it be thought that this is too cryptic or that a vacuous Gundolfian formula[10] is being used to rehearse the distinction between absolute and program music, it is important to specify what is meant, since no feature is more deeply ingrained in the physiognomy of Mahler's work. In the finale of the Sixth, just before the last repeat of the introductory section, which already belongs to the coda, the brass once again intones one of the principal motives of the movement and treats it sequentially, four bars before the final strike-up. These bars contain the feeling of "despite everything!" of success in the face of a doom that the latter can do nothing to diminish. It is a feeling that is expressed with extreme directness; it is as unmistakably present as the spoken word could be, but devoid of every unmusical literariness or anything extraneous to form. What is said is said wholly in the language of music, by virtue of its similarity to music and not through any imitation of images and concepts. No other composer has ever been able to do this to the same degree as Mahler. Hence the utopian cast of his music, as if he had come within an ace of uncovering the ultimate mystery. He promises that music which utters the things inexpressible in words, but which keeps losing its grip on them because it has no words at its disposal, yet can nevertheless express them literally.

A long prehistory provides proof that it is not arbitrary to ascribe this achievement to Mahler. Even those aspects of his symphonies that have been described, following Erwin Ratz, as their "negative space" can be dated back to classicism in a quite unliterary way. A vivid example can be seen in the trio from Beethoven's Fifth. The grim humor in it is not anything whose existence can be disputed. It becomes unambiguous, objectively memorable, in the relationship of the concrete music to the idiom as such. After the double bar line [at the end of the first section of the trio] the principal motive enters, without being able to achieve the strong beat, as it had done earlier. After its quavers, but before the next attack, two crotchet rests gape. The idiom and the preceding first statement of the trio lead us to expect the continuation of the motion as something self-evident, and this expectation is disappointed. The motive's gestural language, fortissimo in the basses, suggests strength. But this strength fails. The block of granite is hurled but falls short. Or perhaps the clumsy giant hand does not venture even to throw it, or else it is not even a granite block in the first place. Without the need to resort to conceptual language, this makes quite evident the futility of strength and indeed its stupidity, as long as it fails to reflect on itself. All that becomes apparent in a flash. You can't put your finger on it, for it vanishes as swiftly as the event in the allegro, even though it is no less firmly defined. We might well say that Mahler's music as a whole, and the negative spaces, above all, take up Beethoven's example and extend it to every imaginable type of expression and, indeed, that they colonize the symphony in its entirety. The extent to which Mahler must have been impressed by that trio can be seen from the scherzo in the Second Symphony.

Among the idiosyncratic features of Mahler's use of rhythm we find isolated notes or, under certain circumstances, accompanying motives in which the flow of the music comes to a halt or, rather, is suspended in midair. We find this as early as the *Urlicht* in the Second Symphony, where, immediately before the A major sidestep to the words "Da kam ein Engelein," a minim E is included that is, strictly speaking, out of place [in an unambiguous B-flat minor passage]. The finale, "Wir genießen die himmlischen Freuden," in the Fourth Symphony is particularly rich in such retarding features. The overall effect is as if everything had been displaced by two crotchets, as if the whole passage had failed to catch up with itself. This is a major source of ambiguity. There is a related effect in the "Von der Schönheit" movement from *Das Lied von der Erde* and the first movement of the Ninth Symphony. Unlike some expressively overextended notes in Wagner or sustained accentuated notes of Beethoven, these do not represent any buildup of power that then motivates a subsequent discharge. Nor are they simply a pause in which the movement temporarily comes to rest, but something different again: they are the seal of permanence, of the music's inability to fight free of itself. The epic sense of form in Mahler's symphonies has penetrated right down to the motivic cell and there resists nonviolently the essentially dramatic onward thrust of the symphony. The difficulties of interpreting such bars correctly—that is to say, in such a way that they acquire their meaning from the way the symphony unfolds, and not from external formal categories, such as tension— are extraordinary. One is tempted to think that the success of performances of Mahler depends on the success of these moments.

Because of their vast scope, Mahler was induced to construct entire symphonies on the principle of correspondence. In the Fifth, for example, the Funeral March in the second movement is elaborated parallel to a theme of the adagietto in the finale, and between these two analogously structured parts the great scherzo acts as a caesura. In a similar way the march rhythm, the harmonic sequence with the cowbells, and individual motivic elements relate the outer movements of the Sixth much more closely than would be the case merely by the use of the major/minor motive. In motivic and thematic terms, a major component of the first theme, as well as of the introduction and coda of the finale, is the retrograde motion of the core motive of the first movement: instead of A—C—B—A, we find A—B—C—A. Finally, the two movements share clearly chorale-like wind stanzas in minims, whose motives do indeed differ radically from each other, but which are brought together by their use of the chorale. Even the Ninth still works with the symmetry of large-scale architecture. The first and last movements are slow; the two are analogous in the disembodiment of their concluding sections. The discovery of techniques similar to those found in film—such as the time lapse seen in the rondo of the Fifth—or of slow motion, which can be seen in the quotations of the episodic theme from the burlesque in the adagio of the Ninth, has redounded to the benefit of Mahlerian composition because of their need for large-scale structuring. But productive though such discoveries turn out to be later on, they pale into insignificance before the exigencies of the here and now of composition. The grand architecture has not yet become fused with the fiber of the music, but, instead, it sketchily frames the details. The parallels give pleasure to those who discover them rather than exercising too much power in terms of a living musical response. There are few things that make the distinction between music and the visual arts as clear as this. The very measures that in Mahler seem to be almost an afterthought are the ones that decide the stature of painters or architects. For too long the theories that have been derived from Mahler's constructs have retained the aura of bricolage. It is only in more recent times that they seem to want to become an integral part of the music itself. This is perhaps the weightiest evidence in favor of the contemporary convergence of painting and music. But Mahler was the first in whose work this convergence was proclaimed, not indeed through any mimesis [*Klangmalerei*], but through the conductor's magisterial gaze, directed at the screen of his compositions.

The more conversant you become with Mahler's work, the clearer the source of his retrograde form becomes, and with that the secret of one of the central formal impulses in his oeuvre. The retrogrades are designed to retrieve something of the vigor of which the open march form had deprived them. This can already be seen in the Third Symphony in the tendency to elaborate the themes of the exposition in reverse order. This is no doubt conditioned by an aversion to the mechanical repetition of even the abstract formal structure, or perhaps in order to establish direct contact between the end of the exposition and the beginning of the elaboration. A further instance can be seen in the finale of the Sixth, where in the recapitulation the sequence of the first and second thematic complexes is reversed and the complex as such is fused with the returning introduction. This tendency toward retrogrades is extended to the point of self-consciousness in the adagio finale of the Ninth, where the final recapitulation makes its entry in an enormous outburst with the second half of the theme and responds with the first only after a moment of extreme tension. The idea of retrograde movement as one of large-scale structure rather than of the treatment of detail is one that Berg may well have borrowed from Mahler, as well as from Schoenberg's *Mondfleck*. His method resembles Mahler's also in that he is less concerned with exact pitch retrogrades—although that does play a considerable role in his music too—than with the effect of retrogression as such. What it may lack in coherence in a constructivist sense, it makes up for by the drastic form it assumes. Behind Mahler's conception of the procedure lies something quite different from the desire to create a stasis in which time is retracted. The quasi-retrograde passages are a form of retrospection, of the transition of the musical present to the realm of memory. A formal intentionality that then makes inroads into the stock of technical devices, as formerly into individual harmonic or timbral significances, arose originally in Mahler's case, too, from an expressive need. This coincided from the outset with an aversion to musical architectonics, a dislike of mere recurrence, as if nothing had happened in the interim, whereas the whole order of music lies in developing the rigorous implications of what has gone before. But whether in the transposition of this experience to the level of the musical material anything decisive has been lost is a question that remains unresolved to this day.

If it is true that every formal aspect, every figure, every question in Mahler's works is precisely what it is and what it should be in the context of the whole, without any trace of the merely conventional, then this compels the composer to revitalize the topoi of the received formal language of symphonic writing and activate them by reawakening the sense of their true purpose and of what they had forgotten as mere topoi. A sense of what this means can be gleaned from certain instrumental mannerisms of Mahler's late phase. The drum roll was a topos designed to use orchestral timbre to create tension, on the dominant, for example. With the passage of time this has become so hackneyed that the tension failed to appear, or else appeared only as mock tension. Mahler needs the device but is forced to rethink it, intensify it beyond its own capacities, renew it so that it may become once again what it may have been on its first appearance in Viennese classicism. The way he achieved this is as simple as it is ingenious. What he does on occasion in the Ninth Symphony is to transfer the drum roll from the kettledrums to the bass drum. This resembles the traditional roll closely enough to leave a similar imprint in the memory. But at the same time, the bass drum has an indefinite pitch, which is closer to mere noise, to something undomesticated and alien to the realm of musical culture. Hence the roll retains much more of the dread than it did on the kettledrums, where it simply evaporated. What had been convention now becomes an event. This is, in general, the fate of conventions in Mahler's music.

It is where Mahler most faithfully keeps to the sonata model for the sake of the traditional idea of integration that his specific formal intentions, his hostility to the schematic, really make themselves felt. The meaning of the prevailing configurations undergoes a significant change. The first movement of the Sixth contains an orthodox transition. But it is designed as a chorale—that is to say, statically and not, as might be expected, something that drives the music forward. Moreover, its color is altered by dissonant clashes. This has immediate consequences both for the structure and for the further development. The chorale cannot lead anywhere. The brutal and dazzling secondary theme that follows is not mediated by it. Precisely because the transition does not culminate in it, even though it stands in the usual place, it comes as a shock. This is intensified because instead of modulating into it, the end of the chorale, the D minor dominant,[11] is followed by the F major tonic, an interrupted progression. The striking feature of the second theme, sensation as character, is not inherent in itself, but springs partly from the formal organization. The latter continues to be affected by it. The surprise effect is unrepeatable. In the recapitulation the second theme appears only in fragments. This is not uncommon in those Mahlerian movements where the themes are unbroken melodies that become overprominent and appear too much as partial wholes in their own right. The surprise element of the second subject is promptly withdrawn from it and is taken up again only in the coda. The movement is sonatalike, as if in defiance, but its form is dictated by the musical content.

One sometimes has the feeling that it would be possible simply to formulate the substance of Mahler's music in words: in it the absolute is conceived, felt, and longed for, and yet it does not exist. He no longer accepts the ontological proof of the existence of God, which all previous music repeated parrot-fashion. All could be well, but in fact all is lost. His nervous, gestural language is a reaction to this situation. But how impoverished, abstract, and false such a jejune formula appears when confronted with the actuality of his work. What it overlooks in its efforts to pin Mahler down is what is unfolded and dedicated within the totality of an experience that does not disclose its secret in selective assertions. Only in this way does its truth-content establish contact with the feeling that leaves such assertions as far behind as the actual meaning of life leaves phrases that purport to sum it up.

I am well aware that the expression on death masks is deceptive. While we imagine that the mask reveals the final facial expression of a life, we know that it merely reflects muscular spasms. But Mahler's death mask, which I first saw at the Centenary Exhibition, is enough to make one doubt such scientific explanations. Other death masks, too, appear to smile. But in Mahler's face, which seems both imperious and full of a tender suffering, there is a hint of cunning triumph, as if it wished to say: I have fooled you after all. Fooled us how? If we were to speculate we might conclude that the unfathomable sorrow of his last works had undercut all hope in order to avoid succumbing to illusion, rather as if hope were not unlike the superstitious idea of tempting fate, so that by hoping for something you prevent it from coming true. Could we not think of the path of disillusionment described by the development of Mahler's music as exemplifying the cunning not of reason but of hope? Is it not the case that in the final analysis Mahler has extended the Jewish prohibition on graven images to include hope? The fact that the last two works that he completed have no closure but remain open translated the uncertain outcome between destruction and its alternative into music.

(1963; GS 16: 323–50)
Translated by Rodney Livingstone

18

Alban Berg

At Christmas 1955, on 24 December, Berg had been dead for twenty years. The period since 1935 had not been one of continuity and steady growth in experience; it was disrupted by catastrophes. People forced to emigrate cannot escape the feeling that long years have been torn out of their lives, and it is easy for them to succumb to the delusion that their present existence is just a continuation of what was destroyed then. That is why it is so difficult to convince oneself that Berg has been gone for so long and that we have to make an effort to remember a man whose absence we have never quite been able to admit to ourselves. A feeling of guilt must come over anyone who, in evoking the memory of Berg, sets a seal on the fact of his death. In addition to its subjective justification, this feeling may also be connected with the life that Berg has been granted since his death, in the afterlife of his works. For ten years, until the end of the war, his memory was expunged from public consciousness in Germany, and likewise in Austria. Following the premiere of the *Lulu* Symphony, which Kleiber dared to put on during the Hitler Reich, he was outlawed as a cultural Bolshevik, and from then on there were probably no further performances of his works. Although there was not anything that the fanatics of racism could have found to object to in him, he scorned to make any concessions to the healthy convictions of the people and to barbarism. After 1945 his music was frequently performed again, but in a very different context. During his lifetime he was a leading member of the avant-garde and would never have felt himself to be anything else. He now finds himself lumped together with others under the label of "modern classics," a label from which he would have recoiled. The kind of reception that would really have enabled him to represent new music in the way that was claimed for him was denied him.

His fate differed from that of the other representatives of musical modernity, however. Today it seems as if the public has made its decision in favor of Berg and against the experts, much as Wagner advocated in *Die Meistersinger*. But this is not entirely accurate either. Even during his lifetime Berg's music was appreciated for its expressive qualities, its human tone, and no doubt also its rich sensuousness, and he was compared favorably with Schoenberg in this respect. Berg always objected to such praise, not simply from loyalty to his older friend, but because he felt it to be based on the misapprehension that he was a conformist. He felt slighted in his claims to radicality. After the Berlin premiere of *Wozzeck* in December 1925 we walked around the town until late into the night, and I had to console him over his success, the greatest of his life. If the audience liked that, he said, there was something wrong. And in fact, the quality that brought him success then is the same one that makes it hard for musicians to accept him today. Although those who denounced him thirty years ago have now fallen silent, he is dismissed today as someone who already belongs to the past. The deepest reason for this rejection is probably that the standards he set for composition are felt to be extremely irksome. People would now like to escape from their constraints and from his insistence on the spontaneity of the imagination, an escape they would justify by appealing to the spirit of the age. At the same time, it was he who was responsible for one of the innovations about which so much fuss is made today, namely, the inclusion of the element of rhythm as a constructive feature. Of all the composers of the Schoenberg school, it was he who was the most willing to involve himself in quasi-geometric formal experiments. It is perhaps not superfluous to remark that as early as *Wozzeck* he constructed an entire scene as a set of variations on a rhythm, and in the twelve-tone *Lulu* this procedure was expanded to a large form with [rhythmic] retrograde elements that he called "Monoritmica."[1] In his later works he generally strives for elaborate symmetries that go from the measure-count proportions of entire movements down to the smallest units of phrase construction. This is particularly true of the Chamber Concerto and the Violin Concerto.—There is a particular hostility toward Berg in Germany among those who belong to the so-called *Sing- und Spielbewegung*[2] and those who advocate both a collectivist attitude on the part of the musician and the contemporary relevance of the seventeenth century. They need only hear a few bars of Berg to start talking automatically of *Tristan*-like late romanticism, as if chromaticism and the leading note were the most important aspects of Berg's mature music, and as if determining what his searching, infinitely subtle sensibility succeeded in making of such elements were irrelevant.

In the light of all this, our task must be to try to correct some of the current misconceptions about him, to compensate for some of the damage that he has suffered at the hands of public opinion, and to eliminate some of the phrases and clichés that have made the living experience of his work so fraught with problems nowadays. I am under no illusions about the difficulty of this task and the small prospects of success. I won't be surprised if tomorrow I read and hear once again that Berg is a neurasthenic late-romantic decadent whose overrefined subjectivity no longer speaks to the younger generation. And I shall be overjoyed if people who hear Berg's music and then read sentences of this kind cease to accept them at their face value, and if those who are still unable to change their views were to stop and think for a single second whether Berg's alleged weakness is not worth more than the security of the present day, in which none of those who talk about it so loudly have any real faith. But nothing would be more misguided than to achieve such modest success by denying those elements of Berg's music that every jackass can hear, to use Brahms's words,[3] and that provide a both cheap and inexhaustible source of pleasure to those who wish to criticize him. What is more important is to be aware of the significance of these elements within the force field of Berg's music, to discover what he has made of them.

The fact is, of course, that Berg's origins do lie in *Jugendstil* and the fin de siècle. His affinity with neoromanticism and aestheticism was powerful enough to have left its mark even on his fragile physical existence. To convince oneself of that it is only necessary to glance at the 1908 photograph of Berg as a young man in Willi Reich's biography.[4] Even the older Berg still retains a resemblance to Oscar Wilde. He was on friendly terms with Peter Altenberg.[5] He would use a word like "secession" as if it were still current, and there are even links with Schreker,[6] for whose *Der ferne*

Klang he had made a piano reduction in his youth. We cannot imagine Berg's music without the element of opulence, of extravagance, especially in his orchestral sound. It has sublimated itself into that synthesis with structure, that seductive and refulgent sensuousness, that gives the instrumentation of the late Berg, above all in *Lulu*, its incomparable aura. The fury that this quality, along with his passionate expressionism, unleashes today obeys a mechanism of repression, to use the language of psychology, which is all too appropriate here. This is because each of the expansive gestures in Berg's music reaches out in search of an unself-conscious happiness that refuses to conform to reality. Such happiness appears unattainable in the regimented condition that grants man happiness only on condition that he conform. It is altogether appropriate if such happiness is made to look either childishly old-fashioned or else, in the contemporary climate of restoration,[7] unworthy of authentic existence. Whoever wishes to hear Berg aright should not begin by asking after every beat whether this is not altogether too personal or whether it also speaks to other people, but rather should follow the logic of the music. He will then find in it more human qualities than in reflecting upon the effects that it may or may not have on others.

This human quality, however, its expressive substance, is diametrically opposed to the Wagnerian, with which insensitive ears confuse it. The degenerate, addicted aspect of Berg's music is not a feature of his own ego. It does not aim at narcissistic self-glorification. Rather, it is an erotic enslavement, the object of which is nothing other than beauty and which calls to mind a nature that has been oppressed and degraded by the taboos of culture. The two great operas, *Wozzeck* and *Lulu*, contain nothing heroic, and in them spirit puts on no airs. Instead their enslaved and lethal love attaches itself to the lower depths, to lost souls, to the half-demented and at the same time helplessly self-sacrificing soldier, to his beloved whose instincts rebel against him and whom he destroys together with himself. Later, that love attaches itself to Lulu, an image from the age of courtesans dressed up in the costume of 1890. She is a woman to whom dominant men succumb and whom they destroy in the course of brutally asserting their dominance. The choice of these texts and the standpoint from which he set them to music, the standpoint of universal sympathy with the oppressed, determines the pattern of his work down to the purest piece of instrumental music. His tone can be described as greathearted. "Compassionate" would be a poor, patronizing word for it. This music gives not alms but total identification; without reservation it throws itself away for the sake of others, something we hear too in the greatest moments of Berg's kindred spirit, Robert Schumann. We become conscious of this Bergian tone as early as the beginning of the development section of the Piano Sonata, op. 1, and then again in the wistful tenderness of the second movement of the *Lyric Suite*, or in the nostalgic quotation, as if gazing backward in recollection, of the Carinthian folk song shortly before the end of the Violin Concerto. Such anachronistic yearning far transcends the unreserved willingness to join in and get on with the job that is acclaimed in so much other contemporary music under the misnomer of vitality. Even the inner structure of the Wagnerian yearning for death has undergone a decisive change in Berg. In Wagner the end of the world was the triumphant consummation of the destructive impulse, transposed into the supreme, unconstrained fantasy of power. In Berg this is translated into a kind of abdication, as if the living subject felt something of the injustice that arises simply because his life depends on stealing a place from someone else, and who would rather give up his life than continue to benefit from the theft. One of Berg's favorite words was "warm-hearted" [*jovial*], and what he meant by this was not small-minded good nature and complacency, but precisely that gesture of selflessness and fellowship. What ultimately divides the tone of his music from Wagner and the rest of the new Germans is an element of acquiescence, a legacy perhaps of the south German or Austrian tradition. It has a strong admixture of nostalgic skepticism and irony and is full of the profound knowledge that there is no hope other than that contained in the gesture of bidding farewell to the world and its goods. If we are to talk about expression, and make judgments about it, we also have to take a view of what is expressed, and in Berg's case this is the reverse of private, subjective self-limitation. It is solidarity with mankind, made concrete as the irresistible approval of what mankind excludes from itself and what therefore stands in unconsciously for the image of a possible humanity. In his case, addiction includes the potential for freedom.

In this spirit, and in opposition to widespread and growing tendencies toward regression, he kept a firm hold on a crucial aspect of operatic form. But his artistic instincts also led him far beyond the empathetic techniques of the musical drama, the illustration of feelings and events by sound. His choice of remote subjects—one from the period before the 1848 Revolution, the other from the 1890s—as well as the fact that he salvaged them as ideas belonging to the past rather than simply attaching his music to them, is significant, for it adds a distancing element to works that he himself called operas. This is matched by the principle of construction that is employed consistently in both works and that confers a certain autonomy on the music, even as it follows the events. This is a principle that can scarcely be claimed for Stravinsky's works for theater, for all their use of miming techniques. In Berg the principle of musical drama, as the translation of music into a wealth of infinitely complex tensions, effectively became one of comprehensive development. In contrast to Wagner, he was the first to introduce into opera the truly dramatic feature of Viennese classicism, its variegated dialectic [*durchbrochene Arbeit*].[8] In his works, and perhaps in them alone, we can see the outlines of a kind of autonomous operatic music emerging from beneath the cloak of the musical drama. It is music that follows its own impulses right through to the end instead of exhausting itself in an ascetic rejection of empathy, and it derives its autonomy from its own internal relationship to the drama that it absorbs. Opera of this type fulfills itself musically, satisfying the logic of its own musical laws, for it does not just run alongside the drama, but follows the contours of all its impulses, developments, contrasts, and tensions. The music is absorbed into the drama more than ever before, and as a direct result it is articulated down to the last note and achieves the autonomy denied it in the old-style, tone-painting musical drama.

That is what distinguishes Berg's relationship to Wagner and to the musical heritage in general from that of the other masters of new music. Just as his compositions seek infinite internal correspondences and are hostile to contrast, so too on the historical plane Berg did not bluntly reject the world of his parents, the late nineteenth century. Loyalty stood at the apex of his moral heaven. Alberich's "Be true" in *Twilight of the Gods* [act 2, scene 1] was something he would quote with emphatic approval, perhaps with a presentiment of the mythical, prehistorical origins of loyalty and also with a sense that loyalty is the quality best suited to twilights of gods. Just as he kept faith with the people and the cause to which he had committed himself freely, rather than under some instinctive compulsion, he also kept faith with the world from which he came. Little characterizes him better than the fact that, at the height of his maturity as a composer, he orchestrated and published the Seven Early Songs, which lie completely outside the confines of everything that had come to be associated so specifically with the Bergian style. He did not shy away from providing insensitive ears with the ammunition to denounce what he wrote subsequently. Berg's development did not consist in his repudiation of his musical heritage. Instead he consumed that heritage, much as in the nineteenth century people of private means lived off their capital. But this also implies that he did not cling to that heritage as if it were his private property. By so consuming it, he ended up destroying it. It is the dual character of this process that defines his uniqueness. The lineaments of his music will be most easily read by those searching to discover what has become of that heritage as a result of this process of dissolving and reconstituting it in the course of composition. Only today, when his constructivism, stripped of his recalcitrant musical language, threatens to relapse into decorative commercialism or to regress to an emphasis on content alien to art, does the truth element in Berg's shy smile and his measured treatment of the past emerge fully. The aspects of his music that do not appear to fit completely with the criteria of stylistic purity and logical consistency are the vestiges of a blindly accepted tradition that he has failed to illuminate. But this musical procedure is legitimated by the way it permeates the world of substance and expression that it confronts. An inexhaustible qualitative wealth characterizes Berg's whole method of composition and flows into it from a past that he does not reject as unmodern. He was undoubtedly very well aware of this tension. With his indescribably proud modesty he once responded to a compliment by saying that his achievement was to have preserved his own personal tone within the twelve-tone technique and its tendency to level out all distinctions. In the same way, when confronted with the critical question of why he almost always allowed elements of tonality to survive in his works, he answered that that was the way he did things and that he was disinclined to change them. We should add that his habit of harking back to the past did not show any signs of diminishing with time; indeed, it is particularly marked in the Alwa sections of *Lulu* and throughout the Violin Concerto. But nothing traditional emerges from his music unaltered. His energy as a composer tests itself on such material indefatigably, and regenerates itself in the process. Despite the junglelike density of its texture, and complementary to it, Berg's music is articulated down to the last note. No other contemporary music, not even that of

Schoenberg, who followed his impulses more spontaneously, is so planned and masterfully worked out as Berg's, no doubt because of his spatial, architectonic gift, in which his sense of articulated order outweighed the flow of feeling. That means that there is not a single movement, no section, no theme, no period, no motive, nor even a single note that fails to fulfill its wholly unambiguous and unmistakable formal meaning even in the most complex of contexts. In this respect he was not so very different from Webern, although the latter's reductive method relieved him of many of the burdens of creating large-scale structures. The more musical production today denies that dimension of composition, that is, the quasi-linguistic, the more Berg's works assume exemplary status for them, first and foremost the *Lyric Suite* for string quartet. However, his gift for the meaningful elaboration of the language of music, for authentic composition—something that has not received proper recognition even today—is nothing other than his highly wrought subjective sensibility and his refined sense of subtle nuance. Berg was able to translate those subjective reactions into the criteria of composition itself, thus displaying a highly civilized, we might even call it French, mastery; his much-criticized subjectivism gave the work its objective validity, the sublime solidity of form, with the consequence that, like Mörike's lamp, it seems "blessed in itself."[9] From the outset, Berg's sensibility was determined by his relationship to objects. The loving and considerate way he treated them arose from a desire to look after created things. It was as if he wished to make good some of the damage done to them by people who altered them for their own purposes. As a forty-year-old he still used his first shaving set and was proud of having looked after it so well that it still looked new. The composer's hand worked with the same care. In his works, the world of prehistoric dreams, the monstrous, and what Goethe termed the dull [*das Dumpfe*] encounter what is brightest and full of sensitive artifice, the beauty of the wealth of forms. This is the riddle of Berg's music. We could scarcely describe it more simply or accurately than by saying that it resembled him.

If we compare Berg with those who were closest to him, with Schoenberg and Webern, and with the development of the radically new music of the last twenty years, it is easy to comprehend his achievement as having formed a link with the past, as securing the connection between the innovations of the moderns and tradition. And in fact the continuity lies closer to the surface in his case than in that of his friends, even though

Schoenberg in particular punctiliously fulfilled the obligations that he had inherited from Bach and Viennese classicism down to Brahms and Wagner. In contrast to Schoenberg's rigor, Berg, we might say, retained a certain urbanity, even in his inclusion of heterogeneous stylistic features, and the internal breadth of his composition gained from this. If in general the influence of Mahler on his school was much greater than appeared on the surface, in Berg's case we can see how often he openly echoes Mahler's intonation, particularly in sections of *Wozzeck* and the Violin Concerto. His ambivalent relationship to the folk song, in which his identification with the victims assumes musical shape, would be unthinkable without the Mahler whose marches[10] resonate with sorrow for the deserter. And Berg's peculiar insatiability ensures that he himself finds it hard to endure the constructive constraints he imposes on himself: hence his constant efforts to extend the limits of sound with doublings, clusters, and parallel progressions, which create an affinity with Debussy that climaxes, above all in *Lulu*, in a veritable impressionist phantasmagoria. His ideal orchestra would have glowed and flashed iridescently, and that was not possible until impressionism had become a historical reality; then the idea of impressionism could be conjured up and made completely available, as if in a memory. We may recollect how the writings of Marcel Proust took possession of the entire technical repertoire of French painting at the moment when these techniques were recalled to mind like something long forgotten. But Berg's oeuvre always has something extraordinary about it, and we would subtly miss the essential point about it if, because of such links to the past, we were to listen to him as if he were the rear guard of modernism. That would be to measure him against a concept of progress that has since become far more dubious than the usual idea that plays the old truths, the eternal values, off against progress. Berg made no such pact with the old values, nor did he stock up on such eternally lasting goods in advance. His music is too strongly dedicated to death for that. However, at every one of its stages music suffers a loss at the hands of progress: the increasing control of its material, the expression of the increasing manipulation of nature, always entails a certain violence. Berg shrank from this, yet simultaneously entrusted himself to progress without reservation. This paradox is promoted by a feature of his musical makeup that prevents him from allowing anything to slip from his grasp and by his determination to retain a grip on anything that might advance his work. It is perhaps an anxiety, related to his affinity for death. But this desire to keep a hold on things is not unlike the attempt to square the circle; it is a piece of quixotry. It means that every one of his works is really an impossibility, attainable only through trickery, a tour de force. He who desires to salvage in progress the very thing that progress destroys must pay an exorbitant price. Berg heroically paid this price. False friends, who knew him well but understood him little, soon realized that an effect of the Schoenberg school had been to add an alien, heterogeneous ingredient to Berg's musical reactions, which were strongly defined early on, and that the fault lines of his work provided ample evidence of this. But these fault lines are the signature of his truth. He risked these fractures—stylistic breaks on which, in pieces like the concert aria "Der Wein" or the Violin Concerto, the clumsiest fingers could be placed—as an act of opposition to a consistency that threatened to devour itself and to a trust in what once had been. In a sense he returned to the past as a sacrifice to the future. Nowadays no artistic totality can be created from itself, and Berg knew that the aesthetic individual is no longer capable of a harmonious act of objectification merely through reliance on his own resources, while every external objectivity stands opposed to him and lacks any authentic power over him. But knowing this, he simply absorbed that antagonistic state of affairs into his work. Indeed, it became its supreme formal principle, as if Berg's boundless need for security preferred to accept the dissolution of his own work, to include the work's internal contradictions in his composition, rather than to throw himself on the mercy of history, which would confront the deluded claims of the work with its internal ruptures. Berg achieved an extreme consistency in composition but sacrificed consistency of style in the process, trusting the monadological eloquence of the work, which absorbs the irreconcilable into itself and forces it to express itself, more than the purity of an idiom in which ineradicable contradictions lie merely concealed. In consequence, alien, external material, even sometimes the traces of the conventional features of commodity music, have been built into this refined and noble music as a permanent source of irritation, even though its finely veined texture permeates them wholly. Not until the last act of *Lulu*, in the procurer scene and the street ballad that can be heard in the attic, did this aspect reveal its true character, that of surrealism. That sounds like dream—not like romantic dreams, but like those dreamed nowadays that depict the return of recent events in a darkened interior while high above

a golden ribbon floats past. Such a tone was always part of Berg's spiritualized music. Stylistic purists imagine themselves superior to such things and
talk about kitsch when it shocks them. They hope to protect themselves
against the shock of the parental world and against a seductiveness that
they feel as strongly as Berg, but they lack the strength to expose themselves to it while retaining their self-control. Thanks to this strength, Berg
has something of what Wedekind, the author of *Lulu,* also possessed. Karl
Kraus praised his *Pandora's Box*[11] by saying that in it trashy poetry became
the poetry of trash, which could be condemned only by certified idiocy.
The greatest works of art do not exclude the lower depths, but kindle the
flame of utopia on the smoking ruins of the past.

(1956; GS 16: 85–96)
Translated by Rodney Livingstone

19

Art and the Arts

In recent times the boundaries between the different arts have become fluid, or, more accurately, their demarcation lines have been eroded. Musical techniques have evidently been stimulated by painting, both by informal techniques and by the constructivism of artists like Mondrian. Much music inclines toward the graphic arts in its notation. Musical notation is becoming similar to autonomous graphic imagery and is even developing a certain autonomy from the composition, most visibly, perhaps, in the works of the Italian artist Sylvano Bussotti, who was a graphic artist before he turned to music.[1] Specific musical techniques, such as serialism, have influenced modern prose, like that of Hans G. Helms,[2] for example, by way of compensating for the retreat from narrative contents. For its part, painting no longer wishes to confine itself to mere surfaces. Having bid farewell to the illusion of spatial perspective, it now presses forward into space on its own account; here we may mention Nesch,[3] or the rampant creations of Bernard Schultze.[4] In Alexander Calder's mobiles, sculpture, which has abandoned the imitation of movement of its impressionist phase, has ceased to remain motionless in all its parts and aspires to make itself temporal, like the aeolian harp, with its principle of random movement.[5]

Musical passages have become interchangeable or have abandoned a set order and hence lost something of their fixed temporal sequencing: they have abandoned any similarity to causal relations. Moreover, sculptors have ceased to respect the boundaries between sculpture and architecture

that had seemed self-evident, since they were based on the distinction between functional and nonfunctional art. Fritz Wotruba recently drew my
attention to the fact that many of his own sculptures start off with the
rudiments of the human figure and then develop in a process of increasing
dematerialization into quasi-architectonic forms—he referred specifically
to Scharoun.[6] As someone accustomed to relating aesthetic experiences to
the realm of art with which I am most familiar, namely, music, I note such
phenomena simply as arbitrary observations; it is not my business to try to
classify them. But they are so numerous and so persistent that one would
have to be blind not to suppose that they are the symptoms of a powerful
trend. I should like to try to understand this development and, in particular, to interpret this process of erosion.

It has the greatest power where it is intrinsic, that is to say, where it
arises from the genre itself. It is not necessary to deny that many works cast
sheep's eyes to one side or the other. When musical compositions borrow
their titles from Paul Klee, we are likely to suspect them of being decorative in nature, the very opposite of the modernity that they imagine they
are laying claim to with such borrowings. Such tendencies are of course
not as disreputable as the routine accusation of snobbery would like us to
believe. The people who complain about fellow travelers are most often
those who never go anywhere themselves. In reality, they are hostile to
artists who are out in front. Immunity to the zeitgeist is no virtue in itself.
It is rarely proof of resistance; it is mainly a sign of provincialism. Even in
the weak form of imitation the impulse to be modern is also an instance of
productive labor.

But the eroding tendency is evidence of something more than flattery or the suspect synthesis whose traces frighten the beholder when they
appear in the name of the *Gesamtkunstwerk*; happenings aspire to be
Gesamtkunstwerke, but only as total anti-art. Thus even though we are
strongly reminded of painting by the dabbing of notes down side by side
in the creation of musical sonorities, these dabbings should be traced back
to the principle of *Klangfarbenmelodie*, with its inclusion of timbres as a
constitutive element, rather than to the attempt to imitate painterly effects. Almost sixty years ago Webern wrote pieces consisting of pointillist-
like groups of notes as a critique of the otiose note-spinning that can so
easily give the illusory impression that something is actually taking place.
And the graphic notations in the invention of which playfulness has a

certain, by no means illegitimate role are a function of the need to record musical events in a more flexible manner than is possible with the traditional signs based on tonality; conversely, they sometimes want to create space for improvisation.

Everywhere here purely musical desiderata are being obeyed. It can scarcely be too hard to discover similar intrinsic motives in the majority of these phenomena of erosion. If I am not deceived, artists who give a further spatial dimension to painting are looking for an equivalent to the organizing principle that disappeared along with perspectival painting. By analogy, musical innovations that scorned what a selective tradition had defined as music sprang up in response to the loss of the dimension of harmony and the forms associated with it. Whatever tears down the boundary markers is motivated by historical forces that sprang into life inside the existing boundaries and then ended up overwhelming them.

This process plays its no doubt considerable role in the antagonism between progressive, contemporary art and the so-called wider public. Where boundaries are violated, fear may easily provoke a defensive reaction to miscegenation. This complex assumed pathological dimensions in the National Socialist cult of pure race and the denigration of hybridity. Whatever fails to abide by the discipline of zones that have once been established is held to be licentious and decadent. This holds even though these zones are not natural but historical in origin, some of them arising as recently as the definitive emancipation of sculpture from architecture, forms of art that had merged again in the age of baroque. The normal mode of resistance to developments that are supposed to be incompatible with a particular genre is familiar to musicians in the form of the question "Is that still music?" For a long time, this was the refrain of the chorus, while music still progressed in accordance with unquestioned, albeit modified, intrinsic laws. Today, however, the avant-garde, when confronted by the philistine question "Is that still . . . ?," takes it quite literally. It sometimes responds with a kind of music that really no longer aspires to be music any more. A string quartet by the Italian composer Franco Donatoni, for example, consists entirely of a montage of noises produced by the four stringed instruments. György Ligeti's very important, highly wrought *Atmosphères* does not recognize any single notes that are distinguishable in the traditional sense. Edgar Varèse's *Ionization*, which was written decades ago, was a prototype of such aspirations, a prototype because despite an almost total renunciation of specific pitch levels, the rhythmic progressions ensure that a relatively traditional musical impression results. The artistic genres appear to revel in a kind of promiscuity that violates some of the taboos of civilization.

At the same time that the blurring of the clean divisions between different genres of art produces anxieties about civilization, this trend also adapts itself, unbeknownst to those who feel the anxieties, to the rationality and civilization that art has always been involved in: in 1938, a professor at Graz University by the name of Othmar Sterzinger published a book entitled *The Principal Features of the Psychology of Art*, dedicating it to "the friends of the arts." The latter plural, touchingly philistine, sheds light on the subject: a profusion of goods on display for the contemplative observer, from the kitchen to the lounge, goods that are then inspected and sampled in the course of the book. In the light of the funereal phrase stating that a wealthy man, now departed, was a friend of the arts and had supported them generously, the impatience of art itself becomes entirely comprehensible when confronted by this profusion. Such impatience regularly attends the no less revolting idea of the enjoyment of art that celebrates its pathetic orgies among people like Sterzinger, namely, the orgies of soulless repetition. Art would prefer to have no more to do with its sensitive friends than is unavoidable for material reasons. "My music is not lovely," grumbled Schoenberg in Hollywood when a film mogul unfamiliar with his work tried to pay him a compliment. Art renounces its culinary side; it became incompatible with its spiritual aspect when it lost its innocence, that of its unity with the composed material, a unity that had become the function of mellifluous sound in the gradual process in which such sound came to dominate the musical material. But now that the culinary element, sensuous charm, has split itself off and become an end in itself and the object of rational planning, art rebels against every sort of dependency upon preexisting materials that are reflected in the classification of art according to different art forms and that resist shaping by the autonomous artist. For the scattered materials correspond to the diffuse stimuli of the senses.

The great philosophers, Hegel and Schopenhauer among them, have labored, each in his own way, at the question of heterogeneous multiplicity and have attempted to provide a theoretical synthesis. Schopenhauer did so in a hierarchical system, crowned by music. Hegel's attempt took the form of a historical, dialectical system that was supposed to culminate in poetry. Neither attempt was adequate. It was obvious that the ranking of works of art did not coincide with the ranking of the different arts. They depended neither on the position of one art in the hierarchy of the arts nor—as indeed the classicist Hegel was careful not to assert—on their historical position in the sense that the later work was the superior one. Such a general assumption would have been as false as its opposite. A philosophical synthesis in the idea of art that would strive to go beyond the simple coexistence of the various arts condemns itself by judgments of the kind made by Hegel about music or by Schopenhauer in his attempt to preserve a niche for historical painting. In return, the actual historical development of art does move toward such a synthesis. Kandinsky's book *On the Spiritual in Art*, whose title amounted for good or ill to a summing up of the latent program of expressionism, was the first to register this process. It is not for nothing that in it technical reciprocity replaces a symbiosis of the arts or their agglomeration in the cause of some intensified effect or other.

The triumph of spiritualization in art, which Hegel anticipated in his discussion of what he called the romantic work of art, was, however, a Pyrrhic victory, like all triumphs. Kandinsky's ambitious manifesto does not shrink from citing bogus evidence, right down to Rudolf Steiner and the fraudulent Madame Blavatsky. In defense of his idea of the spiritual in art, Kandinsky welcomes everything that appealed to spirit in its battle against positivism, even spirits. This cannot be blamed simply on an artist's lack of a firm grounding in theory. There are more than a few artists who have worked at their trade and have felt and still feel the need of theoretical justification. The fact that the objects of their art and their artistic methods no longer seem self-evident leads them to reflect in ways that sometimes go beyond their control. Indiscriminate, half-educated, they take their ideas where they find them.

But my point does not concern individual subjective failings. Even though Kandinsky's book remains faithful to the experience of the moment, the substance of this experience has its dubious side, as well as its truth. This forces him to underpin it with dubious arguments. Since spirit can no longer be satisfied in art with sensuous appearance, it becomes autonomous. Today, just as fifty years ago, the compulsion implied here is one that everyone can reconstruct for himself when he reacts to the sight of sensuous, pleasing works of art, however authentic, by saying "You just can't do that any more."

Such a legitimate and unavoidable process of making spirit autonomous, however, almost inevitably sets spirit at loggerheads, abstractly, as Hegel would have said, with the materials and methods of the works. Spirit is then inserted into the works, as with allegories in times past. Paradoxically, what then decides the sensuous meaning of something spiritual—for example, the symbolic value of colors—turns out to be a matter of convention, the very category against which the entire modern movement in art rebelled. This can be confirmed by the connections between radical art in its early phase and arts and crafts. Supposedly significant colors, sonorities, and so on play their murky part in this. Works of art that rightly devalue sensuous charm turn out to need a sensuous foundation, if they are to be "realized" at all, to use Cézanne's word. The more rigorously and ruthlessly they insist on their spiritualization, the further they distance themselves from what is supposed to be made spiritual. Their spirit seems to hover above it; between spirit and its embodiments whole chasms open up.

The primacy of context that is created in the material by the principle of construction is converted by this domination through the spirit into the loss of spirit, namely of intrinsic meaning. From that point on, all art suffers from this contradiction, and the most serious art suffers the most painfully. Spiritualization, the rational manipulation of artistic methods, seems to drive out spirit as the substantive content of art. What set out to spiritualize the material of art ends up in the naked material as if in a mere existent, just as was explicitly called for by a number of schools—in music, by John Cage, for example. Spirit, which Kandinsky had defended as pristine, as literally true, becomes noncommittal, and is therefore glorified for its own sake: "You must believe in the spirit!" And very much in the same vein, Schoenberg in his expressionist phase found himself unable to dispense with theosophy since theosophy could, as it were, conjure spirit into existence.

In exchange, the individual arts aspire to their concrete generalizations, to an idea of art as such. We can explain this once again with reference to music. With his integrated approach, which attempts to include within itself all possible musical dimensions, Schoenberg gave a powerful impetus to the process of standardizing music. At the level of theory, he expressed this in a doctrine of musical coherence. All the particular aspects of a musical composition were to be subordinated to this; for him the theory of composition was this theory. Much light can be shed on the development of music in the last twenty years in terms of the primacy of the notion of coherence [*Zusammenhang*]. By following Schoenberg's program, consciously or not, this development undermined what had been considered to be music up to that time, even in Schoenberg. He standardized virtually all the musical means of making interconnections that were to be found in the objective, not-yet-explicit history of music, and he did so in the service of the fully organized work. Confronted with the norm of artistic purposiveness, these means were quickly exposed as arbitrary and limited—as special cases of musical coherence, just as tonality had revealed itself to be a special case of the melodic and harmonic forms to which it could have recourse from time to time.

What was of immense importance, following Schoenberg, was for composers to take the step of separating his concept of musical coherence from its traditional assumptions and thereby from everything that had accreted historically in the concept of music. Thus music had even become allergic to such cohesive techniques as free atonality and twelve-note technique, in which the trained ear could still hear the traces of the tonality that such techniques repudiated. It could therefore freely face up to the concept of coherence, independently of the limited shapes that the concept had assumed and that had become an ingrained part of our hearing. The entire output of Stockhausen can be regarded as an attempt to test musical coherence in a multidimensional continuum. Such sovereign mastery, which makes it possible to establish coherence even in an incalculable variety of dimensions, creates from the inside the link between music and the visual arts, architecture, sculpture, and painting. The more the coherence-creating methods of the individual arts spread their tentacles over the traditional stock of forms and become formalized, as it were, the more the different arts are subjected to a principle of uniformity.

Of course, the requirement that the arts should be standardized as art, a requirement whose prototype was the process of integration within the different forms of art, is older than modernity. Robert Schumann coined the epigram that the aesthetics of one art is also the aesthetics of the others. The intention underlying this statement was romantic, and its point was that music should try to animate its different structural elements, which were increasingly seen as clichéd, and make them poetic, much as Beethoven was believed to have done by the generation that followed him and called him a "tone-poet" [*Tondichter*].

In contrast to the modern process of erosion, that romantic standardization placed the accent on subjectivity. Works of art became the impression of a soul—one that was not necessarily identical with that of the composer. It was the language of the self freely expressing itself. This idea brought the arts closer to one another. It could no doubt be shown that the same soul animates all the different arts. But their boundaries were scarcely weakened by this. They remained what they were, and this disparateness is not the least important critical reason for the most recent development.

The problematic aspect of the aesthetic as something animated and of higher rank than its media can be best seen in the typical concept of "mood" [*Stimmung*]. From a certain point on, specifically, the point at which neoromanticism and impressionism were rejected, modernism turned against "mood." But what was so irritating about its amorphous softness was not narcissism—which the reactionary friends of more bracing artistic fare object to in the more differentiated art that they are unable to appreciate—but rather something connected with its objective nature: namely, the absence of resistance at its core. Where art looks for mood in a shapeless, high-handed way, it lacks the element of alterity. Art needs something heterogeneous in order to become art. In the absence of that, the process that every work of art is lacks a target and so just freewheels. The clash between the work of art and the world of objects becomes productive, and the work authentic, only where this clash is allowed to happen and to objectify itself by its friction with the thing it devours. No work of art, not even the most subjective, can be completely identical with the subject that constitutes it and its substantial content. Every work possesses materials that are distinct from the subject, procedures that are derived from the materials of art, as well as from human subjectivity. Its truth content is not exhausted by subjectivity but owes its existence to the process of objectification. That process does indeed require the subject as an executor, but points beyond it to that objective Other. This introduces an element of irreducible, qualitative plurality. It is incompatible with every principle of unity, even that of the genres of art, by virtue of what they express.

If works of art ignore this, they swiftly degenerate into that aesthetic hodgepodge that can be seen in the creations of people who are said to have artistic talent but no leaning toward any particular form of art. It is above all major artists whose gifts are not unmistakably tied to a specific material—I have in mind here Richard Wagner, Alban Berg, and perhaps even Paul Klee—who have every reason to expend their energy submerging a generalized aesthetics in specific artistic material. Nevertheless, that aesthetics survives as an ether, as a reaction that refuses to bow to the all-too-realistic abrasiveness of material discipline. If art gravitates toward dilettantism as long as it remains satisfied with a generalized aesthetics, an art from which the last trace of that ether—the simple fact that someone is an artist—has been expunged simply dries up into philistine handicraft. It is not for nothing that the so-called movement of folk music and youth music was infuriated by that epigram of Schumann's. If the uniform aesthetics is too eager to bypass everything alien to the work of art—in Schumann's music this ominous process is converted into an aesthetic quality, namely an expression of disaster—then the contrary call to roll up your sleeves and do justice to the material of art is mere self-righteousness. It pretends that the heterogeneous aspects of the work of art, and especially those of its practices that have not been filtered through human subjectivity, possess a truth content that they do not have by right.

The conflict between art and the arts cannot be resolved by cutting any Gordian knots. Even in the late romantic period the arts resisted any conclusive standardization of the sort preached in the name of stylistic unity—for *Jugendstil* was nothing more than that. We know that the relationship of great neoromantic poets like Stefan George and Hugo von Hofmannsthal to the fine arts was anything but happy. They thought that they had an affinity with symbolist painters like Burne-Jones, Puvis de Chavannes, and Arnold Böcklin, and Stefan George did not scorn to refer to the impressionists in that contemptuous Wilhelminian phrase about cheeky paint daubers. They failed to recognize that there was more poetic value in impressionist techniques than in the subsequently notorious initiation at the mystical springs.

The fault for this did not lie with their literary eccentricity or the provincial ignorance of poets far removed from what was happening in Paris. More than a few poems by Stefan George contain imagery undeniably close to that of the disastrous painting of the symbolists. But because the best of them achieve their specific vividness in language rather than optically, they turn into something quite different. If you were to translate the autumnal landscapes of his cycle "After the Harvest" into paintings, they would be kitsch. But in their linguistic garb, where the color words have very different values from the physical colors on canvas, some of them succeed in defying obsolescence. Such values are a feature of poetry that poetry shares with music. The respect in which the arts differ essentially, even though their contents and their associations may be very similar, can be seen most clearly in the case of music. The various types of expression in Brahms—old-German ballad, knight in shining armor or waywardly amorous—can be disputed only by people whose musicality lacks that ingredient of extramusical meaning without which music cannot exist. But the fact that these expressive elements are neither encapsulated in an image nor bluntly uttered, but instead just heard in a momentary flash only to disappear a moment later, ensures that they bear no resemblance to the historical myth-making of a writer like Joseph Victor von Scheffel. No criticism could pin the works down to such fleeting emanations of expression; they never protrude awkwardly or crudely from the texture of the music. On the contrary, they dissolve in the pure progress of the work, of a marvelously perfected musical language. This language is ignited by contact with these heterogeneous elements, but not for a single moment is it reduced to them or to their level. If masterpieces need luck in order to come into being at all, then Brahms's good fortune was that his ballads were made into music and not poems. The different arts may aim at the same subject, but they become different because of the *manner* in which they mean it. Their substantial content lies in the relation between the *what* and the *how*. They become art by virtue of this substantial content. But this needs the *how*, their particular language; if it went in search of something larger, beyond the particular form of art itself, it would be destroyed.

Attempts to give a definite answer to the priority of art or the arts come mainly from cultural conservatives. For it is in their interest to reduce art to unchanging factors that are openly or covertly based on the past and that can be used to defame the present and the future. Conservative, and certainly reactionary, thinking always wants to separate the sheep from the goats, and recoils from the idea of objective contradictions in phenomena themselves. They denounce dialectics as sophistry and witchcraft and refuse to countenance the possibility that it might be well founded.

The most resolute German advocate of qualitative distinctions between the arts, distinctions that scarcely allow for the concept of art at all, is Rudolf Borchardt. Borchardt, who inclined toward an extreme archaism, nevertheless paid tribute to Hegel in his essay on Benedetto Croce, although he also displayed his fundamental ignorance of Hegel's thought.

He subscribed to the erroneous belief that it was only in Croce that Hegel had really gone beyond academic squabbles to make his own original contribution. But he failed to observe that Croce had removed the element of true dialectics from Hegel's philosophy, believing that it was dead, and had replaced it with the notion of development that was current around 1900, which flattened everything out to a peaceful juxtaposition of different phenomena. Borchardt's own intention, as expounded in his essay "On Poets and the Poetic," is not afflicted with any sign of dialectic. Appealing to the authority of Johann Gottfried Herder, he attempts to remove the poetic from the realm of art altogether, describing it as a primal language, a "visionary faculty," that transcends the particular arts. Categories like untouchability, divine protection, exceptional status, and sanctification are peculiar to poetry and to poetry alone. In a historical overview, Borchardt sketches his outline of the constantly intensifying conflict between the poetic and the profane world. His watchwords are irrational:

Forget your aesthetics, forget your intelligence; such things have no access to the poetic. They may have access to the artistic. They may have access to literature. But where the poetic appears among you today, it is an integrated whole, as in the days of Solon and Amos, in which you can find the law, religion, music, and in which magic spells can be found as can a living life, a cornucopia, an encyclopedia of the world that is fundamentally different from the encyclopedia of the world provided by science.[a]

I cannot resist interjecting the question of how such an encyclopedic totality is to be reconciled with the Borchardtian arcanum. It is reborn, he continues,

with every poetic mind, and every such mind conceives the wish to acquire a new shape and to transmit it to you, as in times past; in the past tense and the future, but without the present. It is future prediction, as of yore, and like the eternal day of creation it contains the future within itself, not, as the literati proclaim, in the shape of political revolution but as a return to God for the children of God, as in olden times when the poet carried a staff and wore a wreath.[b]

Borchardt has his eye on nothing less than the nonmetaphorical apotheosis of poetry, and "allowing the things that may still dwell among

---

[a] Rudolf Borchardt, *Prosa*, vol. 1, ed. Marie Luise Borchardt (Stuttgart: KGH, 1957), p. 69.
[b] Ibid., pp. 69–70.

you to have their own way, accepting them with shame and reverence however strange they may appear. For they are the Divine in its own forms. Await the revelation and make no attempt to assist it in any way."[c] And according to Borchardt, that is precisely what should happen in the other arts, especially the fine arts. With a rather forced naïveté, he exhorts his reader to attempt

to put himself back once again into the situation of primeval man, who finds himself confronted, on the one hand, by the poet as I have tried to depict him, and, on the other, by the artist, the sculptor, or the painter. You can watch him at his trade. You can stand next to him and watch him create something. See how he pours the molten metal and files it down when it has cooled; see how he draws; and you can see for yourself what his work is supposed to represent. He kneads the clay, and you can see what he is copying, or molding into a model. Associations come to mind; first of all the ability to identify an object, and after that, the aesthetic perception, the categories of rightness, resemblance, beauty. But the point I am concerned with is this: in the eyes of the naive and spontaneous person, the painter and the sculptor are people who have mastered a craft . . . they are people whose work, when you stand next to it and look at it, may be the object of astonished admiration, of joyous applause. But it is no riddle. You can see how it has been made. In the case of the poet, however, you cannot see it. No one has seen it. For the Greeks and for everyone in those primeval times, the sensuous arts lack what I have referred to here: the mystery, the problem. And even if such artists were able to display skills of a very high, or even the very highest, order, what they lacked was intoxication, the consciousness of something quite transcendent. The muse of the fine arts is called not "Muse" but "Tekhnē." What is missing is the demonic, the incalculable.[d]

The pathos here is a little stale; it is the recoil from the disenchanted and reified world. Borchardt's rhetoric cannot justify his insistence on the limits of the phenomenal. The idea that the historical forms of art that have arisen from handicrafts lack the supreme force, the ability, to express the highest realities can be asserted only by someone who wishes to compel handicraft to remain handicraft once and for all, and who is blind to the invisible contained in the visible. The visible process of making does not coincide with aesthetic value, and, on the other side, even the poet may let you peek over his shoulder when he writes. The mystery that Borchardt reserves for poetry is the mystery of all art that says, and yet doesn't

[c] Ibid., p. 69.
[d] Ibid., pp. 46–47.

say, what it says. In all probability, even the origin of the fine arts, the mimetic faculty, contained the opposing element of a supportive rationality, which speaks from archaic sculpture. And there can be no doubt that the fine arts acquired that rational component later on, with the growth of *tekhnē*. Borchardt's antithesis of sculpture as *tekhnē* and poetry is invalid because even in the fine arts language plays a mediating role, something from which Borchardt would like to distance them. Not to mention that music simply does not fit into his dichotomizing approach.

Moreover, what he thinks of as artifactlike, technical features belong with just as much right to poetry and have a crucial part in its success. It is inconceivable that a virtuoso of language like Borchardt, whose plea for poetry must have been made *pro domo*, should have overlooked this and should have attributed everything to inspiration, much like an operetta composer boldly enthusing about Mozart. Borchardt translated Pindar, Dante, and Swinburne into German, the latter in masterly fashion. Would he really want to deny the seriousness of Pindar's artistic skill, which he rather coquettishly labels philistine? Is Dante's work, with its wealth of real and allegorical meanings, nothing more than intoxicating? Is he unable to hear the technical components of Swinburne's musiclike verse, which are separated from their material and which master it by virtue of that separation? The colossus of poetry conjured up by Borchardt's suggestive rhetoric stands on the proverbial feet of clay. It's a joke. The wealth of associations and antitheses deceives us, so that the object Borchardt calls the most serious of all, which he wishes to tell us about, turns out, as soon as we take it seriously, to make a mockery of the attempt to draw definite distinctions between the different arts and, as it were, to fix them ontologically.

The position of Martin Heidegger is at the opposite pole from that of Borchardt, but it is no less ontological, albeit in a more considered fashion. In fact, Heidegger's commentaries on Hölderlin's poems contain passages that take their cue from Hölderlin's own verse. In them he ascribes to the poet, whom he sees as a founder, a prerogative similar to Borchardt's. In this respect both were probably inspired by the George school. But in accordance with the concept of Being that dominates his thought, Heidegger desires unity, to an incomparably greater degree than does Borchardt the artist. His theory that Being has always existed in the world, that it transcends into existing things, does not allow him to despise technology any more than does his old preference for handicraft, the ultimate model for readiness-to-hand [*Zuhandenheit*] in *Being and Time.*

Whereas Borchardt confuses art and religion and suppresses the constitutive element of secularization in works of art, Heidegger's text on the origin of the work of art in *Holzwege* has the merit of providing a sober account of the thinglike nature of objects, a feature that, as Heidegger remarks with justifiable irony, the much acclaimed aesthetic experience cannot ignore. The quality of being a thing and the quality of unity—the unity of rationality, which, however, is swallowed up by Heidegger's concept of Being—these qualities go together. But beyond that, Heidegger takes a further step that Borchardt would find unacceptable. He asserts that all art is essentially poetry and that therefore architecture, painting, and music have to be reducible to poetry.[e] He is not unaware of the arbitrary nature of this statement in its application to the different arts, which are "ontic" beings in his parlance. He escapes from the difficulty by ontologizing the artistic as the "illuminating design of the truth." This is what poetry [*Dichten*] is in the broader sense, while poetry in the sense of writing verse is merely one mode of this.

In contrast to Borchardt, an artist of words, Heidegger specifically emphasized the linguistic nature of all art. However, because of that ontologization, the distinctions between the arts, their relation to specific materials, is elided as a matter of secondary importance. What remains following this subtraction is something quite vague, despite Heidegger's protestations. This vagueness infects Heidegger's metaphysics of art, turning it into a tautology. The origin of the work of art, he maintains emphatically, is art. And, as always in Heidegger, origin is a matter not of genesis in time but of the essence of works of art. His doctrine of such origins adds nothing to what has been originated, nor can it do so, because in that event the doctrine would stain the originated with the stigma of the very existence that the sublime concept of origin wishes to leave behind it. Heidegger rescues the unifying element of art, that which makes it art, but at the price of a situation in which theory reverently falls silent when confronted by the question of what it is. If art is rendered invisible by Borchardt's sudden flight into the claim that theology is its true sphere, in the

---

[e] See Martin Heidegger, "The Origin of the Work of Art," trans. Albert Hofstadter, in Heidegger, *Poetry, Language, Thought* (New York: Harper & Row, 1971), p. 74.

case of Heidegger, art is dissipated in a realm of pure essences without content. As if crushed by the pressure of the attempt by the varieties of art to assert themselves, the unifying aesthetic factor shrinks to what Heidegger once said of Being, namely, that it is ultimately nothing more than itself. Art can be distilled neither into the pure multiplicity of the different arts nor into a pure unity.

In any event, we must dismiss the naive, logical view that "art" is no more than the generic term for the arts, a genus that contains different species within itself. Such a pattern is negated by the heterogeneous nature of the subforms it embraces. The generic term "art" ignores not merely what is accidental but rather what is essential to the arts. It is enough to remind ourselves that historically, at least, one essential difference among the arts has distinguished between, on the one hand, those that are or were based on images and continue to feed on that tradition, that is to say, the imitative or representational arts, and, on the other hand, those, like music, that dispensed with images at least initially, and had them grafted on only gradually, intermittently, and always precariously. There is a further qualitative distinction between literature, which depends upon concepts and cannot dispense with them entirely, even in its most radical form, and the nonconceptual forms of art. Admittedly, music did possess certain conceptlike qualities, as long as it employed the prescribed medium of tonality, that is to say, as long as it employed harmonic and melodic tokens, the few tonal chord-types and their derivatives. However, they were never the defining units of the material they subsumed. Nor did they ever "refer" to anything as a concept refers to the phenomena to which it belongs; they resembled concepts only in that they could only be used as identical forms with the identical function. Differences like these have their own profound implications, but at all events they demonstrate that the so-called arts do not form a continuum that would allow us to provide the entire complex of phenomena with a single unifying label.

Without their knowing it, the arts may erode one another's boundaries in order to abolish the differences between phenomena that go by the same name. The comparison with a musical phenomenon and its development can perhaps elucidate this. An orchestra is no complete totality in itself, no continuum of all possible timbres. This is because there are noticeable gaps between them. Originally, electronics hoped to be able to make good the defective homogeneity of the orchestra, although it was soon realized that it differed from all the traditional sources of sound and thus abandoned the model of the integrated orchestra.

Without doing violence to either of them, we may compare the relation of art to the arts with that of the orchestra to its instruments. Art is no more the concept embracing the arts than the orchestra contains the spectrum of all possible timbres. Notwithstanding this, the concept of art has its truth—and the orchestra likewise contains the idea of a totality of timbres as the goal of its development. In contrast to the arts, art is in the process of formation, it is potentially contained in each art form, just as each must strive to liberate itself from the chance nature of its quasi-natural aspects. *However, such an idea of art in the arts is not positive, it is not anything simply present in them, but must be thought of exclusively as negation.* We have only negatively unified the arts in terms of content, over and above the empty classificatory concept: all recoil from empirical reality, all tend toward the formation of a sphere qualitatively opposed to that reality: historically, they secularize the magic and sacred realms. All require elements taken from the empirical reality from which they distance themselves, yet their products are part of that reality.

It is this that conditions the dual stance of art toward its forms. In tune with their inextinguishable involvement in empirical reality, art exists only in the arts, whose discontinuous relation to one another is laid down by reality beyond the world of art. As the antithesis to empirical reality, by contrast, art is one. Its dialectical nature consists in the fact that it can carry out its movement toward unity simply and solely by passing through multiplicity. Otherwise, its movement would be abstract and futile. Art's relation to the empirical stratum of reality is vital to it. If art bypasses empirical reality, then what it thinks of as its spirit remains external to it, like some outer garment or other. Only if it is immersed in empirical reality can spirit become substance. The constellation of art and the arts dwells within art itself. Substance finds itself stretched out between two poles: the one unifies and is rational, the other is diffuse and mimetic. Neither pole can be eliminated; art cannot be reduced to one of the two, or even to its dualism.

Of course, it would be too anodyne if we were to construct a view of the transition of the arts into art that failed to contain an element of substance, content that was itself nonaesthetic. The history of modern art is largely that of the ineluctable loss of metaphysical meaning. It is undeniable that the arts are unwilling to remain within the confines laid down for them, but by the same token, the impulse of the artists who unresistingly go along with that tendency is closely implicated in that loss of meaning. They adopt it as their own cause, and are stimulated to push further toward that goal. Whether aesthetic theory can discover the term for this or whether, as is most often the case, it throws up its hands in horror and tries to catch up with events depends not least on its insight into the aspect of the artistic spirit that sets out to sabotage meaning. No doubt many go along with a trend that both removes the need for them to make efforts of their own and promises them a substitute for the security that has been undermined by the emancipation of art from its forms throughout the modern period.

It is inevitable that we should find a parallel in the ousting of philosophy in the Anglo-Saxon world by logical positivism: the utter renunciation of meaning of any kind, and even the idea of truth, evidently creates a feeling of absolute, doubt-free certainty, even if it is wholly without content. But this is not the whole story about the intoxication of insatiable disillusionment, for which the notion of the Absurd has meanwhile gained acceptance as a kind of magic spell, or about the self-awareness of one's own contradiction, of mind as the organ of meaninglessness. This experience reaches deeply into many of the phenomena of contemporary mass culture. To ask after their meaning is fruitless because they rebel against the concept of meaning and against the assertion that life is meaningful.

In the realm of aesthetics it is not unusual for the extremes to meet, at the top and at the bottom. For thousands of years, art has conceived of the alleged meaning of life in the imagination and drummed it into people. In its origins, even modernism did not doubt it, as it stood on the very threshold of what is taking place in our day. The work of art that contained its meaning in itself, that was determined by spirit in all its aspects, was the accomplice of what Herbert Marcuse has termed the affirmative nature of culture. Wherever art was a reflection in any sense at all, the illusion of its necessity confirmed that the thing to be reflected had meaning, however tragic or ugly it might turn out to be. The dismissal of aesthetic meaning today goes hand in hand with the dismissal of the work of art as a work that reflects our outer or inner nature. The erosion of the arts is hostile to an ideal of harmony that presupposes, as the guarantee of meaning, what we might call ordered circumstances within the kinds of art. This erosion of the arts wishes to escape from the ideological bias of art, which reaches right down into its constitution as art, as an autarchic sphere of the spirit. It is as if the artistic genres, by denying their own firm boundaries, were gnawing away at the concept of art itself.

The original example of the erosion of art was the principle of montage, which appeared before the First World War in the explosion of cubism and, probably independently of that, in experimenters like Schwitters, and after that in dada and surrealism. However, montage amounts to the disruption, and hence the denial, of meaning in works of art through the invasion of fragments of empirical reality that do not abide by the laws of art. The erosion of the arts is almost always accompanied by the attempt by works of art to reach out toward an extra-aesthetic reality. This element is strictly opposed to the principle of reflecting reality. The more an art allows material that is not contained in its own continuum to enter it, the more it participates in alien, thinglike matter, instead of imitating it. It therefore becomes virtually a thing among things, a something we know not what.

Such not-knowing expresses something with inescapable consequences for art. The loss of meaning that it has adopted as if from a desire to destroy itself, or that it takes as an antidote to save its own life, cannot be its final word. The not-knowing of explicitly absurdist works of art, such as Beckett's, marks a point where meaning and nonmeaning become identical. Admittedly, we would distort this identity if, heaving a sigh of relief, we were to read a positive meaning into his writings. Nevertheless, it is not possible to conceive of a work of art that does not create meaning after all, even if it does incorporate the heterogeneous and turn against its own meaningfulness as a totality. Metaphysical and aesthetic meaning are not one and the same thing, even today. The nonmeaningful realities that find their way into the domain of art in the course of erosion are potentially salvaged as meaningful by art, at the same moment as they fly in the face of the traditional meaning of art. The consistent negation of aesthetic meaning would be possible only if art were to be abolished. The latest significant works of art are the nightmare of such an abolition, even though by their very existence they resist their own destruction; it is as if the end of art threatens the end of mankind, a mankind whose sufferings cry out for art, for an art that does not smooth and mitigate. Art presents humanity with the dream of its doom so that humanity may awaken, remain in control of itself, and survive.

The negativity of the concept of art impinges on its contents. Its own nature, not the impotence of our thoughts about it, forbids us to define it; its innermost principle, that of utopia, rebels against the domination of nature that its definition implies. It does not wish to remain what it once was. How dynamic this makes its relation to the individual arts can be seen from its newest form, the film. The question whether the film is art or not is idle. On the one hand, as Benjamin was the first to show in his essay "The Work of Art in the Age of Mechanical Reproduction," film comes closest to its own essence where it ruthlessly eliminates the attribute of aura that characterized all art before film, that illusion of transcendence guaranteed by its context—to put it another way, where film renounces symbolic and other elements that confer meaning to a degree that could scarcely be imagined by realist painting and literature. Siegfried Kracauer concluded from this that film, as a sort of salvaging of the extra-aesthetic world of things, was made aesthetically possible only by renouncing the principle of style, through the intention-free immersion of the camera in existence in its raw state prior to all subjectivity.

But such a refusal, taken as the a priori premise of filmmaking, is itself a stylistic principle. For all its abstinence from aura and subjective intention, film technique inevitably feeds elements of meaning into the final product: through the script, the photographed images, the camera's point of view, the cutting—methods not unlike those adopted in music or painting, which also want the material to appear naked before the viewer or listener but inevitably preform it in the process. Although film would like to discard its artlike qualities while adhering to the intrinsic laws governing it as a form—almost as if art were in conflict with its own artistic principle—film remains art in its rebellion and even enlarges art.

Such a contradiction, which, incidentally, cannot be worked out in a vacuum because films are dependent upon profit, is the element of all authentically modern art. This indeed may be the secret inspiration of the erosion of the arts. In this sense, the happening is exemplary—even though ostentatious meaninglessness does not necessarily express, or give shape to, the senselessness of existence. Happenings surrender without restraint to the yearning for art to become a reality of its own, in contradiction to its own principle of stylization and its relation to the image. In this way happenings can conduct an aggressive, even shocking campaign against empirical reality, whose equal they wish to become. In their clown-like detachment from the purposes of real life, in the middle of which they are acted out, they are essentially its parody, and parody—for example, parody of the mass media—is what they unmistakably aim to achieve.

The erosion of the arts is a false destruction of art. Art's inescapable nature as appearance becomes a scandal in the face of the overwhelming power of economic and political reality, which makes a mockery of aesthetic appearance even as an idea because it allows no space for the creation of aesthetic substance. That appearance becomes steadily more incompatible with the principle of the rational domination of its material, with which it had been united throughout the entire history of art. While the present situation no longer has room for art—that was the meaning of the statement about the impossibility of poems after Auschwitz—it nevertheless has need of it. For reality without images is the counterpart of another condition without images: the condition in which art disappears because the utopia encoded in every work of art has been fulfilled. In itself art is not capable of such a demise. This is why the arts eat away at one another.

(1967; GS 10.1: 432–53)
Translated by Rodney Livingstone

PART FIVE

A PHILOSOPHY THAT KEEPS ITSELF ALIVE

20

Elements of Anti-Semitism

LIMITS OF ENLIGHTENMENT

I

Anti-Semitism today is for some a question affecting human destiny and for others a mere pretext. For the fascists the Jews are not a minority but the antirace, the negative principle as such; on their extermination the world's happiness depends. Diametrically opposed to this is the thesis that the Jews, free of national or racial features, form a group through religious belief and tradition and nothing else. Jewish traits relate to Eastern Jews, and only to those not yet assimilated. Both doctrines are true and false at the same time.

The first is true in the sense that fascism has made it true. The Jews are today the group that, in practice and in theory, draws to itself the destructive urge that the wrong social order spontaneously produces. They are branded as absolute evil by absolute evil. In this sense they are indeed the chosen people. Now that power is no longer needed for economic reasons, the Jews are designated as its absolute object, existing merely for the exercise of power. The workers, who are the real target, are understandably not told as much to their faces; the blacks must be kept in their place, but the Jews are to be wiped from the face of the earth, and the call to exterminate them like vermin finds an echo among the prospective fascists of all countries. In the image of the Jew that the racial nationalists hold up before the world, they express their own essence. Their craving is for exclusive ownership, appropriation, unlimited power, and at any price. The Jew, burdened with his tormentors' guilt, mocked as their lord, they nail to the cross, endlessly repeating a sacrifice in whose power they are unable to believe.

The other, liberal thesis is true as an idea. It contains an image of the society in which rage would no longer reproduce itself or seek qualities on which to be discharged. But by assuming the unity of humanity to have been already realized in principle, the liberal thesis serves as an apology for the existing order. The attempt to avert the direst threat by minority policies and other democratic measures is ambiguous, as is the defensive strategy of the last liberal citizens. Their powerlessness attracts the enemy of powerlessness. The mode of life and appearance of the Jews compromise the existing universal by deficient adaptation. Their inflexible adherence to their own order of life has placed them in an insecure relationship to the prevailing one. They expected to be sustained by that order without subscribing to it. Their relationship to the dominant nations was one of greed and fear. Yet whenever they sacrificed their difference to the prevailing mode, the successfully adapted Jews took on in exchange the cold, stoical character that existing society imposes on human beings. The dialectical intertwinement of enlightenment and power, the dual relationship of progress to both cruelty and liberation, which has been brought home to the Jews no less by the great exponents of enlightenment than by democratic popular movements, manifests itself in the makeup of the assimilated Jews themselves. The enlightened self-control with which adapted Jews effaced within themselves the painful scars of domination by others, a kind of second circumcision, made them forsake their own dilapidated community and wholeheartedly embrace the life of the modern bourgeoisie, which was already advancing ineluctably toward a reversion to pure oppression and reorganization into an exclusively racial entity. Race is not, as the racial nationalists claim, an immediate, natural peculiarity. Rather, it is a regression to nature as mere violence, to the hidebound particularism that, in the existing order, constitutes precisely the universal. Race today is the self-assertion of the bourgeois individual, integrated into the barbaric collective. The harmonious society to which the liberal Jews declared their allegiance has finally been granted to them in the form of the national community. They believed that only anti-Semitism disfigured this order, which in reality cannot exist without disfiguring human beings. The persecution of the Jews, like any persecution, cannot be separated from that order. Its essence, however it may hide itself at times, is the violence that today is openly revealed.

II

Anti-Semitism as a popular movement has always been driven by the urge of which its instigators accuse the social democrats: to make everyone the same. Those without the power to command must fare no better than ordinary people. From the German civil servant to the Negroes in Harlem, those avidly emulating their betters have always known that they would really gain nothing but the satisfaction of seeing others no better off than themselves. The Aryanization of Jewish property, which in any case primarily benefited those at the top, enriched the masses in the Third Reich hardly more than the wretched booty pillaged from Jewish quarters enriched the Cossacks. The real benefit it brought was a half-understood ideology. That the demonstration of its economic futility heightened rather than moderated the attraction of the racialist panacea points to its true nature: it does not help human beings but assuages their urge to destroy. The actual advantage enjoyed by the racialist comrade is that his rage will be sanctioned by the collective. The less he gains in any other way, the more obstinately, against better knowledge, he clings to the movement. Anti-Semitism has proved immune to the charge of inadequate profitability. For the common people it is a luxury.

Its usefulness for the rulers is evident. It serves as a distraction, a cheap means of corruption, a terrorist warning. The respectable rackets condone it, the disreputable ones carry it out. But the form of the mentality, both social and individual, that manifests itself in anti-Semitism, the primeval-historical entrapment from which it is a desperate attempt to escape, remains wholly obscure. If a malady so deeply embedded in civilization is not properly accounted for by knowledge, the individual, too, though he may be as well intentioned as the victim himself, cannot mitigate it through understanding. The plausibly rational, economic, and political explanations and counterarguments—however correct their individual observations—cannot appease it, since rationality itself, through its link to power, is submerged in the same malady. Whether blindly dealing out blows or blindly fending them off, persecutors and victims form part of the same calamitous cycle. Anti-Semitic behavior is unleashed in situations in which blinded people, deprived of subjectivity, are let loose as subjects. Their actions—for those involved—are lethal yet meaningless reactions, of the kind that behaviorists register but fail to interpret. Anti-Semitism is a well-rehearsed pattern, indeed, a ritual of civilization, and the pogroms are the true ritual murders. They demonstrate the impotence of what might have restrained them—reflection, meaning, ultimately truth. The mindless pastime of beating people to death confirms the drab existence to which one merely conforms.

The blindness of anti-Semitism, its lack of intention, lends a degree of truth to the explanation of the movement as a release valve. Rage is vented on those who are both conspicuous and unprotected. And just as, depending on the constellation, the victims are interchangeable—vagrants, Jews, Protestants, Catholics—so each of them can replace the murderer, in the same blind lust for killing, as soon as he feels the power of representing the norm. There is no authentic anti-Semitism, and certainly no born anti-Semite. The older adults to whom the call for Jewish blood has become second nature are as ignorant of the reason as the young people who have to shed it. The high-placed instigators, who know the reason, neither hate the Jews nor love their own followers. The latter, however, who always go short, economically and sexually, hate without end; they find relaxation unbearable because they do not know fulfillment. Indeed, the organized robbers and murderers are animated by a kind of dynamic idealism. Setting out on their pillages, they construct a grandiose ideology for what they do, with fatuous talk of saving the family, the fatherland, humanity. But since they remain the dupes they secretly suspect themselves to be, their pitiful rational motive, the theft that was supposed to rationalize the deed, is finally discarded entirely, and the rationalization becomes truthful against its will. The obscure impulse that was always more congenial to them than reason takes them over completely. The rational island sinks beneath the flood, and those desperately floundering now appear only as defenders of truth, restorers of the earth, which has to be reformed to its farthest corners. All living things become material for their ghastly duty, which now flinches at nothing. Action becomes a purpose in itself, cloaking its own purposelessness. Anti-Semitism always starts with an appeal to complete the task. Anti-Semitism and totality have always been profoundly connected. Blindness encompasses everything because it comprehends nothing.

Liberalism had granted the Jews property, but without the authority to command. The purpose of human rights was to promise happiness even where power was lacking. Because the cheated masses are dimly aware that this promise, being universal, remains a lie as long as classes exist, it arouses their anger; they feel themselves scorned. They must constantly repress the thought of that happiness, even as a possibility, an idea, and they deny it all the more fiercely the more its time has come. Wherever it appears to be realized amid the systematic deprivation, they must reenact the suppression that has been applied to their own longing. Whatever that reenactment is directed against, however unhappy it may itself be—Ahasuerus and Mignon, exoticism that evokes the promised land, beauty that summons the thought of sex, the animal whose hint of promiscuity condemns it as repulsive—draws down on itself the destructive fury of the civilized, who can never fully complete the painful process of civilization. To those who compulsively control it, tormented nature provocatively reflects back the appearance of powerless happiness. The idea of happiness without power is unendurable because it alone would be happiness. The fantasy of the conspiracy of lascivious Jewish bankers who finance Bolshevism is a sign of innate powerlessness, the good life an emblem of happiness. These are joined by the image of the intellectual, who appears to enjoy in thought what the others deny themselves and is spared the sweat of toil and bodily strength. The banker and the intellectual, money and mind, the exponents of circulation, are the disowned, wishful image of those mutilated by power, an image that power uses to perpetuate itself.

III

The present society, in which primitive religious feelings, new cults, and the legacy of revolutions are peddled in the market; in which the fascist leaders barter the land and lives of nations behind locked doors while the public, lulled by their radio sets, calculate the cost; this society in which even the word that unmasks it doubles as an invitation to join a political racket; in which no longer is politics merely business but business is the whole of politics—this society is scandalized by the Jew, with his obsolete shopkeeper's mannerisms, labeling him a materialist, a haggler, who should make way for the pioneering spirit of those who have elevated business to an absolute.

Bourgeois anti-Semitism has a specific economic purpose: to conceal domination in production. If in earlier epochs the rulers were directly repressive, so that they not only left work exclusively to the lower orders but declared it the ignominy it always was under domination, in the age of mercantilism the absolute monarch transformed himself into the supreme master of manufactories. Production became presentable at court. Finally, as bourgeois, the masters replaced their colorful robes with civilian dress. Work is no disgrace, they said—the more rationally to take possession of that of others. Aligning themselves with the productive elements, they remained the parasites of old. The factory owner ventured and raked in like a great merchant or banker. He calculated, procured, bought, sold. In the market he competed with the merchants and bankers for the profit due to his capital. But he grabbed not merely from the market but from the source: as a functionary of the class system he took care not to go short of the fruits of his workers' labor. The workers had to deliver as much as possible. Like a true Shylock he insisted on his contract. By virtue of owning the machines and materials, he forced the others to produce. He called himself the producer, but he and everyone secretly knew the truth. The productive work of the capitalist, whether he justified his profit as the reward of enterprise, as under liberalism, or as the director's salary, as today, was the ideology that concealed the nature of the labor contract and the rapacity of the economic system in general.

That is why people shout, "Stop thief!"—and point at the Jew. He is indeed the scapegoat, not only for individual maneuvers and machinations but in the wider sense that the economic injustice of the whole class is attributed to him. The factory owner has his debtors, the workers, under observation in his factory and can check their performance before he parts with his money. They find out the true nature of the exchange only when they see what they can buy with it: the smallest magnate has access to a quantity of services and goods available to no ruler before him; but the workers receive what is called the cultural minimum. Not content with letting the market tell them how few goods can be theirs, the salesman sings the praises of those they cannot afford. Only the relationship of wages to prices expresses what is withheld from the workers. With their wages they have accepted the principle of just remuneration. The merchant presents them with the promissory note they have signed on behalf of the manufacturer. The merchant is the bailiff for the whole system, taking upon himself the odium due to the others. That the circulation sphere is responsible for exploitation is a socially necessary illusion.

The Jews had not been the only people active in the circulation sphere. But they had been locked up in it too long not to reflect in their makeup something of the hatred so long directed at that sphere. Unlike their Aryan colleagues, they were largely denied access to the source of added value. Only at a late stage and with difficulty were they allowed to gain ownership of the means of production. To be sure, in the history of Europe, and even in imperial Germany, baptized Jews had reached high positions in administration and industry. But they always had to justify this with redoubled devotion and diligence, and stubborn self-denial. They were admitted only if, through their behavior, they tacitly adopted and confirmed the verdict on the other Jews: that is the purpose of baptism. All the great achievements of their prominent members were not enough to allow Jews to be admitted to the peoples of Europe; having been prevented from putting down roots they were then criticized as rootless. They always remained the protected Jews, dependent on emperors, princes, or the absolutist state. These patrons were economically more advanced than the rest of the population. To the extent that they could make use of the Jew as an intermediary, they protected him against the masses who had to foot the bill for progress. The Jews were the colonizers of progress. Having helped as merchants to disseminate Roman civilization throughout Gentile Europe, they became, in keeping with their patriarchal religion, representatives of urban, civic, and finally industrial conditions. As bearers of capitalist modes of existence from country to country they earned the hatred of those who suffered under that system. For the sake of the economic progress that today is their downfall the Jews were from the first a thorn in the side of the craftsmen and farmers whose status capitalism undermined. Now it is their turn to bear the brunt of its exclusive, particularist character. They, who always wanted to be first, are left far behind. Even the Jewish head of an American entertainment trust is hopelessly defensive amid his wealth. The caftan was the ghostly residue of ancient civic dress. Today it is a sign that its wearers have been flung to the margins of a society that, now wholly enlightened, is exorcising the spirits of its prehistory. They who propagated individualism, abstract law, the concept of the person, have been debased to a species. They who were never allowed untroubled ownership of the civic right that should have granted them human dignity are again called "the Jews" without distinction. Even in the nineteenth century the Jew remained dependent on an alliance with the central authority. The general law, protected by the state, was the guarantor of his safety, and the exceptive law the specter that ensured his docility. He remained an object, dependent on grace and favor, even when claiming his rights. Trade was not his vocation; it was his fate. The Jews were the trauma of the knights of industry, who have to masquerade as productive creators. In the Jewish jargon they detect what they secretly despise in themselves: their anti-Semitism is self-hate, the bad conscience of the parasite.

IV

Nationalist anti-Semitism seeks to disregard religion. It claims to be concerned with purity of race and nation. Its exponents notice that people have long ceased to trouble themselves about eternal salvation. The average believer today is as crafty as only cardinals were in former times. To accuse the Jews of being obdurate unbelievers is no longer enough to incite the masses. But the religious hostility that motivated the persecution of the Jews for two millennia is far from completely extinguished. Rather, anti-Semitism's eagerness to deny its religious tradition indicates that that tradition is secretly no less deeply embedded in it than secular idiosyncrasy once was in religious zealotry. Religion has been incorporated as cultural heritage, not abolished. The alliance between enlightenment and power has debarred from consciousness the moment of truth in religion while conserving its reified forms. Both circumstances finally benefit fascism: the unchanneled longing is guided into racial-nationalist rebellion, while the descendants of the evangelistic zealots are converted into conspirators of blood communities and elite guards, on the model of the Wagnerian knights of the Grail. In this way religion as an institution is partly meshed directly into the system and partly transposed into the pomp of mass culture and parades. The fanatical faith on which leader and followers pride themselves is no other than the grim doctrine that was earlier used to discipline the desperate, except that its content has gone astray. That content lives on only as hatred of those who do not share the faith. Among the "German Christians,"[1] all that remained of the religion of love was anti-Semitism.

Christianity is not only a regression beyond Judaism. The latter's God, in passing from a henotheistic to a universal form, did not entirely shed the features of the nature demon. The terror originating in remote preanimist times passes from nature into the concept of the absolute self, which, as its creator and ruler, entirely subjugates nature. Despite the ineffable power and splendor in which such alienation clothes it, that ruler is still attainable to thought, which becomes universal through this very relationship to something supreme, transcendental. God as spirit is the principle opposed to nature; it not only stands for nature's blind cycle, as do all the mythical gods, but offers liberation from it. But in its remote abstractness, the incommensurable has at the same time become more terrible, and the pitiless statement "I am who am," which tolerates nothing beside itself, surpasses in its inescapable power the blinder and therefore more ambiguous judgment of anonymous fate. The God of Judaism demands what he is owed and settles accounts with the defaulter. He enmeshes his creatures in a tissue of debt and credit, guilt and merit. In contrast, Christianity emphasized the moment of grace, although that, too, is contained in Judaism, in God's covenant with men and in the Messianic promise. It softened the terror of the absolute by allowing the creature to find itself reflected in the deity: the divine mediator is called by a human name and dies a human death. His message is: fear not; the law yields before faith; love becomes greater than any majesty, the only commandment.

But by virtue of the same moments by which it lifted the spell of nature religion, Christianity is producing ideology once again, in a spiritualized form. To the same degree as the absolute is brought closer to the finite, the finite is made absolute. Christ, the incarnated spirit, is the deified sorcerer. The human self-reflection in the absolute, the humanization of God through Christ, is the *proton pseudos* [first substitution]. The progress beyond Judaism is paid for with the assertion that the mortal Jesus was God. The harm is done precisely by the reflective moment of Christianity, the spiritualization of magic. A spiritual essence is attributed to something that mind identifies as natural. Mind consists precisely in demonstrating the contradiction inherent in such pretensions of the finite. Bad conscience is therefore obliged to present the prophet as a symbol, the magical practice as transubstantiation. It is that which makes Christianity a religion, and, in a sense, the only one: an intellectual link to something intellectually suspect, a special sphere of culture. Like the great Asiatic belief systems, pre-Christian Judaism was hardly separable from national life, from collective self-preservation. The reshaping of the heathen ritual of sacrifice not only took place in worship and in the mind but determined the form of the labor process. In providing the schema for the latter, sacrifice becomes rational. The taboo is transformed into the rational organization of the work process. It regulates administration in war and peace, sowing and harvesting, food preparation and slaughter. Although the rules may not arise from rational reflection, rationality arises from them. The effort of primitive peoples to free themselves from immediate fear engendered among them the institution of ritual; this was refined by Judaism into the sanctified rhythm of family and national life. The priests were appointed to watch over the proper observance of custom. Their function within the power structure was clearly displayed in theocratic practice; Christianity, however, wanted to remain spiritual even where it aspired to power. In ideology it repudiated self-preservation by the ultimate sacrifice, that of the man-god, but thereby relegated devalued life to the sphere of the profane: it abolished the law of Moses but rendered what was theirs unto both God and Caesar. Secular authority is either confirmed or usurped, while Christianity acquires a license to manage salvation. Self-preservation is to be conquered though the imitation of Christ—by order. In this way self-sacrificing love is stripped of its naïveté, severed from natural love, and turned to account as credit. The love mediated by ecclesiastical knowledge is presented as immediate love, in which nature and the supernatural are reconciled. Therein lies its untruth: in the fraudulently affirmative interpretation of self-forgetting.

That interpretation is fraudulent because the church depends for its existence on people's belief that they will attain salvation by following its teaching, whether that teaching demands works like the Catholic version or faith like the Protestant, yet cannot guarantee that goal. The nonbinding nature of the religious promise of salvation, the Jewish and negative moment in the Christian doctrine, by which magic and finally the church itself are relativized, is tacitly ignored by naive believers, for whom Christianity, supranaturalism, becomes a magic ritual, a nature religion. They believe only by forgetting their belief. They convince themselves of the certainty of their knowledge like astrologers or spiritualists. That is not necessarily worse than spiritualized theology. The old Italian lady who with devout simplicity consecrates a candle to St. Gennaro to protect her grandson in the war may be closer to the truth than the high priests and pontiffs who, untainted by idolatry, bless the weapons against which St. Gennaro is powerless. To the simple, however, religion itself becomes a substitute for religion. Christianity had some awareness of this from its earliest days, but it was only the paradoxical Christians, the antiofficial thinkers from Pascal through Lessing and Kierkegaard to Barth, who made it the keystone of their theology. In this awareness they were not only the radical Christians but the tolerant ones. The others, who repressed that knowledge and with bad conscience convinced themselves of Christianity as a secure possession, were obliged to confirm their eternal salvation by the worldly ruin of those who refused to make the murky sacrifice of reason. That is the religious origin of anti-Semitism. The adherents of the religion of the Son hated the supporters of the religion of the Father as one hates those who know better. This is the hostility of spirit hardened as faith in salvation for spirit as mind. What is vexatious for the Christian enemies of the Jews is the truth that withstands evil without rationalizing it, and clings to the idea of unearned beatitude in disregard of worldly actions and the order of salvation that allegedly bring it about. Anti-Semitism is supposed to confirm that the ritual of faith and history is justified by ritually sacrificing those who deny its justice.

V

"I simply can't abide you—so don't forget it," says Siegfried to Mime, who is trying to win his love. The stock reply of all anti-Semites is the appeal to idiosyncrasy. Society's emancipation from anti-Semitism depends on whether the content of that idiosyncrasy is raised to the level of a concept and becomes aware of its own senselessness. But idiosyncrasy attaches itself to the peculiar. The universal, that which fits into the context of social utility, is regarded as natural. But anything natural that has not been absorbed into utility by passing through the cleansing channels of conceptual order—the screech of stylus on slate that sets the teeth on edge, the *haut goût* that brings to mind filth and corruption, the sweat that appears on the brow of the diligent—whatever is not quite assimilated, or infringes the commands in which the progress of centuries has been sedimented, is felt as intrusive and arouses a compulsive aversion.

The motifs that trigger such idiosyncrasy are those that allude to origin. They re-create moments of biological prehistory: danger signs that made the hair stand on end and the heart stop. In the idiosyncratic aversion individual organs escape the subject's control, autonomously obeying fundamental biological stimuli. The self that experiences itself in such reactions—rigidity of the skin, muscles, and limbs—is not quite master of them. For a few moments they mimic the motionlessness of surrounding nature. But as what is mobile draws closer to the immobile, more highly developed life to mere nature, it is also estranged from it, since immobile nature, which living creatures, like Daphne, seek with utmost agitation to become, is capable only of the most external, spatial relationships. Space is absolute alienation. Where the human seeks to resemble nature, at the same time it hardens itself against it. Protection as petrified terror is a form of camouflage. These numb human reactions are archaic patterns of self-preservation: the tribute life pays for its continued existence is adaptation to death.

Civilization replaced the organic adaptation to otherness, mimetic behavior proper, firstly in the magical phase, with the organized manipulation of mimesis, and finally in the historical phase, with rational praxis, work. Uncontrolled mimesis is proscribed. The angel that, with fiery sword, drove humans out of paradise and onto the path of technical progress is itself the symbol of that progress. The severity with which, over the centuries, the rulers have prevented both their own successors and the subjugated masses from relapsing into mimetic behavior—from the religious ban on graven images through the social ostracizing of actors and gypsies to the education that "cures" children of childishness—is the condition of civilization. Social and individual education reinforces the objectifying behavior required by work and prevents people from submerging themselves once more in the ebb and flow of surrounding nature. All distraction, indeed, all devotion has an element of mimicry. The ego has been forged by hardening itself against such behavior. The transition from reflecting mimesis to controlled reflection completes its formation. Bodily adaptation to nature is replaced by "recognition in a concept,"[2] the subsuming of difference under sameness. However, the constellation under which sameness is established, both the direct sameness of mimesis and the indirect sameness of synthesis, the adaptation of the self to the thing in the blind act of living no less than the comparison of reified elements in scientific conceptualization—that constellation remains terror. Society perpetuates the threat from nature as the permanent, organized compulsion which, reproducing itself in individuals as systematic self-preservation, rebounds against nature as society's control over it. Science is repetition, refined to observed regularity and preserved in stereotypes. The mathematical formula is consciously manipulated regression, just as the magic ritual was; it is the most sublimated form of mimicry. In technology the adaptation to lifelessness in the service of self-preservation is accomplished no longer, as in magic, by bodily imitation of external nature, but by automating mental processes, turning them into blind sequences. With its triumph human expressions become both controllable and compulsive. All that remains of the adaptation to nature is the hardening against it. The camouflage used to protect and strike terror today is the blind mastery of nature, which is identical to farsighted instrumentality.

In the bourgeois mode of production the ineradicable mimetic heritage present in all praxis is consigned to oblivion. The pitiless ban on regression appears like an edict of fate; the denial is so total that it is no longer registered consciously. Those blinded by civilization have contact with their own tabooed mimetic traits only through certain gestures and forms of behavior they encounter in others, as isolated, shameful residues in their rationalized environment. What repels them as alien is all too familiar.[a] It lurks in the contagious gestures of an immediacy suppressed by civilization: gestures of touching, nestling, soothing, coaxing. What makes such impulses repellent today is their outmodedness. In seeking to win over the buyer with flattery, the debtor with threats, the creditor with supplication, they appear to translate long-reified human relationships back into those of personal power. Any emotion is finally embarrassing; mere excitement is preferable. All unmanipulated expression appears like the grimace that the manipulated expression—of the film actor, the lynch mob, the führer's speech—always was. Undisciplined mimicry is the brand burned by the old domination into the living substance of the dominated, and is inherited through an unconscious process of imitation in early childhood from generation to generation, from the Jewish rags-and-bones man to the banker. Such mimicry provokes anger, because it puts on show, in the face of the new relationships of production, the old fear that one has had to forget in order to survive them. It is the compulsive moment in behavior, the rage of the tormentor and of the tormented, reappearing indistinguishably in the grimace that triggers the specific rage of civilized people. Impotent appearance is answered by deadly reality, play by seriousness.

[a] See Sigmund Freud, "The Uncanny," in *The Standard Edition of the Complete Psychological Works of Sigmund Freud,* trans. James Strachey, ed. James Strachey in collaboration with Anna Freud (London: Hogarth, 1953–74), 17: 219ff.

The grimace seems like playacting because, instead of performing serious work, it prefers to portray displeasure. It appears to evade the seriousness of life by admitting it without restraint: therefore it is false. But expression is the painful echo of overwhelming power, violence that finds utterance in complaint. It is always overdone, no matter how heartfelt it may be, because, as in each work of art, the whole world seems contained in every plaintive sound. Only activity is proportionate. It, and not mimesis, can bring an end to suffering. But its consequence is the rigid, unmoved visage, culminating, at the end of this age, in the baby faces of the practical men, the politicians, priests, managing directors, racketeers. The strident voices of fascist rabble-rousers and camp commanders show the reverse side of the same social condition. The screaming is as cold-blooded as business. Even the plaintive sounds of nature are appropriated as an element of technique. The bellowing of these orators is to the pogrom what its howling Klaxon is to the German flying bomb: the cry of terror that announces terror is mechanically switched on. The screamers deliberately use the wail of the victim, which first called violence by its name, and even the mere word that designates the victim—Frenchman, Negro, Jew—to induce in themselves the desperation of the persecuted who have to hit out. They are the false likeness of the terrified mimesis. They reproduce within themselves the insatiability of the power of which they are afraid. Everything must be used, everything must belong to them. The mere existence of the other is a provocation. Everyone else "gets in the way" and must be shown their limits—the limits of limitless horror. No one who seeks shelter shall find it; those who express what everyone craves—peace, homeland, freedom—will be denied it, just as nomads and traveling players have always been refused rights of domicile. Whatever someone fears, that is done to him. Even the last resting place shall be none. The despoiling of graveyards is not an excess of anti-Semitism; it is anti-Semitism itself. Those evicted compulsively arouse the lust to evict them even here. The marks left on them by violence endlessly inflame violence. Anything that wants merely to vegetate must be rooted out. The chaotically regular flight reactions of the lower animals, the patterns of swarming crowds, the convulsive gestures of the tortured—all these express what wretched life can never quite control: the mimetic impulse. In the death throes of the creature, at the furthest extreme from freedom, freedom itself irresistibly shines forth as the thwarted destiny of matter. It is against this freedom that the idiosyncratic aversion, the purported motive of anti-Semitism, is ultimately directed.

The psychic energy harnessed by political anti-Semitism is this rationalized idiosyncrasy. All the gesticulations devised by the führer and his followers are pretexts for giving way to the mimetic temptation without openly violating the reality principle—with honor, as it were. They detest the Jews and imitate them constantly. There is no anti-Semite who does not feel an instinctive urge to ape what he takes to be Jewishness. The same mimetic codes are constantly used: the argumentative jerking of the hands; the singing tone of voice, which vividly animates a situation or a feeling independently of judgment; and the nose, that physiognomic *principium individuationis*, which writes the individual's peculiarity on his face. In the ambiguous partialities of the sense of smell the old nostalgia for what is lower lives on, the longing for immediate union with surrounding nature, with earth and slime. Of all the senses the act of smelling, which is attracted without objectifying, reveals most sensuously the urge to lose oneself in identification with the Other. That is why smell, as both the perception and the perceived—which are one in the act of olfaction—is more expressive than other senses. When we see we remain who we are; when we smell we are absorbed entirely. In civilization, therefore, smell is regarded as a disgrace, a sign of the lower social orders, lesser races, and baser animals. The civilized person is allowed to give way to such desires only if the prohibition is suspended by rationalization in the service of practical purposes, real or apparent. One is allowed to indulge the outlawed drive if acting with the unquestionable aim of expunging it. This is manifested in the practical joke. It is a wretched parody of fulfillment. The mimetic function is sneeringly enjoyed as something despised and self-despising. Anyone who sniffs out "bad" smells in order to extirpate them may imitate to his heart's content the snuffling that takes its unrationalized pleasure in the smell itself. Disinfected by the civilized sniffer's absolute identification with the prohibiting agency, the forbidden impulse eludes the prohibition. If it crosses the threshold, the response is laughter. That is the schema of the anti-Semitic reaction. The anti-Semites gather to celebrate the moment when authority lifts the ban; that moment alone makes them a collective, constituting the community of kindred spirits. Their ranting is organized laughter. The more dreadful the accusations and threats, the greater the fury, the more withering is the scorn. Rage, mockery, and poisoned imitation are fundamentally the same thing. The purpose of the fascist cult of formulae, the ritualized discipline, the uniforms, and the whole allegedly irrational apparatus is to make possible mimetic behavior. The elaborate symbols proper to every counterrevolutionary movement, the death's heads and masquerades, the barbaric drumming, the monotonous repetition of words and gestures, are so many organized imitations of magical practices, the mimesis of mimesis. The führer, with his ham-actor's facial expressions and the hysterical charisma turned on with a switch, leads the dance. In his performance he acts out by proxy and in effigy what is denied to everyone else in reality. Hitler can gesticulate like a clown, Mussolini risk false notes like a provincial tenor, Goebbels talk as glibly as the Jewish agent whose murder he is recommending, Coughlin[3] preach love like the Savior himself, whose crucifixion he impersonates for the sake of yet more bloodshed. Fascism is also totalitarian in seeking to place oppressed nature's rebellion against domination directly in the service of domination.

This mechanism needs the Jews. Their artificially heightened visibility acts on the legitimate son of Gentile civilization like a kind of magnetic field. In being made aware, through his very difference from the Jew, of the humanity they have in common, the rooted Gentile is overcome by a feeling of something antithetical and alien. In this way the tabooed impulses that run counter to work in its dominant form are converted into conforming idiosyncrasies. Against this the economic position of the Jews, the last defrauded fraudsters of the liberal ideology, offers no reliable protection. Because they are so eminently suited to generating these inductive psychic currents they are unresistingly allocated to such functions. They share the fate of the rebellious nature for which fascism substitutes them, being put to use with the perspicacity of the blind. It makes little difference whether the Jews as individuals really display the mimetic traits that cause the malign infection or whether those traits are merely imputed. If the holders of economic power have once overcome their fear of employing fascist agents, in the face of the Jews the harmony of the national community is automatically established. They are sacrificed by the dominant order when, through its increasing estrangement from nature, it has reverted to mere nature. The Jews as a whole are charged with practicing forbidden magic and bloody rituals. Disguised as an accusation, the subliminal craving of the indigenous population to revert to mimetic sacrificial practices is joyously readmitted to their consciousness. Once the horror of the primeval age, sent packing by civilization, has been rehabilitated as a rational interest through projection onto the Jews, there is no holding back. It can be acted out in reality, and the evil that is acted out surpasses even the evil content of the projection. The popular nationalist fantasies of Jewish crimes, of infanticide and sadistic excesses, of racial poisoning and international conspiracy, precisely define the anti-Semitic dream, and fall short of its realization. Once things have gone so far, the mere word "Jew" appears like the bloody grimace whose image—skull and mangled cross in one—is unfurled on the swastika flag; the fact that someone is called a Jew acts as a provocation to set about him until he resembles that image.

Civilization is the triumph of society over nature—a triumph that transforms everything into mere nature. The Jews themselves, over the millennia, have played their part in this, with enlightenment no less than with cynicism. As the oldest surviving patriarchy, the incarnation of monotheism, they converted taboos into maxims of civilization while the others were still enmeshed in magic. The Jews appeared to have success-fully achieved what Christianity had attempted in vain: the disempower-ment of magic by means of its own strength, which, as worship of God, is turned against itself. They have not so much eradicated the adaptation to nature as elevated it to the pure duties of ritual. In this way they have preserved its reconciling memory, without relapsing through symbols into mythology. They are therefore regarded by advanced civilization as both backward and too advanced, like and unlike, shrewd and stupid. They are pronounced guilty of what, as the first citizens, they were the first to subdue in themselves: the susceptibility to the lure of base in-stincts, the urge toward the beast and the earth, the worship of images. Because they invented the concept of the kosher, they are persecuted as swine. The anti-Semites appoint themselves executors of the Old Testa-ment: they see to it that the Jews, having eaten of the Tree of Knowledge, unto dust shall return.

VI

Anti-Semitism is based on false projection. It is the reverse of gen-uine mimesis and has deep affinities to the repressed; in fact, it may itself be the pathic character trait in which the latter is precipitated. If mimesis makes itself resemble its surroundings, false projection makes its surroundings resemble itself. If, for the former, the outward becomes the model to which the inward clings, so that the alien becomes the intimately known, the latter displaces the volatile inward into the outer world, branding the intimate friend as foe. Impulses that are not acknowledged by the subject and yet are his, are attributed to the object: the prospective victim. For the ordinary paranoiac the choice of victim is not free; it obeys the laws of his illness. In fascism this behavior is adopted by politics; the object of the illness is declared true to reality, the system of delusions the reasonable norm in a world that makes deviation neurosis. The mechanism that the totalitarian order takes into its service is as old as civilization. The sexual impulses suppressed by humanity survived in both individuals and peoples and asserted themselves in the imaginary transformation of the surrounding world into a diabolic system. Those impelled by blind, murderous lust have always seen in the victim the pursuer who has driven them to desperate self-defense, and the mightiest of the rich have experienced their weakest neighbor as an intolerable threat before falling upon him. The rationalization was both a ruse and a compulsion. The person chosen as foe is already perceived as foe. The disorder lies in the subject's faulty distinction between his own contribution to the projected material and that of others.

In a certain sense, all perception is projection. The projection of sense impressions is a legacy of animal prehistory, a mechanism for the purposes of defense and obtaining food, an extension of the readiness for combat with which higher species reacted actively or passively to movements, regardless of the intention of the object. Projection has been automated in man like other forms of offensive or defensive behavior that have become reflexes. In this way his objective world has been constituted as a product of "an art concealed in the depths of the human soul, whose real modes of activity nature is hardly likely ever to allow us to discover, and to have open to our gaze."[b] The system of things, the fixed universal order of which science is merely an abstract expression, is, if Kant's critique of knowledge is applied anthropologically, the unconscious product of the animal tool in the struggle for existence—it is the automatic projection. In

[b] Immanuel Kant, *Critique of Pure Reason*, trans. Norman Kemp Smith (London: Macmillan, 1973), p. 183 (B 180f.).

human society, however, where both the affective and the intellectual life grow complex with the formation of the individual, projection must be increasingly controlled; individuals must learn both to refine and to inhibit it. As economic compulsion teaches them to distinguish between their own thoughts and feelings and those of others, a distinction emerges between outer and inner, the possibility of detachment and of identification, self-consciousness and conscience. More precise reflection is needed to understand this controlled form of projection and its degeneration into the false projection that is essential to anti-Semitism.

The physiological theory of perception, which has been despised by philosophers since Kant as naively realistic and as a circular argument, holds the world of perception to be a reflection, guided by the intellect, of the data received from real objects by the brain. According to this view, punctual indices, or impressions, are registered physiologically and then ordered by the mind. Although the Gestalt people may insist that the physiological substance receives not merely points but structure, Schopenhauer and Helmholtz, despite or even because of the circularity of their view, knew more about the intermeshed relationship of subject and object than is reflected in the official logical consistency of the schools, whether neopsychological or neo-Kantian: the perceptual image does indeed contain concepts and judgments. Between the actual object and the indubitable sense datum, between inner and outer, yawns an abyss that the subject must bridge at its own peril. To reflect the thing as it is, the subject must give back to it more than it receives from it. From the traces the thing leaves behind in its senses the subject re-creates the world outside it, the unity of the thing in its manifold properties and states; and in so doing, in learning how to impart a synthetic unity not only to the outward impressions but to the inward ones, which gradually separate themselves from them, it retroactively constitutes the self. The identical ego is the most recent constant product of projection. In a process that could be accomplished historically only when the powers of the human physiological constitution were fully developed, this self has emerged as a unified and, at the same time, an eccentric function. But even as an autonomously objectified subject it is only what the objective world is for it. The inner depth of the subject consists in nothing other than the delicacy and richness of the outer perceptual world. If this intermeshing is broken, the self petrifies. If it is confined, positivistically, to registering the given without itself giving, it shrinks to a point, and if, idealistically, it projects the world out of the bottomless origin or its own self, it exhausts itself in monotonous repetition. In both cases it gives up the ghost—in this case the mind or spirit. Only mediation, in which the insignificant sense datum raises thought to the fullest productivity of which it is capable, and in which, conversely, thought gives itself up without reservation to the overwhelming impression—only mediation can overcome the isolation that ails the whole of nature. Neither the certainty untroubled by thought, nor the preconceptual unity of perception and object, but only their self-reflective antithesis contains the possibility of reconciliation. The antithesis is perceived in the subject, which has the external world within its own consciousness and yet recognizes it as Other. Reflection on that antithesis, therefore, the life of reason, takes place as conscious projection.

The pathic element in anti-Semitism is not projective behavior as such but the exclusion of reflection from that behavior. Because the subject is unable to return to the object what it has received from it, it is not enriched but impoverished. It loses reflection in both directions: as it no longer reflects the object, it no longer reflects on itself, and thereby loses the ability to differentiate. Instead of the voice of conscience, it hears voices; instead of inwardly examining itself in order to draw up a protocol of its own lust for power, it attributes to others the Protocol of the Elders of Zion. It overflows at the same time as it dries up. It invests the outside world boundlessly with what is within itself; but what it invests is something utterly insignificant, an inflated accumulation of mere means, relationships, machinations, a grim praxis unilluminated by thought. Domination itself, which, even as absolute power, is inherently only a means, becomes in untrammeled projection the purpose both of oneself and of others, purpose as such. In the sickness of the individual, humanity's sharpened intellectual apparatus is turned once more against humanity, regressing to the blind instrument of hostility it was in animal prehistory, and as which, for the species, it has never ceased to operate in relation to the rest of nature. Just as, since its rise, the human species has manifested itself toward others as developmentally the highest, capable of the most terrible destruction; and just as, within humanity, the more advanced races have confronted the more primitive, the technically superior nations the more backward, so the sick individual confronts the other individual, in megalomania as in persecution mania. In both cases the subject is at the center, the world a mere occasion for its delusion; it becomes the impotent or omnipotent quintessence of what is projected onto it. The opposition of which the paranoiac complains indiscriminately at every step is the result of the lack of resistance, of the emptiness that the encapsulated subject generates around itself. The paranoiac cannot stop. The idea, having no firm hold on reality, insists all the more and becomes the fixation.

Because paranoiacs perceive the outside world only insofar as it corresponds to their blind purposes, they can only endlessly repeat their own self, which has been alienated from them as an abstract mania. This naked schema of power as such, equally overwhelming toward others and toward a self at odds with itself, seizes whatever comes its way and, wholly disregarding its peculiarity, incorporates it in its mythic web. The closed circle of perpetual sameness becomes a surrogate for omnipotence. It is as if the serpent that told the first humans "Ye shall be as gods" had kept his promise in the paranoiac. He creates everything in his own image. He seems to need no living thing yet demands that all shall serve him. His will permeates the whole universe; nothing may be unrelated to him. His systems know of no gaps. As astrologer, he endows the stars with powers that bring about the ruin of the unsuspecting, whether it is the ruin of others in the preclinical stage or of his own ego in the clinical stage. As philosopher, he makes world history the executor of inescapable catastrophes and downfalls. As completely insane or absolutely rational, he annihilates those marked down as victims either by the individual act of terror or by the well-considered strategy of extermination. In this way he succeeds. Just as women adore the unmoved paranoid man, nations fall to their knees before totalitarian fascism. The paranoid element in the devotees responds to the paranoiac as to the evil spirit, their fear of conscience to his utter lack of scruples, for which they feel gratitude. They follow the man who looks past them, who does not treat them as subjects but hands them over to the operations of his many purposes. Like everyone else, these women have made the occupation of greater or lesser positions of power their religion, and themselves the malign creatures society takes them for. And so the gaze that reminds them of freedom must strike them as that of the over-naive seducer. Their world is inverted. But at the same time they know, like the ancient gods who shunned the gaze of the faithful, that something lifeless resides behind their veil. In the trusting look of the nonparanoid they are reminded of the spirit that has died in them, because they see outside them only the cold means of their self-preservation. To be touched in this way awakens in them shame and rage. Yet the madman does not reach them, even though he may stare them in the face like the führer. He merely inflames them. His proverbial gaze straight into the eyes, unlike the free gaze, does not preserve individuality. It fixates. It binds others to one-sided loyalty, by confining them to the windowless, monadic fortress of their own person. It does not awaken conscience, but prematurely imposes responsibility. The penetrating look and the one that goes past you, the hypnotic and the disregarding gaze, are of the same kind: in both, the subject is extinguished. Because in both looks reflection is absent, the unreflecting are electrified by them. They are betrayed: the women cast away, the nation incinerated. Thus, the self-encapsulated figure remains a caricature of divine power. Just as his lordly gesture is entirely without creative power in reality, so, like the devil, he lacks the attributes of the principle he usurps: mindful love and freedom secure within itself. He is malignant, driven by compulsion, and as weak as he is strong. If divine omnipotence is said to draw creation unto itself, this satanic, imagined omnipotence draws everything into its impotence. That is the secret of its rule. The compulsively projecting self can project nothing except its own unhappiness, from the cause of which, residing in itself, it is yet cut off by its lack of reflection. For this reason the products of false projection, the stereotyped schemata of both thought and reality, bring calamity. For the ego, sinking into the meaningless abyss of itself, objects become allegories of ruin, which harbor the meaning of its own downfall.

The psychoanalytic theory of pathic projection has identified the transference of socially tabooed impulses from the subject to the object as the substance of that projection. Under the pressure of the superego, the ego projects aggressive urges emanating from the id—which, through their strength, are a danger to itself—as malign intentions onto the outside world, and succeeds in ridding itself of them as reactions to that outside world, either in fantasy by identification with the alleged malefactor or in reality by ostensible self-defense. The proscribed material converted into aggression is usually homosexual in nature. Through fear of castration, obedience toward the father preempts castration by adapting the conscious emotional life to that of a little girl, and hatred of the father is repressed as endless rancor. In paranoia, this hatred is intensified to a castration wish expressed as a universal urge to destroy. The sick subject regresses to an archaic confusion between love and dominance. It is concerned with physical closeness, with taking possession, finally with relationship at any price. Because it cannot acknowledge desire within itself, it assails the Other with jealousy or persecution, as the repressed sodomite hounds the animal as hunter or driver. The attraction stems from excessive attachment or develops at first sight; it can emanate from great figures, as in the case of malcontents and murderers of presidents, or from the most wretched, as in the pogrom itself. The objects of the fixation are replaceable like father figures in childhood; whatever it hits on fits its purpose; the delusion of relatedness strikes out unrelatedly. Pathic projection is a desperate exertion by an ego that, according to Freud, has a far weaker resistance to internal than to external stimuli: under the pressure of pent-up homosexual aggression the psychic mechanism forgets its most recent phylogenetic attainment, the perception of self, and experiences that aggression as an enemy in the world, the better to master it.

This pressure acts also, however, on the healthy cognitive process as a moment of its unreflecting naïveté, which tends toward violence. Wherever intellectual energies are concentrated on an external intention, wherever it is a matter of pursuing, ascertaining, grasping—of exerting those functions that have been sublimated from the primitive overpowering of animals into the scientific methods of controlling nature—the subjective process is easily overlooked in the schematization, and the system is posited as the thing itself. Objectifying thought, like its pathological counterpart, has the arbitrariness of a subjective purpose extraneous to the matter itself and, in forgetting the matter, does to it in thought the violence that later will be done in practice. The unconditional realism of civilized humanity, which culminates in fascism, is a special case of paranoid delusion that depopulates nature and finally nations themselves. In the abyss of uncertainty, which every objectifying act must bridge, paranoia installs itself. Because there is no absolutely compelling argument against materially false judgments, the distorted perception in which they lurk cannot be healed. Every percept unconsciously contains conceptual elements, just as every judgment contains unclarified phenomenalistic ones. Because imagination is involved in truth, it can always appear to this damaged imagination that truth is fantastic and its illusion the truth. The maimed subject lives on the element of imagination immanent in truth by ceaselessly putting it on show. Democratically, he insists on equal rights for his delusion, because, in fact, not even truth is stringent. While the citizen may admit that the anti-Semite is in the wrong, he requires the victim to be guilty too. Thus Hitler demands the right to practice mass murder in the name of the principle of sovereignty under international law, which tolerates any act of violence in another country. Like every paranoiac he takes advantage of the hypocritical identity of truth and sophistry; the distinction between them is as uncompelling as it nevertheless is strict. Perception is possible only insofar as the thing is already apprehended as determinate—for example, as a case of a genus or type. It is a mediated immediacy, thought infused with the seductive power of sensuality. It blindly transfers subjective elements to the apparent givenness of the object. Only the self-conscious work of thought—that is, according to Leibnizian and Hegelian idealism, only philosophy—can escape this hallucinatory power. As, in the course of cognition, thought identifies the conceptual moments that are immediately posited in perception and are therefore compelling, it progressively takes them back into the subject and strips them of their intuitive power. In this process every earlier stage, including science, turns out to be, in comparison to philosophy, a kind of percept, an estranged phenomenon permeated with unrecognized intellectual elements; persistence at this stage, without negation, forms part of the pathology of cognition. The subject that naively postulates absolutes, no matter how universally active it may be, is sick, passively succumbing to the dazzlement of false immediacy.

Such blindness is, however, a constitutive element of all judgment, a necessary illusion. Every judgment, even negative, is reassuring. However much a judgment may stress its own isolation and relativity for the purpose of self-correction, it must assert its own content, no matter how cautiously formulated, as something not merely isolated and relative. That constitutes its nature as judgment, whereas the clause merely entrenches a claim. Truth, unlike probability, has no gradations. The negating step beyond the individual judgment, which rescues its truth, is possible only insofar as it takes itself to be truth and in that sense is paranoid. True derangement lies only in the immovable, in thought's incapacity for the negation in which, unlike the fixed judgment, thought actually consists. The paranoid over-consistency, the bad infinity of never-changing judgment, is a lack of consistency in thought; instead of conceptually carrying through the failure of the absolute claim and thereby continuing to qualify his or her judgment, the paranoiac clings obdurately to the claim that has caused the judgment to fail. Instead of going further by penetrating its subject matter more deeply, thought places itself entirely in the hopeless service of the particular judgment. The latter's irresistibility is the same as its intact positivity, and the paranoiac's weakness is that of thought itself. For reflection, which in the healthy subject breaks the power of immediacy, is never as compelling as the illusion it dispels. As a negative, reflective movement not directed straight ahead, it lacks the brutality inherent in the positive. If the psychic energy of paranoia stems from the libidinal dynamic laid bare by psychoanalysis, its objective impregnability is founded on the ambiguity inseparable from the objectifying act; indeed, the latter's hallucinatory power will have been originally decisive. To clarify, it can be said in the language of natural selection theory that during the formative period of the human sensorium those individuals survived in whom the power of the projective mechanisms extended most deeply into their rudimentary logical faculties, or was least moderated by the premature onset of reflection. Just as, even today, practically fruitful scientific enterprises call for an unimpaired capacity for definition, for shutting down thought at a point designated by social need, for demarcating a field, which is then investigated in the minutest detail without passing outside it, paranoiacs cannot step outside a complex of interests designated by their psychological fate. Their mental acuteness consumes itself within the circle drawn by their fixed idea, as human ingenuity is liquidating itself under the spell of technical civilization. Paranoia is the shadow of cognition.

So calamitous is the mind's tendency to false projection that, as the isolated schema of self-preservation, such projection threatens to dominate everything that goes beyond self-preservation: culture. False projection is the usurper in the realm of freedom as of culture; paranoia is the symptom of the half-educated. For such people, all words become a system of delusion, an attempt mentally to occupy the regions to which their experience does not extend, violently to give meaning to a world that makes them meaningless, but at the same time to denigrate the intellect and the experience from which they are excluded and to burden them with the guilt really borne by the society that has brought about that exclusion. The half-educated, who, unlike the merely uneducated, hypostatize limited knowledge as truth, cannot endure the breach between inward and outward, individual fate and social law, appearance and essence, which for them is heightened to unbearable levels. To be sure, their suffering does contain an element of truth, compared to the mere acceptance of the given to which superior understanding has sworn allegiance. Nevertheless, the half-educated reach out stereotypically in their fear for the formula that suits their need, now to justify the disaster that has happened, now to predict the catastrophe still to come, which is sometimes disguised as a regeneration. The explanation, in which their own desires appear as an objective power, is always as external and meaningless as the isolated event itself, at once feeble-minded and sinister. The obscurantist systems of today bring about what the devil myth of the official religion enabled people to do in the Middle Ages: to imbue the outside world with an arbitrary meaning, which the lone paranoiac now constructs according to a private schema shared by no one, and which only for that reason appears actually mad. Relief is provided by the dire conventicles and panaceas that put on scientific airs while cutting off thought: theosophy, numerology, naturopathy, eurythmy, teetotalism, Yoga, and countless other sects, competing and interchangeable, all with academies, hierarchies, and specialist jargon, the fetishized officialese of science and religion. When confronted by an educated public, they remained apocryphal and disreputable. But today, when education itself is withering for economic reasons, unprecedented conditions are created for the paranoia of the masses. The belief systems of the past, which were embraced by the populace as self-contained paranoid forms, had wider meshes. Just because they were so rationally elaborated and specific, they left room, at least above them, for culture and mind, which, conceived as spirit, were their true medium. Indeed, to an extent they counteracted paranoia. Freud calls neuroses—even rightly in this instance—"asocial formations"; "they endeavor to achieve by private means what is affected in society by collective effort."[c] Those belief systems retain something of the collectivity that preserves individuals from pathological symptoms. The sickness is socialized: in the intoxication of the communal ecstasy—indeed, as itself a community—blindness becomes a relationship and the paranoid mechanism is made controllable, without losing the power to strike terror. Perhaps that was one of the major contributions of religions to the survival of the species. Paranoid forms of consciousness tend to give rise to leagues, factions, rackets. Their members are afraid to believe their madness on their own. Projecting it, they everywhere see pros-

[c] Sigmund Freud, *Totem and Taboo*, in *Standard Edition*, 13: 73.

elytizing and conspiracy. The established group has always taken a paranoid stance toward others; in this the great empires, indeed, organized humanity as a whole, are no better than headhunters. Those who were excluded from humanity against their will, like those who excluded themselves from it out of longing for humanity, knew that the pathological cohesion of the established group was strengthened by persecuting them. Its normal members relieve their paranoia by participating in the collective one, and cling passionately to the objectified, collective, approved forms of delusion. The *horror vacui* with which they devote themselves to their confederacies welds them together and gives them their almost irresistible power.

With bourgeois property, education and culture spread, driving paranoia into the dark corners of society and the psyche. But since the real emancipation of humanity did not coincide with the enlightenment of the mind, education itself became sick. The less social reality kept pace with educated consciousness, the more that consciousness itself succumbed to a process of reification. Culture was entirely commoditized, disseminated as information, which did not permeate those who acquired it. Thought becomes short-winded, confines itself to apprehending isolated facts. Intellectual connections are rejected as an inconvenient and useless exertion. The developmental moment in thought, its whole genetic and intensive dimension, is forgotten and leveled down to what is immediately present, to the extensive. The present order of life allows the self no scope to draw intellectual or spiritual conclusions. Thought, stripped down to knowledge, is neutralized, harnessed merely to qualifying its practitioner for specific labor markets and heightening the commodity value of the personality. In this way the self-reflection of the mind, which counteracts paranoia, is disabled. Finally, under the conditions of late capitalism, the half-educated condition has become the objective spirit. In the totalitarian phase of government its exponents reinstate the provincial charlatans of politics, and with them the system of delusion, as the *ultima ratio*, imposing it on the majority of the administered, who have already been softened up by big politics and the culture industry. The absurdity of the present system of rule is so transparent to healthy consciousness that it needs sick consciousness to keep itself alive. Only those suffering from persecution mania can tolerate the persecution that domination inevitably becomes, provided they are allowed to persecute others.

In fascism, where the responsibility for wife and child painfully inculcated by bourgeois civilization is being obscured by the individual's insistent conformity to regulations, conscience is being liquidated in any case. Contrary to the ideas of Dostoyevsky and the German apostles of inwardness, conscience consisted in the self's devotion to something substantial outside itself, in the ability to make the true concerns of others one's own. This ability involves reflection as an interpenetration of receptivity and imagination. Because the abolition of the independent economic subject by big industry—partly by absorbing free entrepreneurs and partly by transforming the workers into objects of trades unions—is irresistibly eroding the basis of moral decisions, reflection, too, must wither. The soul, as the possibility of guilt aware of itself, decays. Conscience is deprived of objects, since individuals' responsibility for themselves and their dependents is replaced—although still under the old moral title—by their mere performance for the apparatus. The internal conflict of drives, in which the agency of conscience is formed, can no longer be worked through. If internalized, the social injunctions not only would be made both more binding and more open but also would be emancipated from society and even turned against it; instead, the individual identifies himself or herself promptly and directly with the stereotyped scales of values. The exemplary German woman, who has a monopoly on femininity as the true German man has on masculinity, and their counterparts elsewhere, are conformist, asocial human types. Despite and because of its obvious deficiency, the system of power has become so preponderant that powerless individuals can avert their fate only through blind compliance.

In face of such power, it is left to chance—guided by the Party—to decide where despairing self-preservation is to project the guilt for its terror. The Jews are the predestined target of this guided chance. The circulation sphere, in which they once held positions of economic power, is vanishing. The liberal form of commercial enterprise once endowed fragmented wealth with political influence. Now, no sooner emancipated, its owners are merged with the state apparatus and placed at the mercy of capital powers that have outgrown competition. No matter what the makeup of the Jews may be in reality, their image, that of the defeated, has characteristics that must make totalitarian rule their mortal enemy: happiness without power, reward without work, a homeland without frontiers, religion without myth. These features are outlawed by the ruling powers because they are secretly coveted by the ruled. The former can survive only as long as the latter turn what they yearn for into an object of hate. They do so through pathic projection, since even hatred leads to union with the object—in destruction. It is the negative of reconciliation. Reconciliation is Judaism's highest concept, and expectation its whole meaning. The paranoid reaction stems from the incapacity for expectation. The anti-Semites are realizing their negative absolute through power, by transforming the world into the hell they have always taken it to be. A radical change would depend on whether the ruled, in the face of absolute madness, could master themselves and hold the madness back. Only the liberation of thought from power, the abolition of violence, could realize the idea that has been unrealized until now: that the Jew is a human being. This would be a step away from the anti-Semitic society, which drives both Jews and others into sickness, and toward the human one. Such a step would fulfill the fascist lie by contradicting it: the Jewish question would indeed prove the turning point of history.[4] By conquering the sickness of the mind that flourishes on the rich soil of self-assertion unhampered by reflection, humanity would cease to be the universal antirace and become the species that, as nature, is more than mere nature, in that it is aware of its own image. The individual and social emancipation from domination is the countermovement to false projection, and no longer would Jews seek, by resembling it, to appease the evil senselessly visited on them as on all the persecuted, whether animals or human beings.

VII

But there are no longer any anti-Semites. The last of them were liberals who wanted to express their antiliberal opinions. By the end of the nineteenth century the old-style conservative aloofness of the nobility and the officer corps toward the Jews was merely reactionary. The people abreast of the times were the Ahlwardts and the Knüppelkunzes.[5] They drew their followers from the same groups as the führer, but their support came from troublemakers and malcontents throughout the country. When people voiced anti-Semitic attitudes, they felt they were being bourgeois and rebellious at the same time. Their nationalistic grumbling was still a distorted form of civil freedom. The beer hall politics of the anti-Semites exposed the lie of German liberalism, on which it fed and whose demise it finally brought about. Even though they used their own mediocrity as a license to subject the Jews to beatings in which universal murder was already latent, they were economically farsighted enough to weigh the risks of the Third Reich against the advantages of a hostile form of tolerance. Anti-Semitism was still a competing motif within a range of subjective choices. But the outcome related specifically to it. The whole chauvinistic vocabulary was implied from the start in the adoption of the *völkisch* thesis. Anti-Semitic views always reflected stereotyped thinking. Today only that thinking is left. People still vote, but only between totalities. The anti-Semitic psychology has largely been replaced by mere acceptance of the whole fascist ticket,[6] which is an inventory of the slogans of belligerent big business. Just as, on the ballot paper of the mass party, voters are presented with the names of people remote from their experience for whom they can vote only *en bloc*, the central ideological concepts have been codified into a small number of lists. One has to opt for one of them *en bloc* if one's own position is not to seem as futile as splinter votes on polling day in face of the statistical mammoths. Anti-Semitism has practically ceased to be an independent impulse and has become a plank in the platform: anyone who gives fascism its chance subscribes to the settlement of the Jewish question along with the breaking of the unions and the crusade against Bolshevism. The anti-Semite's conviction, however mendacious it may be, has been absorbed into the preconditioned reflexes of the subjectless exponents of a particular standpoint. When the masses accept the reactionary ticket containing the clause against the Jews, they are obeying social mechanisms in which individual people's experiences of Jews play no part. It has been shown, in fact, that anti-Semitism's prospects are no less good in "Jew-free"[7] areas than in Hollywood itself. Experience is replaced by cliché, the imagination active in experience by diligent acceptance. The members of each class have to absorb their quota of guidelines on pain of rapid downfall. Just as they need to be instructed on the technical merits of a particular aircraft, so do they, too, on their allegiance to one of the prescribed agencies of power.

In the world of mass production, stereotypes replace intellectual categories. Judgment is based no longer on a real act of synthesis but on blind subsumption. If, at an early historical stage, judgment consisted in the swift decision that immediately unleashed the poisoned arrow, in the meantime exchange and the institutions of law have taken their effect. The act of judgment passed through a stage of deliberation that afforded the judging subject some protection from brutal identification with the predicate. In late-industrial society there is a regression to judgment without judging. When, in fascism, the protracted legal process was replaced by an accelerated procedure in criminal trials, up-to-date people had been economically prepared for this development. They had learned to see things unreflectingly, through ready-made thought models, the *termini technici* that provide them with iron rations following the decay of language. The perceiver is no longer present in the process of perception. He or she is incapable of the active passivity of cognition, in which categorial elements are appropriately reshaped by preformed conventional schemata and vice versa, so that justice is done to the perceived object. In the field of the social sciences, as in that of individual experience, blind intuition and empty concepts are brought together rigidly and without mediation.[8] In the age of the "three hundred basic words" the ability to exercise judgment, and therefore to distinguish between true and false, is vanishing. Thinking, where it is not merely a highly specialized piece of professional equipment in this or that branch of the division of labor, is suspect as an old-fashioned luxury: "armchair thinking." It is supposed to "produce" something. The more superfluous physical labor is made by the development of technology, the more enthusiastically it is set up as a model for mental work, which must not be tempted, however, to draw any awkward conclusions. That is the secret of advancing stupidity, on which anti Semitism thrives. If, even within the field of logic, the concept stands opposed to the particular as something merely external, anything that stands for difference within society itself must indeed tremble. Everyone is labeled friend or foe. The disregard for the subject makes things easy for the administration. Ethnic groups are transported to different latitudes; individuals labeled "Jew" are dispatched to the gas chambers.

The indifference to the individual expressed in logic draws its conclusions from the economic process. The individual had become an impediment to production. The lack of synchronicity between technical and human development, the "cultural lag" that used to exercise the minds of sociologists, is beginning to disappear. Economic rationality, the vaunted principle of the smallest necessary means, is unremittingly reshaping the last units of the economy: businesses and human beings. The most advanced form at a given time becomes the predominant one. Once, the department store expropriated the old-style specialist shop. The latter, having outgrown mercantilist regulation, had absorbed initiative, control, and organization within itself and become, like the old mill and smithy, a little factory, a free enterprise. Its mode of operation was complicated, expensive, risky. Competition therefore replaced it with the more efficient, centralized form of retail shop, the department store. The psychological small business—the individual—is meeting the same fate. It came into being as the power cell of economic activity. Emancipated from the tutelage of earlier economic stages, individuals fended for themselves alone: as proletarians by hiring themselves out through the labor market and by constant adaptation to new technical conditions, as entrepreneurs by tirelessly realizing the ideal type of *homo oeconomicus*. Psychoanalysis has portrayed the internal small business that thus came into being as a complex dynamic of unconscious and conscious elements, of id, ego, and superego. In its negotiations with the superego, the ego, the agency of social control within the individual, keeps the drives within the limits set by self-preservation. The areas of friction are large, and neuroses, the incidental expenses of such a drive economy, inevitable. Nevertheless, this complex psychical apparatus made possible the relatively free interplay of subjects that constituted the market economy. In the era of large combines and world wars, however, the mediation of the social process by innumerable monads is proving obsolete. The subjects of the drive economy are being psychologically expropriated, and the drive economy is being more rationally operated by society itself. The individual no longer has to decide what he or she is supposed to do in a given situation in a painful inner dialogue between conscience, self-preservation, and drives. For the human being as wage earner the decision is taken by a hierarchy extending from trade associations to the national administration; in the private sphere it is taken by the schema of mass culture, which appropriates even the most intimate impulses of its forced consumers. The committees and stars function as ego and superego, and the masses, stripped of even the semblance of personality, are molded far more compliantly by the catchwords and models than ever the instincts were by the internal censor. If, in liberalism, the individuation of a section of the population was necessary for the adaptation of society as a whole to the state of technology, today the functioning of the economic apparatus demands that the masses be directed without the hindrance of individuation. The economically determined direction of the whole society, which has always governed the mental and physical constitution of human beings, is causing the organs that enabled individuals to manage their lives autonomously to atrophy. Now that thinking has become a mere sector of the division of labor, the plans of the authorized experts and leaders have made individuals, who plan their own happiness, redundant. The irrationality of the unresisting and eager adaptation to reality becomes, for the individual, more reasonable than reason. If, previously, the bourgeois had introjected the compulsions of conscience and duty into themselves and the workers, now the entire human being has become at once the subject and the object of repression. In the progress of industrial society, which is supposed to have conjured away the law of increasing misery it had itself brought into being, the concept that justified the whole—the human being as person, as the bearer of reason—is going under. The dialectic of enlightenment is culminating objectively in madness.

This is also a madness of political reality. As a dense web of modern communications, the world has become so standardized that the differences between diplomatic breakfasts in Dumbarton Oaks and Persia have to be specially devised as an expression of national character, while actual national peculiarity is experienced primarily by the millions hungering for rice who have fallen through the narrow meshes. Although the abundance of goods that could be produced everywhere and simultaneously makes the struggle for raw materials and markets seem ever more anachronistic, humanity is nevertheless divided into a small number of armed power blocs. They compete more pitilessly than the firms involved in the anarchy of commodity production ever did, and strive toward mutual liquidation. The more senseless the antagonism, the more rigid the blocs. Only the total identification of the population with these monstrosities of power, so deeply imprinted as to have become second nature and stopping all the pores of consciousness, maintains the masses in the state of absolute apathy that makes them capable of their miraculous achievements. As far as any decisions are still left to individuals, they are effectively decided in advance. The irreconcilability of the ideologies trumpeted by the politicians from the different camps is itself just one more ideology of the blind constellation of power. Ticket thinking, a product of industrialization and its advertising, is being extended to international relations. Whether a citizen chooses the communist or the fascist ticket depends on whether he happens to be more impressed by the Red Army or the laboratories of the West. The reification by virtue of which the power structure, made possible solely by the passivity of the masses, appears to those same masses as an iron reality, has been consolidated to the point where any spontaneity, or even the ability to conceive of the true state of affairs, has necessarily become an eccentric utopia, an irrelevant sectarianism. Illusion has become so concentrated that to see through it objectively assumes the character of hallucination. To vote for a ticket, by contrast, means to practice adaptation to illusion petrified as reality, which endlessly reproduces itself through such adaptation. The reluctant voter is therefore ostracized as a deserter. Since Hamlet, hesitation has for modern people been a sign of reflection and humanity. The wasted time at once represented and mediated the gap between individual and universal, as circulation does between consumption and production in the economy. Today individuals receive their tickets ready-made from the powers that be, as consumers receive their automobiles from the sales outlets of factories. Conformity to reality, adaptation to power, no longer are the result of a dialectical process between subject and reality but are produced directly by the cogs and levers of industry. The process is one of liquidation instead of sublation, of formal instead of determinate negation. The unleashed colossi of production have subdued the individual not by granting him or her full satisfaction but by extinguishing the subject. Precisely therein lies their perfect rationality, which coincides with their insanity. The extreme disproportion between collective and individual eliminates tension, but the untroubled harmony between omnipotence and impotence is itself unmediated contradiction, the absolute antithesis of reconciliation.

For this reason the psychological determinants of the individual—which have always been the internal human agencies of wrong society—have not disappeared with the individual itself. However, these character types are now being assigned to their mathematically exact positions within the coordinates of power. Both their efficiency and their coefficient of friction are included in the calculation. The ticket acts as a gearwheel in this process. Anything in the old psychological mechanism that was compulsive, unfree, and irrational is precisely adjusted to it. The reactionary ticket that includes anti-Semitism is suited to the destructive-conventional syndrome. It is not so much that such people react originally against the Jews as that their drive-structure has developed a tendency toward persecution, which the ticket then furnishes with an adequate object. The "elements of anti-Semitism" once derived from experience and now rendered inoperative by the loss of experience reflected in ticket thinking, are remobilized by the ticket. Being already corrupted, these elements also provide the neo-anti-Semite with the bad conscience and thus with the insatiability of evil. Just because the psychology of the individual can now construct itself and its content only from the synthetic schemata supplied by society, contemporary anti-Semitism takes on its empty but impenetrable character. The Jewish middleman fully becomes the image of the devil only when economically he has ceased to exist. Victory is thus made easy, and the anti-Semitic family man becomes the spectator, exempt from responsibility, of an irresistible historical tendency, intervening only when called to do so by his role as an employee of the Party or the Zyklon gas factories. As they designate obsolete sections of the population for extermination, the administrations of totalitarian states are merely the executors of economic verdicts passed long ago. Members of other branches of the division of labor can look on with the indifference of people reading newspaper reports on clean-up operations at the scene of yesterday's catastrophe. The peculiarities for the sake of which the victims are killed have long been effaced. Those who fall within the terms of the decree as Jews have to be identified by means of elaborate questionnaires, now that the antagonistic religions that once differentiated them have been successfully remodeled and assimilated as cultural heritage under the leveling pressure of late-industrial society. The Jewish masses themselves are no more immune to ticket thinking than the most hostile youth organization. In this sense fascist anti-Semitism is obliged to invent its own object. Paranoia no longer pursues its goal on the basis of the individual case history of the persecutor; having become a vital component of society it must locate that goal within the delusive context of wars and economic cycles before the psychologically predisposed "national comrades" can support themselves on it, both inwardly and outwardly, as patients.

The tendency according to which anti-Semitism now exists as only one item on an interchangeable ticket gives irrefutable reason to hope for its end. The Jews are being murdered at a time when the leaders could replace the anti-Semitic plank in their platform just as easily as their followers can be transplanted from one location of wholly rationalized production to another. The development that leads to ticket thinking is based, in any case, on the universal reduction of every specific energy to the one, identical, abstract form of labor, from the battlefield to the studio. However, the transition from those conditions to a more human state cannot take place, because benign and malign tendencies suffer the same fate. The

freedom on the progressive ticket is as far removed from the existing political power structures, to which progressive decisions necessarily lead, as
hostility to the Jews is external to the chemical cartel. To be sure, the psychologically more humane are attracted to freedom, but the advancing loss
of experience is finally turning even the supporters of the progressive ticket
into enemies of difference. It is not just the anti-Semitic ticket that is anti-
Semitic, but the ticket mentality itself. The rage against difference that is
teleologically inherent in that mentality as the rancor of the dominated
subjects of the domination of nature is always ready to attack the natural
minority, even though it is the social minority that those subjects primarily
threaten. The socially responsible elite is in any case far harder to pin down
than other minorities. In the murky intertwinement of property, ownership, control, and management, it successfully eludes theoretical definition. The ideology of race and the reality of class both equally reveal only
an abstract difference from the majority. But although the progressive
ticket tends to produce something worse than its content, the content of
the fascist ticket is so vacuous that it can be maintained as a substitute for
something better only by desperate efforts on the part of the deceived. Its
horror is that of the blatant but insistent lie. While it admits no truth by
which it might be measured, its absurdity is so monstrous as to bring truth
negatively within reach, so that it can be kept apart from those deprived of
judgment only by their total abstention from thought. Enlightenment itself, having mastered itself and assumed its own power, could break
through the limits of enlightenment.

(1947; GS 3: 192–234)
Translated by Edmund Jephcott

21

Selections from *Metaphysics:*
Concept and Problems

Lecture Fourteen, "The Liquidation of the Self"
(15 July 1965)

At the end of the last lecture I attempted to explain why temporal elements decisively affect our thinking about metaphysics, and have a bearing on metaphysical experience itself. And I should like to say to you straightaway that it would be mistaken to take these comments in a purely subjective sense—as meaning that it is more difficult to have metaphysical experiences under present conditions. That would be a complete misunderstanding of what I wish to communicate to you in words that inevitably are far too insipid. Naturally, the subjective difficulty also exists, but given the intertwinement between subjective experience and the objective in this sphere, the two cannot be separated as neatly as it might appear to a naive, unreflecting consciousness, which says that all this just depends on how one happens to feel toward metaphysics today, but changes nothing at all in its objective contents. My thesis is directed against precisely this attitude, and you will only understand me correctly if you take what I have to say in the strong and far from innocuous sense in which it is meant. You will have noticed from my analyses and expositions of Aristotle's *Metaphysics* how far this whole metaphysics is filled by the affirmative side—forgive me, something can hardly be filled by a "side"—how fundamental the affirmative moment is to this whole conception of metaphysics. You will therefore have seen how far the theory that, even without a divine influence, being is teleologically orientated toward the divine by its own nature—however far that may imply that which is meaningful. From this Aristotle draws the conclusion—I mention this to make fully clear the metaphysical problem that concerns me here—that matter, ὕλη as that which is represented by possibility, must be endowed with some kind of purposiveness; and he argues this even despite the fact that it is in some contradiction to his own doctrine of possibility as wholly abstract and indeterminate. In the face of the experiences we have had, not only through Auschwitz but through the introduction of torture as a permanent institution and through the atomic bomb—all these things form a kind of coherence, a hellish unity—in the face of these experiences the assertion that what is has meaning, and the affirmative character that has been attributed to metaphysics almost without exception, become a mockery; and in the face of the victims it becomes downright immoral. For anyone who allows himself to be fobbed off with such meaning moderates in some way the unspeakable and irreparable things that have happened by conceding that somehow, in a secret order of being, all this will have had some kind of purpose. In other words, it might be said that in view of what we have experienced—and let me say that it is also experienced by those on whom it was not directly perpetrated—there can be no one, whose organ of experience has not entirely atrophied, for whom the world *after* Auschwitz, that is, the world in which Auschwitz was possible, is the same world as it was before. And I believe that if one observes and analyzes oneself closely, one will find that the awareness of living in a world in which that is possible—is possible *again* and is possible *for the first time*—plays a quite crucial role even in one's most secret reactions.

I would say, therefore, that these experiences have a compelling universality, and that one would indeed have to be blind to the world's course if one were to wish *not* to have these experiences. In view of them, the assertion of a purpose or meaning that is formally embedded in metaphysics is transformed into ideology, that is to say, into an empty solace that at the same time fulfills a very precise function in the world as it is: that of keeping people in line. No doubt metaphysics has always had its ideological aspects, and it is not difficult to demonstrate in detail in what ways the great metaphysical systems have functioned ideologically. But unless I am mistaken, something like a qualitative leap has taken place at this point. That is to say that, although the old metaphysical systems transfigured the existing order by insisting on this moment of meaning, they always had the moment of truth at the same time; they tried to understand that which is, and to gain certainty about the enigmatic and chaotic. And one could always demonstrate in the older metaphysics, no less than in their ideological character, this moment of truth, this increasing power of reason to understand what is opposed to it, and not to be content with mere irrationality. This can be seen most splendidly in the metaphysics of St. Thomas Aquinas, which is an attempt to bring Christian doctrine into agreement with speculative thought, and therein has the potential to transform what is merely posited and inculcated dogmatically into a kind of critique—however positive this critique may have been in the Thomist philosophy. That is now finished. Such an interpretation of meaning is no longer possible. And I believe I have already said[1] that it seems to me an achievement of Jean-Paul Sartre that should not be overlooked—although I regard his philosophy as very incoherent and not really adequate as a philosophical structure—that he was the first to formulate this realization without any embellishment. In this he went far beyond Schopenhauer, who, of course, was a pessimist in the usual sense and vehemently opposed the affirmative character of metaphysics (as you probably know), especially in its Hegelian form. Nevertheless, in his work he turned even this negativity into a metaphysical principle, the principle of the blind Will, which, because it is a metaphysical principle and therefore a category of reflection, contains the possibility of its own negation by human beings. Thus, he also posits the idea of the denial of the Will to Live,[2] a denial that, in view of what has been and continues to be perpetrated on the living and can increase to an unimaginable degree, is an almost comforting idea. I mean that, in a world that knows of things far worse than death and denies people the shot in the neck in order to torture them slowly to death, the doctrine of the denial of the Will to Live itself has something of the innocence for which Schopenhauer criticized the theodicies of philosophers.

After the Lisbon earthquake, Voltaire, who had been a follower of Leibniz, abandoned Leibniz's interpretation of the world as the best of all possible worlds and went over to the empiricism of the most progressive figure of that time, Locke.[3] Admittedly, Leibniz's dictum is not so optimistic as it seems but refers only to the optimum, the minimum optimum. But what, in the end, is such a limited natural catastrophe compared to the natural catastrophe of society, spreading toward totality, the actuality and potentiality of which we face today—when socially produced evil has engendered something like a real hell? And that situation affects not only metaphysical thought but, as I showed you in relation to the moment of meaning, the content of metaphysics itself. And perhaps I may add at this point that there seems to me to be hardly anything more contemptible, hardly anything more unworthy of the concept of philosophy, of what philosophy once wanted to be, than the mood, especially widespread in Germany, that amounts to a belief that, just because the absence of meaning is unbearable, those who point out that absence are to be blamed. This mood leads people to draw from the postulate that life in a world without meaning cannot be endured the conclusion that (because what should not be cannot be) a meaning must be constructed: because, after all, *there is* a meaning. If I may reveal to you what I really meant by the "jargon of authenticity,"[4] I was not just criticizing this or that linguistic cliché—I should not have taken those quite so tragically. What I was really attacking—and if you pick up that little book I would ask you to be quite clear on this point—is precisely the supposition of a meaning on the sole grounds that there must be one since otherwise one could not live: this supposition of a meaning as a *lie*. And in Germany this supposition seems to me to have slipped into the language to a worrying degree, so that it is no longer made explicitly in thought. That is the reason why I attacked a certain linguistic form so energetically in that book.

Briefly, therefore: the traditional compatibility between metaphysical thought and intramundane experience has been shattered. As I indicated by the comparison between Voltaire's situation and our own, there has been a kind of switch from quantity to quality. The millionfold death has acquired a form never feared before, and has taken on a very different nuance. "Nuance"—the word alone is a disgrace in the face of what one would like to say, for which language truly lacks words; it actually cannot be said. And that is the strongest proof of how much these things can now be understood only in material terms. Today something worse than death is to be feared. Perhaps I might draw your attention in this context to an essay on torture by Jean Améry, an author otherwise entirely unknown to me, in the latest issue of *Merkur*.[5] The philosophical backbone of the essay, existentialism, does not accord with my own views, but the author does quite admirably express the changes in the rock strata of experience that have been brought about by these things. The change I have in mind can also be expressed, perhaps most simply, by saying that death, in the form it has taken on, no longer accords with the life of any individual. For it is a lie to say that death is an invariant at all times; death, too, is a quite abstract entity; death itself can be a different thing in very different times. Or, one might say, if you will not take my literary references amiss, that there is no longer an epic or a biblical death; no longer is a person able to die weary, old, and sated with life. Another aspect of the situation I am trying to indicate to you is that old age, with categories such as wisdom and all that goes with it, no longer exists, and that old people, insofar as they are condemned to become aged and too weak to preserve their own lives, are turned into objects of science—the science of gerontology, as it is called. In this way age is seen as a kind of second minority, so that something like a program of euthanasia carried out by some future form of inhumanity, of no matter what provenance, becomes foreseeable. Thus, the reconciliation of life, as something rounded and closed in itself, with death, a reconciliation that was always questionable and precarious and, if it existed at all, was probably a happy exception—that reconciliation is out of the question today.

I would say that the approach adopted in *Being and Time*—and here I'd like to make a few more comments on the "jargon of authenticity"—is perhaps nowhere more ideological than when its author tries to understand death on the basis of "Dasein's possibility of Being-a-Whole,"[6] in which attempt he suppresses the absolute irreconcilability of living experience with death, which has become apparent with the definitive decline of positive religions. He seeks, in this way, to rescue structures of the experience of death as structures of *Dasein*, of human existence itself. But these structures, as he describes them, existed only within the world of positive theology, by virtue of the positive hope of resurrection; and Heidegger fails to see that through the secularization of this structure, which he at least tacitly assumes in his work, not only have these theological contents disintegrated, but without them this experience itself is no longer possible. What I really hold against this form of metaphysics is the surreptitious attempt to appropriate theologically posited possibilities of experience without theology. I hasten to add, to avoid misunderstandings, however unlikely, that in view of the historical state of consciousness my remarks should not, of course, be construed as a recommendation of theology, simply on the grounds that, under the protection of religion, it was allegedly easier to die. Now, if one is speaking of the form of death that exists under the absolute controllability of people, including their mass annihilation, one will have to say that from an intramundane standpoint the change signifies that the process of adaptation to which people are subject is posited as *absolute*—just as torture is an extreme form of adaptation. Words such as "brainwashing" already indicate that by these horrifying means, which include the electric shock treatment of the mentally ill, human beings are to be standardized by force. Any slight difference, any deviation they still possessed in relation to the dominant tendency—that too must be eradicated.

In other words, the change that we are experiencing in metaphysics is on the most fundamental level a change in the self and its so-called substance. It is the liquidation of what the old metaphysics sought to encompass by a rational doctrine of the soul as something existing in itself. Brecht has characterized this experience, though in a very uncertain and ambiguous way, with his formula "A man's a man."[7] I would just point out (but will not be able to go into this in detail in these lectures) that it is here, in the question of the liquidation of the self or the ego, in the question of depersonalization, that the most unfathomable problems of metaphysics are concealed; for this ego itself, as the incarnated principle of self-preservation, is involved in the context of social guilt right to its innermost core. And in its social liquidation today the self is only paying the price for what it once did by positing itself: repaying the debt of its guilt. This is a horizon of metaphysical speculation that I can only touch on here, since one cannot speak at all seriously about these things without knowing at least whether the concept of the person itself, into which, for so many—for example, Martin Buber, who died recently—the metaphysical substance has withdrawn and concentrated itself, is not precisely the node that needs to be removed in order to liberate that which might be different in human beings. One should not, therefore, regard the liquidation of the ego that we are witnessing today as absolutely evil and negative, since to do so would probably be to make into the principle of good and bad something that itself is entangled in evil, and that bears within it a historical dynamic that prevents it from being hypostatized. For people chained to the blind principle of self-preservation under the prevailing social conditions of production, however, this liquidation of the ego is what is most to be feared. And in the present situation, in order to recognize the dialectic between the ego and its disintegration that I have just touched upon, or to gain any insight into present conditions, what is called for is precisely that unyielding and unerring strength of the ego in the face of the predominant tendency that is obstructed by the historical tendency, and that is realized in fewer and fewer people now. What meets its end in the camps, therefore, is really no longer the ego or the self, but—as Horkheimer and I called it almost a generation ago in *Dialectic of Enlightenment*[8]—only the *specimen*; it is, almost as in vivisection, only the individual entity reducible to the body or, as Brecht put it,[9] the torturable entity, which can be happy if it has time to escape that fate by suicide. One might say, therefore, that genocide, the eradication of humanity, and the concentration of people in a totality in which everything is subsumed under the principle of self-preservation are *the same thing*; indeed, that genocide is absolute integration. One might say that the pure identity of all people with their concept is nothing other than their death—an idea that, most surprisingly and remarkably, though with a quite different, reactionary accent, is anticipated in the theory in the *Phenomenology of Spirit* by which Hegel equates absolute freedom with death.[10] I do not need to engage polemically with the denunciation of the French Revolution, which Hegel had in mind at that point; but it is the case that the early Hegel, with his unparalleled speculative power, had an inkling of the fact that absolute self-assertion and the absolute negation of all that lives, and thus, finally, genocide, are the same thing, at a time—more than one hundred and fifty years ago—when nothing of that kind was foreseeable within the actual historical perspective. In this connection, a formulation—reported by Kogon in his book on the "SS state" that was said to have been used by SS henchmen against earnest Bible scholars moments before their end, made an indelible impression on me. They are said to have told them: "Tomorrow you shall wind from this chimney as smoke to the heavens."[11] That is no doubt the most exact formulation of the satanic perversion of the metaphysical idea and of the substance of metaphysics itself that we are forced to witness today.

When I said that these experiences affect everyone, and not only the victims or those who narrowly escaped them, I did not mean only that the experiences I have tried to characterize are of such terrible violence that no one whom they have touched, even from a distance, so to speak, can ever escape them—as Améry says very convincingly in his essay, no one who has once been tortured can ever forget it again, even for a moment.[12] By saying that I also referred to something objective, and, again, my intention in pointing this out is that you should not simply equate the things I am speaking of today with the subjectivity of the person who experiences them. A situation has been reached today, in the present form of the organization of work in conjunction with the maintenance of the existing relations of production, in which every person is absolutely fungible or replaceable, even under conditions of formal freedom. This situation gives rise to a feeling of the superfluity and, if you like, the insignificance of each of us in relation to the whole. That is the reason, located in the objective development of society, for the presence of the feeling I have referred to, even under conditions of formal freedom. I am trying, inadequately as ever, to express these changes for you today, because I have the feeling that to speak of metaphysics without taking account of these things would really be nothing but empty verbiage. In my view, these experiences have such deep objective reasons that they are actually untouched even by political forms of rule, that is, by the difference between formal democracy on the one hand and totalitarian control on the other. That, at least, is how matters have appeared up to now. But we must also be well aware that, just because we live under the universal principle of profit and thus of self-preservation, the individual has nothing more to lose than himself and his life. At the same time—as Sartre has shown in his doctrine of the absurdity of existence—the individual's life, though it is all he has, has become, objectively, absolutely unimportant. Yet what he must know to be meaningless is forced on him as the meaning of his life; indeed, a life that is really no more than the means to the end of his self-preservation is, by that very fact, bewitched and fetishized as an end. And in this antinomy—on the one hand the debasement of the individual, of the self, to something insignificant, his liquidation, and on the other, his being thrown back on the fact that he no longer has anything but this atomized self that lives our life—in this contradiction lies the horror of the development that I regard it as my duty to present to you today.

I once said that after Auschwitz one could no longer write poetry,[13] and that gave rise to a discussion I did not anticipate when I wrote those words. I did not anticipate it because it is in the nature of philosophy— and everything I write is, unavoidably, philosophy, even if it is not concerned with so-called philosophical themes—that nothing is meant quite literally. Philosophy always relates to tendencies and does not consist of statements of fact. It is a misunderstanding of philosophy, resulting from its growing closeness to all-powerful scientific tendencies, to take such a statement at face value and say: "He wrote that after Auschwitz one cannot write any more poems; so either one really cannot write them, and would be a rogue or a cold-hearted person if one did write them, or he is wrong, and has said something that should not be said." Well, I would say that philosophical reflection really consists precisely in the gap, or, in Kantian terms, in the vibration, between these two otherwise so flatly opposed possibilities. I would readily concede that, just as I said that after Auschwitz one *could not* write poems—by which I meant to point to the hollowness of the resurrected culture of that time—it could equally well be said, on the other hand, that one *must* write poems, in keeping with Hegel's statement in his *Aesthetics*[14] that as long as there is an awareness of suffering among human beings there must also be art as the objective form of that awareness. And, heaven knows, I do not claim to be able to resolve this antinomy, and presume even less to do so since my own impulses in this antinomy are precisely on the side of art, which I am mistakenly accused of wishing to suppress. Eastern-zone newspapers even said I had declared my opposition to art and thereby adopted the standpoint of barbarism. Yet one must ask a further question, and this is a metaphysical question, although it has its basis in the total suspension of metaphysics. It is, in fact, curious how all questions that negate and evade metaphysics take on, precisely thereby, a curiously metaphysical character. It is the question whether one can *live* after Auschwitz. This question has appeared to me, for example, in the recurring dreams that plague me, in which I have the feeling that I am no longer really alive, but am just the emanation of a wish of some victim of Auschwitz. Well, the bleaters of connivance soon turned this into the argument that it was high time for anyone who thought as I did to do away with himself as well—to which I can only respond that I am sure those gentlemen would like nothing better. But as long as I can express what I am trying to express, and as long as I believe I am finding words for what otherwise would find none, I shall not, unless under extreme compulsion, yield to that hope, that wish. Nevertheless, something said in one of the most important plays by Sartre, which for that reason is hardly ever played in Germany, deserves to be taken immensely seriously as a metaphysical question. It is said by a young resistance fighter who is subjected to torture, who asks whether or why one should live in a world in which one is beaten until one's bones are smashed.[15] Since it concerns the possibility of any affirmation of life, this question cannot be evaded. And I would think that any thought that is not measured by this standard, that does not assimilate it theoretically, simply pushes aside at the outset that which thought should address—so that it really cannot be called a thought at all.

Lecture Fifteen, "Metaphysics and Materialism" (20 July 1965)

I do not wish to recapitulate or sum up what I said in the last lecture, but would remind you that we arrived at the idea that the question whether it is still possible to live is the form in which metaphysics impinges on us urgently today. Without being a follower of Spengler one might well compare this situation to that of the philosophy of late antiquity, in which, in response to the same question, people fell back on expedients such as ataraxy, that is, the deadening of all affects, just to be capable of living at all. I cannot undertake a critique of Stoicism here. There is undoubtedly much that impels us toward the Stoic standpoint today, as appears very clearly in some motifs of Heidegger, especially in his early work. But I would say that even this standpoint, although it emphatically embraces the idea of the freedom of the individual, nevertheless has a moment of narrow-mindedness in the sense that it renders absolute the entrapment of human beings by the totality, and thus sees no other possibility than to submit. The possibility of seeing through this situation as a context of guilt concealed through blinding, and thus of breaking through it, did not occur to that entire philosophy. Stoicism did, it is true, conceive for the first time the idea of the all-encompassing context of guilt, but it did not discern the moment of necessary illusion in that context—and that, I would say, is the small advantage that we, with our social and philosophical knowledge, enjoy over the Stoic position. It should be said, at any rate, that the guilt in which one is enmeshed almost by the mere fact of continuing to live can hardly be reconciled any longer with life itself. Unless one makes oneself wholly insensitive one can hardly escape the feeling—and by feeling I mean experience that is not confined to the emotional sphere—that just by continuing to live one is taking away that possibility from someone else, to whom life has been denied; that one is stealing that person's life. Similarly, a society that in its absurd present form has rendered not work but people superfluous predetermines, in a sense, a statistical percentage of people of whom it must divest itself in order to continue to live in its bad, existing form. And if one does live on, one has, in a sense, been statistically lucky at the expense of those who have fallen victim to the mechanism of annihilation and, one must fear, will still fall victim to it. Guilt reproduces itself in each of us—and what I am saying is addressed to us as subjects—since we cannot possibly remain fully conscious of this connection at every moment of our waking lives. If we—each of us sitting here—knew at every moment what has happened and to what concatenations we owe our own existence, and how our own existence is interwoven with calamity, even if we have done nothing wrong, simply by having neglected, through fear, to help other people at a crucial moment, for example—a situation very familiar to me from the time of the Third Reich—if one were fully aware of all these things at every moment, one would really be unable to live. One is pushed, as it were, into forgetfulness, which is already a form of guilt. By failing to be aware at every moment of what threatens and what has happened, one also contributes to it; one resists it too little; and it can be repeated and reinstated at any moment.

It is not my style to justify philosophy just because it is my job, if one may put it so paradoxically. I am aware, heaven knows, how dubious it is to occupy oneself with philosophy in a world like the one in which we live. But—since one always seeks justification for what one does—there is, perhaps, a certain justification for occupying oneself with philosophy in that, as the one form of knowledge that has not yet been departmentalized, split into branches, reified, it seems to me to represent the only chance, within the boundaries of this departmentalized world, of making good at least a part of what, as I have tried to explain to you, is otherwise denied. If one is not oneself capable at each moment of identification with the victims, and of alert awareness and remembrance, philosophy, in the necessary forms of its own reification, is perhaps the only form of consciousness that, by seeing through these matters and making them conscious in a more objective form, can at least do *something*, a small part of that which we are unable to do. And it must be admitted that to do this in a universal way would by far overtax the strength of any individual person. Yet it must be said—when circling around the problems of metaphysics in this connection, as I am doing now—that the world in which we live arouses a kind of mistrust toward philosophy from a different point of view from the one I have set out up to now. The fact is that the deeper philosophy grows and the further it is removed from the surface of the merely existent, the harder it becomes to free oneself of the feeling that, through its depth and re-moteness from mere existence, philosophy is also growing remote from the way things really and actually are, *comment c'est,* as Beckett puts it.[1] One has the feeling that the depth of philosophical reflection, which is neces-sary as a resistance to all the illusion with which reified consciousness sur-rounds us, at the same time leads away from the truth, since one some-times suspects that this same existence, which it is the inalienable impulse of philosophy to penetrate and go beyond, is the only thing that exists and is worth reflecting upon *at all.* The considerations concerned with the cri-sis of the concept and of meaning, and the impossibility of restoring mean-ing to existence, which I set out in the last lectures, point in exactly this di-rection. And I believe that you need only to apply these considerations to the question I am presenting to you at this moment and you will quite eas-ily see the problem that, on the one hand, any construction of a meaning, however constituted, is forbidden to us, but that, on the other, the task of philosophy is precisely to *understand,* and not simply to reflect, what hap-pens to be, or to copy it, to use Kant's expression. This has placed philoso-phy in a true quandary. One sometimes has the feeling that the prevalent positivist science is right in capturing only the most superficial and trivial and thus the most external relationships with its classifying procedures, whereas essence, once disclosed, aims at depth. As a metaphysical thinker, that is, someone who cannot do otherwise than seek to understand, one is sometimes overcome by the eerie suspicion that understanding itself is an illusion that one ought to be rid of, and that precisely the superficial mind, which merely registers facts, which one resists with every fiber of one's be-ing, may in the end be right. One must, as it were, include common sense and human triviality in metaphysical meaning; one must incorporate it in speculation as the principle that ensures that the world merely is as it is and not otherwise, if the depth of speculation is not to be false, that is, a depth that confers an *illusory* meaning.

By contrast, however, the joy of thought, which motivates us to think on metaphysical matters in the first place and to raise the questions I have discussed in the course of these lectures, is simply the joy of eleva-tion, the joy of rising beyond what merely is. And one of the most painful thoughts that can afflict someone who engages in philosophy is that, in giving way to this joy of philosophizing—in refusing to be bargained out of truth by mere being—one is being lured into a demonic situation by this very truth. If the pedestrian replacement of knowledge by the mere registering, ordering, and summarizing of facts were to have the last word against the elevation of thought, truth itself would really be a chimera, and there would be no truth, for truth would be no more than the practicable summarizing and arranging of the merely existent. The suspicion that I am expressing here and that, I would say, is an indispensable *moment* of philosophical speculation, is that trivial, positivist awareness may today be closer to the *adaequatio rei atque intellectus* than sublime consciousness. I believe that the only way out of this dilemma would be to reflect on the idea of truth itself, and to grasp truth, not as an *adaequatio*, not as a mere measuring against factual circumstances, but as a procedure adopted toward a being of a quite different nature and dimension, and tied to a quite different procedure of consciousness than mere registration. But in the face of this pedestrian or positivist motif that mind really consists in nothing other than counting the feet of the millipede—and I can say that everything I think is just one single resistance to that conception of mind—the impulse opposed to it can probably survive only by adopting the principle: renounce, that you may gain. That is to say, one will survive not by preserving some so-called higher spheres, or what I would prefer to call nature reserves, which reflection is not allowed to touch, but by pushing the process of demythologizing, or enlightenment, to the extreme. Only in this, if at all, is there any hope that the philosopher, through his self-reflection, will not end by consummating triviality, the consummation of which is absolute horror. For no matter how one may view the works of Hannah Arendt, and I take an extremely critical view of them, she is undoubtedly right in the identification of evil with triviality.[2] But I would put it the other way round; I would say, not that evil is trivial, but that triviality is evil—triviality, that is, as the form of consciousness and mind that adapts itself to the world as it is, that obeys the principle of inertia. And this principle of inertia truly is what is radically evil. I would say, therefore, that if metaphysical thinking today is to have any chance, and is not to degenerate into claptrap about a "new protectedness" [*neue Geborgenheit*][3] and suchlike nonsense, it will have to cease being apologetic and pointing to something one can hold onto and never lose, and think against itself. And that means that it must measure itself against the ultimate, the absolutely unthinkable, to have any right to be a thinking at all.

NB

Ladies and Gentlemen, in the last lecture I spoke about Auschwitz and said that because of the things that happened there—for which I used only the name "Auschwitz," although, of course that name stands for something unthinkable beyond the unthinkable, namely, a whole historical phase—metaphysics has been changed in its innermost motifs. I could, if you like, give this a moral-philosophical twist and say that Hitler has placed a new imperative on us: that, quite simply, Auschwitz should not be repeated and that nothing like it should ever exist again. It is impossible to found this imperative on logic—it has that in common with the Kantian imperative. When Kant states that his own imperative is simply given, that assertion doubtless contains all kinds of grimly authoritarian and irrationalist elements, but also—as I tried to explain to you in my lectures last semester[4]—an awareness that the sphere of right action does not coincide with mere rationality, that it has an "addendum."[5] I believe that an attempt to state as a general law why Auschwitz or the atom bomb or all those things that belong together here should not be repeated would have something utterly feeble about it because it would transfer into the sphere of rationality, which is ultimately the secondary sphere of mind, the right to a jurisdiction that it can only usurp. It is also the case—and this does belong within that sphere—that as soon as one attempts to apply logic here one is drawn into an insoluble dialectic. Consider one of the dreadful semicolonial wars that are so characteristic of our time, in which one party—and one can always toss a coin to decide which one it is—tortures and commits dreadful atrocities, so that the other is also forced to torture, as it claims, to prevent its opponent from doing so. I do not wish to explore the validity or otherwise of such considerations, but just to say that as soon as one attempts to provide a logical foundation for a proposition such as that one should not torture, one becomes embroiled in a bad infinity, and probably would even get the worst of the logical argument, whereas the truth in this proposition is precisely what falls outside such a dialectic. And I do not think you will misunderstand this statement as advocating a form of irrationalism or a belief in some natural law directly accessible to intuition. All that is far from my intention. What I wish to point out is this practical moment, which does not coincide with knowledge but is constitutive of moral philosophy. The extralogical element to which I am appealing—to make this quite clear and to rule out any irrationalism—is really that which is conjured away by philosophy and rationalism. But what they conjure away is not irrational moments or values, as is claimed, but the converse: it is quite simply the moment of aversion to the inflicting of physical pain on what Brecht once called the torturable body[6] of any person.

If I say to you that the true basis of morality is to be found in bodily feeling, in identification with unbearable pain, I am showing you from a different side something that I earlier tried to indicate in a far more abstract form. It is that morality, that which can be called moral, i.e. the demand for right living, lives on in openly materialist motifs. The metaphysical principle of the injunction "Thou shalt not inflict pain"—and this injunction is a metaphysical principle pointing beyond mere facticity—can find its justification only in the recourse to material reality, to corporeal, physical reality, and not to its opposite pole, the pure idea. Metaphysics, I say, has slipped into material existence. Precisely this transition of metaphysical questions and, if I might state it so grandly, of metaphysics itself to the stratum of the material is what is repressed by the conniving consciousness, the official yes-saying of whatever ilk. As a child, I believe, one still knows something about this stratum—with the dim knowledge children have of such things. It is the zone that later materialized literally in the concentration camps; as a child one had an inkling of it in subliminal experiences—as when the dog-catcher's van drove by, or suchlike things: one knew that that was the most important thing of all, that was what really mattered, the zone of the carcass and the knacker. And this unconscious knowledge—that that was the most important thing to know—is, no doubt, hardly less significant than infantile sexuality, which, as Freud has demonstrated, is extremely closely related to this sphere and has a very great deal to do with it. I would say that this feeling that the most wretched physical existence, as it confronts us in these phenomena, is connected to the highest interests of humanity has hardly been thought through properly up to now, but has been only skirted by thought. I believe the education we undergo as students is perhaps the only place where we find out anything about these matters—in anatomy in the study of medicine. And the terrible excitement that that zone arouses in students in their first semester—all this seems to point to the fact that that is where the truth is hidden, and that the most important thing of all is to divest ourselves of the civilizing mechanisms that, again and again, blind us to that sphere. It is almost as if philosophy—and most of all the great, deep, constructive philosophy—obeyed a single impulse: to get away from the place of carrion, stench, and putrefaction. And just because of this distance, which gains its depth from that most wretched place, philosophy is no doubt in perennial danger of itself becoming something just as thin, untrue, and wretched. I would remark in passing that the reflections I am presenting to you, however fragmentary they may be, may perhaps help you to understand why the dramas of Beckett, which, as you know,[7] seem to me to be the only truly relevant metaphysical productions since the war, constantly end up in this sphere. And the cheap jibe that Beckett can never get away from urns, refuse bins, and sand heaps in which people vegetate between life and death—as they actually vegetated in the concentration camps—this jibe seems to me just a desperate attempt to fend off the knowledge that these are exactly the things that matter.

If one realizes that everything we call culture consists in the suppression of nature and any uncontrolled traces of nature, then what this culture finds most unbearable are those places where it is not quite able to control natural manifestations, where they intrude persistently into its own domain, as in the case of the dark stratum I just spoke about. It might be said that culture banishes stench because it itself stinks—which Brecht once formulated in the truly magnificent and inspired statement that humanity up to now had built itself an immense palace of dogshit.[8] I believe that culture's squalid and guilty suppression of nature—a suppression that is itself a wrongly and blindly natural tendency of human beings—is the reason why people refuse to admit that dark sphere. And if one really wants to cure philosophy of its ideological, dissembling character, which has reached an almost unendurable level today, then this is probably the τόπος νοητός, the point of recognition, where that transformation should be achieved. If what I have tried to explain—in extreme terms—about the concept of culture is true, and if it is the case that philosophy's only *raison d'être* today is to gain access to the unsayable, then it can be said that Auschwitz and the world of Auschwitz have made clear something that was not a surprise to those who were not positivists but had a deep, speculative turn of mind: that culture has failed to its very core. This was also stated by Marx in the magnificent formulations in his drafts for *Capital*, which he later suppressed, in which he spoke of the narrow-mindedness of all culture up to that time.[9] The same idea was, of course, expressed by Nietzsche, who, because his attention was fixated on the cultural superstructure, peered more deeply into it than any other. The reason can be seen most clearly in the fact that philosophy, art, and rational science have not really impinged on human beings, to whom they are necessarily addressed as their ideal subject. I recall a visit to Bamberg, when the question was raised whether the spectacle of the indescribably beautiful and intact town, partly medieval and partly baroque, had had even a slightly beneficial influence on the people living there. If I only mention the word "Bamberg," I think the question answers itself.[10]

But when I speak of culture, more is at stake than its failure in relation to human beings, for the autonomy that culture has acquired cannot be canceled simply by demanding that it should now address itself to human beings, that it should be something for them or give something to them. Culture, especially in its great manifestations, is not some kind of social, pedagogical institution, but has its truth—if it has any—only within itself. And it can fulfill what might be its meaning for human beings only by *not* thinking of them but by being purely and consistently formed within itself. However, such is the blindness of the world's course that any such tendency is generally held against culture as a lack of love, a failure to adapt in the specific way people require. But, leaving that aside, I believe that untruth is also lodged in the autonomous zones of mind. And if I give such prominence to what can be criticized in the products of the objective mind, in a way that may make some of you uncomfortable, I do so because I believe it essential, in liberating human beings from the veil of ideology, to make them aware of the moment of untruth precisely where it mistakes itself for truth, and mindlessness for mind. We see this perhaps most clearly in the area that, many years ago, directly after my return from America, I called the resurrected culture,[11] a culture that was rehashing its traditional values of truth, beauty, and goodness as if nothing had happened. For this whole sphere of resurrected culture is itself precisely the refuse, the rubbish from which, as I said earlier, culture is trying to escape. This resurrected culture resembles the ruins it has cleared away; having removed them it then reinstalled itself on them in the wretchedly makeshift way that is symbolically revealed by the outward image of our rebuilt cities. This culture has now become *wholly* the ideology that, through the division between mental and physical work, it has always *partly* been. In the face of this, one is caught in an antinomy; for anyone who pleads for the preservation of this culture makes himself an accomplice of its untruth and of ideological illusion in general; but whoever does not do so and demands the creation of a *tabula rasa* directly promotes the barbarism over which culture had elevated itself and which the mediations of culture had actually moderated. Not even silence leads out of this circle, since he who keeps silent, who says nothing at all—and, heaven knows, the temptation to do that is strong enough—not only attests to his incapacity to say what needs to be said, but interprets this subjective incapacity as permitting a serene detachment with regard to objective truth. The abolition of culture as perpetrated in the Eastern bloc, that is, culture's transformation into a mere instrument of power, only combats like with like, since culture has always been enmeshed with power. But this abolition is not, itself, better than culture, but even worse, since it strangles even the element of promise and hope that culture had contained and that went beyond the ever-sameness of control and turns it back into direct oppression—while trying to convince people that this state of direct oppression is freedom. In pointing to this cultural and philosophical antinomy, therefore, I believe I have also expressed a political one.

Lecture Sixteen, "Consciousness of Negativity" (22 July 1965)

I am afraid you may be thinking[1] that I have adjourned the discussion of metaphysical subjects by inquiring into the possibility of saying anything about those subjects. But that inquiry has been not into a particular subject, of whatever kind, as happens in the current idealist theories, but into culture itself. I appear to be measuring metaphysics by the state of culture, making the answers to so called metaphysical questions depend on a consciousness of the historico-cultural situation, whereas, according to current notions, which endow metaphysics with an absolute truth transcending all human conditionality, no such constitutive relationship should be attributed to that kind of consciousness. I think I owe it to you, therefore, to say something about the intertwinement between what is commonly called culture and metaphysical questions. You will have noticed that at some crucial points in my argument—and the discussion I am carrying on at present is what people call a methodological discussion—I have *not* drawn the currently accepted, epistemological conclusion from the intracultural experiences of metaphysics: that while the consciousness of the absolute depends on the given state of cultural consciousness, the absolute itself is untouched by it. I think it may be useful here, while we are inquiring into the possibility of metaphysics, to provide a decisive clarification of this point, so that you do not have the impression that I am evading the crucial issue or trying to muddy the waters with inconsistent thinking. My position is as follows: such a question—how the things that have happened were possible—not only has an epistemological or nosological influence on the question about the nature of metaphysics but really and *directly* affects the metaphysical answers. I believe, in other words, that the metaphysical thesis of the inherent meaning of the world, or of a cosmic plan underlying everything that happens, must be called into question at the very moment when a meaningful connection can no longer be established between what has happened and the metaphysical ideas. The moment one falls back on the wholly abstract notion of the world's inscrutable ways—and the attribution of inscrutable ways to anything has always been calamitous—the assumption of metaphysical meaning itself (and not just our consciousness of it) is shattered. For I believe that we have nothing except our reason, that we have no option but to measure by our concrete experience, and that within the constellations that now define our experience all the traditional affirmative or positive theses of metaphysics—I think I can put it most simply like this—simply become blasphemies.

There are many people who, in the face of the resulting despair, take refuge in theology. I think it should be said that the demand this places on them and on their concept of the absolute—the implication that these things[2] could be located within the meaning of the absolute itself—effectively demonizes the absolute. This possibility was already implicit in dialectical theology as the doctrine of the "wholly Other," which turns God into an abyss.[3] It then irrupted, with overwhelming force, into the work of Kafka, where traditional theological categories are measured against experience in a way that turns them into their opposite, a sinister mythology or demonology.[4] That is what I had in mind. And for that reason I ask you to understand that the connections between culture and metaphysics that I now propose do not relate to the spectacles we look through or the glass window behind which we are trapped,[5] but that the events I have referred to relate directly to reality at its most essential level. They bring about a switch from quantity to quality, in that while such horrors have always been present, and theological justification has always found it desperately difficult to come to terms with them, what earlier appeared mysterious and unfathomable only in individual cases has now become so much a part of the objective and universal course of the world that, in the face of the preponderance of this objective order, any attempt at harmonization with the so-called cosmic plan or providence necessarily degenerates into lunacy. The theology of crisis—the name given to the dialectical theology going back to Karl Barth's commentary on the Epistle to the Romans[6]—detected the fateful intertwinement of metaphysics and culture with that against which they abstractly and impotently protested. It is undoubtedly the enormous merit of all these thinkers—Emil Brunner,[7] Ebner,[8] Friedrich Gogarten,[9] and some others apart from Barth (although there were others whose thought took a sinister turn)[10]—to have recognized that the immanence of culture, and the amalgamation of cultural categories and ideas with metaphysical ones, has the tendency to deprive these ideas themselves of their objective truth, to reduce them to the level of the subject, or to mind (*Geist*), as the ancestor of this movement, Kierkegaard, called it. Kierkegaard also said that such tendencies "mediate" the ideas, although, if you will forgive me the pedantry, he entirely misunderstood the Hegelian concept of mediation, which is a mediation *within the extreme itself.* Kierkegaard understood this concept of mediation from outside, as a kind of bridge between the absolute and the finite, contingent human mind. This intertwinement of self-deceiving culture and an inner decay of the metaphysical ideas was registered with extraordinary honesty and rigor by the dialectical theologians. But (as is demonstrated in the still unpublished book of Hermann Schweppenhäuser),[11] they were denied the fruits of their insight, or remained trapped in a subjectivist position—the position they most vehemently opposed—by believing that the answer lay in the notion of the absolutely different and indeterminate, which they opposed to the decay of metaphysics. This concept of the absolutely Other, they thought, was what was needed. What can be said about this concept of the absolutely Other is that either it remains entirely indeterminate and abstract, so that it cannot perform what it is supposed to perform, or it takes on determinants that are themselves subject to the criticism of these theologians, since they are determinants of immanence, or, finally—and this is the path taken by most of these thinkers—this content is summoned up from outside, in a dogmatic and arbitrary leap, so that the dialectic that forms the core of this theological standpoint is at the same time revoked by it. The fact is that the principle of the absolute spirit, which is a curiously indifferent determinant existing between transcendence and the quintessence of the human mind as its own most comprehensive totality, tirelessly destroys what it purports to express. It ceaselessly absorbs into itself what it seeks to formulate as the absolute, which is supposedly impervious to such assimilation. For this reason—and on this point Hegel, if you like, needs to be taken beyond himself—its supreme concept, the absolute, in which everything is supposed to come to rest, becomes dialectical within itself, so that spirit, in becoming absolute for itself, is at the same time, by virtue of everything that is, absorbed into the mind as a human entity, thus destroying the transcendence or absoluteness of the idea that it asserts.

    I believe that the first conclusion to be drawn from this—which was *not* drawn by the dialectical theologians, who, despite the doctrine of the absolutely other, continued to use the traditional words of theology without interruption—is that noble, elevated words (and things such as Auschwitz cannot be thought except in words, if I may repeat the point) can no longer be used. This is not only for the reasons I have already set out—that lofty words have become simply incommensurable with experience—but for the, if you like, far more devilish reason that it is characteristic of evil today to appropriate the most noble and elevated words for its own use. It is practically the trademark of totalitarian movements that they have monopolized all the so-called sublime and lofty concepts, while the terms they use for what they persecute and destroy—base, insectlike, filthy, subhuman, and all the rest—they treat as anathema. And the dissimulating tissue or spell I have spoken of is so tightly woven that anyone who refuses to conform, and thus truly stands for otherness, is almost always disparaged as base, while ideals have, to an almost inconceivable degree, become a screen for vileness. And one of the most important goals (apart from those I have already mentioned) that I set myself in my text on the "jargon of inauthenticity," if I might allude to it again, was to analyze this mechanism and to show concretely how the sublime, elevated traditional words have become a cover for baseness, exploitation, oppression, and evil. One would need to be a very superficial and, if you like, a very nominalistic linguistic philosopher to deny that this experience of being unable to take certain words into one's mouth—which you can all have and which was probably first registered, though in a very different way, in Hugo von Hofmannsthal's "Chandos" letter[12]—also says something about what the words stand for. I believe that one of the crucial points on which the theory I advocate, and of which I can present you at least some sizable fragments in these lectures, differs from the currently prevalent one is my view that the historical-philosophical fate of language is at the same time the historical-philosophical fate of the subject matter to which it refers. This is supported, incidentally, by a viewpoint which was by no means foreign to German idealism, and especially to Wilhelm von Humboldt: that language constitutes thought no less than thought language. This insight has in the meantime been trodden so flat by nominalism that few people can remember it, although any reflection on thought can show you to what degree thought is as much mediated by language as vice versa. Karl Kraus's entire work can be understood as demonstrating that the fate of language is the history of the decay of the contents embodied in language, so that the decline of language within bourgeois society is for him an index of what has become of the great ideas themselves.

I can perhaps clarify what I am saying here, and what is constitutive of the standpoint toward metaphysics that I am trying to outline for you in these last lectures, by telling you a story about something that happened, I believe, last year. I was on holiday in the company of a writer whom I value highly for his moral integrity; he had spent many years in a concentration camp—a Jew, one of the persecuted—and had had the strength to record and objectify the things he had seen in the camps. And he is one of the few to whom we owe it that, thanks to his report, we can render the only service to the victims of which we are still capable: not to forget them.[13] I went walking with this man—we were in high mountains—and when the talk turned to Beckett he revealed an extremely violent affect against that writer, giving vent to the comment: "If Beckett had been in a concentration camp he probably would not write these despairing things; he'd write things that gave people courage." I believe that the confusion manifested in this remark—the subjective motivation of which I fully understand and respect after what that man had gone through—throws light on the specific character that ideology has taken on in dealing with metaphysical concepts today. There is an American saying that there are no atheists in the trenches; the old German proverb that danger teaches us to pray points in the same direction—and, fundamentally, this heroic man had argued in a very similar way. This argument is illogical because the situations in which people are forced to think "positively" simply in order to survive are themselves situations of compulsion, which force people back on pure self-preservation, and on thinking only what they need to in order to survive in such a situation, to a point where the *truth content* of what they think is hopelessly undermined and utterly destroyed. It is possible that, had Beckett been in a concentration camp, he would not have written *The Unnamable* or *Endgame*, but I do not think it possible that this would have made what he wrote better or truer. The idea you will come across again and again in this context, that one has to give people something, has to give them courage—all these things are conditions that *restrict* the thinking of truth, but that may well bring down on someone who thinks the truth the odium of inhumanity, as I demonstrated to you earlier. But I also think that this mode of thinking, this demand placed on thought, does an injustice to the people in whose honor it is ostensibly made. Although this demand is seemingly made out of a charitable concern for the victims, in fact it reduces them to the objects of a thinking that manipulates and calculates them, and assumes in advance that it is giving them what they need and want. By the evaluation manifested in such ostentatiously noble injunctions, the people they pretend to serve are in reality debased. They are treated by metaphysics in fundamentally the same way as by the culture industry. And I would say that the criterion to be applied to any metaphysical question today is whether it possesses or does not possess this character of connivance with the culture industry. I recall, by contrast, that when, many years ago, immediately after the war, while we were still in America, Horkheimer and I read together Kogon's book on the "SS state,"[14] although it was the first to give us a full idea of what had happened, our mutual reaction was to experience the reading as something immensely liberating. And I am democratic enough to believe that what we experienced could be the same for all who concern themselves with these things, except that most people are so in thrall to current notions that they lack the courage for such an experience. If there is any way out of this hellish circle—and I would not wish to exaggerate that possibility, being well aware of the weakness and susceptibility of such consciousness—it is probably the ability of mind to assimilate, to think the last extreme of horror and, in the face of this spiritual experience, to gain mastery over it. That is little enough. For, obviously, such an imagination, such an ability to think extreme negativity, is not comparable to what one undergoes if one is oneself caught up in such situations. Nevertheless, I would think that in the ability not to feel manipulated, but to feel that one has gone relentlessly to the furthest extreme, there lies the only respect that is fitting:

a respect for the possibility of the mind, despite everything, to raise itself however slightly above that which is. And I think that it really gives more courage (if I can use that formulation) if one is *not* given courage, and does not feel bamboozled, but has the feeling that even the worst is something that can be thought and, because it falls within reflection, does not confront me as something absolutely alien and different. I imagine that such a thought is probably more comforting than any solace, whereas solace itself is desolate, since it is always attended by its own untruth.

There is a passage in Kant, in the theory of the dynamically sublime in *Critique of Judgment*, where he speaks of the feeling of the sublime. It is a remarkable passage, one of those in which Kant no longer uses the rococo diction of the eighteenth century but takes on, even in his language, the tone of the great German and English lyric poetry that emerged about 1780. In it he speaks of the feeling of the sublime as a peculiar vibration between the powerlessness felt by the empirical person in the face of the infinitude of natural forces, and, by contrast, the joy of mind, as the essence of freedom, in being superior to and stronger than this natural power.[15] Compared to the spacious grandeur that such a theory still has in Kant, we are now, heaven knows, crowded together on a tiny island. And what I am trying to express today certainly does not presume to reclaim for the self even a remnant of the autonomy and dignity that Kant was able to assert. But something of it still remains, though impalpable and extremely confined—and lies perhaps in the fact that the possibility of any change depends on the ability to become aware of the ultimate negativity, which is the negativity located in the fundamental strata and not just in ephemeral surface phenomena. Perhaps changes can be made today only through thoughts that do not directly aim at change. And it is characteristic that whenever one seriously expresses thoughts that do not address the question "Yes, but what am I supposed to *do*, here and now?"—one is regularly met with a howl of rage[16] (it can also be a silent howl) that respects no demarcation lines, political or otherwise, simply because it is unbearable *not* to give oneself up to some praxis or other. This is rationalized, and very well rationalized—it's difficult to say anything against it—by the argument: "Well, is the world supposed to stay as it is, with all its horrible possibilities? Should one not do something against it?" I honor this need; I would be the last to dare to say anything against it. I only ask you to consider, Ladies and Gentlemen, whether the compulsion to do something here and now, and the tendency to fetter thought that it contains, does not bring thought to a standstill precisely where it ought to go further, in order to reach the place where something can really be changed. When I once said—in an ironic and melancholy sense—that this is the time for theory, I meant only that. The spell that binds us today consists not least in the fact that it ceaselessly urges people to take *action* that they *believe* will break the spell; and that it prevents the *reflection* on themselves and the circumstances that might *really* break it. I believe that there is a precise correlation between these two phenomena: on the one hand, the rage that comes over people in the face of—shall we say?—reflection without consequences, and, on the other hand, the moment of liberation contained in such reflection. Those who appeal for action, for the sake of human beings, cheat them of their right, even if they believe the opposite—depriving them of their own possibility, their humanity. I give the same answer to those who accuse me of a "lack of love for human beings," because I give no guidelines for praxis and offer no consolation. I warn them that when there is talk of a lack of love there is almost always a desire that this love be somehow directed toward evil. And in the face of that, Strindberg's words in *Black Banners* are undoubtedly true: "How could I love good if I did not hate evil?"[17]

If one really understands the world of today as one of total entrapment, in the way I have tried to set out for you, I do not know how one could be uncritical, how one could adopt an attitude of unqualified love in the face of what is. But, of course, by confessing this one makes oneself the target of all the instincts and affects that are ready to be unleashed, with a great feeling of moral justification, against anything that tries to stretch out its head or its feelers even a little way. The desire for the existing culture to be swept away and an absolutely new start to be made has been very strong in Germany since the catastrophe. And I believe that the question of the position of metaphysics today has much to do with this desire—in that there has been a belief that, if only the debris of this culture could be finally cleared away, access could be gained to the original truth to which metaphysics points and which, according to this view, has been merely concealed by culture. This demand for a new beginning places the metaphysical thinker in a somewhat precarious position; he is rather like the women who picked over the rubble in the first years after the war. You are so young that most of you will probably not have heard of those women, who were once a familiar sight. The idea of a new start was extraordinarily compelling. Such tendencies had existed even before Hitler. There is, however, a curious ambivalence in this: on the one hand, critical thought—ideas of the kind I have set out for you in these lectures—is branded as destructive, and the pack is let loose on it; but at the same time the concept of destruction is monopolized by the same people who have used it negatively against others. I am thinking here of Herr Heidegger, who believed himself the true, that is, the positive, destroyer, who, by demolishing all the waste products of civilization, all the alienated, reified thinking, would open the way to the rightly prized authenticity of things. However, it was proved by subsequent events—irrevocably, I would say—that this attempt to demolish culture, this destruction carried out in the hope of gaining direct access to the absolute once everything that was mere θέσει had disappeared, led directly to barbarism and fascism. Now there is much to be criticized in culture (and I do not think that I could be suspected of adopting an apologetic or affirmative stance toward it)—not in its so-called degenerate manifestations but in its actual concept. But while culture has undoubtedly failed, through its own fault, and is being punished for that, the straightforward barbarism that is brought into being through its failure is always even worse. It is, I would say, a metaphysical fallacy into which I should like to prevent you from falling to believe that, because culture has failed, because it has not kept its promise, because it has denied human beings freedom, individuality, true universality, because it has not fulfilled its own concept, it should therefore be thrown on the scrap heap and cheerfully replaced by the cynical establishment of immediate power relationships. One of the most dangerous errors now lurking in the collective unconscious— and the word "error" is far too weak and intellectual for it—is to assume that because something is not what it promises to be, because it does not yet match its concept, it is therefore worse than its opposite, the pure immediacy that destroys it. On these grounds too, therefore, for reasons arising from the dialectical nature of culture, the abstract separation of culture from metaphysics that is taken for granted today cannot be endorsed.

Lecture Seventeen, "Dying Today" (27 July 1965)

I spoke in the last lecture about the interconnection of metaphysics and culture, and said that the spectacular failure of culture today had radically undermined the possibility of metaphysics. But I would now like to add—not only to prevent misunderstanding but because completeness of thought requires it—that the failure of culture does not give thought a kind of free passage to some natural state. It cannot do so because the failure of culture stems from its own naturalness, if I might put it like that; it is the result of its own persistent character as a natural entity. This culture has failed because it has clung to mere self-preservation and its various derivatives in a situation in which humanity has simply outgrown that principle. It is no longer confined by direct necessity to compulsive self-preservation, and is no longer compelled to extend the principle of mastery over nature, both inner and outer nature, into the indefinite future. On the other hand, it is idle and futile for thought to attempt now to appropriate metaphysics as a collection of pure categories that are immediate to consciousness, since knowledge can never disown its own mediatedness, or, in other words, its dependence on culture in every sense. Philosophy is itself a piece of culture, is enmeshed in culture; and if it behaves as if it were rendered immediate by some allegedly primal questions that elevate it above culture, it blinds itself to its own conditions and truly succumbs to its cultural conditionality; in other words, it becomes straightforward ideology. There is no knowledge that can repudiate its mediations; it can only reflect them. Both the alleged primal experiences and the threadbare categories of culture as something man-made are inalienably mediated and have their own negativity in this mediation. As long as culture lives on in a world arranged like ours, in which, whether in South Africa or Vietnam, things happen of which we know and only with difficulty repress the knowledge that they happen—in such a world, culture and all the noble and sublime things in which we take delight are like a lid over refuse. But nature, insofar as we believe we can share in its original qualities independently of culture, is no more than a projection of the cultural desire that everything should remain unchanged; that we should stay in the good, untrue old days, in the "aeon,"[1] to speak with Schelling, in which, as Kafka put it, no progress has yet taken place.[2]

That, I believe, is the framework within which one should think about the complex of ideas I have spoken about in these last lectures, in which I no longer took Aristotle's text as my starting point but directly presented some of my own reflections. I have already spoken repeatedly about this complex, which concerns the question of death. Death juts into culture, into the network of civilization, as something entirely alien, which cannot be mastered even with the best connections, and in the face of which one cannot cut a powerful figure. And because, if I may put it like this, culture has not integrated death—or, when it has done so, it has made itself as ridiculous as it is shown to be in Evelyn Waugh's novel *The Loved One*,[3] for example—philosophy has used death, expressly or tacitly, as the gateway through which to break into metaphysics. This has not just happened since Heidegger, by the way; it has always been said that death is the true spur to metaphysical speculation, that the helplessness of people in the face of death provides the impetus for thoughts that seek to penetrate beyond the boundaries of experience. The metaphysics of death seems to me in principle impotent—but not in the sense that one should not reflect on death. Curiously, Heidegger sought to use reflection on death to discourage, precisely, reflection on death,[4] and it is one of the quaintest features of his philosophy that, on the one hand, it gains its concept of authenticity, and thus its central speculative motor, through reflecting on what he calls the structure of death, but, on the other, he was furious with anyone who, as he contemptuously put it, "brooded" on death:[5] as if what he did was even slightly different from such brooding; indeed, as if any thought about death—which, of course, is something closed off and impenetrable to thought—could possibly be anything other than brooding. I bring this point to your attention only to show you how inconsistent his thought is, and how much, even on such a central matter, it is organized by privilege and the need for control. What appears to me to be the impotence of the metaphysics of death is not the fruitlessness of brooding, which Heidegger criticized, or the belief that in the face of death only a posture of tight-lipped readiness, or some such thing, was seemly. Incidentally, very similar formulations are to be found in Jaspers, in their cultivation of the heroic possibilities of death these two seemingly so antithetical thinkers got along very well. Heidegger's metaphysics is impotent, either because it necessarily degenerates into a kind of propaganda for death, elevating it to something meaningful, and thus, in the end, preparing people to receive the death intended for them by their societies and states as joyfully as possible—just as Professor Krieck[6] declared at this university during the Third Reich that only the sacrificial victims would make "you," meaning the students, free; or because—leaving aside this aspect of the death metaphysics, which justifies death as the meaning of existence—any reflections on death are of such a necessarily general and formal kind that they amount to tautologies, like the definition of death as the possibility of the absolute non-being of existence, which I quoted in *The Jargon of Authenticity*,[7] or another, less well-known formulation of Heidegger's, in which he solemnly announces that, when we die, a corpse is left behind.[8]

I believe that this insufficiency of consciousness in the face of death, its inability to extract the alleged meaning from it, has to do not only with the absolute inaccessibility of what is being talked about. I believe that if we leave aside the truly unfathomable question whether one can talk meaningfully about death at all, something else is in play, which is really connected with consciousness, and perhaps with the present state of consciousness, with history. Perhaps I might remind you once again—and this is probably one of the strongest arguments against the attempt to wring a metaphysics from death—that although nature, in the form of death, juts into society and culture as something not yet integrated, nevertheless the experience of death, the side that it turns toward us, the living, is undoubtedly determined in part by society. Dying, if not death, is certainly a social phenomenon, and if anyone took the trouble to investigate how people die, that person would find as many mediations of culture in this side of death that is turned toward us as in any other phenomena. But what I mean is something different, that human consciousness clearly is not capable of withstanding the experience of death. I am unsure whether we are dealing here with a kind of biological fact that extends back beyond our human and conscious history, or whether it is something historical. At any rate, it is the case that, in contrast to the other *animalia* known to us, humans are clearly the only ones that in general have a consciousness of the fact that they must die. But it seems to me—and I suspect that for reasons connected with social arrangements our mental organization is not equal to this knowledge—that although, with this knowledge, we have, if you like, elevated ourselves so far above nature that on this crucial point we can reflect on our natural origin, on the other hand, we are still so governed by nature on this same point, so attached to our interest of self-preservation, of self-perpetuation, that we can have this experience only in a curiously abstract form. I'd like to be very cautious here: if we were to bring vividly to mind, at each moment, that we must die . . . In any case, this is not a discovery of mine; in book 4 of Schopenhauer's *The World as Will and Representation* there is a passage in which he notes with surprise how untroubled people are, in the general course of their lives, by the thought of their mortality.[9] He explains this by the veil of Maya, and thus by the *principium individuationis*. I would say, rather, that there is a kind of internal antagonism in this, that people are, as it were, unequal to their own minds—an antagonism, moreover, which, if you consider the actual arrangement of the world in relation to the potentials over which human beings now have control, is being incessantly reproduced and intensified. Our consciousness has clearly remained too weak to withstand the experience of death; too weak because it is too much in thrall to the biological life of which consciousness is itself a kind of derivative, a diverted energy. Because consciousness imagines itself, in its forms, in the forms of pure thought, to be something eternal, it fortifies itself against anything that might remind it of its own unsteady floor, its own frailty. One might add to this an idea that Ernst Bloch has expressed again and again with extraordinary emphasis in our time;[10] apart from the motif of utopia, with which it is intimately connected, it is perhaps the decisive motif of Bloch's metaphysics: that in the world in which we exist there is not a single human life that remotely matches what each of us *could* be. It is, incidentally, an old thought, conceived in the Enlightenment by Helvetius, although in him it was still accompanied by the illusion that education was all that was needed to change this and to make us, if I might put it like this, equal to our own possibility, to attain an identity between our potentiality and our actuality.[11] We know now, of course, that the mechanisms preventing us from doing so extend deeply into the organization of the very self that Helvetius, and the Enlightenment thinkers in general, believed could be changed and perfected simply by becoming conscious. I would say that only if we were truly ourselves, only if the infinite possibility that is radically contained in every human life—and you may think me an old-fashioned Enlightenment thinker, but I am deeply convinced that there is no human being, not even the most wretched, who has not a potential that, by conventional bourgeois standards, is comparable to genius—only if such a state were reached, in which we were really identical to that which we are not but which we deeply know we could become, though we may want to believe the contrary—only then might we have the possibility of being reconciled to death. Only then, probably, would we be equal to the experience of death, and as long as that possibility is attributed to any other condition, it is merely a lie. So deeply, I would say, is the metaphysics of death, unlike the distorted version of it concocted by a static ontology, bound up with history and with the deepest strata of humanity's historical life.

The metaphysics of death, as practiced today, is, it seems to me, much more a vain solace for the fact that human beings have lost what may at earlier times have made death endurable: the unity of experience. I would say, in general, that the problematic feature of all the resurrected metaphysical systems, which one would probably need to destroy to be free to reflect on these matters without ideology, is that they act as a kind of substitute; and that what is most deeply suspect in the popular metaphysical systems of today is that they always convey the message, even if peripherally and as if from far off, that things are not really so bad. That is to say, they try to reassure people about certain essentialities that, precisely, have become problematic. I am referring here, above all, to *time*. There can be little doubt that the awareness human beings have of time, and the very possibility of a continuous experience of time, has been deeply disrupted. And it seems to me to be a precise response to this situation, though actually a mere reflection of it, that the current metaphysical systems are now attempting to rescue this conception of time, which is no longer accessible to experience, and to present temporality as a constituent of existence itself. These systems therefore have a tendency to conjure up what is no longer experienced. And that is the true reason—which goes much deeper than a superficial, so-called sociological interpretation—why the current metaphysical thinkers sympathize in this curious way with archaic conditions no longer important to society, especially with agrarian conditions or those of a simple, small-town barter economy. The so-called epic death, which is presented in Heidegger's doctrine of death as a necessary moment of the "wholeness of existence," and which is really at the root of all these death metaphysics, is no longer possible, because such a wholeness of life no longer exists. In my introduction to Walter Benjamin's *Schriften*[12] I attempted to express the idea that a concept such as "the life's work" has become problematic today because our existence has long ceased to follow a quasi-organic law immanent to it, but is determined by all kinds of powers that deny it such an immanent unfolding; and that a belief in such a wholeness of life, to which death might correspond as something meaningful, already has the character of a chimera. But I should like to go further. It has doubtless become obvious by now that the notion of wholeness is a kind of ersatz metaphysics, because it attempts to underpin the assertion of meaningful being or meaningful life

(v) with the positivist credentials of something immediately given, as in *Gestalt* theory. But I should like to go a step even beyond that. For it might be

vid ↓ asked whether that kind of epic wholeness of life, the biblical idea that Abraham died old and sated with life, whether this wishful image of a life stretching out in time so that it can be narrated, and rounded off in its own death, was not always a mere transfiguration. I cannot escape the suspicion that wherever such a harmony between a self-contained life and death appears to have existed in the past, the life of those to which the harmony is attributed was subjected to so inordinate a burden, was, as one is apt to say today, so alienated from them, that they did not even get so far as to perceive the heterogeneousness of death, and integrated themselves with death out of a kind of weakness. Consequently, the idea of a complete life, meaningful within itself, must probably be abandoned with the conception of the epic death—for catastrophes always have the power to draw into themselves remote realities and events from the distant past. If mortally weary people take an affirmative view of death, it is most likely the case that death relieves them of a burden. The reason for the allegedly positive relationship to death taught by these metaphysics is none other than the one that comes forcibly to mind today, and that I already mentioned: that the life in question amounted to so little that there was little resistance to its ending.

[n.b.] It is remarkable, all the same, that we are so little able to incorporate death, since, in view of our continuing state of nonidentity with ourselves, the opposite might be expected. And even the power of the instinct of self-preservation—if one wishes to speak of an instinct here; Freud did sanction it by introducing the concept of the ego drives[13]—seems to me insufficient to explain it, if it is taken on its own. As far as I am able to observe these matters, it is the case that it is precisely the people who are not old and frail who put up no resistance to death, who experience it as contingent and, in a curious way, accidental. If a very large number of people fall victim to accidents today, in comparison to earlier times, this seems to me to indicate something structural in the experience of death: that to the precise extent that we are relatively autonomous beings aware of ourselves, we experience death, or even a serious illness, as a misfortune that comes upon us from outside. At the same time, however, it is also the case that, when people die very old, their great age often does not appear as something joyous. I am speaking here of the intramundane aspects of death, which reflection on death cannot ignore, but in which it has shown itself curiously uninterested up to now. I am not speaking here of the discomforts associated with old age in the epic ideal. But, as far as my experience extends, there is also something immeasurably sad in the fact that, with the decline of very old people, the hope of *non confundar*, of something that will be preserved from death, is also eroded, because, especially if one loves them, one becomes so aware of the decrepitude of that part of them that one would like to regard as the immortal that one can hardly imagine what is to be left over from such a poor, infirm creature, which is no longer identical with itself. Thus, very old people, who are really reduced to what Hegel would call their mere abstract existence, those who have defied death longest, are precisely the ones who most strongly awaken the idea of absolute annulment. Nevertheless, this experience of death as something fortuitous and external—rather like an illness one has been infected with, without knowing its source—does contain a moment connected with the autonomy of mind. It is that, because the mind has wrested itself so strongly from what we merely are, has made itself so autonomous, this in itself gives rise to a hope that mere existence might not be everything.

If one does not cling to the thesis of the identity of subject and object taught by idealism; if the subject, mind, reflecting itself critically, does not equate itself to, and "devour," everything that exists, it may happen that the mind, which has become as unidentical to the world as the world has become to it, takes on a small moment of not-being-engulfed-in-blind-contingency: a very paradoxical form of hope, if you like. And the very curious persistence of the idea of immortality may be connected to this. For this idea seems to me to manifest itself more substantially where consciousness is most advanced than in the official religions. Even as a child I was surprised how little attention was paid to these last things—just a few pages in a Protestant hymn-book, for example—whereas one would expect them to be the only ones that mattered to a religion. I would remind you here of the magnificent passage in Marcel Proust depicting the death of the writer Bergotte, who was Anatole France, in which, in a truly grandiose, regenerative, mystical speculation, the writer's books, displayed by his deathbed, are interpreted as allegories of the fact that, on account of its goodness, this life was not wholly in vain.[14] You will find something similar in the writings of Beckett, who is, of course, anathema to all affirmative people and in whose work everything revolves around the question of what nothingness actually contains; the question, one might almost say, of a topography of the void. This work is really an attempt so to conceive nothingness that it is, at the

same time, not *merely* nothingness, but to do so *within* complete negativity.[15] But that, too, should be said with extreme gentleness and circumspection. And it is perhaps no accident that in the passage of Proust
I have just referred to the writer chooses a formulation that bears a curious resemblance to those of Kafka, with whom he has nothing directly in
common. I attempted to explore this connection in "Short Commentaries on Proust," in the second volume of *Notes to Literature*,[16] and I do
not want to speak of it now. But the less people really live—or, perhaps
more correctly, the more they become aware that they have not really
lived—the more abrupt and frightening death becomes for them, and the
more it appears as a misfortune. It is as if, in death, they experienced
their own reification: that they were corpses from the first. Such an experience was expressed in the most diverse passages of expressionist poetry,
by Benn[17] and Trakl, taking a curiously identical form in writers otherwise at opposite poles. The terror of death today is largely the terror of
seeing how much the living resemble it. And it might therefore be said
that if life were lived rightly, the experience of death would also be
changed radically, in its innermost composition.

That is probably the most extreme speculation by which I can
demonstrate, at least as a possibility, the link I am trying to explain in
these last lectures between the historical, immanent sphere and what are
called the great metaphysical categories. Death and history form a constellation. Hamlet, the first wholly self-aware and despondently self-reflecting
individual, experienced his essence as something absolutely transitory. In
him the absolute experience of the individual as the self, and the experience of its absolute transience, that the rest is silence, coincided. By contrast, it is probably the case today that, because the individual actually no
longer exists, death has become something wholly incommensurable, the
annihilation of a nothing. He who dies realizes that he has been cheated of
everything. And that is why death is so unbearable. I will close by pointing out that in this fact that the horizon of death has been displaced in the
curious way I have just indicated, what I might call the good side of the
decline of the individual is manifested. It is that the experience of the nullity of the individual not only reveals our ego weakness, our functionaliza-
tion, but also takes away something of the illusoriness and guilt that have
always persisted in the category of individuation, up to the threshold of
this age.

Lecture Eighteen, "Metaphysical Experience"
(29 July 1965)

Ladies and Gentlemen, when one of these lecture series reaches its
end, it seems to be a natural law—or an unnatural one—that one has not
remotely covered the ground one had intended to. That is the case with
me. That is to say, I have been able to present you only fragments of what
is contained in the manuscript "Reflections on Metaphysics," on which I
have been basing the second half of the series,[1] and have not got nearly as
far as I had hoped. That is due in part to the difference between the forms
of written and spoken expression. When one writes, one is obliged to present the matter as clearly and precisely as possible, and can permit oneself
extreme concentration for the sake of clear expression. When one is talking to living people it would be absurd, and professorial in the bad sense,
to cling to the fiction that one can express pure thought, and one must do
one's best, following one's own innervations, to make things clear to the
people one is talking to. This does, however, have the disadvantage that
when people like you come to listen to a person like me, you will almost
inevitably be disappointed, as you will expect from what I write to hear
something much more pithy than is possible in a spoken lecture. In short,
one is, in educated language, in an aporia; in less educated language: however you do it, it's wrong. And so, in full awareness of this fragmentariness,
I would say to you today that what I have told you, in the form I have told
it, can do no more than encourage you to think further on it for yourselves, and especially to free yourselves from a collection of clichés and
ideas that have been foisted on you. To expect these lectures to have given
you a comprehensive account of how or in what form metaphysics, or its
opposite, is possible today would be a foolish presumption. And I should
like to make it quite clear that I have no such pretension.

I spoke at different points about the concept of metaphysical experience,[2] and perhaps it would not be a bad thing to say a few more words
about it in this last lecture. What I mean by metaphysical experience certainly cannot be reduced to what are called primal religious experiences.
The reason is simply that if one spends a little time studying the stratum
of theology that claims to have access to such primal experiences—that is,
in crude terms, the mystical stratum, which places such primary experience
higher than any codified theology—one becomes aware of something very

peculiar and, I must say, very surprising. It is that mystical texts, and descriptions of fundamental mystical experiences, by no means have the primary, immediate quality one might expect, but are very strongly mediated by education. For example, the intricate interrelationships between gnosticism, neo-Platonism, the cabala, and later Christian mysticism give rise to an area of historicity that is equal to anything in the history of dogma. And it is certainly no accident that the corpus in which the documents of Jewish mysticism are brought together more or less disconnectedly, the cabala, bears the title of tradition. Far less emphasis is put on a primary, immediate vision than one imagines; far more attention is paid to the τόποι of so-called religious experience than to pure subjectivity than might be supposed. What the reasons might be I do not want to discuss; that is really a matter for the philosophy of religion. I shall content myself with one observation, that almost all the mystical speculations that exist find their support in so-called sacred texts, which in the eyes of mystical-metaphysical thinkers become symbolic in the sense that they mean something quite different from what is said in them. For example, in the famous interpretation of the first chapter of Genesis, as set out in the book "Sohar," the history of the creation of the world is interpreted as a history of the inner process of creation that took place within the divinity itself.[3] This is, incidentally, the model for the speculations of Schelling, which, in a later phase, became famous under the name of positive philosophy.[4] I do not wish to say anything about the truth of these matters; but I should like at least to make you aware of a problem.

Through our philosophical and, above all, our academic education—as long as it is based on the model, however latent, of the natural sciences—we have become tacitly accustomed to an irreconcilable antithesis between tradition and cognition. It is no accident that the most vehement invective against tradition is to be found in the two philosophers who mark the beginning of what is called modern philosophy, Descartes and Bacon, who emancipated themselves from tradition. It is, however, questionable (and I shall only raise the question here) whether the idea underlying this position—that tradition, what is not known at first hand, should be spurned in the face of the immediacy of lived experience—whether this motif, which we take almost for granted, is really so valid, in view of the fact that many such traditional elements are unknowingly contained in knowledge we regard as *not* traditional, but as pure, autonomous cognition. One might be inclined to think that the subject supposedly capable of cognition as a kind of *actus purus*, as a piece of pure actuality—and this, implicitly, is the epistemological ideal of the whole of modern philosophy—is an abstraction that does not correspond to any actual subject of cognition; and that the traditional, that is, the historical moment, not only permeates supposedly authenticated knowledge far more deeply than is generally admitted, but actually makes that knowledge possible. One might even suppose that the moment I have repeatedly brought to your notice under the heading of the mediatedness of thought is contained in this traditional moment, in the implicit history that is present within any cognition. And it is probable (at any rate, I should like to think so today) that the crucial threshold between this and positivist thinking lies in the question whether thought is aware of this inalienable traditional moment contained within it, whether knowledge reflects it within itself or whether it simply denies it—which is not to assert, of course, that knowledge should simply abandon itself to this traditional moment. The criticism that has been leveled at tradition has its reasons and its legitimacy, heaven knows. But it is also naive in believing that it can divest itself entirely of this moment. The truth probably lies in a kind of self-reflection that both recognizes the inalienable presence of the traditional moment within knowledge, and critically identifies the dogmatic element in it—instead of creating a *tabula rasa* on both sides, as now, and thus succumbing either to dogmatism or to a timeless and therefore inherently fictitious positivism. You will perhaps understand that, for this reason, I am unwilling to attach metaphysical experience to religious experience as firmly as is generally asserted; I am unwilling to do so, above all, because this kind of experience, as handed down by very great figures of Catholicism, such as St. John of the Cross, hardly seems to be accessible any longer, given the assumptions regarding the philosophy of history under which we live today. On its actual truth content I will hold my peace.

A more decisive contribution to these matters, I believe, is made by Marcel Proust, whose work, as a precipitate of experience and an exploration of the possibility of experience, should be taken extremely seriously from a philosophical point of view. I would mention in passing that the separation between art and so-called scholarship in the sphere in which we are now moving is entirely without substance and is a mere fabrication of the division of labor. I mean—the idea that Herr Bollnow should be qualified to contribute seriously to a discussion on metaphysics while Marcel Proust should not—well, I would just mention that idea to you without commenting further. I do not wish to reproduce Proust's theory of meta-physical experience to you here. I would just point out that perhaps one of the clearest manifestations of what I am concerned with here is the way in which certain names can vouch for that experience. In Proust they are the names of Illiers and Trouville, Cabourg and Venice.[5] I myself have had a similar experience with such names. When one is on holiday as a child and reads or hears names like Monbrunn, Reuenthal, Hambrunn, one has the feeling: if only one were there, at that place, that would be it. This "it"—what the "it" is—is extraordinarily difficult to say; one will probably be able to say, following Proust's tracks here too, that it is happiness. When one later reaches such places, it is not there either, one does not find "it." Often they are just foolish villages. If there is still a single stable door open in them and a smell of a real live cow and dung and such things, to which this experience is no doubt attached, one must be very thankful today. But the curious thing is that, even if "it" is not there, if one does not find in Monbrunn any of the fulfillment that is stored up in its name, neverthe-less, one is not disappointed. The reason, if I am interpreting it correctly, is that—and you must forgive me if I ramble a bit in this lecture, in just the way that Kant forbids[6]—one is, as it were, too close, one is inside the phenomenon, and has the feeling that, being completely inside it, one can-not actually catch sight of it.[7] Once, many years ago, in *Minima Moralia*, I wrote about thanking and gratitude, which have their dignity—and I did not mean dignity in the idealist sense—because the giving of thanks is the only relationship that consciousness can have to happiness, whereas the person who *is* happy is too close to it to be able to have any standpoint to-ward it within consciousness.[8] At such moments one has a curious feeling that something is receding—as is also familiar from an old symbol of hap-piness, the rainbow—rather than that one has really been done out of it. I would say, therefore, that happiness—and there is an extremely deep con-stellation between metaphysical experience and happiness—is something within objects and, at the same time, remote from them.

But as I mention this example to you, I become aware of how ex-traordinarily precarious such speculations are. I have just picked out a stra-tum of these experiences quite arbitrarily; another, perhaps far more cru-cial one, is the experience of *déjà vu*, the feeling When did I see that before? that can be induced by a certain type of children's book. In such ex-periences one succumbs to the conditions of the empirical world; one suc-cumbs to all the fallibility that attaches to one's own psychology, one's wishes, one's longing. All metaphysical experiences—I should like to state as a proposition here—are fallible. I would say, in general, that all experiences that have to be lived, that are not mere copies or reconstructions of that which is in any case, contain the possibility of error, the possibility that they can completely miss the mark. And, in much the same way as I indicated earlier with regard to the concept of tradition, it may be one of the ψευδῆ, the deceptions in which scientific-idealist thinking has enmeshed us, that we believe a piece of knowledge to rank higher the less it is liable to failure, to disappointment. It might well be that, according to this criterion, everything that really matters would be excluded as unworthy of being known; whereas in truth—so it seems to me—only what can be refuted, what can be disappointed, what can be wrong, has the openness I have spoken of;[9] that is, it is the only thing that matters. It is in the concept of openness, as that which is not already subsumed under the identity of the concept, that the possibility of disappointment lies. And I should like to say that within the meaning of these reflections on the possibility of metaphysics there lies a peculiar affinity to empiricism. For empiricism, with its emphasis on empirical sources, implies an element of metaphysics at least in the sense that the *essential* knowledge is seen as that which does *not* coincide with concepts, but which, as it were, falls accidentally into my lap, and thus always includes the possibility that it *might not* do so. Such knowledge therefore has an inherent fortuitousness, from which it derives an element of meaning that, according to the prevalent logic, is excluded precisely by the concept of the accidental. Fallibility, I would say, is the condition of the possibility of such metaphysical experience. And it seems to attach most strongly to the weakest and most fragile experiences.

Yet, from the extreme doubtfulness of what I have just said, a doubtfulness that, I believe, is indispensable to thought if it wants to be anything at all, you might gain a critical insight that, from the opposed standpoint, sounds highly heretical. You all know that the critical theory of society, and especially its popularized form in the modernistic vulgar theology of today, is fond of adducing the Hegelian and Marxian concept of *reification*, and that, for it, only what is entirely exempt from reification can be counted as knowledge or truth. But if you bear in mind the peculiarly fallible and unavoidably problematic nature of metaphysical experience that I have described, the concept of reification may, in a complementary way, take on a meaning that is far from purely derogatory. It is a meaning in which, as in

Marx, the whole of idealism is contained, in that the assumption is made that even that which is not I, which is not identical, must be able to resolve itself entirely, as it were, into the actual, present I, into the *actus purus*. That none of this is plain sailing, that these questions are not so simple—Hegel undoubtedly had an inkling of this in his later phase. And the traits of reactionary harshness we find so disturbing in Hegel are certainly connected to the realization that the moment of the complete dissolution of all objectivity in what might be called the living subject also contains a deceptive element, in the absolute presence of the subject in that which it is not. When I said earlier that pure mystical experience is a somewhat dubious matter, that it is far less pure and inward and far more concretely objective than one would expect from its concept, I was referring to this same deception.

What I am saying to you appears to be in sharp contradiction to the idea that cognition should necessarily be fallible if the resulting knowledge is to be worthy of being thought. And I would not presume, and certainly not in the miserably few minutes we have left, to resolve this contradiction. I would say, however, that precisely the polarity I am referring to—that, on the one hand, it is a condition of metaphysical experience that it can miss the mark, that it can be quite wrong; and that, on the other, it requires an objective moment, antithetical to it and incapable of being assimilated to it—that these two motifs together form the dialectical figure, the dialectical image,[10] through which alone one can, perhaps, gain awareness of what is meant by the concept of metaphysical experience. The objective categories of theology are not only—as it appears from Hegel's early theological writings published by Herman Nohl[11]—residues of the positive moment, which are then resolved into subjectivity, into life, in a process of increasing dialectical identification, but actually complement the weakness of immanent dialectics: they reclaim, in a sense, what is not assimilated by the dialectic and would, as the merely Other, be devoid of any determination. Thus, not only the ossified society but also the moment of the *primacy of the object*, which I have repeatedly mentioned,[12] was precipitated in the objectivity of the metaphysical categories. And between these two moments—on the one hand, the flashes of fallible consciousness that I illustrated by the example of place names, and, on the other, the primacy of the object—there seems to me to exist a curious constellation. True, it is one that is discharged abruptly at certain moments, rather than being a merely contemplative entity that could be grasped as a kind of categorial structure of a so-called matter of fact. If everything objective is volatilized by consciousness—and this applies especially to metaphysical objects—thought regresses to the subjectivism of the pure act. It then finally hypostatizes the mediation carried out by the subject itself, as a kind of pure immediacy. This may help to explain the quite significant fact that Kant, who attempted in the *Critique of Practical Reason* to interpret metaphysical ideas as a full participation of the subject, indeed, as nothing other than pure reason itself, finally moved almost imperceptibly to a position where he sought for that subjectivity precisely the objective correlatives that he had previously criticized and radically excluded. It is a remarkable fact that, in this way, even the concept of the highest good and the concept of humanity are resurrected in the *Critique of Practical Reason*.[13] But despite all this it has to be said that, in the course of advancing enlightenment, the possibility of metaphysical experience is tending to become paler and more desultory. If one reads Proust today, the accounts of such metaphysical experience, which play such an enormous role in his work—although even there they are far more bare and limited than one might expect—have a romantic moment through which they are already exposed to criticism. It is as if the joy of finding that somewhere some such thing as life were possible at all—and this is the counter-motif to reification—had lured the subject of the experience into directly equating these surviving traces of life with the meaning of life itself.

As a result, one will have to pursue metaphysical experience into a stratum that originally was extremely alien to it. For in reality it now survives only negatively. I would say—and this must be understood very strictly and made into a kind of canon for metaphysical thinking itself—that the form in which metaphysical experience still manifests itself with any compelling force today is not that which has made itself suspect as a sphere of romantic wishing, but is the experience that leads to the question: Is that all? It is the experience that, if I might speak for once like an existentialist, perhaps bears the greatest resemblance, among the "situations" we pass through,[14] to the situation of fruitless waiting: that is no doubt the form in which metaphysical experience manifests itself most strongly to us. It made an unforgettable impression on me when my composition teacher, Alban Berg, told me more than once that what he regarded as the crucial and most important parts of his own work, and the ones he liked best, were the bars in which he expressed situations of fruitless waiting. He experienced these things so deeply that they reached the threshold of consciousness, although, heaven knows, that is not required of an artist. But the authenticity of even this is not guaranteed, for where there is no longer any life, where immediacy has been so truly abolished, as in the world in which we exist, the temptation is doubly strong to mistake the remnants of life, or even the negation of the prevailing condition, for the absolute.

We reach here, if you like, the crucial distinction between the considerations I have been presenting to you and the Hegelian philosophy to which these considerations owe so much. It lies in the fact that Hegel's philosophy contains a moment by which that philosophy, despite having made the principle of determinate negation its vital nerve, passes over into affirmation and therefore into ideology: the belief that negation, by being pushed far enough and by reflecting itself, is one with positivity. That, Ladies and Gentlemen, the doctrine of the positive negation, is precisely and strictly the point at which I refuse to follow Hegel. There are other such points, but in the context of this discussion this is the one to which I should refer. One might be inclined to think that if the present situation is really experienced as negatively as we all experience it, and as only I have taken it upon myself, as a kind of scapegoat, to express it (that is the only difference separating me from other people), one might think that by *negating* this negativity one had already attained the positive; and that is a very great temptation. And when I told you that the form of determinate negation is the only form in which metaphysical experience survives today, I myself was moving at least in the direction of that idea. But this transition is not itself compelling: for if I said that the negation of the negation is the positive, that idea would contain within itself a thesis of the philosophy of identity and could be carried through only if I had already assumed the unity of subject and object that is supposed to emerge at the end. If, however, you take seriously the idea I put forward earlier today, that the truth of ideas is bound up with the possibility of their being wrong, the possibility of their failure, you will see that this idea is invalidated by the proposition that, merely by negating the negation, I already have the positive. In that case[15] one would be back in the sphere of false, deceptive, and, I would say, mythical certainty, in which nothing can be wrong and in which, probably for that reason, everything one said would be all the more hopelessly lost. For thought there is really no other possibility, no other opportunity, than to do what the miner's adage forbids: to work one's way through the darkness without a lamp, without possessing the positive through the higher concept of the negation of the negation, and to immerse oneself in the darkness as deeply as one possibly can. For one thing is undoubtedly true: I told you that, where there is no longer life, the temptation to mistake its remnants for the absolute, for flashes of meaning, is extremely great—and I do not wish to take that back. Nevertheless, nothing can even be experienced as living if it does not contain a promise of something transcending life. This transcendence therefore *is*, and at the same time *is not*—and beyond that contradiction it is no doubt very difficult, and probably impossible, for thought to go.[16]

In saying that, Ladies and Gentlemen, I have the feeling that I have reached the point where the insufficiency of my own reflections converges with the impossibility of thinking that which must nevertheless be thought.[17] And all I hope is that I may have given you at least an idea of that convergence.

Translated by Edmund Jephcott

Credits

We are grateful to earlier publishers of the following essays for permission to include them in this collection.

"The Meaning of Working through the Past." In Theodor W. Adorno, *Critical Models: Interventions and Catchwords*, trans. Henry W. Pickford, pp. 89–104. New York: Columbia University Press, 1998. © 1998 Columbia University Press. Reprinted by permission of the publisher.

"Education after Auschwitz." In Adorno, *Critical Models*, pp. 191–204. © 1998 Columbia University Press. Reprinted by permission of the publisher.

Selections from Theodor W. Adorno, *Minima Moralia: Reflections from Damaged Life*, trans. Edmund Jephcott. London: Verso, 1994.

"Progress." In Adorno, *Critical Models*, pp. 143–60. © 1998 Columbia University Press. Reprinted by permission of the publisher.

"Cultural Criticism and Society." In Theodor W. Adorno, *Prisms*, trans. Samuel Weber and Shierry Weber Nicholsen, pp. 17–34. Cambridge, Mass.: MIT Press, 1981. © MIT Press, 1981.

"*Crowds and Power*: Conversation with Elias Canetti," which appears here in English translation for the first time, was originally published as Theodor W. Adorno, "*Masse und Macht*: Gespräch mit Elias Canetti." In Elias Canetti, *Die gespaltene Zukunft*, pp. 66–92. Munich: Carl Hanser Verlag, 1972.

"Heine the Wound." In Theodor W. Adorno, *Notes to Literature*, vol. 1, ed. Rolf Tiedemann, trans. Shierry Weber Nicholsen, pp. 80–85. New York: Columbia University Press, 1991. © 1991 Columbia University Press. Reprinted by permission of the publisher.

"Notes on Kafka." In Adorno, *Prisms*, pp. 245–71. © MIT Press, 1981.

"Commitment." In Adorno, *Notes to Literature*, 2: 76–94. © 1991 Columbia University Press. Reprinted by permission of the publisher.

"Trying to Understand *Endgame*." In Adorno, *Notes to Literature*, 1: 241–75. © 1991 Columbia University Press. Reprinted by permission of the publisher.

"Mahler." In Theordor W. Adorno, *Quasi una Fantasia*, trans. Rodney Livingstone, pp. 81–110. London: Verso, 1992.

"Alban Berg." In Theodor W. Adorno, *Sound Figures*, trans. Rodney Livingstone, pp. 69–79. Stanford, Calif.: Stanford University Press, 1999.

"Elements of Anti-Semitism: Limits of Enlightenment." In Max Horkheimer and Theodor W. Adorno, *Dialectic of Enlightenment*, ed. Gunzelin Schmid Noerr, trans. Edmund Jephcott, pp. 137–72. Stanford, Calif.: Stanford University Press, 2002.

Selections from Theodor W. Adorno, *Metaphysics: Concept and Problems*, ed. Rolf Tiedemann, trans. Edmund Jephcott, pp. 103–45. Stanford, Calif.: Stanford University Press, 2001.

Translators' and Editors' Notes

Throughout the text, words that appeared originally in English have been italicized and designated with the symbol [E]. At times, Adorno uses an English term, then immediately glosses it in German. In such instances, the German has been supplied in brackets.

INTRODUCTION

1. Theodor W. Adorno, note in a school exercise book without a cover, in *Frankfurter Adorno Blätter IV*, ed. Theodor W. Adorno Archiv (Munich: Edition Text und Kritik, 1995), p. 7.

2. The volume and page numbers in parentheses in the text refer to Theodor W. Adorno, *Gesammelte Schriften*, ed. Rolf Tiedemann in collaboration with Gretel Adorno, Susan Buck-Morss, and Klaus Schultz (Frankfurt am Main: Suhrkamp, 1970–86). [The quote in Tiedemann's original German is from GS 6: 355; we have used the version of the statement in *Metaphysics: Concept and Problems*, p. 435 in the present volume.—Trans.]

3. Theodor W. Adorno, "Selections from *Minima Moralia*," Chap. 3 in the present volume, p. 46.—Trans.

4. Theodor W. Adorno, "The Meaning of Working through the Past," Chap. 1 in the present volume, p. 5.—Trans.

5. Ibid., p. 13.—Trans.

6. Detlev Claussen, "Nach Auschwitz: Ein Essay über die Aktualität Adornos," in *Zivilisationsbruch: Denken nach Auschwitz*, ed. Dan Diner (Frankfurt am Main: Fischer Taschenbuch, 1988), p. 55. Claussen was probably the first and for a long time almost the only thinker to point to the importance of Auschwitz in Adorno's philosophy.

7. G. W. F. Hegel, *Elements of the Philosophy of Right*, ed. Alan Wood, trans. H. B. Nisbet (1991; reprint, Cambridge: Cambridge University Press, 1996), p. 21.

8. See Eckart Goebel, "Das Hinzutretende: Ein Kommentar zu den Seiten 226 bis 230 der *Negativen Dialektik*," in *Frankfurter Adorno Blätter IV*, pp. 109ff.

9. Günther Anders, *Ketzereien,* 2d ed. (Munich: Beck, 1991), pp. 242–43: "Adorno's dictum that after Auschwitz poems can—in the sense of 'may'—no longer be written, can be confirmed. His statement must probably even be extended to say that we can no longer believe, thank, or pray—likewise in the sense of 'may.' And that still to be religious after Auschwitz is evidence of mindlessness and is immoral."

10. Theodore W. Adorno, "Cultural Criticism and Society," Chap. 7 in the present volume, p. 160.—Trans.

11. Ibid., p. 162.—Trans.

12. It appears that Paul Celan saw the matter in a similar light. Why otherwise would he have been so keen to persuade Adorno to write a study of his poems? And in the posthumous *Aesthetic Theory,* Adorno discusses Celan in these words: "This poetry is permeated with the shame of art in the light of the suffering that withdraws from both experience and sublimation. Celan's poems wish to express an acute horror by remaining silent. . . . The infinite discretion of Celan's radicalism gives him strength. The language of the lifeless becomes the last source of consolation for the death of meaning of every kind" (Adorno, *Gesammelte Schriften,* 7: 477).

13. Kafka said this about psychology.—Trans.

14. One representative of this intelligentsia believes that the "reconstruction of myth" could "play a role" in giving us an "insight into the truth of cruelty. Adorno called it suffering." (Karl-Heinz Bohrer, ed., *Mythos und Moderne: Begriff und Bild einer Rekonstruktion* [Frankfurt am Main: Suhrkamp, 1983], preface, p. 7.) This synthesis of conflicting ideas and the implied attempt to secure for Adorno a niche in the new mythologies are obscenities that can scarcely be surpassed.

15. The Ilisus is one of two rivers watering the Athenian plain. The allusion here is to Socrates' famous description of that idyllic landscape at the opening of Plato's *Phaedrus.* The verse from Celan's poem "To stand . . ." ("Stehen") can be found in Paul Celan, *Selected Poems,* trans. Michael Hamburger (Harmondsworth, Middlesex: Penguin, 1996), pp. 232–33.—Trans.

16. Adorno to Max Horkheimer, letter of 5 August 1940, Max-Horkheimer-Archiv, Stadt- und Universitätsbibliothek Frankfurt am Main, Sign. VI 1A.24.

17. The present anthology includes some, though admittedly not many, texts of an earlier date, the end of the 1920s. These are texts that in the judgment of the editor may be said to be "anticipations" of a philosophy that shed its "dreamlike" qualities only later on.

18. To be sure, on a pragmatic level such an analysis can be correct. See the conclusions to which Raul Hilberg comes in his historical research: "The machinery of destruction, then, was no different from organized German society as a whole; the difference was only one of function." (Raul Hilberg, *The Destruction of*

the European Jews, revised and definitive ed. [New York: Holmes and Meier, 1985], 3: 994.) Philosophy, however, is not historiography.

19. Adorno, "Selections from *Minima Moralia*," Chap. 3 in the present volume, p. 90.—Trans.

20. Theodor W. Adorno, "Elements of Anti-Semitism," Chap. 20 in the present volume, p. 421.—Trans.

21. Ibid., p. 420. Adorno's German phrase is *kategoriale Arbeit*, translated by Jephcott as "intellectual categories." A more literal translation would be "work on categories."—Trans.

22. Ibid., p. 391.—Trans.

23. Theodor W. Adorno, "Reflections on Class Theory," Chap. 4 in the present volume, p. 94.—Trans.

24. Adorno, "Selections from *Minima Moralia*," Chap. 3 in the present volume, p. 39.—Trans.

25. A contradiction between the two theories, one that can scarcely be resolved, lies in the difference of perspective. Adorno's "prehistory" attempts to examine origins from the standpoint of modernity, while Canetti enters into the spirit of the "so-called primitive" in order to "shed light unsparingly on himself" (Elias Canetti, *Die Stimmen von Marrakesch: Das Gewissen der Worte* [Munich: Carl Hanser, 1995], p. 119). On the other hand, Adorno and Canetti agree in their interest in "primal images" and in their use of the concrete as a starting point. Whether in conversation Adorno "vainly tried" to make Canetti's allegedly "ideal" images material or "to update" them by bringing them into conjunction with questions similar to those of scientific terminology is something that readers can easily determine for themselves. They can also decide whether there is anything more than resentment behind the statement that "for all the brilliance of his intimidating talent for abstraction, Adorno gives the impression of a moderator who associates everything with everything else, whereas Canetti is the man with intellectual dignity" (Karl-Heinz Bohrer, "Der Stoiker und unsere prähistorische Seele: On *Masse und Macht*," in *Wortmasken: Texte zu Leben und Werk von Elias Canetti* [Munich: Carl Hanser, 1995], p. 94).

26. See Theodor W. Adorno, *Problems of Moral Philosophy*, ed. Thomas Schröder, trans. Rodney Livingstone (Stanford: Stanford University Press, 2000), p. 94.

27. Adorno, "Elements of Anti-Semitism," Chap. 20 in the present volume, p. 392.—Trans.

28. Ibid., p. 394.—Trans.

29. On the theory of the "block," which Adorno developed in connection with the Kantian critique of reason, see Theodor W. Adorno, *Kant's 'Critique of Pure Reason,'* ed. Rolf Tiedemann, trans. Rodney Livingstone (Stanford: Stanford University Press, 2001), pp. 175ff. [For the Kafka epithet, see Franz Kafka,

"Reflections on Sin, Suffering, Hope and the True Way," in *Dearest Father: Stories and Other Writings*, trans. Ernst Kaiser and Eithne Wilkins (New York: Schocken Books, 1954), pp. 38–39: "The more horses you harness to the job, the faster the thing goes—that is to say, not tearing the block out of its base, which is impossible, but tearing the straps to shreds, and as a result the weightless, merry journey."—Trans.]

30. The Melusine story concerns a beautiful woman anxious to keep from the man who loves her the secret that she is really a mermaid. In Goethe's version, her secret is that she is really a queen of the dwarfs, a fact her lover discovers when he finally peers into the mysterious chest. See book 3, chap. 6, of *Wilhelm Meisters Wanderjahre.*—Trans.

31. In the preface to Hegel's *Phenomenology*, "science" (Hegel's term for philosophy) "is the artful device which, while seeming to refrain from activity, looks on and watches how specific determinateness with its concrete life, just where it believes it is working out its own self-preservation and its own private interest, is, in point of fact, doing the very opposite, is doing what brings about its own dissolution and makes itself a moment in the whole" (G. W. F. Hegel, *The Phenomenology of Mind*, trans. J. B. Baillie [London: Allen & Unwin, 1964], p. 114).

32. See, for example, the great footnote relating to the Kantian schematism of the pure concepts of the understanding in Theodor W. Adorno, *Against Epistemology: A Metacritique*, trans. Willis Domingo (Oxford: Blackwell, 1982), p. 143n (original in Adorno, *Gesammelte Schriften*, 5: 147–48); also in Adorno, *Kant's Critique of Pure Reason*, p. 275.

33. In all probability Adorno the materialist was encouraged by Benjamin to adopt the theological idea of the revocation of past suffering, an idea that flies in the face of materialism. We should remind ourselves above all of the second thesis of Benjamin's "Theses on the Philosophy of History," where Benjamin writes that the past has "a claim on the *weak* messianic power with which we have been endowed, like every generation before us. That claim cannot be settled cheaply. Historical materialists are aware of that" (Walter Benjamin, *Illuminations*, ed. Hannah Arendt, trans. Harry Zohn [London: Jonathan Cape, 1970], p. 256).

34. Celan, *Selected Poems*, pp. 140–53. See n. 15 above.—Trans.

35. Walter Benjamin, *Selected Writings*, vol. 1, *1913–1926*, ed. Marcus Bullock and Michael W. Jennings (Cambridge, Mass.: Harvard University Press, 1996), p. 356, trans. Stanley Corngold.

1. THE MEANING OF WORKING THROUGH THE PAST

NOTE: This essay was first delivered as a lecture to the Deutschen Koordinierungsrat der Gesellschafter für Christlich-Jüdische Zussammenarbeit (German Social Council for Coordinating Collaborative Work between Christians and Jews), Wiesbaden, 1959. All numbered notes in this chapter are by the translator.

1. *Aufarbeitung* is here translated "working through" and requires clarification, since it does not wholly coincide with the psychoanalytical term "working through" (*Durcharbeitung*), though it is related. Its common meaning is that of working through in the sense of dispatching tasks that have built up and demand attention, catching up on accumulated paperwork, etc. It thus conveys the sense of getting through an unpleasant obligation, clearing one's desk, etc., and some politicians and historians with less sensitivity to language than Adorno began using the term in reference to the need to reappraise or "master" the past (the German for the latter being *Vergangenheitsbewältigung*, which connotes both confrontation and overcoming). At the outset of the essay Adorno contrasts "working through" (*aufarbeiten*) with a serious "working upon" (*verarbeiten*) of the past in the sense of assimilating, coming to terms with it.

2. Adorno's reply to the highly critical appraisal of the postwar Frankfurt Institute's *Gruppenexperiment* by the respected, conservative psychologist Peter R. Hofstätter, who defended what Adorno had disparagingly called the "positivist-atomistic" method of orthodox opinion survey (which defines public opinion as the sum of individual opinions). Hofstätter reinterpreted the material to indicate that by the study's own standards only 15 percent of the participants could legitimately be considered authoritarian or undemocratic, a percentage fully comparable to that in any other Western country: there was no "legacy of fascist ideology" in Germany, no danger from the right. Furthermore, Hofstätter attacked the study's authors as totalitarian moralists and idealists themselves. He described the qualitative analysis (Adorno's contribution to the study) as "nothing but an accusation, or a demand for genuine mental remorse" and countered that "there is simply no individual feeling that could satisfactorily correspond to constantly looking at the annihilation of a million people"; therefore "the indignation of the sociological analyst" seemed "misplaced or pointless," because, according to Hofstätter, moral reflection on personal guilt was a private affair. (Peter R. Hofstätter, "Zum 'Gruppenexperiment' von Friedrich Pollock: Eine kritische Würdigung," *Kölner Zeitschrift für Soziologie und Sozialpsychologie* 9 [1957]: 97–104).

Adorno's reply is no less polemical: "The method is declared to be useless so that the existence of the phenomenon that emerges can be denied." According to him, Hofstätter's criticism indicates the appeal to collective narcissism: "Hofstätter considers 'it is hardly possible that a single individual could take upon himself the horror of Auschwitz.' It is the victims of Auschwitz who had to take its horror upon themselves, not those who, to their own disgrace and that of their nation, prefer not to admit it. The 'question of guilt' was 'laden with despair' for the victims, not for the survivors, and it takes some doing to have blurred this distinction with the existential category of despair, which is not without reason a popular one. But in the house of the hangman one should not mention the noose; one might be suspected of harboring resentment" (Theodor W. Adorno, "Replik zu Peter R.

Hofstätters Kritik des Gruppenexperiments," *Kölner Zeitschrift für Soziologie und Sozialpsychologie* 9 [1957]: 105–17; reprinted in Theodor W. Adorno, *Gesammelte Schriften,* ed. Rolf Tiedemann in collaboration with Gretel Adorno, Susan Buck-Morss, and Klaus Schultz (Frankfurt am Main: Suhrkamp, 1970–86), 9.2: 378–94, quotations from pp. 392–93).

3. Radio version: "I do not wish to go into the question of neo-Nazi organizations. From the communication by Harry Pross you've learned more, and more starkly, about it than presumably most of us knew. Those of us who have gathered here see very little of what we want not to happen again—the fact that we do not want it already separates us from the others. But I consider. . . ."

4. Radio and first published versions continue: "Compared with this, the continued existence of radical-right groups, which by the way during the last weeks suffered a severe rebuff from the voters of Bremen and Schleswig-Holstein, seems to me to be only a surface phenomenon."

5. See *Gruppenexperiment: Ein Studienbericht,* revised by Friedrich Pollock, vol. 2 of *Frankfurter Beiträge zur Soziologie,* commissioned by the Institute for Social Research [Institut für Sozialforschung], ed. Theodor W. Adorno and Walter Dirks (Frankfurt am Main: Europäische Verlagsanstalt, 1955).

6. Radio version: "You all, ladies and gentlemen, are familiar with. . . ."

7. Radio version adds: "or at least it is hardly reflected upon."

8. Radio and first published versions have "naive" instead of "lax."

9. The reference is to Mephistopheles' reaction to Faust's death in part 2, after the latter finally says, "Abide, you are so fair! [*Verweile doch, du bist so schön!*]," when contemplating his intentions for bettering the lot of humanity:

> MEPH.: Now it is over. What meaning can you see?
> It is as if it had not come to be,
> And yet it circulates as if it were.
> I should prefer—Eternal Emptiness.
> (J. W. von Goethe, *Faust,* trans. Walter Kaufmann [New York: Doubleday, 1961], pp. 468–71, ll. 11595–603)

10. See several essays included in the following collections: Hermann Heimpel, *Der Mensch in seiner Gegenwart: Acht historische Essais* (Göttingen: Vandenhoeck & Ruprecht, 1954, 1957); *Kapitulation vor der Geschichte? Gedanken zur Zeit* (Göttingen: Vandenhoeck & Ruprecht, 1956, 1957, 1960).

11. Radio and first published versions interject the following paragraph:

> This German development, flagrant after the Second World War, coincides with the lack of historical awareness [*Geschichtsfremdheit*] in the American consciousness, well known since Henry Ford's "*History is bunk*" [E], the nightmare of a humanity without memory. It is no mere phenomenon of decline, not a reaction of a humanity that, as one says, is

flooded with stimuli and cannot cope with them. Rather it is necessarily connected to the advancement of the bourgeois principle. Bourgeois society is universally situated under the law of exchange, of the like-for-like of accounts that match and that leave no remainder. In its very essence exchange is something timeless; like ratio itself, like the operations of mathematics according to their pure form, they remove the aspect of time. Similarly, concrete time vanishes from industrial production. It transpires more and more in identical and spasmodic, potentially simultaneous cycles and hardly requires accumulated experience any more. Economists and sociologists, such as Werner Sombart and Max Weber, have ascribed the principle of traditionalism to feudal forms and the principle of rationality to bourgeois forms of society. But this means nothing less than that recollection, time, memory is being liquidated by advancing bourgeois society itself, as a kind of irrational residue, similar to the way advancing rationalization of the industrial means of production reduces along with the remains of the artisanal also categories like apprenticeship [the radio version interjects: "that is, the gaining of experience"]. If humanity divests itself of memory and breathlessly exhausts itself in continually conforming to what is immediately present, then in doing so it reflects an objective developmental law.

12. For instance: "Here came to consciousness and received its plain expression, what *German* is: to wit, the thing one does for its own sake, for the very joy of doing it; whereas Utilitarianism, namely, the principle whereby a thing is done for the sake of some personal end, ulterior to the thing itself, was shewn to be un-German." Wagner goes on, first, to identify this "German virtue" with the highest principle of Kantian aesthetics, the autonomy of art, and, second, to advocate this principle as a national policy "which assuredly presupposes a solid ordering of every nearer, every relation that serves life's necessary ends" (Theodor W. Adorno, "German Art and German Policy," in his *Richard Wagner's Prose Works*, trans. William Ashton Ellis, vol. 4, *Art and Politics* [London: Routledge & Kegan Paul, 1895; reprint, New York: Broude Brothers, 1966], pp. 35–148, quotation from pp. 107–8). See also Adorno's "On the Question: 'What Is German?,'" in *Critical Models: Interventions and Catchwords*, trans. Henry W. Pickford (New York: Columbia University Press, 1998), pp. 205–14.

13. See Franz Böhm's preface to *Gruppenexperiment*, the published results of a study undertaken by the Institute for Social Research exploring ideologies of various population groups in postwar Germany:

> What is it then that produces the shock when reading the present investigation?
> I would like to think that it is a double aspect.

First of all the overly clear perception that alongside the so-called public opinion, which expresses itself in elections, referenda, public speeches, newspaper articles, radio broadcasts, the platforms of political parties and groups, parliamentary discussions, political meetings, there is also a *nonpublic opinion*, whose contents can diverge very considerably from the contents of the actual public opinion, whose statements, however, circulate alongside the statements of the public opinion like the monetary units of a *second currency*—indeed, they have perhaps a more fixed and stable rate than the values of actual public opinion, which we flaunt according to propriety in public, especially for the audience abroad, and of which we imagine they represent our own and only currency, as though they expressed what we really mean to say, although, after all, they are only formal expressions we use when we are wearing our Sunday clothes. Yes, it almost appears as though what circulates about us as public opinion represents the sum of those (mutually contradictory) opinions we wish people would believe are our true opinions, whereas nonpublic opinion is about the sum of those (likewise mutually contradictory) opinions that we actually have.

Second, the likewise overly clear perception of what the nonpublic opinion actually looks like. So that is what many of us actually think!

In other words: the one shock results from the perception that we have *two currencies of opinion*, each encompassing a whole bundle of diverse opinions. And the other shock overcomes us when we look at the values comprising the unofficial opinion. (Franz Böhm, "Geleitwort," in *Gruppenexperiment: Ein Studienbericht*, pp. xi–xii)

See also Franz Böhm, "Das Vorurteil als Element totaler Herrschaft," in vol. 17 of *Vorträge gehalten anläßlich der Hessischen Hochschulwochen für staatswissenschaftliche Fortbildung* (Bad Homburg vor der Höhe: Verlag Dr. Max Gehlen, 1957), pp. 149–67.

14. First published version is more cautious: "Certainly one may hope that democracy is more deeply rooted. . . ."

15. Radio and first published version: "with Western democracy" instead of "with the West."

16. Radio and first published version: "deadly serious" instead of "obvious."

17. *Wir Wunderkinder*: a film satire of the so-called economic miracle in West Germany, it depicts the unprincipled career of a small-town operator during four decades of German history: first a dashing Nazi leader, then a successful financier in postwar West Germany, his unswerving self-interest and opportunism ensure his success. Directed by Kurt Hoffmann; 1958 Filmaufbau.

18. *KdF* = *Kraft durch Freude* ["Strength through Joy"], National Socialist recreational organization (whose name supposedly was invented by Hitler him-

self) set up in imitation of a similar Italian organization, *Dopolavoro*, founded by Mussolini for the purpose of stimulating workers' morale. A new form of industrial relations and mass tourism, the *KdF* program encompassed package holiday tours on its own ocean liners and via the state railway system as well as subsidized theater and concert performances, exhibitions, sports, hiking, folk dancing, and adult education courses. The organization, part of the German Labor Front (*Deutsche Arbeitsfront*), received massive state subsidies for the purpose of demonstrating the enlightened labor policies of the National Socialists in eliminating classes within the Third Reich.

The *KdF* comprised the following offices: (1) the "After Work" department organized theater performances, concerts, etc., as well as political education courses for ca. 38 million people (1933–38); the "Sport" department organized factory sports for "military training" and "racial perfection"; the "Beauty of Labor" department sought to improve working conditions and the aesthetic contours of the workplace; the "Military Homes" department promoted contacts to the armed forces and the State Labor Service; the department of "Tour, Travel, Vacation" until 1938 organized vacation trips for ca. 10 million people. As the German Labor Front put it in 1940, "We did not send our workers off on vacation on our own ships or build them massive sea resorts just for the fun of it. . . . We did it only in order for them to return to their workplaces invigorated and with a new orientation."

19. Sigmund Freud, *Massenpsychologie und Ich-Analyse* (1921); English in *The Standard Edition of the Complete Psychological Works of Sigmund Freud*, trans. James Strachey, ed. James Strachey in collaboration with Anna Freud (London: Hogarth, 1975), 18: 67–143.

20. Radio and first published version: "automatically" instead of "pharisaically."

21. Radio and first published version: "features of horror" instead of "grotesque features."

22. Radio and first published version: "Just as the witch trials took place not during the high point of Scholasticism but during the Counter-Reformation, that is, when what they wanted to reinforce was already undermined, so too has nationalism first become completely sadistic and destructive in an age in which it was already toppling."

23. In his article "Anti-Semitism and Mass Psychopathology," in *Anti-Semitism: A Social Disease*, ed. Ernst Simmel (New York: International Universities Press, 1946), Simmel draws on Le Bon and Freud to arrive at the following interpretation:

> By identifying himself with the mass, the individual in his retreat from reality employs the same escape mechanism as the psychotic, i.e., regression to that infantile level of ego development when the superego was still represented by external parental power.
>
> However, through this temporary regression he gains one advantage the individual psychotic does not have. The submergence of his ego into

the group enables him to overcome his actual infantile impotence toward reality; he attains instinct freedom with the power of an adult. *This circumstance allows him, by way of a mass psychosis, to return to reality, from which the individual psychotic must flee.* (p. 47)

Summarizing the parallelisms between a collective psychosis and an individual psychosis, we can say: The mass and the psychotic think and act irrationally because of regressively disintegrated ego systems. In the individual psychotic mind the process of regression is of a primary nature and is constant. In the collective psychotic mind regression is secondary and occurs only temporarily. The reason for this is that in the individual psychotic, the ego breaks with reality because of its pathological weakness, whereas *in the mass member, reality breaks first with the ego.* This ego, by submerging itself into a pathological mass, saves itself from individual regression by regressing collectively. *Flight into mass psychosis is therefore an escape not only from reality, but also from individual insanity.*

This insight gives us our answer to the enigmatic question why apparently normal individuals can react like psychotics under the spell of mass formation. *Their ego is immature* as a result of superego weakness. The immature individual who, under the stress of environmental circumstances, is on the verge of losing contact with reality can find his way back to it when his ego, carried by the spirit of the group, finds opportunity for the discharge of pent-up aggressive instinct energies into the object world. (pp. 49–50)

24. Radio and first published version: "the self-reflection" instead of "the autonomy."

25. Radio version adds: "They experience their own autonomy in a certain sense as a burden."

26. Radio version interjects: "if it hasn't always been so."

27. Radio and first published version: "objects" instead of "subjects."

28. Radio version interjects: "to use an example Franz Böhm likes to adduce. . . ."

29. First published version has "anti-Semitism" instead of "fascism," and the radio version continues here: "In our work this is that danger for which in America they use the saying '*preaching to the saved*' [E] [*also, denen predigen, die ohnehin bereits gerettet sind*]."

30. Snub of Heideggerian existentialism.

31. Radio version interjects: "subjectively, that is, the appeal to individuals. . . ."

32. Radio version interjects: "individuation, that is, that it concerns this specific girl and not everyone."

33. See #233 of La Rochefoucauld's *Maximes* (1678):

Afflictions give rise to various kinds of hypocrisy: in one, pretending to weep over the loss of someone dear to us we really weep for ourselves, since we miss that person's good opinion of us or deplore some curtailment of our wealth, pleasure, or position. The dead, therefore, are honoured by tears shed for the living alone. I call this a kind of hypocrisy because in afflictions of this sort we deceive ourselves. There is another hypocrisy, less innocent because aimed at the world at large: the affliction of certain persons who aspire to the glory of a beautiful, immortal sorrow. Time, the universal destroyer, has taken away the grief they really felt, but still they obstinately go on weeping, wailing, and sighing; they are acting a mournful part and striving to make all their actions prove that their distress will only end with their lives. This miserable and tiresome vanity is usually found in ambitious women, for as their sex precludes them from all roads to glory they seek celebrity by a display of inconsolable affliction. There is yet another kind of tears that rise from shallow springs and flow or dry up at will: people shed them so as to have a reputation for being tender-hearted, so as to be pitied or wept over, or, finally, to avoid the disgrace of not weeping. (La Rochefoucauld, *Maxims*, trans. Leonard Tancock [London: Penguin, 1959], pp. 67–68)

34. Radio version and first published version have the following addition to the conclusion: "Whatever aims at the more humanly decent organization of the whole, be it theoretically or practical-politically, is at once also resistance against the relapse."

2. EDUCATION AFTER AUSCHWITZ

NOTE: This essay was first delivered as a lecture on Hessischen Rundfunk (Hessian radio), Frankfurt am Main, 1968. All numbered notes in this chapter are by the translator.

1. Sigmund Freud, *Massenpsychologie und Ich-Analyse* (1921) and *Das Unbehagen in der Kultur* (1930); English: in *The Standard Edition of the Complete Psychological Works of Sigmund Freud*, trans. James Strachey, ed. James Strachey in collaboration with Anna Freud (London: Hogarth, 1975), 18: 67–143 and 21: 59–145, respectively.

2. First published version: "helpless" and "helplessness" instead of "desperate" and "desperation."

3. *Die vierzig Tage des Musa Dagh* (1933), by Franz Werfel. Set in Syria in 1915, the novel recounts the resistance offered by the Armenians against more numerous and better equipped Young Turk forces. The Armenian forces entrench themselves on the mountain Musa Dagh for forty days and, on the verge of being over-

whelmed, are rescued by an Anglo-French naval squadron. English: Franz Werfel, *The Forty Days of Musa Dagh*, trans. Geoffrey Dunlop (New York: Viking, 1934).

4. See the essay "The Meaning of Working through the Past," Chap. 1 in this volume, pp. 3–18.

5. First published version: "resistance, rebellion" instead of "spiteful resentment."

6. The German translation of Sartre's title is *Tote ohne Begräbnis*. See Jean-Paul Sartre, *Morts sans sépulchre*, in *Théatre*, vol. 1 (Paris: Gallimard, 1946). English: Jean Paul Sartre, *The Victors*, in *Three Plays*, trans. Lionel Abel (New York: Knopf, 1949).

7. Eugen Kogon, *Der SS-Staat: Das System der deutschen Konzentrationslager* (Frankfurt am Main: Europäische Verlagsanstalt, 1946); numerous reprints. English: Eugen Kogon, *The Theory and Practice of Hell: The German Concentration Camps and the System behind Them*, trans. Heinz Norden (New York: Berkley, 1950).

8. First published version: simply "has not yet succeeded," without the comparative.

9. See Max Horkheimer and Theodor W. Adorno, *Dialectic of Enlightenment*, trans. Edmund Jephcott (Stanford: Stanford University Press, 2002), esp. pp. 192–96.

10. See William Graham Sumner, *Folkways: A Study of the Sociological Importance of Usages, Manners, Customs, Mores, and Morals* (Boston: Ginn, 1906). See also *Soziologische Exkurse: Nach Vorträgen und Diskussionen*, vol. 4 of *Frankfurter Beiträge zur Soziologie* (Frankfurt am Main: Europäische Verlagsanstalt, 1956), p. 157; and Theodor W. Adorno, *Einleitung in die Soziologie* (Frankfurt am Main: Suhrkamp, 1993), p. 77; English: Theodor W. Adorno, *Introduction to Sociology*, ed. Christoph Gödde, trans. Edmund Jephcott (Stanford: Stanford University Press, 2000), p. 43. Adorno planned to have Sumner's book translated into German when he returned to Frankfurt after the war.

11. *Rauhnächte*: hazing ritual during the nights of Christmastide; *Haberfeldtreiben*: old Bavarian custom of censuring those perceived by the community as (often moral or sexual) reprobates who have been overlooked by the law. See Adorno, *Einleitung in die Soziologie*, p. 65, where Adorno speaks of "Oberbayerische Haberfeldtreiben" in the context of the conceptual opacity of Durkheim's *faits sociaux* (*Introduction to Sociology*, 36).

12. See Friedrich Nietzsche, *Beyond Good and Evil*, trans. Walter Kaufmann (New York: Vintage, 1966), numbers 82, 210, 260, 269; idem, *The Gay Science*, trans. Walter Kaufmann (New York: Random House, 1974), number 26; idem, "On the Old and New Tablets," no. 29, in *Thus Spake Zarathustra*, trans. Walter Kaufmann (New York: Viking, 1966), p. 214.

13. Wilhelm Boger was in charge of the "escape department" at Auschwitz and took pride in the fact that it had the fewest escapes of any concentration camp. As

one of the twenty-one former SS men brought before the "Frankfurt" or "Auschwitz" trials (1963–65), Boger was accused of having taken part in numerous selections and executions at Auschwitz as well as having mistreated prisoners so severely on the "Boger swing" (a torture device he invented) during interrogation that they subsequently died. The court found him guilty of murder on at least 144 separate occasions, of complicity in the murder of at least 1,000 prisoners, and of complicity in the joint murder of at least 10 persons. Boger was sentenced to life imprisonment and an additional five years of hard labor.

14. First published version: "objects" instead of "material."

15. See Adorno's interpretation of "The 'Manipulative' Type," in Theodor W. Adorno, Else Frenkel-Brunswik, Daniel J. Levinson, and R. Nevitt Sanford, in collaboration with Betty Aron, Maria Hertz Levinson, and William Morrow, *The Authoritarian Personality*, Studies in Prejudice, ed. Max Horkheimer and Samuel H. Flowerman (New York: Harper & Brothers, 1950), pp. 767–71.

16. See part 3 of "Egoism and the Freedom Movement: On the Anthropology of the Bourgeois Era" (1936), in Max Horkheimer, *Between Philosophy and Social Science: Selected Early Writings*, trans. G. Frederick Hunter, Matthew S. Kramer, and John Torpey (Cambridge, Mass.: MIT Press, 1993).

17. Original reflections on "L'inhumaine" in Paul Valéry, "Rhumbs," in *Œuvres II*, ed. Jean Hytier (Paris: Gallimard, 1960), pp. 620–21.

Cf. Adorno's review of recent German translations of Valéry, "Valéry's Abweichungen," in Theodor W. Adorno, *Noten zur Literatur*, in his *Gesammelte Schriften*, ed. Rolf Tiedemann in collaboration with Gretel Adorno, Susan Buck-Morss, and Klaus Schultz (Frankfurt am Main: Suhrkamp, 1970–86), 11: 158–202. See esp. pp. 177–78, where Adorno cites the passage as translated by Bernhard Böschenstein (*Windstriche* [Frankfurt am Main: Insel Verlag, 1959], reprinted in Paul Valéry, *Werke*, vol. 5, *Zur Theorie der Dichtkunst und vermischte Gedanken*, ed. Jürgen Schmidt-Radefeldt [Frankfurt am Main: Insel Verlag, 1991]). The English version of Adorno's essay ("Valéry's Deviations," in *Notes to Literature*, trans. Shierry Weber Nicholsen [New York: Columbia University Press, 1991] 1: 137–73, here p. 153) quotes Valéry from the *Collected Works of Paul Valéry*, ed. Jackson Matthews, Bollingen Series 45, vol. 14, *Analects*, trans. Stuart Gilbert (Princeton, N.J.: Princeton University Press, 1970], p. 190): "The revolt of common sense is the instinctive recoil of man confronted by the inhuman; for common sense takes stock only of the human, of man's ancestors and yardsticks; of man's powers and interrelations. But research and the very powers that he possesses lead away from the human. Humanity will survive as best it can—perhaps there's a fine future in store for inhumanity" (translation corrected).

18. The "technological veil," as Adorno and Horkheimer first conceived it, is the "excess power that technology as a whole, along with the capital that stands behind it, exercises over every individual thing" so that the world of the commodity,

manufactured by mass production and manipulated by mass advertising, comes to be equated with reality per se: "Reality becomes its own ideology through the spell cast by its faithful duplication. This is how the technological veil and the myth of the positive is woven. If the real becomes an image insofar as in its particularity it becomes as equivalent to the whole as one Ford car to all the others of the same range, then the image on the other hand turns into immediate reality" ("The Schema of Mass Culture" [1942], trans. Nicholas Walker, in Theodor W. Adorno, *The Culture Industry: Selected Essays on Mass Culture*, ed. J. M. Bernstein [London: Routledge, 1991], p. 55; original in Adorno, *Gesammelte Schriften*, 3: 301). Adorno used the concept throughout his works, e.g., the 1942 text "Reflexionen zur Klassentheorie" ("Reflections on Class Theory," Chap. 4 in the present volume, p. 108–9 original in *Gesammelte Schriften*, 8: 390) and the 1968 text "Spätkapitalismus oder Industriegesellschaft," where he defines it as follows: "The false identity between the organization of the world and its inhabitants, an identity created by the expansion of technology, amounts to the affirmation of the relations of production, for whose beneficiaries we seek today almost as vainly as for the proletarians, who have become all but invisible" ("Late Capitalism or Industrial Society?," Chap. 5 in the present volume, p. 124; original in *Gesammelte Schriften*, 8: 369).

19. Radio version is stronger here: "If I may voice a suspicion here, concerning how this fetishization of technology comes about, then I would like to say that people who cannot love, that is, those who constitutively, essentially, are cold, must themselves negate even the possibility of love, that is, withdraw their love of other people from the very outset, because they cannot love them at all, and at the same time apply to means whatever has managed to survive of their ability to love."

20. See Adorno's qualitative evaluation of the clinical interview with "Mack," the exemplary subject prone to fascism as presented in Adorno et al., *Authoritarian Personality*, p. 789; see also pp. 55, 802

21. According to Aristotle, "man is by nature a political animal. And therefore men, even when they do not require one another's help, desire to live together," where "common advantage" and "friendship as political justice" hold states together. See Aristotle, *Politics*, 1278b16–25, and *Nicomachean Ethics*, 1155a21–28 and 1160a9–14.

22. David Riesman, *The Lonely Crowd: A Study of the Changing American Character* (New Haven, Conn.: Yale University Press, 1950).

23. Radio version and first published version continue as follows: "Similar behavior can be observed in innumerable automobile drivers, who are ready to run someone over if they have the green light on their side."

24. Charles Fourier, *Le Nouveau Monde industriel et sociétaire; ou, Invention du procédé d'industrie attrayante et naturelle distribuée en séries passionnées* (1829). En-

glish: Charles Fourier, *The Passions of the Human Soul, and Their Influence on Society and Civilization*, trans. Hugh Doherty (London: Hippolythe Baillière, 1855).

25. Radio version: "First of all, it is necessary to learn about the objective and subjective mechanisms that led to this, as well as to learn about the stereotypical defense mechanisms that prevent working against such consciousness."

26. First published version: "then people perhaps will not give vent to these traits so unrestrainedly." Radio version: "When one no longer has the feeling that countless people are all similarly waiting for outrages to be committed, rather, when one knows that they are deformations and the entire cultural consciousness is permeated with the intimation of the pathogenic character of these traits, then people will perhaps not give vent to it so unrestrainedly."

3. SELECTIONS FROM 'MINIMA MORALIA'

NOTE: All notes except those for "The Paragraph" were added by the publisher of the original English translation, New Left Books (London). A few new addenda by Rodney Livingstone are provided in brackets.

Grassy seat
TITLE: Allusion to the lines of a well-known German song: "Der liebste Platz den ich auf Erden hab', / das ist die Rasenbank am Elterngrab" ("The dearest spot I have on earth / is the grassy seat by my parents' grave").

How nice of you, Doctor
TITLE: *Herr Doktor, das ist schön von Euch.* humble thanks of an old peasant to Faust for consorting with a popular crowd at Easter (Goethe's *Faust*, Part One).

Refuge for the homeless
1. Friedrich Nietzsche, *Werke*, ed. Karl Schlechta (Munich: C. Hanser, 1955), 2: 154; English: Friedrich Nietzsche, *The Joyful Wisdom* (Edinburgh, 1910), p. 203.

Savages are not more noble
1. Rudolf Carnap (1891–1970), leading philosopher of neopositivism, who emigrated to the U.S.A. in 1936. Matthias Grünewald (ca. 1470/80–1528), late Gothic painter, and Heinrich Schütz (1585–1672), early baroque composer—both of intense religious inspiration.

2. August Bebel was cofounder and leader of the German Social-Democratic Party from the Franco-Prussian War to the eve of the First World War.

3. Hans Driesch (1867–1941), vitalist philosopher and biologist, author of "The Science and Philosophy of the Organism." Heinrich Rickert (1863–1936), neo-Kantian philosopher and subjectivist exponent of a value-oriented epistemology.

Back to culture

1. Mosse Verlag and Ullstein Verlag were the two largest press combines of German-Jewish capital in the Weimar Republic, controlling newspapers, magazines, and publishing houses. Both were taken over by the Nazis.

2. Hans Fallada (1893–1947), social novelist of reportorial realism, whose works enjoyed great popular success in the last years of the Weimar period and who continued to write novels in Germany under the Nazi regime.

Invitation to the dance

TITLE: *Aufforderung zum Tanz*: title of the piano solo that was the first modern dance music of the post-Napoleonic epoch, composed by Carl Maria von Weber in 1819.

On the morality of thinking

1. Nietzsche, *Werke*, 2: 152–53; English: Nietzsche, *Joyful Wisdom*, p. 201.

A word for morality

1. David-Friedrich Strauss (1808–74), biblical critic and ideologist, who rallied to Bismarck after 1866 and advocated evolutionism as a philosophical substitute for Christianity in *Der alte und der neue Glaube* (1872).

People are looking at you

TITLE: Modification of the title of a book by Paul Eipper (1891–1964), an author of animal stories, *Tiere sehen dich an* (*Animals Are Looking at You*).

Pseudomenos

TITLE: The Greek term for "liar," which gave its name to the logical puzzle invented by Eubulides, often known as the Cretan paradox, of him who says: "All men are liars."

The paragraph

NOTE: This section is missing from the English translation of *Minima Moralia* and has been translated for this volume by Rodney Livingstone.

1. The—now almost wholly obscure—reference is to a notorious case of 1913, in which Ernst Wagner, a head teacher from Degerloch near Stuttgart, killed his wife and their four children and then set out to burn down the entire village of Mühlhausen an der Enz. He was put into a mental institution, Heilanstalt Winnental, where he lived into the 1930s. He claimed at that time that he had been the first National Socialist in his area. Two years after his death, 396 patients from the asylum were taken off to Grafeneck and Mauthausen, where they were killed as

part of the Nazi euthanasia program. The novelist Hermann Hesse based his story "Klein und Wagner" on the incident. I am grateful to Frau Sabine Giebeler, of the Lektorat Landeskunde Baden-Württemberg, and the librarians of the Stadtteil-bücherei Degerloch for this information.—R. L.

Passing muster

1. Carl Schmitt (born 1888), authoritarian legal theorist and philosopher of the state, who acquired official status during Nazi rule.

Picture-book without pictures

TITLE: Title of a work by Hans Christian Anderson.

Monad

1. Jakob Burckhardt, *Griechische Kulturgeschichte* (Berlin, 1902), 4: 515–16.

Bequest

1. Walter Benjamin, *Illuminations*, ed. Hannah Arendt, trans. Harry Zohn (London: Jonathan Cape, 1970), p. 258.

Late extra

1. Notion of Walter Benjamin: the whole passage here on Baudelaire and the concept of the "new" is constructed in implicit contrast to Benjamin's interpretation of them in *Charles Baudelaire—A Lyric Poet in the Era of High Capitalism* (London: New Left Books, 1973). For an English translation of Adorno's famous critique of Benjamin's views, see "Letters to Walter Benjamin," *New Left Review* 81 (Sept.–Oct. 1973). [These letters can also be found in Ernst Bloch et al., *Aesthetics and Politics* (London: New Left Books, 1977), pp. 110–41. A different translation is given in Theodor W. Adorno and Walter Benjamin, *The Complete Correspondence 1928–1940* (London: Polity, 1999), nos. 39, 47, 110, and 111.—R.L.]

Boy from the heath

TITLE: *Der Heideknabe*: a ballad by Hebbel (1844) in which every misfortune feared by the boy of the title invariably befalls him.

Il servo padrone

TITLE: Allusion to the title of the comic opera by Giovanni Pergolesi, *La Serva Padrone* (*The Maid as a Mistress*, 1733).

The bad comrade

TITLE: *Der böse Kamerad*: allusion to the song "Der gute Kamerad" ("The Good Comrade"), popularized by the Nazis. [The song is by the romantic poet Ludwig Uhland.—R.L.]

Juvenal's error

TITLE: Allusion to Juvenal's remark "Difficile est satiram non scribere" ("It is difficult not to write satire"). [Satire 1, 30.—R.L.]

Consecutio temporum

TITLE: "Sequence of tenses."

1. Hedwig Courths-Maler (1867–1950), best-selling novelist of popular sentimental romances.

2. Allusion to *Die Gartenlaube*, an illustrated family magazine of patriotic-conservative tendency in the late nineteenth century.

Toy shop

1. See Karl Marx, *Capital* (Moscow: International Publishers, 1961), 1: 55ff.

2. Ibid., p. 56.

Novissimum organum

TITLE: Superlative rendering of the title of Bacon's treatise *Novum Organum*.

1. Marx, *Capital*, 1: 622.

2. Georg Lukács, *History and Class Consciousness*, trans. Rodney Livingstone (London: Merlin, 1971), p. 100.

Knackery

1. Charles Péguy, *Men and Saints*, trans. Anne Green and Julian Green (New York: Pantheon, 1944), p. 98.

Don't exaggerate

1. Karl Marx, *Grundrisse* (Harmondsworth, Middlesex: Penguin, 1973), p. 88.

4. REFLECTIONS ON CLASS THEORY

NOTE: All numbered notes in this chapter are by the translator.

1. Throughout this essay, Adorno uses the term "theory" as a code word for "Marxism" or "dialectical materialism."

2. This refers to a meeting between Franz von Papen and Hitler at the home of the Cologne banker Kurt von Schroeder on 4 January 1933. The negotiations

that gave Hitler the support of sections of German industry and finance were initiated at this meeting; they would culminate in his appointment as chancellor at the end of the month. The mention of bribery refers to properties that were given to President Hindenburg in the summer of 1933 and to his son, some years before, in 1927. These gifts were then linked to a scandal in which government subsidies for agriculture in the East were said to have been diverted into the pockets of the Junkers and perhaps also the Hindenburg family. In his play *Arturo Ui*, Brecht uses the idea of Hindenburg's fear of exposure to explain why he acquiesced in Hitler's appointment, to which he had earlier been bitterly opposed.

3. This reference to "the author of *Psychology of Socialism*" is not entirely clear. It is conceivable that Adorno was thinking of Gustave Le Bon, whose *Psychologie du socialisme* appeared in Paris in 1899. Many of Le Bon's attitudes—his anti-Semitism and racism, for example—fitted in easily with fascism. His major work, *Psychologie des foules* (*The Crowd*) had a direct influence on both Hitler, who copied passages from it directly into *Mein Kampf*, and Mussolini, with whom he corresponded. Nevertheless, there is no evidence that in his old age (he died in 1931) he adopted fascist views. A stronger case can be made that Adorno's reference is to Hendryk (Henry) de Man, whose book, also entitled *Psychologie du socialisme*, appeared in English translation in 1928. When the Germans invaded Belgium in 1940, de Man, who was president of the Socialist Party, made an official declaration praising Hitler and claiming that the arrival of the Nazi troops meant the "liberation of the working class."

The "sociologist of political parties," to whom Adorno also refers here, was Robert Michels (1876–1936). His chief work, *Political Parties*, appeared in English in 1915, translated from the Italian edition of *Zur Soziologie des Parteiwesens in der modernen Demokratie*.

5. LATE CAPITALISM OR INDUSTRIAL SOCIETY?

NOTE: This talk was given as the keynote lecture to the Sixteenth Congress of German Sociologists on 8 April 1968 in Frankfurt am Main.

1. According to Marx's Eleventh Thesis on Feuerbach, "The philosophers have only interpreted the world, in various ways; the point is to change it."—Trans.

2. The slogan *formierte Gesellschaft*, the "unified" or "formed" society, comes from Ludwig Erhard, the conservative West German federal chancellor (1963–66). The term expressed his desire for a harmonious society from which egotistical behavior and factionalism would be eliminated. Although rather vague, the concept mobilized the opposition of the Left, which thought it constituted a call for a return to a rigidly organized, hierarchical society with fascist overtones.—Trans.

6. PROGRESS

NOTE: All numbered notes in this chapter are by the translator.

1. Throughout this essay Adorno plays on the double meaning of *Menschheit*, which, like its usual translation, "humanity," can signify an abstract principle as well as the sum of existing human beings (that is, "humanness" on the one hand, "humankind" on the other). In the first "model" of *Negative Dialectics*, in a section entitled "Ontical and Ideal Moments," Adorno explores this ambiguity of *Menschheit* in Kant's moral theory, concluding, "Kant must have noticed the double meaning of the word 'humanity,' as the idea of being human and as the totality of all men; he introduced it into theory in a manner that was dialectically profound, even though playful. His subsequent usage vacillates between ontical manners of speech and others that refer to the idea. . . . He wants neither to cede the idea of humanity to the existing society nor to vaporize it into a phantasm" (Theodor W. Adorno, *Negative Dialectics*, trans. E. B. Ashton [New York: Seabury, 1973], p. 258). In this essay *Menschheit* is consistently translated as "humanity" to preserve the doubleness. By contrast, German *Humanität*, which also occurs in the essay, derives from the Latin *humanitas*, and signifies not the ontic human species but rather the ideal of humane refinement as a mark of civilization; it is translated as "humanitarianism."

2. Here, as in his essay on Kafka in *Prisms* ("Notes on Kafka," Chap. 11 in the present volume; see also *Gesammelte Schriften*, 10.8: 229), Adorno's partial quotation neglects Kafka's emphasis on the mutual implication of progress and belief. Kafka's aphorism is quoted in its entirety by Benjamin in "Franz Kafka: On the Tenth Anniversary of His Death": "'To believe in progress is not to believe that progress has already taken place. That would be no belief.' Kafka did not consider the age in which he lived as an advance over the beginnings of time. His novels are set in a swamp world. In his works, created things appear at the stage Bachofen has termed the hetaeric stage. The fact that it is now forgotten does not mean that it does not extend into the present. On the contrary. it is actual by virtue of this very oblivion" (Walter Benjamin, *Illuminations*, ed. Hannah Arendt, trans. Harry Zohn [London: Jonathan Cape, 1970], p. 130).

3. "Und wer's nie gekonnt, der stehle weinend sich aus diesem Bund," from Friedrich Schiller's ode "An die Freude" (1786).

4. First published version has: "For the element of enlightenment within it, that of demythologization, which terminates. . . . "

5. "Und alles Drängen, alles Ringen / Ist ewige Ruh in Gott dem Herrn," from "Zahme Xenien VI," translated in *Goethe: Selected Verse*, ed. David Luke (New York: Penguin, 1981), p. 280.

6. "The fact that the subjective purpose, as the power over these processes (in which the *objective* gets used up through mutual friction and sublates itself), keeps itself *outside of them* and *preserves itself* in them is the *cunning* of reason.

"In this sense we can say that, with regard to the world and its process, divine Providence behaves with absolute cunning. God lets men, who have their particular passions and interests, do as they please, and what results is the accomplishment of *his* intentions, which are something other than those whom he employs were directly concerned about" (G. W. F. Hegel, *The Encyclopedia Logic: Part I of the Encyclopedia of Philosophical Sciences, with the Zusätze*, trans. T. F. Geraets, W. A. Suchting, and H. S. Harris [Indianapolis: Hackett, 1991], p. 284. German: G. W. F. Hegel, *Enzyklopädie der philosophischen Wissenschaften I, Werke* (Frankfurt am Main: Suhrkamp, 1970), 8: 365 (209 and Zusatz). See also *Wissenschaft der Logik II, Werke*, 6: 452 ("C. Der ausgeführte Zweck") and *Philosophie der Geschichte, Werke*, 12: 49 and 119.

7. I.e., the fifth and sixth theses.

8. See the fifth proposition of Kant's "Idea for a Universal History":

> *The greatest problem for the human species, the solution of which nature compels him to seek, is that of attaining a civil society which can administer justice universally.*
>
> The highest purpose of nature—i.e. the development of all natural capacities—can be fulfilled for mankind only in society, and nature intends that man should accomplish this, and indeed all his appointed ends, by his own efforts. This purpose can be fulfilled only in a society which has not only the greatest freedom, and therefore a continual antagonism among its members, but also the most precise specification and preservation of the limits of this freedom in order that it can co-exist with the freedom of others. The highest task which nature has set for mankind must therefore be that of establishing a society in which *freedom under external laws* would be combined to the greatest possible extent with irresistible force, in other words, of establishing a perfectly *just civil constitution*. For only through the solution and fulfillment of this task can nature accomplish its other intentions with our species. Man, who is otherwise so enamoured with unrestrained freedom, is forced to enter this state of restriction by sheer necessity. And this is indeed the most stringent of all forms of necessity, for it is imposed by men upon themselves, in that their inclinations make it impossible for them to exist side by side for long in a state of wild freedom. But once enclosed within a precinct like that of civil union, the same inclinations have the most beneficial effect. In the same way, trees in a forest, by seeking to deprive each other of air and sunlight, compel each other to find these by upward growth, so that they grow beautiful and straight—whereas those which put out branches at will, in freedom and in isolation from others, grow stunted, bent and twisted. All the culture and art which adorn mankind and the finest social order man creates are fruits of his unsociability. For it is compelled by its own nature to discipline itself, and

thus, by enforced art, to develop completely the germs which nature implanted ("Idea for a Universal History with a Cosmopolitan Purpose," trans. H. B. Nisbet, in Immanuel Kant, *Political Writings*, ed. Hans Reiss, 2d ed. [Cambridge: Cambridge University Press, 1991], pp. 45–46).

9. Adorno alludes to Heidegger's *Kant und das Problem der Metaphysik* (1929); English: Martin Heidegger, *Kant and the Problem of Metaphysics*, trans. J. S. Churchill (Bloomington: Indiana University Press, 1962).

10. See Walter Benjamin, "Theological-Political Fragment," in his *Reflections: Essays, Aphorisms, Autobiographical Writings*, ed. Peter Demetz, trans. E. Jephcott (New York: Schocken, 1978), pp. 312–13.

11. Adorno here alludes to a seminar presentation made by one of his students, Karl Heinz Haag, which has been preserved in the Adorno Archive in Frankfurt. Haag later briefly touches on some aspects of this paper in his *Der Fortschritt in der Philosophie* (Frankfurt am Main: Suhrkamp, 1983), esp. pp. 37–39.

12. See Arthur Schopenhauer, *The World as Will and Representation*, trans. E. F. J. Payne (New York: Dover, 1969), 1: 185 (36, on art):

> Whilst science, following the restless and unstable stream of the fourfold forms of reasons or grounds and consequents, is with every end it attains again and again directed farther, and can never find an ultimate goal or complete satisfaction, any more than by running we can reach the point where the clouds touch the horizon; art, on the contrary, is everywhere at its goal. For it plucks the object of its contemplation from the stream of the world's course, and holds it isolated before it. This particular thing, which in that stream was an infinitesimal part, becomes for art a representative of the whole, an equivalent of the infinitely many in space and time. It therefore pauses at this particular thing; it stops the wheel of time; for it the relations vanish; its object is only the essential, the Idea. We can therefore define it accurately as *the way of considering things independently of the principle of sufficient reason*, in contrast to the way of considering them which proceeds in exact accordance with this principle, and is the way of science and experience.

And in chapter 41, "On Death and Its Relation to the Indestructibility of Our Inner Nature": "There is no greater contrast than that between the ceaseless, irresistible flight of time carrying its whole content away with it and the rigid immobility of what is actually existing, which is at all times one and the same; and if, from this point of view, we fix our really objective glance on the immediate events of life, the *Nunc stans* becomes clear and visible to us in the center of the wheel of time" (ibid., 2: 481).

13. Adorno surely relies here on the severely abbreviated version of the essay "Die Rückschritte der Poesie" ("The Regression of Poetry"), by Carl Gustav

Jochmann (1789–1830), which Walter Benjamin published with an introduction in *Zeitschrift für Sozialforschung* 8 (1939/40): 92–114. Benjamin presented what originally appeared as the fourth of five sections constituting Jochmann's anonymous book *Über die Sprache* (Heidelberg: C. F. Winter, 1828). Jochmann makes the distinction between material progress in the natural sciences and the lack of progress in the "spiritual domain": whereas the natural sciences progress in terms of technical ability, knowledge, and the domination of nature, the intellectual "internal development" operates in the opposite direction, as the destruction of reigning prejudices, as the reinvestment of the world with imagination. The investment through fantasy was the chief characteristic of lyric poetry, and Benjamin's excision of this section of Jochmann's text misled Adorno to think that Jochmann had prophesied the end of art (see Walter Benjamin, *Gesammelte Schriften* [Frankfurt am Main: Suhrkamp, 1972–89], 2.3: 1393; and Theodor W. Adorno, *Ästhetische Theorie*, in his *Gesammelte Schriften*, 7: 501).

14. First published version has a slightly different sentence: "it is the Hegelian 'Furie des Verschwindens,' which plunges one concept after another into the Orcus of the mythical."

15. See "On the Tarantulas" and "On Redemption," in Friedrich Nietzsche, *Thus Spake Zarathustra*, trans. Walter Kaufmann (New York: Viking, 1966), pp. 99–102, 137–42.

16. First published version: "behavior" instead of "attitude."

17. Adorno here both invokes and corrects Walter Benjamin's theory of the "dialectical image," the cognitive armature of the studies composing his unfinished *Arcades Project* [*Passagenarbeit*] Benjamin, who Adorno felt was too much under the sway of the surrealists, had suggested that juxtapositions of historical material in "constellations" would release the archaic dream and wish images lodged in the collective unconscious at the threshold to modernity. In a now renowned exchange of letters, Adorno rejected the theory's implied idealism: "If you transpose the dialectical image into consciousness as a 'dream,' then not only has the concept been disenchanted and made more tractable, it has also thereby forfeited precisely the objective interpretive power which could legitimate it in materialistic terms. The fetish character of the commodity is not a fact of consciousness but rather dialectical, in the eminent sense that it produces consciousness" (*Aesthetics and Politics: Debates between Bloch, Lukács, Brecht, Benjamin, Adorno*, ed. Ronald Taylor [London: New Left Books, 1977; Verso, 1980], pp. 140–41). Indeed the present essay can be considered a practical exposition of Adorno's viewpoint.

18. Karl Marx, *Critique of the Gotha Programme: With Appendixes by Marx, Engels, and Lenin* (New York: International Publishers, 1970).

19. First published version: "is one with" instead of "reinforces."

8. THE JARGON OF AUTHENTICITY

NOTE: This chapter is an essay-length version of the book that was published with the same title in 1964. The book appeared in English as *The Jargon of Authenticity*, translated by Knut Tarnowski and Frederick Will (London: Routledge & Kegan Paul, 1973). I have consulted their version in making my own translation.—Trans.

1. *Jugendstil* is the German variant of the style of decorative art, architecture, and design prominent in western Europe and the United States from about 1890 until the First World War. Generally known outside the German-speaking countries under the name of "Art Nouveau," it was characterized by intricate linear designs and flowing curves based on natural forms.—Trans.

9. 'CROWDS AND POWER': CANETTI

NOTE: This conversation about Canetti's book *Masse und Macht* (Hamburg: Claassen, 1960) was recorded for North German Radio on 21 February 1962. Carol Stewart's English translation of Canetti's book appeared with the title *Crowds and Power* (London: Victor Gollancz, 1960).—Trans.

1. See Gustave Le Bon, *Psychologie des foules* (Paris: Félix Alcan, 1895); the English translation appeared with the title *The Crowd: A Study of the Popular Mind* (London: T. Fisher Unwin, 1920).—Trans.

2. See Sigmund Freud, *Massenpsychologie und Ich-Analyse* (1921); *Group Psychology and the Analysis of the Ego*, trans. James Strachey, in *The Standard Edition of the Complete Psychological Works of Sigmund Freud*, ed. James Strachey in collaboration with Anna Freud (London: Hogarth, 1975), 18: 67–143..

10. HEINE THE WOUND

1. Heinrich Heine, *Heine's Prose and Poetry*, trans. M. M. B. (New York: Dutton, 1934), pp. 27–28.—Trans.

12. COMMITMENT

NOTE: All numbered notes in this chapter are by the translator.

1. Jean-Paul Sartre, *What Is Literature?* (London: Methuen, 1967), p. 4.

2. Jean-Paul Sartre, "Parce qu'il est homme," *Situations* II (Paris: Gallimard, 1948), p. 51.

3. Jean-Paul Sartre, *No Exit*, in *No Exit and Three Other Plays* (New York: Vintage, 1955), p. 47.

4. Sartre, *What Is Literature?*, p. 46.

5. Ibid., p. 34.

6. "We know very well that pure art and empty art are the same thing and that aesthetic purism was a brilliant manoeuvre of the bourgeois of the last century

who preferred to see themselves denounced as philistines rather than as exploiters" (ibid., p. 17).

7. Cf. Jean-Paul Sartre, *L'Existentialisme est un humanisme* (Paris: Nagel, 1946), p. 105.

15. SCHUBERT

NOTE: All numbered notes in this chapter are by the translator.

1. Rudolf Hans Bartsch (1873–1952) was a popular Austrian novelist. His *Schwammerl*, a sentimental version of Schubert's life, appeared in 1912.

2. The *Dreimäderl* house is a charming remnant of Biedermeier Vienna (1803). According to legend, Schubert is supposed to have been in love with three girls who lived there. However, it is thought more likely that the name only goes back to Berté's 1916 operetta, *Das Dreimäderlhaus*, which makes use of melodies taken from his songs. Versions of this operetta, to which Adorno refers here, enjoyed great success in English under the title "Lilac Time" in Britain (1922) and "Blossom Time" in the United States (1921). There were film versions in 1934 and 1938, both with Richard Tauben.

3. For greater clarity, Deutsch numbers have been added for Schubert's works wherever possible.

4. "Frozen Tears," from *Die Winterreise.*

16 WAGNER'S RELEVANCE TODAY

NOTE: All numbered notes in this chapter are by the translator.

1. Lorenz's *Bogenform* (a *Bogen* is an arch) is a ternary form, A-B-A or any variation of that; the *Bar* is A-A-B.

2. Carl Spitzweg (1808–85) was an artist known for his whimsical, anecdotal paintings on subjects such as the Poor Poet, the Bookworm, and the Love Letter. Highly atmospheric, they embody the spirit of the Biedermeier age.

17. MAHLER

NOTE: All numbered notes in this chapter are by the translator.

1. Looking at Mahler from a German perspective, Adorno thinks of Austrian as a deviation from German, even though the Austrian musical tradition is not a deviation but the core.

2. The Viennese Ringstrasse replaced the old city walls, which were demolished in 1860. A number of imposing public buildings constructed in various historical styles were built between then and the end of the century. They included the opera house, the principal museums, and the parliament building.

3. A reference to Maxim Gorky's play of that name, which was set among the outcasts of fin-de-siècle Russian society, as well as to Dostoyevsky's *The Insulted*

and the Injured, a novel set in St. Petersburg, which depicts the miseries of the modern city.

4. The "way of the world" (*Weltlauf*) is a Hegelian term based on a contrast between the everyday world, with its multitude of more or less selfish purposes and actions, and "ideal life."

5. See the last chapter in Franz Kafka's *America*.

6. In *Aesthetic Theory* Adorno refers to periods in which art and mathematics were closely related. In such a period art emphasizes internal logical consistency. It follows from this that "by way of their logical character, artworks are determined objectively in themselves without regard to their reception" (Theodor W. Adorno, *Aesthetic Theory*, trans. Robert Hullot-Kentor [Minneapolis: University of Minnesota Press, 1997], p. 137).

7. This poem from *Des Knaben Wunderhorn* describes the fate of a Swiss soldier who is overcome with homesickness when he hears an Alpine horn. He tries to desert, but is caught and shot.

8. For Adorno, "negative" is a laudable quality, opposed as it is to "affirmative"—that is, conformist art—and to "positive," that is, positivistic science.

9. Alfred Roller (1865–1935) was a set designer. He worked with Mahler on redesigning the Vienna Opera in the spirit of Wagner's ideal of a *Gesamtkunstwerk* (1903–7). Carl Moll (1861–1945) was one of the cofounders and key figures of the Viennese Secession.

10. Friedrich Gundolf (1880–1931) was a well-known literary critic associated with the circle around the poet Stefan George.

11. This should read "the A minor dominant."

18. ALBAN BERG

NOTE: All numbered notes in this chapter are by translator Rodney Livingstone and Rick Graebner.

1. See Alban Berg, *Lulu*, act 1, scene 2, m. 669, "Du hast eine halbe Million geheiratet." "Monoritmica" is a five-part rhythmic canon, the second half of which reverses the tempo sequence of the first half. According to Robert Morgan, there are only two strict retrogrades in *Lulu*, and "Monoritmica" is not one of them; see David Gable and Robert P. Morgan, *Alban Berg: Historical and Analytical Perspectives* (Oxford: Clarendon, 1991), p. 124. According to Douglas Jarman, "Monoritmica" makes clear the connection between the *Hauptrhythmus* and its retrograde; see *The Music of Alban Berg* (London: Faber & Faber, 1979), pp. 104–5.—R.G.

2. A movement that grew out of the turn-of-the-century Youth Movement, which promoted a healthy, back-to-the-land ideology, encouraging hiking and camping as a way of countering the unhealthy life of the new industrial towns. It was, naturally, associated with music and began with a cult of folk songs, often played on the guitar. Subsequently, educators like Fritz Jöde and Hermann

Reichenbach urged the young to put their guitars aside and turn to Bach instead. They were also responsible for a revival of Bach's predecessors. After 1933 the movement was integrated into Nazi organizations. Attempts were made to revive it after 1945.

3. It is said that when Brahms was told that the finale of the First Symphony resembled the "Ode to Joy," he retorted, "any jackass may discover a resemblance to Beethoven's Ninth Symphony." See David Brodbeck, *Brahms: Symphony No. 1* (Cambridge: Cambridge University Press, 1997), p. 65; his source is Max Kalbeck, *Brahms*, 4 vols. in 8, 2d rev. ed. (Berlin, 1915–21; reprint, Tutzing: H. Schneider, 1976), 3: 109.

4. Willi Reich, *The Life and Work of Alban Berg*, trans. C. Cardew (London: Thames & Hudson, 1965).

5. Peter Altenberg (1859–1919) was a well-known figure of Viennese café life at the turn of the century. As a writer he specialized in short forms—essays, impressionist sketches, and autobiographical pieces. He was on friendly terms with some of the major figures of the period, such as Karl Kraus and Arthur Schnitzler, and is often thought to embody the aestheticist and bohemian values of the day.

6. Franz Schreker achieved instant success with his three-act opera *Der ferne Klang* (*The Distant Sound*), which was first performed in 1912. The hero of the opera, Fritz, sets out in search of the "distant sound," which will make him famous and enable him to win his beloved Grete and make her his bride. She runs away, though, and becomes a prostitute, whereupon Fritz spurns her. They experience an ecstatic reconciliation on his deathbed, and he recognizes that the "distant sound" he had looked for is in reality enduring love. Schreker was seen as a leading modernist at the time, but his career was destroyed by the Nazis. Interest in his works has been gradually reviving, with some notable performances and recordings.

7. Adorno is referring here to the conservative tendencies that gained ground in West Germany under Adenauer in the 1950s and 1960s. Related to that is Adorno's scathing attack on the influence of Martin Heidegger's brand of existentialism, which appeared in 1964 under the title *Jargon der Eigentlichkeit*, published in English as Theodor W. Adorno, *The Jargon of Authenticity*, trans. Knut Tarnowski and Frederic Will (London: Routledge & Kegan Paul, 1973); see also the essay version, "The Jargon of Authenticity," Chap. 8 in the present volume, pp. 163–81.

8. *Durchbrochene Arbeit*, often translated as "filigree openwork," is a term frequently used by Adorno in these essays and generally. It refers to the division of voice function among different voices. According to the *Riemann Musik-Lexikon, Sachteil* (Mainz: B. Schott, 1967), p. 246 (s.v. "durchbrochene Arbeit"), it occurs in the late Beethoven, in Brahms, and in Mahler and culminates in the *Klangfarbenmelodie* of Schoenberg's op. 16, no. 3.—R.G.

9. The reference is to Eduard Mörike's poem "Auf eine Lampe" ("On a Lamp"), which ends with the words "Ein Kunstgebild der echten Art. Wer achtet sein? / Was aber schön ist, selig scheint es in ihm selbst" ("A work of art of the genuine kind. Who heeds it? / But whatever is beautiful appears blessed in itself"). This poem has been much commented on by philosophers, including Heidegger, as well as by Adorno. The last lines are often taken to be a rendering of Hegel's definition of beauty in the *Aesthetics*.

10. Presumably a reference to such songs as "Der Tambourg'sell" and "Zu Straßburg auf der Schanz," which Mahler set in the *Des Knaben Wunderhorn* collection and elsewhere.

11. The libretto of Berg's *Lulu* was a conflation of two plays by Frank Wedekind, *Erdgeist* (Earth spirit, 1895) and *Die Büchse der Pandora* (Pandora's box, 1904). Karl Kraus, the Viennese satirist, was a great defender of Wedekind, who was constantly in trouble with the censorship of the day. The essay Adorno refers to is "Die Büchse der Pandora," which appeared in Kraus's magazine *Die Fackel*, no. 182 (9 June 1905). At the play's premiere, Kraus read his essay aloud as a kind of preface and also acted the part of one of Lulu's more exotic clients in the last scenes, where she is reduced to prostitution.

19. ART AND THE ARTS

NOTE: All numbered notes in this chapter are by the translator.

1. Sylvano Bussotti (1931–) is an Italian composer who began as a graphic artist. Starting in 1958 he became closely involved in the post-Webernian music of the Darmstadt summer schools, where he associated with and learned from Boulez, Cage, Nono, and others. His own music, some of which was interpreted by Cathy Berberian, was notorious for a variety of provocations.

2. Hans G. Helms, born in 1932 in Mecklenburg, was a writer for radio, working mainly on political and sociological topics. However, in 1975 he published *John Cage: Talking to Hans G. Helms on Music and Politics*.

3. Rolf Nesch (1893–1975) was a printmaker and sculptor from Esslingen, who later moved permanently to Oslo. He was influenced by *Die Brücke* and Ernst Ludwig Kirchner, as well as Munch. As a sculptor, he was known for his *Materialbilder*, which often incorporated found objects, in the style of Kurt Schwitters.

4. Bernard Schultze, born in 1915, was a painter, draughtsman, and sculptor strongly influenced initially by expressionism and surrealism, in particular the work of Alfred Kubin and James Ensor. After 1945 he worked in the spirit of Tachism and Jackson Pollock.

5. Alexander Calder (1898–1975) was an American sculptor and a leading exponent of kinetic art. He is best known for his mobiles, such as *The Circus* (1926–32), which are both modernist and rooted in popular art.

6. Fritz Wotruba (1907–75) was an Austrian sculptor and architect who lived in exile in Switzerland during the war, then returned to Vienna after 1945. Among other work, he designed the costumes and set for a production of Stravinsky's *The Soldier's Tale* in 1948. Hans Scharoun (1893–1972) was an architect with left-wing views who became the municipal architect in Berlin after 1945. Among his best-known buildings are the Siemensstadt development in Berlin in the late 1920s and the Berlin Philharmonie (1956–65).

20. ELEMENTS OF ANTI-SEMITISM

NOTE: All numbered notes in this chapter are by the translator.

1. The Protestant movement "Deutsche Christen" sought a union between Church and National Socialism.

2. Immanuel Kant, *Critique of Pure Reason*, trans. Norman Kemp Smith (London: Macmillan, 1973), pp. 79ff. (B 103).

3. Charles Edward Coughlin was a Catholic priest and demagogic anti-Semitic radio preacher.

4. This is an allusion to Marx's "Zur Judenfrage," in Karl Marx, *Aus den Deutsch-Französischen Jahrbuchern* (1843–44).

5. Hermann Ahlwardt, author of anti-Semitic pamphlets, was a Reichstag deputy at the end of the nineteenth century; for years his appearances were accompanied by uproar and scandal. Hermann Kunze was a teacher at the Cadet School, chairman of the Deutsch-Soziale Partei, and anti-Semitic demagogue; his nickname [*Knüppel*, stick, cudgel] resulted from the frequent brawls at his meetings.

6. A ticket is a single list of a party's candidates in the American electoral system.

7. From the National Socialist term *judenrein*.

8. This is an allusion to Kant's proposition "Thoughts without content are empty, intuitions without concepts are blind" (*Critique of Pure Reason*, p. 93 [A 51]).

21. SELECTIONS FROM 'METAPHYSICS'

Lecture Fourteen, "The Liquidation of the Self"

1. See Theodor W. Adorno, *Metaphysics: Concept and Problems*, ed. Rolf Tiedemann, trans. Edmund Jephcott (Stanford: Stanford University Press, 2001), Lecture Thirteen, p. 101.

2. Schopenhauer's "doctrine of the denial of the Will to Live," which forms part of his system relating to moral philosophy, is to be found in Arthur Schopenhauer, *The World as Will and Representation*, trans. E. F. J. Payne (New York: Dover, 1966), bk. 4, vol. 1, 68 (pp. 378ff.), and vol. 2, chap. 48 (pp. 603ff.); see also Arthur Schopenhauer, *Parerga and Paralipomena*, trans. E. F. J. Payne (Oxford: Oxford University Press, 1974), vol. 2, chap. 14 (pp. 312ff.).

3. On 1 November 1755 the Portuguese capital was devastated by an earthquake in which a quarter of its inhabitants lost their lives. Voltaire, deeply shaken, wrote his "Poème sur le désastre de Lisbonne, ou examen de cet axiome: *tout est bien*":

O malheureux mortels! ô terre déplorable!
O de tous les fléaux assemblage effroyable!
D'inutiles douleurs éternel entretien!

. . .

Quel crime, quelle faute ont commis ces enfans
Sur le sein maternel écrasés et sanglans?
Lisbonne qui n'est plus eut-elle plus de vices
Que Londres, que Paris, plongés dans les délices?
Lisbonne est abîmée, et l'on danse à Paris.

. . .

Ce monde, ce théâtre et d'orgueil et d'erreur,
Est plein d'infortunés qui parlent de bonheur.

. . .

Nos chagrins, nos regrets, nos pertes sont sans nombre.
Le passé n'est pour nous qu'un triste souvenir;
Le présent est affreux s'il n'est point d'avenir,
Si la nuit du tombeau détruit l'être qui pense.
Un jour tout sera bien, voilà votre espérance:
Tout est bien aujourd'hui, voilà l'illusion.

Voltaire's "Poème"—which, with another "sur la loi naturelle," was published as a book—was condemned and burned in 1759. Rousseau's "Letter on Providence" is dated 18 August 1756; he later commented rather aptly on it in his *Confessions*:

> Struck by seeing that poor man, weighed down, so to speak, by fame and prosperity. Bitterly complaining, nevertheless, against the wretchedness of this life and finding everything invariably bad, I formed the insane plan of bringing him back to himself and proving to him that all was well. Though Voltaire has always appeared to believe in God, he has really only believed in the Devil, because his so-called God is nothing but a malicious being who, according to his belief, only takes pleasure in doing harm. (Rousseau, *The Confessions*, trans. J. M. Cohen [Harmondsworth, Middlesex: Penguin, 1953], pp. 399–400)

And: "In the meantime Voltaire has published the reply that he promised me. It is nothing less than his novel *Candide*" (ibid., p. 400).

4. See Theodor W. Adorno, *The Jargon of Authenticity*, trans. Knut Tarnowski and Frederic Will (London: Routledge & Kegan Paul, 1973); see also "The Jargon of Authenticity," Chap. 8 in the present volume.

5. Jean Améry, "Die Tortur," *Merkur* 208, vol. 19, no. 7 (July 1965): 623ff., reprinted in a revised version in Jean Améry, *Jenseits von Schuld und Sühne: Bewältigungsversuche eines Überwältigten*, 2d ed. (Stuttgart: Klett-Cotta, 1980), pp. 46ff.

6. See Martin Heidegger, *Being and Time*, trans. John Macquarrie and Edward Robinson (New York: Harper & Row, 1962), div. 2, "Dasein and Temporality," chap. 1, "Dasein's Possibility of Being-a-Whole, and Being-Towards-Death" (pp. 279ff.). Also see these comments by Heidegger: "The 'end' of Being-in-the-world is death. This end, which belongs to the potentiality-for-Being—that is to say, to existence—limits and determines in every case whatever totality is possible for Dasein" (ibid., pp. 276–77) and "When Dasein reaches its wholeness in death, it simultaneously loses the Being of its 'there'" (p. 281); also Adorno's critique in *Jargon of Authenticity*, pp. 130ff.

7. See Bertolt Brecht, *A Man's a Man*, in *"Baal," "A Man's a Man," and "The Elephant Calf,"* trans. Eric Bentley (New York: Grove, 1964), pp. 117ff. On the status of the text of the play, written in 1924–26, see Bertolt Brecht, *Gesammelte Werke in acht Bänden* (Frankfurt am Main: Suhrkamp, 1976), 1: 363n and p. 4.

8. See, for example, the chapter on the "culture industry":

> Where the culture industry still invites naive identification, it immediately denies it. It is no longer possible to lose oneself in others. Once, film spectators saw their own wedding in that of others. Now the happy couple on the screen are specimens of the same species as everyone in the audience, but the sameness posits the insuperable separation of its human elements. The perfected similarity is the absolute difference. The identity of the species prohibits that of the individual cases. The culture industry has sardonically realized man's species being. Everyone amounts only to those qualities by which he or she can replace everyone else: all are fungible, mere specimens. As individuals they are absolutely replaceable, pure nothingness, and are made aware of this as soon as time deprives them of their sameness. (Max Horkheimer and Theodor W. Adorno, *Dialectic of Enlightenment*, trans. Edmund Jephcott [Stanford: Stanford University Press, 2002], pp. 116–17)

The reduction of the individual to the mere specimen of its species is one of the central ideas in *Dialectic of Enlightenment*. In "Elements of Anti-Semitism," where the theory of logic is traced right to the extermination camps, the formulation "specimen" is, however, lacking:

> In the world of mass production, stereotypes replace intellectual categories. . . . If, even within the field of logic, the concept stands opposed to the particular as something merely external, anything that stands for difference within society itself must indeed tremble. Everyone is labeled

friend or foe. The disregard for the subject makes things easy for the administration. Ethnic groups are transported to different latitudes; individuals labeled "Jew" are dispatched to the gas chambers. ("Elements of Anti-Semitism," Chap. 20 in the present volume, pp. 420–21)

Regarding the text of the lecture see the parallel passage in *Negative Dialectics*: "That in the concentration camps it was no longer an individual who died but a specimen—this is a fact bound to affect the dying of those who escaped the administrative measure" (Theodor W. Adorno, *Negative Dialectics*, trans. E. B. Ashton [New York: Seabury, 1973], p. 362). And see especially the conclusion of the book: "The smallest intramundane traits would be of relevance to the absolute, for the micrological view cracks the shells of what, measured by the subsuming cover concept, is helplessly isolated and explodes its identity, the delusion that it is but a specimen" (ibid., p. 408).

9. See Brecht's poem "On the Suicide of the Refugee W.B.": "So the future lies in darkness and the forces of right / Are weak. All this was plain to you / When you destroyed a torturable body" (Bertolt Brecht, *Poems 1913–1956*, ed. John Willett and Ralph Manheim [London: Methuen, 1976], p. 363).

10. See the section "Absolute Freedom and Terror": "The sole work and deed of universal freedom is therefore *death*, a death too which has no inner significance or filling, for what is negated is the empty point of the absolutely free self. It is thus the coldest and meanest of all deaths, with no more significance than cutting off a head of cabbage or swallowing a mouthful of water" (G. W. F. Hegel, *Phenomenology of Spirit*, trans. A. V. Miller [Oxford: Oxford University Press, 1977], p. 360).

11. See Eugen Kogon, *Der SS-Staat: Das System der deutschen Konzentrationslager*, 2d ed. (Stockholm: Bermann-Fischer, 1947). The quotation, also to be found, though not attributed, in Adorno, *Negative Dialectics* (see p. 362), has not been traced; however, a similar passage has been found: "Someone called out to a Jew: 'It's now 12 o'clock. At 12.05 you'll be with Jehovah!' It didn't take even five minutes" (translated from Kogon, *Der SS-Staat*, p. 94).

12. Améry describes being tortured:

> Now there was a cracking and splintering in my shoulders which I have not forgotten to this day. . . . Anyone who has been tortured remains tortured. The torture is burnt into him inextinguishably, even if no clinical or objective traces can be found. . . . Finally I became unconscious—and it was over for once. It is still not over. . . . You cannot rid yourself of torture any more than you can rid yourself of the question about the possibilities and limits of the power to resist it. (Améry, "Die Tortur," pp. 632, 634, and 636)

And at the end of the essay he writes:

As far as any knowledge remains from the experience of torture beyond that of mere nightmare, it is that of a great amazement, and of being a stranger in the world, which cannot be compensated by any later human communication. Astonishment at the existence of the Other which asserts itself boundlessly in torture, and at what one can oneself become: flesh and death. That life is fragile, and that it can be ended "with a bare bodkin"—that truism has always been known. But that a living human being can be made half-and-half the prey of death while still alive is only experienced under torture. The shame of such annihilation can never be effaced. Anyone who has been tormented remains defenselessly exposed to fear. *It* henceforth wields its scepter over him. It—and also what is called *ressentiment*, which remains behind and has not even the chance to condense into a desire for revenge—and to be purged. From there, no one looks out onto a world in which the principle of hope holds sway. (Ibid., p. 638)

That is the text to which Adorno refers. Améry later intensified it still further in a book version: "Anyone who has been subjected to torture cannot again feel at home in the world. The shame of annihilation cannot be expunged. The trust in the world, which collapses partly with the first blow but only fully under torture, is never regained" (Améry, *Jenseits von Schuld und Sühne*, p. 73).

13. Adorno made the statement first in the essay "Kulturkritik und Gesellschaft," of 1949 (Adorno, "Cultural Criticism and Society," Chap. 7 in the present volume, p. 162). For a discussion and interpretation, see Rolf Tiedemann's introduction to the present volume, "Not the First Philosophy, but a Last One," pp. xv–xvii.

14. On the proposition in question, see Theodor W. Adorno, *Kant's 'Critique of Pure Reason,'* ed. Rolf Tiedemann, trans. Rodney Livingstone (Stanford: Stanford University Press, 2001), pp. 269–70 n. 8.

15. See Sartre, *Morts sans sépulture*, tableau 4, scene 3:

HENRI: Est-ce que ça garde un sens de vivre quand il y a des hommes qui vous tapent dessus jusqu'à vous casser les os? Tout est noir. (*Il regarde par la fenêtre.*) Tu as raison, la pluie va tomber. [Do you still feel alive while men beat you until they break your bones? It's very dark. (*He looks out of the window.*) You are right, it's going to rain.] (Jean-Paul Sartre, *La p . . . respectueuse . . . suivi de Morts sans sépulture: Pièce en deux actes et quatre tableaux* [Paris: Gallimard, 1972], p. 210)

Lecture Fifteen, "Metaphysics and Materialism"

1. The title of Beckett's last novel (Paris, 1961), frequently quoted by Adorno in *Aesthetic Theory*.

2. See Hannah Arendt, *Eichmann in Jerusalem: A Report on the Banality of Evil,* rev. ed. (New York: Viking, 1964).

3. An allusion to the book with the same title by Otto Friedrich Bollnow (Stuttgart, 1956); see Adorno, *Jargon of Authenticity,* pp. 9–10 and passim; see also "The Jargon of Authenticity," Chapter 8 of this volume, pp. 172–73.

4. See Adorno, *Metaphysics,* Lecture Eleven, p. 171 n. 7.

5. On the category of the addendum, see Adorno, *Negative Dialectics,* pp. 226ff.; see also Eckart Goebel, "Das Hinzutretende: Ein Kommentar zu den Seiten 226 bis 230 der *Negative Dialektik,*" in *Frankfurter Adorno Blätter IV,* ed. Theodor W. Adorno Archiv (Munich: Edition Text und Kritik, 1995), pp. 109ff.

6. See Lecture Fourteen, and *Negative* n. 9, above in this chapter.

7. Here Adorno is referring to his essay on Beckett's *Endgame* (see "Trying to Understand *Endgame,*" Chap. 13 in the present volume pp. 259–94; original in Adorno, *Gesammelte Schriften,* 11: 281–321.). Adorno's interest in Samuel Beckett is now documented fully in *Frankfurter Adorno Blätter III,* ed. Theodor W. Adorno Archiv (Munich: Edition Text und Kritik, 1994).

8. Similarly, in Adorno's *Negative Dialectics*: "It [culture] abhors stench because it stinks—because, as Brecht put it in a magnificent line, its mansion is built of dogshit. Years after that line was written, Auschwitz demonstrated irrefutably that culture has failed" (p. 366). The passage in Brecht has not been traced.

9. Not traced.

10. Not traced.

11. See the essay "Die auferstandene Kultur," of 1950, reprinted in Adorno, *Gesammelte Schriften,* 20.2: 453ff.

Lecture Sixteen, "Consciousness of Negativity"

1. One or more sentences appear to be missing at the start of the lecture; at any rate, the source text begins: "*Ich meine damit konkret, Sie könnten denken.*"

2. For "these things" read "Auschwitz or the atom bomb or all those things that belong together here" (see Lecture Fifteen above in this chapter, p. 440).

3. The category of the "wholly Other" was introduced by the Marburg Protestant theologian Rudolf Otto (1869–1937), who defined the numinous, the *mysterium tremendum,* and finally the divine itself with this term; however, the thing referred to as the *mysterium,*

> that is, the religious mystery, the genuine *mirum,* is, to express it perhaps most aptly, the "wholly other," the *thateron,* the *anyad,* the *alienum,* the *aliud valde,* the alien and perplexing thing that falls outside the realm of the familiar and understood, and thus outside the "homely," setting itself up in opposition to it and therefore filling the mind with petrified amazement. (Rudolf Otto, *Das Heilige. Über das Irrationale in der Idee des Göttlichen und sein Verhältnis zum Rationalen* [1917: Munich, 1991], p. 31)

Otto finds moments of the wholly Other especially in mysticism: "Mysticism contains essentially and primarily a theology of the *mirum,* the 'wholly Other'" (ibid., p. 36). Horkheimer appears to have responded affirmatively to this category in his last years; at any rate, he did not object to the publication of a conversation on theology and critical theory with the title "Die Sehnsucht nach dem ganz Anderen" (see Max Horkheimer, *Die Sehnsucht nach dem ganz Anderen: Ein Interview mit Kommentar von Hellmut Gummior* [Hamburg: Furche, 1970). However, all he actually said was, "Critical theory contains at least one idea about the theological, the Other" (Max Horkheimer, *Gesammelte Schriften,* vol. 7, *Vorträge und Aufzeichnungen 1949–1973* [Frankfurt am Main: S. Fischer, 1985], p. 398), and he spoke of "the point on which Judaism is of such interest to me: the identification not with the *Other* but with *the others*" (ibid., p. 401). Elsewhere, he describes theology as "the expression of a yearning," "a yearning for a state in which the murderer might not triumph over the innocent victim" (ibid., p. 389). Adorno would have subscribed to this.

    4. Cf. Adorno's "Notes on Kafka":

> Kafka's theology, if one can speak of such at all, is antinomian with respect to the very God that Lessing defended against orthodoxy, the God of the enlightenment. This God, however, is a *deus absconditus.* Kafka thus becomes, not a proponent of dialectical theology, as is often asserted, but its accuser. Its "absolute difference" converges with the mythic powers. Totally abstract and indeterminate, purged of all anthropomorphic and mythological qualities, God becomes an ominously ambiguous and threatening deity, who evokes nothing but dread and terror. His "purity"—patterned after the mind—which expressionist inwardness sets up as absolute, re-creates the archaic terror of nature-bound man in the horror of that which is radically unknown. Kafka's work preserves the moment in which the purified faith was revealed to be impure, in which demythologizing appeared as demonology. (Adorno, "Notes on Kafka," Chap. 11 in the present volume, p. 235)

That Adorno had a no less critical attitude toward the restitution of the theology of the enlightenment can be seen from his correspondence with Paul Tillich of 1964. Tillich had asked him: "What do you think about the new phase of theology which—following Heidegger and Bultmann's philosophy of language—replaces all ontology with the '*word* of God'? With Heidegger they let language be as the 'house of being,' but without any 'being' in the house!" (Paul Tillich to Adorno, undated [c. early Oct. 1965], in the Theodor W. Adorno Archiv, Frankfurt am Main). From Adorno's reply:

> The word-of-God theology in the sense you refer to, which, by the way, had been prepared by Heidegger since his "turning point," I reject no less

than you do. The mystical conception of language of which it is so reminiscent has meaning only in the context of a positive theology. Otherwise the philosophy of language becomes something like a fetishism of language. What is the word of God supposed to mean without God? No, that won't do, and not only will it finally lead to a resurrection of the liberal-secular moralization of theology, but these theologians will make common cause with the logical positivists, for whom language has a very similar function, namely, to replace the subject. (Adorno to Paul Tillich, 9 Oct. 1965, in the Adorno Archiv)

5. Probably an allusion to the metaphor used by Kleist to describe his acquaintance with "the new, so-called Kantian philosophy" (see Adorno, *Kant's 'Critique of Pure Reason,'* pp. 251–52 n. 8).

6. See Karl Barth, *Der Römerbrief* (1st version 1919, 2d version 1920), 15th ed. (Zurich: Evangelischer Verlag, 1989).

7. The text source reads "Konstantin Brunn," but undoubtedly the Zurich Professor of Systematic and Practical Theology Emil Brunner (1889–1966) is meant; he was one of the cofounders of dialectical theology and was also a participant, with Adorno and Horkheimer, in the so-called Frankfurt conversation of 1931 on the "meeting" of Protestant theology with the proletariat and with secular culture. See "Das Frankfurter Gespräch," in Paul Tillich, *Briefwechsel und Streitschriften: Theologische, philosophische und politische Stellungnahmen und Gespräche,* ed. Renate Albrecht and René Tautmann (Frankfurt am Main: Evangelisches Verlagswerk, 1983), pp. 314ff.

8. Ferdinand Ebner (1882–1931), an Austrian primary school teacher and Catholic linguistic philosopher, was a member of the circle associated with the periodical *Der Brenner.*

9. Friedrich Gogarten (1887–1967), a Protestant theologian and pupil of Ernst Troeltsch. Since 1933 Gogarten had held a chair at Göttingen.

10. Adorno is thinking primarily of Gogarten, who wrote in 1933 on the "unity of Gospel and national character," arguing that "we must strive, bound by God's words, to perceive in the great events of our days a new task that our Lord has set for our Church" (quoted in Erich Trier [review], "Friedrich Gogarten, *Einheit von Evangelium und Volkstum?*" [Hamburg: Hanseatische Verlagsanstalt, 1933], in *Zeitschrift für Sozialforschung* 3, 2 [1934]: 307).

11. Adorno is referring to Schweppenhäuser's doctoral thesis, not published until 1967, and especially to the last chapter, entitled "Postscript." See Hermann Schweppenhäuser, *Kierkegaards Angriff auf die Spekulation: Eine Verteidigung* (1967), 2d, revised version (Munich, 1993).

12. First published in 1902; now in Hugo von Hofmannsthal, *Prosa II,* ed. Herbert Steiner, *Gesammelte Werke in Einzelausgaben* (Frankfurt am Main: S. Fischer, 1959), pp. 7ff.

13. Adorno is speaking of H. G. Adler (1910–88) and his book *Theresienstadt 1941–1945: Das Antlitz einer Zwangsgemeinschaft: Geschichte Soziologie Psychologie* (Tübingen: Mohr, 1955). On H. G. Adler, also see Adorno, *Gesammelte Schriften*, 20.2: 495; on Beckett's statement referred to in the following text, see Adorno, *Negative Dialectics*, pp. 367–68.

14. See Lecture Fourteen, p. 504 n. 11, above. In a letter of 24 May 1947, Horkheimer reported on his reading of *Der SS-Staat*; see Max Horkheimer, *Gesammelte Schriften*, vol. 17, *Briefwechsel 1941–1948* (Frankfurt am Main: S. Fischer, 1996), p. 814.

15. The passage Adorno is referring to is in § 28 of *Critique of Judgment*:

> Nature considered in an aesthetical judgment as might has no dominion over us, is *dynamically sublime*. If nature is to be judged by us as dynamically sublime, it must be represented as exciting fear. . . . But we can regard an object as *fearful*, without being afraid *of* it; viz. if we judge of it in such a way that we merely *think* a case in which we would wish to resist it, and yet in which all resistance would be altogether vain. [Adorno annotated the last sentence in his copy with: "*Critique of Judgment*: rather: the image mediates the fear concealed in reality."] Bold, overhanging, and as it were threatening, rocks; clouds piled up in the sky, moving with lightning flashes and thunder peals; volcanoes in all their violence of destruction; hurricanes with their track of devastation; the boundless ocean in a state of tumult; the lofty waterfall of a mighty river, and such like; these exhibit our faculty of resistance as insignificantly small in comparison with their might. But the sight of them is the more attractive, the more fearful it is, provided only that we are in security. (*Kant's Kritik of Judgment*, trans. J. H. Bernard [London: Macmillan, 1892], pp. 123–25)

Adorno annotated the last paragraph in the margin: "Like the poetry of the young Goethe." See Adorno, *Beethoven: The Philosophy of Music*, ed. Rolf Tiedemann, trans. Edmund Jephcott (Stanford: Stanford University Press, 1998). p. 169 and 241 n. 284.

16. Part of the sentence has been omitted from the text source.

17. August Strindberg's novel *Black Banners* (see A. Strindberg, *Schwarze Fahnen* [Munich, 1916], p. 254).

Lecture Seventeen, "Dying Today"

1. Allusion to Schelling's writings on "Die Weltalter" (see the reference in Adorno, *Metaphysics*, Lecture Two, pp. 150–51, n. 6), on which Adorno and Horkheimer had held their advanced philosophy seminar in the winter semester of 1960–61.

2. See Franz Kafka, *Nachgelassene Schriften und Fragmente II in der Fassung der Handschriften*, ed. Jost Schillemeit (Frankfurt am Main: S. Fischer, 1992), p. 123: "To have faith in progress does not mean to have faith that any progress has yet taken place. That would not be faith."

3. Published in London, 1948.

4. Conjectural reading.

5. See 53 of *Being and Time*:

> if by "Being towards death" we do not have in view an "actualizing" of death, neither can we mean "dwelling upon the end in its possibility." This is the way one comports oneself when one "thinks about death," pondering over when and how this possibility may perhaps be actualized. Of course such brooding over death does not fully take away from it its character as a possibility. Indeed, it always gets brooded over as something that is coming; but in such brooding we weaken it by calculating how we are to have it at our disposal. (Heidegger, *Being and Time*, pp. 305–6; see Adorno, *Jargon of Authenticity*, p. 131, where this formulation is quoted)

6. The National Socialist Ernst Krieck (1882–1947), professor at the Pädagogische Akademie in Frankfurt am Main since 1928, had become rector of the Johann Wolfgang Goethe-Universität in 1933. In a report on Arnold Gehlen, Horkheimer refers to the same quotation when he compares Gehlen's theory of institutions with "Krieck's thesis" "that only sacrifice makes us free, sacrifice for its own sake" (Max Horkheimer, *Gesammelte Schriften*, vol. 18, *Briefwechsel 1949–73* [Frankfurt am Main: S. Fischer, 1996], p. 420). Whether the quotation is correctly attributed to Krieck, in whose work it has not been traced, seems doubtful in view of a passage in *Jargon of Authenticity*: "In 1938 a National Socialist functionary wrote, in a polemical variation on a Social Democratic phrase: 'Sacrifice will make us free'"; the source given is Herbert Marcuse's critique in *Zeitschrift für Sozialforschung 7* (1938): 408. However, Marcuse's critique is of a book by Franz Böhm, *Anti-Cartesianismus: Deutsche Philosophie im Widerstand* (Leipzig, 1938). Since a review of a book by Krieck begins on the next page, a lapse of memory by both Horkheimer and Adorno seems likely.

7. Cf. Adorno, *Jargon of Authenticity*, p. 138: "Death is the possibility of the absolute impossibility of Dasein." (Quoted from Heidegger, *Being and Time*, 50.)

8. Adorno probably has a passage from § 47 of *Being and Time* in mind:

> Yet when someone has died, his Being-no-longer-in-the-world (if we understand it in an extreme way) is still a Being, but in the sense of the Being-just-present-at-hand-and-no-more of a corporeal Thing. . . . The *end* of the entity *qua* Dasein is the *beginning* of the same entity *qua* something present-at-hand. . . . From a theoretical point of view, even the corpse which is present-at-hand is still a possible object for the student of

pathological anatomy, whose understanding tends to be oriented to the idea of life. (Heidegger, *Being and Time*, pp. 281–82)

9. See the following passage from 54:

Man alone carries about with him in abstract concepts the certainty of his death, and yet, most strangely, this certainty arouses anxiety in him only at isolated moments when some cause brings it vividly to his imagination. Against the mighty voice of nature reflection can do little. In man too, as in the animal that cannot think, prevails the certainty sprung from his innermost consciousness, that he is nature, is the world itself, so that no one is noticeably troubled by the idea of their certain and never distant death, but each carries on his life as if he must live for ever. (Arthur Schopenhauer, *Sämtliche Werke*, vol. 1 [Darmstadt, 1982], pp. 388–89)

10. In his essay on Bloch's *Spuren* (in *Traces*, trans. Anthony A. Nassar [Stanford: Stanford University Press, forthcoming]), Adorno connects this motif to the sections entitled "Störende Grille" and "Weiter geben" ("Disturbing Whim" and "Passing It Forward") in that work:

In *Traces*, whose constitutive texts are developed out of the experience of individual consciousness, the rescuing of illusion has its center in what Bloch's *The Spirit of Utopia* [trans. Anthony A. Nassar (Stanford: Stanford University Press, 2000)] called *Selbstbegegnung*, encounter with the self. The subject, the human being, is not yet himself at all; he appears as something unreal, as something that has not yet emerged from potentiality, but also as a reflection of what he could be. Nietzsche's idea of the human being as something that has to be overcome is modified to become nonviolent: "for the human being is something that still has to be invented." (Theodor W. Adorno, "Ernst Bloch's *Spuren*: On the Revised Edition of 1959," in *Notes to Literature*, ed. Rolf Tiedemann, trans. Shierry Weber Nicholson [New York: Columbia University Press, 1991], 1: 205)

The reason for his nonidentity with himself, however, is the materialistic one

in a society of universal exchange human beings are not themselves but agents of the law of value; for in previous history, which Bloch would not hesitate to call prehistory, humankind has been object, not subject. "But no one is as he intends to be, and certainly not what he represents. And everyone is not too little but rather from the outset too much for what they became." (Ibid, 1: 295)

11. On the function of education in the social philosophy of Helvétius, see Max Horkheimer, "Vorlesung über die Geschichte der neueren Philosophie," in his *Gesammelte Schriften*, vol. 9, *Nachgelassene Schriften 1914–1931* (Frankfurt am Main: S. Fischer, 1987), pp. 362ff., and the dissertation by Günther Mensching,

supervised by Adorno and Horkheimer, *Totalität und Autonomie: Untersuchungen zur philosophischen Gesellschaftstheorie des französischen Materialismus* (Frankfurt am Main: Suhrkamp, 1971).

12. See Adorno, *Notes to Literature*, trans. Shierry Weber Nicholson (New York: Columbia University Press, 1992), 2: 181–82).

13. In Freud's early theory of the drives, the concept of the ego drives is used synonymously with that of the self-preservation drives and contrasted to the sexual drives:

> These instincts are not always compatible with each other; their interests often come into conflict. Opposition between ideas is only an expression of struggles between the various instincts. . . . A quite specially important part is played by the undeniable opposition between the instincts which subserve sexuality, the attainment of sexual pleasure, and those other instincts, which have as their aim the self-preservation of the individual—the ego-instincts. As the poet has said, all the organic instincts that operate in our mind may be classified as "hunger" or "love." (*The Standard Edition of the Complete Psychological Works of Sigmund Freud*, trans. James Strachey, ed. James Strachey in collaboration with Anna Freud, vol. 11 (1910) [London: Hogarth, 1962], pp. 213–14)

According to Freud's later theory, which operates with the antithesis of the Eros and death drives, the self-preservation drives are a special case among the Eros drives.

14. Cf. Marcel Proust, *Remembrance of Things Past*, trans. C. K. Scott Moncrieff (London: Chatto & Windus, 1957), *The Captive*, part 1, pp. 243ff. The passage, which Adorno also interprets in his "Short Commentaries on Proust" (Adorno, *Notes to Literature*, 1:174–84), influenced his thinking about immortality more than anything else. Bergotte dies while visiting an exhibition where he wanted to study "a little patch of yellow wall" in Vermeer's *View of Delft*:

> He was dead. Permanently dead? Who shall say? Certainly our experiments in spiritualism prove no more than the dogmas of religion that the soul survives death. All that we can say is that everything is arranged in this life as though we entered it carrying the burden of obligations contracted in a former life; there is no reason inherent in the conditions of life on this earth that can make us consider ourselves obliged to do good, to be fastidious, to be polite even, nor make the talented artist consider himself obliged to begin over again a score of times a piece of work the admiration aroused by which will matter little to his body devoured by worms, like the patch of yellow wall painted with so much knowledge and skill by an artist who must for ever remain unknown and is barely identified under the name Vermeer. All these obligations which have not their sanction

in our present life seem to belong to a different world, founded upon kindness, scrupulosity, self-sacrifice, a world entirely different from this, which we leave in order to be born into this world, before perhaps returning to the other to live once again beneath the sway of those unknown laws which we have obeyed because we bore their precepts in our hearts, knowing not whose hand had traced them there—those laws to which every profound work of the intellect brings us nearer and which are invisible only—and still!—to fools. So that the idea that Bergotte was not wholly and permanently dead is by no means improbable. (Proust, *Remembrance*, pp. 250–51)

15. See the sketch of the essay planned by Adorno on "L'Innommable": "Is nothingness the same as nothing? That is the question around which everything in B[eckett] revolves. Absolutely everything is thrown away, because there is hope only where nothing is kept back. The fullness of nothingness. This the reason for the insistence on the zero point." And: "The positive categories, such as hope, are the absolutely negative ones in B[eckett]. Hope is directed at nothingness" (source: Rolf Tiedemann, "'Gegen den Trug der Frage nach dem Sinn': Eine Dokumentation zu 186 Adorno's Beckett-Lektüre," in *Frankfurter Adorno Blätter III*, pp. 73, 44).

16. See Adorno, *Notes to Literature*, pp. 182–84. Regarding the comparison between Proust and Kafka: "Here . . . we find a statement which, at least in the German version, has echoes of Kafka. It is: 'the idea that Bergotte was not wholly and permanently dead is by no means improbable'" (ibid.; see Proust, *Remembrance*, p. 251).

17. The name of the first poet mentioned was not understood by the secretary; possibly Heym should be conjectured.

Lecture Eighteen, "Metaphysical Experience"

1. See Adorno, *Metaphysics*, Lecture One, p. 147 n. 1 and Lecture Thirteen, pp. 175–76 n. 9. On 29 July 1965, when Adorno gave the last of the lectures on metaphysics, the first manuscript version of "Meditationen zur Metaphysik," which he had begun to dictate on 3 May 1965, was completed. It was still entitled "Zur Metaphysik," but starting with the second version, dating from 18 May 1965, it was called "Meditationen zur Metaphysik." While Adorno also refers in his notes to "Metaphysische Thesen," no other reference to "Reflexionen zur Metaphysik" as a title has been traced.

2. See Adorno, "Metaphysics," Lecture Four, pp. 15ff., and Lecture Thirteen, pp. 101–2; also Lecture Fourteen above in this chapter, p. 428 passim.

3. Adorno knew of the Sohar speculations through Scholem; see the latter's translation of the first chapter and especially the introduction to the translation, in *Die Geheimnisse der Schöpfung: Ein Kapitel aus dem Sohar von G[erschom]*

Scholem (Berlin: Schocken, 1935). See Adorno's letter of 19 April 1939 to Scholem, in Theodor W. Adorno, "Um Benjamins Werk: Briefe an Gerschom Scholem 1939–1955," in *Frankfurter Adorno Blätter V*, ed. Theodor W. Adorno Archiv (Munich: Edition Text und Kritik, 1998).

4. As early as 1804 Schelling used the term "positive philosophy" to refer to his own philosophy, equally opposed to rationalism and empiricism; this philosophy was not content with reason—regarded as "negative" in relation to the real—but was directed toward the real itself: "The positive philosophy . . . does not take as its starting point what is merely present in thought, or anything occurring in experience. . . . Its principle is found neither in experience nor in pure thinking. It can thus set out only from the absolutely transcendent" (Friedrich Schelling, *Philosophie der Offenbarung 1841/42*, ed. Manfred Frank, 3d ed. [Frankfurt am Main: Suhrkamp, 1993], p. 146). Scholars have treated Schelling's late thought, which he himself claimed to be both an "existential philosophy" and a foundation for a "philosophical religion," as verging on the apocryphal, if not on obscurantism; only recently has it also been seen as an attempt to overcome idealism. In his reference to the theological speculation in the cabala Adorno probably had in mind an essay by Jürgen Habermas that discusses connections between Schelling on the one hand and the Sohar, Isaak Luria, and Jakob Böhme on the other. See Jürgen Habermas, "Dialektischer Idealismus im Übergang zum Materialismus—Geschichtsphilosophische Folgerungen aus Schellings Idee einer Contraction Gottes," in his *Theorie und Praxis: Sozialphilosophische Studien* (Neuwied: Luchterhandi, 1963), pp. 108ff.

5. The place names in Proust have been conjectured, since the source text contains only omission marks.

6. Adorno is thinking of a passage in the chapter on amphiboly in the *Critique of Pure Reason*: "The critique of this pure understanding . . . does not permit us . . . to stray into intelligible worlds; nay, it does not allow of our entertaining even the concept of them" (Immanuel Kant, *Critique of Pure Reason*, trans. Norman Kemp Smith [London: Macmillan, 1973], p. 294 [A 289, B 345]). See also Adorno, *Kant's 'Critique of Pure Reason,'* pp. 6–7.

7. On the constellation of happiness and place names in Adorno, see Adorno, *Negative Dialectics*, p. 373, and Adorno, *Beethoven*, p. 197 n. 1.

8. See Theodor W. Adorno, "Second Harvest," in *Minima Moralia*, trans. Edmund Jephcott (London: New Left Books, 1974), p. 109.

9. See Adorno, *Metaphysics*, Lecture Nine, p. 68.

10. Adorno took over the concept of the dialectical image from Benjamin, but characteristically remodeled it in his own theory. On Adorno's use of the term, see Rolf Tiedemann, "Begriff Bild Name: Über Adornos Utopie der Erkenntnis," in *Frankfurter Adorno Blätter II*, ed. Theodor W. Adorno Archiv (Munich: Edition Text und Kritik, 1993), pp. 92ff.

11. See G. W. F. Hegel, *Theologische Jugendschriften*, following the manuscripts, ed. Herman Nohl (Tübingen: J. C. B. Mohr, 1907).

12. Not in this lecture, at least the surviving part; but see Adorno, *Negative Dialectics*, pp. 173ff., and Adorno, "On Subject and Object," *Critical Models: Interventions and Catchwords*, trans. Henry W. Pickford (New York: Columbia University Press, 1998), pp. 245–58.

13. In this connection see Adorno, *Kant's 'Critique of Pure Reason,'* pp. 76ff and 172–73.

14. The concept of the "situation" was endowed with the value of a category by Jaspers; it was emphasized less by Heidegger, but most of all in the existentialism of Sartre; see the section "Freedom and Facticity: The Situation," in Jean-Paul Sartre, *Being and Nothingness*, trans. Hazel E. Barnes (London: Methuen, 1972).

15. Meaning: with the idea of the negation of the negation as a positivity attained.

16. At the conclusion of his last lecture Adorno had reached page 20 of his notes (see Theodor W. Adorno Archiv, Vo 10806) and thus almost the end of the fourth of the "Meditations on Metaphysics" (see Adorno, *Negative Dialectics*, p. 375). However, the notes for the lecture continue some way beyond this point, including the first third of the fifth "Meditation" (ibid., pp. 376–77). Since Adorno clearly meant to take the lecture to at least that point, the remaining notes—some of which Adorno had, however, already dealt with outside the planned sequence at the end of the lecture—will be listed here, as they were noted down (the small type clearly indicates later additions, as distinct from the main text):

> The despair at what is is spreading to the transcendental ideas.
>
> Paradox is passing over into slander (a tendency already found in Kierkegaard, in his attitude to poverty).
>
> In Kant the—unrealizable—metaphysical ideas were supposed, at least, not to collide with reason; absurd today. NB. Their anthropocentrism and cosmology. Ambiguity of the Copernican revolution.
>
> False elevation of the fate of metaphysical ideas to a metaphysics.
>
> The deception that despair guarantees the existence of what is hopelessly lost. The howls of religious joy over despair. Alleluia!
>
> Just as socially the means replace the ends, metaphysically the lack replaces what is lacking.
>
> The truth of what is absent is becoming indifferent; it is asserted because it is good for people, as a heart-warmer. A curious inversion, in relation to the situation of Epicureanism; that too is subject to a historical dialectic.
>
> Metaphysics is turning into pragmatism.
>
> The truth of negation must not be subverted as positivity.

The real criticism of Hegel: it is untrue that the negation of the negation is the positive. (Projection of consequential logic onto the absolute. Dissolution of the nonidentical into identity.)

The question of the "meaning of life."

The associated idea that it is what the questioner gives to life.

But meaning ought to be objectively beyond all doing; otherwise false, a mere duplication.

All metaphysics aims at something *objective*.

Subjects imprisoned in their constitution; metaphysics means reflection on how far they can see beyond the prison of their selves.

Any other question about meaning is an advertisement for the world.

The Nazis: the world *has* a meaning. The terrorist element in this idealism's lapse into the question of meaning condemns it retrospectively: it already contained the untruth of the mirroring.

Mirroring is the primary phenomenon of ideology.

The *totality* of the question of meaning as a spell.

If a suicidal person asks about the meaning of life, the helpless helper will be unable to name one.

If he attempts to do so he can be convicted of talking rubbish.

Life that had meaning would not ask about it; it shuns the question.

But abstract nihilism just as untrue.

It would have no answer to the question: Why, in that case, are you yourself alive?

To aim at the whole, to calculate the net profit of life, is precisely the death that calculation seeks to evade.

Where there is meaning, it is in the open, not in what is closed in on itself.

The thesis that life has no meaning is, as a positive statement, as false as its antithesis; true only as a blow against empty affirmation.

The close affinity of Schopenhauer to the German idealists.

The rekindling of nature religions; the blind will as demon.

The *truth* in monotheism against Schopenhauerian irrationalism.

Regression to the stage before the awakening of genius amid the mute world.

Denial of freedom; this makes the escape by the back door in Book 4 [of *The World as Will and Representation*] so feeble.

Total determinism no less mythical than the totalities in Hegelian logic.

The *totum* is the totem. (Theodor W. Adorno Archiv, Vo 10806–10808)

17. Regarding Adorno's paradox of the "impossibility of thinking that which must nevertheless be thought," see Kierkegaard: "The paradox is not an admis-

sion, but a category, an ontological determination, which expresses the relationship between an existing, cognizant mind and the eternal truth" (Søren Kierkegaard, *Die Tagebücher*, ed. Hayo Gerdes, vol. 2 [Düsseldorf: E. Diederichs, 1963], p. 80 [VIII, A 11]). But see also Adorno's critique in *Negative Dialectics*: "The theological conception of the paradox, that last, starved-out bastion, is past rescuing—a fact ratified by the course of the world in which the *skandalon* that caught Kierkegaard's eye is translated into outright blasphemy" (p. 375).

Index of Names

Chapter titles in this volume appear for selected names.

Cultural Memory in the Present

Michael Naas, *Taking on the Tradition: Jacques Derrida and the Legacies of Deconstruction*

Herlinde Pauer-Studer, ed., *Constructions of Practical Reason: Interviews on Moral and Political Philosophy*

Jean-Luc Marion, *Being Given: Toward a Phenomenology of Givenness*

Theodor W. Adorno and Max Horkheimer, *Dialectic of Enlightenment*

Ian Balfour, *The Rhetoric of Romantic Prophecy*

Martin Stokhof, *World and Life as One: Ethics and Ontology in Wittgenstein's Early Thought*

Gianni Vattimo, *Nietzsche: An Introduction*

Jacques Derrida, *Negotiations: Interventions and Interviews, 1971-1998*, ed. Elizabeth Rottenberg

Brett Levinson, *The Ends of Literature: Post-transition and Neoliberalism in the Wake of the "Boom"*

Timothy J. Reiss, *Against Autonomy: Global Dialectics of Cultural Exchange*

Hent de Vries and Samuel Weber, eds., *Religion and Media*

Niklas Luhmann, *Theories of Distinction: Re-Describing the Descriptions of Modernity*, ed. and introd. William Rasch

Johannes Fabian, *Anthropology with an Attitude: Critical Essays*

Michel Henry, *I am the Truth: Toward a Philosophy of Christianity*

Gil Anidjar, *"Our Place in Al-Andalus": Kabbalah, Philosophy, Literature in Arab-Jewish Letters*

Hélène Cixous and Jacques Derrida, *Veils*

F. R. Ankersmit, *Historical Representation*

F. R. Ankersmit, *Political Representation*

Elissa Marder, *Dead Time: Temporal Disorders in the Wake of Modernity (Baudelaire and Flaubert)*

Reinhart Koselleck, *The Practice of Conceptual History: Timing History, Spacing Concepts*

Niklas Luhmann, *The Reality of the Mass Media*

Hubert Damisch, *A Childhood Memory by Piero della Francesca*

Hubert Damisch, *A Theory of /Cloud/: Toward a History of Painting*

Jean-Luc Nancy, *The Speculative Remark (One of Hegel's bon mots)*

Jean-François Lyotard, *Soundproof Room: Malraux's Anti-Aesthetics*

Jan Patočka, *Plato and Europe*

Hubert Damisch, *Skyline: The Narcissistic City*

Isabel Hoving, *In Praise of New Travelers: Reading Caribbean Migrant Women Writers*

Richard Rand, ed., *Futures: Of Derrida*

William Rasch, *Niklas Luhmann's Modernity: The Paradox of System Differentiation*

Jacques Derrida and Anne Dufourmantelle, *Of Hospitality*

Jean-François Lyotard, *The Confession of Augustine*

Kaja Silverman, *World Spectators*

Samuel Weber, *Institution and Interpretation: Expanded Edition*

Jeffrey S. Librett, *The Rhetoric of Cultural Dialogue: Jews and Germans in the Epoch of Emancipation*

Ulrich Baer, *Remnants of Song: Trauma and the Experience of Modernity in Charles Baudelaire and Paul Celan*

Samuel C. Wheeler III, *Deconstruction as Analytic Philosophy*

David S. Ferris, *Silent Urns: Romanticism, Hellenism, Modernity*

Rodolphe Gasché, *Of Minimal Things: Studies on the Notion of Relation*

Sarah Winter, *Freud and the Institution of Psychoanalytic Knowledge*

Samuel Weber, *The Legend of Freud: Expanded Edition*